W9-CEI-226

OUR AGE

ALSO BY NOEL ANNAN

Roxburgh of Stowe
Leslie Stephen – The Godless Victorian

OUR AGE

English Intellectuals Between the World Wars— A Group Portrait

❦

NOEL ANNAN

Random House
New York

 Published in the United States by Random House, Inc., New York. Originally published in Great Britain by George Weidenfeld and Nicolson Limited, London, in 1990.

Excerpts from "An Ancient to Ancients" by Thomas Hardy are from *The Complete Poems of Thomas Hardy,* edited by James Gibson (New York: Macmillan, 1978).

Grateful acknowledgment is made to the following for permission to reprint previously published material:

GERALD DUCKWORTH AND COMPANY, LTD: Excerpt from *Maurice Bowra,* edited by Lloyd Jane. Reprinted by permission of Duckworth.

THE UNIVERSITY OF CHICAGO PRESS: Excerpt from *Journey to the Frontier* by Peter Stansky and William Abrahams, published by The University of Chicago Press. Reprinted by permission of The University of Chicago Press.

Library of Congress Cataloging-in-Publication Data

Annan, Noel Gilroy Annan, Baron.
Our age : English intellectuals between the world wars—a group portrait / by Noel Annan. p. cm.
ISBN 0-394-54295-9
1. Great Britain—Intellectual life—20th century. I. Title.
DA566.4.A665 1991 941.085—dc20 90-52887

Manufactured in the United States of America
24689753
First American Edition

To Gabriele

Doch hängt mein ganzes Herz an dir,
Du graue Stadt am Meer;
Der Jugend Zauber für und für
Ruht lächelnd doch auf dir, auf dir,
Du graue Stadt am Meer.

THEODOR STORM

'People have thought that it was the duty of the historian to judge the past and instruct the present for the benefit of the future. The present essay is more modest. It merely wants to show what it was really like.'

LEOPOLD VON RANKE

Contents

PART IV

Introduction

IN 1978 STEPHEN Graubard, the editor of *Daedalus*, the journal of the American Academy of Arts and Sciences, asked me to write an article on generations in Britain: and out of it came this book. But it might not have been written had it not been for the generosity of the Leverhulme Trust which awarded me an Emeritus Fellowship for two years. Like many other scholars I owe the Trust much and am very grateful. I am also indebted to University College London for inviting me to give the Lord Northcliffe Lectures in 1985 which I have subsequently used in writing this book.

My greatest debt is to Daniel Bell. During his year as visiting American professor at the University of Cambridge he read more than half of an earlier draft of this book and his voluminous comments made me glimpse what a better book it might have been had he written it. Indeed so many friends have encouraged, and so many writers have stimulated me, that I cannot list them. But I should mention among old friends my mentor, George Rylands; Francis Haskell among younger friends; and among more recent friends Samuel Hynes. I owe much to Shirley Letwin for our talks over the years full of excellent provocation. John Grigg read two of the chapters on politics and saved me from several errors; and so did Eric Roll.

I must thank the librarians, and their staffs, of the House of Lords, the London Library and the University of London for their willingness and resourcefulness. I am also indebted to George Simson for inviting me to lecture at the University of Hawaii and for allowing me to reprint material that appeared in *Biography* which he edits. The editors of the *London Review of Books*, the *Times Literary Supplement*, the *New Statesman and Society*, the *Spectator*, the *Listener*, *Encounter*, the *Sunday Times*, the *Sunday Telegraph*, and the *Observer* have kindly permitted me to quote from articles that appeared in their pages. And I am particularly grateful to Robert Silvers of the *New York Review of Books*, a prince among editors, for inviting me to write for him over the past twenty years.

Once again Douglas Matthews, librarian of the London Library, has come to my aid and compiled the index, and Patrick Hunter my classics tutor at Stowe, meticulous as ever, has read the proofs: I owe them much, as I do my editor Rosemary Legge. Harriet Croxton, who typed the text from my handwritten manuscript, deserves a medal. My daughter Juliet gave me invaluable professional advice, yet I owe most to Gabriele, my wife, to whom I dedicate this book.

NOEL ANNAN

PART I

CHAPTER 1

Our Age

1

IF YOU HAD asked Maurice Bowra, the most famous Oxford don and wit of his day, how old someone was, as like as not he would have replied: 'Our Age'. He meant by this anyone who came of age and went to the university in the thirty years between 1919, the end of the Great War, and 1949 – or, say, 1951, the last year in which those who had served in the armed forces during the Second World War returned to study. To him they were all one generation.

'Our Age'. But who are 'we'? Bowra meant those who make their times significant and form opinion. He would have thought of poets, writers, artists and dons. He would have added some politicians, civil servants, diplomats and, grudgingly, priests. He would have included animators – those who liberate their contemporaries by their vitality, exuberance and spontaneity even though they themselves may leave nothing but memories behind. He would have thought of certain women, dons such as Elsie Butler and Enid Starkie, or life enhancers like Barbara Hutchinson, Ann Fleming, Pamela Berry or Joan Eyres-Monsell. But to be a genuine member of Our Age it was not enough to be well-born, or well-known, or pleasure-loving. Nor was it enough to be a scholar. He liked people to be quick, intelligent, and to delight in general ideas.

It goes without saying that he expected them to come from the upper or middle classes, to grow up in a public school and go to Oxford or Cambridge. He should have added the London School of Economics. These were the three places where ideas fermented. Of course other universities possessed influential scholars and scientists and lively students. In London the institutions that amalgamated to form Imperial College rivalled Cambridge as a scientific powerhouse after the war. University College London, a university within a university, excelled in science and engineering as well as being the foremost stronghold of what can be called British Museum scholarship. At Manchester there was Namier, at Bristol Powell; Edinburgh and Glasgow each had a distinctive culture; and there were a score of lively departments before the war in the Victorian civic universities. But just as after the war in America Harvard, Berkeley, Chicago, Columbia and MIT were the campuses that made the running for the young, so the ancient universities and LSE are the ones to watch in identifying Our Age. And since Our Age belonged to the educated classes I have chosen these three places to illustrate the kind of people they were.

Maurice Bowra was the acknowledged leader of the Oxford Wits, that group of undergraduates in the twenties sometimes dubbed the Children of the Sun and identified with Harold Acton and Evelyn Waugh. John Sparrow, warden of All Souls', pictured Bowra at the Last Judgement:

> He'll seize the sceptre and annex the throne,
> Claim the Almighty's thunder for his own,
> Trump the Last Trump and the Last Post postpone . . .
> Then shall we supplicate at Heaven's high bar:
> 'Be merciful.' You made us what we are,
> Our jokes, our joys, our hopes, our hatred too,
> The outrageous things we do, or want to do –
> How much of all of them we owe to you!

But Bowra was by no means the only don to gather a circle about him. There was Sligger Urquhart, unemphatic but most charismatic of Balliol dons, who invited to his Swiss chalet a succession of talented and gentle undergraduates for reading parties. Some became dons like the classical scholar Roger Mynors, others civil servants like John Maud who was permanent secretary of the Ministry of Education after the war. There was the master of Balliol, Sandie Lindsay and Douglas Cole who were the mentors of future Labour ministers such as Hugh Gaitskell. There was always a Union set, led by such debaters as the future Conservative ministers David Eccles and John Boyd-Carpenter; and in the early forties the remarkable trio of Labour contenders, Roy Jenkins, Tony Crosland and Denis Healey. As the years succeed each other you can see an unbroken succession of types. Ken Tynan with his winning effrontery and talent for publicity appears as genuine an animator as Harold Acton.

But it is also true that the tastes and concerns of my generation changed with the decades: everyone knows how the young of the thirties differed from those of the twenties. The mood became more serious and later more political. Auden was homosexual, as were many of the Wits, but he cared nothing for their social climbing and extravagance. Nor did the circle of the philosophers, Freddie Ayer, John Austin, Isaiah Berlin, and the writers Arthur Calder-Marshall, Goronwy Rees and Stephen Spender. They had less in common with the Wits than with their juniors, the even more politically minded generation of the historian Christopher Hill, the philosopher Stuart Hampshire, and the art historian and editor Ben Nicolson.

To move from Oxford to Cambridge is like moving from a gallery displaying the paintings of Veronese and Rubens to one in which are hung the austere simplicities of Piero della Francesca. Cambridge did not pride itself on being the mother of statesmen or an enclave of the metropolis. No Cambridge college could compete in promoting its outstanding undergraduates with the Christ Church Mafia under its *capo*, that quintessential Establishment figure, J.C.Masterman. Oxford's tentacles stretched through the ministries into the secret intelligence and security services. Oxford was always news; the disputes of its dons and the frolics of its undergraduates regaled the London press. Cambridge's bleak motto was: *nil admirari*; and its tone of voice was impersonal, less playful, witty and mondain, the dry biscuit served with the Oxford Madeira. Many of the ablest students at Cambridge studied mathematics or science, and the most striking names were to be found in the laboratories – in the Cavendish under Rutherford where the atom was split or among Adrian's physiologists, or in the unit where the structure of DNA was discovered. It was in the laboratories rather than in the humanities that the earliest marxists were to be found. Bernal and Haldane, and such sympathizers as Gowland Hopkins and Waddington, preached the gospel that scientists, guided by scientific principles, should replace politicians and run public affairs.

Scientific method was never far from the minds of those who taught the humanities. According to Bury, history was 'a science, no less and no more', and Housman regarded the establishment of the text as the only reputable activity for classical scholars. The philosophers were proud of their isolation: Wittgenstein was more talked of in Oxford than in Cambridge. Even the English faculty was susceptible to science: I.A.Richards in the twenties was propounding a psychological theory of appreciating poetry based on the satisfaction of 'appetencies'. The economics tripos consisted of a one-year introduction to weed out the businessmen and discourage the weaklings; and a tough two-year course followed. It so stretched the survivors that those who graduated with first-class honours were accepted as professional economists. To help him write the *General Theory* Keynes assembled what he called his circus in which the performers were Richard Kahn, Joan and Austin Robinson, James Meade and Piero Sraffa. It was arguably the most remarkable group in the humanities in Cambridge between the wars.

But despite those great Cambridge Whig historians, Macaulay and Trevelyan, most dons in the humanities were stout Conservatives. The history faculty was a nest of Tories and Christians, out of which tumbled the fledgling Conservative ministers Rab Butler and Iain Macleod. In the thirties, when marxism appealed to numbers of intelligent undergraduates, no don lectured on Marx until 1938. The don who did so was Michael Oakeshott, and that name is significant. Cambridge was to produce two of the most important deviants of my generation, men who repudiated nearly all its beliefs and assumptions. Oakeshott challenged their philosophical and political traditions, and set out a new agenda for Conservatives. The second deviant, F.R.Leavis, launched a crusade against its moral and literary ethos.

Indeed Cambridge more than Oxford was the temple of the arts. Before the war the choirs of King's, St John's and the influence of the musicologist Edward Dent produced a level of performance of a different order from that of Oxford. So did the dramatic performances of the Marlowe Society from those of the OUDS. George Rylands at King's drilled his undergraduate actors and actresses to think, while they were speaking, what the Elizabethan and Jacobean blank verses meant instead of ranting or throwing away the lines. They learnt how to respect the interplay of rhythm and metre of the lines – a discipline that after the war was to transform for three decades the speaking of verse at Stratford and on the London stage.

What could be further from the colleges of these ancient universities than the London School of Economics? Between the wars it was the only institution to take all the social sciences seriously. There the majority of the students came from grammar schools and many of the Indians who were to rule their country in the first thirty years after independence had studied there or at Cambridge. Harold Laski, who belonged to the pre-1914 generation, was their guru as he was for hundreds of students who went to the school. His confident belief that he could reconcile parliamentary democracy with marxism gave the impression that the LSE, founded by the Webbs, was the powerhouse of socialism. Certainly there were other supporters of the Labour party on the faculty. There was Tawney; the old Fabian Graham Wallas; the sociologist Tom Marshall; and the expert on public administration Willie Robson. Certainly the students were as raucously marxist in the thirties as their contemporaries at Oxford and Cambridge.

But from its foundation LSE had been a chapel of many faiths. Laski was a propagandist for socialism, but Hugh Dalton in the twenties and Tom Marshall in the thirties were scrupulous and unbiased teachers. The left, teaching social studies, were balanced by the neo-classical economists Lionel Robbins, Arnold Plant, Hayek and Hicks; and the tyrannical Liberal Beveridge, the school's director, was as far removed from socialism as Karl Popper or Malinowski, the most distinguished anthropologist in the country. Robbins acted as a gatekeeper monitoring possible marxist infiltration. Without consulting any of his colleagues Beveridge was on the point of giving refuge *en bloc* to the Institute for Social Research at Frankfurt then in flight from Nazi Germany. Robbins stopped him. Yet LSE was remarkable for being far more willing than Oxford and Cambridge to take a chance in making an appointment. No one quite knew what exactly were the antecedents of Munia Postan, a refugee from Soviet Russia, and he himself seemed unable to decide which version he had settled for; but he was a brilliant economic historian and one of the most stimulating members of a famous dining club, the Tots and Quots, founded by Gip Wells (son of H.G.) and Solly Zuckerman. Where but at LSE would Richard Titmuss have got a post to become eventually a professor of social administration, when he had no degree nor educational qualification of any kind, since he left school at fourteen?

So here is the portrait of a generation – at least of some of them. And this book is about their beliefs and assumptions, their achievements and failures, in morality, politics and intellectual pursuits.

2

HOW DID ONE get accepted as a member of Our Age? In the same way that most people have always got accepted – by ability, by family connections and knowing somebody. Even in the more open society of the United States many entered Wall Street and Washington through the Ivy League. Birth still counted for something. In 1962, in Macmillan's time, the descendants and collaterals of four Victorian peers (Devonshire, Lansdowne, Abercorn and Marlborough) included the prime minister, foreign secretary, lord chancellor and six other ministers; the ambassador to Washington; the governor and former governor of the Bank of England; seven directors of merchant banks; and the proprietors of *The Times*, *Observer* and *Daily Mail*. Some members of Our Age came from this milieu. David Cecil for one.

But far more came from another aristocracy – the intellectual families that intermarried in the nineteenth century and were in full flower between the wars. These families produced a disproportionately large number of eminent men and women and a fair share of those of not outstanding ability but who occupied top posts in academic and cultural life. There was the Macaulay-Cripps-Hobhouse-Babington-Booth-Beatrice Webb clan; a great-niece of Beatrice Webb was to marry Victor Rothschild. There was the Arnold-Trevelyan-Huxley-Darwin-Wedgwood clan which contained members of the Keynes, Vaughan-Williams, Sidgwick, Cornford and Barlow families. Or the Fry-Hodgkin-Haldane-Mitchison-Butler-Faber-Adam Smith connection. Or the Stephen-Venn-Elliott-Strachey-Barnes-Shuckburgh strain, and so on. These intellectuals were not an intelligentsia burning to overthrow institutions. Whereas in the nineteenth century their grandfathers disliked the jaunty Palmerston, and still more imperialism, by the mid-twenties they had become more seducible by upper-class graces. Nevertheless, they threw up their share of left-wing activists. J.B.S. Haldane and his sister Naomi Mitchison; John Strachey and his sister Amabel Williams Ellis; Vanessa Bell's sons, Julian and Quentin; and John Cornford who, like Julian Bell, was killed in the Spanish Civil War. Dozens of their children became the radicals of the thirties.

You did not have to belong to the intellectual aristocracy to realize that family connections and intermarriage were an entrée to Our Age. John Lehmann and Christopher Isherwood were cousins of Graham Greene; Evelyn Waugh of Claud Cockburn. Right-wing Roy Campbell married the sister of a communist whose other sister married a partner of Lawrence and Wishart, the publishers of the Communist Party. Kathleen Raine married the marxist apostle Hugh Sykes Davies and then ran off with Charles Madge who later married the first wife of Stephen Spender.

But more important than their family connections was the old school tie. Our Age made a point of not wearing it – the Etonians excepted – and, as we shall see, turned against the public school ethos. But the tie was a cultural bond and anyone who reads the literary historian Valentine Cunningham's (see p. 50) account of the intellectuals in the thirties will see how many of the household names of Our Age went to the same school: seven at Winchester, three at Wellington, four at Lancing, three at Repton, eight at Gresham's Holt, five at Marlborough and fifteen at Eton. Cyril Connolly, Cecil Beaton, George Orwell and Gavin Maxwell were at the same prep school; Auden and Isherwood were at another; the novelists Anthony Powell and Henry Yorke at a third; Cecil Day Lewis and Basil Wright (the maker of documentary films) at a fourth. The experiences they shared at school were reinforced by their experiences at university.

This similarity of upbringing explains in part why, whether they became revolutionaries or conformists, they spoke in an unmistakable tone of voice. Auden's early poetry is full of schoolboy jokes and allusions. They dedicated their works to each other as if their clique was unique. That was why the culture of Our Age was to be pilloried by their successors as class-bound, arrogant, snobbish and chained to the public schools and Oxbridge, even when they were reacting against the class structure and its institutions. That was why Leavis denounced their works as coterie culture.

Those on the inside track were astonished when contemporaries who came up the hard way accused them of belonging to a gilded elite. Did not debates in the Union, graced by ministers speaking on the paper, partly exist to introduce young aspirants to those who had made it in politics? Was there anything sinister about your sixth-form master recommending you to the don who was to direct your studies and who had directed his? Four years later that don would write a testimonial of such solicitude on your behalf to the civil service commissioners, or to a publisher or some other concern, that only the most skilled recipient could guess by its omissions or elided compliments what feathers this swan was missing or what symptoms it showed of turning into a goose.

There was one trait that marked the difference between the youth of Our Age at Oxford and Cambridge and the youth of those in the fifties and sixties. The manners of Our Age were public school manners; and it was easier to be accepted if you adopted their manners, dressed like them, spoke with their accent and learnt their language and jokes. The grammar school boy who came up to sit for the scholarship exams with fountain pen clipped into his breast pocket, in school blazer or with the collar of his open-necked shirt worn outside the coat, would change the way he dressed in order to conform. If he learnt to adapt no one cared what school he had gone to. Brains and originality would always open doors. Grammar school boys found no difficulty in becoming dons. But in the fifties and sixties the scene changed. The manners of the grammar school boys became ascendant and the public school boys found themselves at a disadvantage. The grammar school boy was freer, more successful with girls, more self-confident and street-wise. The manners of LSE replaced those of the Christ Church peer and the Trinity flat cap. Too much should not be made of such trivia. Public and grammar school boys alike who despised upper-class manners could move into the world of Fabian summer schools or splinter groups of the left. There was the network of bookshops – Harold Monro's Poetry Bookshop, Collet's for progressives, shops off Charing Cross Road, Covent Garden and Clerkenwell, and premises where the *Daily Worker* was printed and the *New Statesman* edited. To clamber downwards was more exciting to numbers of Our Age than to scramble up. Bliss was it in that dawn of the thirties to run away from public school and arrive at the Parton Street Bookshop, where the anti-public school magazine *Out of Bounds* was published, there to confront the sweaty, white face of sixteen-year-old Esmond Romilly and to announce, 'I'm Toynbee of Rugby.'

But one half of Our Age found few ladders to help them climb. They were the women. Read the diaries of Chips Channon or Harold Nicolson or the memoirs of dozens of civil servants and dons, such as that of the outsiders from South Africa or Canada like Solly Zuckerman or Harry Ferns, and you can see how young men got on. But women had few helping hands. They made it by talent alone unless they had beauty as well as brains. In those days few fathers thought it was as natural for their daughters as for their sons to go to university. Or were willing to pay the fees. In the upper classes it was still thought odd for a girl to want a job let alone excel in a profession. In the middle classes the obstacles Arnold Bennett charted for Hilda Lessways still stood. Yet the women of Our Age were on the threshold of triumph. At the end of their era a range of jobs from the old stand-by of advertising to fashion, design, publishing, and above all public service were at last open to them. But it was the successors of Our Age who were the beneficiaries of the change.

3

MY GENERATION PLAYED its times in a minor key. We were not as original as our heroic predecessors before 1914. Our scientists and mathematicians were original. But not our philosophers, economists or visionaries. Perhaps it was impossible in so short a time for another revolution in mood and ideas to take place. We played variations on our predecessors' themes. Our Age produced no socialists comparable in invention and importance to Shaw, Wells, the Webbs and Tawney, no writers of the stature of T.S.Eliot or Joyce or D.H.Lawrence, no thinkers of the originality of Russell or Keynes.

We lived under the shadow of two movements that affected all Europe: modernism and collectivism. Modernism affected the way we regarded life and hence our literature and art. It was a movement that both admired and rejected science. English philosophers became engrossed by the discovery of exact truth and many intellectuals were convinced that we could improve the conditions under which we lived by applying the methods of science to social problems. At the same time philosophers declared there were large tracts of experience in which it was difficult, probably impossible, to say anything truthful. Modernism flooded into the estuary vacated by the retreating tide of orthodox theories. How could anyone say he was the master of his fate and the captain of his soul after Freud had analysed the unconscious? Modernism had begun as a destructive movement undermining the rules of academies, law courts and all forms of authority. The champions of irrationalism like the Dadaists did not much affect us and we were a little astonished in the sixties when at last, in very different forms, irrationality crossed the Channel. But the resounding disputes about modernist art and literature had one effect. They inspired us with the mission to transform philistine Britain into a country in which the arts were enjoyed and artists respected as in other European countries. George Steiner said he was amazed that we could have such simple faith in the healing power of art when the executioners in the concentration camps gassed Jews and yet enjoyed Beethoven. But the posthumous quartets or the septet Opus 20 are not agents of salvation. Great art expresses a vision of life and makes life more significant.

Every generation turns on its fathers; but the Great War, which most of Our Age considered was a war that could have been avoided and should have been stopped, made us preternaturally critical of what one of our number, Alan Taylor, called the Establishment – the network of people and institutions with power and influence who rule the country. Every activity breeds its own Establishment, the Jockey Club, the benchers of the Inns of Court, the General Council of the TUC; but whereas the committee of the MCC wields some influence over cricket, it does not contribute much to the government of the country. On the other hand those whom Montesquieu called *les grands décisionaires* do: the cabinet, the leading members of the Houses of Parliament, the judiciary, the leaders in the City of London and the Confederation of British Industry, and many of the chairmen – there must be thousands of them – of quangos, tribunals, professional bodies, welfare, cultural and educational organizations and the like. The Establishment is always willing to move things along a little, make small adjustments to the way things are run, but opposes major change. It has strong links, some would say is identical, with the *bien pensants* who regard themselves as the guardians of morality and manners.

But the Establishment is protean; it can change its shape. Under Labour governments the trade union bosses became more important and new faces appeared. Intellectuals are affronted if anyone suggests they belong to it, but quite a few do. As we grew up, however, there was no question that the following belonged to it, apart from the Sovereign, the royal family and the court: the editor of *The Times*; the director-general of the BBC and some other editors, publishers and media men; a few vice-chancellors, even the odd bishop. In particular it includes men and women who have held a multitude of public appointments during their lifetime.

Such a man, for instance, was Lionel Robbins. Ostensibly, Robbins was a professor at the LSE and an economist. In fact he was also chairman of the boards of the *Financial Times* and the National Gallery, and he sat on the boards of the Tate Gallery, the Royal Opera House and the Royal Economic Society. He served as president of the British Academy and was a life peer. Or consider Cyril Radcliffe, a lawyer who, without ever having been a puisne judge, was promoted direct to be a law lord. In the war he was director-general of the Ministry of Information and after it he was called in to determine the boundary line between India and Pakistan on partition and again in Cyprus; the chairman of two enquiries into taxation of profits and income; of the monetary and credit system: and of three enquiries into security. He was on the Court of the University of London and chairman of the British Museum trustees.

Though very different in temperament Robbins and Radcliffe had much in common. They were sagacious, believed themselves to be liberal, were in fact sound conservatives on most issues, were loyal to any institution with which they were connected and regarded those who criticized it as ignorant, malignant or ill-informed. Yet as they grew older it was inevitable that some of Our Age, like myself, who had fancied themselves as needlers of the Establishment, began to run institutions. Or they became executives, spoke as pundits, rose to the top of their profession; and in so doing found they had to speak for the profession or institution instead of solely for themselves. To their dismay they found themselves regarded as part of the Establishment. A few managed to escape the stigma of siding with Old Corruption. Jeremy Hutchinson, the finest advocate in his time at the criminal bar, after he took silk more often than not appeared for the accused and continued to strike terror into the hearts of police officers in the witness box. But even he, fearless in his criticism of judges, joined the chorus of outrage in the Inns of Court when it was proposed to reform the bar.

The Establishment is in part a journalist's myth. There is certainly no inner mafia manipulating affairs to its own advantage. Indeed the evidence suggested that management was not their forte. Nevertheless, a sizeable segment of my generation, even when they found themselves in the Establishment, revolted against its stuffiness and self-satisfaction. They regarded themselves as belonging to what Maurice Bowra called the Immoral Front. The adherents of the Immoral Front were in favour of extending personal liberty far further, and they were not deterred by the arguments that to lift this or that restriction would 'weaken society' or 'corrupt the young'. If someone said, 'People should be stopped from doing that' the Immoral Front insisted that authority should justify its laws and conventions. If the young wanted to demonstrate, or utter absurd views, or do disgusting and disobliging things, or make love with their own sex or in heaps, we might think they were idiotic or ill-mannered; but, if they were entitled to do so, we saw no reason to stop them; or if a law did exist to stop them we asked: was it wise and humane and on what grounds did society issue this prohibition? Frequently the grounds were slight. Perhaps it was because so many of us were aware of the advantages they started with in life that they were so hostile to the ethos of their elders.

We grew up under the shadow of collectivism. The left had no difficulty in believing that the state should intervene to promote the greater social justice: in the case of socialists state intervention was part of a coherent theory of politics concerning the ownership of the means of production and class conflict. But Conservatives, too, appealed to their history to justify some measure of state intervention – to the factory acts that curbed the mill-owners and protected the workers. The post-war Conservatives were keen to show they had taken to heart Disraeli's aphorism of the Two Nations. Conservative and Labour politicians had their differences about the extent of the free market and the method of state intervention. But both were consumed by the guilt that the war implanted in the West. America felt guilt about the blacks and the Continent about collaboration and the persecution of the Jews. Britain felt guilt about class. Conservatives felt guilt about their treatment of the miners and the harshness of the cuts in social benefits during the Depression. Labour felt guilt about their divisions in the inter-war years that led to the General Strike and the ineffectiveness of their opposition to Hitler. Both parties wanted to make the trade unions partners in government, both wanted to maintain full employment. Both agreed that palpable injustices and differences in the life chances of the well-to-do and of the poor could be diminished by public expenditure and redistributive taxation; and the agents to bring about change were the bureaucracies of central and local government under the control or their elected ministers and councillors.

The experience or memories of capitalism's cataclysm, the Depression of 1931, ate into our consciousness. We wanted a job that was secure. So government service, teaching and the professions were our first choice.

Satirical employers used to complain that those they interviewed did not ask what their prospects were but what their pension was likely to be. Collectivism seemed to be a way of making life safer for everyone and less susceptible to the roulette wheel of the market.

The will was suspect. Had not two of the sages we read, Shaw and E.M. Forster, told us that imposing one's will has disastrous effects? We were only too ready for the captains and the kings to depart: we had seen far too much of Great Men. We made an exception of Churchill: whatever his faults this great man was not pompous or censorious – indeed was all his life a rebel against the Establishment. Yes, leadership was needed but it should be exercised through persuasion and example. We did not neglect power. But we made the mistake of thinking it could always be tamed: surely reconciliation was always possible through trade-offs. The army was right to tell its officers that their first duty at the end of the day was to see their men got a hot meal; should not the upper classes and the managers concern themselves with the welfare of the manual workers? Yes, policies had to be formed, but not according to some ideology: we had had enough of ideologies in Nazi Germany and the Soviet Union. Time and again we quoted the mythical old don who told us that nothing we had learnt in our studies would be of the slightest use to us, but in acquiring this useless knowledge we had learnt, he hoped, to spot spurious arguments and specious charlatans. Conviction was a dubious blessing. 'Lord, I disbelieve,' wrote one of our gurus, E.M. Forster, praising Erasmus and Montaigne, 'help thou my unbelief.' Our Age were often sceptics, but self-confident sceptics.

Our belief in giving the greatest possible freedom to people in their private lives, and in the way they expressed that life through the arts, conflicted with our belief in the duty of the state intervening to prohibit factories being built in the heart of the countryside or to compel parents to send their children to school. The fact that this conflict existed confirmed us in our belief that men of good will must sit down together and work out sensible solutions to their problems. The brave new world was to be a pluralist world. People should acknowledge that there was no single model of belief and behaviour, such as that of the gentleman in bygone days. Freedom and tolerance demanded that each must find his own level and ideals. Tolerate rebels because they were quite likely to be the innovators of the next decade. Tolerate irreverence. It was a positive virtue to tweak the Establishment and keep it on the hop. In this way, so we hoped, the next generation would not fall into self-hatred as the young communists of the thirties had done.

We wanted all classes in society to enjoy what formerly had been the privileges of the rich. We rejoiced in the fifties as travel became cheaper and the package tour to Spain became a recognized mass holiday. We liked seeing clothes become less formal. We saw in the clothes the Teds wore in the fifties a sign of working-class independence. (They had forgotten the Edwardian Knuts.) Something of the contempt of the modernist movement for the routine of office and factory lingered on. Men and women were owed parties, leisure enjoyment by virtue of having to work; and one objective in one's work was to mix as much pleasure as possible with the job through the expense account or the discovery of an obligation to travel. And similarly there was a disinclination to take too severe a view of the Spanish practices among the workforce, overmanning and moonlighting: what were they but the analogue of directors' lunches and perks? But our generation was not composed solely of vulgar hedonists. They believed in spreading Arnold's sweetness and light. They thought that if the authorities supported the arts people would realize what intense joy the greatest works of man could bring to their lives. The cardinal virtue was no longer to love one's country. It was to feel compassion for one's fellow men and women.

These were some of the commonest *mentalités* of Our Age; and they were to look very different by the time we were bowing out. We were not spared by intellectuals in the next generation. We were regarded by some of them as bumptious and insolent: men who had far too high an opinion of their own abilities. We were so snobbish and conceited that we held the comfort and pleasures of others of no account when set beside the need to advertise our own superiority. Why should we have been so contemptuous of authority, why sneer at the police and head teachers? No wonder the dons were so upset and looked so ridiculous when their own authority was challenged in the seventies by student militants. How easy to write those self-satisfying letters to the press protesting against some breach of liberty in another country when we sat like budgerigars in our gilded cage secure against the injustices of the world. To such critics our conceit in presuming to lay down the law was breathtaking. Did we never consider how trivial and insignificant our world was? Waugh, Leavis and Oakeshott, each in his own tone of voice, taught our successors how to rough us up.

4

INTELLECTUALS DEFINE THE *mentalités* of a generation. And yet how can one speak of a common set of assumptions when intellectuals belong to so many different hostile tribes? Rationalists regarded appeals to tradition as obscurantist and arbitrary; technocrats applied the scientific method – statistical techniques, n-dimensional geometry and the theory of games – to solve social problems; marxists and structuralists maintained that the scientific method would not tell us how to analyse or change society; revolutionaries, the descendants of the Jacobins, regarded the world as a battlefield between good and evil and preferred to see the heavens fall rather than justice be cheated; populists distrusted the official culture taught in schools and believed ordinary people were wiser than the elites; the authoritarian intellectuals who regarded the free intellect to be the greatest danger to mankind: these were the descendants of Plato who would have censored poetry and executed atheists, or of Li-Tsu who wanted to burn all books. And to one side of the intellectuals stood bohemians and hippies who said people should opt out.

Indeed do generations really exist? Many professional historians doubt it. For them generations are too transient and ill-defined to be credible. Since babies are always being born and since the birthrate fluctuates, what justification is there for separating any particular cohort in the age group from its predecessors? Generations overlap: so to try and distinguish one from the other is fruitless. In that inspired essay, *Portrait of an Age*, G.M.Young reminded us that, at the height of what he called the Victorian noontide and W.L.Burn the age of equipoise, men were struck by religious doubt at the very time when the churches had found a new fervour and pews were filled; when liberalism appeared beyond challenge, socialism emerged to challenge and overtake it; when imperialism became a national policy, England's oldest colony Ireland broke into terrorist revolt. The fact that people write as if generations existed, they say, is no proof that they do. Once upon a time educated people believed in witchcraft.

And yet this sense of belonging to a particular peer group who share common assumptions about their own society, and who are convinced they are different from their fathers, never fails to fascinate men's minds. They discuss which goals in life are worth striving for, which ways of attaining those goals are despicable and which noble. Distinct and hallmarked, they feel themselves to be the apostles of a new age. Young men felt so in Europe after the French Revolution, and again in England in the 1830s at the time of the Oxford Movement, romanticism and philosophic radicalism. In Russia in the 1840s repression and despair begot the age of the 'superfluous men'. The generation in Britain, formed by popular culture in the 1960s, recognize each other at a glance: John Betjeman spotted that pop music had become the poetry of that generation. At such times the old are alarmed by the intensity of feeling among the young. Hannah More declared that the French Revolution had encouraged sons and daughters to adopt 'something of that spirit of independence and disdain of control which characterize the time', and she foretold that when the discussion of the rights of man at last palled, people would discuss the rights of women and then 'the rights of youth, the rights of children, the rights of babies'. The generation gap is no modern phenomenon. Gloucester in *King Lear* utters his lament: 'In cities, mutinies, in countries, discord, in palaces, treason; and the bond crack'd twixt son and father ... there's son against father ... there's father against child. We have seen the best of our time.'

Perhaps the best argument for believing that generations exist – despite the argument about witchcraft – is this. People have always thought they did. The Preacher in Ecclesiastes said 'One generation passeth away and another generation cometh.' And this is what Glaucus says when he encounters Diomede in battle on the plains of Troy and Diomede asks him who he is. 'Great son of Tydeus, why do you ask whom I sprang from? As the generations of leaves, so are the generations of men. The leaves are scattered by the wind on earth and the living wood brings other leaves to birth and the season of spring comes round again. So one generation of men flowers and another passes away.'

There are at least four models for writing the history of a generation. You can explain it in terms of the literature and art it creates. Or you can depict its political expression and conventions. Or you can study the behaviour of its members when they were young. Or you can plot its development by examining each cohort as it emerges from childhood, the education each receives and the jobs each chooses or fails to get.

I intend to tell the story of my generation in a different way. What did we revolt against and who helped us to form our beliefs? What events influenced us as we grew up? When we did grow up and were in a position to put those beliefs into practice, did we do so? Indeed when some of us entered the Establishment, how did we behave? The contribution we made to the intellectual life of the country concerns me. So too does our contribution to politics. All the more so since, as we began to bow out, we heard some of our number repudiate our assumptions, and we suffered the mortification of being blamed for the political and economic decline of our country.

5

AS I TELL the tale I hear once again the question: 'Yes, but who are *we*?' Lionel Trilling was once taken to task for referring to what 'we' thought or felt. He could hardly have meant, his critic said, Americans in general. What was his 'we' but 'a very narrow class consisting of New York intellectuals as judged by his brighter students in Columbia'?

In this book I am concerned almost wholly with the educated classes, what Coleridge called the clerisy – a different status group from an intelligentsia. The educated classes are certainly not confined to intellectuals. They include enlightened public servants, articulate businessmen, certainly some trade union leaders, politicians of all parties: people who reflect on life and relate their calling to other walks of life. I do not attempt to include all those born in the first quarter of this century. If they were to be included I should be writing a history of mid-twentieth-century Britain. In effect I concentrate on intellectuals, on those who formed opinion and those who tried to put those opinions into practice.

In the end the observations in this book are mine and I cannot claim they reflect the judgement of anyone other than myself. They would have been very different if they had been made by a sound supporter of any political party or by someone committed to all liberal and progressive causes. They cannot be criticism because I was not trained to be a literary critic, though I read the critics for edification much as our ancestors in the eighteenth and nineteenth centuries read sermons. I studied history; and the historian, if he judges at all, judges with different eyes and different criteria from the critic. Yet they cannot be history: history is written by those who have made a critical study of the sources. At times I mention my own experience, but this book is not a memoir. This book is the impression I as an individual have formed of the part of my own times that I know something about, and it has no other validity.

My impression is influenced by certain beliefs formed when I was an undergraduate at King's College Cambridge. I became fascinated by the struggles of medieval philosophers to reconcile the wisdom of the ancient world with theology. How could Aristotle's physics, and hence his theory of being, be reconciled with dogma about the nature of God? The Islamic teacher at Cordoba, Averroes, put forward a solution: there were two truths, philosophic truth and theological truth. The orthodox Christian schoolmen could not accept that this was so, and by a supreme effort of reasoning Aquinas managed to reconcile Aristotle with patristic and Platonic tradition: double truth was pronounced heretical. But then I studied another thinker who persuaded me that Averroes was right. Machiavelli showed that no statesman could rule and remain faithful to Christian virtues. Any ruler who did so would be defeated by other rulers or turned off his throne by his own subjects. The fact that Machiavelli went on to write a questionable 'Machiavellian' text book, *The Prince*, was irrelevant. It did not affect his great insight. He had shown that there was an irreconcilable conflict between two ways of life – the life of personal relations, the inner life in which we ask, 'How shall we live?'; and the life of politics, of getting and gaining, of using power to attain good ends, but ends that are public and not personal.

As undergraduates do, I found heroes. Machiavelli was one. Among the medievalists Occam was another. I caught the glint of his famous razor: don't invent concepts, terms, names, he said to me, in order to get round intellectual difficulties as second-rate sages do. My third hero was Hume. Hume told me we assume that certain convictions hold good because we could not live in a civilized manner unless they did; and that is why we often declare that they must be true. But they are not true. We can never prove something is valuable or right. It is in the end our desires, our 'passions' as Hume called the emotions, that guide our reason; and our reason obeys them. You cannot prove that men and women have natural rights, any more than you can prove that men will create a just society by following their own self-interest.

The way these matters are put has moved on since Hume. It may well be true that what we call knowledge is not true but a reflection of our own interests. But that is why, like Hume, we need to be sceptical, tolerant and practise detachment even if we cannot achieve it. That is why I have never believed in the beneficence of collectivism, or of individualism, or theories of rights or utility. But I am not sceptical of the value of reason. If challenged, I give reasons and ask if my challenger can give me better reasons to the contrary. Sometimes I am persuaded he can, sometimes not. For many years I have believed that good ends conflict: they do not always conflict because sometimes they can be reconciled. But more often than not they do. It is a vulgar error to argue that, if one does not believe in absolute moral principles, one is denying that good and evil, right and wrong, exist. Civilized human beings always acknowledge the existence of moral principles, and part of their claim to be civilized rests in their acknowledgement that these principles can change and have to be adjusted simply because good ends conflict. In politics an end that seems good today may turn out to be fatal to pursue a few years later. The English politician nearest, perhaps, to my heart (and our analogue to Rochefoucauld in literature) is Halifax the Trimmer. This was the man who fought the bill to exclude Charles II's brother James from the throne in bitter debates in Parliament with Shaftesbury's mob howling for his head – and was rewarded by his Sovereign's amused comment, 'Why, 'tis better than the play'; and then was foremost a few years later in sending for William of Orange when James's policies seemed to be leading to the establishment of a Catholic absolutist monarchy.

These are the explanations I offer for such conclusions as I come to about my generation. But I am part of it, I do not stand above it. I share most of its failings and few of its virtues. In my readers' orisons be all my sins remembered.

CHAPTER 2

The Insufferable Ideal

1

THE IDEAL THAT Our Age was taught to admire when they were children was the ideal of the English gentleman. The ideal of those pre-1914 days has been caricatured for so long, and sometimes so amusingly, that one forgets this was the ethos that Churchill invoked in 1940. It went back to the eighteenth century. Wellington embodied it, Waterloo exhibited it. According to this code an Englishman should be guided by an overpowering sense of civic duty and diligence. Every man's first loyalty should be to the country of his birth and the institution in which he served. Loyalty to institutions came before loyalty to people. Individuals should sacrifice their careers, their family, and certainly their personal happiness or whims, to the regiment, the college, the school, the services, the ministry, the profession or the firm. Service was an acknowledgement that there are other communities or territories which it was now the duty of the British to rule. Ruling other men and other races did not mean discovering and complying with their wishes. Their wishes would almost certainly be self-interested pleas for ephemeral ends often a mask for the duplicity of would-be politicians, demagogues and agitators. While the rest of the world feared the will to power that was behind the missionary force of the Empire, the British, whose administrators exported the life of the motherland in their clothes, their food, their sport and pipe-smoking, could never be brought to admit they were in danger. They were indignant when told that they exploited idealistic movements such as anti-slavery and Zionism as ways of getting others to do their work for them, or that they betrayed idealists such as E.D.Morel in the Belgian Congo or T.E.Lawrence in Arabia. Plutarch gave them examples of the type to admire: Lycurgus rather than Pericles, Julius Caesar rather than Pompey or Brutus; never Cleon or Catiline.

The gentleman was someone who developed his latent qualities by engaging in gentlemanly pursuits. An officer acquired an eye for country by riding to hounds, and thus learnt the art of moving his infantry platoon into dead ground to hide them from the enemy. Provided he excelled as a sportsman and played games fearlessly, his men would follow him anywhere. At Waterloo, officers courted danger to encourage their men in much the same way as naval officers at Trafalgar strolled up and down the quarterdeck regardless of sharpshooters or grapeshot. In the early days both of the Boer War and the Great War to take cover was thought to be a bit iffy. A gentleman disguised his abilities as much as he disguised his emotions: not to do so was to show side and drop one's guard. When Tony Chenevix Trench, later a public school headmaster, emerged from a Japanese prisoner of war camp, he was greeted by his brother with the words, 'Oh, I didn't expect to find you alive.' The key to recognition was good manners – unceremonious, relaxed behaviour designed to put friends at ease. The temptation to intellectualize about one's calling was unwise and people who had theories needed to be watched. To reduce tradition and custom to dry principles, to become too reliant on technology, was to forget that character was more important than hare-brained schemes. Men should be judged by their conduct rather than their ideas. Mark Antony was an example of self-indulgence and that weakness of character which tempts a man to desert duty for pleasure. Women were a potential snare and they should be treated warily. But good women were romantic objects and, because they were good, could be treated as such. The young were full of good stuff but callow. They would be all the better for being snubbed and put in their place.

People wanted to show that they too knew what leisure pursuits to follow, what manners to copy. This was how others could recognize that you were incorporated within society. Perhaps it is not going too far to say that a man and his family came to be regarded as citizens by the degree to which they were able to conform to the code of the governing class and to the part of the country they belonged. Before 1914 you had to assimilate as far as your means allowed to the governing class's way of life to be received within the social pale. Servants indicated status, and it is astonishing how many of those with modest incomes and jobs had servants until one remembers that kitchen ranges, coal fires instead of central heating, the copper instead of a washing machine, created so much work that there was a real inducement to economize on consumer goods and employ servants. A housemaid needed to be paid only thirty pounds a year. Clothes no less than servants were the clue to your social standing. A hat was a symbol of being socialized. That was one reason why even the poorest wore one: they were staking a claim to being a citizen even if they had no vote. Only the self-confident could neglect the requirements of fashion, like the Cecils who dressed in shapeless garments or the intellectuals who climbed mountains and communed with nature on thirty-mile walks. Invited in 1929 to Bicton for a country house party, Alan Pryce-Jones, twenty-one years old and impecunious, descended for dinner wearing a black tie to find the other men wearing tail coats. 'Which footman have you got?' asked his uncle and host when he apologized. 'It is not the fault of the footman,' he replied, 'I haven't brought a white tie.' Putting a hand on his shoulder, his host proposed the only remedy.

'My dear fellow, sack your man.' He was not invited again.

Many were the foreigners who analysed the cult of the gentleman. One of the more astute, Wilhelm Dibelius writing after the Great War, was struck by how Britain was both highly individualized and highly socialized. British historians saw their country's history as the lives of its great men; British journalists did not write *exposés*, they interviewed people; British novels were about personalities; their elections were contests between people; even their wars were fought not against other nations but against Napoleon or the Kaiser. Beneath the surface seethed curious passions that sometimes overflowed into their literature and art or into sentimentalism for criminals, animals or revolutionaries abroad. But this sentimentalism was kept in check by their institutions. The public schools frowned on Blake, Byron, Shelley and Swinburne. The British were not governed by objective codes. There was no code of honour safeguarded by the duel: only strict libel laws. There was no legal code: jurisprudence was despised. In their law courts counsel conducted the case, not the judge. The judge was interested solely in guilt or innocence, not in the truth; and justice was impartial but class-ridden.

Many were the writers who praised the ideal of the gentleman. The mass of Victorian authors, whose novels were serialized in the periodicals, such as Charlotte Yonge or Wilkie Collins, Kingsley, Le Fanu, Ouida, the great George Eliot herself, were portraying gentlemanliness, whatever other themes they had in mind. Even Henry James, who found the stereotype inadequate, tried to redefine it and suggest a new degree of sensitivity. Shirley Letwin maintained this was the theme that fascinated Trollope who explored it throughout his novels. Perhaps his most perfect gentleman was a woman. Madame Max Goesler refused to marry the old Duke of Omnium not because his family would oppose it, nor even because she was not in love. She refused the duke because he would not have chosen her in his younger days and to accept him now would be to take advantage of the weakness of his old age. She would lose her self-respect. Whether Phineas Finn was a true gentleman was a nice question – he was certainly not a true lover and lacked 'something in individuality and was accordingly too much a friend to everybody'. What saves him is his honesty, his refusal to break a promise. He stands by what he said in the heat of a political argument about Irish tenant right even though he knows it would lose him office; and he marries his childhood sweetheart even if it means ending his parliamentary career. Marriages of convenience are not evil; they often work. Those that do not work fail because the husband or wife determines to dominate and hence insult the other's individuality; Mrs Proudie is determined to become the bishop herself. Flirting is one of a gentleman's joys in life; but neither party should get infatuated. Men and women should stand up for themselves in love, and love means sex – the lovers in *Framley Parsonage* 'longed for each other and they were not ashamed to say so'. But promiscuity or jealousy are vulgar aberrations.

Like Dickens, Trollope thought that making money and decent ambition in life were desirable: his gentry and clergy talk money all the time. His crooked financiers were guilty not because they pursued wealth but because they overrode the law and morality. But if a gentleman goes in for politics he should not act the prig when he finds he has to bribe his electors. Compromise and dissimulation are part of the game. You stand by your leader even if you don't like him because personal likes or dislikes should be beneath a gentleman in politics. It is ignoble to claim you are a fly caught in the wheel of history or whine that you had a hard upbringing. Nor is it corrupt to show deference to rank and position. No doubt there are plenty of silly, vain and pompous aristocrats in Trollope's pages but formal differences in society will always exist. The deference a scientist might show to a Nobel Prize winner or a journalist to his editor is no more than tribute to sagacity and know-how. Social distinctions are not barriers, they are signposts which can be disregarded for good cause; but in a country which had no signposts it would be hard to find one's way.

There were other virtues that the true gentleman required. He should not be too spontaneous in his conduct. That virtue which Castiglione had so admired had become suspect. Like a game fox a man should run straight. Predictability was a virtue. To strain to be original was a sign of side, conceit, vanity and showing off. To be determined to distinguish oneself from one's fellows was considered disagreeable. A dandy could get by, an aesthete was fishy. Of course, the notion of the gentleman was bound up with social status: indeed it held within it the assumption that a gentleman was responsible for others, for his tenants, the soldiers under his command, his flock in the parish, his servants: but only rarely the hands in his mill. He would command, but off-duty he would be courteous.

In his entertaining book on the subject Philip Mason maintains that Protestant Christianity set so impossibly high a standard of conduct that the cult of the gentleman had to be substituted to provide a realizable ideal. There has to be a place for the scholar gentleman, the officer gentleman and the sporting gentleman as well as for the Christian gentleman. But Dibelius thought the English had overcome this difficulty by socializing religion. Whereas German Protestants put sincerity first and tried to overcome worldliness by piety, English Protestants put good habits before piety and church organization before dogma and spiritual issues. It is true that the British considered their toleration of religious differences as yet another example of the superiority of British over continental life. No *Kulturkampf* here or political division between free thinkers and *croyants*. But religion reflected social differences. Relations between church and chapel were not all that cordial and their antagonism plagued national education. Apart from the old recusant families, Roman Catholics were regarded with suspicion and, since most of them were penniless Irish immigrants, as dishonest and dirty. Too many distinguished men and women were agnostics or sceptics for them to be ostracized, but many posts in official and semi-official life were expected to be filled by communicating members of the Church of England.

Among the differences between the years before the Great War, and the years after 1945, was one not often noted. Intellectuals then counted for little. It was not that men of intellect were divorced from politics. Gladstone kept up with classical and theological scholarship, Balfour was the author of a philosophical work and there were other prime ministers, Rosebery and Asquith, who were well read. Victorian life seems peopled with sages, theologians, scientists, editors, philosophers, economists and learned men. But their direct influence on current affairs was limited and it was not they but the upper-class politicians, administrators and servants of the state who set the agenda. When Our Age was growing up the ruling class ignored the intellectuals. Baldwin, Chamberlain, Simon, MacDonald and Snowden were impervious to the change of mood after 1918.

Most of the educated classes were not disaffected. They were accepted as gentlemen. Most of the dons before 1914 were conservative by inclination and even the radicals were anchored in the security of their fellowship. The welfare economist A.C.Pigou was at home in the post-1906 Liberal Party. G.M.Trevelyan believed that radicalism should be bracing: his copies of Hardy's poetry were scored with sardonic exclamations deploring the poet's lack of manliness – Meredith was a better tonic. The Edwardian dons had got what English intellectuals usually want, security of tenure in a prestigious institution at Oxford or Cambridge or in the universities at London or Manchester; and by the reforms of the seventies and eighties they could now marry and need not take holy orders. Science, engineering, economics and history came into the curriculum. Even after the Great War posts were few and fine scholars often had to teach in the public and grammar schools. But for those who studied the humanities there was always the world of letters and publishing as an alternative. The intellectuals had no need to become republicans or reject parliamentary government or identify with some revolutionary or dissident body, still less with the working class.

The new educated classes of the left, Hobson, Hobhouse, Gilbert Murray, the Hammonds, Graham Wallas, Nevinson and H.W.Massingham were reformers. Nothing gave H.G.Wells greater pleasure than to cheek the upper classes, but in 1914 both he and Shaw supported the British declaration of war. Parents, teachers, managers and foremen, above all the older generation, were vested with an authority and respect that would be regarded as astonishing today. After all, Britain had not yet become a mass society. Large parts of the population had still to be incorporated into it. Before 1918 no woman had the vote and universal male suffrage was still a novelty. The welfare state was in its infancy and much scorned. Too many of the ruling class still considered workers as objects whom they had to take into account, 'hands' to be laid off or taken on but for whom they were not responsible. Only Bohemians or the descendants of the Victorian magsmen, macers and gonophs, the outcasts, vagabonds and street-dealers whom Mayhew described in his famous book on the London poor, rejected the society into which they were born. Our Age were told time and again by their elders that life was serene. Their elders boasted that Britain was not threatened with revolution as the French had been in 1871, nor had they seen their sovereign assassinated as the Russians had seen Alexander II. They knew they were the richest nation in the world. Apart from the concert of Europe, who else existed? Only the United States and Japan. The feeble states of South America or Turkey, the sick man of Europe, did not really count. China and Persia were fiefs and the rest of the world was divided among the Europeans.

The serenity was misplaced. Astute observers at home warned that Britain was losing its industrial supremacy and was indifferent to its ill-educated population. Acute observers abroad declared that the solidarity of British life was an illusion. The American historian Brooks Adams (brother of Henry) forecast the departure of Britain from the historical stage. The steel production of the United States and Germany was overtaking that of Britain; and the Boer War had revealed Britain's inefficiency as a world power. Conrad heard the tumult beneath the surface of that thin crust men called civilization – the anarchist world of the secret agent or of Henry James's Hyacinth Robinson. But there was one writer in particular who was aware how thin the crust was and who redefined the gentlemanly ethos, and it was often through his eyes that Our Age was told to admire it. That was Kipling.

Kipling wanted his generation to recall how much the gentleman owed to society. He valued the independence of the individual – as an artist how could he not? But the individual left on his own, isolated and lonely, disintegrated. Particularly in India where men and their wives died young, where to take one's work seriously could end in madness because government, unlike in England, never achieved results. What prevented such a society from going over the precipice? Kipling answered: religion, law, custom, convention, morality – the forces of social control – which imposed upon individuals certain rules which they broke at their peril. Conventions enabled men to retain their self-respect and even to live together under appalling circumstances. Those who break the conventions must be punished. Numbers of Kipling's stories contain scenes in which the individualist, the eccentric, the man who offends against the trivial rules of the club, are tarred and feathered with gleeful brutality. If the offender is not brought to heel, society will suffer. It is not worth spending much effort, Kipling thought, debating whether the customs, morality and religion of the place you live in are right or wrong.

His contemporary, the anthropologist James Frazer, was informing the learned public that religion and magic were a kind of primitive science which would vanish as scientific knowledge spread; but for Kipling, as for Max Weber, religion was a social fact.

These forces of social control, as Kipling admitted, were harsh. The harshness could be alleviated by belonging to in-groups. These in-groups protect the individual, give him privacy, identity and self-confidence. They are the family, the school and the craft or profession you follow. These in-groups, too, teach us our place. We all need a course of indoctrination to find our place and, if we have come up in the world, to be taught it. But when the individual has proved himself in his in-group, and so long as he is not in the strict sense of the word an eccentric, then the more daring his behaviour and the more abundant his action, the greater is the addition of joy in the world. Stalky was the prototype of this socialized individualism. He acted beyond the formal law of school or army regulations and possessed the gift of seeing himself from the outside in relation to society. In Kipling's world action revitalized man. That was the obverse of the suffering it caused. And suffering was inevitable. Political action is often not a choice between good and evil but between lesser and greater evil.

Social realities interested Kipling. The liberal pictures man as choosing goals to pursue and asks whether or not he is free to pursue them. Kipling thought that men and women were forced to accept those goals which their group or clan in society chose for them and only when they had accepted these constraints were they free to exercise their individuality and take it for a trot. He is not unlike Durkheim who saw the individual as a bolt which might snap if the nut of society held it too tightly, or by being too loose allowed it to vibrate. Excessive integration as in the officer caste in the army could be as dangerous as imperfect integration.

Brought up in a society untouched for generations by civil wars, revolution or economic disaster, Kipling's English contemporaries were never compelled to consider why society still continues to hang together. But in India Kipling was forced to consider it. He believed that man achieves happiness when he comprehends where he himself fits into the scheme of things. He has to realize that spring cannot for ever be spring and that winter succeeds autumn. Since men continue to nurse illusions they must be taught the terms on which they are allowed to rise. Subject the upstart, therefore, to a course of indoctrination to bring his ambition within bounds and turn his children into gentlemen. Whereas for most of the greatest writers society, with its rules, conventions, customs, morality and taboos surrounding the sacred, is the enemy and their characters in fiction are depicted as locked in heroic combat with them, for Kipling they are a *donnée* with which mankind has to come to terms or perish.

Kipling therefore defined a gentleman differently from Trollope. His gentleman has come down in the world, is harsher, more meagre, with fewer graces and more limitations. The gentleman has now become the manager, the colonial administrator, the engineer and the skilled worker. You feel his gentleman is more beleaguered. He is threatened from above by the politicians, threatened from below by the lower orders who now have the vote, and threatened by the new barbarians in Europe. In the fable of England he wrote for his children Kipling scanned the future with anxious eyes. Would the wall of British civilization fall again before the democratic hordes of little men and the barbarians, the Prussian Winged Hats? Were not the younger rulers like Churchill tainted by the same ambition that made Roman generals overthrow the emperor? Were not the financiers manipulating trade and industry to their own ends, were not luxury and wealth corrupting the ruling class and turning their children into flannelled fools at the wicket? What would be England's fate – an England rent by class warfare and in a few years' time to be meditating civil war in Ireland? Other writers were also scanning the future. *Heartbreak House*, *Howards End* and *Puck of Pook's Hill* are meditations of a socialist, a liberal and a conservative, troubled by England's destiny.

2

IDEAL TYPES ARE nearly always in real life debased. The nuances, the distinctions, which make the ideal noble or desirable get worn down or neglected, and people turn against the crude stereotype in disgust. One way of seeing how the ideal got distorted is to read popular fiction which consists of stereotypes; and in the case of the gentlemanly ideal this means reading the works of those writers who created what Richard Usborne called Clubland Heroes.

No one debased Kipling's code of the gentleman more doggedly than Sapper. H.C.McNeile purloined his plots from Kipling and Conan Doyle and even so ran out of material as the yarns repeat themselves; his characters were stereotypes, the tone facetious, but his vitality and self-assurance are undeniable. Throughout his early war stories (*Sergeant Cassidy*, *Shorty Bill*, *Jim Brent*, *No Man's Land*), written in praise of the courage and humour of the infantry, ran that theme dear to the hearts of Kipling's generation. The army disciplines brash young officers to put the regiment before themselves and trains gormless clerks and men from the lower classes to behave like the Breed. Looking in August 1914 at a gaggle of Knuts and their girls on the seafront 'in very tight trousers and very yellow shoes with suits obviously bought off the peg who wandered about with ladies of striking appearance', a regular officer embarking at Folkestone for active service in France says, 'I wonder if we are looking at the passing of the breed.' But such gloomy thoughts are dispelled: after the war 'the duke and the labourer will have stood side by side and will have found one another men. No longer self the only thing: no longer a ceaseless grouse against everybody and everything: no longer an instinctive suspicion of the man one rung up the ladder.' There will be joy for those who return to the women who have endured more than the men; and there will be for a woman whose man did not return the knowledge that 'he was glad to pay that final price and is waiting for you – waiting with a trusty band of friends, happy, contented and proud'.

Sapper's fame rested on his Bulldog Drummond books, but it is in his short stories that one sees what he believed a gentleman to be. A gentleman was lean, fit, and had a head of iron for alcohol. He can spot a card-sharper in an instant because he had made himself a master at that art the better to frustrate crooks. He can also spot a young man who looks, and indeed may be, a fine specimen of the Breed, but who has a yellow streak. Good looks can conceal that weakness. Sapper's heroes are cheerful and ugly, 'only his eyes themselves deep-set and steady . . . redeemed Drummond's face from being what is known in the vernacular as the Frozen Limit'. Jack Delawney was a good-looking boy but his best friend Jerry Dixon recognized that he had a yellow streak and when he wavered about going over the top in Flanders Jerry had to shoot him dead. As a gentleman, Dixon felt he could not then marry Jack's sister. Desmond Brooke had 'brains, money, charm and tact' and would be elected to Parliament, but when the horse in the dogcart bolted he showed the yellow streak and jumped out leaving his girl to be rescued and marry the bumbling, freckled, silly chump, Stubby.

A gentleman suspects anyone who knows about art, music or literature. He plays cricket, is scratch at golf and has a fine seat on a horse. If a girl misjudges you, never enlighten her. Your friends may say, 'You damned quixotic fool', but until she says, 'What a blind little fool I was', a gentleman is in honour bound to let her think the worst: let her continue to believe you are a gaol-bird or that you made her wastrel husband drunk to lower him in her eyes. If you have a job in the City, you make it plain that you spend the hours drawing on the blotting paper. If someone asks what Jim Maitland does, he is told, 'Why, man, he lives. He lives: he doesn't vegetate like nine out of ten of us have to. He never forgives and never forgets.' A manly tear may rise to the eye only to be suppressed by loud blowing of the nose, for emotion and intimacy are dangerous and unwise. Did not Kipling write, 'If neither foes nor loving friends can hurt you, / If all men count with you but none too much'? And does not Sapper write, 'Like most of us he detested being called by his Christian name promiscuously'?

A gentleman of the Breed knows the infallible signs of the right sort of girl. 'Drummond glanced at her feet . . . being an old stager; she was perfectly shod.' The best girls are 'white (or pure gold) . . . clean through' and are called Joan Barstairs, Sylvia Clavering, Joan Prettyman, Sylvaine Lankaster, Sybil Deering. Denise Morgan was 'the very incarnation of sweet girlhood'. A gentleman should display a keen interest in such girls and say about the one he is determined to marry, 'All I know is that she looked as if the sun had come from heaven and kissed her and had then gone back again satisfied with his work.' But he would never dream of seducing a virgin or looking at another man's wife unless she was married to a sadistic wrong 'un. There is a right way and a wrong way to woo, and a gentleman only woos the right sort. Young Thompson, who is so disliked by the mess that he is made to face a subaltern's court martial, 'poodle-fakes to excess with the wrong people which, for the benefit of the uninitiated, may be interpreted as implying that he consumed buns to excess in the boudoirs of dubious females'.

Girls who are topping or absolute fizzers are not vapid. They spar with their men, keep their manners in order and can go beagling mile after mile. The line between permissible and outrageous conduct in fizzing girls is certainly narrow. Madge Saunderson bets the air-ace Captain Seymour VC six pairs of gloves to five hundred of his special cigarettes that he won't climb a smokestack. She does so in order to prove that Peter Benton has got a yellow streak and won't dare to rescue him when he pretends to have vertigo. But the pretence becomes reality and Benton has to climb the stack to rescue Seymour. For such conduct the famous surgeon tells Madge she ought to be publicly horse-whipped through the streets of London. (Did Sapper have Lady Diana Manners in mind and the death of Sir Denis Anson, drowned in the Thames on a boat party for a dare? She was not at all like a topping fizzer.) On the other hand, it is in order for Molly Tremayne or Molly Gollanfield to make their horses bolt on purpose to test their men. For a time it is feared each in rescuing his girl has broken his back, but no; both girls marry their men and the knowing forgive them. The line between Madge and the two Mollys seems a bit hard to draw. A gentleman will always be courteous, whatever the woman's reputation. Drummond is gallant with Carl Peterson's delectable mistress, Irma; though a foreigner, she had a sense of humour. But a gentleman will refer to women who are 'rotten to the core' as 'a terrific chutney' – women like the Comtesse de Gramont who had a predilection for captivating young men, married or not.

In recent years Bulldog Drummond has been called hard names, fascist among them, and the educated classes have recoiled from the Black Gang's propensity to beat up and kidnap communist trade unionists (though it is true that in the immediate post-1918 years first Chicherin, and later the Comintern, were indeed trying to promote sedition and industrial unrest). But Sapper's characters reveal how the gentlemanly ideal is being interpreted in the heartland of the middle classes. For with all his chatter to duchesses about slaughtering birds up north and dropping in for tea at the Carlton, Drummond by the mid-1920s can no longer have any pretensions to be considered upper class. He had revealed what class he really belongs to by joining the Ancient Order of Frothblowers and singing their anthem. Indeed he represents that special status group in the suburbs of the twenties, the dedicated motorist, consisting partly of demobilized officers who ran their own garages and spent the evenings driving to a road house on the new arterial roads to monitor the performance of a super-charged, drop-head coupé or comparing the merits of Delages and Sunbeams with eight-cylinder Marmons.

Richard Usborne chose another writer John Buchan, who had a more reputable pretension to describe the manners of the governing classes, as it was beyond doubt that he joined them. All his gentlemen have something in common. Each is a success. Buchan peopled a world in which everyone glows in the pursuit of public success. He makes a point of telling you just how many runs each man has scored in the long-playing cricket match called life in which men establish their reputation. Medina was the 'best shot after his Majesty' in England; an explorer had 'mushed and tramped over most of the Arctic and there are heaps of mountains and wild beasts named after him'; there was another of whom 'few men were his equal in classical scholarship'. Sandy Arbuthnot was 'one of the two or three most intelligent people in the world'. Even the minor characters are labelled by their achievements: 'seriously spoken of for India', 'the richest man in the world'. In a fine essay Gertrude Himmelfarb defended Buchan by reminding us that he admitted there was a price to be paid for success. His characters suffer from introspection and self-doubt: revolutionaries falter in their attempts to overthrow law and order, leaders question their ability to lead, 'fatigue and lassitude' overcome his gentlemen: they recover only when they toughen themselves by physical hardship on mountain and moor. However, unlike Sapper's characters, Buchan's heroes and villains lie dead upon the page and the best way to see what he contributed to the gentlemanly ideal is to look at his life.

Since the Act of Union Scotsmen of brains and push turned their backs on the unattractive side of Scots life, the mawkish, rhetorical, self-righteous, unctuous society, pilloried in literature from Holy Willie's prayer to *The House with the Green Shutters*. They sought their fortune in England, the Empire or America. Their parents and teachers kept an eye on them to see they did not assimilate too smoothly to English ways; but they were proud that in their country a man could be seen to rise by his merits and not by his birth. To seek success was part of the national myth. Buchan simply set out to be successful in the classic Scots way.

First move. Educated at a fine Glasgow grammar school, Buchan enters the university there at seventeen. In his first term he goes up to Gilbert Murray at the end of his lecture and asks what Latin translation of Democritus was used by Francis Bacon; he would like to know because he is preparing an edition of Bacon's essays. Shrewd. On to Oxford with glowing testimonials from Murray where he keeps himself by his writing as much as by winning prizes and scholarships. The publisher, John Lane, makes him his literary adviser and, already in *Who's Who* giving his profession as 'under-graduate', he ends with a first in Greats, many useful upper-class friends and the entrée to great houses and London society. Then off to South Africa after the Boer

War to join Milner's kindergarten of dashing young administrators engaged in the pacification of the country. Having broken into the world of affairs he marries on his return a Grosvenor. Fails to wangle a job under Cromer in Egypt. Friends worried that he won't declare himself for one or other political party: finally plumps for the Tories. In the Great War becomes director of propaganda. Fails to get a knighthood. Bestsellers pour out at the rate of one a year, romances with imperial settings and of secret service doings. Soon he is in Parliament representing the Scottish universities. Becomes an intimate friend of Baldwin and later, in the days of the National Government of Ramsay MacDonald, fails to get into the cabinet or even a ministry. Turns to writing biographies and historical works. Sends sons to Eton. Represents the Sovereign as high commissioner of the General Assembly of the Church of Scotland. Asked in 1935 to perform in similar style as governor-general in Canada. Mackenzie King wants him to come as a commoner, but Buchan writes 'an immediate peerage might revive mother'. It revives him. Much liked in Canada, supports appeasement, writes autobiography in which he says: 'I never went to school in the conventional sense for a boarding school was beyond the narrow means of my family.' A martyr all his life to an ulcer. Dies of a stroke on eve of his return home in 1940.

What went wrong? The gentlemen of the Establishment are cold-hearted judges of men. 'How do you handicap him?' is the phrase used when they want to sum up a man's usefulness. The phrase is characteristic of the contempt by men of the world for genuine personal relations. Buchan was far abler than many of those who got office, he had wider sympathies and put into words most effectively the kind of generous, imperial vision which many Conservatives imagined inspired them. Unlike Sapper he did not despise the intellect, but in his view a man should get his first without visible effort and he would be wise to have no truck with modernism. Like Sapper he did not hide in his books his distrust of Jews or contempt for blacks. But Conservatives don't like literary gents. In wartime they put them in charge of propaganda – Duff Cooper was to follow in Buchan's footsteps – and in peace they are suspect even when, like Buchan, they flatter them by romanticizing their kind of politics. It was not that he was too liberal for them, or never acquired the House of Commons manner. He simply wasn't their kind of man. But he could be of use as a front man, and that was what they made him. When Leo Amery said that Buchan was not really interested in politics, he meant that Buchan had not the talent for the real work in Parliament – the pursuit of a line of policy and the determination to convince others that this is the line to follow. Just as Richard Hannay was always willing for Blenkiron or Sandy to give him orders, Buchan wanted to work for others. Thus when the Tory knights looked at Buchan in the paddock and marked their card, they gave him few points for toughness and even fewer for the talent of practising politics and getting what he wanted. Apprenticeship under Milner in South Africa was a poor training for British politics. It was colonial administration; little negotiating skill was needed. In Parliament Buchan was not even an influence. His real role was to be that of the confidant and hand-holder of his chief and of his fellow Scot, MacDonald. He made MacDonald feel happier.

But there was in him a profounder weakness. The great romantic artists of the nineteenth century discovered new truths about personality and the nature of life. Buchan's romanticism was a device which enabled him to evade truth: it was a cocoon of words and ideas which insulated him from the world that intrigued him so greatly. This would have surprised him. His novels are full of characters drawn from life. Richard Hannay was based on Ironside, who rose to be Chief of the Imperial General Staff; Sandy Arbuthnot was a portrait of the improbable Aubrey Herbert and later of the scarcely less probable T.E.Lawrence. But Buchan's yarns are full of sentences which mean practically nothing. The Kaiser is described as 'a human being ... who had the power of laying himself alongside other men'. The wicked Medina is 'a god from a lost world'. The modern girl is 'a crude Artemis but her feet were on the hills'. The villainess, Hilda von Einem, 'mad and bad she might be but she was always great'. His villains have to be more than wicked: they have to be the personification of evil, dark forces, masters of diabolic mechanisms. He was appalled by Henry VIII's ruthlessness. Nevertheless he said he 'could not blind himself to his power. Power of Mammon, power of Anti-Christ, power of the Devil maybe, but born to work mightily in the world.'

As a result when he had to make up his mind about someone who also worked mightily in the world and could certainly have been considered as a power of the Devil, he decided that Hitler was just 'tom-foolery'. Buchan's trouble was that he could not help looking on the bright side of life. All his friends were luminous swans, all his political colleagues were wise and sensible. The fact that he did not paint his villains irremediably black and confessed that his heroes had dark nights of the soul is hardly here nor there. His prose indicates a deep-seated revulsion from attempting to tell the truth. That was why all his generous impulses were vitiated – towards the unemployed and the unimportant, towards America, towards Zionism and Jewish causes despite the conventional upper-class anti-semitism in his books. He did not fawn on aristocrats but he could not resist the appeal of ancient titles. 'You have no idea of the bores we had to put up with,' said one of his sons, 'because their ancestors had fought at Crécy.' He understood much of what was wrong in English upper-class rule, so did Baldwin; but just as Baldwin was too indolent to try and change it, Buchan was gooey about it. No wonder the Tory knights thought so little of him. They were immune to flattery. Self-flattery was what they liked.

Buchan was imbued with another emotion with which the heart of the gentleman was supposed to throb: love and veneration for the Empire. The Empire was ever present in the mind of my generation as they grew up. The yarns they were given as pre-teenage presents, the history they were taught at school, the Wembley Exhibition, the Ottawa agreements, Empire Day itself were symbols of a reality. Half Britain's trade was with the Empire. So were two thirds of her overseas investments. The gentleman believed that Britain's imperial mission was Roman in its nobility. The Pax Britannica had ended generations of barbarous internecine fighting between tribes and sects. Slowly but surely the natives would be civilized. Other nations might mock Britain's hypocrisy; but the gentleman regarded that charge with the contempt it deserved. Were not the colonies ruled with a minimum of force? Indeed, the mandates accepted from the League of Nations at Versailles were more trouble than they were worth: but it was the duty of a great imperial power to shoulder these burdens. The word 'empire' was frequently coupled with the word 'heritage'. It was a sacred trust that children must learn to cherish. These English-speaking countries were nearer to our hearts and our interests than the jabbering European states. The dominions were shining examples of the imperial spirit. Had they not given their sons to die on Flanders fields, on Vimy Ridge and Gallipoli?

These sentiments were not in fact shared by the country. Politicians believed they were true and saw the Empire as vital to Britain's own security. The country had always been bored with the Empire: on this matter a gulf yawned between the mass of the population and the ruling class. There were few imperialists among us, even among the sons of politicians: though Julian, the son of a great imperialist, Leo Amery, was an exception. It was indeed the discrepancy between the romance of Empire and its practice that became a cliché in our mentality. High in their mythology of villains were Cecil Rhodes, General Dyer and others who in their eyes had tricked unsuspecting natives into parting with their own, or had mown down opposition and pleaded the higher dictates of preserving the peace.

3

THE GENTLEMANLY IDEAL always looks somewhat odd when it is contrasted with the way gentlemen behave. The life of London political circles or among the more vigorous of the gentry has in some respects not changed all that much in the past hundred years. There have always been fast, loose, raffish sets. At the turn of the century there were those in the shires who sat over their port drinking toasts to fucking and fox-hunting just as in London there was the Marlborough House set who expected their hostesses in country houses to know who was whose mistress and how to allocate bedrooms accordingly. The ever-entertaining topic of who is sleeping with whom still occupies the mess at Wellington or Knightsbridge Barracks as it delights the parties of the beau monde. In the nineteenth century the rows were more scandalous because the conventions were far stricter. When in 1876 the Prince of Wales' friend Lord Aylesford threatened to divorce his wife who intended to elope with the Marquess of Blandford, the Marquess's brother Lord Randolph Churchill rushed to his defence and tried to blackmail the prince by threatening to publish his innocent but flirtatious letters to Lady Aylesford. The prince called out Lord Randolph. In an insulting letter Churchill refused to fight. For eight years the prince, who had been his close friend, cut Churchill dead in public. No one could be sure whether the code was being extended or broken.

But there were fashionable sets which interpreted gentlemanly behaviour in other ways. There was the set which included the Lyttelton brothers, the Tennant sisters, the Wyndhams (brother and sister), Balfour, Brodrick, Curzon and Cust. The Souls found the philistinism of London society intolerable. Margot Tennant used to say that royalty called clever men prigs, clever women advanced, Liberals socialists, the uninteresting pleasant, and the interesting intriguers. Thanks to the Souls, said Lady Violet Bonham Carter, it was 'no longer smart to be exclusive or fashionable to be dull'. She considered the Souls to be 'unconventional but neither fast nor loose'. Instead of bridge they spent evenings playing party games and to turn a set of light verses became a desirable accomplishment. Serious discussion was not encouraged but the Souls set a fashion in being well read and able to quote from the poets. That tradition continued in the salons of Emerald Cunard and Sibil Colefax that Our Age visited. It was continued by Diana Cooper and Ann Fleming.

The Souls posed a problem for the gentlemanly ideal. How should a gentleman prize success? The younger set of Winston Churchill, F.E.Smith and Max Aitken were not ashamed to display ambition, and F.E.Smith told schoolboys at their speech days to seize life's glittering prizes. The gospel of success, the blue ribands of school and university life, the showmanship that went with achieving them, were to nauseate us. But others preached a more austere version of the gentlemanly code. There were aristocratic families who were as respectable as Victoria's court and unaffected in their Christian piety. The Cecils at Hatfield and the Woods in Yorkshire, both ardent High Church families, were not the only noble families which lived with sobriety and without ostentation. Behind them stood the legions of the respectable middle classes. Men of this persuasion regarded the young Winston Churchill and F.E.Smith as too much like buccaneers ready to lay athwart the vessels of weaker men and plunder them. No one could deny that Churchill was born a gentleman but many in the upper classes doubted whether he was one. He was too ambitious, too vehement, too given to self-advertisement, too intoxicated by words and grandiose schemes, too ready to change parties when he saw the wind set to blow that way. Such criticism overlooked Churchill's sense of history and breadth of vision, his fine patriotism, his instinct for the British people and their needs, his genuine comprehension of Britain's interests as a great power. But when Churchill was young – and long after those days – he was thought to be too ambitious and harum-scarum, to lack gravitas and virtu.

At no time was the antipathy between these two interpretations of the gentlemanly ideal more obvious than in 1922. Lloyd George's coalition cabinet was perhaps the most talented and formidable in this century, even remembering the Wilson cabinet of 1966. Why then did Bonar Law and the Conservatives decide to bring it down? And why a few months later when Bonar Law, stricken with cancer, resigned was Baldwin rather than Curzon asked by the King to succeed him? There were many reasons, but one surely was that in the view of respectable upper and middle-class opinion the country was being governed in an ungentlemanly way. Should the prime minister sell peerages, baronetcies and knighthoods on such a scale and according to such a precise tariff as Lloyd George had done? And should he pocket the proceeds on the grounds that he needed a personal fighting fund for the forthcoming general election? No wonder brokers such as Maundy Gregory sprang up and claimed that for a commission he could obtain such honours. Brilliant as the lord chancellor might be in reforming the anachronistic land law, and negotiating peace in Ireland, was such an alcoholic fit to be the keeper of the King's conscience? Did one trust that Churchillian impetuousness which might have involved the country in war against Turkey? Did one want Max Beaverbrook dropping in at 10 Downing Street to discover which companies of non-ferrous metals had got concessions following the negotiations between the British and Australian governments and then coolly demand to telephone from No. 10 his brokers to profit from the information? That new *éminence grise* of the Conservative Party, John Davidson, private secretary first to Bonar Law and then to Baldwin, always refused to spend a night at Beaverbrook's country house. 'I didn't like the house or the way it was run,' he said. Davidson was determined to sweep away the cobwebs from the dirtier corners of the wizard's castle. When Lloyd George fell, Davidson proceeded to stop the sale of honours by penetrating Maundy Gregory's organization. He broke him, got him sent to prison and then provided a secret pension for the rest of Gregory's life provided he lived in France and kept his mouth shut.

Baldwin and Davidson came under fire from the old guard of their party who thought them soft on India and colonial government and softer still towards the trade unions during the General Strike. On both these issues they clashed with Churchill and defeated him. In fact Davidson was anything but soft towards socialism. He paid spies in the Labour Party, hired an official from MI5 to organize a Conservative Party intelligence service, raised hush money to damp down scandals in his own house and did what he could to set them alight among his Labour opponents. Lloyd George had scarcely bothered to hide his contempt for the King. But in Davidson's book no gentleman should slight the monarch, and he re-established good relations with the palace and the secret service. Naturally he was one of the first to suspect Mrs Simpson. Baldwin and Davidson revived Buchan's ideal of homespun honesty; but their smooth ruthlessness in dealing with their opponents was in the best traditions of Sapper.

In the early twentieth century, then, the gentlemanly ideal was looking somewhat moth-eaten. By then it was omitting too much of what is vital to human existence. It excluded the saints and idealists. It excluded those who dedicate themselves to some good cause – who are often the most fearful bores but are the salt of the earth. It was hostile to spontaneity. Spontaneity makes actions attractive because they are not calculated actions. Prudence is no doubt a Cardinal Virtue; but one can't help thinking that a world governed by her and her sisters, Temperance, Fortitude and Justice, would be dispiriting.

The political implications of the gentlemanly code also became clearer. There was much to be said for minimalist Whig rule or even for the tranquillity which Salisbury maintained after the duel between Gladstone and Disraeli. There was even more to be said for the respect for political liberty which made England a haven for refugees from European autocracies. But there was also a lot to be said against it. The gentlemanly habit of never moving to reform institutions, until it was impossible any longer to delay, left England by the end of the nineteenth century with the least adequate system of public education in western Europe, with universities far behind those of Germany and France, with sparse public support for the arts and scholarship, with an antiquated legal system, and with wretched provision for the poor.

So long as the poor are individuals with whom they speak face to face, gentlemen are at ease with them – far more so than intellectuals, because the gentlemen of those days were unembarrassed by their difference in status. But they became deeply embarrassed by the undifferentiated poor with their grinding problems caused by bad housing, bad upbringing, bad health, bad schooling. Nor did they much like those measures intended to give other classes or groups in society possibilities in life. The ladies Trollope admired denounced degrees for women, jobs for women, votes for women. The gentlemen he admired were ready to put down the irrepressible working-class boy or the outspoken son of a manufacturer who dared to criticize the traditional way of doing things. They thought of them as bounders disturbing the social arrangements which would continue to serve the nation well, regardless of the fact that the terms of trade for England were changing.

The gentlemanly code rested on a sense of superiority, at its best unostentatious and delightful in expression, but unshakeable. Moderate though their abilities were they judged others by their superficial manners of speech, accent or dress. There was something insufferable in maintaining that whate'er is best administered is best when those who maintain it have not much talent for administration. People began to question their right to govern because so few of them had acquired the art through the rough and tumble of managerial or entrepreneurial life. It was not so much that gentlemen governed, as every group must, in their own interest. Not even, as every group does, that they convinced themselves their own interest was identical with the interests of the country. It was that with such a deep scepticism of 'ideals' they had no criterion of action other than abiding by time-honoured practices that were becoming obsolete in their fathers' time. That was why the new ideas of Lloyd George liberalism or Fabian socialism or modernism in art seemed so outrageous.

When people think they have discovered the source of their discontents, they search for something that symbolizes it. Our Age found such a symbol in the public schools.

CHAPTER 3

The Public Schools

1

HOW WAS THE gospel of the gentleman spread? The first seeds were sown in the family but the prep schools and public schools, to which boys of the upper and middle classes were sent to board, introduced them to the customs and ideals of their social class in their simplest form.

My own prep school was in no way distinguished. Unlike the forcing house to which Cyril Connolly and George Orwell were sent, no boy had won a scholarship to any public school for years and no sprig of the nobility ever crossed its threshold. We were middle-class boys, the sons of businessmen and civil servants. Not that some did not make a name for themselves later in life. Among my contemporaries was a future president of the Royal Academy, an ambassador and three members of MI6, one of whom became its head, the legendary 'C'. In the bottom form one was taught manners and the way to write a letter and address an envelope. The limit of the school's ambition in work was to defeat the Common Entrance exam and in games to defeat the other prep schools in Seaford – and there were then a lot of them. Mathematics was taught disgracefully by a lumbering mountain of a man, geography by a lively retired naval officer and French by a negligent Belgian refugee from 1914 days who, having found a cosy billet, had decided to stay put. The only subject taught with spirit in the top two forms was Latin. Mr Ryves was short and wiry with a red moustache and a peppery temper. All compositions had to be dated in Latin; Kennedy's famous gender rhymes and examples of figures of speech (zeugma, hendiadys) had to be learnt by heart. We learnt to recognize well-known pitfalls in translation: *uter* a leathern bottle, *uter* which of the two: or (*malo* I would rather be, *malo* up an apple tree, *malo* than a mast at sea, *malo* in adversity). We stood up to construe orally Livy and Caesar, Ovid and Vergil in T.E.Page's light blue editions and we had the licence to make only one false concordance in the interminable twelve-week terms; a second mistake he punished by a spanking on the bare behind with a fives bat. He was a fierce disciplinarian out of class and, unlike the headmaster and his partners who owned the school, was never jocular and never unbent – except once a year in July when he took those leaving the school for a long walk across the downs to Alfriston and allowed himself to be teased by us as we capered round him. The day ended by eating an enormous strawberry tea, returning in the dusk for a late-night bathe. At the end of a winter term after we had struggled to identify the Greek accusative and other syntactical niceties in the second book of the *Aeneid* we were told to shut our books and he would take up his Conington and, while we sat quiet as mice, read that translation of the passages we had stumbled over. The noble lines echoed in our ears. The inescapable and incomprehensible end of Laocoon, the cruel death of Priam slithering in the blood of his son who had been killed before his eyes by the man who was to murder him – this was why one read Vergil.

One subject was, however, taught thoroughly. That was Christianity. Every morning there were prayers, two services on Sunday and each night the silent appeal to God kneeling by the bedside. Not for us the bland harmonies and pieties of the *English Hymnal*, still less Broad Church complacencies such as 'Hills of the north rejoice, Rivers and mountains sing ...' The plaintive melodies of *Hymns Ancient & Modern*, packed with the dogmas and unction of the Christian faith, moved the heart. Those hymns portrayed a world full of sin and implored us to struggle to fight to do good. We sang of ourselves as a happy band of pilgrims with Jesus as our fellow, and the angels of light singing to welcome us, the pilgrims of the night. We sang of the Blood that Jesus spilt and let that Blood our pardon buy. The hymns told us we were journeying through a vale of tears and should yearn for the joys of Paradise and Jerusalem the golden with milk and honey blest. Sometimes we sang with a light heart about the troops of Midian who prowled and prowled around and, as Christians, were exhorted to up and smite them. Sometimes a stanza was as hard to construe as Ovid. For years I puzzled over the meaning of John Henry Newman's theological aphorism:

> O generous love! that He Who smote
> In Man for man the foe,
> The double agony in Man
> For man should undergo.

Every day we heard the noble cadences of the Prayer Book and Bible, every week in class passages of the Old and New Testament were expounded and the moral revealed. '"So Absalom stole the hearts of the men of Israel." What does that mean, boys? It means he *curried favour*.' The headmaster, a bluff, hearty joker, read the Gospels in prayers till we knew the parables by heart. On the rare occasions Mr Ryves took Sunday evening prayers he would read for a quarter of an hour or longer some blood-curdling story from the Old Testament. The school was a temple of altruism and purity. No word of smut was ever heard, no sexual misdemeanour ever occurred; the faintest sign of deviancy, eccentricity or departure from the norm was punished with ridicule, ostracism or the fives bat. Every hamper from home was impounded and shared among one's fellows. At half term parents would be asked to take out with their own boy the sons of those whose parents lived abroad or could not come. Books brought from home were vetted to see if they were suitable and the library was filled with that chronicler of Empire G.A.Henty and Percy Westerman's *A Sub in a Submarine*, or the romances of Seton Merriman and Dumas.

Lessons conveyed moral tales. Charles II who let the Dutch burn the English fleet in the Medway was much despised. We were often told that history showed one incontrovertible truth. The ascetic, disciplined, God-fearing children from the hills, or the desert, or the north, hardened by austerity, swept down and destroyed the fat, self-indulgent children of the plains. But if the invaders became etiolated by the pleasures of soft living, they in their turn would fall, the prey of some new marauder. That was why one had to Fear God and Honour the King – these words hung in a classroom in letters of brass taken from the wardroom of a cruiser. In the two minutes silence one tried hard to think of the million dead of the British Empire. From time to time as a special treat a silent film of the raid on Zeebrugge was shown to frenzied cheering. Our history lessons resounded with the names of Havelock and Outram and the infamous deeds of Suraj-ad-Doulah and the Nana Sahib who are today heroes to Indian schoolchildren; and what the masters omitted was taught by the yarns of Henty whose heroes in *With the Allies to Peking*, in *The Dash for Khartoum* or *Through the Sikh War* can ride a hundred miles on horseback, scale a hill fort, capture a dacoit and his band and never shrink from shedding blood.

We emerged from the school as patent prigs with punctilious manners. Spontaneity was at a low ebb until nature reasserted itself. Drummed into us in the simplest terms were the ground rules for decency and duty. Wherever we journeyed or whatever we came to believe, the training we received nagged at the mind and required an answer. From the age of eight what should have grown by instinct had become a code of behaviour. This code had been defined and refined for over a century. It was the official code of the public schools.

2

THE PUBLIC SCHOOLS, praised and denounced, succoured by benefactors and consigned to destruction by reformers, are a unique British institution – though exported with variations to the dominions, to India and to New England. Until 1914 they dominated secondary education. Whereas France and Prussia had established a system of national education, England had relied on private enterprise. Their expansion coincided with the railway age: without railways the boarding schools could not have multiplied on such a scale. They needed reform: the buildings were insanitary, their curriculum narrow and the boys' lives brutal. The reform of the public schools was part of the Victorian reform of morals. The men who reformed them – Butler at Shrewsbury, Arnold at Rugby – wanted their pupils to be honourable and God-fearing and to share their own delight in developing their accuracy and taste through construing classical texts. But they had more pressing problems. How could one mitigate the guerilla warfare between masters and boys which flared every so often into open rebellion and riot? How could the leisure hours spent by the boys in poaching and smashing the neighbours' property be turned to better account? How could one convert into school rules the jungle law of boy-made customs and brutalities by which they governed themselves? How could one stop drunkenness, savage bullying, cribbing and other conspiracies to do the minimum of work, when the schoolboy code operated which forbade sneaking and condoned lying to masters? How could one stop the sexual orgies?

The headmasters had first to restore order. Only men of towering personality could have restored it. Hooligans and bullies the boys might be, nor were they to be cowed by the birch; but they were often impressionable, warm-hearted and craved affection. They could be awed by sermons or by death – and at least one of their schoolfellows would die at the school each year. They could be moved to tears by a headmaster's earnest appeal to their honour and decency. The personality of the headmaster was crucial. Those who were weak soon resigned or their school sank into oblivion. The portrait in school stories of the doctor in billowing gown, thunderous in wrath at some schoolboy iniquity, is a testimony to the stature of the autocrats who reformed the schools. They had to be autocrats. They had to insist that the headmaster alone, and not the governors, was responsible for discipline. Two boys at Wellington, barely fourteen years old, whose mothers were sisters and lived close together, went to bed in the holidays with one of their maids. This came to light when it was discovered that the elder boy had caught a venereal disease from the maid. Edward Benson, the headmaster and later archbishop, asked their mothers to withdraw them, but since the offence took place in the holidays the mothers appealed to the governors. The governors told Benson they were astonished by his severity. They regarded what the boys had done as part of the natural process of growing up. Benson got his way only by a stratagem and nine months later resigned.

But on one matter the headmasters had their way. They restored order by decreeing senior boys themselves the prefects, and they, not the masters, should supervise what boys did outside the classroom. And here they ran into a dilemma. The best scholars, the sixth, ought to wield authority. The diminutive Walter Leaf, at the age of fifteen, half-dead with fright, caned a boy twice his size, but most headmasters came to realize that a boy's authority rested on the respect his schoolfellows had for him. That respect did not depend on his ability to translate Helen's lament over the dead Hector; they respected him for doing well what they themselves liked doing; and that was playing games.

By the end of the century the cult of games had transformed the schools.* For some years the old schoolboy pursuits of birds' nesting, botanizing, collecting caterpillars or butterflies and country walks continued. For some years the headmasters who encouraged games, such as Frederick Temple at Rugby, saw to it that athletes who shirked their work were kept in detention within earshot of the match they should have played in. But Temple also showed that a dropped catch was as unforgivable to him as a false concord. From there it was a short step to preaching in chapel against the 'sins of intellectuality', and for the boys to deduce that education was not hard work but hard play. The notion of the plant a public school required changed, and soon schools were buying land for playing fields. Harrow's eight acres in 1845 had risen by 1900 to 146, Marlborough's two to sixty-eight, Uppingham's two to forty-nine. Edward Bowen, a housemaster at Harrow, wrote 'Forty Years On', the most famous of all school songs, and when Rosebery lay dying the 'Eton Boating Song' was played to him on a gramophone by his instructions. No school seemed to be orthodox unless it resounded to refrains such as 'Up bonny Browns for House and for Cup, For the sake of the School play up, play up', or to the more curious exhortation to 'Come and put your flannels on and let the fun begin'. Soon the symbols of athleticism began to appear, the fezes, blazers, scarves, caps, shirts and ties; the awarding of colours; and the stringent rules determining who could wear what hat and at what angle, walk arm in arm with whom down what street; and, if alone, whether only one or both hands could be put in pockets. Dressed in sombre black for work, the bloods during the afternoon peacocked about in radiant plumes loaded with emblems of their achievements like generals in full dress uniform.

As in fairy tales the djinn who has been coaxed out of his bottle refuses to return to it, so the imp of organized games changed the face of the schools in ways which those who had first beckoned to it could hardly have credited. The pale bewhiskered young usher in holy orders competent in Latin syntax was replaced by a stalwart assistant master who kept a page or two ahead of his class but could teach the knack of getting the ball back from a ruck. Oxford and Cambridge had followed the lead from the schools. Some young tutors among the dons, weary of the riotous behaviour of idle pass-men,

* Cotton of Marlborough is credited more than any other for seeing that games enabled boys to treat masters as allies instead of enemies. The legend is not quite accurate. There had been fine cricketers among masters, such as Charles Wordsworth at Winchester, and the Eton and Harrow match dates from 1821; but even the founder of muscular Christianity, Charles Kingsley, put country pursuits and athletic feats far beyond games. It was not until the sixties that organized games began to dominate the schools. Team games always had greater prestige than athletics or fives or racquets which Thring at Uppingham considered selfish pursuits. Malim at Wellington in the thirties condemned tennis and golf as insufficiently painful.

encouraged their charges to go in for athletics, then games and above all to row. By the end of the century to wear the tie of Vincent's or the Hawk's Club was a passport to any number of jobs, particularly in schoolmastering. 'Boys always respect a Blue. Keep a tight hand. No fraternizing', was the bleak message the headmaster of Rossall gave to an Oxford graduate when appointing him to the staff.

It was not only the public school boys who were games mad. The nation too was intoxicated by cricket and football. Packed proletarian crowds cheered Huddersfield United. At Leeds they applauded as connoisseurs an audacious late cut by Ranji or watched Wilfred Rhodes varying without mercy his pitch, pace and spin. Games became the natural metaphor for moralists. We could hold on to the Empire, said the Chief Scout, only if we played up and did not loaf like slackers. Newbolt's *Vitai Lampada* was the most memorable of hundreds of execrable verses comparing life to a game with the Great Scorer recording our tally in which sin was to take your eye off the ball. When the war came, the versifiers assured the nation that victory would be ours because, having learnt to play up, face fast bowling on a bumpy pitch and in a blinding light, our men would face bullets and shells without flinching.

Another change took place that was to make life at a public school more of a prison. As games became more important so did the houses into which the school was divided, because it was through the house that games were organized. It was a matter of indifference to a housemaster whether a boy could master Greek iambics and construe Tacitus. But it was vital to him to have as prefects boys whose skill at games made them admired and obeyed. Power shifted from the headmaster to the housemasters.* The boarding houses introduced new rigidities and loyalties into school life. A boy was often prohibited from speaking to a boy in another house until he became a member of a school team; and as it was also forbidden to speak to those senior to him, Harold Nicolson found that in effect he spent his schooldays confined to the company of a handful of contemporaries who went up the school with him. The house was also responsible for teaching a new boy the tabus and rituals of the tribe. He had to learn the tribe's language – school slang – within a few weeks or he (or his initiator) was beaten. He had to be competitive in the race to get grace and favour but he must never show competitiveness. Intellectual preciosity, even an interest in politics or literature (which if modern was likely to be subversive), or any subject other than the cricket county championship or the England XV was suspect. Housemasters watched over their charges with ever increasing zeal. Visits to places outside the school

* At the turn of the century it was the housemasters' names that passed into public school lore: Trant Bramston at Winchester, T.E. Brown at Clifton, Durnford at Eton, men who became the walking chronicles of the school, receiving dozens of letters each term from their old boys and for lack of pensions running their houses until into their seventies.

were prohibited during such free time as a boy had. He did not have much. The obsession in late Victorian and Edwardian times with illicit sex bred a new theory that boys should be sent to bed physically tired and every minute of the day should be occupied by a specific school activity. No longer were the beer and game pie suppers of Tom Brown's days permitted: rich fare might inflame desire. Even the family came to be regarded as a mollycoddling institution. The school was there to insulate those boys rising in society from the vulgarisms of their parents. Women in any shape, even that of mother and sister, were unwelcome visitors; and the only feminine shapes to entrance boys' eyes were the ample form of the matron and the housemaster's wife, who lived on the other side of the impenetrable green baize door.

At the time Our Age entered the public schools they inculcated two ideals: manliness and loyalty. Sparta had replaced Athens as the ideal city state and not for nothing did Loretto and Sedbergh choose as their motto 'Spartam nactus es, hanc exorna'. In Bowen's house at Harrow no boy might have an armchair, a fire or a warm bath. A boy had to endure the headmaster's birch or the prefect's cane without flinching or crying, however unfair and however savage the beating might be. The dread of waiting to be beaten and the ritual of being called up and sentenced was almost as bad as the agony of the beating itself. Loyalty was the supreme asset which investment in a public school education produced. And it was a transferable asset. It guaranteed devotion to regiment, college, hospital, the civil and colonial service or to Jardine Matheson. The Officers' Training Corps was the symbol of loyalty to the greatest entity – the nation.

These were the schools who sent into the world, as E.M. Forster said, boys 'with well-developed bodies, fairly developed minds and underdeveloped hearts'. For boys who were clever, retiring, intellectual, nondescript, late developers, rebels, boys who were learning to flex their minds, their wits, their will and show that they did not accept good form opinion, they were a Gehenna. And not only the tough character-building schools, not only the top twenty, but the two most famous, synonymous with grace and learning, treated small boys brutally. Winchester had the highest all-round academic standing of any of the schools, yet the pressure there to conform and not appear spree was intense. No junior ventured an opinion until he had twenty men junior to himself. The bright little Kenneth Clark chattered to other Wykehamists in the train on the way to his first day at school. That evening he was summoned by the prefect in his house, told to 'sport an arse' and was beaten for breaking a rule he did not know existed. Precocious athletes and scholars alike were put down. *Nil admirari* was balanced by *non licet*. The complexity of Winchester rules and notions, some of them irrational, was supposed to train the young to develop ingenuity in argument. You could evade punishment if you showed that the rule you were accused of breaking did not in fact apply in your case. No wonder Winchester was renowned for producing civil servants and proconsuls skilled in the art of drafting for their minister answers to parliamentary questions that came as close as possible to accuracy without actually telling the truth.

Nor did Eton differ. Cyril Connolly's account of the torments he suffered as a small boy in College was memorable. The lesson that boys drew from the chapel and the classics was, so Cyril Connolly thought, the Gospel of the Jealous God. 'Human beings are perpetually getting above themselves ... and when they reach this state of insolence or hubris, they are visited with some catastrophe, the destruction of Sodom or the Sicilian Expedition, the fate of Oedipus or Agamemnon ... everything in life has to be paid for. All [they] can do is to walk delicately, to live modestly and obscurely like the Greek Chorus and to pay careful attention to omens for misfortunes never come alone.' *Enemies of Promise*, so far from being a unique indictment, came at the end of two decades of protest by the boys of Our Age. In newspaper articles they denounced their schools. And nowhere more unsparingly than in the public school novel.

3

THE PUBLIC SCHOOL novel is an astonishing phenomenon. England is the only country where this peculiar genre exists. Just as the ideal of the gentleman was the theme of so many Victorian novels, the institution which was designed to educate and civilize gentlemen, too, was mirrored in fiction. For fifty years the flow of novels idealizing the schools swelled until after the Great War the stream became a torrent – a muddy torrent.

There were in effect two streams: the novel and the yarn. The school yarn was written for boys and girls younger than public school age. Talbot Baines Reed wrote the *Fifth Form at St Dominic's* and *The Adventures of a Three Guinea Watch* which were widely read. The most preposterous and best known were the long-running soap operas at Greyfriars and St Jim's, composed by Frank Richards. They were read with derision by boys who were destined for public schools and goggle-eyed by those who weren't. (The sociologist of education Brian Jackson reported that in the 1960s some working-class families' notion of grammar schools came straight from Billy Bunter.) More typical were John Finnemore's Teddy Lester books. Between 1898 and 1928 Finnemore published fifty-seven books of adventure. The Teddy Lester yarns came out in the early 1900s. The formula is the same in every book. There is always a gang of bullies in the house who are too self-indulgent to train hard and therefore always doomed to let down the side, and too caught in the toils of drinking or betting or billiards to change their ways, however often they are flogged by the head. Gnawed with envy of Teddy and his friends, they plot to get them cut off by the tide, or sandbagged by bargees, or accused of stealing gold medals. At times they seem to have success within their grasp as Teddy and his chums are caught out of bounds or are late for lock-up. Not once but twice the Doctor orders Teddy to spend his last night in the infirmary before being expelled, but on one occasion Teddy spots a fire and on another bags some burglars as the Doctor calls to his butler, 'Awake Benson! Arise Benson! The house is being assailed. Let us deal with the intruders.' In every book the bullies are unmasked publicly, flogged and expelled.

Never in any of the books is there ever a reference to form work or learning. Teddy and his Japanese chum Ito go up the school always winning the house match by a try in the last minute or a run in the last over. The prefects are weak sixth-formers who let discipline slip into the hands of the bullies. Pages and pages celebrate the whoppings, the touchings-up and the birching of the chums or their tormentors when they are in the end exposed. The chums always take their gruel without a murmur, Ito displaying true Japanese bushido; the bullies squirm, yell and beg for mercy. Japes, resourcefulness when in trouble, the stiff upper lip and honour, which burns so bright that it dazzles the reader, are the virtues Finnemore praises. So successful were the Teddy Lester stories that they were reprinted as late as 1941 and 1953.

The public school novel is another matter. It was written about an identifiable school for adult readers. The first of note was J.A.Froude's tale of Westminster, *Shadow of the Clouds* (1847), but the most famous in Victorian times were *Tom Brown's Schooldays* (1857) and *Eric or Little by Little* (1858). There was Vachell's well-known story of Harrow *The Hill* (1905); E.W. Hornung, the creator of Raffles, wrote in praise of Uppingham as Charles Turley did for Cheltenham, Desmond Coke for Shrewsbury, Ian Hay for Fettes and Lionel Portman for Wellington. Kipling wrote *Stalky and Co* in praise of his old school, but it was praise which sent shivers down the spines of headmasters. Kipling saw his school as a microcosm of society. To survive in it as individuals boys have to learn how to exploit the social system in which they exist. The secret is to learn the difference between appearance and reality. The good form hero schoolboy, the flannelled fool at the wicket, may *appear* to be the ideal type; but he is not. The *real* public school type is the cynical Stalky. The heavy, priggish housemaster Prout, always banging on about house spirit and playing the game, is contrasted with the realists Hartopp and the chaplain, who expect boys to crib and bully. Real enthusiasm for letters is to be found, not among the sixth-form swots, but in Beetle, avidly reading his way through the head's French yellow-backs and the metaphysical poets.

Real education is what the boys teach each other in ways which the masters cannot. Schooling gives men the means to hurt their enemies more effectively and to acquire this power is a painful process of learning 'all the Armoured Man should know, Through his seven secret years ...' Kipling sent up the system and its ideology but he praised the product. It was the public school boys who ran the Empire.

But the tide began to turn. In 1913 Arnold Lunn wrote a novel about Harrow and his hero is the antithesis of Vachell's worthy. Cynical and unlikeable, he has one object: to revenge himself on his enemies when he gets to the top of the school and at last has power, the power to make masters fawn and his juniors flatter. He gloats that the bloods, less omniscient than he, do not realize that when they leave Harrow their power and prestige will vanish and life will be a long anticlimax. The second novel was Alec Waugh's classic *The Loom of Youth*. Waugh took the lid off homosexual romance in the schools and the grotesque importance given to winning at games. He saw the real struggle in the schools to be between the stimulating, unorthodox sixth-form master (in Waugh's time at Sherborne it was S.P.B.Mais who died in penury at a great age) and the phalanx of housemasters who fight his influence and badger the headmaster to get rid of him.

And yet perhaps no novel better explains the resentment which many intellectuals of Our Age were to feel against the public schools than a series of volumes which purport to be the diary of a boy, Aubrey Fowkes, in Yoll's House at Portlow School.*

When he arrives there in 1914 Aubrey is a sensitive, plucky boy who likes reading poetry and novels and had been good at games at his prep school. In his first term he is bullied almost beyond endurance. 'It was the unfriendliness too that hurt me as much as being bombarded by pellets and ink and pencils.' The bosers, or prefects, beat him but his chief tormentor is the heavyweight champion of the school, 'Pestie,' who terrifies everyone including the house prefects. Catching Aubrey writing his diary Pestie nicknames him 'Scribe-boy' and gets a bigger boy to rough him up. But the boy meets his match in Aubrey who fights him. 'You've got more guts than I thought, Scribe-boy,' says Pestie and makes him take up boxing. In the ring he is knocked about even more; but, now, Pestie becomes someone whose favour he tries in desperation to gain. He ends by loving the bully.

Meanwhile nostalgia has become his favourite emotion. Here he is writing the day before his fourteenth birthday.

I then made a boat out of a sheet of paper I'd bought specially for the purpose – and when I remembered how I'd been taught to make paper boats by my nurse, tears clotted my eyes. I wrote on my boat the magical word *thirteen*. I've always fancied thirteen – it sounds so beautifully swish . . . thirteen is just the spiffy spifficient age. Before I launched my boat I said to it, Paperboat, I made you. You were my

* Each volume covers a year of his life (except for the two volumes when he is sixteen). They were published by the Fortune Press between 1937 and 1947. Later volumes covered the years from eight to thirteen, and then nineteen, and appeared during 1948–54. Their style is more suspect and too near to the diaries of his public school days: so they may have been invented or edited. As indeed all of them may have been: but they read as if based on authentic diaries.

idea. Now you're going to be swept away from me on the water and you will never see me again. But I'll remember you, paperboat. You are my thirteen and you're going to carry away part of me. Then I leant over the bank and launched it ... Farewell, paperboat. Farewell my thirteen. Farewell for ever and ever.

The only friend he makes is a greater muff than himself. By the time he is fifteen his skill at games has gone and his self-confidence has collapsed. By sixteen he no longer seems to be so lively and the diary is fuller of school slang and the prose is less inventive or dull. Ragging has become the chief pleasure in life. By seventeen the diary consists of accounts day after day of the latest maul in the yard where the boys kick a podge (football) around. He needs encouragement and never gets it, he needs stimulation and scarcely a master notices him. He never becomes a boser. By now he is a vague socialist, sympathizes with strikers, cannot endure the Officers' Training Corps and has to leave early to cram for Cambridge. After all these years, this lively thirteen-year-old has not got exemption from School Certificate. 'I failed badly at games at Portlow and I've never been the same since.' But Portlow has left him with an obsession: bottoms. Beatings, marks on bottoms, the slope of bottoms continue to fascinate him. At Cambridge anyone to whom he finds he can talk about this topic becomes his friend. Pestie and the bosers marked him for life.

In the twenties, my own generation changed the tone of the public school novel. The hero is no longer a good-natured fellow who gradually begins to feel that possibly one might doubt Christianity and think Arnold Bennett more important than Dickens. The names of the novels tell their own tale: *Out of Step*, *The Day Boy*, *The Shadow of the Chapel*, *Death of a Hero*, *Unwillingly to School*. The new hero is the sensitive intellectual who as a pacifist refuses to join the Officers' Training Corps and finds himself in revolt against the philistinism and the upper-class official ethos. In 1919 Mais followed his pupil Alec Waugh and wrote *The Education of a Philanderer* and from then on books about the schools poured from the press. No year passed without one being published. In 1922 six, in 1926 five, in 1930 five, in 1934 four. On the London stage Young Woodley fell in love with his housemaster's wife – but compared with the revelations of the novel that was a comparatively healthy emotion. Books appeared with titillating titles such as *Virgin Sinners*. Eton was exposed by John Heygate, Lancing by Leonid Bely, Stowe by Richard Heron Ward. Alert schoolboys, reading each novel as it appeared, enjoyed identifying the school whose disguise could often be penetrated by the giveaway slang. The age of Almamatricide had begun.

The press began to run articles on the future of the schools. Then in 1934 Esmond Romilly ran away from Wellington, a school which Cuthbert Worsley, then a junior master, described as 'philistine to a degree almost unimaginable ... there was no literary society, no political club, no acting'. Aged sixteen, a nephew of Winston Churchill and already in touch with communists and supporters of every progressive and soundly subversive cause, Romilly got the full treatment from Fleet Street when he published *Out of Bounds* and arranged for agents in a number of schools to circulate his broadsheet there. For Romilly the schools were part of the organized hypocrisy of capitalism and progressive manifestoes featured the public schools – their reform, their abolition. The young assistant masters of the twenties encouraging boys to read Strachey, Robert Graves and Huxley were succeeded in the thirties by a new breed asking their rebellious charges what they thought of pacifism, fascism and communism. In the same year that Esmond Romilly hit the headlines, Graham Greene published an anthology of reflections, *The Old School Tie*. William Plomer talked of the irrelevant drudgery he experienced at Rugby, but the most critical essay was Auden's denunciation of his school, Gresham's Holt. There boys were placed on their honour and, he said, the masters had either silted up or were scoutmasters who identified the welfare of the school with the welfare of the boys. Anthony Powell was more merciful to Eton which, so he said, told boys, 'If you don't learn some sort of civilized behaviour, England will become uninhabitable.' Characteristic of those times was his comment that a bad house was made worse 'when the non-Aryan proportion in its membership seemed to many unnecessarily high'.

Not all the clever intellectuals were miserable all their days. Boys who had a gift for language or enjoyed mastering the rules of syntax and grammar flourished; and by the turn of the century they were taught by masters who in these days would have been dons – excellent scholars such as T.E. Page at Charterhouse, or North, Hillard and Botting who edited classical textbooks, or G.G. Coulton who taught at several schools and in the end got his fellowship. Sometimes one master would make all the difference. William Plomer remembered one at Rugby who lent him Turgenev; Harold Nicolson at Wellington found an oasis of civilization in Talboys who taught history. The fact that the cleverest boys were together in College House at Eton meant that there would always be some of similar tastes and sense of humour to mitigate the affronts to a boy's dignity delivered by the other boys who despised them as tugs. In the first decade of the century Maynard Keynes and Ronald Knox both enjoyed their days in College. Indeed Knox enjoyed them so much that, like hundreds of other schoolboys, he was never as happy again. For this was the most extraordinary phenomenon of the schools. At that impressionable age when emotion is so strong, the joys and sorrows of school life stamped themselves so deeply upon the mind that no other loyalties and loves later in life seemed comparable. They were struck by the disease Cyril Connolly diagnosed as the theory of Permanent Adolescence in which 'the experiences of boys at the great public schools, their glories and disappointments are so intense as to dominate their lives and to arrest their development. ... For my own part,' he continued:

> I was long dominated by impressions of school. The plopping of gas mantles in the classrooms, the refrain of psalm tunes, the smell of plaster in the stairs, the walk through the fields to the bathing places or to chapel across the cobbles of School Yard evoked a vanished Eden of grace and security ...

Perhaps this was why numbers of intellectuals erased from their memory their sufferings and came in middle and old age only to remember the golden evenings. Connolly acknowledged that Eton could put a case against him. He pictured the holy shade of Henry VI who had founded the college reproaching him. Why did he complain of being unhappy as a small boy and then complain of being happy when he got into Pop and became court jester to the school bloods? If he had been less vain and less bereft of guts, he would not have let success get the better of him. 'You imply our education is no use to you in after life. But no education is. We are not an employment agency; all we can do is to give you a grounding in the art of mixing with your fellow men.'

After the Great War some new public schools were founded which took account of the criticism of the old order. Indeed radical schools like Dartington and Bembridge were inspired by their hostility to public school education. Others played variations: Rendcomb admitted boys of different class, T.F. Coade at Bryanston and Kurt Hahn at Gordonstoun taught new ideals of social responsibility. I was lucky enough to go to Stowe, where J.F. Roxburgh reinterpreted the ideal. He accepted the system – houses, prefects, fagging and the rest. But he wanted the school to be less dominated by the worship of games and less regimented. Unless boys had leisure how could they develop individuality and originality, how could they learn on their own, learn to paint or read something other than set books? There were to be no absurd boy-made rules about dress or who could walk where. Indeed there were to be as few rules as possible: but what there were had to be kept. He wanted the public schools to stop neglecting literature and the visual arts – to make Dr Arnold share his pedestal with his son Matthew.

Did he succeed? Partially. Only a few of his housemasters really understood him. There were, as there always will be, clever rebellious boys who could not fit in and sensitive creatures who suffered at the hands of their insensitive tough contemporaries. There was a house where the head prefect beat a boy because his shoelaces were untied, and others where life was dreary and callous. But there were some lively young masters: my English tutor was T.H. White, a severe teacher who introduced us to I.A. Richards's criticism, ridiculed our snob culture and tried to shock clever boys into responding to poetry instead of copying critics or firing off epigrams. George Rudé, later one of the band of French Revolution historians, skilfully veiling his marxism, analysed the corruption of the Third Republic in France and taught us German by letting us read that delightful anti-capitalist children's book *Emil und die Detektive*. The science tutor gave gramophone recitals of symphonies and *The Ring* on Tuesday nights; and to sing Constant Lambert's *Rio Grande* was a welcome variant on the *Messiah*. My tutor, William McElwee, was one of the many gifted sixth-form history teachers of the day from John Edward Bowle at Westminster to Bert Howard at Alderman Newton's Leicester. My own housemaster was young and believed in freedom. I enjoyed playing games so I had enjoyable schooldays. Never was any member of my generation less disgruntled. But many of them were.

Stowe was not alone in attracting good men to teach. In the early thirties three to four thousand out of two million white-collar jobs disappeared and numbers of the writers of Our Age found the easiest way of getting a job was to apply to the agency and wait, as Auden put it, for the 'postman to bring, / Typed notices from Rabbitarse and String'. Valentine Cunningham (see p. 8) logs eighteen of the intellectuals of those days who taught in public or prep schools – among them Grigson, Day Lewis, Cowper Powys, Betjeman and Upward. So much did they become part of the schools, he says, that even when they declared how monstrous these class-ridden institutions were, they could not cut the umbilical cord. From the Oxford Wits came Evelyn Waugh's *Decline and Fall* and Henry Green's *Blindness*, and Auden and his fellow poets wrote using schoolboy slang and allusions. Louis MacNeice defended himself by saying that at any rate he and they wrote from experience: they knew about changing rooms and playing fields and not about champagne and brothels. The generation that succeeded us chided them and did not accept this excuse for remaining such dogged Old Boys.

No separate chapter is needed for the girls' boarding schools. It was never obligatory to send daughters away to school as it was for boys. In Victorian times education even among cultivated families was not regarded as essential for girls. Beatrice Webb's father was a generous benefactor to his impoverished nieces and enabled them to go to university because for them better educational qualifications meant the difference from being a teacher or a secretary to being a governess. But he did not consider his own daughter needed such an insurance policy. She would have her own fortune. Only a few of the girls' public schools in these times had pretensions to scholarship. Accomplishments were what they prized; and devoted, gifted teachers waited often for years for a bright girl to appear eager to master language or numbers. The ideal of the schools was to produce girls of character who would serve the nation in some voluntary work or other. Just as the first women dons were determined to show that girls could be as meticulous scholars as men and worked their poor charges far harder, so the games mistresses of the boarding schools wanted their girls to display at lacrosse the same ruthlessness as rugger players. They too would have uniforms and wear ties and straw boaters: or, most advanced, they would be draped in jibbahs, with a flower embroidered on the bosom as a concession to individuality – the choice of deadly nightshade brought reproof. They too would sing school songs, and 'Wimbledonia, Fair and Free' fluted from the hall of Roedean. Modelled on the boys' public schools, these establishments were so aware of feminine mission that they became enveloped in ridicule. Arthur Marshall, a connoisseur of the school stories of Angela Brazil, immortalized them in his monologues, and the Girls of St Trinian's exploited the theme.

Some will think it absurd to concentrate on the public schools when all over the country there were grammar schools. The great direct grant schools, as historic as any public school, gave a sterner education. But despite the fact that boys in day schools had a life of their own over weekends and learnt sooner to meet the problems of adolescence, many grammar schools modelled themselves on the public schools. During the years when Our Age grew up, the public schools and Oxford and Cambridge were still setting the goals in English education. The scholarship exams which the colleges had arranged in an attempt to enable boys from less well-to-do homes to go to these universities were hijacked by the public schools who saw in them a bunch of blue ribands for their best scholars and an excellent advertisement for their prowess in teaching.

And yet – singular irony – if one asks what was the most enduring legacy Britain gave to the twentieth century, it was something which owed much to the pre-1914 public school spirit. It was not parliamentary democracy or representative institutions. Still less was it the rule of law. It was organized games. That was what Britain gave to countries in Asia, Africa, South America and even Europe. No other country so hallowed games in its national life as the British, and in the main it was public school men who institutionalized athletics, rugger, cricket, tennis and golf. Even in its early years the most international sport of all, football, owed something to the amateur public school sides of the Corinthians and the Casuals. The public school man felt a pang when a professional foul was regarded as an acceptable tactic.

CHAPTER 4

Modernism

1

TWO MOVEMENTS IN ideas moulded the consciousness of Our Age. They challenged the culture of the gentleman and forced us to come to terms with them. These were the movements of modernism and pacifism.

Modernism was the shrine of an idea that was to haunt us for life – the idea of man's alienation from his society. The modernists believed art should portray society as disintegrating and decomposing. If society is dehumanized, why depict people as recognizable human beings? They should squint out of paintings like the deformities they had become, they should look like the machines that had destroyed them. The artist's duty was to express his consciousness of living in an insane society. Let the sound of atonalist music grate on the ear of the fuddy-duddies longing for soothing harmonies, let cubism bewilder those expecting the customary representation of nature, let the flow of consciousness replace those solid four-square characters who delighted the readers of George Eliot. Modernism should reject both the ideal world of romanticism and the hard solid world of Tolstoy's art. It is not the moral of the story but the way you tell it that counts. Art is there to bear witness to the disaster of the industrial city. It was the city that had dehumanized society and established degrading social relationships where human beings lived cheek by jowl yet had never been so lonely. Surrounded by neighbours they felt insecure. Begotten by the city, the modernist movement was driven like Oedipus to murder its father. The artist should show his contempt for the life of commerce in which people calculate the consequences of their actions and preach the hypocrisies of prudence. If art can change men and women, as evangelical religion once claimed to do, all the more reason why art should not represent the unregenerate world of reality. The artist does not exist to praise 'decent, godless people: their only monument the asphalt road, / And a thousand lost golf-balls.'

Modernists valued Style, Experiment, Originality and Mockery.

Modernism meant a revolution in style: and an epic revolution at that. I remember hearing C.S.Lewis, one of the earliest members of our generation, a contemporary of Bowra, give his inaugural lecture after his uneasy translation from Oxford to Cambridge. Lewis loathed modernism. He was, he declared, one of the last survivors of a vanishing epoch. No change, not that of Antiquity to the Dark Ages, nor the replacement of the Age of Reason by Romanticism, was comparable to the transformation made by modernism. No other age had 'produced work which was, in its own time, so shatteringly and bewilderingly new, as that of the cubists, the Dadaists, the surrealists and Picasso . . . Modern poetry is new in a new way, almost in a new dimension'. If C.S.Lewis and many others had not felt that to be so, modernism would have failed as a movement. Modernists wanted to shock and to outrage; and through that outrage awake people into seeing the world about them in a new way. Like the French Romantics you created a scandal, you proclaimed your belief in nothing; or in something absurd that would be scorned by the scientific – for instance, alchemy or the occult.

Why was it so important to find the right style? Many artists of modernity dreamt that there was a Palace of Art and they could find the path to it only by discovering the right style. How can the artist escape the bondage of social conventions and the laws of nature? By abstracting reality. Abstract painting sets both the artist and the beholder free. At last the artist is free to roam in a higher world and art to convey meanings and intuitions never previously imagined. The world no longer makes art: art creates the world. The artist shows us his mind and goes on for ever telling us what his mind imagines at a particular moment. He rejects mimesis: he is now free to invent his own world.

Enormous importance, therefore, was attached to experiment and originality. *Neuheit stand auf dem Programm.* How else could one shock the bourgeois? Who can forget Diaghilev, the greatest impresario of modernism, saying to the best known of all its sprites: '*Etonne-moi, Jean*'? As we entered middle age, we were to experience the fearful effects of this command to be original. The first effect was to separate the artist from the mass of society. The avant-garde outdistanced the army it was leading. On marched the artists. They were not marching to any known land, they were marching to discover new countries beyond the horizon of their fellow men and women. Desperate to follow them an elite corps broke away from the army to join them. The elite ended by being as isolated as the artists as they strove to keep pace with the change in styles. You come to love an artist only when you have struggled to understand his latest puzzling novelty: and love, not respect, is what an artist wants. What he does not want is the plaudits of democratic voters who if they had their way would vote art out of existence. Not only Eliot and Pound despised democracy. For D.H.Lawrence humdrum people didn't matter. They must never be given a clue about the direction art might take. Modernism would commit suicide if it ever settled for one style. For a composer or painter or poet to become predictable would be a sign of approaching death.

The second effect of the search for originality was ennui. After a while novelty becomes a drug and stronger shots have to be taken to overcome ennui. The artist must for ever develop or die. In each phase of his work he must change almost beyond recognition. He starts by stripping the furniture he lives with of varnish, paint and polish. Out went the lush epithets of the past and the theory of poetry that justified them. Poetry did not mean turning loose the emotions but escaping from them. The consequences were curious. If art is to have no moral purpose, to make no spiritual pretensions, to display no decorative furbelows, what can it be but acrobatics? We watch entranced as the poet swings on the trapeze and somersaults, hanging on now with one hand and now the other. But he is in danger. As every artist has to prove that he owes nothing to any other or indeed to his own past, the devoted soldiers of the avant-garde flag, bewildered and exhausted by the effort to capture so many strong points. Experiment no more.

Nevertheless, in their assault upon the bourgeois citadel, the modernists rediscovered the most effective method of demolition. One method is to use invective and destroy the enemy's fortifications by the sheer weight of bombardment. Another is to use reason to shell first one redoubt and then another until your enemy is left without defences. But the most devastating method is to undermine his Maginot line by burrowing under it. You tunnel first with ridicule, then with mockery, insinuation, derision, flippancy and satire; and suddenly the defences of bourgeois society collapse. The English delude themselves that they alone have a sense of humour. It was the French who perfected *la blague*. It was invented, said the Goncourt brothers, in the ateliers, the joke which threw doubt on everything, poisoned faith and murdered respect. In many manifestations of modernism, the spoof, the lark, the snigger and the knowing smile, grotesque mirth and hilarious laughter, send up reality. And soon they send up art itself. Dada laughs, what is there left to laugh about? Does Picasso laugh at us for taking all his paintings as high art or is he saying there is no such thing? Surrealism despatched its victims by bizarre association. In a café André Breton dismissed that Bloomsbury Francophile, Raymond Mortimer, with the words: '*Allez-vous-en, affreuse bergère.*' Before mockery religion quailed, respect dissolved and faith failed. Nor does the form which mockery takes have to be harsh. In England Lytton Strachey's feline prose tore the skin of middle-class respectability.

If originality was a prime sacrament in the cult, it was inevitable that some modernists would contradict others. The very names of its movements – cubism, futurism, imagism and vorticism, Dadaism and surrealism – were denials of what preceded them. If Pound was sickened by the culture of London, Joyce was inspired by Dublin, and Léger and the Italian futurists celebrated the city's technology and the civilization of the aircraft and motor car. If Eliot takes pains to redefine tradition and the poet's relation to it, manifesto after manifesto stamps on the face of the past. Does modernism have classical or romantic antecedents, is it Apollonian or Dionysian? Modernists may scoff at theorists, yet who can doubt that the cubists or the constructivists of *die neue Sachlichkeit* were cerebral?

And yet was there not also in modernism a contempt for logic and reason? When regimental sergeant major of the Comintern, Willi Muenzenberg, recruited some veterans of modernism to join the party, they resembled the awkward squad of slapstick comedy. With the exception of Aragon, the transformation of surrealists into good party members was always suspect. Suspect, too, to the high priests of marxism who regarded modernism as another stage in the decomposition of the corpse of capitalism. *Guernica* and the Dove of Peace were welcomed as propaganda but Stalin's response to Picasso or atonalist music was no different from Hitler's. A movement which delighted so much in the individual's own exclamation when confronted with life was always going to be regarded by politicians with suspicion: particularly when the exclamation was so batty. As time passed the search became more desperate to go beyond consciousness, to explore the irrational, to prefer dream and perhaps schizophrenia, to submit to Zen or yoga to release oneself from the thrall of the reasoning mind until one entered a world created by acid and heroin. The most determined revolté among the Beatles, John Lennon, became the hero of doing one's own thing; and he was shot dead by someone who did it.*

Defining modernism becomes a kind of sport. To some critics the word takes on the magical powers of a fetish and they turn the hounds onto those modernists who are accused of betraying the cause. For abandoning the style of *The Waste Land* for that of *The Four Quartets,* Eliot is cast for the role of Actaeon and torn limb from limb. The hunt becomes ever more disorganized if you try to define when modernism began. Throw the hounds into that covert and any number of foxes will run because none of the earths have been stopped. In Scandinavia and in Germany they start running thirty years before they run in France. If you try to run the original fox to ground, you are in for a long day in the saddle. Off goes the hunt past Rimbaud and de Nerval, past Poe and the inconsequential Sterne. Then on back to Villon

* Roger Shattuck, one of the best analysts of modernism, denied this was so. In a book combining learning and agility he made an ingenious refutation. So far from despising science, some modernists reflected the new science of quantum mechanics and electromagnetic wave theory. Did not Valéry take Leonardo as a culture hero? And did not Leonardo's description of the air being full of radiant lines crossing and interweaving without one ever entering the path of another prefigure field theory, the outcome of Clerk Maxwell's electro-magnetism? Valéry and Monet rejected the Romantic belief that man's mind combined two faculties, reason and imagination. The mind was one and irregularities and unpredictability were as evident in physics as in art. What did Monet do in his old age painting at Giverny but break down the molecules of waterlilies and wisteria into fields of light instead of painting individual objects as they appeared? Perhaps only when we are drunk or drugged and unstrung by excess do we perceive things as they really are. Only middle-class intellectuals consider science and art to be opposed: in fact scientists and artists see things alike. Is Shattuck's evidence conclusive? The new physics was as skilfully vulgarized as physics had been in Newton's day when the mercantilists made great play with the theory of gravitational forces; but physics did not become unpredictable after Einstein and Heisenberg published. The change was from strict determinism to probability: probability still was able to predict in large numbers. Delightful though the picture is of artists in the Dome or Coupole poring over the Proceedings of the Royal Society, it seems somewhat far-fetched.

and hounds are still going hard when they reach Catullus. That is what happens if you confuse a mood with a change of style.

2

THERE IS, HOWEVER, considerable agreement on the date modernism arrived in England. Its finest critics, Frank Kermode, Roger Shattuck, Malcolm Bradbury and Richard Ellmann are pretty much in agreement. Ellmann saw Oscar Wilde as an undoubted member of the movement and Kermode accepts that there are signs of the impending explosion in Edwardian times. But he will not date it before 1907, the year Picasso painted *Les Demoiselles d'Avignon*. There is the annus mirabilis of 1922 when there appeared Yeats's *Later Poems*, *The Waste Land*, *The Duino Elegies*, *Ulysses*, *Aaron's Rod*, *Jacob's Room* and the *Tractatus*. All agree that it could not possibly be put later than 1925, the year Eliot published his first collection of poems and Virginia Woolf *Mrs Dalloway*. A special plea could be made for 1913 when London first heard *Le Sacre du Printemps*. That excellent conductor of ballet, Constant Lambert, was to recognize it was not simply the animal vitality of *Le Sacre* that amazed the London audience. The melodic line and its harmonic setting, unlike the music of the past, were at war with each other: the relation between them, he said, seemed to resemble 'more that between the unfortunate yokel in the dock and the cynical barrister prosecuting him'. Bowled over by the ballet the young Osbert Sitwell opened the conversation with Diana Manners at a formal dinner party by asking her what she thought of Stravinsky, not at that time the natural gambit to play when meeting a beauty for the first time. But then Diana Manners, the reigning beauty of the Asquith and Grenfell set and under siege by Duff Cooper, was already setting a new style in upper-class circles. To drink whisky and soda in public would be thought common, but she drank vodka and absinthe in private and asked openly at parties which would be the soporific for the night – morphia or 'jolly old chlorers'.

Virginia Woolf was quite certain when modernism began. 'In or about December 1910, human character changed ... All human relations shifted – those between masters and servants, husbands and wives, parents and children. And when human relations change there is at the same time a change in religion, conduct, politics and literature.' In picking that date she had in mind the post-impressionist exhibition which Roger Fry and her sister Vanessa had helped to organize. Perhaps she remembered the ball to celebrate it when she and Vanessa scandalized the press by appearing as Gauguin girls, bare-shouldered and bare-legged swathed in African sailcloth. Next summer she was to bathe naked in Byron's pool with Rupert Brooke at Cambridge, and go camping with him in Devon unchaperoned. In the spring before the exhibition her sister had begun an affair with Roger Fry and said she did not see why the women in Bloomsbury should not have the same freedom as the homosexual men. This happened shortly after another freedom had been established in Bloomsbury – the freedom to say in mixed company things that formerly had been said only by men to men. On August 11, 1908, Lytton Strachey saw a stain on the front of Vanessa Bell's skirt and had said to her, 'Semen?'

The abuse hurled at Bloomsbury for organizing the post-impressionist exhibition marked their first clash with the cultural Establishment. Why did Sickert dismiss Cézanne as a failure, why did Tonks, who had championed the impressionists, revile cubism? Why did intelligent artists shout, 'Drink or drugs?' when Fry showed them a Matisse? No doubt because those crude colours and distortions of the human body affronted people who had been accustomed to the 'beautiful' paintings of Leighton and Alma-Tadema. The Fauves contradicted their conception of civilized life, of the dignity of man and the desirability of women. The exhibition rejected the Victorian obsession with beauty – that beauty which, as Quentin Bell said, cascaded over every object in the home and emerged in the shape of stucco moulding, buttons, beading, Berlin wool, lincrusta, papier-mâché, buttresses, cherubs, scroll-work and foliage. They rejected the idea popularized by Diderot and developed by Ruskin and Arnold that beauty grows out of the side of morality. In making this connection Ruskin had seemed to imply that art arises from a kind of social anxiety or ostentation and not from delight in the visible world.

Fry argued that the artist laboured under only one obligation – to express his own sensibility. But it was the way Fry argued that was intriguing. Bloomsbury did not react to the vituperation with manifestoes. They tried to seduce their opponents by reason. Fry would start by telling his baffled listeners that the reasons they admired Piero or Vermeer or Poussin were precisely the same as the reasons that persuaded all enlightened men and women such as they to admire Picasso and Matisse. When they began to examine the things common to all painting – colour, plasticity, perspective, form – the difference between them and him turned out to be minimal. Just as Darwin had his bulldog in T.H.Huxley, Fry had Clive Bell. Bell enjoyed outraging the benighted. 'To appreciate a work of art,' Bell wrote, 'we need bring with us nothing from life, no knowledge of its ideas and affairs, no familiarity with its emotions.' Yet when Bell developed his doctrine of significant form he displayed very much the same respect for persuasion by reason. Fry and Bell created a criterion for judging both old masters and the modernists. Sentimentalism, literary overtones and rhetoric were condemned in the distant as well as the immediate past: they preferred Piero and Vermeer to Michelangelo and Bernini, and Constable to Turner. Above all among the moderns, they loved Cézanne for his serenity and for the architectonics of his painting that they so admired.

Roger Fry's influence as a critic of art was as great as that of Pound and Eliot in poetry. No one had spoken with such authority since Ruskin. He gave Our Age a formula for defending modern art and abstract art in particular.

First he declared that there was no right or wrong way of judging a painting, and the declaration was all the more telling because he admitted he had for long thought academics and ateliers were right in thinking that rules could be established even if they had picked the wrong rules. He next maintained that when we look at a painting it is the combination of colours and forms which induces an aesthetic emotion; not the objects or the event the painting depicts. What the painting is intended to represent is strictly speaking irrelevant. 'You see this important mass of colour here,' he said during a lecture indicating with his pointer the body of Christ on the cross. Fry was disinterested. He not only dissented from fashionable taste and was unenthusiastic about Turner or the Pre-Raphaelites. He dissented from the advanced taste of Sickert and Tonks: he did not care for the impressionists: they offended his sense of design. Nor were Piero and Cézanne the only artists he regarded as models: he made people look at Scythian, and pre-Columbian, and African art.

Fry's position as arbiter did not survive the Second World War. The recently dead – he died in 1933 – have a brief life as ghosts, then the grave closes over them: few return. It was not that the Academicians or Dougal McColl made a comeback, but by then the art historians, two of them English members of Our Age, had imposed their authority. Fry painted. He was an unsuccessful painter but he had got his hands dirty and was perhaps nearer in spirit to the Slade School at University College London than to the Slade chair at Cambridge to which, just before he died, he was belatedly elected after Oxford had twice rejected him. A clear but uninspired writer, he was an incomparable lecturer who filled the Queen's Hall in London.

Fry was displaced as the leading authority on art by Kenneth Clark, a scholar who was justifiably sniffy about some of Fry's writing, particularly on Flemish art. Only Clark among art historians of his day had the courage and the knowledge to have written his book on *The Nude*. Clark too had a flair for haute vulgarization and was to hold millions on television with his series on civilization – a considerably more convincing account than Clive Bell's notion of civilization. Clark showed what mettle there was in the Oxford Wits.

The second art historian who became an arbiter was Anthony Blunt. He was fired by Fry's enthusiasm for Poussin and made that painter his own specialism. Abandoning the crude marxism of his pre-war writings, he taught his students to judge painters by relating them to the social forces of the time. He was determined as director of the Courtauld not to allow that institution to become a finishing school for debutantes. One of the achievements of our generation was the emergence of a succession of art historians – Ellis Waterhouse, John Pope-Hennessy, Francis Haskell, Michael Jaffe, Michael Levey among them – who rivalled their colleagues in America and Europe and superseded Tom Boase and the amateurs of the inter-war years. But an example was set for them by the great refugee art historians from Germany: Pevsner, Wilde, Wittkower and the egregious Edgar Wind. They showed what training in philology and classical scholarship could bring to the subject. Above all there was Ernst Gombrich. *Art and Illusion* replaced Fry's *Vision and Design* as the book that made us look at art in a new way. And yet once again we have to admit that no achievement of theirs was quite as remarkable as that of Roger Fry. He did for the visual arts what T. S. Eliot and the English faculty at Cambridge were to do for English literature. He drew a new map.

In the days of the post-impressionist exhibition London was a duller city than Paris. It lacked Viennese cafés and the atmosphere an intelligentsia finds congenial. Writers who settled there moved on to Paris. Even Henry James who years ago had chosen London rather than Paris was saddened in his old age by the relentless preference of Londoners for middlebrow theatre and literature. Edmund Gosse succeeded Andrew Lang as the leading bookman and groomed Jack Squire to succeed him. Writers who challenged Victorian conventions were liable to have their books destroyed by magistrate's order and might even find themselves in the courts. And in what other European university of Oxford's distinction would a professor of literature think to discredit Zola and Ibsen in a friend's eye by showing him their photographs and asking him to compare them with those of 'any decent midshipman'?

Pound and Eliot. They were the heart of modernism for Our Age. All the great names of the movement gathered about Pound: Joyce, Eliot, Hulme, Wyndham Lewis, Lawrence, H. D. Aldington. He even had a link to Bloomsbury through David Garnett. This is the authentic world of modernism, the poetry shop, the little magazine, the lightning birth and death of passionate movements each with its manifesto, its stance, its outbursts of contemptuous hostility to the world at large. The manifesto of Pound's imagism today seems mild. Poets were to avoid rhetoric, preaching, ornament, metaphor, metronomic metre, ideas. Above all they should banish the palpitating ego. The ideal now was to make precise statements of classical brevity and impersonality, and to pare down, winnow and refine their utterances.

> Like a skein of loose silk blown against a wall
> She walks by the railing of a path in Kensington Gardens,
> And she is dying piece-meal
> Of a sort of emotional anaemia.

This is when Milton and the Romantics began to be rejected and the obsession with truth led to inarticulacy.

The next movement Pound was to plunge into was Wyndham Lewis's vorticism. In June 1914 the first number of *Blast* appeared:

BLAST years 1837 to 1900. Curse abysmal inexcusable middle-class, also aristocracy and proletariat. WRING THE NECK of all sick inventions, born in that progressive white wake. Blast their weeping whiskers, hirsute rhetoric of eunuch and stylist, sentimental hygienics, Rousseau-isms (wild nature cranks) fraternizing with monkeys, DIABOLICS, raptures and roses of the erotic bookshelves culminating in purgatory of Putney.

In a few lines, all social classes and Darwin and Swinburne were clubbed, and the vorticists took to gang warfare among the modernists. The gang to be carved up was the futurists led by Marinetti who praised speed, machines, youth, war, called for the destruction of museums and deified the new woman. That meant the vorticists consigned the suffragettes to oblivion.

The image of the vortex was well-chosen. The futurists pictured men driving forward at breakneck speed. The vorticists pictured human beings revolving in a circle, the energy they generated mounting in intensity. The image was of a whirlpool which broke up the smooth surface of conventional painting and indeed of artistic life which was to swirl as first one then another destructive artist stirred things up. At the end of his life Lewis was to say, 'Vorticism, in fact, was what I, personally, did and said at a certain period,' but initially it was for him a movement in painting and sculpture in which Gaudier-Brzeska and he were the progenitors. Irritated as Lewis was by futurism's celebration of the machine, it was odd that he treated human beings as machines and thought puppets were more human. The hard carapace of bone that he painted in his portraits reflected his own harshness. His hatred of others amused Arnold Bennett. 'One of his minor purposes is to disembowel his enemies who are numerous for the simple reason that he wants them to be numerous.' Invective was nothing new in the world of letters; one thinks of Churton Collins thumping the wretched Gosse. But the particular strain of violence that Wyndham Lewis bred was an interesting mutant and he infected several men of letters of Our Age with it, notably Geoffrey Grigson.

When people contrast the a-political twenties with the thirties they forget that Pound was as committed as Auden – committed to social credit economics, to anti-usury, anti-capitalism, anti-semitism and to the spiritual destruction of democracy. But he wrote *Mauberley* and what some regard as the greatest poem of the Second World War – the competition is not all that strong – *The Pisan Cantos.* His dedication to writing fascinated the modernists among Our Age: Cyril Connolly's prose style owes a good deal to Pound's poetry. Yeats was the better for knowing him and (one of the great bibliographical facts in the modernist movement) Pound improved *The Waste Land* rearranging the order of words and making enormous excisions. Few animators and teachers did what he did: he learnt from one whom he had tutored – Eliot taught him to be serious. And his tribute to Eliot when he read that poem, which expressed his feelings so well, was touching: 'Complimenti, you bitch. I am wracked by the seven jealousies.'

It is hard to think of any single poem that had such an electrifying effect upon the young as *The Waste Land.* 'What can convey,' wrote Connolly, 'the veritable brain-washing, the total preoccupation, the drugged and haunted condition which this new poet induced in some of us? We were like new-born goslings for ever imprinted with the image of an alien and indifferent foster parent, infatuated with his erudition, his sophistication, yet sapped and ruined by the contagion of his despair.' It was not only the Georgians who melted away: so did the Sitwells who had been the fashionable models of modernity for the Oxford Wits. No one then knew how the poem expressed not just Eliot's despair with the modern world but the anguish of the failure of his first marriage. What they saw was the mastery of different styles of speaking, each voice realized to perfection. And as the years passed his poetry reached new heights until it culminated in *Four Quartets.*

The generation that succeeded ours did not have the experience of growing up at a time when a great poet was publishing, who changed the style of poetry as Wordsworth had, and when each new publication did not diminish but added to his reputation. As each *Quartet* appeared during the war in its paper cover you were humbled. Eliot's modesty and gentleness reminded you of other worlds of sin, repentance and death whether or not you were a Christian. He did not call you to righteousness as the left-wing poets of the thirties did. He asked you to live a little less trivial a life. In my own adolescence Yeats had become vatic, Hardy was dead, but here was this astonishing voice using language in a way no other poet had ever used it before, yet the rhythms and cadences were so exact that no one, it seemed, could doubt it was poetry. Sensibility – what people think important or feel intensely – is always changing. But a new mode of expressing sensibility is something only a genius invents. Even in those days his disapproval of liberalism, his noble Christianity, his less than noble distaste for those lesser breeds without the law of white Anglo-Saxon, Anglo-Catholic society seemed irrelevant. Eliot taught me that opinions, prejudices, beliefs are an inescapable part of a vision of life, but to be moved and touched by that vision does not mean you have to sign a contract with the poet and implement all its clauses.

Eliot became the cult hero of modernists in Fitzrovia. Our generation fathered an enormous number of the progeny of modernism – the little magazines. These tumbled into the world edited by Americans in Paris, and Americans in Chicago and New York and also Americans in London where Eliot himself was to edit the *Criterion.* Many others, such as the *Dial,* the *Little Review, Wheels* or *transition* were edited by Eliot's contemporaries; but later Edgell Rickword, Grigson, Bronowski, Lehmann and Leavis became the leading editors trying to change the face of literature and criticism. Oxford officially ignored modernism as no literature after the early romantic poets was then studied in the school of English, but no don was needed to make Eliot a sensation. At Cambridge Leavis believed that he alone, derided and abused, had the courage in 1929 to publish an appreciative article on Eliot. In fact

Dadie Rylands, Joan Bennett and Muriel Bradbrook, among the younger dons, and Forbes and Potts among the older, spent hours of tutorials discussing Eliot's poetry with their pupils.

Eliot's criticism was another matter and F.L.Lucas at King's ridiculed Eliot's *obiter dicta* on Shakespeare, Goethe and Keats. For Leavis Eliot's criticism was as crucial as his poetry. Throughout his life Leavis never stopped expressing his pain that Eliot abandoned, apparently without thought, positions he had captured and which for Leavis were crucial. Leavis knew Eliot spoke with the authority of a saint and was astonished that the saint should not have recognized that in Leavis he had a theologian able to turn the saint's gnomic utterances into coherent dogma. As the years passed, and the saint failed to pronounce a benediction, Leavis made many disobliging references to Eliot's character, and found in D.H.Lawrence a more heroic modernist – someone who could not be captured by the vogue and who detested the culture of his times.

Lawrence fulfilled another destiny. When the American historian of ideas, Robert Wohl, looked at the leaders among the young in Europe in 1914 he found they were self-conscious generationalists. They believed theirs was a generation which for the first time in history could change the world because they had a clear objective and knew how to achieve it. Science, progress, even reason itself were illusions and therefore useless. Destruction must precede change. Only then could creation follow. The future lay with doers not thinkers, with a few bright, animated spirits who understood the nature of life; not with the masses or the old aristocratic and bourgeois elites. The intellectual must never accept the limitations imposed on man's freedom of action by geography and biology. He must recognize the inescapable destiny and would be judged by how he responded to that destiny.

Wohl studied these ideas through the lives of Massis and Montherlant in France, Junger in Germany and Ortega y Gasset in Spain. When he came to England he was perplexed, but chose as nearest to these continentals Rupert Brooke. He picked the wrong man. The real analogue was D.H.Lawrence. Lawrence did not, like Brooke and the others, welcome the Great War as purification. He despised democracy as the politics of the mob mind and communism as the embodiment of envy; determined never to be at the disposal of society; believed in the self as the final arbiter of every question, moral or political; and trusted in primitivism and emotion as the best path to follow in his search for a faith in which love and power would be united.

Lawrence was the most vocal of all the writers before the Great War in celebrating 'life'. He faced strong competition. Novelists and playwrights worked that word for all it was worth. Jonathan Rose showed how Samuel Butler, that liberator of the Edwardians, popularized the idea of a life force which was taken up by dozens, Shaw and Hulme among them. Some used it as a synonym for self-realization, others used it to distance themselves from the nineties; others, such as Henry James and Conrad, invoked 'life' as the gift of free will. Joyce used it to mean liberation from sexual hang-ups. Forster pictured his heroes awakening to life and breaking out of repressive conventions of sex and class. Wells, Maugham and Compton Mackenzie declared that life acquires meaning through fighting the mechanistic world. But it was Lawrence who more than any of them invoked life. He invoked it in *The Rainbow*, Rose assures us, 330 times or even 516 if one counts 'live', 'living', 'alive' and 'liveth'. For Lawrence life came to mean rebirth. The sexual act does not just enable men and women to reproduce their kind. It awakens them to the possibilities of existence.

His contemporaries were puzzled by him. Eliot coupled Lawrence (wrongly) with Wyndham Lewis. Both rushed into friendships that ended in insults, rows and rebuffs. Both had to dominate and demanded submission. To think as they did was not enough; their friends had to feel as they did. Both Lawrence and Lewis resented their poverty, the gifts or loans from patrons. Both raged that they had to rely on middle-class publishers and editors for their earnings. Frieda, the lazy, sexy aristocrat, shook Lawrence out of his puritan manners; but unlike Lewis he was, for all his hatred of the middle classes, full of good middle-class feelings, shocked by pornography, shamed by having to beg and wheedle, and proud of keeping a spick and span home.

There was another aristocrat who was as contemptuous as Lawrence for the conventions and boiled with rage against the Great War. The split between Bertrand Russell and Lawrence was taken by Leavis to be a crucial division in which Lawrence must be seen as the champion of 'life' against the cold, brittle philosopher and his Bloomsbury friends, who were all, said Lawrence, 'dead, dead, dead'. Everyone knows what Lawrence thought of Russell, but Russell's reaction to Lawrence is not much quoted. He began by liking Lawrence's fire, his energy and passion, and he even wondered whether Lawrence might be right about Keynes and the rest, but, 'Gradually I discovered that he had no wish to make the world better but only to indulge in eloquent soliloquy about how bad it was.' Russell disliked Lawrence's contempt for democracy and his Caesarism. 'I came to feel him a positive force for evil and he came to have the same feeling about me.' Russell could not endure the craziness:

> He is undisciplined in thought and mistakes his wishes for facts. He is also muddle-headed. He says 'facts' are quite unimportant, only 'truths' matter. London is a 'fact', not a 'truth'. But he wants London pulled down. I tried to make him see that that would be absurd if London were unimportant, but he kept reiterating that London doesn't really exist, and that he could easily make people see it doesn't, and then they would pull it down. He was so confident of his powers of persuasion that I challenged him to come to Trafalgar Square at once and begin preaching. That brought him to earth and he began to shuffle. His attitude is a little mad and

not quite honest, or at least very muddled. He has not learnt the lesson of individual impotence . . .

Lawrence, so powerful, so touching, so maddening, was a great but ambivalent figure for Our Age. A few followed Russell and saw Lawrence as infected by the same madness as the Nazis. Others such as Eric Bentley considered such a judgement as crude and insensitive. He placed Lawrence among the hero-worshippers with Nietzsche, Wagner and Shaw; but dispassionate critics were puzzled when they took Lawrence's advice to trust the tale not its teller. Which tale? The marvellous appeal to romantic dictatorship in *The Plumed Serpent* and *Kangaroo*? Or the genius of his early poems and half a dozen of his novels and the short stories? Leavis sanitized Lawrence and declared neither Eliot nor Forster could hold a candle to him. Lawrence divided our generation as much as he did his own. The last word was with Forster. When Lawrence died Forster said he 'was the greatest imaginative novelist of his generation'. And when Eliot asked Forster what exactly he meant by those three words, speaking with all Eliot's authority as a critic, Forster diminished Eliot by saying he didn't know: 'Only that there are occasions when I would rather feel like a fly than a spider, and the death of D.H.Lawrence is one of these.' These were our spiritual fathers.

Modernism did not sweep all before it between the wars. Probably more members of Our Age remained true to Rupert Brooke and Georgian literature. They were those who were haunted by the disappearance of rural England. The past bewitched post-Victorian writers. Galsworthy wrote of the passage of time, Belloc and Chesterton about the lessons to be learnt from history, even Wells began to ask how history conditions ideas. Reverence for the past is at the root of Hardy, of E.M.Forster, too, and of Edward Thomas. The Georgians were obsessed with the countryside, with country ways, with flowers and dells and harvest home. They saw the home counties being submerged by metroland and suburbia. The team of shire horses breasting the hill as they ploughed the land – that image so beloved by Stanley Baldwin – was being displaced by the tractor: arable was shrinking as farmers, in desperation at the collapse of the price of grain, as bad in the thirties as it had been in the eighties of the last century, put the land down to grass and abandoned marginal farms.

Inspired by Hardy and Housman, or by the threnodies of George Sturt, Adrian Bell and A.G.Street, whose *Farmer's Glory* drew a memorable contrast between farming in his father's days and his own, a stream of books extolling farming and country pursuits flowed from the press. Mary Webb's novels were Baldwin's favourite reading and so grotesque did these evocations of rural life become that Stella Gibbons was moved to write *Cold Comfort Farm.* Schoolmasters were still enthusiastic Tennysonians and Rupert Brooke's 'Grantchester' their approved modern poem. Novelists wove together themes

about the supernatural and the natural, simple yet intricate as the smocking on a child's frock. At times they were interwoven with fantasy like David Garnett's *Lady into Fox* or Sylvia Townsend Warner's *Lolly Willowes* about a woman living in the country who discovers she is a witch.

When T.H.White was a schoolmaster, he scorned the clever boys whom he thought insincere show-offs: he preferred those boys who knew how to ride or with whom he could catch snakes or go ferreting. Boys have a cruel eye. The clever wrote satires on him and the country-born waited for him to show his inexperience at things they had been bred to do. 'I am beginning to find,' he wrote, 'there is something horrible about boys in the mass: like haddocks.' His troubled heart was moved by the beauty of the English countryside and the dignity of the countrymen who farmed it. He wrote a diary about his experiences in learning to love it called *England Have my Bones.* But when the war came Ireland had his bones, where he retired to write his Arthurian cycle *The Once and Future King,* a pacifist reinterpretation of Mallory. He sentenced himself to do the only thing that gave his life meaning, learning to hunt, fish, shoot, loose hawks and fly an airplane. Young writers were still Georgians and by no means followers of Dorothy Richardson's exploration of the stream of consciousness. In his autobiography Denton Welch in the forties was to write passages such as:

> I looked at the flying clouds and the last leaves still trying to cling to the branches. The sun was making all the decay rich and lovely. Only the stream we crossed seemed cruel, still. The cold scum whirled under the bridge and reappeared with evil bubbles pushing through it.

In 1935 the Spencer Society published the poem of Christopher Gandy, a Cambridge freshman:

> There is a hunger in me for what is old
> Delicate and distant; a boy in bronze
> Who lay a thousand years on the sea floor
> Curling hair, smooth thighs crusted green.
> A thousand years the sun shone dimly on him
> Broken by the shadow of weeds, then darkness
> Of a shoal of tunnies; a great garden statue
> Dug on a torpid afternoon in Rome
> From the damp earth; he slept for an age
> And will sleep for another, vine-entangled hair
> Resting on cool hand; I sit and watch;
> My eyes wave; the lovely mouth
> Seems almost to breathe; perhaps I can take
> His sleep from him and he my waking.

CHAPTER 5

Pacifism

1

NOTHING SHOOK THE faith of Our Age in the ethos of the gentleman more than the self-destruction of Europe in what was for years to come to be known as the Great War. For a century England had not known what a continental war was: the Crimean War, the Indian Mutiny, colonial campaigns and the Boer War were all interludes which after humiliating beginnings turned in the end into heart-warming victories. Nor had England known a citizen war as had France, Germany or the United States. The experience of a war in which citizens were conscripted was all the more strange. To the casual observer it appears to be on a smaller scale for the British than the Second World War when the only continent to escape was South America, and at one point the armies fought as far east as the Caucasus and a separate war was being fought in the Pacific and Indian Oceans. In Europe the vast displacements of population, the devastation of cities by bombing, the annexation of whole countries by occupying troops, the massacre of the Jews and the subsequent shift in the balance of power may have seemed to us to be far more significant than the stalemate of the trenches. But to our fathers the Great War destroyed ancient continental dynasties and empires, created new states, and moved financial power from the City to Wall Street. It destroyed their peace of mind. They were haunted by the spectre of social revolution. And there was one great difference between the two world wars. Far fewer of Our Age were killed than our fathers.

The Great War was more gruesome. On the Western Front five out of every nine in the army were killed, missing or wounded. All over the country stand dumb testimonies to the sense of the annihilation of a generation. The Cenotaph represents the tongue-tied grief of the Anglo-Saxons just as the kilted Highlander on the march in Scottish towns the defiant grief of the Celt. Every school and college inscribed the names of the boys who never grew to be men. Each seems to ask: what would he have been, what would he have done? If you enjoy church-crawling in England – stopping on a drive to look at the churches in villages through which you are passing to enjoy the mixture of medieval styles or lament the Victorian restoration or to read the family names on the tombs in the chancel and transepts and the lapidary inscriptions com-

memorating those long dead – you will always find a memorial to men killed in the war of 1914–18, long lists of names even in tiny villages often bearing the bathetic words, 'Their name liveth for evermore.' Sometimes that memorial is flanked by a tablet to the officer son of the squire who never returned to live at the 'big house' and whose family have long since disappeared.

Every village has such a memorial, but you may well search in vain for a similar inscription to those who were killed in the Second World War. It was in Britain that the idea of honouring an 'unknown warrior' sprang up. Of the thousands of unidentifiable corpses several were exhumed from the vast cemeteries in Flanders, and one was chosen to be brought back and reinterred 'known only to God' in Westminster Abbey. First France and then country after country followed suit. Until 1939 the dead were commemorated by a two minutes' silence during which traffic stopped and people stood silent in the streets at the very time and date the ceasefire sounded on the Western Front.

Some historians have argued that as the British lost only seven hundred thousand men while France with a comparable population lost twice as many and Germany proportionately also double, the legend of a lost generation in which the 'best' men died was false. In fact thirty per cent of those between twenty and twenty-four in 1914 were killed and in the first two years of the war over forty per cent of the professional class joined up. In the first two years it was the middle and upper classes who were able financially to afford to join up and impelled by their ideals to do so. The losses of officers compared to other ranks was high in the army and vastly higher in the Royal Flying Corps. A subaltern was the most lethal of ranks. But the loss of non-commissioned officers had as debilitating an effect on business and industry after the war. Nor will it do to say that the British invented the legend to cover up the brutal fact that Britain after 1918 was no longer the first power in the world. The shock of the losses stunned the British; and the lesion of trench warfare and its toll never healed.

From then until now people have asked themselves how it could have occurred. The explanations, each of which gathered supporters, were these. It was a war caused by the contradictions of capitalism. Or it was an imperialist war caused by the struggle for colonies. Or it was caused by the rulers in Europe as a deliberate diversion from their domestic troubles beleaguered as they were by restive national minorities, militant trade unions and other opponents, such as the suffragettes, within their borders. Or it was caused by the generals abetted by armaments manufacturers elbowing the politicians aside. Or it was an accident due to the fact that none of the military machines had a reverse gear – once mobilization was ordered and troops began to move by rail, they could not be halted because to do so would be to throw the timetables into confusion and reveal to the enemy that country's strategic dispositions. Or it was caused because each nation was advised by its pundits that the struggle would be short and sharp, over by Christmas, and would end in victory. Kitchener alone predicted the war would last three years. The incredulous cabinet received the prediction in silence.

Not all these explanations have worn well. James Joll, our most sagacious analyst of international relations for these years, has shown that the evidence often points the other way. So far from politicians staging a diversion, most feared that war would provoke disaffection and even insurrection: had not the International declared that no worker would support a war? Bankers, as always, deplored anything which created instability and the head of the most famous banking house in Europe, Nathan Rothschild, implored *The Times* not to advocate military support for France. German manufacturers had no incentive to welcome a war with Britain, their best customer. Even Krupps, Creusot and Vickers stood to lose more than they would gain if international trade in armaments was suspended. The least sensational explanation – what A. J. P. Taylor called war by timetable – carries most weight. The civilians lost control of their armies especially in Russia, Austro-Hungary and Germany where civilian control was weakest.

But these explanations in themselves do not account for the failure of the statesmen to control events. They do not explain why the war was greeted with such enthusiasm. For one of the waves of emotion which overwhelmed the sea wall was the willingness of so many to accept war as a solution to the problems of their times. The fears and fantasies that moved the actions of statesmen were wider than those generated by offensive-defensive alliances and strategic plans. It was not only the old men who in Owen's words were willing like Abraham to slay 'his son, / And half the seed of Europe one by one'. It was the sons themselves. John Keegan described the innate inarticulate patriotism of working-class and lower-middle-class Britons who, like their German and French contemporaries, believed in their country's superiority to others. They had a sense of belonging not merely to Britain but to their churches, chapels, benefit clubs, Scout troops, Boys Brigades, schools, cricket and football teams, cycling clubs, and their City offices.

When on 28 August Derby launched the idea that Pals battalions should be formed and that 'those who joined together should serve together', the response in Manchester alone was prodigious. Three hundred battalions, nearly a quarter of a million men, were raised on those terms. Many joined for a lark, for release from a dreary job, and were cheered on their way by portly mayors and pretty women and by vast crowds filled with local pride. The troubles in Ireland disappeared overnight. So did the militant strikers. The idealism of the public school boys who, as former members of the Officers' Training Corps, were at once commissioned as officers was as intense. Like the young Ernst Junger in Germany, Rupert Brooke saw the war as a torrent of spring that would cleanse the country. Others more cynical, like Saki or Montherlant, welcomed the destruction of a society that seemed to them hypocritical, cowardly and without virtú.

In modernism itself, though the writers and artists were to be after 1918 among the most caustic critics of the war, that strong, destructive streak got full play. T.S.Eliot praised Hulme for being the antithesis of the tolerant, democratic mind; Pound and Wyndham Lewis were already on their way to the state of mind in which they were to praise Mussolini or Hitler. In the 1960s and seventies the young in the West were to feel the same. Never before had adolescents enjoyed such freedom, prosperity or advantages. But to them society seemed corrupt, too tolerant, too much given to the habit of applying reason to social problems instead of recognizing that the dark forces at play beneath the surface of society made such discussion irrelevant.

One profession in particular in Britain emerged discredited by the war. This was the military. Not so in countries whose armies had been defeated. In Russia the Red Army was greeted as a victorious force which had defeated the enemy within and the foreign interventionists without. In Germany there was bitter anti-war feeling which produced one of the most widely read books, *All Quiet on the Western Front*, and inspired the paintings of George Grosz. But the legend of the stab in the back and the very limitations on von Seeckt's army imposed by the Versailles Treaty encouraged many Germans to retain pride in their army. In their eyes Hindenburg had led the army back to the Fatherland unbroken and undefeated. The young diplomat Bill Cavendish-Bentinck, sent on an allied mission in 1920 to inspect the handover of the Polish Corridor to Poland, chatted to the German officer commanding the frontier guard. The officer said: 'You made a very hard treaty with us but it will be as it was after the battle of Jena, the spirit of the army will remain secretly alive in gymnastic associations, fire brigades, associations for this and that. In a few years you will get tired of sitting on us, we will rearm: *und dann wird ein Führer erscheinen.' 'Wer soll erscheinen, ein Hohenzollern?' 'Ach, nein, irgendjemand – und danach der Revanchekrieg.'*

But in France and Britain opinion somersaulted. During the war it had been hostile to Lloyd George and the frocks for interfering in military matters. Now Haig and his generals, who had not scrupled to intrigue against their political masters, began to be denounced for launching futile offensives on the Western Front. The tiny British army, unlike the great continental ones, never had a professional corps of staff officers. In peacetime it had a handful of divisions and hence few commanding officers of the rank of general. Wellington in the past, Brooke and Montgomery in the future, lamented the lack of generals competent to command an army corps or a division. There were some competent generals in the Great War, but (except for the Australian Monash) few had imagination, none had genius. Contempt for the military mentality became a cliché. The young men of Our Age found a theme that was to be worked and overworked in the years to come.

'Good morning; good morning!' the General said
When we met him last week on our way to the line,
Now the soldiers he smiled at are most of 'em dead,
And we're cursing his staff for incompetent swine.
'He's a cheery old card,' grunted Harry to Jack
As they slogged up to Arras with rifle and pack.

* * * *

But he did for them both with his plan of attack.

No longer were generals praised for winning the war. They were blamed for losing the lives of those who had won it and the politicians blamed for losing the peace. When Colonel Blimp was invented by David Low, he became a national figure. In 1963 Joan Littlewood staged her anti-militarist revue *Oh, What a Lovely War.* To do so she had to skip the Second and return to the Great War to depict the Blimps enjoying themselves oblivious of the carnage. In his celebrated study *The Great War and Modern Memory* Paul Fussell argues that an innocence about war dissolved for ever the old way of regarding national events, and created a new form of modern consciousness. Irony, which replaced that innocence, reflected the way men remembered the events of the Great War. Our metaphors, our choice of language, our tendency to polarize issues are legacies of those days. The supercilious staff officers of war became the clubmen, bookmen, industrialists and politicians of peace. Such simplification was to madden George Orwell who on his return from Spain found that 'the very people who for twenty years had sniggered over their superiority to war hysteria were the ones who rushed straight back into the mental slum of 1915'. They called anyone who did not toe the party line a spy, they retold atrocity stories, they sniffed out anti-fascists just as the Special Branch in the Great War had winkled out pro-Germans and pestered Frieda Lawrence. After the Great War the generation that fought muttered they had been fooled and betrayed. We were determined never again to be fooled. Some of us thought that there was one way certain to prevent ourselves from being so. That was to embrace pacifism; and in no country after 1918 did the pacifist movement gain such support as in Britain. It was the first sustained political revolt against the ethos of the gentleman.

2

THERE HAD FOR long been a pacifist tradition in Britain generated first by the Quakers and sustained by other nonconformist communions. In Victorian times it flourished for one good reason. Unlike any continental country

Britain, thanks to the navy, was invulnerable to invasion. In no other European country could John Stuart Mill have written his 'Essay on Liberty'. National security hardly figures in its argument. Moreover, whereas other continental powers had conscript armies, Britain had never compelled any citizen to bear arms and pacifists were not, as they often were on the Continent, socialists sustained by the ideas of international brotherhood. Liberals and radicals recalled how during the Crimean War John Bright begged Palmerston to negotiate and hushed the House of Commons when he spoke of the anxious homes awaiting the next mail. 'The Angel of Death has been abroad throughout the land; you may almost hear the beating of his wings ... he takes his victims from the castle of the noble, the mansion of the wealthy and the cottage of the poor and lowly.'

Until Belgium was invaded – and British security threatened by the loss of the Channel ports – Lloyd George, Simon, Harcourt and Beauchamp in the cabinet were opposed to supporting France. The Liberal press threatened any minister who voted for war that his career would be finished; and when war came Morley and Burns resigned from the cabinet. Ramsay MacDonald and the leaders of the Labour Party had protested at a mass meeting on 2 August against any attempt to support Tsarist Russia, but three days later the parliamentary Labour Party supported the government's motion to vote war credits and MacDonald resigned as leader. He, Philip Morrell, Norman Angell, Charles Trevelyan, E.D. Morel and Arthur Ponsonby formed a pacifist committee demanding the opening of negotiations.

'War is always bad for Liberals,' said the young Winston Churchill, then in 1900 a Tory; and for those suckled on Mill, on the Bulgarian atrocities and the Midlothian campaign, on the belief in the inevitability of progress so long as parliamentary democracy could be established within the civilized world, the declaration of war was a disaster. Their vision of life was shattered. The fragments were to be splintered still further as the Liberal government found it could not conduct a war on Liberal principles. In the Boer War, people had been free to oppose the war and to refuse to play any part in it. Now every principle of individual liberty was mocked by conscription and censorship, and it was a Liberal government that was imposing these constraints. The bill to introduce conscription in January 1916 produced a new kind of pacifist. These were not men and women who thought war *per se* was wicked or who objected themselves to taking life. They declared that since the British went to war to put an end to militarism, it was wrong in effect to establish militarism in Britain. This was the line which that long-lived progressive Fenner Brockway took when he declared militarism to be the enemy and not merely German militarism. The bellicose speeches of ministers, the insensitivity of the tribunals set up to consider the cases of conscientious objectors, the way war propaganda menaced reason and democracy made the wholly a-political Duncan Grant regard the war as 'utter madness and folly'. To some members of the educated classes the war was an affair from which they were entitled to opt out rather as today nuclear disarmers declare boroughs to be nuclear-free zones.

Pacifism had curious and far-reaching consequences upon the educated classes. It divided those returning from the trenches. We remember today the war poets revolted by the way the war was depicted on the London stage or in *Punch* when they contrasted it with the realities of enfilade fire and creeping barrages. We forget the large numbers who thought that pacifism was likely to lose what the war had been fought for. Pacifism checked the feminist movement. Immediately war was declared the Pankhursts enlisted the suffragettes, and young women began to hand out white feathers to men of military age. Those who fought and returned disillusioned saw women and old men as the two groups who, themselves safe from danger and death, drove them back to the trenches.

Pacifism also chipped the reputation of pre-war progressives. Those who fought at the front were not challenged, particularly if like Tawney they declined to rise above the rank of sergeant. But the elders who did not fight but supported the war lost part of their following. Shaw, as clever and paradoxical as ever, enraged both sides. The playwright Henry Arthur Jones never spoke to him again; and Robert Blatchford, the old socialist, denounced him as a renegade Irish alien betraying England. They did so because Shaw mocked the British for being as much governed by Junkers as Prussia. He lost his name with those who rejoiced to see the Tsarist government fall in Russia. Shaw urged Kerensky to fight on because only by the defeat of Prussia could British imperialism be defeated. That jocular, self-assured, provocative voice declared that the Kaiser was as much within his sovereign right to declare war as Britain was right to resist him; Germany must be smashed but those who did the smashing were either criminals or rascals.

Samuel Hynes has argued that the war dispersed the pre-war avant-garde. Certainly wartime censorship changed the relations between writers and the state. Few of them had had many dealings with the state in pre-1914 England. Now it perturbed them. They were compelled to submit to some sort of war service, and if they protested their work might be censored or they were threatened by prosecution. Particularly distasteful were the exhortations to do this and not to do that; to find that one could no longer get a drink in a pub at any time of day as one could on the Continent; to be badgered to 'take the pledge' and not to drink alcohol for the duration as the King did and Lloyd George, who persuaded him to do so, did not. The mood was to opt out. Disarmament and open diplomacy were the most spectacular ways of opting out of the discredited politics of the balance of power. Above all, one must opt out of the life and language of deceit and moral suasion.

The pacifists bequeathed their demonology to my generation. Their fiends were as numerous as those in *Paradise Lost.* High in the diabolic hierarchy came profiteers and armaments manufacturers, generals out for medals and slippery politicians evading disarmament. Newspaper proprietors had particularly long and twisted tails. Had they not gulled the public with their propaganda and stories of atrocities? It became common to declare that the stories of atrocities committed by German troops as they advanced through Belgium were deliberate lies concocted to make a negotiated peace impossible. (Some of them were false; but by no means all.) Paul Fussell constructed a table of 'high diction' words such as a 'steed' for horse and 'breast' for chest, a diction of euphemisms compounded from Henty's yarns and the poetry of Tennyson and Bridges (and, he could have added, the Edwardian Bookmen). This was why the earliest members of our generation were so deflationary. They learnt deflation from Richard Aldington, C.E.Montague and Robert Graves who wrote of the death of heroes, disenchantment with the world the war had created and their resolve to say goodbye to it. Later Beverley Nichols came out as a pacifist; we bore the news with stoic resolution.

For a decade no one wanted to relive the horrors of the Great War. And then R.C.Sherriff's *Journey's End* startled West End audiences. He showed a subaltern no more than a boy breaking down under shell fire and the company commander whom he idolized able to carry on only by taking to the bottle. The new gambit was to show how divisions between nations were artificial and could be transcended if human beings asserted themselves. Many admired movies such as Pabst's *Kameradschaft* in which a coal-mining disaster brought French and German miners together in the common cause of saving their mates. Or there were plays such as *Miracle at Verdun* (which T.H.White produced at my school) in which the dead soldiers of both countries rose from their graves to protest at the crimes politicians committed, and were still committing, in their names. The stock hero of the public school novel was time and again portrayed as being punished for refusing to join the Officers' Training Corps. The OTC with its field days and summer camps, which the Nazis were to declare was evidence of British militarism, became in fact something of a school joke.

Bertrand Russell was to be the hero of those who denounced war, the man who went to gaol for prejudicing Anglo-American relations in 1917 by saying that American soldiers would be used as strike-breakers since they were accustomed to playing that role in their own country; the man whom Trinity, to the scandal of the younger fellows away at the war, had deprived of his college lectureship; the man whose No Conscription meetings were broken up by an old-fashioned mob brandishing boards spiked with nails while the police stood by leaving Russell to his fate. (According to Russell they were deaf to the pleas that he was an eminent philosopher and intervened only when told he was the brother of an earl.) Before 1914 he had been only occasionally interested in politics – his most notable contribution being his book on German social-democracy in which he declared his aversion to marxism and faith in radicalism, neither of which he was to renounce. Those were the years which brought him lasting fame as an analytical philosopher. But after 1914 he resembled Timon of Athens.

There was, he admitted, no necessary connection between his views on these subjects and those he held on logic and epistemology. He endorsed the divorce between the two made by Hume 'with whom I agree so largely on abstract matters and disagree so totally in politics'. Was he, he asked himself, justified in holding such a view? Yes, he was, he declared. Whenever he found his opinions and emotions in unity, he knew he must be right. Strange to say he usually found they were so.

Writing in a prose whose lucidity was equalled by its elegance, Russell assumed that men behaved rationally, chose their goals and figured out the way of obtaining those goals, as if none of the impersonal forces of history that the continental sociologists had identified had any influence. If men failed to reach their goals that must be because evil or misguided rulers had impeded them. What stood in the way of the prevention of war, the control of the birthrate and the improvement of living standards? 'Only the evil passions of human minds,' he replied. Russell, a child of the Enlightenment, wrote as if human nature was changeless and men of all nations animated by the same ideas. He had little sense of history. 'In the middle ages,' he wrote, 'teaching became the exclusive prerogative of the Church with the result that there was little progress either intellectual or social.' To introduce symbols into logic is one thing: to introduce them into politics is another. Why not in an international dispute, he argued, substitute x, y and z for Germany, Russia and Britain? By doing so emotion would be subtracted from both sides of the political equation and the correct answer would emerge. He could write about nuclear weapons: 'It is, however, just possible, that mankind may prefer to survive and prosper rather than perish in misery.' As if 'mankind' – which is incapable of choosing – had any such choice!

Russell struck another note that can be heard by those who listen to my generation. He hated and distrusted authority: the enemy of teachers, the police, civil servants and the whole 'insolent aristocracy of jacks in office'. Did one 'regret that Pitt failed to catch and hang Tom Paine? For my part I was brought up in childhood to execrate Pitt and I see no reason to change.' He denounced 'the system' which demands we show loyalty to our country, impose discipline upon children and repress our sexual drives. He was a Whig holding advanced Victorian views and he saw no reason why he should not express what he thought about war, fiscal reform, marriage, the suffrage, education and euthanasia. Unlike Lawrence he considered protest should end in political action of some kind but he was not much good at organizing such action. He was too forthright an individual to succeed in the role of organization even on committees where one has to tack and veer. He did veer on one matter. He admitted that his experiences in the twenties when he and his second wife ran a progressive school taught him that 'a very definite and forceful exercise of authority' was needed if the weaker children were not to be bullied. Still, it can be argued Russell popularized the notion that small children should not be disciplined with military vigour; and that it is better to let them learn that their own ill-behaviour brings unhappiness than to stop them behaving spontaneously.

How far Russell was consistent is a matter for debate. He was a utilitarian. He opposed war in 1914 because he did not believe it would make the world a better place. He supported it in 1939 because he thought Hitler would make it a very much worse place. Yet his pamphlet 'Which Way to Peace?' argued that truth would be the first casualty in war; that in a war pacifists would be executed and a military dictatorship would be established. Britain should hand over her colonies to Hitler, disarm and the Nazis would look ridiculous. The atom bomb was another example of a rapid reassessment of utility. He at first advocated dropping the bomb on Russia in certain circumstances. Later he denied he had said any such thing – the report was a communist fabrication designed to discredit him.

Russell was always vain and perhaps the fear that he was becoming respectable – and therefore by his definition wicked – made him deviate from the truth. He got rid of the incubus of sin by becoming a member of the most extreme wing of the nuclear disarmament movement which was committed to civil disobedience. That was in line with his conduct in the Great War. It was also in line with his utilitarianism to decide that the triumph of communism would be less disastrous for mankind than the continued possession of weapons by America and this country which, if used, would result in appalling destruction. It was a blow to his vanity that the authorities did not oblige by making him a martyr. As de Gaulle said of Sartre, '*On n'arrête pas Voltaire.*'

Russell's name will live, like that of Occam, for his contribution to logic. He was, however, revered by progressives among Our Age for his writing on most advanced causes and for his belief that politics should be governed by the same principles as govern relations between decent human beings. His popular work *Marriage and Morals* won the Nobel Prize for literature and his writings during and after the First World War, naive or not, were read with attention and devotion. Freddie Ayer revered him, and one of the most subtle and radical of the philosophers of Our Age, Richard Wollheim, wrote in 1968 that Russell had been 'triumphantly right on nearly all the major issues of the day', arriving at 'correct and human views, far in advance of thinkers no less liberal but ostensibly more expert than himself'. He thought that in imaginativeness and prescience Russell made 'most other views about the state of the world seem puny and squalid'. This was the year when his son, the historian Conrad Russell, remembered Russell, beside himself with rage over the Vietnam War which proved (so he thought) that liberal, scientific man had sunk lower than the beasts, saying he could not 'vote for the Liberal Party because it was the party of Sir Edward Grey'. The politics of rational man are for ever fascinating. Conrad Russell preferred to praise his father for the blessings he gave to Our Age. He said Russell had made life safe for agnostics and atheists, he made it possible for couples who were not married to live together without censure and for anyone to make the maximum use of contraception. Standing for Parliament, as he once did as a candidate for Women's Suffrage, he made it possible for a woman to become prime minister and women's rights to be acknowledged. Above all he kept alive the radical tradition that rejects marxism and the egalitarian tradition of the Labour Party that rejects the class war and syndicalism.

In fact the contest for freedom from conformity to Christian belief was won by the generation of Bertrand Russell's father – Lord Amberley was a high-minded agnostic. The other two claims are just. Russell drew the sting from the words fornication and adultery which are heard more these days in the law courts than from the pulpit. But the very fact that he spoke and behaved as if one man's ideas could shame the world gave his ideas the force they had for our generation.

But those seriously interested in politics or even in social questions found his simplistic views and his failure to understand the impersonal forces of history naive.

CHAPTER 6

The Change in Manners and Morals

1

'AFRAID OF, NO; marginally bored with, yes' was the caption of one of Mark Boxer's pocket cartoons. No wonder Edward Albee took Virginia Woolf's name as a ploy intellectuals used to put down the middlebrows. By the 1980s people became irritated by the flow of autobiography, biography, diaries, letters, collections of ephemera and even newsletters of reminiscences that fed a stream of studies on Bloomsbury in hardback, paperback and holograph. And yet for many of us Bloomsbury were the liberators or the enragers – a group whom you could not ignore unless you were submerged in politics; and even then you had to find reasons for dismissing them. The animosity they aroused is testimony to their influence. They influenced more than most of our views on manners and morals.

They were certainly not consistent modernists. Strachey disliked post-impressionist art, thought Clive Bell's *Art* (1913) nonsense, and was at heart a mild conservative. Rum, too, that such an admirer of French literature should usually refer to Frenchmen as frogs. While Leonard Woolf and Forster scolded British officials for snubbing Africans and Asians, Virginia referred to them as darkies and Strachey called them gollywogs. Bloomsbury grew up in the heyday of imperialism and displayed that faint contempt for Jews so characteristic of their class. Leonard Woolf himself, who was an assimilated Jew more hostile to Jehovah than to Jesus, saw nothing odd in touring in his car through Germany in 1935. Virginia praised Joyce in public for experimenting and finding a new form for the novel but in private expressed disgust for *Ulysses* and called it an 'illiterate and underbred book'. Forster dismissed it too. James and Alix Strachey were psychoanalysts but Bloomsbury dismissed Freud. Virginia Woolf's novels and Fry's criticism were certainly avant-garde but what marked the group as modernists was their pride in being highbrow and their distrust of authority. For Leonard Woolf their first duty was to pillory the monarchy, vested interests, the upper classes, suburbia, the church, the army and the stock exchange, to question everything and respect nothing. Whatever explanation authority gave in self-justification was likely to be lies. From this came our distaste for the Establishment. In his commonplace book Forster quoted Acton: 'Every villain is followed by a sophist with a sponge.'

They wanted to live their lives regardless of the conventions of class, family and of national myths. The Victorian sages had declared that people should do this, and not do that: they owed this duty here and that there. This was anathema to Bloomsbury. The only way, Desmond MacCarthy concluded, to decide what a person was like was to 'trust your personal feelings towards him'. As everyone knows Moore, not God, was their interpreter and he had made it plain. For them the great discovery was that there was not much connection between being good and doing good. Although Moore contended the rightness of actions depended on the eventual good they produced, they considered that good states of mind which valued friendship and art were infinitely more important than other more humdrum virtues. Philosophers have expressed amazement that Keynes and Strachey could have misinterpreted Moore, but Moore himself had argued how exceptionally difficult it was ever to show that one had a *duty* to perform a particular action. To be sure of that one would have to know exactly all the effects of the action in the future; how valuable the action would be; and whether – supposing it could be shown to be valuable – how much more valuable the action would be than all its alternatives. The terms 'right' and 'wrong' were only ways of arriving at good or bad ends. What is the end to which you owe a duty? Answer that, and you will see whether you really do owe it. So many of the self-evident laws of behaviour, therefore, looked silly to these young dogs. Desmond MacCarthy recalled that they thought it more important to have the right feelings than to concern themselves with the unforeseeable consequences of actions. It is true that Leonard Woolf remembered the endless arguments they had about the consequences actions could have upon society. They did discuss what part one ought to take in practical politics. But even Woolf accepted it was the states of mind concerned with friendship and art that were most discussed. Their understanding of personal relations bore no resemblance to those self-conscious attempts to build fellowships like the early Fabians or Eric Gill, or guilds like Penty and Chesterton, or slum settlements like Toynbee. Friends were the barrier against worldliness. In those days Bertrand Russell maintained that only a particular union with one chosen woman could banish the intolerable loneliness of life in society. Bloomsbury disagreed. Forster took the title of his second novel from Shelley and said one should not 'with one chained friend, perhaps a jealous foe, / The dreariest and the longest journey go'.

'Personal relations,' wrote Morgan Forster, 'are the most important thing for ever and ever, and not this outer life of telegrams and anger.' He was the one to question the 'wall of newspapers and motor-cars and golf-clubs' which, if it fell, would reveal nothing but panic and emptiness. Each novel was a tract. Don't lie about your feelings: trust your sexual desire, even if you are a well-bred young girl overwhelmed with the advice of well-bred ladies, says *A Room With A View*. The inner life alone is real and pays off, people are real not ideas about them, says *The Longest Journey*. Think clearly not conventionally and act out your feelings: no passion can be wrong nor thought dangerous if it is honest. Renounce religion, dogmatic atheism, class, respectability and you will be saved; you will never experience Agape, spiritual love, unless you have first satisfied Eros, sexual desire.

Well known though Forster was after the Great War it was not until *A Passage to India* (1924) that he became a guru. In that novel, his undisputed claim to fame, he admitted that the tidy scheme of morality in pre-1914 England which his first four novels had explored no longer made sense. When he was younger Greece was the symbol of truth: now India told him truth was far more complex and odd. Passion and money were no longer the main motive forces of life; religion was one such force in India, and the moral judgements he had made about the struggle within the genteel Edwardian middle class seemed irrelevant in India. Rose Macaulay once twitted him for having been too much a Kingsman in the past, and Forster admitted to his Anglo-Indian friend Malcolm Darling that she had made a point. 'King's stands for personal relationships and these still seem to me to be the most real things on the surface of the earth, but I have acquired a feeling that people must go away from each other (spiritually) every now and then, and improve themselves if the relationship is going to develop or even endure ... the King's view over-simplified people: that I think was its defect. We are more complicated, also richer, than it knew, and affection grows more difficult than it used to be, and also more glorious.'

Some among Our Age like Forster for his faults. He was sentimental. He was detached and ironic, but hinted that Pan could be seen in the woods if only you opened your eyes. He sentimentalized the virtues he wanted to praise, like Charlie Chaplin exploiting the little man who thwarts the fates and authority. There was a further reason: he epitomized the sexually inhibited young Englishman. Forster knew and felt *Sehnsucht*, longing for the loved one. He could not express uninhibited passion and yet this was what his mind told him was desirable in itself and essential to success with a lover.

Music was the outlet for his emotions. His taste in music was the exact opposite of what might have been expected. He did not like what he regrettably called Mozartian tinkling, and particularly disliked madrigals, that staple entertainment by the choir at King's. Music for him meant uninhibited passion – Beethoven, Brahms, Strauss, Wolf. Within him were longings and visions resembling Michelangelo's 'Last Judgement' or Giorgione's 'La Tempesta'. But as a novelist he was a Le Nain. Occasionally a purple passage broke through, but it sounded out of place. As he ends the long evocation of England in *Howards End* 'lying as a jewel in a silver sea, sailing as a ship of souls, with all the brave world's fleet accompanying her towards eternity', it is like the second act of Strauss's *Ariadne auf Naxos* where two operas are being sung at the same time. His novels implore the intellectual to let go, yet at the same time they present the intellectual as a muff. Forster made muffiness into a cult. The muff tied to his mother, the muff who cannot endure male heartiness, the muff disheartened by bullies at school who finds in his Oxbridge college the dons who tell him that the life of books and art and friendship is superior to the duplicities of the world of affairs – this kind of person became the stereotype for many first novels between the wars. I.A. Richards noted this. He said Forster's 'real audience is youth caught at that stage when rebellion against uncomfortable conventions is easy because the cost of abandoning them has not been counted'.

Forster's reputation continued to mount during the thirties and the Second World War. Here was incorporated dislike of the public schools, dislike of gentlemanly snobbery, disbelief in belief. Liberals liked his rebuke to the marxists for dividing humanity into the good who wore red shirts and the bad who wore black. And the left liked him for distinguishing fascists from communists, who at least intended to do good. Had he not mocked the allegation, dear to the heart of *The Times*, that if we 'had all played less in the twenties and theorized less in the thirties, the jelly of civilization would have slid out of its mould and stood upright in a beautiful shape'? Was he not right to give no more than two cheers for the democracy which had led to Munich and regarded mass unemployment as a normal facet of life? Our Age liked his definition of the aristocracy as one not of power but of 'the sensitive, considerate and the plucky' – that included men and women from any social class. For three decades young intellectuals took Forster's aphorisms to heart. Almost immediately after he died in 1970 in his nineties the reaction set in.

Forster was a disciple of Lowes Dickinson, not of Moore, and hence stood a little to one side of Bloomsbury. Moore gave Bloomsbury a manner as well as a method – his silences, his eyes opening wide in astonishment at some point put to him and the eyebrows shooting up as he said, 'I *simply* don't understand *what* he means.' The Bloomsbury style of argument bore no relation to Victorian pontification. You made assertions but never justified them to the benighted, all you did was to raise your eyebrows. The only way to dissent from a Bloomsbury judgement was to make a counter-assertion and raise your eyebrows even higher. By raising your eyebrows you showed that no enlightened person could hold such benighted views. You did not earnestly contradict people who justified cruel actions on the grounds that you can't make an omelette without breaking eggs. To do so would be to pontificate like a Victorian. Judgement was an act of disdain. Disdain for words such as honour or indecency which were bandied about by those who were too lazy or frightened to face where a rational argument might lead them.

The master of this style was Lytton Strachey. A killing silence followed any remark he considered boorish or *funeste*. The world, he lamented, was not governed by reason. In a dialogue he invented, Locke says, 'If men were told the truth, might they not believe it? Let Rulers be bold and honest, and it is possible that the folly of their Peoples will disappear.' Diogenes: 'A pretty Phantastick Vision. But History is against you.' 'And Prophecy,' says Moses. 'And Common Observation,' adds Diogenes. 'Look at the world at this moment and what do we see? So long as it endures the world will continue to be ruled by cajolery, by injustice and by imposture.' Locke replies, 'If that be so, I must take leave to lament the Destiny of the Human Race.'

2

HE HAD CAUSE to lament the destiny of the human race. The Great War cemented Bloomsbury. They did not – like Russell – oppose it in 1914. At first Clive Bell wondered whether to join a non-combative unit. Strachey even felt a mild patriotism and thought Russell alienated public opinion. But as the hysteria rose he saw the very people who turned nasty against Fry and Bell for organizing the post-impressionist exhibition now turning nasty against anyone who did not warm to the war. In 1916 Strachey attended some lectures by Russell and wrote: 'Governments, religion, laws, property, even Good Form itself – down they go like ninepins – it is a charming sight!' Lloyd George, he said, deserved to be castrated in public at the foot of Nurse Cavell's statue. Nor did he lack courage of a kind; he sent up the tribunal which heard his application to be exempt from war service – and in the Great War such tribunals were very different from the fair-minded bodies that sat in the Second World War. The inflation of his Cambridge blue air cushion, the rug about his knees, the piping voice denying that he objected to all wars but only to this one, the pause as he surveyed the three of his sisters who had accompanied him before answering what he would do if a German soldier had attempted to rape one, and the skilful reply ('I should endeavour to interpose my body between the two'), with its hint of homosexual enjoyment, passed into the mythology of modernism.

Meanwhile deadly as ever Strachey was undermining Keynes. He suspected him of enjoying too much his work at the Treasury, the delights of Garsington and his friendship with Asquith. Early in 1916 Strachey cut out a press report of a militarist speech by a cabinet minister and put it on Keynes's breakfast plate with the comment: 'Dear Maynard, why are you still in the Treasury?' By the end of 1917 the poison had worked. When Lansdowne's proposals for peace talks had been rejected Keynes wrote to Duncan Grant, 'I work for a Government I despise for ends I think criminal.' He went to Versailles carrying a burden of personal guilt hoping to make reparation but despondent of the outcome from the first. As a comparatively junior official he had little chance of influencing affairs; Lloyd George, with whom he had crossed swords at the Treasury, disliked him; and as he watched reason and justice so often defeated he became ill with rage and misery.

Thus was the stage set for the delivery of two polemics that were classics for Our Age. Keynes's *The Economic Consequences of the Peace* expressed his contempt for the folly of governments and the venality of their leaders who had not the courage to ignore their countrymen's evil screams for revenge. He predicted that the double dealing at Versailles and the economic disorder caused by reparations would destroy prosperity in Europe, rot confidence in capitalism and destabilize democracy in Germany. Later in a marvellous passage he pictured Clemenceau, old and yellow with cynicism, sitting beside Lloyd George, a Welsh witch chanting spells that would beguile that non-conformist minister, Woodrow Wilson, into believing that his Fourteen Points remained intact when in fact they were being torn to tatters.

It is, of course, true that Keynes did not allow himself to take into account the political realities at Versailles. Keynes never considered the political and social forces that weighed upon his three villains. He did not realize they were prisoners. He could not allow that Lloyd George was the prisoner of the Conservative Party, or that Clemenceau – an exceptionally open-minded Frenchman married to an American wife – was the prisoner of France, whose northern provinces had been devastated and who had lost twice as many soldiers in the war as Britain. Keynes knew little about foreign countries, let alone the American Constitution. To him it was clear: reason, fair dealing and decency had been defeated by the Bloody Old Men.

Our Age was to see a reprise of the irrationality which Keynes so detested. In 1945 when the American and British governments were pondering what to do when they occupied Germany, there arrived in Whitehall the plan put forward by Morgenthau, the secretary to the US Treasury. It proposed Germany should be pastoralized and everyone in official and economic life down to the middle executive rank of, say, bank manager, should be expelled from their posts for having supported or connived at Nazism. Among the officials at the British Treasury was Edward Playfair who had been at King's. He saw at once that the proposals which had landed on his desk were like the settlement at Versailles, not only bad but mad. Why should Britain pay vast sums to feed the unemployable population of a deindustrialized and destabilized Germany in order to satisfy a demand, however comprehensible, for revenge? This time the forces of reason prevailed.

The second polemic was *Eminent Victorians* in which Strachey satirized the culture whose apotheosis was the Great War. The elaborate essay on Gordon was an attack on imperialism and power politics. It was also an attack on Messianic Christianity – the Christianity of those evangelical bishops who preached hatred of the Germans. But there was another form of Christianity which Strachey thought was equally insidious. That was the form exemplified by Cardinal Manning, the worldly wise, scheming prelate of the Church of Rome. Next he chose Dr Arnold as the hero of the public schools which turned out the Christian gentlemen who had fought unthinkingly in the war. Finally, Strachey struck at the one great movement that had salved the conscience of Victorian England – he struck at humanitarianism. He did not deny that Florence Nightingale's work was magnificent. He simply removed the picture of the lady with the lamp and drew in its place the portrait of a commanding, ruthless bird of prey destroying anybody standing in her path whether friend or foe, who treated human beings not as sentient beings but as objects to be manipulated to her ends – whose nature had been misunderstood even by her family. 'It was not a swan that they had hatched,' he wrote, 'it was an eagle.'

Strachey was saying something about public life that affected Our Age. He said that generals, headmasters, archbishops, even great authoritarian ladies who defeated generals through their machinations and treated human beings like objects, lost their own humanity in pursuing success. By suppressing her genuine erotic nature Florence Nightingale had transformed herself into a megalomaniac who, so far from inaugurating a new era in the care of patients, set her face against the findings of medical science. By becoming a mountainous prig Arnold had missed the opportunity to give boys a human education. By treating Newman with contempt Manning showed that in the church, as well as in the state, power drives out love. By his longing for fame Gordon destroyed himself and, in the concluding words of Strachey's diabolical book which were intended to make the reader think of the Great War, 'it had all ended very happily – in a glorious slaughter of twenty thousand Arabs, a vast addition to the British Empire, and a step in the peerage for Sir Evelyn Baring'.

Historians never mention Strachey's name without a curse. Trevor-Roper summed up professional opinion when he said 'his only achievement was to trivialize history and empty it of its real content in order to raise a few complacent titters from the radical chic of his times'. That odd clergyman at Trinity, F.A.Simpson, convicted Strachey of attributing self-seeking motives to Manning when the text from which Strachey was working gave clear evidence to the contrary. The critics are even more severe – Leavis denounced Bloomsbury for thinking Strachey a great writer and he spoke of Strachey's snigger. (Strachey never sniggered: he mocked.) And no professional biographer would endorse Strachey's method of 'lowering a little bucket into the vast ocean of material' to bring up a delicious *specimen* of evidence in order to transfix the butterfly he was mounting in his collection. And yet the dispassionate American historian and biographer of Macaulay, John Clive, praised Strachey for noticing how the social and psychological strains and stresses of the age erupted in individual neurosis and confusion.

Strachey was right to expose the stupidity and vulgarity of those times; and was his judgement on Manning, Gordon and Florence Nightingale so much at fault?

But then *Eminent Victorians* is neither history nor biography. It is a polemic designed to undermine the Victorian Establishment and its culture. It did so by treating life as a comedy – which Our Age found irresistible. Matthew Arnold had dismayed true Victorians by his flippancy; Max Beerbohm drew a cartoon of Arnold's niece Mrs Humphry Ward as a child saying, 'Why, Uncle Matthew, oh, why, will you not be always wholly serious?' Fun – the marvellous inventions of Dickens, the lyrics of W.S.Gilbert, the fancy of Lewis Carroll and the fantasy of Edward Lear – the Victorians accepted. Far less acceptable in the pre-1914 world were the paradoxes of Shaw and Chesterton, Belloc's verses, Wells's impudence, Saki's venom and Firbank's camp. No one could accuse Strachey of good, clean fun. Ridicule, a difficult weapon to handle, was his choice in the duel. Ridicule of His Most Catholic Majesty Philip II as he lay dying: 'And so, in ecstasy and in torment, in absurdity and in greatness, happy, miserable, horrible and holy King Philip went off to meet the Trinity.' Life was both tragic and comic and he considered scholars to be more comic than tragic. For him the spectacle of Horace Round writing at his home in Brighton a series of articles which convicted the omniscient Professor Freeman of inaccuracies of fact and misreading of authorities became particularly piquant when Round denounced this irascible pedant for imposing on the learned world the word 'Senlac' as the correct name for the Battle of Hastings.

> The effect of these articles on Freeman was alarming; his blood boiled, but he positively made no reply. For years, the attacks continued, and for years the professor was dumb. Fulminating rejoinders rushed into his brain only to be whisked away again – they were not quite fulminating enough. The most devastating article of all was written, was set up in proof, was not yet published; it contained the exposé of "Senlac", and rumours of its purpose and approaching appearance were already flying about in museums and common rooms. Freeman was aghast at this last impertinence; but still he nursed his wrath. Like King Lear he would do such things – what they were yet he knew not – but they should be the terrors of the earth. At last, silent and purple, he gathered his female attendants about him, and left England for an infuriated holiday. There was an ominous pause; and then the fell news reached Brighton. The professor had gone pop in Spain.

'I am afraid my biography will present a slightly shocking spectacle', Strachey confessed to Mary Hutchinson; and it was indeed Michael Holroyd's biography that first revealed the hours of homosexual intrigue Keynes and Strachey spent as undergraduates pursuing the ideal of what they called the Higher Sodomy. That was to be a love that was simultaneously physical, spiritual and intellectual, a combination of qualities that put it in their view in a different class from heterosexual love. There were many liaisons in Bloomsbury but they did not consider themselves to be promiscuous. One or both of the protagonists must have experienced that longing for the other that is called love. In this they differed from Russell or H.G.Wells who set out in their maturity to make any pretty woman who took their fancy. The trouble in Bloomsbury was that Duncan Grant, like the girl in *Oklahoma* who can't say no, experienced that state of mind so continuously and with so many people, and was so thoughtless, mischievous, selfish, disorganized and enchanting, that he created havoc among his friends. Strachey was lonely and for years miserable in love; but he did not deviate from the ideal.

At a conference of French intellectuals at Pontigny Strachey was woken from slumber by being asked point-blank what in his opinion was the most important thing in the world. He uttered a single word: 'Passion'. He was racked with passion and once said that he longed to throttle his lovers with luxury. Yet he learnt in middle age to rise above jealousy and become the diplomatic pacifier. My generation was taught by Bloomsbury that the conquest of jealousy was the mark of civilized behaviour. In love wounds would be inflicted; that was inevitable. But the desire to wound back in revenge must be resisted. No one should blame you for feeling jealous: if you feel, you feel. But you can be blamed for doing spiteful and malicious actions. Vanessa Bell was wounded by her husband's infidelities, but she did not quarrel with his mistresses. She in turn disentangled herself from her affair with Roger Fry with such skill that he felt hardly a pang even though he had been displaced by the ubiquitous Duncan Grant. Vanessa took a proprietary interest in Maynard Keynes and therefore did not take kindly to Lydia Lopokova who would wander over and interrupt her painting. In the same way her sister Virginia, who had a proprietary interest in Clive Bell, never took to Mary Hutchinson. But in neither case did they give way to jealousy. When Virginia Woolf had her fling with Vita Sackville-West, Leonard let the affair take its course: but he watched over her health and warned Vita that she had a problem on her hands.

But should one always let an affair takes its course? Bunny Garnett, who had been one of Duncan Grant's loves and was present at the birth of his and Vanessa's daughter Angelica, waited until Angelica grew up. Then he went into action and married her. Garnett was the one predator in Bloomsbury. Vanessa and Duncan saw what he was at. But, true to their convention, they did nothing about it. They stood aside and watched the sacrifice of the lamb to the wolf in the pack.

In the end Joyce became the god of the experimental novel, but before the Second World War Virginia Woolf was its goddess and nearer to the morality of Our Age. Her upper-class characters bolster the way things go on, denouncing the Irish or the miners or rebellious natives, those who threaten their way of life. She did not romanticize the death of war heroes in *Jacob's Room*. That book was her attempt to destroy the legend that had gathered about Rupert Brooke. It was also about the society that destroyed him – the complacent provinciality of Cambridge, the Hellenism of Lowes Dickinson, the contempt for women and the impersonal state that demanded Brooke's death. Throughout her life she saw the Establishment saying that life must go on even if thousands of young men have to die – and her death can be seen as an unconscious protest at it. That is what Mrs Dalloway says. But need things go on in that way?

She became the patron saint for the feminists of Our Age and still more for their children. Who strangled women's liberty? She told them it was the patriarchal family. It turned girls into spinsters ministering to ageing parents; or into wives ministering to husbands round whom the household must revolve; or into mothers burdened with every kind of obligation to cousins and aunts beyond their own children: the patriarchal family where children, none of whom have privacy or a room of their own, are estranged from their parents who have married late to enable the wife to live 'in the style to which she is accustomed': the patriarchal family where servants were not human beings to talk to but hands separated by architectural devices from the family to live in a world below stairs: the patriarchal family where there was no honest talk because so many subjects were unsuitable for women or children, and a child had to use coconut language to talk about the unmentionable such as M-ker, O-ker, N-ker, E-ker, Y-kernut – Money. Above all there was the hypocrisy about sex: no mention ever of mésalliances or buggers. And without truthfulness about feelings what was there left in private life?

Almost alone among the major writers of the time she spoke for women. She stood in particular against the phallic Lawrentian vision of life, and encouraged novelists like Elizabeth Bowen and Rosamond Lehmann to write about the sufferings of women. In the 1970s she became a cult figure, and militant feminists regarded her father, her half-brothers, her husband and her nephew who wrote her biography as fiends who had one object in view – to imprison and torture her and justify these actions. Mad? – she was not mad. That was the invention of those determined to repress her outburst of resentment against her imprisonment. Leonard Woolf, counting the dates of Virginia's periods because he had detected a correlation between delay in menstruation and her bursts of manic depression, became transformed from the devoted husband into an anal monster whose so-called concern for her health was on a par with his habit of keeping meticulous accounts, logging the number of miles he drove, recording the date he had his hair cut, the number of bushels of apples yielded by each tree in his orchard, the events of every day for fifty years and their exact expenditure and earnings. For the feminists none of her books outshone the two feminist volumes, *A Room of One's Own* and *Three Guineas*.

It says something about my generation that these were the two volumes that embarrassed them. They thought them silly. Queenie Leavis's review of *Three Guineas*, 'Caterpillars of the Commonwealth Unite', stands high in the annals of modern invective. For Our Age Virginia Woolf was the protagonist of the experimental novel, a self-conscious artist ready to twit the Grand Old Men of letters like Arnold Bennett. She also impressed them as the protagonist of the private life. She seemed to prove that the mind, which gave shape to feelings, was the ultimate in life and art. The miseries of adolescence and the falsities of public affairs and institutions were as nothing compared to the integrity that demanded you should detect exactly what you felt and should then, having realized what sort of a person you were, live up to it. She even gained a few supporters in Oxford; David Cecil considered her superior to Forster.

Were Bloomsbury snobs? Our Age were divided on the matter. It would be very hard to find anyone less satisfied with their own class or less envious of a higher class than Forster, Leonard Woolf or Desmond MacCarthy. Certainly they were clear what class they belonged to – the intellectual aristocracy. Keynes believed that was the class which ought to take the essential decisions in government; Bell that civilization depended on leisured rentiers. They knew the currency of the London *beau monde*, the world of politics, titles and money, to be rhinestones not diamonds. Keynes flirted with that world in the Great War and moved in it again in the Second World War ('I never could resist a Cecil'); Strachey was for a time dazzled by Ottoline Morrell and enjoyed being lionized, but the malice of his comments upon the circles of Garsington, the Asquiths and Emerald Cunard show how much he kept his distance. Virginia Woolf, too, liked to flit in and out of Mayfair, but her essay, 'Am I a Snob?' pleads that everyone, herself included, is compromised by worldliness. Compromised but not deluded. Poor Lady Colefax and her rival hostesses are consigned to the wilderness, 'as coarse as usual and dull'. She had a sharp eye for social differences and thought herself several cuts above the young women adherents of Bloomsbury such as Barbara Hiles, or Carrington or Alix Strachey. She knew that class and money shape an individual and Forster called her snobbery courageous. 'She was a lady, by birth and upbringing, and it was no use being cowardly about it, and pretending that her mother had turned a mangle, or that Sir Leslie had been a plasterer's mate . . .'

She had guilt, the American critic Alex Zwerdling thinks, about her inherited income that enabled her to keep servants and she could not get on with them as she would have liked. She would not pretend she could relate to people of the lower classes and she could not describe them in her novels. She was unfair to those who tried to change their state. To her Mrs Humphry Ward had all the insensitivity of the charitable. She saw Beatrice Webb as 'an industrious spider surrounded by earnest drab women and broad-nosed, sallow, shock-headed young men, who all looked unhealthy and singular and impotent'. She could enjoy a pacifist meeting in which H.G.Wells, who had been defending the war, was punctured emitting squeaks of rage. 'The jingoes were defeated by the cranks ... It was a splendid sight to see.' But she would not identify with those 'gnomes who as always creep out on these occasions – old women in coats and skirts with voluminous red ties and little buttons and badges attached to them – crippled, stammering men and old patriarchs with beards'. She would not step out of her class nor out of her group. She knew precisely where she was and thought that the break Bloomsbury had made in manners was right. She liked a world where young men did not talk of engagements and marriages but of their own sexual adventures; yet did not use four-letter words. Yes, she minded a bit what people said of her blue dress, unlike her sister who cut the cable and dressed down to the point where to have gone any further would have led to indecency. But Virginia would retrieve without batting an eyelid a hairpin that she dropped in her soup, lick it and reinsert it into the ruin that passed for a coiffure.

Forster summed up the virtues and failings of his friends in Bloomsbury by saying:

> Essentially *gentlefolks*. Might occasionally open other people's letters but wouldn't steal, bully, slander, blackmail or resent generosity as some of their critics would ... The only genuine *movement* in English civilization though that civilization contains far better and more genuine individuals. But unkind despite irritable protests to the contrary: Orlando regards centuries of flesh and spirit as fresh fuel for her bonfire and death can only be laughed at ... Contempt for the outsider plays a very small part and rests on inattention rather than arrogance. Once convinced he is not a figure of fun, it welcomes and studies him, but the rest of humanity remains in a background of screaming farce as before ...
>
> Meanwhile the intellect – thinking and talking things out – goes steadily ahead, 'things' looking rather like small xmas trees when they come into the room and trees minus their leaves and decorations when they are carried out. The final bareness isn't tragic, the horrors of the universe being surveyed in physical comfort and suffering only apprehended intellectually ...

Did Bloomsbury have much influence on Our Age? Some say very little and regard them as overrated and insignificant. What did they say that was not being said by dozens of others? Probably between the wars a few of Bloomsbury's ideas were adopted by a large number of people and a large number of them by a few. For instance, Bloomsbury set a style of life for intellectuals. They began to buy country cottages. In the days before labour-saving devices were invented and electricity reached the villages, the cottages were stark enough. For years the Woolfs lived with outdoor sanitation and a copper for the weekly wash. (Leonard Woolf was so stingy that he used discarded galleys as lavatory paper.) But other intellectuals took country cottages without any prompting from Bloomsbury. There were, however, others who, disapproving of Bloomsbury, argued that their influence was enormous and destructive of British culture. Leavis claimed that Bloomsbury wrapped its tentacles round British culture. Desmond MacCarthy was succeeded as literary editor of the *Nation*, David Garnett and Raymond Mortimer of the *New Statesman and Nation*; and Mortimer succeeded MacCarthy as lead reviewer in *The Sunday Times*. Among the early members of Our Age were the music critic Eddy Sackville-West, Vita's cousin. John Lehmann became an editor of a series on the BBC's Third Programme which was run by George Barnes, half-brother of Mary Hutchinson. Later Lehmann edited *New Writing* and the *London Magazine*. Joe Ackerley, a close friend of Morgan Forster, became editor of the *Listener*. Roger Senhouse, Lytton Strachey's beloved, was a publisher and a partner in Secker and Warburg. Shove, Lucas and Rylands were dons at King's. The term Bloomsbury came to be a synonym for what Leavis called 'metropolitan culture' that included virtually anyone of Our Age who worked in the media. It was, in fact, as we shall see, a term used to mark off one social class from another.

Of course there were others subverting Establishment morality – not only in Chelsea and Hampstead but in every provincial city. But subversion was not confined to the progressives. There was one who was subverting it in Mayfair. He had been a successful playwright, moving in the best circles before the Great War. After his divorce in the twenties he moved somewhat to the side of the best circles. This was Somerset Maugham, the guru of café society. He told the rich and literate how and where to travel, where to buy their clothes, how to win at bridge and what kind of male sensibility and looks excites animal lust in women. He gave them the illusion that they too were cosmopolitan. His stories told the upper classes that they ought to be less intolerant of queer fish since among themselves there were quite a number who suddenly could resist no longer and broke out of their conventions, went off, not just with somebody's wife, but the last sort of woman whom you would think they would choose; they seduced a waitress, or went to live with a Tahitian girl to get free.

Deceit was part of the jungle he explored. He discovered the boredom and corruption of communities such as the rubber planters in Malaya, and conveyed through the caddishness of its officials or businessmen the decline of the British Empire itself. Standing outside his stories as the modest but worldly-wise commentator, Maugham fancied himself to be the analogue of his brother the judge: he was 'summing up' his times. Academic critics refused to rank him among the giants, and bitter with gall he sneered at Henry James's style and modern art. He had learnt from Maupassant how to tell a short story and his pride in his craftsmanship and contempt for contemporaries who could not hold their readers' attention was understandable. He justified his vision of the world as that of the classic French nineteenth-century writers: the world is pitiless and revenges itself on the deviant, well-known men and women are vile, you either play along or drop out. In Larry Darrell the American hero of *The Razor's Edge* Maugham invented a character that was to become a model in the sixties: the young artist who turns to India for religion and drops out. Maugham never offended society by revealing his homosexuality; but equally he never bothered to conceal it. He had never been good at suppressing his envy but he had suppressed his meanness. In his nineties he lost control of both as other men lose control of their bladder and their wits.

Then among the father figures of Our Age was Aldous Huxley, who knew Bloomsbury well through his visits to Garsington but was never one of them. He was an indisputable son of Oxford. 'Only connect', wrote Forster, hoping that if people made the effort they would lose some of their insensitivity. Aldous Huxley's novels can be read as Oxford's denial of Cambridge hopes. His tortured intellectuals never connect. And yet it would be easy to show how he popularized several of Bloomsbury's ideas – the importance of travel, for instance, which became a fetish for our generation. The educated classes felt themselves to be more part of Europe then than they do today and 'Dear Abroad' was Mexico, China, Iceland, the Levant, for Graham Greene Africa. No one was ever more of an intellectual than Huxley. He influenced more intellectuals in their youth among Our Age than Bloomsbury. Alan Pryce-Jones once said, 'Huxley gave us our intellectual colours.' By spotting the allusions to books you had not read you felt you had won your cap in the XV. How could one not be dazzled by the incomparable erudition in science as well as literature? How could one not be secretly glad to have learnt through the discomfiture of his callow young men and women how to be less callow oneself? One had the illusion of listening to one of those 'healers in country-houses at the end of drives' whom Auden blessed. Few schoolboys who were trying to be sophisticated could resist the appeal of this modern Thomas Love Peacock.

3

THERE WAS ONE last gift that we prized. We wanted to be amused and to be amusing. Not only the intellectuals. Our philistine members wanted to regard life as a rag in order to forget the Great War. It was the pleasure-loving philistines who made the morality of the pre-war world tremble before cocktails, motor racing, necking, gate-crashing and pyjama parties; when society began to crumble before café society; when musical comedy stars devastated audiences with their charm as well as their looks and conjured up a world of innocence, bliss and fun; when American styles began to titillate

Europe and Hollywood provided dream worlds for the pinched middle classes and the deprived working classes. Many Oxford and Cambridge colleges were only too glad to supplement their numbers by admitting thick, indolent, agreeable athletes in the hope they would play at Twickenham, or row on the Tideway or represent the university at Lord's: some even remained in residence year after year trying in vain to pass the entrance exam, Smalls or Little-go, so that they could formally enter the university and read for a pass degree.

One Englishman of the pre-war generation symbolized this frank, unthinking schoolboy world. He became our supreme entertainer, amusing America almost as much as his countrymen. He had been one of the bowler-hatted crowd working in a bank before the Great War like T.S.Eliot. But there the comparison ended. He played games with style, glowed with self-confidence and missed what his characters called the 'Varsity only because his father lost most of his money. Unlike Eliot he did not last long in the bank. In a rag he profaned the mysteries of Lombard Street. Like a curate defiling a Bible, he tore the front page out of a ledger. He was sacked on the spot.

No author probably had such a wide audience as P.G.Wodehouse. If you had not read at eleven his school stories, or met Psmith at fourteen and learnt how to enrage housemasters and prefects, or sympathized at seventeen with Lord Emsworth and his pigs, or seen yourself as Bertie Wooster attended by Jeeves, you were a dull pooky fellow. Wodehouse revived light English prose. He was the only Englishman who saw how the American vernacular revitalized the English language. Wodehouse's metaphors and similes replaced the epigram. There was the 'whacking big fish lying on the carpet and staring up at me in a rather austere sort of way as if it wanted a written explanation and apology'. There was 'when Aunt is calling to Aunt like mastodons bellowing across primeval swamps'. Adoring public school life he remained the irrepressible fifth-former to the end of time to whom highbrows, Freud, aunts, magnates, club bores and the Right Hon. 'who looked as if he had been poured into his clothes and had forgotten to say "When!"' were God-given targets for ragging.

Wodehouse irritated earnest progressives, who saw him as a buffoon pandering to nostalgia and romanticizing the most effete elements in the upper classes. He was also dismissed by the literary sages: Leavis was enraged when Oxford gave him an honorary degree. He had edited his school magazine at Dulwich, and the editors of all university and school magazines with pretensions to humour between the two wars tried to imitate him. In his first novel Evelyn Waugh has passages of pure Wodehouse. '"We class schools, you see, into four grades: Leading School, First Rate School, Good School and School. Frankly," said Mr Levy, "School is pretty bad."'

Despite the fun Wodehouse had at the expense of education he could turn out a copy of Greek or Latin verse at Dulwich with the best of them. But then education for my generation often itself resembled a game. Skill in turning out hexameters produced the age of the crossword, the acrostic, the palindrome, the anagram, the clerihew, the parody and the *New Statesman* competition. The art of light verse that Ronald Knox had brought to perfection flourished. The classical curriculum had even more exalted achievements. It trained cryptographers who deciphered enemy traffic with all the skill of Housman in emending a corrupt text. The succinct and killing Whitehall minute was perfected. During the Second World War the British often gained points in negotiation with the Americans despite their inferiority in strength because they drafted documents more lucidly. Keynes gave offence in Washington by contending that American officialese was written in Cherokee, a language that had survived the colonial period and which, to placate Red Indian susceptibilities, had been adopted as the language of government.

Boys in the sixth form were praised if they could acquire another accomplishment. They were encouraged to polish their essays and employ epigram and paradox. To be dull was to lack intellectual flair, fire, imagination. Those who acquired these arts revolved like a Catherine wheel, sparks flying; but as often as not the firework spluttered to a halt and one could see the wheel still turning incandescent for a while until it too became extinct. No one could have guessed from the middle-aged man what the promise of his youth had seemed to be.

Such a boy was Geoffrey Madan, who wrote a description of Eton in Herodotean Greek so perfect that it was 'sent up for play' and the school got a half holiday. Taken up for his looks and his wit he was eighteen when the Great War began, returned to Oxford after it, left in boredom and retired into a lifetime of obscurity. Two friends edited his notebooks after his death, a collection of epigrams and aphorisms by others. His own anagram, 'R.C.Saint's life? O No!' out of 'less fornication', or his epigram of an excruciating bore, 'Alive, in the sense that he can't be legally buried', or the aphorism 'There are people who should be careful to amortize the charm of their youth' are the genuine article. In Madan's notebooks you can see the delight the young of Our Age had in spotting the ludicrous. 'Lunch party given by Lady Colefax to meet the mother of the Unknown Warrior.' Or, 'The Bishop of Gloucester begins an article on Christian doctrine, "The Apostles' Creed need not detain us long."' The master aphorist from whom some of us learnt was Russell's first brother-in-law Logan Pearsall Smith. From the starting gate of classics or history at school shot out the first string of racehorses to set the pace. They were the Oxford Wits.

At this point warning bells begin to ring. Historians and critics are compelled to use shorthand terms to impose some sort of intelligible order upon their material: they refer to the Lake Poets, the Spasmodics and the Pre-Raphaelites in the nineteenth century. Such groups – like Bloomsbury – exist, but they change their nature or melt away as the years pass, and the set of individuals within them goes each on his own way. Many are the books, written in the thirties and forties, which explain human beings by categorizing them. Some use physical categories. You could divide your friends into Kretschmer's types: the pyknic which he thought exhibited a cyclothymic temperament prone to manic depressive psychosis: and the asthenic allied to schizoid or schizophrenic states. Realizing that not all cyclothymes were short and compressed and not all schizoids weedy and weak, he added a pyknic-athletic and an asthenic-athletic type. Or you could follow Sheldon. After measuring and marking a thousand students at Chicago University on a seven-point scale Sheldon decided there were three types of extreme physique, endomorphs, mesomorphs, ectomorphs and three corresponding types of temperament: viscerotonics, somatatonics and cerebrotonics.

Individuals were a mixture of these types: even Aldous Huxley the ultra-ectomorph had muscles and intestines. Some people preferred Joan Evans's delightful game of dividing people into introverts or extroverts, slow or quick. According to which you were you admired this or detested that artist, you decorated your rooms in a particular way and either lived among the objects that recalled your past or chose objects for their intrinsic aesthetic value. Psychology gave way to sociology. David Riesman analysed our times as an age when inner-directed man, who regardless of opposition homed on to his goal aided by the gyroscopic of his conscience implanted within him, was being ousted by other-directed man who acted only when he had read on his radar screen the blips of other people's approval. If medieval tradition-directed man failed he felt shame; if inner-directed man failed he felt guilt; if other-directed man failed he felt anxiety at losing the approval of his peers.

Martin Green played the game of categories when he came to write about the Oxford Wits and divided them into dandies, rogues and naïfs. The dandies and aesthetes were led by Harold Acton and Brian Howard; the rogues by Robert Byron, Randolph Churchill and – at a later date and at Cambridge – by Guy Burgess; and the naïfs by Auden and Spender. Under these categories he tried to subsume English culture between the two wars. Against the Wits he set the puritans who recalled Englishmen to serious life: Leavis and Orwell. Somewhat naturally the categories proved unequal to the task and burst. So did Martin Green. Returning to England in the liberating days of the sixties he began to wonder whether he had been right in seeing these Children of the Sun as responsible for Britain's decadence. Worse still he actually met Harold Acton and was charmed off his perch. Might not the Wits have been the source of Britain's present vitality? Perhaps Firbank and not Leavis was the man to follow. Green brought together a lot of entertaining material about the Wits and he was indeed right to see some of them as dandies

– that tributary of talent which fascinated Baudelaire and whose stream one can follow back through the decadents of the Yellow Book, through the young Disraeli and Dickens and the Regency bucks to the Restoration rakes and the bejewelled Elizabethan poetasters.

The Wits have been much romanticized as a set; and they themselves have gilded the legend by their own writings – Waugh and Powell in their novels, Harold Acton and Connolly in their memoirs.* But they were not a set. They were not a self-conscious group of friends like Bloomsbury. They might resemble an apostolic succession but, spread out across the decade, they spoke with different voices and went different ways. Maurice Bowra was at their head partly because he was older – he went straight from school into the artillery during the war – and partly because this convivial, gregarious and powerful classical scholar reminded his generation that Eliot's poetry was part of European modernism, the movement that numbered Valery, Rilke, George, Cavafy, Blok – and Yeats. Greek lyric poetry remained the first of his loves: but Pasternak, Quasimodo, Neruda and Seferis spoke of him with gratitude as their interpreter. Bowra was, however, more than a scholar. He was an uninhibited conversationalist and made the joke in bad taste acceptable. He embodied the spirit of those who wanted to be done with the war and good form. Pleasure, vitality and spontaneity were his delight: caginess, philistinism, pretentiousness and pomposity his prey. He distrusted the Establishment, was the friend of freedom and the young, the enemy of drabness and the *bien pensants*. Prigs or prudes detested him and feared the sharpness of his retorts.

He considered himself with justice as the leader of the Immoral Front, and he liberated successive years of undergraduates by his unbridled talk about people, sex, poetry and art. The power of his personality, his overwhelming voice and his lightning play with words dominated those who gathered in his rooms in Wadham. His mannerisms were imitated by his admirers. Osbert Lancaster took over his voice and manner of speech lock, stock and barrel. Bowra's penchant for litotes which he indulged in speech (but never in his businesslike and workaday prose) such as 'far from jolly', 'by no means

* Robert Boothby and Roy Harrod came up to Oxford in the same year as Bowra but they were two years younger – too young to have fought in the Great War. In 1922 Evelyn Waugh and the movie buff John Sutro appeared, as did the much courted historian Richard Pares. Cyril Connolly, Kenneth Clark, Robert Byron, Eddy Sackville-West and Bobby Longden were a year younger. Harold Acton and Brian Howard arrived about the same time as Graham Greene, Patrick Kinross and Claud Cockburn who was later to edit *The Week*. The novelists Anthony Powell and Henry Yorke (Henry Green) were contemporaries of Peter Quennell and Tom Driberg. John Betjeman and John Sparrow, later to be warden of All Souls', came up in 1925: Christopher Sykes, Waugh's biographer, was a year younger. The next year Osbert Lancaster, wittiest of cartoonists, and Alan Pryce-Jones, who later edited *The Times Literary Supplement* in one of its best periods, make their bow. Some did not stay at Oxford all that long: Pryce-Jones was sent down after two terms for gross idleness. This roll-call does not include those who made a name for themselves acting in the OUDS, nor those like Hamish Erskine and Mark Ogilvie-Grant who appear in memoirs as members of Comus's rout.

bad', litter the pages of Anthony Powell's memoirs. In one of Powell's volumes one finds sprouting 'the decision to marry could hardly be regarded as less than rash on both sides'; or 'something by no means to be dismissed as negligible'; or 'not much less than staggered', or 'by no means at that moment overwhelmed with invitations I unhesitantly accepted', or 'could not have been more agreeable'; or 'nothing from which to dissent'. Even Evelyn Waugh's letters echo Bowra's figures of speech.

The Oxford Wits might visit Garsington but they owed nothing to Bloomsbury. In fact they disliked Bloomsbury, thought its inhabitants dowdy, middle-class, lacking in vitality and insufficiently cosmopolitan and modernist. Forster in particular they thought an old maid and a pious moralist. Bowra resented the fact that his rumbustiousness had not been appreciated at Garsington and Powell rarely lost an opportunity to denigrate Virginia Woolf whom he considered inferior to Ivy Compton-Burnett. Whereas for Strachey French literature reached its apogee under Louis Quatorze and Louis Quinze, the Wits praised Radiguet, Cocteau and Apollinaire. Bloomsbury ventured into the fashionable world and withdrew. The Wits took it as a world to conquer. They were voluble crusaders. Harold Acton left a memorable account of his campaign to smite the philistines. Clad in grey bowler, lamé shirt and Oxford bags he first swept from the scene unwanted allies, languid Bunthornes, lily in hand, invoking the beauty of chalcedonies and chrysoprases. Next he banished Georgian poetasters praising yokels and linnet-infested thickets. 'We wanted Dawns not Twilight. We must blow the bugle and beat the drums and wake the Sleeping Beauty.' Not Greece but Italy, not the Florence of the Medici, but the Naples of Pergeloni, Pergolesi, Carracciolo and the Bourbons was the city to be praised.

The Wits, unlike Bloomsbury, lived for pleasure. They liked novelty in pleasure: jazz, cocktails, the gramophone. In the pages of *The Unquiet Grave* Cyril Connolly, a dedicated hedonist, listed the delights of places, food, sunshine, clothes, trees, the memories of lovemaking and attributed to this delight his vanity, remorse, boredom and angst. E.M.Forster said of Connolly that he gave pleasure a bad name. The Wits were also intensely competitive. To be at least as clever as the next, to be invited to all parties of note, to give a party unique in its originality, panache, expense and outrage was their ambition. Waugh rarely lost an opportunity to bludgeon Connolly after he had made his name as a reviewer; and he bore a grudge against Robert Byron whose violence, hatreds and rages were more sensational than his own. Most competitive of all in his insolence was Brian Howard. He pursued peers for two reasons. For snobbery certainly, but also from a genuine mission to educate and capture them for modernism and if possible to go to bed with them. He liked to dominate: he had a gift for sensing what would ridicule and wound his adversary.

The Oxford Wits were undismayed by the charge of snobbery. That was part of the competitiveness that animated them. The Wits were worldly: as undergraduates they learnt to have an eye on London and a foot in it. They did more than lampoon the stuffy and conventional: they invaded their parties and haunts. It was all very well to be clever and amusing but could one also capture the citadels of the well-born and the rich? Could one move to the point of refusing invitations from Maud Cunard or Sibil Colefax? Connolly admitted, 'We were greatly impressed in a ninetyish way, by money and titles and the necessity of coming into closer contact with them.' You were expected to move at ease among the upper classes not only in England but on the Continent, Almanach de Gotha in hand. Three of the Wits – Evelyn Waugh, Anthony Powell and Henry Yorke – recorded their progression over the years: their novels astonish by being records of their social lives, their party-goings, their debts and their contemporaries' dedication to the bottle.

They mocked parochial England. You were expected to know the work of those continental artists, writers and musicians who composed the true avant-garde. In Victorian days the educated were assumed to read French literature and the learned German poetry and philosophy. The Wits took the Continent of Europe as their playground, and after the Second World War Alan Pryce-Jones transformed *The Times Literary Supplement* into a periodical that published special numbers on the literature and thought of America and various European countries. If the Wits were inspired by any of the pre-war generation it was by the Sitwells. Edith Sitwell was their Cumaean sibyl, Osbert their model for effrontery and showmanship, the artist and Guards officer who had a Horner for lover and who could move from atelier to salon, from artists to the ancient aristocracy – always supposing that the aristocrats were not insufferable bores. The Sitwells encouraged the Wits not to be scholars – not to tame their enthusiasms by pedantry or theories – to be partisan, skilled in vendetta and maestros in publicity. They encouraged them to amuse others with fantasy, satire and parties.

And yet perhaps the Sitwell who had the most lasting influence upon Our Age and posterity was the third of the siblings. By his books on Portuguese and South German baroque and rococo architecture Sacheverell Sitwell helped to rehabilitate styles which had languished in outer darkness since Ruskin and won no plaudits from Roger Fry. Soon the young Wit Roger Hinks began to study Caravaggio, and travellers penetrated the Bamberg countryside to discover Vierzehnheiligen and Banz. The Wits removed cataracts from the eyes of their generation. Bloomsbury detested Victorian art. But the Wits, who had no theory of aesthetics like Fry or Bell, exalted taste and revelled in Victoriana. Harold Acton's rooms were filled with Victorian bric-à-brac. Evelyn Waugh's first publications were on the Pre-Raphaelites and Rossetti, and throughout his life he collected examples of Victorian furnishing far more startling than anything Betjeman ever praised.

In 1929 Kenneth Clark published his first significant work on the Gothic Revival. He declared that the Victorians were not feeble imitators but vigorous, imaginative, ingenious creators who revived a style not simply because it was romantic or beautiful but because they thought it embodied the moral principles by which life should be lived. Reflecting on his book twenty years later Clark recollected that in those days Keble was regarded as the ugliest building in the world, Ruskin an execrable influence and the revival 'produced nothing which the "sensitive eye" (a favourite feature of the 1920s) could rest on without pain'. In those days beauty had nothing to do with rules, with associations nor with the subject represented: least of all did it depend on morals – but lay in some mysterious combination of shapes and colours. Scrupulous as ever Clark admitted the real reason that his book contained no chapter on Street or Butterfield was because 'I had too little understanding of real Gothic architecture to be a confident judge of its later variants or . . . the wholehearted enthusiasm which was needed to swim against the current of informed opinion'.

In 1949 Clark was to praise John Betjeman for recognizing the force of Voysey and Comper, and for rescuing the Victorian decorative arts from obloquy. He could have added Osbert Lancaster's name who by that time was commenting in prose and drawing on the variations in architectural style. None of the Wits except Bowra, Clark and Sparrow could have been called a scholar, and perhaps for that reason they had more influence than they could ever have had by settling to a lifetime of research. They made the arts cosmopolitan and pluralist: you could pick and choose your favourites. Horace and Vergil, Villon and Montaigne, La Fontaine, Rochefoucauld and Baudelaire, Pope and Dryden, Rimbaud and Don Juan were Connolly's choices for their 'love of life and nature, lack of belief in the idea of progress, interest in, mingled with contempt for, humanity'. Anyone who had his eye on succeeding in money-making or politics was suspect. In Anthony Powell's *roman fleuve* the characters who try to be efficient or moralists or who want to change things or who want power – like G. Watkin, the assistant bank manager turned company commander, above all the odious Widmerpool – in the end fail. They are foiled by fate.

There was one further characteristic of some of the Wits. More than half of them were at one time or another homosexual. And the time has now come to examine a conspicuous feature of our generation: why did homosexuality become such a cult?

CHAPTER 7

The Growth of the Cult of Homosexuality

1

OUR AGE IS remarkable for being a generation which made homosexuality a cult. The practice itself was not remarkable. The first King of England who was almost certainly homosexual was William Rufus: the chronicles record Anselm rebuking him. Richard I is said to have picked up the practice in the Holy Land, Edward II was Marlowe's hero, James I and the inscrutable William III were noted by their contemporaries for their interest in young men. Vanbrugh regarded his marvellous Lord Foppington with faint contempt, and Wycherley, Swift and Smollett found homosexuals, the 'Mollys', ridiculous or despicable. Later the Society for the Reformation of Manners were to recruit informers to harry them. The gallows or the pillory were the reward for the working class, exile and ostracism for the upper class – such as the suspect William Beckford or the delinquent Bishop of Clogher who, caught *flagrante delicto*, skipped bail. But Louis Crompton's conjecture about Byron is probably wrong: it is as unlikely the poet left England for fear of exposure as it is likely he was looking forward to picking up boys in Greece.

In some sense the illicit homosexual was a distorting mirror of the immoral heterosexual world of mistresses, courtesans and prostitutes. Young men found a protector who either paid them or gave them a good time or advanced them in society. Certain professions and occupations were habitual hunting grounds – the Brigade of Guards and ratings in the Royal Navy; in the eighteenth century scullions, in late Victorian times messenger boys, and in the mid-twentieth-century interior decorators and hairdressers.

It was in the late nineteenth century that homosexuality first showed signs of becoming a cult. At first the cult was celebrated clandestinely: only later in the mid-twentieth-century was it practised openly. The cult was European. It flourished in Proust's Paris, Freud's Vienna and in the Berlin of Sacher-Masoch. In Wilhelm II's court the Kaiser's friend Prinz von und zu Eulenburg was forced out of public life after a libel case; and Alfred Krupp's cavortings on Capri caused comment. In London Lady Henry Somerset (Virginia Woolf's aunt) left her husband because he found the footmen more attractive than her; and in 1889 his younger brother Lord Arthur Somerset fled the country when a homosexual brothel in Cleveland Street was discovered. Lord Euston, the heir to another duke, was implicated but found innocent, and rumours flew about that Prince Eddy, in direct succession to the throne and Lord Arthur's intimate, was also involved. Meanwhile the Marquess of Queensberry tried to flog Lord Rosebery in the belief that he was perverting his eldest son, and the Prince of Wales in his role as arbiter of society did what he could to restore the peace. A few years later Queensberry's son committed suicide. Little wonder then that, when Queensberry's younger son Lord Alfred Douglas revelled in his friendship with Wilde, the Marquess ran true to form. So did his son; and egged his lover on to bring the fatal libel suit. There was even an *éminence grise* suspect among Edward VII's most confidential entourage, that discreet and formidable operator behind the scenes, the second Lord Esher.

The cult took a peculiar form in England though one can find parallels in Germany, and there is a hint of it in *Le Grand Meaulnes*. This was the romantic friendship. It was canonized by Tennyson's *In Memoriam* and eulogized by Disraeli in an astonishing passage that described the intense emotion boys feel for each other. In England it flourished because the public schools acted as a hothouse for its growth. The public schools had been notorious for a very different expression of homosexuality. During the 1850s most of the well-known schools witnessed scenes that Victorian memoirs referred to by such dissembling phrases as 'boundless depravity'. John Addington Symonds did not dissemble. In his memoir (unpublished until nearly a century after his death) he recorded that at Harrow 'the talk in the dormitories and studies was incredibly obscene. Here and there one could not avoid seeing acts of onanism, mutual masturbation and the sport of naked boys in bed together. There was no refinement, no sentiment, no passion, nothing but animal lust.' Every boy of good looks was given a female nickname. He was then 'recognized either as a public prostitute and as some bigger fellow's bitch' unless he was discovered to be 'not game'. Boys would prowl from house to house, and Symonds recalled the powerful brigand who came after his prey, a 'plump fair-haired boy whom we dubbed Bum Bathsheba because of his opulent posterior parts'.

It was such scenes that the reforming headmasters determined to eradicate – or at least drive underground; though at all schools there were periods and certain houses in which a boy would never encounter anything untoward. What took the place of orgies was the romantic friendship in which the older boy made himself responsible for the younger and each could exercise a moral influence over the other. Charles Kingsley praised 'the old tale of Jonathan and David, Socrates and Alcibiades and Shakespeare and his nameless friend'. Tom Hughes, much as he admired Kingsley, did not altogether agree. In *Tom Brown's Schooldays* he referred to 'pretty white-handed, curly-headed boys, petted and pampered by some of the big fellows, who ... did all they could to spoil them ... for this world and the next'. In a later edition remonstrances from well-wishers made him add a footnote that there 'were many noble friendships between big and little boys'. No wonder he made the addition. He had immortalized such a friendship. He depicted Dr Arnold himself making Tom take little Arthur under his wing; and the 'young master' at the end of the book tells Tom at the cricket match against the MCC that the friendship has been the making of them both. The young master was a sketch of Cotton; and when Cotton was headmaster of Marlborough, he preached a sermon on unselfish love between boys as pure as that for the disciple whom Jesus loved. Sewell of Radley preached on the same text (John XXIII.23). Dickens knew how boys felt about each other. Steerforth nicknames David Copperfield 'Daisy' and regrets his little friend has no shy pretty sister who would look like David and enslave him. In Farrar's famous novel Eric and his friend Upton are shown discussing how best to translate an image from Aeschylus when they are interrupted by a master who is 'particularly angry' when he sees Upton's arm encircling Eric's shoulder; but the good master who tries to save Eric from ruining himself approves of the friendship.

Aeschylus ... Did the classics reinforce scripture? Or did they subvert it? Since Boethius men had tried to reconcile Plato with Christianity, and Victorian schoolmasters and dons carried on the struggle of reconciling Matthew Arnold's contrasts of Hebraism and Hellenism. Jowett's painstaking attempt led him to be suspected of infidelity. To Pater, Plato was the dramatic artist, the aesthete aware that love involves 'an exquisite cultivation of the senses ... ever on the watch for those dainty messages that lovers sent to eye and ear'. The first sacred text of Victorian Hellenism was Pater's essay on Winckelmann; and John Addington Symonds was at least as influential as Pater. Ancient Greece exerted a tyranny over English intellectuals. They identified their own country, the incidents in their lives and their fantasies with the tales of Homeric heroes and the swains of Theocritus. On board ship off the Dardanelles Patrick Shaw-Stewart, who belonged to the Raymond Asquith and Julian Grenfell circle, wrote a poem which ended 'I will go back this morning / From Imbros over the sea; / Stand in the trench, Achilles, / Flame-capped and shout for me'.

Clever schoolboys quoted the encomium in Plutarch pronounced by Philip of Macedon in tears over the band of the three hundred Theban lovers as they lay dead on the battlefield of Chaeronea, and Hellenists liked to quote a third-century inscription found on a stone in Athens. 'Lysitheos declares he loves Mikion more than all the boys in the city because he is brave.' In his memoirs Symonds recollected how coming back late from the theatre aged only seventeen he picked up the *Phaedrus*, read it and followed it by reading the *Symposium* until dawn broke; and some years later Forster pictured in *Maurice* his buttoned-up public school boy, Clive Durham, discovering in the *Phaedrus* that he was possessed by 'a passion which we can direct towards good or bad'.

Our Age inherited a world in which a few schoolmasters treated boys as equals and friends. In Victorian times G.H.Shorting at Rugby and Graham Dakyns at Clifton taught receptive and good-looking pupils something more than the grind of syntax. Most famous of all was William Cory Johnson. An eccentric who nevertheless held his division spellbound, a patriot who would break off a lesson with, 'Brats! The British army' and expect the boys to rush to the window when a company of Guards from Windsor marched by, he was the author of the haunting Victorian translation of Callimachus:

> They told me, Heraclitus, they told me you were dead,
> They brought me bitter news to hear, and bitter tears to shed.

Johnson's life at Eton was a succession of romantic friendships, among them the young Rosebery and Regy Brett, who became Lord Esher. Johnson's letters to his loves were as abandoned in their phraseology as they were misleading in the inferences that could be drawn from them. He might caress and kiss a favourite pupil but he almost certainly never had him. Unfortunately for him there was a scandal and some boys were expelled; in the aftermath a letter fell into the hands of the boys' parents; and with the expulsion of the boys the headmaster asked Johnson, too, to leave. A few years later another Eton master, Oscar Browning, was also manoeuvred into leaving by the headmaster, who had found an excuse to get rid of this troublesome colleague after he had displayed too keen an interest in the young George Curzon. (Curzon's father, who was Lord Scarsdale, wrote a letter of remonstrance to the headmaster – in defence of Browning.) Johnson and Browning were not the only Eton beaks to form such friendships. Esher's tutor Ainger and another housemaster, A.C.Benson, each had a succession of friends.

The same change in the relationship between dons and undergraduates was under way at the turn of the century. Some felt that undergraduates should no longer be ignored or snubbed and put down by their elders. They were to be taken up and encouraged. This was particularly true of King's where, in the days when it had been an Etonian preserve, the younger dons had been at school with the undergraduates and hence knew them. One fellow, in particular, was unbridled – the absurd, insanely touchy Oscar Browning who on leaving Eton retired to King's where he entertained the undergraduates and helped dozens of young sailors, soldiers, errand boys and others down on their luck. Browning was entirely indifferent to public opinion and thought nothing of startling a friend by sending him a set of Alcaics in honour of the penis with translation attached. It was he who brought out of their shell Lowes Dickinson and Sheppard, and Lowes Dickinson in turn brought out Forster. Dickinson's private papers, edited in 1973 by

Dennis Proctor, the last of his loves, give a moving account of the frustration and anguish of unrequited love, all the more difficult to satisfy physically as he found sexual satisfaction only through being trampled on.

The tradition of the bachelor don persisted for many years – certainly throughout the period when Our Age went up to Oxford and Cambridge. We forget today that, although dons were at last permitted to marry by the reforms of 1882, it was some years before any but the middle-aged took advantage of the change of statute. To be a married don meant keeping up a position and running a house with at least two servants. Since the agricultural depression of the seventies, which had cut college revenues to the bone, few fellows could afford to marry until their late thirties. In those days a fellow was lucky if he could scrape together £150 a year, an income which was supplemented by free rooms and dinner. The girls in the women's colleges lived a segregated existence heavily chaperoned; and girls outside Cambridge appeared only on rare occasions like the college balls at the end of the summer term.

When I went up to King's as an undergraduate in 1935, the two greatest colleges were full of bachelor dons who had been young in the nineties. At Trinity the most famous of all, A.E.Housman, was still alive. There was the philosopher C.G.Broad, with his penchant for Scandinavians. There was Winstanley, the historian of Victorian Cambridge, there was the American medievalist Gaillard Lapsley, and the gentle Evennett. F.A.Simpson was to be seen on summer days at the town bathing place or prowling around the gardens, nail scissors in hand, snipping shoots off plants; and Andrew Gow used to find the university library a convenient place to cultivate new friendships. At King's there was the founder of welfare economics, A.C.Pigou, who was much put out when someone hinted that his choice of good-looking undergraduates to accompany him to the Alps or the Lake District might be ill thought of. There was the University Librarian Scholfield; and the ancient historian Adcock would invite undergraduates to play golf at Brancaster where they found that there was no lock to the bathroom door. Most eccentric of all in his conversation and behaviour was the Provost, J.T.Sheppard.

Nor was Oxford different. Sligger Urquhart at Balliol, and Dundas, a contemporary of Keynes in College at Eton, drew amused comment at Christ Church for the curious and searching questions he put to undergraduates. At Magdalen before the Great War there was a set consisting of Edward Spencer Churchill, R.P.Jones, F.G.Hamilton (nicknamed Juggins, Ma and Pa respectively), J.H.Morris and L.R.McClure, all of whom died unmarried: they paid unsuccessful court to an exceptionally good-looking contemporary Tommy Brooke, among whose other admirers was Cosmo Lang, the future archbishop.

What are we to make of these romantic friendships and the Hellenist dons and schoolmasters so frank about their loves? Did they or didn't they? Impossible to be sure. Some left letters and journals written in such passionate language that today one might imagine that they were describing everything except what occurred in bed. And yet it can be safely said about most of these bachelors that they were never guilty of any homosexual act that was criminal according to the law of the land. Some, such as Oscar Browning, probably went to bed with a few of the soldiers or working-class boys he knew. All his life Esher had crushes on boys, the most sensational being for his younger son. He knew Arthur Somerset and Loulou Harcourt, who tried to seduce both his son and his daughter. Can one believe he never enjoyed the shady company they kept? Did Esher live a secret life finding physical satisfaction in other attachments than those which meant so much to him and which his wife understood and tolerated? Yet no evidence exists that he did anything of the sort. He remained a powerful influence, able to remove barnacles from the Admiralty and establish a General Staff in the War Office. No hostess dreamt of closing her doors to one who had been the confidant of Queen Victoria, the close adviser of Edward VII and was on the best of terms with Queen Mary.

2

OUR AGE WERE well aware that homosexuality flourished in Church as well as State. Charles Williamson was on holiday at Baden with William Johnson when their companion, another Etonian, suddenly died. Williamson was shattered. He became religious, converted after a few years to Rome, joined the Oratorians – until he discovered sometime later that he had no vocation. The passion that today flows into idealistic causes and political action in Victorian times got canalized into religion. Love of friends was not all that far from love of God, from sacrifice, dedication and vows. Writing to a monk troubled by his love for a friend, the Provincial of the English Dominicans said, 'You love him because you love him, neither more nor less, because he's lovable. You won't find any other sincere reason however hard you try ... Enjoy your friendship, remember it in your Mass and let him be a third in it ... Oh, dear friendship, what a gift of God it is. Speak no ill of it.'

The Oxford Movement throbbed with passionate friendships. John Henry Newman adored Hurrell Froude, Newman himself had a devoted lover in St John, and Frederick Faber was spellbound by the future lord chancellor, Roundell Palmer. Throughout his life Faber's capers made eyebrows shoot up. There was something more to Kingsley's famous attack on Newman than a difference of doctrine. Did not Kingsley, that vigorous believer in the divine origin of physical love, the bard of Anglo-Saxon manliness that found its fulfilment, not only in braving the elements at sea in freezing north winds, but in prolonged encounters in bed with an awakened, responsive wife in every part of whose nakedness he revelled, did not the manly Kingsley see his sexual antithesis in the feminine, seductive, alluring, sinuous Newman, the movements of whose body seemed to reflect the writhings of that subtle mind? Numbers of homosexuals were spikes, dedicated Ritualists, others converts to Roman Catholicism. Oscar Wilde, flirting with fashion as an undergraduate, waltzed towards Catholicism – and then, to make matters even, reversed to finger freemasonry. His homosexual acquaintance, André Raffalovich, himself a convert, recalled that on the day when Wilde was to be received into the church there arrived at the Brompton Oratory, not Wilde, but a large bunch of lilies. Faced with a choice between alternatives Wilde discovered that the most agreeable thing to do was choose both.

This *mélange* of ritualistic religion, ambivalent aestheticism and Hellenism found its most curious expression in yet another circle: the paedophiles.* Their labyrinthine connections have been traced in a fine monograph by the learned Timothy D'Arch Smith, who showed how the Uranian groups were linking themselves to other homosexual circles or devotees of romantic love. For the paedophiles the choirboy supplanted the messenger boy. Among them were the novelists of boy love, Forrest Reid and Howard Sturgis; there were Gleeson White, the friend of Baron Corvo and of Norman Douglas, and the rationalist lawyer E.S.P.Haynes who shared Swinburne's taste for flagellation. There were sinister figures like Aleister Crowley or squalid ones like Swinburne's acquaintance Simeon Solomon. Most of the paedophiles, too, were probably innocent of any criminal act, trying only to open the eyes of the young to nature and the arts. In their ephemeral magazines the paedophiles lamented how fleeting boyhood was, how guilty they were in thinking strange thoughts, and how delightful it was to catch a glimpse of forbidden nakedness. They wrote about the martyrdom of boys, rather as baroque painters depicted St Sebastian in ecstasy impaled by arrows. They wrote in a private language. D'Arch Smith suggested that one of the versifiers among the paedophiles, John Gambril Nicholson, in his sequence of fifty sonnets entitled *Love in Earnest*, gave Wilde the play upon words for his one undisputed work of genius.

> My little Prince, love's mystic spell
> Lights all the letters of your name
> And you, if no one else, can tell
> Why Ernest sets my heart on flame.

In the nineties one member of the fraternity might ask another, 'Is he musical?' or 'Is he earnest?', code words for homosexual as 'gay' is today. It is pleasant to think of Wilde, as he surveyed the first-night audience at the Haymarket,

* There was a paedophile cult in America, *vide* the anonymous editor of two volumes of poetry, *Men and Boys* (New York 1924) and *Lads of the Sun* (New York 1928); but despite Preston Caulfield's daydreams and fears it was not, I think, culturally significant.

remembering that the most outrageous joke in his play was concealed in the title.

To Our Age the poetry of these paedophiles was preposterous. One of them, the Rev. E.E.Bradford, ended his days in a rectory in Norfolk and was somewhat bewildered to be visited by licentious Oxford undergraduates led by John Betjeman who knew his verse by heart. Betjeman admired, as an example of Victorian topographical poetry, the first line of one of his poems, 'The institute was radiant with gas.' That poems ends: 'Common boys / Have great temptations and few wholesome joys.' Boys – how to chat them up and get off with them – was his special concern.

> No bird or brute's more shy than the boy bather
> In Belton Cove. If in a sheltered nook
> He's run to earth, he eyes the bold intruder
> With startled look.
>
> You'd best begin by talking of the weather
> Or asking if the water's hot or cold
> Then when you've had that little chat together
> He'll grow more bold . . .
>
> His coat comes off again, his trousers follow,
> And by the time his sunburnt body's bare
> He'll laugh and chatter, whistle, shout and hollow,
> As free as air.

That comes in a volume called *The Kingdom of Heaven Within You*. The good parson was unshakeable in his faith that such friendships kept boys, particularly working-class boys, from coarser and more sinful pleasures.

> Our yearning tenderness for boys like these
> Has more in it of Christ than Socrates.

Perhaps even more astonishing were the verses of John Leslie Barford.

> Soldier boys, sailor boys, scout cubs and rovers
> I am of each the inveterate lover,
> Boys of rough trade and the laddies of leisure
> All give me equal and infinite pleasure.
>
> Boys are the leaven the stodge of me lightening
> Lamps everlasting my gloominess brightening
> Pages in chocolate, purple and blue
> Who as they handle the tray or the cue
> Tightly be-buttoned their plump form display
> (Laws should forbid it the prurient say).

But what would the prurient have said about two poems which he wrote, the one entitled 'The Dormitory Talks' and the other 'The Playing Field Talks'? Here is the playing field talking:

Sweet was the summer, and though for their matches
Cruelly they cut me and rolled me full sore,
Stabbed me and mocked with disfiguring patches
All their ill-treatment I cheerfully bore.

When after chapel beloveds and lovers
Strolled arm in arm through my night-cap of dew
Close in a love that's more close than a brother's
Little they spoke – but their secret *I* knew!

In some respects the Victorians were less prurient and more innocent than their descendants in England today. Today, if a man followed the normal Victorian practice of swimming naked in a river, he would be arrested for indecent exposure. Certainly the press notices of Bradford's volumes of verse displayed no alarm. 'Of the love of man for man, and occasionally of man for boy, Mr Bradford is a steadfast, and occasionally an eloquent advocate.' Or more succint: 'Cheery and wholesome' – *The Times*.

But not all such paedophile poetry was trash. Gerard Manley Hopkins wrote 'The Bugler's First Communion'.

A bugler boy from barrack (it is over the hill
There) – boy bugler, born he tells me, of Irish
        Mother to an English sire (he
shares their best gifts surely, fall how things will)

This very very day came down to us after a boon he on
My late being there begged of me, overflowing
        Boon in my bestowing,
Came, I say, this day to it – to a First Communion.

Then though I should tread tufts of consolation
Days after so I in a sort deserve to
        And do serve God to serve to
Just such slips of soldiery Christ's royal ration.

One of the most striking manifestations of boy culture was a movement that became worldwide. The hero of the defence of Mafeking in the South African war, Baden Powell, admired the Boers for those crafts that had made them such tough opponents. Their eye for country, their knowledge of how to live off it, to stalk their prey and improvise devices were gifts which he thought boys ought to develop; and these gifts should be joined to other virtues such as honour and truthfulness. Like others at the time Baden Powell had been dismayed by the large number of volunteers who had been turned down for military service because they were physically unfit, and he conceived how boys could be made physically fit and better citizens. Foreigners saw the Scouts as a paramilitary organization founded by a soldier who pretended with characteristic British hypocrisy that they were civilians when, in fact, they wore a uniform, went to camp and learnt skills an infantryman would covet. Yet in fact the Scouts were quite different from the cadet corps that had grown up in the public schools. Unlike the Boys Brigade and other youth movements, the Scouts did not march to bands and were spurned by the dictators of the twentieth century. The very uniform of the Scouts, the hat capable of carrying water, the toggle, the bare knees, set it apart from paramilitary organizations.

The Scouts were a paradox. Baden Powell was the shameless proponent of British racial superiority to other nations, but the Scouts became international and multiracial. Baden Powell spent his life in an army in which the chasm between officers and other ranks was profound, yet he thought of the Scouts as classless: boys of rough trade were to mix with the laddies of leisure. He was not so innocent a Victorian bachelor (until his late fifties) that he did not know what boys camping in tents might get up to, and he preached a high-flown purity denouncing masturbation and misuse of the 'racial organ'. But inevitably some active homosexuals were scoutmasters, often athletic, upstanding men who, after a few years in the movement, would make a miserable appearance in a court of law asking for thirty-seven previous offences to be taken into account in addition to those they were charged with against the boys in their troop.

The notion that men could live with a working-class lover came to them from Edward Carpenter, who was a model monogamist. Lowes Dickinson wrote of him: 'He believes and practises the physical very frankly. How it is that public opinion hasn't managed to get him to prison and murder him is a mystery.' The mystery, perhaps, lay in his tact, his charm and his cunning use of words. His book *The Intermediate Sex* (1908), which was to sell a hundred thousand copies in half a dozen languages, was only one of many which tried to make homosexuality scientific and respectable by calling it 'contrasexuality' or 'similisexualism' or 'intersexuality'. No word or hint of impropriety ever sullied his page while in fact he was endorsing numbers of outrageous acts. He popularized the term 'Uranian' and began a chapter with the statement that 'Urning men and women' are those 'on whose book of life nature has written her new word which sounds so strange to us'. Carpenter pleased feminists by denouncing the ancient Greeks for treating women as serfs and suggesting that marriage was both carnal and capitalist in its preoccupation with property and class. Forster may have got from Carpenter his idea of a democratic aristocracy composed of 'the sensitive, the considerate and the plucky'; and his novel *Maurice* ends with the hero set up, as Carpenter was, with his working-class friend.

By the end of the century numbers of these cells began to float together and, whatever their inclinations, members of Our Age were likely to encounter one or other as they grew up. There was A. C. Benson's set which in the nineties included Howard Sturgis, the American Etonian and author of *Belchamber*, who lived at Windsor with his inseparable companion known as 'the Babe'. Sturgis had been charmed by Benson's head of house, Percy Lubbock, as were Oliffe Richmond and Frank Salter, later a don at Magdalene. When Benson became master of that college his diaries record a legion of young men to whom he became attached – Edward Horner, George Mallory, Geoffrey Madan, Francis Ogilvy and Dadie Rylands. Sturgis entertained his guests while doing embroidery, and Henry James was often there. James had been in love with the sculptor Henrik Andersen and with a young man about town, Jocelyn Persse. Like Benson he was to be taken with the young Hugh Walpole. Then there was the cell that formed around John Addington Symonds: his literary executor Horatio Brown, Charles Kains Jackson, the publisher of Uranian poetry, the Cambridge bibliographer Charles Sayle and his playmate A. T. Bartholomew, who collected all the material for the life of F. R. Rolfe that A. J. Symons was to write. Another adherent was Proust's translator Scott Moncrieff; another Samuel Butler's literary executor, Festing Jones; another the art critic Gleeson White who revived the rondeau form in verse writing. One of the largest cells had as its chief Robbie Ross: through him More Adey, Ronald Firbank, Charles Shannon, Charles Ricketts and Wilde's sons, Vyvyan and Cyril Holland were connected.

Wilde's sentence and degradation confirmed homosexuality as the unmentionable subject, but he was too much of a personality, a star performer, reckless and courting destruction, to disappear into obscurity. In prison he found the new role of martyr and (semi) penitent. Through *The Ballad of Reading Gaol* and *De Profundis* he spoke for the cause. It was hardly surprising that some young men considered talk about a love that dared not speak its name silly and affected. In the Apostles of Lytton Strachey's day at Cambridge there was probably more talk than achievement, the exquisite hare eluding the timorous hounds. Strachey was both dominant and submissive. He dominated his friends by the strength of his personality and his power of ridicule and contempt, but in love he wanted to submit: in middle age he acted out fantasies in which Roger Senhouse was Nero or his fagmaster and he a slave or a timid small boy. He was the one person who could dominate Keynes. When they were young and before he had learnt to control his jealousy, Strachey played Madame de Merteuil in *Les Liaisons Dangereuses* to Keynes's Valmont. Pursuing an old Eton flame, Bernard Swithinbank, Keynes reported that 'things ended only in a semi-embrace'. By return of post Strachey turned on him. 'How you can throw away your opportunities in the way you do I can't conceive. Glances, imaginations, half embraces – really, I give you up! ... I really did hope there would be something fine; – and then your "nerves give way". Pooh!' Keynes replied, 'My dear, I have always suffered and I suppose I always will from a most unalterable obsession that I am so physically repulsive that I've no business to hurl my body on anyone else's.'

Nevertheless Keynes hurled his body to some effect on Arthur Hobhouse and Duncan Grant; and Strachey, racked with jealousy, resembled the marquise when she writes her final ferocious letter to Valmont: '*Quand j'ai à me plaindre de quelqu'un, je ne le persifle pas; je fais mieux; je me venge.*' He nicknamed Keynes 'Pozzo di Borgo', ridiculed him, called him lascivious and incapable of true love, 'a safety-bicycle with genitals', and by spreading malice among their friends struck at the jugular. For what Keynes wanted even more than sex was affection. Theirs was a relationship that was to be paralleled many times among Our Age between the wars.

3

THERE WAS YET another facet to the homosexual demand that Our Age examined. An austere poet of the English countryside was to publish a book even more influential than *Dorian Gray*. This was *A Shropshire Lad*. Housman's unrequited love for Moses Jackson inspired these poems and they evoked the mood of many dons and bachelors who fell in love with the young and knew nothing would come of it. Perhaps something did in the end come of it. Robert Graves thought so and Housman's scrupulous biographer, Norman Page, admitted it was more, rather than less, likely that Housman towards the end of his life had a gondolier in Venice and rough trade in Paris. That is of trivial importance compared with the impact his poetry had for several decades. When Housman died Cyril Connolly deprecated his inflated reputation. The heavens opened. 'Late for the funeral, Mr Connolly at least had the satisfaction of arriving in time to spit upon the grave before the mourners departed,' wrote John Sparrow. Housman's laurels will remain unwithered: he had a faultless ear. And yet there was something in Connolly's riposte to his critics when he asked them to consider how long it was since they read Housman and what age they were at the time, 'for he is a poet who appeals especially to adolescence, and adolescence in a period when one's reaction to a writer is often dictated by what one is looking for rather than what is there'. Many who read Housman were looking for a dramatization of the love of comrades, and his *Last Poems* (1922) brought tears to the eyes of those of his generation who had seen the young men they loved killed in the Great War.

Housman exemplifies another strain in the homosexual fraternity. For him, a conservative in politics, an ascetic and a patriot, a soldier's red coat not only showed off his masculinity but was an emblem of protection and self-sacrifice. Here was a young man who would never meet him, still less know Housman's feelings for him, but who would die for Housman in battle. His own safety, his ease of life, the very leisure he enjoyed to edit the text of Manilius depended on this young man, who in the Great War formed part of the army of mercenaries, as Housman called Kitchener's volunteers, who 'saved the sum of things for pay'. It was a different relationship from Edward Fitzgerald idealizing his sailor friend Posh Fletcher or Oscar Browning helping soldiers and sailors. It was much nearer to Proust's Robert de Saint-Loup admiring the courage of young men each of whom was prepared to sacrifice his life for the other in the Great War. Saint-Loup thought of himself as serving in a masculine order of chivalry remote from women. And characteristically Proust adds that the falsehood in such sentiments consisted in the fact that those who harboured them did not want to admit to themselves that they were rooted in physical desire. Proust also detected another trait in the Housmans of this world. To show how virile they were they had to hide their heart of gold under gruffness. Or they would explode with anger at any sign of sentimentality. Parting was excruciating but they would do anything rather than appear to feel grief. The conservative homosexual Baron de Charlus admired German as well as French soldiers, as T.E.Lawrence admired the Bedouins. Saki went further and turned his back on his languid, unbearable Bassingtons and their pretty protégés. Before he was killed by a sniper, he denounced 'boys of the lap-dog breed ... who belong to no sex who ... should be treated as something apart, not altogether British'.

The austere homosexual was to be found more on the Continent than in England: in Montherlant, Wittgenstein, and especially in the Stefan George Kreis in Germany. The spirit was fierce, even puritanical. Those possessed by it wanted to purify society, rid it of worldliness, shabbiness and equivocation and, while idealizing young men, to protect them from the corrupting influence of women.

> Du schlank und rein wie eine flamme
> Du wie der morgen zart und licht
> Du blühend reis vom edlen stamme
> Du wie ein quell geheim und schlicht.

Slender, clean, delicate, noble, secret and simple – these are the adjectives George chose to describe his ideal of youth. That fierce purity flares up again in the relationship between Birkin and Gerald in *Women In Love* where the violent clash between the women and the men is paralleled by the two men wrestling in anger as if they have to be bound together by a sexual sacrament. But to cite Lawrence is to raise yet another ambiguity. The champion of outspoken physical love of man for woman was obsessed by the penis and by the masculinity that he feared he lacked and projected into the heroes of his later novels.

No one should generalize about homosexuality without considering the current idea of womanhood. The growth of the homosexual cult in late Victorian times was in part a reaction against the romantic ideal of spiritual woman lifting carnal man upwards to a higher life. *Das Ewig-Weibliche zieht uns hinan* ... The convention that women were passive, suffering, loving, redeeming creatures created impossibly lofty barriers almost as impregnable as the gowns, petticoats, bustles and appurtenances of women's fashions. The dismay some young men felt faced with the ideal of the innocent, child-bearing wife and home-bound mother was matched by their distaste for the melodrama of courting a mistress, or for the saunter to the brothel and the fear of venereal disease. They felt defrauded if a girl had to be either a plain-speaking, plain-looking blue-stocking, or a demure and dutiful wife. It is true that George Meredith imagined a new kind of woman in his novels, the girl of spirit, wit, sensitivity and imagination with whom to be in love would be a delight and to live with in marriage a perpetual pleasure; and perhaps Margot Asquith was an awful warning of what happened when Meredith's dream was realized.

Of course, there were witty and companionable women: today it is not their stuffy philistine contemporary critics but the Souls who shine in memoirs of those times. More often than not the Victorian girl was replaced by the self-satisfied, uneducated, conventional Edwardian girl, whom Forster knew so well, corseted by the conventions of her class and determined, come what may, to impose her will. No wonder American girls so often made the most desirable matches: they were spunky and liked to please. The fault, too, lay with the shy, buttoned-up young Englishmen. Cut off from women for thirty-four weeks of the year in their youth, and taught at school to repress their emotions, they did not know how to chat up girls and make them feel cherished. Their gaucherie was a subject of mockery on the Continent and in America. They seemed to regard heterosexual relations as a choice between bores and whores.

Lesbianism, the disdainful riposte for male insensitivity towards women, was not so much unknown as unrecognized. No one commented at the sight of Edith Simcox or Elma Stewart prostrating themselves at George Eliot's feet and calling themselves her daughters; or paid much attention to Violet Paget writing under her pseudonym of Vernon Lee. There was nothing in London life that at all resembled the salon where Natalie Barney and Romaine Brooks entertained in Paris. There was no rich American heiress such as the Princesse de Polignac, or the later expatriates Gertrude Stein and Alice B. Toklas, no poetess such as the exquisite Renée Vivien, no star of the demi-monde as Liane de Pougy, no circle like Paris-Lesbos where Colette embraced 'Maisy', the Marquise de Balboeuf. Later in the twenties there were to be well-known lesbians among minor figures in the arts: Dottie Wellesley, Ethel Smythe, Beatrix Lehmann, Dorothy Sayers, and there was the famous elopement of Violet Trefusis with Vita Sackville-West. But there was no cult comparable to that of the homosexuals.

There was one homosexual who did not conceal his hatred of women. H.H.Munro – Saki – was a familiar homosexual type: rueful, self-mocking, intolerant. His characters may marry but never embrace or show affection, and prefer to kill rather than cherish women and children. The one woman who succeeds in overcoming a young faun's 'unaffected indifference to women' and rejoices to see him weaned from what a knowing reader is meant to infer are homosexual pleasures, is gored by a hunted stag and dies to the sound of a brown-faced boy laughing at her fate. Yet, Michael Levey observed, although the heroes of his stories are good-looking men of eighteen – 'if they are ever in love, it is with themselves' – the reader overlooks their homosexuality, dazzled by the brutality of the action, the epigrams and the strenuous immorality of the tales. 'This story has no moral,' is Saki's note to the *The Unbearable Bassington*. 'If it points out an evil at any rate it suggests no remedy.' The nastiness, the studied rudeness, the practical jokes, the delight in imagining suffragettes being thrown to lions in ancient Rome, take one's mind off the sadness of the writer who, unable to grow up, revenged himself upon life.

CHAPTER 8

The Cult Flourishes

AS WITH SO much else the change in moral fashion came after the Great War. Compare those pre-war university novels, *The Babe B.A.* by E.F. Benson and Compton Mackenzie's *Sinister Street,* with Beverley Nichols's *Patchwork* or the satire upon its precious hero *Oxford Circus* written by Raymond Mortimer. The homosexuals of the twenties came out of the closet and into the drawing room. They did not – or very few of them did – 'come out', i.e. write manifestoes and boast of what then was criminal conduct. But many did not try to hide the difference between them and the other guests – in their manners, their tone of voice or their clothes. One no longer had to admire chi-chi or pose lily in hand or court choirboys. Homosexuality became a way of jolting respectable opinion and mocking the Establishment. What better way was there to declare one's hostility for the official mores of society than to take a whirl among homosexuals? Homosexuality had all the thrill of being illicit (as taking drugs has today) and all the pleasure of being certain to outrage the older generation.

The aesthetes at Oxford and Cambridge could hardly help being outnumbered by the game-playing hearties; but their parties, their appearance and their extravagance made the news. Answering some journalist, John Betjeman once said with pardonable exaggeration, 'Everyone was queer at Oxford in those days.' People tend to think of Evelyn Waugh's Ambrose Silk and Anthony Blanche, the unforgettable painted and powdered queens he described in his later novels, as caricatures of Brian Howard; but like so many of Waugh's fantastical characters it was a meticulous portrait. Cambridge was a little less flamboyant. A distinction used to be drawn between 'good Trinity', the susceptible older dons who formed romantic attachments – and didn't – with 'bad Trinity', a few of the younger fellows such as Dennis Robertson – who did. At King's the dons were more uninhibited and there were mutterings among old Kingsmen about the college's reputation. The innuendoes of the brochure read out after Founder's Feast became so hair-raising that after one such night the headmaster of Westminster, who had been present as a guest, saw to it that for years no boy from that school applied for entry. Recollecting those days when he was a young don, Patrick Wilkinson judged that homosexuality 'had ceased to have any moral overtones. In the general absence of women homosexual affairs were natural and common and passionate relationships accepted ... In the end most of the participants got married, often soon after going down.' Any shrewd observer of public school life would agree. Those who got involved at school in homosexual activities, from the house tart to the predatory prefect, were likely to be highly sexed boys who on leaving their monastic establishment moved at once to girls. Those who became life-long homosexuals were as often as not at school frustrated and obsessed by the belief that they were ugly and the beloved unattainable.

The literary world was a natural place for the cult to flourish. The *New Statesman* was not exclusively homosexual but it certainly provided a haven in the literary pages under Raymond Mortimer for contributors such as Cuthbert Worsley, as did the *Listener* under Joe Ackerley. The theatre, the cabaret, design and fashion were other professions in which homosexuals excelled. In Britain John Fowler became renowned for interior decoration, Oliver Messel for his stage designs, Norman Hartnell for his fashion house, and Cecil Beaton for photography. Diaghilev and his lovers in the Russian ballet had made the cult familiar before the war. Now after the war, unknown though the fact was to the matinée audiences of suburban ladies, their idol Ivor Novello and the most prolific and versatile *jeune premier* actor and composer, Noel Coward, were homosexuals. Great was the disgust of the impresario Bronson Albery when he found his new young stars enticed to work for H.M.Tennant's by the rising impresario Binkie Beaumont. Some of the better known on the stage between the two wars were Max Adrian, Gyles Isham, Henry Kendall, Charles Laughton, Ernest Milton, Esme Percy, Eric Portman, Ernest Thesiger and Frank Vosper. Some married for appearance's sake, others because they were bisexual. Cecil Beaton, for instance, had affairs with women, among them Adèle Astaire, Coral Browne, Doris Castlerose, Lilia Ralli and Greta Garbo.

One needs to be wary in drawing conclusions. Transvestism might be thought to be conclusive proof of inversion until one thinks of the tradition of pantomime, the principal boy and the Widow Twanky, or of that Victorian comedy *Charley's Aunt* – or for that matter the artists in drag who delighted working men's clubs up and down the country. Certainly Douglas Byng's success in the thirties rested on the comedy of sex transference. Arthur Marshall, who was particularly cherished by the theatrical profession, had a special flair for innuendo with his impersonations of schoolmistresses and hospital matrons. In the thirties his reviews in the *New Statesman* contained outrageous allusions; by the 1980s it had become possible to say or print almost anything, and he had become one of the favourite humorists on television and radio and wrote a column for that pillar of conservatism the *Sunday Telegraph*.

In the twenties when comedy, incongruity, innuendo and humour were so highly regarded, the cult of homosexuality attracted the young because homosexuals were so often beyond question gay. Noel Coward's good manners, the taste with which he conducted his vigorous sex life, the wit and spontaneity of his jokes opened all doors to him. Certain types of humour were relished by homosexuals: for instance, the spoof play or novel. It had a long ancestry. Noticing that the French, whenever they wrote about English life, misspelled most proper names and misunderstood every social nuance, Swinburne wrote stories and plays in French with unbelievable plots. He surpassed himself in one play, *La Soeur de la Reine.* Queen Victoria has abandoned herself to shameless and nameless practices and is blackmailed by her former lover Lord John Russell. But, she declares, she will have him executed like the headmaster of Eton who had been unwise enough to hint that she could be compared to Messalina. In one scene Victoria bewails her fall from virtue: *'Ce n'était pas un milord, ni même Sir R. Peel. C'était un misérable du peuple nommé Wordsworth, qui m'a récit des vers de son Excursion d'une sensualité si chaleureuse qu'ils m'ont ébranlé – et je suis tombée.'*

This was the model for Lytton Strachey's *Ermyntrude and Esmerelda* and his plays in which, like baroque opera, the role of the principal male part was played by a girl and the heroine, to escape a fate worse than death, dressed up as a boy. The gods and goddesses each coming to the aid of a mortal assume disguises concealing their gender with the result that lovers explode in indignation on finding themselves deceived in the act of love. But such squibs were set off only in private. The lord chamberlain was still censor of the theatre. In the late thirties he passed one sketch in a Farjeon revue, in which the curtain rose on an exquisite young man holding a bunch of flowers who sang a song beginning, *Joli garçon c'est moi, oui, oui*, only 'on the express understanding that he should remain still and make no movement associated on the stage with what are commonly known as panzies' (sic).

In the ephemeral music of the educated classes – which was played in magazines, periodicals, plays and cabarets (though never on Reith's BBC) – certain melodies unmistakable to keen ears began to be heard. There were themes that became stereotypes between the two wars and which had homosexual overtones: the theme of *le petit poète*, of the sensitive young man misunderstood by the harsh moralists among his elders; there was Nicky in Noel Coward's *The Vortex* or Gielgud's first Hamlet. Some have tried to carry this theory of themes further through the concept of 'camp'. Christopher Isherwood in *The World in the Evening* compared camp to Lao-Tzu's Tao: camp was worthless unless it sprang from genuine and serious emotion. It made fun about its object but never of it. Classical ballet was a camp genre for expressing love, baroque art a camp fashion for expressing religion. Susan Sontag went over the top when she called camp the music of Mozart and Richard Strauss, the paintings of Georges La Tour, the poetry of Pope, the comedies of Congreve and – bizarre conceit – the leadership of General de Gaulle. She was somewhat more convincing when she cited as hallmarks of camp the determination to convert the serious into the frivolous, to use artifice and exaggeration, to prefer judgements of taste to moral judgements, to sentimentalize the past, to value the decorative styles like rococo, to praise the sensuous and the extravagant, to decry character and sincerity and exalt personality and style, to rise to pathos but never tragedy. Camp refused to limit art to a few great works. Merit does not vanish if a work is in bad taste or spoilt by vulgarity. All these traits, she argued, can be found in the work of some homosexuals.

The work of the pioneers of sexology in Berlin and Vienna at the turn of the century, Freud, Krafft-Ebing and Magnus Hirschfeld, which set out the case histories of their patients, only started to circulate at all widely in the twenties. People then began to realize that sizeable numbers of solid citizens led bizarre private lives. Compared with sado-masochists and fetishists, many homosexuals seemed almost normal in their behaviour. But it was the revelation of the tortures of these patients living double lives which sometimes ended in suicide that helped to change public opinion. Hirschfeld campaigned for this change in Europe, lecturing at international conferences and becoming a best seller. In May 1933 the Institute for Sexual Science was destroyed by the Nazis, and Hitler's execution the next year of Roehm and his young adjutants revealed that there were those who considered that Hitler was the sort of man this country needed.

But despite the attractions of Berlin and Hamburg it was Paris, the cultural capital of Europe, that was the international capital of the fraternity: the Paris of Gide, Montherlant, Poulenc, Satie, Aragon, Breton, Radiguet; and of those indefatigable impresarios Jean Cocteau, Bébé Berard and Jacques Lacretelle. Vienna and Berlin produced the analysts of homosexuality, but from Paris came the novel that made the most powerful impression on the young men of the twenties and thirties. Proust's great work was the only serious major work of art to address itself to the subject. Faint and few, said Macaulay, are those who are in at the death of the Blatant Beast; and just as the early Victorians who read *The Faerie Queen* flagged, so readers laid down *La Prisonnière* and *Albertine Disparue*, wearied by the labyrinthine jealousies. Raymond Mortimer, who read Proust in French, considered him to have made a positive addition to knowledge with his diagnosis of love as a malady of the imagination. Today we admire Proust's delineation of an aristocracy bereft of political power and taste; or we discuss the general laws that govern human behaviour that he laid down in the tradition of La Rochefoucauld or La Bruyère. But for Our Age in their youth he was the first major writer to create openly homosexual characters. Proust reminded us that men who pursue women may well take time off to have affairs with men; and Baron Charlus, declining into fantasy, is one of the unforgettable characters in fiction. Proust himself was attracted only by heterosexual men; and that is why in the novel love is never reciprocated. For many homosexuals who experienced the desolation of unrequited love and the journey year in, year out, in search of a companion, Proust spoke the truth.

These homosexuals often found sexual satisfaction only outside their own class. They admired virile, tough, working-class men – men who appeared to be normal heterosexuals – and very often were normal. Sometimes they would be younger men and their lovers took pleasure in giving them a good time, educating them, making them companions without spoiling them. Joe Ackerley found 'working-class boys more unreserved, and understanding, friendship with them opened up interesting areas of life, hitherto unknown'. Others preferred older men, father figures heavily moustached, affectionate, commanding and dependable. But probably the majority of those homosexuals who specifically wanted to have sex with working-class men were out for casual encounters. They might have two or three steadies, a sailor who could be depended on to come up from Portsmouth when his ship had returned from a cruise, or a regular frequenter of a well-known pub, but most of the time they would be on the search for fresh faces. Some homosexuals cannot endure the possibility of a stable relationship. For them encounter, courtship, consummation and parting all have to be achieved in a single evening. And yet, familiar as these types were, to categorize them as specifically homosexual would be a mistake. There were plenty of examples of heterosexual men who craved working-class women: for instance the Victorian Alfred Munby who married his cook and amassed a collection of photographs of working-class women. Nor can anyone who reads that cold, anonymous work *My Secret Life* doubt that womanizers can be as inveterate cruisers as homosexuals and as obsessed with victory from the casual encounter.

But the cult of homosexuality had wider and more disturbing repercussions. There were the usual grumbles among theatre impresarios, actors, publishers and reviewers that a homosexual ring had wrecked their plans or blocked their advancement, but there was a more serious charge. Bowra invented the nickname 'Homintern' for the fraternity, and its experienced members constructed a sign language, a private code signalling complicity and connivance. To belong to a fraternity enjoying the same jokes, at once secret and illicit, courting danger of prosecution, and able to believe if they so wanted that they engaged in a conspiracy against the rest of society, were reasons why the cult became so fashionable. Wilde delighted in seeing how many subtle allusions he could make to the secret vice which could be read by the unsuspecting in a harmless way yet allow the initiated reader to infer that Lord Henry Wotton had seduced Dorian Gray. The Uranians operated the equivalent of a samizdat or clandestine press; their ephemera circulated in the shops of Charing Cross Road where pornographic books were sold.

Perhaps homosexuals disliked each other more venomously than rival heterosexual men do; but if one were in danger of exposure, for whatever kind of misdemeanour and illegal act, other members of the cult would rally round. It was a freemasonry that reached into the upper echelons of the elite. This was particularly true of Britain where clubability is at such a premium. It became a mark of civilized behaviour not to exclude or penalize a man for being homosexual. But homosexuals could, if they were unscrupulous, play upon the decent, liberal demand for tolerance yet at the same time threaten anyone in their circle or profession who had ever been homosexual. In his play *Another Country* Julian Mitchell pictures the young Guy Burgess at school in danger of being beaten by a prefect: he threatens to tell their housemaster what the prefect had been up to with a small boy. And Robert Cecil made the cunning suggestion that Anthony Blunt called off his bullies at Marlborough by just such a threat. Blunt was a master of manipulating other people and had an eye for any indiscretion that could be used to disarm a potential enemy. He also had an eye for those in government circles whose loyalty to the Homintern he could rely on – such as Harold Nicolson, a man who had no truck with communism but who did not hesitate to correspond with Guy Burgess after he had fled to Moscow. Nicolson saw that as an act of loyalty to the in-group and to the ideal of friendship in defiance of the Establishment. The Soviet agents who recruited the spies knew, as good marxists, that social structures and institutions give protection to those who were to lead double lives and nowhere more so than in England where the clubs of public school, Oxford and Cambridge colleges, the small top civil service grade, the scientific community and, not least, the homosexual fraternity interlinked.

For it was in the thirties the cult of homosexuality met a competitor for shocking the elder generation. You could choose between joining the Comintern or the Homintern – unless, like Guy Burgess, you joined both. The finest vignette of Oxford homosexual culture, a masterpiece of humour which charted the progress of Brian Howard from aesthete to communist, was Cyril Connolly's *Where Engels Fear to Tread.* It was matched by Bowra's unpublishable parody of Eliot entitled *Old Croaker* which mourned his friend, the Kingsman Adrian Bishop. It traced Bishop's passage from the days he used to pick up boys at Silhouette or Cosy Corner in Berlin ('Prevent us, oh Lord, prevent us, / In all our wooings') to the day when he entered a monastery disgusted with life.

There was one famous partnership that united the homosexual and the political worlds. Auden and Isherwood became folk heroes of the left at the universities in the late thirties. About their homosexuality they were matter-of-fact. Like Morgan Forster, whose friend and admirer they became, they could not go to bed with men of their own class; but unlike him they also had a hang-up about their own countrymen. The reason Isherwood gave for discovering his sexuality is a classic statement of the morality of Our Age. He met a psychoanalyst, John Layard, who told him,

> There is only one sin: disobedience to the inner law of our own nature. This disobedience is the fault of those who teach us as children to control God (our desires) instead of giving Him room to grow. The whole problem is to find out which is God and which is the Devil. And the one sure guide is that God always appears unreasonable while the Devil appears to be noble and right. God appears unreasonable because he has been put in prison and driven wild. The Devil is conscious control and is therefore reasonable and sane.

Isherwood added: 'Life-shaking words'. Homosexuality fitted in with Isherwood's detestation of the Establishment. Yes, he preferred boys because he liked their shape, their voices, the small movements they made. Yes, girls might be beautiful and he could feel romantic about them, but they were part of the church, the law, the press and professional life. Far from mellowing into an autumnal tolerance, he became more and more unable to believe in the sincerity of any moral attitude other than his own. The growth of the movement of Gay Liberation rejoiced his heart. He liked to imagine a time when heterosexuals would be on the run. 'On to victory' became his motto.

In the thirties no one of any sophistication could have doubted that Isherwood, the creator of Mr Norris, was himself homosexual: whereas only those who had known Auden at Oxford or moved in his circles knew the truth about him. And yet it was Auden who made Isherwood, his senior, recognize his destiny and went to bed with him as an act of friendship rather than for sexual attraction. When Auden went up to Oxford in the year of the General Strike, homosexuals were aesthetes. Auden, who dismissed the sonnets of Lord Alfred Douglas and the poetry of the Sitwells as beneath serious notice, was not an aesthete. He had no wish to be an Oxford Wit. He was already a professional poet and his homosexuality was not an adornment of his nature but a routine expression of his attitude to life. Homosexuality had become normal.

It had become normal, but not in the world of good form. If a homosexual were compromised he was dead to official life. Sometimes he preferred to be really dead. Lewis Harcourt, the Liberal minister, is thought to have taken an overdose of sleeping tablets to avoid prosecution: he was involved with the son of Mrs Willie James, Edward VII's mistress. Victor Grayson, at one time a Labour MP, disappeared and Lord Beauchamp, hounded by his despicable brother-in-law Bendor, Duke of Westminster, fled into exile in 1931 and did not dare return, for fear of prosecution, for his son's funeral. Forster did not publish *Maurice* in his own lifetime even when it became possible to do so.

Anyone of Forster's generation was circumspect, even though the Victorians were losing their innocence. Whenever Pater found that some homoerotic passage in his works was being interpreted for what indeed it was, he was as likely as not to excise it in a second edition. Henry James was as explicit as he ever allowed himself to be in *The Turn of the Screw* when he depicts Miles going off for hours with Peter Quint and being expelled for corrupting the other boys at school; and his governess recognizes that this occurred because he had done something 'against nature'. James's portrait of the aesthete Gabriel Nash in *The Tragic Muse* is covered in veils. Only Howard Sturgis referred in unmistakable terms to the subject in *Belchamber*. The hero has to lie to extricate his younger brother from a scrape at Eton that his sinister and charming cousin refers to as 'a great massacre of the innocents' when a number of boys are expelled to the bewilderment of their parents. In good form Edwardian society, homosexuality might be mentioned with contempt in the smoking room but never in the drawing room. Women like Ada Leverson (Wilde's Sphinx) or Vanessa and Virginia Stephen who enjoyed the society of homosexuals were very rare. Such empathizers, sneered at as fag-hags, were more a phenomenon of Our Age.

Until long after the Second World War no one would hint that a famous actor or writer was homosexual. The silence was so pervasive that when Lionel Trilling wrote the first important critical study of Forster in 1944, he did not know Forster was homosexual and did not allude to the homoerotic themes in his work. Even in the 1950s none who wrote on Auden mentioned that the lines 'Lay your sleeping head, my love, human on my faithless arm' were addressed to a homosexual. It was possible to convey that Diaghilev or Cocteau were homosexual but to do so was to run the risk of a libel suit: as it did when Liberace brought a successful action against a newspaper. In 1968 Goronwy Rees challenged Leonard Woolf to say why he had concealed in his volume of reminiscences the homosexuality of some of his Bloomsbury friends. Woolf replied that as he himself was not homosexual it was irrelevant to his relations with them. And he added, 'When I wrote it was still unusual to reveal facts which might be painful to living people unless it was absolutely vital to mention them.' It was a pity Gertrude Himmelfarb did not remember this exchange when she denounced Bloomsbury's morals and was ill-considered enough to suggest that its members were hypocritical 'in concealing from the public the wickedness they flaunted in private'. It is difficult to know what she meant. Did she expect Strachey to have committed a homosexual act in Hyde Park on a Sunday morning or Vanessa Bell and Duncan Grant to have declared their adultery in a letter to *The Times*? She went on to condemn Roy Harrod's commemorative biography of Keynes published five years after his death for the 'deliberate suppression of his sexual proclivities and activities' – at a time when there were still alive Keynes's father, mother, widow and his anti-homosexual brother who, as one of the two trustees of his brother's papers, would have stopped the publication of an explicit biography. And so Our Age became enveloped in a paradox. Among the well-educated classes homosexuality was a topic publicized in the public school novel as well as in Isherwood's tales from Berlin, a topic on which reformers wrote earnest articles replete with statistics. Yet at the same time it was still often spoken of as an aberration, a phase in adolescence, a deformation, even a psychological disease.

Nothing could illustrate this better than the treatment of the great Alexandrian poet Constantine Cavafy. Immediately after the Great War, E.M. Forster had written an article praising the poetry of a certain 'Greek gentleman in a straw hat standing absolutely motionless at a slight angle to the universe'. In 1949 Bowra praised Cavafy for recreating moments of history but, like Forster, made no reference to his homosexual poems. The professor of modern Greek at Oxford, the eccentric Richard Dawkins, remembered for the cackle and hoot which he emitted when his friends told him their latest scandalous encounters, used to hand them copies of his translations of Cavafy; but he too kept silent. Then in 1951 his successor John Mavrogordato published his edition with an introduction by Rex Warner who said nothing except that Cavafy found beauty 'in what to many would seem to be unlikely places'. Here was one unlikely place.

> It must have been one o'clock at night
> or half-past one.
>
> A corner in a taverna,
> behind the wooden partition:
> except for the two of us the place completely empty.
> A lamp barely gave it light.
> The waiter was sleeping by the door.
>
> No one could see us.
> But anyway, we were already so worked up
> we'd become incapable of caution.
> Our clothes half-opened – we weren't wearing much:
> It was a beautiful hot July.
>
> Delight of flesh between
> half-opened clothes;
> quick baring of the flesh – a vision
> that has crossed twenty-six years
> and now comes to rest in this poetry.

Cavafy's memories did not resemble Housman's yearnings. They described what homosexual encounters were like. In an unforgettable tone of voice that defied the maxim that poetry is untranslatable, he spoke without sentimentality or cynicism about the nostalgia of such short-lived affairs:

While looking at a half-grey opal
I remember two lovely grey eyes
It must be twenty years ago I saw them . . .
We were lovers for a month
Then he went away to work, I think in Smyrna
and we never met again.

Those lovely grey eyes will have lost their charm
– if he's still alive;
That lovely face will have spoiled.
Memory, keep them the way they were
And memory, whatever you can bring back of that love,
Whatever you can bring back tonight.

Cavafy was unrivalled at describing the brevity of love and the bitterness at losing a boy – 'Tamides left me, he went off with the Prefect's son to earn himself a villa on the Nile, a mansion in the city'. He knew about love as an obsession for 'one of the many unknown and shady young types, who have dropped in there' at the taverna and for whom, week after week, his lover sits waiting for him to reappear.

Of course, he tries not to give himself away,
But sometimes he almost doesn't care.
Besides he knows what he's exposing himself to,
He's come to accept it. Quite possibly this life of his
will land him in a devastating scandal.

And yet although Cavafy came to be regarded as unique in European poetry – an international figure in the way that his compatriots Palamas and Sikelianos were not – it was not until the sixties that Auden wrote an article which spoke about his homosexual poems. Auden said that, although poems made by human beings are no more exempt from 'moral judgement than acts done by human beings', the moral criterion is not the same. The poet bears witness to the truth and it is not the business of a witness to pass verdict. Cavafy told the truth. He neither bowdlerized nor glamorized nor giggled. He would not pretend that he felt guilty about those moments of physical pleasure he recalled. Auden went on to say that, irrelevant though it was to our judgement of the poems as poetry, Cavafy's readers may well wonder what happened to these companions of his whom he picked up. The experience for Cavafy might not be harmful and trivial; but for them? Just as Proust called homosexuality a vice, so Auden regarded it as a sin for which the sinner will find himself accountable for the direction the life of his lover takes.

Homosexuality was to become subsumed as a topic in the liberation movement of the fifties and sixties. People began to study the subculture of British life.

It was a homosexual, Colin MacInnes, who was the first to write about the black West Indian culture that by then was established in London. The discrepancy between what went on and what could be stated about it in public became too ludicrous to continue. The determination grew to say everything about anything – about royalty and politicians as well as celebrities. Most of Our Age adopted the prudent argument: why stop a minority from doing what they want? There is enough suffering in private life; why not diminish it? When a marriage has run on to the rocks, why try to identify one guilty party? Why pretend hanging deters murderers when statistics show otherwise and you run the risk of hanging the wrong person? Tolerance, in particular of homosexuals: was it not the mark of totalitarian states to treat such men harshly?

Isherwood recalled in his autobiography that he rejected communism when he came to realize that Stalin persecuted homosexuals. Among the first to have been flung into the concentration camps in Nazi Germany had been the working-class boys and their lovers in the intelligentsia. (Not, of course, the famous actor Gustav Grundgens whom Goering protected but required to marry the actress Marianne Hoppe. Berliners declared that above their marital bed hung the epitaph by Simonides on the Spartans at Thermopylae: 'Here obedient to their laws we lie.') Liberals turned the argument about loyalty against the state. Why was it that, despite the perennial flotsam of anti-semitism which never quite disappears, Jews in Britain were loyal to the state? Was it not because centuries of pogroms and persecution made them feel little loyalty to certain Continental countries, whereas in Britain they were not subject to grave social, let alone civil, disabilities? But homosexuals were so subject.

The reformers had to hand a modern version of the Christian doctrine of predestination. Freud had explained that children who failed to identify with their fathers became fixated on their mothers and, when adults, became homosexuals; and his followers later argued that men became homosexuals because their mothers had dominated them as their father distanced himself. Thus homosexuals were predestined to be what they were and could not grow out of the adolescent homosexuality that most boys experience. Was it right to punish them? Then after the war the sociologists reinforced the psychoanalysts. Kinsey argued that since so high a proportion of the men he interviewed had at some time had a homosexual experience, the practice had to be regarded as natural a form of sexuality as heterosexuality. Housman had published a coded poem ending 'Keep we must, if keep we can, These foreign laws of God and man'; and his unpublished verse on the trial of Oscar Wilde was often repeated by homosexuals: 'They are sending him to prison for the colour of his hair.' As reformers of the law often do, they turned to Bentham. In one of Bentham's least-known pleas for reform (written in 1774, though it had to wait until 1931 for publication by C.K.Ogden), he argued, 'This crime, if crime it is to be called, produces no misery in society.'

It also began to be recognized how much homosexuals enriched the nation's culture. Hardly surprising since by the sixties the best known English-born poet, the outstanding composer, the most famous choreographer, and the most prestigious painter – Auden, Britten, Ashton and Bacon – were all known to be homosexuals. The generation which had admired so many dazzling performances by homosexuals on stage and screen, and the brilliance of men in academic, scientific and professional life who had remained conspicuously unmarried – this generation was now coming to power. War loosens sexual restraints and, encouraged by Shaw and Wells, Russell and Bloomsbury, Our Age determined to liberate John Bull and Britannia from the Victorian sexual prison.

CHAPTER 9

Our Age Reforms the Law

1

THE INTELLECTUALS AMONG Our Age who thought the laws on homosexuality would be liberalized were in for a shock. The contest in the twenties between the hearties and the aesthetes in the universities was still in full swing, but by the fifties the hearties were in a position to fling the aesthetes not into the fountain but into prison. David Maxwell-Fyfe, fresh from his triumphant cross-examination of Goering at Nuremberg, had returned convinced that Britain should take the lead in uniting Europe. On other matters he was less enlightened. A Scot on the make at Oxford, he had learnt that the way up in Chamberlain's circle was through undeviating rectitude; and he continued to display rectitude when made home secretary. His permanent secretary was Frank Newsam, a handsome womanizer and reactionary – an English Pobedonostsev.

When Theobald Mathew, a Roman Catholic, was appointed in 1944 Director of Public Prosecutions, the number of convictions for the commonest homosexual offence, gross indecency, rose from eight hundred cases before the war to 2,300 in 1953. Like the prefects of a slack house at a public school these three, aided by a new commissioner of police, determined to pull the place together: and they had a pretext. Homosexuality had become a political issue. When Guy Burgess decamped the indignation of the popular press knew no bounds. How was it possible for such a notorious homosexual to have been cleared by security or kept in his post in the foreign service when his drunkenness and lechery were known to so many of his colleagues and acquaintances? Was it not axiomatic that all homosexuals, being open to blackmail, should be classed as unfit for any confidential employment? To convince America that Britain recognized homosexuals as criminal deviants and a risk to security the Home Office determined to make an example of them whenever a suitable opportunity arose.

Maxwell-Fyfe was more intelligent than Joynson-Hicks, the puritanical home secretary of the 1920s, but he was determined to loose the police on to these deviants. The police needed no urging: they had for years used *agents provocateurs* in public lavatories and few were the homosexuals who could stand up to the bullying in the police station where they were urged to plead guilty before a magistrate in the hope that a fine would settle the matter. Only hard-bitten journalists, such as Tom Driberg, who was twice caught and never charged, knew enough to threaten to fight the case through the courts and take it to a jury. (The only time before the war when he faced a jury he was acquitted and his employer, Beaverbrook, kept the case out of the newspapers.) First a Labour MP, William Field, had to resign his seat. Then John Gielgud was fined for a misdemeanour. The next year, 1954, Lord Montagu, who had reported a case of theft to the police, was accused of an 'indecent attack' on two boy scouts. The police altered the date in his passport which recorded a visit to France in an attempt to destroy his alibi. Montagu was acquitted but was arrested at once with two of his friends and charged with offences against servicemen in the RAF. Telephones were tapped, searches made without warrant, the Crown committed forgery and the Director of Public Prosecutions, Theobald Mathew, assured the RAF men that however many offences they had committed they would not be prosecuted. Mathew later sat gloating in court when the accused were sentenced.

In 1958 a Conservative MP, Ian Harvey, was convicted of an offence in Hyde Park, and he too left public life. Intelligent opinion was by no means ranged against Maxwell-Fyfe. Before the war Firbank's prose and Norman Douglas's life succeeded in outraging the *bien pensants.* That fine old codger, G.M.Young, a Victorian and proud of it, borrowed from Robert Byron Strachey's *Eminent Victorians* and handed it back to the lender with the words 'We are in for a bad time.' 'What went wrong with the twenties?' he asked and Byron had replied, 'It was just foul.' Wyndham Lewis took a bludgeon and Geoffrey Grigson vitriol to punish Strachey and the frivolity of homosexual culture. Nor were homosexuals themselves blind to the hypocrisies of the cult. In his novels Angus Wilson exposed the corruption and self-deception in homosexual society. Proust always spoke of homosexuality as a vice and a pit of self-destruction. David Eccles argued the administrative case against homosexuals: he admitted (though he later tried to withdraw the admission) that homosexuals would be considered without question always to be a security risk.

The drive against 'male vice', which brought such a satisfactory increase in prosecutions, won support in Parliament where denunciations of homosexuality rivalled those at Wilde's trial. The medical journal, *The Practitioner,* explained that discipline must come before happiness and sexual vice meant 'the slow death of the race': perhaps a camp on the island of St Kilda for the afflicted would 'strengthen their resolve' in a 'natural and bracing climate'. Even those who pleaded for an enquiry did so on the grounds that homosexuality was a disease that needed medical treatment rather than prison. When Bob Boothby asked the home secretary to institute an enquiry, Maxwell-Fyfe said that as long as he held office the law would remain unchanged. Soon the Home Office had cause for celebration. More homosexuals were prosecuted, several murderers were hanged, and five prosecutions were brought against reputable publishers for disseminating obscene literature.

The aesthetes of Our Age were not going to be silenced by the counter-attack of the hearties. They were encouraged in 1955 when Forster wrote an article in the *New Statesman* pointing out that in one police court alone six hundred cases of male soliciting had been heard and in his gentle teasing way asked what could be done about it. Imprison them? That was to sweep it under the carpet. Treat them medically? The numbers, even of the willing, would be overwhelming. Hang them? A holocaust each generation was perhaps too alarming a prospect. Could there then not be a change in the law to legalize such behaviour in consenting adults? In order to divert such criticism the Home Office at last set up a committee under Jack Wolfenden, then vice-chancellor of the University of Reading, to consider homosexuality and prostitution. The committee made two main recommendations. The law should be changed to permit adult homosexuals to make love in private provided both consented; and prostitutes should be prevented from plying their trade on the streets. Predictably the government decided to reject the first and implement the second.

Much play was made by liberals of the hypocrisy of condoning prostitution so long as it was invisible. Were tarts worse than their clients? Nevertheless, liberals ignored the fact that the prosperity of the fifties had created a minor social problem. Shaw had depicted Mrs Warren's profession as the most dramatic example of Ricardo's theory of surplus value in capitalist society. But in the fifties it became clear that prosperity as well as poverty induced girls to solicit on the streets – the prosperity that enabled many more men to seek casual sex. In an article Wayland Young quoted a prostitute who had realized the potentialities of her peachy behind as saying: 'I'd been working in that factory for five years before I realized I was sitting on a fortune.' At that time the *Strich* stretched from Lisle Street in Soho to Queensway, a distance of nearly five miles in practically every section of which girls accosted passers-by, or predatory men harassed the indignant women residents of the area. Young took his readers, as many longer and less entertaining books had done from Mayhew's day, on a Cook's tour of prostitution – street walkers, call girls, scrubbers, fly-me girls in Chelsea willing to go to Tangier, Ibiza or Cannes, ponces, police courts – and predicted that soon there would be girls who set out to get laid by a newsworthy personality and then report back to the editor of the newspaper paying for the story. There was no cure, he said, but perhaps there might be less prostitution if we all discussed sex more. His wish was to be granted. Sociological studies such as *Women of the Streets* (1955) began to appear; but when Eileen McLeod published her study in 1982 she called it *Working Women.* The change in title was significant.

It was significant because women were acquiring more rights. They benefited by the reform of the divorce laws. Asquith had set up a Royal Commission in 1909 under Lord Gorell. It took years for its recommendation – that adultery should not be the sole cause for divorce – to be enacted. Week after week in *Punch* Alan Herbert depicted the absurdities of the law, of having to be discovered by a chambermaid in a Brighton hotel having breakfast in bed with an accommodating lady spied upon by private detectives and the Queen's proctor, but it took the Second World War to make divorce cheap and available for the citizen soldiers. In 1951 Eirene White moved a bill to enable desertion to be cause for divorce but was persuaded to withdraw it on the promise that another Royal Commission would be set up. Its chairman, the judge Lord Morton, and its members proved to be of unexampled blandness.

The reports of committees of enquiries often receive rough treatment, but none can have elicited such a blistering analysis as that made by O.R. McGregor in his book *Divorce in England* (1957). McGregor, who had learnt his sociology at the LSE, was outraged by the amateur, slipshod, antediluvian way the members of the commission had set about their task. They simply invited large numbers of individuals and organized bodies to expound their opinions about divorce. Opinions . . . there was no lack of them. But practically none of these opinions was based on fact, on evidence acquired from statistics or from opinion polls. The Headmasters' Conference said that it was better for a child to have a 'real home' than to have none, even if it was a boxing ring where father and mother slugged each other. No mention was made of the fact that, far from having 'none', many children of divorced parents had a home since two thirds of the parents remarried. The Association of Headmistresses did supply figures. Over sixty per cent of five hundred cases of maladjustment could be attributed to broken homes and similar disturbances. Yet it emerged that only 0.1 per cent of the 90.5 of those sufficiently maladjusted to be referred to child guidance clinics came from homes broken by divorce. The commission's search for evidence, said McGregor, 'produced one of the most impressive selections of unsupported cliché ever subsidized by the tax payer'.

It was an unrepresentative body. Thirteen of its members were connected with the law; and lawyers are the most self-intoxicated and oblivious to the public needs of any profession in England. Not a single member was known to favour change: all were 'impartial' members of the upper middle classes. A psychiatric social worker, who provided evidence of a decline in religious influence and practice in regard to divorce, was asked by Morton whether she thought that 'a good thing or a bad thing'. She answered that her own opinion was irrelevant to the objective picture she was presenting. But not to the judge. 'It is a matter of opinion,' concluded McGregor, 'whether the Morton Commission is intellectually the worst Royal Commission of the twentieth century, but there can be no dispute that its report is the most unreadable and confused.' From this time social investigators – 'sociologists' as they were vulgarly called – were not to be denied. Their findings were quoted in every serious enquiry and analysed by statisticians and social investigators in universities and periodicals.

Women had longer to wait than homosexuals for reform of the laws that restricted their freedom. Eventually the doctrine of the matrimonial offence, the guilty party, was abandoned, desertion as due cause after two years legalized, and one spouse was no longer able to oppose a divorce after five years' desertion. But the Matrimonial Property Act (1970) declared that the wife's work in the house or at work should be regarded as a financial contribution to the family; indeed, the provision that enabled a divorced wife to obtain part of her husband's capital soon led to tales of designing harpies fleecing their husbands on divorce of a sizeable part of their capital inheritance. The legislation recognized women as individuals in their own right.

So did the legislation on abortion. The laws on abortion and illegitimacy, whose effect Rosamond Lehmann depicted in *The Weather on the Streets*, created misery and shame in a population many of whom still ignored birth control. Yet abortion was an issue that revealed, as none other did, the division on sexual morality. The old guard, supported by the Roman Catholic Church, believed sexual reform threatened the stability of society. The family needed to be protected as it was crucial to a good society. Sexual intercourse should take place only within marriage: the key to overpopulation was self-control and continence. The headmaster and future Conservative minister, Rhodes Boyson, thought sexual freedom had led to isolation and despair. Sexual deviance was a sickness which the state had a right to punish. On contraception they diverged: but many Catholics favoured contraception rather than the graver sin of abortion. On the other side, the party of reform thought society tough enough not to be endangered by abortion. To them the prevention of unwanted children strengthened rather than weakened the family. They favoured, as their opponents did not, equality between the sexes and tolerated sexual deviancy. They considered that individuals have the right to control fertility. The reformers were, however, outflanked by the small vocal group of feminist-marxists who proclaimed that sexual unhappiness had its origins in the capitalist system: only when the social order had been restructured and the nuclear family destroyed would problems such as overpopulation be seen to be irrelevant and nonexistent. In sexual freedom lay health, and female as well as male homosexuality should be welcomed. Above all a woman's body was her own to do with as she saw fit and no one should try to diminish this right.

The influence of the churches was waning by the sixties – less than half of marriages were solemnized in a church – and the churches themselves were divided on sexual morality. The rise of the student estate, the acceptance of premarital sex, the thalidomide calamity which revealed that to abort a deformed foetus would be illegal, encouraged a pressure group to form and exploit any news items of the old-style back-street abortion. Their opponents had the more difficult task of campaigning to preserve the status quo. But the Catholic lobby was powerful enough and the Society for the Protection of the Unborn Child argued that abortion on demand ran contrary to medical interests; and their appeal to the natural conservatism of the medical profession did not fail. When David Steel was able to introduce his bill in 1967, its passage was eased by the support the home secretary, Roy Jenkins, gave it. The American women's movement had won a signal victory when the Supreme Court ruled that the decision to abort should be left to the woman and her attending physician in the first three months of pregnancy. The British Act did not in the end give women the right to choose an abortion: the medical practitioners controlled abortion. Nor could women necessarily get an abortion free of cost on the health service. But women from other countries travelled to Britain to obtain an abortion. Many could not get it in their own.

2

NEITHER DIVORCE NOR abortion would have gathered the same impetus but for an event in 1960 that was to symbolize the determination of Our Age not only to change the laws but to exploit the change. One of the minor irritants of intellectual life was the censorship of literature effected by the laws of obscenity. In the fifties elderly respectable publishers found themselves to their horror in the dock at the Old Bailey under laws that had made Britain the laughing stock of Europe as the works of authors ranging from Tolstoy and Ibsen to Joyce and Lawrence were prosecuted.

Roy Jenkins was the politician of Our Age who did more than any other to increase personal liberty. He determined when in opposition to amend the law of obscenity; and with the help of two robust Conservatives, Tony Lambert and Hugh Fraser, he tried to persuade in 1956 the new home secretary, Rab Butler, to do so, since Butler at least understood what literature was which his predecessor Gwilym Lloyd George did not. But Butler showed no signs of bringing in legislation after a select committee had examined the matter, and had acquiesced in his party's decision to block Jenkins's bill. He had not reckoned with Alan Herbert, the old campaigner for liberalizing the laws on divorce and obscenity. Herbert threatened to stand in a by-election and split the Conservative vote. This concentrated Butler's mind. He allowed an unopposed second reading but intended to rewrite the bill in committee, leaving in the provisions the police desired and striking out the clauses which ensured that the work should be considered as a whole and could be defended by calling expert witnesses as being in the interest of the public good. Yet in another respect Butler was very much a man of Our Age. He preferred negotiation and compromise to a rough-house; eventually in 1959 the bill became law in much the form Jenkins wanted.

It was to be tested almost at once. Whatever Jenkins's bill was meant to do, it was intended to protect serious literature. Yet the very next year Allen Lane's decision that Penguin books should publish *Lady Chatterley's Lover* was challenged by the tireless Theobald Mathew, still Director of Public Prosecutions. For the first time expert witnesses were called, critics of impeccable academic standing such as Graham Hough, Joan Bennett and Helen Gardner, old and young members of provincial universities, and Richard Hoggart from Leicester; among the ancients, Rebecca West supplied the *son* and E.M.Forster the *lumière*, and a medley of journalists, writers, publishers, clergymen, schoolmasters and dons, such as myself, brought up the rear, thirty-five in all. John Robinson, the modernist Bishop of Woolwich, informed the court that for Lawrence, as for Christians, the sexual act was sacred, 'the flesh was completely sacramental of spirit'. Christians, so Archbishop Temple had said, did not make jokes about sex any more than they did about Holy Communion. Precentor Tytler said that phallic was a word 'taken over from a pagan world and had been baptized by Christians and made into a sacred word'. Their evidence amazed a number of pagans and certainly amazed the prosecuting counsel Mervyn Griffith-Jones. He was even more amazed when Richard Hoggart maintained that Lawrence was at heart a puritan. Griffith-Jones sneered at him for giving a lecture but Hoggart refused to be put down. He gave the impression of being patient, clear, devoted to truth and decency; and Bernard Levin judged him to be the most effective of all the witnesses.

The trial delighted my generation. They enjoyed Griffith-Jones asking the jury to consider whether the book was one they would wish 'your wife and your servants to read'. He seemed to rely on the argument that since the book glorified an adulterous relationship and would be far too cheap and easy to buy and contained four-letter words it would corrupt people. His concern for the morals of the lower orders was matched by his contempt for them; and the judge himself in his summing up interpreted the new act in such a way that the defendants had to prove the book's merits were so high that they made an identifiable contribution to the public good. Judge and counsel argued in vain. The jury was not convinced and set Lady Chatterley free. The grammar school extra-mural lecturer from Leicester had worsted the Treasury counsel from Eton and Cambridge; Osbert Lancaster and the cartoonists enjoyed themselves; and the media chortled.

Perhaps they chortled too loud. For Leavis that sound was the triumph of a new and hateful orthodoxy of enlightenment. Enraged by the annexation of an author whom he considered his own property, Leavis accused the witnesses of producing the grotesque argument that the book promoted respect for marriage (none did). Lawrence was a sick man when he wrote it: how otherwise could he have offended his own fine sense of pudeur? Leavis complained that Lawrence made Mellors drop into dialect, although Mellors was not a true son of the soil but an intellectual.

It was not Leavis, however, who created the sensation. It was the warden of All Souls'. In a remarkable article in *Encounter* John Sparrow denounced the witnesses as either stupid or humbugs. 'Strange experts they must have been', to fail to understand that in one episode Lawrence described Mellors buggering Connie. Why had the witnesses defended this sadistic act? Was anal intercourse now to be regarded as sacred? How could Gerald Gardiner for the defence plead that in this book 'there is no kind of perversion at all'? If Lawrence was so honest why was he so secretive and allusive? On this last point Sparrow found an ally in an old Scrutineer supporter of Leavis, D.W.Harding, who, reviewing the Penguin edition with respect, admitted that in this episode Lawrence was 'as discreetly allusive as the most respectable of novelists'. (In fact Sparrow was not the first to draw attention to this passage: as early as 1929 a young Cambridge don had made the point.) Sparrow also won support from an unexpected quarter. Colin MacInnes, a high priest of the liberation movement, attacked the witnesses for 'being trapped by ignorance, vanity or by fatal good intentions'. They had dishonoured Lawrence by appearing: better that the book had remained banned than Lawrence's vision should have been distorted by this hateful trial.

Sparrow's hour of triumph was short-lived. He found himself lapped by waves of laughter. Alastair Forbes observed that he had become the warden of All Holes. Perhaps the laughter was deserved. As a barrister Sparrow knew well enough that in England a criminal trial is not a search for truth. It is concerned with guilt or innocence. There was no obligation upon Gardiner to draw the jury's attention to an episode that was unfavourable to his cause when prosecuting counsel had been so inept as to miss the point. Nor was it true that the expert witnesses were so inexpert as to miss it too. In conference before the trial, Graham Hough and Joan Bennett raised the matter with Gerald Gardiner. What should they say if challenged? Gardiner asked them whether it was not possible to interpret the passage in other ways: could it not, for instance, be argued that Lawrence was describing normal sexual intercourse from behind? In the divorce courts it had long been recognized that sexual acts which would be cruel if done with an inexperienced young bride would not be judged to be so in the case of a mature woman, especially if these acts gave satisfaction to both lovers. Hough argued that the witnesses did not have to endorse every act of lovemaking described in the book. The point at issue was whether a great writer should be prohibited from expressing his vision of love in print. Did it not cross Sparrow's mind that the book on trial was not *Lady Chatterley's Lover* but John Stuart Mill's *Essay on Liberty*?

Within a few years almost anything could be published. It is true that *Fanny Hill,* which is undoubtedly pornographic but delectable reading, was prosecuted successfully, and no one would publish the autobiographical *My Secret Life* that the American scholar Steven Marcus had used in writing about the 'other' lives of Victorians. But then the ban on *Last Exit to Brooklyn* was overthrown on appeal and the Crown became unwilling to bring further prosecutions as juries refused to convict. Not only the homosexual elaborations of Genet and Burroughs, but *L'Histoire d'O, Candy* and a torrent of hard pornographic books poured on to the market. For some years the demand outstripped the supply. When the Crown failed to indict *Inside Linda Lovelace* it became clear that literary censorship – until the Jenkins Act is repealed or modified – appeared to have gasped its last.

One of the first initiatives Roy Jenkins took when he became home secretary was to end the censorship of the theatre, and he asked me to open a debate in the House of Lords and move that a Select Committee of both houses should be appointed to review the lord chamberlain's authority over stage plays. The absurdities of the censorship were deployed. The lord chamberlain, advised by a staff of retired Guards officers, censored all plays and dictated even what gestures might be permitted on stage. Four-letter words on radio or in print were unknown, nor were they heard at dinner parties. Before the war a West End vehicle *When Parents Sleep* was thought pretty daring when a character spoke of something going arse over tip. Striptease joints were subject to no censorship whereas a serious dramatist could expect to lose a considerable sum if his play was banned outright by the lord chamberlain. Even if it was permitted to be staged at a theatre club with a small auditorium, it would be open to prosecution. It emerged in the course of the select committee hearings that most anti-American plays would as a matter of policy be banned. The list of writers whose plays had at one time or another been banned was startling. So were some of the anomalies. The lord chamberlain had no power to censor a play written before the date on which Walpole gave him this power. So Restoration drama and Shakespeare were exempt but Aeschylus or Aristophanes in translation were not.

The abolition of the lord chamberlain's powers transformed the British theatre for a while. Artaud's theatre of cruelty and Beckett's theatre of absurdity burst upon the public and, to the satisfaction of some aficionados, in Edward Bond's play *Saved* a baby was stoned to death in its pram. Meanwhile Kenneth Tynan, who had created a storm by saying 'fuck' on television, now produced *Oh! Calcutta!,* which contained some exceedingly funny sketches in a revue given to celebrating the delights and absurdities of the sexual act; he later declared that he saw no reason why the act should not be performed on stage instead of being simulated; but then Tynan thought nothing should ever be prohibited from being produced. Finally in 1967 – the same year the Abortion Act was passed – *Hair* was produced with a chorus of boys and girls in full frontal nudity before an audience which one night contained the young Princess Anne.

Our Age had hoped that Butler could be persuaded to move on the Wolfenden recommendations about homosexuality, but he was no more disposed to do so than he had been to reform the laws of obscenity. Once again it was Roy Jenkins who got his cabinet colleagues to agree to find time for a private members' bill and put the Home Office behind it. Eight years after Wolfenden had recommended changes in the law an off-beat and courageous peer, 'Boofy' Arran, had introduced a motion in the House of Lords calling for reform; only four spoke against the motion. Thereupon he introduced a bill to change the law. On this occasion the luminaries of the law, Field Marshal Montgomery and the Chief Scout were among those who opposed it and the roar of 'not content' when the lord chancellor asked whether the house was willing to give the bill a second reading was deafening. To Arran's surprise a steady stream of peers passed through the content lobby, almost double the number of those who opposed the bill. The bill now went to committee and the fight began in earnest. Owing to procedural difficulties Arran had to introduce his bill no less than three times (I remember on one of those making my maiden speech to support him). The Chief Scout feared the country would go the way of Greece and Rome; the Field Marshal favoured the age of consent being fixed at eighty; the sometime attorney general, Lord Dilhorne, taunted the Archbishop of Canterbury by asking whether he favoured legalizing the act of buggery; a former lord chief justice, Rayner Goddard, warned the house of the existence of buggers' clubs and another peer declared that he had seen a member of one of them 'shamelessly flaunting the club tie'.

Goddard was not without a certain grim sense of humour. A week later he told Arran that none of the letters he received gave him support: all asked for the addresses and telephone numbers of the clubs. Even on the third reading Dilhorne rose to get sodomy excluded from the bill. He brought upon himself a crushing retort from Barbara Wootton. 'I ask myself, what are the opponents of this bill afraid of? They cannot be afraid that these disgusting practices will be thrown upon their attention because these acts are legalized only if they are performed in private ... I can only suppose that the opponents of the bill will be afraid that their imagination will be tormented by visions of what will be going on elsewhere. Surely, if that is so, that is their own private misfortune, and no reason for imposing their personal standard of taste and morality on the minority of their fellow citizens who can find sexual satisfaction only in relations with their own sex.'

When the sexual offences bill was about to pass, Arran made the sort of Establishment speech beloved in legislatures – no cause for jubilation, let alone celebration; a note of triumph would be most out of place – saying if there was nothing bad in being homosexual there was certainly nothing good, and so on. A number of his supporters winced but they felt that for Our Age matters had ended satisfactorily and might rest there. But matters never rest.

CHAPTER 10

Reaping the Whirlwind

1

RUSKIN TILLED THE soil, Pater sowed the seed and Wilde reaped the whirlwind. We were now to reap ours. In the years between the wars when they were young, the young in every class faced sexual taboos and a wall of silence. Sexual matters were not discussed in the media. Menstruation, masturbation, clitoris, were not words used by journalists nor were four-letter words spoken on the stage. The comedians of my generation had to be masters of allusion, which to their successors seemed arch and unamusing. The years in which we grew up were not years of innocence, they were years of ignorance. Ignorance expressed itself in pregnancies, bungled illegal abortions, illegitimate children, ostracism from the family, suicide from shame, shotgun marriages and unconsummated unions where one partner did not know how to dispel frigidity in the other, or discovered that he or she was homosexual.

The wall of silence and ignorance crumbled in the fifties and sixties. What had once been the arcana of the bright young things of the twenties, dancing the Charleston and the Black Bottom, or of the languid sophisticates of the thirties driving home at dawn humming the tune of Noel Coward's 'The Party's Over Now', became common knowledge to millions. How did it happen? Partly by the invention of medical technology. The pill gave women a greater freedom to make love than the condom, the coil or the cap. If they fell prey to anxiety there were tranquillizers, if they were depressed there were purple hearts. But the media struck the new note. The old distinctions between high and low culture were being erased. *The Times* under William Rees Mogg was a different paper from *The Times* under William Haley, as the *Sun* of the eighties with its page-three nudes was different from Hugh Cudlipp's *Daily Mirror* or Arthur Christiansen's *Express*. The love life of popsies and bimbos, toyboys and spies, became the circulation builders. Television and the Italian cinema spread ideas that suddenly appeared realizable as affluence spread and the consumer boom grew. The austerity Stafford Cripps had to impose – and the enjoyment of that austerity that Edith Summerskill displayed when she rebuked those who wanted French cheese to be imported – vanished in the inflationary budgets of the sixties and seventies. British wealth was not increasing at the rate of its competitors' but still it was increasing. Full employment meant that the young left school to enter jobs that seemed secure and from their parents money filtered down to those still at school. Teenage culture was transformed as Carnaby Street and King's Road opened their doors in provincial cities.

The moralists themselves changed. They no longer stood on the rock of righteousness; they asked what were the likely consequences of a sexual act; and after the pill the consequences so dreaded between the wars receded. Other consequences took their place and the nation saw sights and heard stories from television and newspapers that Lytton Strachey would scarcely have envisaged. Philip Larkin's well-known verse that 'sexual intercourse began in 1963 ... between the end of the Chatterley ban, and the Beatles first LP' was meticulously accurate. In the summer of that year London was regaled by rumours of a minister waiting at a dinner party clad only in a lace apron and of a cabinet minister said to be the 'headless man' in a photograph produced by the Duke of Argyll as evidence of adultery by the duchess. In order to prove his innocence the cabinet minster submitted to an examination of his genitals by a Harley Street consultant. Hard on its heels followed the scandal of the decade. The Profumo affair, like the Chatterley trial, showed how the gap had widened between public opinion and the conventions of the Establishment. By this time the Establishment accepted that men in public life slept with each other's wives or had a steady mistress and might as a result land in the divorce courts. It did not accept that they might pick up girls casually at parties or through the network that passes on names and phone numbers. Jack Profumo when secretary of state for war had the bad luck to have an affair with a twenty-one-year-old girl who knew a Soviet naval attaché. She claimed (though in his report Denning, the Master of the Rolls, disbelieved her) that he too was her lover. Worse still she was a girl who would say anything to hit the headlines. Profumo had the misfortune, when woken from sleep and challenged by his colleagues, to deny the story, and the bad judgement, when cornered by his political opponents who were out for his blood, to repeat his denial to the House of Commons. When the truth came out he was driven from office and political life in disgrace. The moralists who condemned him so roundly for lying did not add that such would have been his fate had he told the truth.

The Establishment was both apoplectic and vindictive. The wretched go-between in the case, Stephen Ward, was first harassed and then stood trial on the charge of living off immoral earnings. He was convicted on dubious evidence and committed suicide. The sanctimonious tone of Denning's report suggested that, like many a judge, he was not all that aware of how men and women behave. Quintin Hogg denounced Profumo on a BBC programme calling him a liar several times in scarcely as many minutes. The editor of *The Times*, William Haley, saw the affair as the result of Macmillan's shameless hedonism ('You've never had it so good'). He was repelled by the desire for instant gratification demanded by the girl in Kingsley Amis's novel *I Want It Now*. One MP opined that the Queen should not suffer the affront of having to receive Profumo in person to surrender his seals of office. The Queen did not endorse this Pecksniffian morality. She wrote to thank Profumo for his service and said how sorry she was that his career had ended in this unhappy way.

The effect of the post-Wolfenden legislation had been to supplement the street walker by the call girl; and a wider public became aware of what services were on offer. In the late fifties curiously worded notices appeared in newsagents' windows. Next to those which offered help with typing or removals were those which quoted phone numbers and promised French lessons or advertised a chest of drawers, or simply a black shiny mackintosh. When the police intervened a man called Shaw published a magazine called the *Ladies' Directory* retailing the call girls' phone numbers and the services offered. The laws were stretched and he was found guilty on appeal, one law lord dissenting, for publishing a document against the public interest. But for two decades other specialist magazines were sold to enable couples to find other couples with similar taste. The publishers waged a war of ingenuity against the police. In the art of making the explicit inexplicit, they used such abbreviations as AC/DC, sub-dom and water games, or referred to humiliation and bondage.

As the sociologists got to work people learnt to distinguish between close couples, i.e. monogamous homosexuals and open couples, i.e. those who lived together but were promiscuous, between the functionals or swinging singles and the dysfunctionals or asexuals. Hostesses gave parties for men and women dressed from head to foot in rubber or in black leather and chains, some wearing gas masks. Nor were parties only for the kinky. For businessmen wanting straight sex, the evening trip in a river boat awash with call girls and champagne, or the furnished flat hired for the evening for communal sex, became features of the affluent life of wife-swapping and key parties celebrated by John Updike in America. Businessmen are too busy to become enslaved to passion, some even too busy to have affairs: in these parties they found a convenient surrogate. The obsession that Vronsky felt for Anna, or Adolphe for Eléonore, or Heathcliff for Cathy disappeared into the past. The object in life now became to depersonalize sex and to move into a world of fantasy with the help of cannabis or amyl nitrate. And yet one would be wise to recall *Lolita* which is about passion, obsession, love; about a lover who breaks the conventions of advanced enlightened society as much as Vronsky did.

The distinction between prostitutes and extramarital sex became blurred. It never has been clear cut. How was one to categorize the behaviour of the aristocratic girl who expected her air fare and expenses to be paid and to receive a present for going to the south of France or the Caribbean for a holiday? Was her compliant husband living off her immoral earnings? Prostitution began to appear in a different light. The cliché of miserable women and their sordid clients, as high-toned as a religious tract, found a competitor in the merry tales of transvestism, bondage and fantasy. Not all the courtesans were rapacious harpies. Some of the most successful resembled the much admired Victorian demi-mondaine Skittles. Lower in the social scale Cynthia Payne was convicted for keeping a disorderly house where clients brought luncheon vouchers for the food, drink and kinky practices she provided. There elderly men could find pleasure in being humiliated, dressed as a maid or being pelted with mud (simulated by the contents of a Hoover bag mixed with vaseline). But a second prosecution was thrown out by a jury and she became a tolerated folk heroine. Like the old woman who lived in a shoe and had so many children she didn't know what to do, Cynthia Payne made them pay for their broth without any bread and whipped them all soundly and put them to bed.

The cinema exploited the change in taste. John Trevelyan as chief censor to the board now permitted nudity. One of the few concessions made to the past was the cutting of the shot in *Last Tango in Paris* where Brando tells the infatuated girl to reach for the butter to lubricate her bottom and stick her finger up it. Meanwhile a profitable trade developed in pornographic films and later videos. They were less explicit in London than in Amsterdam, Hamburg, Copenhagen and New York, but illegal imports from those cities satisfied those who felt deprived. More and more of Soho was taken over by cinemas showing hard or soft porn and by strip clubs and sex shops. The British Museum has always prided itself on maintaining its Private Case collection of erotica compiled under the eye of honorary curator, E.J.Dingwall, among whose publications were *Very Peculiar People* (1950) and *Some Human Oddities* (1974), whose recreations were listed as 'studying rare and queer customs'. But even that department of the library must have gathered only a fraction of the trash pornography that was now on sale. No longer did a schoolboy have to penetrate the recesses of booksellers' shops in the Charing Cross Road to read copies of forbidden books. They were on sale on bookstalls. Many of them used the device of pretending to be case studies such as a psychiatrist might compile.

Thus it was that London and Paris exchanged roles. Fifty years ago Paris still held its traditional role. The Folies Bergère, the sexual latitude of Montparnasse and, for those with stranger tastes, the Boeuf sur le Toit, the Rue de Lappe and Le Monocle, were accepted by a French public which made fun of English prudery and hypocrisy. By the sixties the Parisian cinema and television were under strict surveillance. The Olympia Press no longer published there. Night life was more discreet and *les jeunes filles du gratin* were sent to learn English in Ireland by their parents apprehensive that in England their hosts' children would take them to parties at which fornication and drugs were the mode.

But a more curious phenomenon confronted us. Before our eyes we saw the culture of the young transformed. American missionaries invaded Britain, but they in no way resembled the evangelist Aimée Semple Macpherson (whose sermons Our Age in their youth had played for amusement on the gramophone). These missionaries were the hippies preaching Flower Power. You should do your own thing, drop out of square society, turn your friends on with cannabis and LSD, practise honesty, live for fun and, if authority intervenes, love it until it relents. There were various sexual manifestations like Yoko Ono's film of 365 naked bottoms or the pornographic pop group called the Galaxy which played what it called erectile music. The rebellious among Our Age in the thirties had been strict political rebels, puritans, ascetic in their uniform of corduroy trousers, sports jackets and big knotted ties, intellectual in their marxist concerns. The new rebels wore exotic, sometimes expensive, clothes and their target was authority in all its forms. They were cynical and confident, their enemies were not capitalists so much as the universities, colleges or institutions such as the Arts Council or the Greater London Council.

At the heart of the counter-culture was not sex, but drugs, particularly cannabis and LSD, which the young argued were less harmful than the drug my generation often used to excess – alcohol. Most lawyers and medical pundits, as could have been predicted, opposed the sale of the hallucinogens, for the same reasons that the government had already legislated to curb the sale of amphetamines like benzedrine and purple hearts. But some reputable doctors – Anthony Storr and Nicholas Malleson among them – questioned whether cannabis smokers were likely to become juvenile delinquents or heroin addicts. What was wrong with producing a state of euphoria, or a mystical experience, and why infuriate the young with police raids and prosecutions? Why jail Keith Richards and Mick Jagger for a first offence of possessing cannabis, why give John Hopkins of the editorial board of *International Times* nine months if not to make an example of the Rolling Stones as a group, and to silence a paper which advised its readers 'if you can't turn your parents on, turn on them'? Some among Our Age enjoyed a second adolescence, began to smoke pot at weekends, got rid of their wives and married their secretaries or their student pupils. They began to grow their hair long and took to beards.

My successor as provost of King's seized an opportunity to praise the unorthodox. Edmund Leach created a minor sensation with his Reith Lectures of 1967. We are participants in history, he said, and scientists who pride themselves on preserving detachment betray their calling. We should welcome a spot of anarchy and twit the scientists who have set up a pecking order in which the most exact and abstract enquiries – mathematics and physics – are mostly highly praised, and engineering and sociology are treated as scum. 'One of our fundamental troubles – particularly we British – take it for granted that there is something intrinsically virtuous and natural about law and order.' In fact we are getting more not less conformist every day. Crime is decreasing: the statistics show that more crimes are detected and more crimes are manufactured by Parliament. At a time when most people thought the young were in their heyday, Leach thought they were having a pretty rough time at the hands of judges and moralizing journalists. He considered that they, not their elders, showed the better judgement in rebelling against the Vietnam War, the bomb and hypocrisies of our society such as the class system and the family 'with its narrow privacy and tawdry secrets'. Far from being the basis of good society the family 'is the source of all our discontents'. It is in the family that we see the evils of competitiveness – trying to live at a certain economic level – and that competitiveness is intensified in grammar schools, examinations and universities. We should cooperate, we should structure education to discover unorthodox geniuses: instead our schoolmasters cram us with facts instead of teaching us 'how to enjoy the pleasures of civilization'. The dons who are innovators are rarely over forty: why not compulsory early retirement for the rest? (Leach was not heard to applaud Conservative university policy in the eighties.) He concluded:

> Every manifestation of national consciousness is an evil; respect for tradition is an evil; every vested interest is at all times open to challenge ... These phrases imply a political philosophy of continuous revolution, a permanent disrespect for all forms of bureaucracy ... You can go on believing that the world ought to be an orderly place even though the quite obvious absence of order fills you with terror, or you can revel in the anarchy and thereby recover your faith in the future instead of hankering after a long dead past.

Leach achieved his purpose. *Encounter* denounced the lectures as an intellectual disaster, the earnest threw up their hands in horror and the sensible smiled sadly at such characteristic progressive sentiments. The lectures caricatured the liberalism of his generation; but caricatures resemble their originals and the reason Leach gave when he asked his contemporaries to act like gods, confidently and with a show of purpose, was revealing. It was not that the Homeric gods were more likely to achieve their private ambition than mere men who have to bow to fate. But gods have much more fun. That was the authentic voice of our generation.

The academic profession was making its contribution to the new age in another way by uncovering the secrets of the Victorians. One of the first disclosures was made by a young Canadian scholar, Phyllis Grosskurth, who persuaded the London Library to allow her to use material from the autobiographical fragment left by John Addington Symonds (hitherto only seen by favoured readers such as Raymond Mortimer). Now it became clear why Vaughan had resigned as headmaster of Harrow and refused ever to accept preferment in the church: Symonds had told his father that Vaughan had made love with one of the boys, and the father threatened to expose Vaughan. In studies, such as Steven Marcus's *The Other Victorians* (1964) or Ronald Pearsall's *The Worm in the Bud* (1969), the skeletons in the cupboard of our forefathers tumbled out, some long known but never documented, others showing that however hard people try to cover the traces of their past some document or reminiscence gives them away.

In 1980 Phyllis Grosskurth's research revealed what Havelock Ellis was really like. A stream of women flowed through Ellis's life. The particular act which gratified him was to see girls pee. Not on him. In front of him, preferably standing up. In those days of long skirts his mother had amused herself by performing in front of him and in the street, and for the rest of his life he remained obsessed by what went on under those skirts. That was why he named his steady companion Françoise Lafitte 'Naiad' and another, with the titillating name of Winifred de Kok, 'Dryad'. He was proud to have given the practice in the literature of sexology the name of Undinism and achieved final ecstasy by getting Françoise to pee in Oxford Circus.

2

'IN ALL CUPID'S pageant there is presented no monster,' says Troilus. 'Nor nothing monstrous either?' asks Cressida. 'Nothing but our undertakings,' he replies. 'when we vow to weep seas, live in fire, eat rocks, tame tigers ... this is the monstrosity in love, lady, that the will is infinite, and the execution confined, that the desire is boundless and the act a slave to limit.' The calculating, cool-headed Greek adventuress knew better than the romantic Trojan. Was *le vice anglais* a monster? The publication of Swinburne's *Lesbia Brandon* reminded readers how much a part of English underground life were the poet's favourite fantasies of being birched as a schoolboy. Swinburne had been introduced to the flagellation brothel in St John's Wood by a kitchen boy whom he heard reciting *Paradise Lost* – clearly someone who would make a sound recommendation.

Some attributed this English obsession to the Protestant reverence for the Old Testament, but Jewish communities were not noted for their ferocity in wielding the rod. In Tsarist Russia parents used the birch and soldiers and criminals were flogged rather than executed, but the practice does not seem to have aroused flagellomania. Huffy schoolmasters denied that there was any connection between flagellation and sexual excitement, although treatises by Meibom in the seventeenth, Rousseau in the eighteenth and Krafft-Ebing and Freud in the twentieth century established such a connection beyond doubt. The defence of the practice in British schools amazed foreigners. A debate on corporal punishment in Parliament would attract a swarm of back-benchers murmuring like bees after hibernation. Indeed, where but in England could one find a bishop arguing in the House of Lords in defence of a headmaster of a reform school that the photograph of a boy's bottom, produced in evidence as showing excessive severity, must have been faked because the bruising was shown as equally severe on either side of the anal cleft: whereas anyone with experience knows that a pliant cane will mark less severely on the left side as it whips round the right cheek? Where else would one see a slogan painted on a wall, by some fanatical supporter of corporal punishment, BRING BACK THE BIRCH – to which, hope springing eternal, a suppliant and willing victim had added the word PLEASE? Small wonder that during the sixties the number of establishments offering what they called correction multiplied and the police moved in. But as fast as they closed down one torture chamber and burnt the racks and cages, the cat o'nine tails, the rows of whips and straps, the monstrous dildos, the tweezers and other blood letting appliances, another sprang phoenix-like from the ashes. Clearly, such places satisfied what in Leavis's jargon was called a 'felt need'.

A sense of proportion should be observed. Dr Johnson defended whipping on the ground that boys know where they are with such a punishment. Better that than telling some boys that they are superior to others or putting them on their honour. Many public school boys would have agreed: they accepted corporal punishment as a matter of course and were neither affected by it there or later in life. Sado-masochism lives deep in the psyche of the human race and whipping is not the only action to satisfy certain human instincts. The Latin for 'I beat' is *verbero*: but the passive 'I am beaten' is a different verb in the active voice *vapulo* (Lewis and Short make the learned conjecture that the word comes from *vappo*, butterfly, and evokes the image of the fluttering and twitching of a trapped insect).

Some men and women get positive pleasure from watching a victim writhe. And from this springs the propensity of men to torture each other. The Assyrians impaled their captives, the Romans crucified them, the Inquisition burned them, the Elizabethans disembowelled, hanged and dismembered them. During our own times hideous tortures have been inflicted in so many countries by the agents of the state on its victims, some in revenge for the cruelties practised by the revolutionaries who want to destroy the regime. To contemplate this odious spectacle – the perennial enjoyment of men in seeing other men twist and scream in torment and watching their bodies twitch in death – makes one regard Swinburne's fantasy that he was a boy again at Eton held down on the block for a swishing as an innocent daydream.

But now that Our Age was in power, the pressure for reform mounted. One theme of the school novels, it will be remembered, had been the unfairness of being beaten for trivial offences. And the report of the Public Schools Commission, set up by the Labour government, urged that corporal punishment should cease. In particular, the beating of boys by boys should stop at once. The existence of the commission, rather than its report, brought about change. Eton, as usual, retreated with measured pace: the headmaster replaced the birch by a cane. Throughout the schools senior boys declined to beat their juniors. Now new boys, like Christian emerging from the Valley of the Shadow of Death, found that the tyrants who used to inhabit the cave were powerless: the Pope of Dr Keate and the Pagan of countless prefects in the past sat biting their nails and kicking the broken canes that littered the ground.

Even so the practice did not at once expire. The magistrates in the seventies on the Isle of Man exploited its semi-independent judicial system and sentenced a half-witted boy to be birched to the evident satisfaction of the islanders. Not until the courts of the European Community ruled that Britain was in breach of European law did beating cease in state schools. In accepting the ruling the Conservative government tried to legislate that it would still be legal for children to be caned provided parents gave their consent. The prospect of a school in which one set of hooligans were caned while their companions in mischief mocked their discomfiture was sufficiently grotesque for the House of Lords to vote against the clause in the bill. Eventually another ruling in the courts in 1987 upheld the right of schoolmasters in independent schools to cane boys on the grounds that the parents were under no obligation to send their sons there and must accept whatever punishment the schools decreed. No one faced the real trouble. Teachers in the state schools needed protection from young thugs (and sometimes from their parents), and few had the courage to devise ways of legally punishing parents for the outrageous conduct of their children at school.

3

REFORMERS, MARCHING AT the head of their pressure group, caught sight as they rounded the bend of a rival pressure group marching towards them. The Society for the Protection of the Unborn Child was only one of a number of groups which argued that the right to life of the child superseded that of the mother. Were we to stay silent when over 150,000 babies could be saved by reducing the limit of pregnancy to twenty weeks? Stories ran in the press of nurses revolted by the sight of squirming foetuses exhibiting the symptoms of pain as their chance of life was extinguished. Margaret Thatcher thought the law should be amended and her first leader of the house, Norman St John Stevas, led the Catholic opposition to abortion which culminated in a bill being introduced to amend the Act of 1967. The bill was in the end withdrawn, but the campaign never died down. The anti-abortionists mounted new attacks in parliament and a handful staged sit-ins in hospital operating theatres.

This division of moral opinion was paralleled on other issues. There were two camps and each felt threatened by their allies as much as by their enemies. The first was composed of those who distrusted conventional wisdom and valued exuberance, pleasure, freedom, individuality and independence, and detested the dim, grey, mediocre majorities always ready to disapprove and find excuses to stop people living as they chose. They pointed out that, though people said sex today was being commercialized, it always had been commercialized. What difference in intention was there between Loretta Young in a pre-war film stepping out of her skirt to reveal a shining slip and the convention on the screen today which decreed that a man should wear underpants and a woman knickers when they went to bed together? They denied that the young were corrupted by nudity or even porn. It was part of the 'illegal' literature that had always circulated in schools. (Before the war copies of the *Daily Worker*, hidden under gym tunics and in knickers, circulated in girls' boarding schools under the code name of 'Diana Wynyard'). It was a pity if some people were shocked but it was never wise to frame the laws upon the highest factor of shockability. No one was compelled to buy the product, and if it obtruded, well, so did a great number of other products which were more obnoxious. Brian Rix's Whitehall farces or the gross humour of old music hall entertainers are among the simplest and lowest forms of culture. They do not enrich history, like art, because they are ephemeral; but they enrich life.

Nevertheless this camp was embarrassed by its allies. When Frank Longford opened a Lords debate in the seventies on pornography some of his opponents denied that any increase of pornography had taken place. They even argued that strip clubs were closing for lack of custom and the moral quality of films was improving: there was no obligation, they said, to see or read descriptions of physical sex. Yet anyone who went to the cinema or read run-of-the-mill novels could not avoid them. Then they said that the young were more honest than their elders in their desire to see and experience everything, and (of course) that there had never been a finer generation. The very meaning of the word obscenity should be changed so that it would come to mean sadism, unemployment and poverty.

After this you felt Longford was right to cling like a drowning man to Tynan's definition of pornography as that which is intended to induce an erection and gives sexual pleasure. Longford and Tynan were at any rate agreed upon the meaning of the word; only what Tynan called good Longford called evil. No one should take what a barrister says in court as a scrupulous attempt to tell the truth, but John Mortimer in his defence of *Oz* magazine in 1971 put forward three astonishing arguments. It was not possible, he said, to be a writer if you were prevented from exploring any area of human activity; obscenity could not be identified; and it was good for us all to be nauseated and outraged by what we saw and read – regardless apparently of the nature of the outrage. In a fine flight of rhetoric he asked whether Socrates was again to be condemned to death for corrupting the morals of the people. Some libertarians argued that the trial of *Oz* was political on the ground that the sexually obscene passages were part of a political protest against the Establishment. Others said that violence or sex on television had a 'cathartic effect' upon the viewers. The underground went a few steps further. They supported porn for the same reasons that they advocated violence, taking drugs and hatred of the police. Regarding society as despotic and contemptible they intended to destroy it. To disseminate pornography, particularly to children, would so outrage the Establishment that it would be forced to confront them.

No wonder an opposing camp formed. It maintained that it was no less liberal than the other camp. Why, they asked, had their opponents changed their tune since the Chatterley trial? The reformers then took the line that all they wanted was to prevent serious works of art from being bowdlerized and they were as much in favour of prosecuting pornography as anyone. This camp believed that the verdict on the editors of *Oz* was just and showed the good sense of the jury who drew a sensible distinction between the two counts of the indictment. (The sentences passed by the judge were quite another matter.) In order, therefore, to prevent the brutalization of art a line had to be drawn somewhere, or the simulated sex of *Oh! Calcutta!* could develop into public displays of sexual intercourse of every variety – why not audience participation? There would never be agreement on where exactly the line should be drawn – whether *Portnoy's Complaint* should or should not fall within the pale. Conspicuous outrage is a well-known Veblenian law in fashion, but all societies set limits to it. Does drawing a line involve hypocrisy? Or is it like the gilt vase the old Jewish *Mohel* put in his shop window? When asked why he put it there if his profession was the circumcision of infants, he replied 'What else should I put there?'

Some social controls are bound to operate on sexual behaviour. No society exists without them. Accordingly this camp rested its case on the need to uphold an ideal – the sanctity and dignity of life. And since at the centre of life is love of which the sexual act is only a part, to degrade and insult sex is to injure life itself and poison what is most precious in society. George Steiner denounced Maurice Girodias and his Olympia Press for invading our sexual privacy and insulting the language of love. David Holbrook argued that pornography debased not only language but feeling. Pamela Hansford Johnson, married to C.P.Snow, wrote a book about Ian Brady and Myra Hindley who tortured and murdered children and buried their bodies in the Yorkshire moors. Brady possessed a library of pornography and sadistic works. From his own evidence they affected his life – and if his life why not his crimes? Did he not lend his brother-in-law *Justine* to educate him in the delights of sadism? When Bernard Levin trounced her for ignoring research that cast doubt on the link between reading and doing, Goronwy Rees asked Levin whether he would have taken the same line on reading *Der Stürmer* and the persecution of the Jews in Nazi Germany. Those in this camp were indignant when they were accused of betraying liberalism. They saw no reason why they should not be on the same side as Father Trevor Huddleston or Norman St John Stevas, and they objected to being told to toe a party line. For such reasons Tolstoy quarrelled with Turgenev who made the mistake of demanding that his friends should endorse his progressive notions. 'Just look at him,' said Tolstoy, 'walking up and down the room and waggling his democratic haunches on purpose each time he goes by.'

Nevertheless, this camp was as embarrassed as the other by some of their allies. Mary Whitehouse and Frank Longford gave the impression of trying to reimpose the Hays code, and Malcolm Muggeridge, who thought D.H.Lawrence was at the root of all evil, was an odd bedfellow for that fervent Lawrentian David Holbrook. Yet in fact Longford was batting on an easy wicket. The body of opinion that can be mustered to demand stricter safeguards is far larger than the libertarian party. The Establishment does not take defeat lightly, and thirty years after the Jenkins Act was passed judges and the police had curbed what the Establishment considered were excesses. Blue cinemas vanished and only the softest of porn was on view; bookshops were raided and the contents impounded.

This happened elsewhere. Times Square, the Kurfurstendamm and the Champs Elysées, like Soho, were sanitized. Most dogged of all was Mary Whitehouse who formed a pressure group to clean up television. For years she was abused and ridiculed by the media; but if she failed in her objective she discredited the media by showing up their arrogance. She got help from an unexpected, and probably to her unwelcome, quarter. A puritan, a new Labouchere, appeared in the shape of Richard Ingrams the editor of *Private Eye*. Undeterred by libel actions, which he lost with regularity but without gross inconvenience (since the circulation figures grew ever more buoyant and the production costs of cyclostyled copies remained negligible), he pursued people rumoured to be engaged in an extramarital affair with remorseless savagery. *Encounter* had for some years been questioning the permissive society, and the *Spectator* followed the same line in the eighties. The tabloids had always been hot on the scent. The British press had always had a keen nose for indiscretions of those in public life, and the retribution which they brought about astonished continental politicians. President Mitterrand said that, if he had to lose ministers for the misdemeanours that forced Margaret Thatcher's colleagues to resign, he would be reduced to presiding over a cabinet of homosexuals. In the seventies a newspaper printed the story of a minister photographed in bed smoking pot with two call girls: but in the eighties the trap sprung on Jeffrey Archer, who was said to have gone to a hotel with a street walker, snapped on the newspapers. The damages awarded to Archer must have made even hardened editors wince.

In America such matters are left to the courts to decide. In Britain it was then the fashion to set up committees of enquiry, and two of them passed verdicts. I was chairman of the first – the Committee on the Future of Broadcasting. We reproved the broadcasters for neglecting their own guidelines on television violence and being indifferent to research which suggested that children were particularly vulnerable to it. Even if the findings of the researchers were uneven in quality and ambiguous in inference, the broadcasters should respect the public's concern about violence. We were also concerned about sex. The committee did not take the view that those who protested against the amount of sexual innuendo on TV should be written off as fuddy-duddies who knew little about art and less about life; and it noted that when figures so widely different in upbringing and outlook as Kenneth Clark, David Holbrook and Mary Whitehouse protested, the broadcasters should recognize the force of their arguments. We thought the utilitarian principle embodied in the Obscenity Act, which claims you must prove someone has been depraved or corrupted by the work in question, was inadequate for television. It was inadequate because the evidence could never be overwhelming enough. Even blameless acts such as sexual intercourse between husband and wife would be regarded as indecent if shown on television beamed into the family sitting room. Michael Swann, the chairman of the BBC governors, circulated the chapter that dealt with these matters and another on political impartiality to the top executives in the BBC. The broadcasters ignored them.

The second committee under the philosopher Bernard Williams, then provost of King's, endorsed this distinction. It recommended that the offence of depravity and corruption should be abandoned. The law ought to be based not only on the harm which books or films might do: it should also be based on the legitimate desire of the public not to be offended. Material should be prohibited only if one could reasonably assume it was likely to do harm, e.g. to the young. So the printed word should be neither prohibited nor restricted because it cannot be *immediately* offensive and because opinions and ideas should not be censored. But on other material the criterion of what might be considered offensive by a reasonable person should apply. Apart from certain gross material it should not be prohibited; but it should be restricted. The showing of pictures or a performance of a cruel and indecent nature should be restricted whatever intrinsic merit it might possess. A board should censor or restrict what could be shown. In other words, as in the Wolfenden recommendations on prostitutes, the public should be protected against the offensiveness of sex shops and strip shows by restricting their advertisement. Bernard Williams's report was the first statement of the liberal case on these matters, and it did not accept the coarse utilitarianism of the progressives. Equally it did not reassure the *bien pensants*. In the House of

Lords Patrick Lauderdale, a high churchman, appointed himself the tripos examiner of the former Knightbridge professor of moral philosophy at Cambridge, and awarded Williams an alpha double plus for casuistry and a delta double minus for his conclusions. Reform of the law of obscenity did not come high in the priorities of the Conservative government.

4

THERE WERE TWO pressure groups which overlapped and startled Our Age, though one of them would not have startled Virginia Woolf. The women's liberation movement taught the gays how to campaign, but the two movements were not to be spoken of in the same breath. The women's movement was far more important. It was also more political. Lesbianism was not an issue because one of the few rights women did not have to fight for was the right to sleep together. The stereotype of the butch woman with monocle and tie was succeeded by the cool elegant predator who stole Childie away from Sister George in the successful West End comedy. There was no striking increase in militant lesbianism. Most accepted Simone de Beauvoir's sensible line that it was either a way of escaping from something or a way of accepting something about oneself. French women did not think of lesbianism as being concerned with butch and fem types: Courbet's enchanting painting of two girls together makes it seem a normal affectionate relationship. In the sixties and seventies Our Age was to see girls accepting reciprocal tenderness as natural; and since women want things done to them, desiring solicitude, affection, attention, languor, care, some found it easier to satisfy their desires with their women friends whether or not they had men as lovers.

Like the suffragettes, the feminists had a militant wing. Germaine Greer made the running with *The Female Eunuch* (1970) in describing men's odious ways. Men expected, rather like Lawrence and Freud, male dominance to go unquestioned. Or else, like Don Juan, they expected submission to cold hearts and hot loins. And sometimes there would be an outburst from Andrea Dworkin against husbands: what was normal sexual intercourse but rape? But it was the women's movement that gathered evidence that violent sex on the screen led to sexual assault. Hold the video recording on the one frame that gave the most electrifying image, and then fantasize: that, they surmised, was what rapists in the eighties did. 'To be presented with the unthinkable makes the unthinkable possible,' said Fay Weldon. 'So rape becomes something young men do on their night out.'

The British feminists were better tempered than their American sisters, less bitter and less submissive to the tyranny of heavy rap sessions. They did not need to be cheered by symbolic bonfires of bras. The patriarchal family came in for a pasting, and some complained that the sexual liberation of the sixties had merely increased the number of men who were interested primarily in making yet another woman. But the feminists were more intent on equal rights and equal pay. They knew that a woman in a job had a different requirement from a man, a nursery for her small child, or holidays at a time when the kids would be having theirs. They could see that the barriers had fallen in higher education – though David Eccles had to overrule Lionel Robbins and appoint two women to his committee when Robbins refused to have any on it. Women now demanded that the state should no longer assume they were housewives and their earnings, if any, were pin money. The state should recognize the single parent. It should also recognize that only five per cent of families relied on a single breadwinner. Even the Department of Health admitted that if women had stopped working the number of families below the poverty line would have trebled. It was a Labour government that brought in the bills for equal pay and against discrimination and set up an Equal Opportunities Commission to enforce the new regulations. As usual the machinery creaked: the commission needed a silver tongue if it was to persuade businesses not to discriminate against women, and it also needed a rough tongue to force its enemies through the courts to redress wrongs. The conflict between the two requirements exhausted the commission. Industrialists impeded the law, and male trade unionists denounced the women's claims as divisive of This Great Movement of Ours.

The feminist movement did not have the success it deserved. Our Age did not contemplate imitating American practice. There the law on affirmative action required institutions to show that women and blacks got a proportion of jobs; and many a dean or head of department in an American university groaned to English guests that he could no longer ask fellow scholars for confidential reports on candidates since candidates now had the right to see such reports. He ran the chance of being prosecuted under the law for making an untoward remark in committee on the merits of this or that candidate. Was it any wonder that the time now taken to make an appointment was inordinate or that the best candidate no longer got the job?

In Britain there was no Bakke case. If a white student was better qualified than a black he got the university place. Women faced an intolerable dilemma in academic life. The British academics were intent on preserving the freedom of individuals and bodies within the university to judge who was the best candidate for a post. Our Age came down on the side of Mill's essay on liberty and not on his essay on the subjection of women. With evident distaste Our Age accepted the newspeak of chairperson but they refused to make special provisions to enable a wife to return to an academic post after her family were of school age or to acknowledge that a woman who reared a family could not have such an impressive list of publications as a man. In Cambridge, for instance, the refusal (or inability) of committees to appoint women to university posts created an anomaly in a university in which nearly half the students were women. Anything resembling a quota was abhorrent to both sides. When Margaret Thatcher was secretary of state for education she suggested it was time quotas of women in medical schools should be abolished: they had in fact been imposed originally to ensure that at least a handful of women could qualify as doctors.

Perhaps what mattered most to feminists was the camaraderie of the struggle, the meeting that had given a new way of looking at life, the faith in sorority. It was just such a feeling that buoyed up the activists of all kinds from CND and the Greenham Common women to the marchers and demos and student sit-ins, the feeling of solidarity that makes light of the fact that the great aims of the movement have not yet been achieved.

The other movement that startled us was gay liberation. When Dr Kinsey published his report, Lionel Trilling looked at it with a sardonic eye. Had the good doctor ever asked himself what the word homosexuality meant? Suppose a society considered homosexuality to be the form of sexuality that should be dominant. Suppose people accepted it to be as good a way of life as heterosexuality. Would such a society differ from one that might tolerate individual homosexuals but still regarded homosexuality as an aberration and something society should not encourage? Our Age, homosexual and heterosexual alike, for the most part agreed.

Suddenly in the seventies a new kind of homosexual culture sprang to life. The impetus came, as many impulses did that offered alternative ways of life, from America, in particular from San Francisco where gays had taken over a part of the city in which, so it was said, even the police were gay. The language of American homosexuals was adopted; their aspirations too. What had been a tragic handicap was now to become a glorious alternative. The new gays despised us for conceding that homosexuality was a misfortune or at least an aberration calling for tolerance and understanding. They demanded to be acknowledged as homosexuals. They insisted that homosexuals should come out and a few, in an odious display of intolerance, threatened to expose those who didn't. Their right to any job, to teach in schools, to adopt a child, even perhaps to be given and taken in marriage, should be the same as any other citizen's. The enterprising radical leader of the Greater London Council, Ken Livingstone, a master at mocking and infuriating the Establishment, realized that gays had votes. He made grants from public funds in London treating them as he treated other interest groups such as blacks; and by politicizing homosexuality reawakened the hatred and contempt for it that is never far below the surface. We blinked. Who were these hard-left creatures in dungarees, trumpeting *Time Out* values, sporting pink triangle badges and glowering instead of camping? Whether or not homosexuals liked it they were now in politics.

Just how far they came to realize in 1988. In that year some boroughs under militant left-wing control circulated among school teachers books that suggested a homosexual father and his lover could bring up a small girl and that teenagers could enjoy homosexual experiences with adults. These books found their way into the Inner London Education Authority's resource list. The government accordingly introduced a clause into its local government bill forbidding local authorities to promote homosexuality. Many of Our Age thought this was an unnecessary piece of legislation. Only six out of some fifteen hundred local authorities had listed the books and public opinion was already forcing these authorities to reconsider the matter. The clause was interpreted as an encouragement to busybodies, humbugs and queer-bashers to bring prosecutions. The theatrical profession pulled out the stops and pleaded that what had happened to Lady Chatterley would happen to a production of *The Importance of Being Earnest*; the militant gays got the row they wanted and organized demos; and the government gave hostages to those who had said it was ruled by Mary Whitehouse and determined to put the clock back. Those who predicted the clause would lead to absurdity were right. In May 1989 Kent County Council, with immense self-satisfaction, banned a performance at a school of Benjamin Britten's opera *Death in Venice*.

Yet only a short time before this Margaret Thatcher's government had reacted admirably to one of those strange impersonal forces in history that are beyond human control; and which could well have been taken to be a judgement on the new sexual freedom. There is a famous passage in which Gibbon described the behaviour of 'the virgins of the warm climate of Africa who permitted priests and deacons to share their bed and glorified amidst the flames their unsullied purity. But insulted Nature sometimes vindicated her rights and this new species of martyrdom served only to introduce a new scandal into the Church.' Grave moralists were now to hint that, insulted by human promiscuity, Nature was taking her revenge. In America some homosexuals were assailed in the eighties by a strange virus (HIV) which attacked the T-cells of the body and broke down the body's system of immunity to disease. When the destruction reached mammoth proportions the victim was diagnosed as suffering from Acquired Immune Deficiency Syndrome (AIDS), a condition in which the body's system of immunity collapsed leaving the patient incapable of resisting diseases such as pneumonia or cancer.

The virus probably came from central Africa and Haiti and struck in particular those homosexuals who were wildly promiscuous and enjoyed anal and oral sexual intercourse. For five years after the identification of AIDS hardly a mention of its effects occurred on screen or in the press. It was, in fact, homosexuals and their doctors, some of whom were also homosexual, who raised the alarm. In America there were some anti-homosexual reactions. Politicians began to oppose legislation designed to reduce discrimination against homosexuals; moralists to denounce the medical research aimed at finding a cure for AIDS on the grounds that it endorsed buggery and the bathhouses where homosexuals met; movie stars to demand that the star playing opposite them be tested for HIV; Protestants to express fears that the communion cup could be transformed into a poisoned chalice; or – as was inevitable – members of the public to dread that the same disease could be transmitted by lavatory seats.

By the time AIDS spread to Britain the reaction was less frenzied. To Malcolm Muggeridge who, after a lifetime of enjoyment, had rebuked the Edinburgh students in the sixties for revelling in pot and sex, and in the eighties when a Catholic convert kept repeating 'God is not mocked', it seemed indeed as if the God of the Old Testament had visited his erring people with a plague to recall them to the paths of virtue. But the churches did not take this line. Nor, much to their credit, did the government or the Establishment. Royalty visited the sufferers in hospital who take long to die and knew that in their time there was no cure. The government displayed commendable sang-froid, treated the disease as a public health hazard and funded homosexual organizations as front-line troops in the battle. The minister charged with the supervision of both programmes returned from his first meeting saying that as far as he could see there was nothing left in sex that was safe other than bondage and flagellation; but in fact he set in train a programme of research and a campaign to enlighten the public. The public were told not to be chaste but to be prudent. They were told the good news as well as the bad – that AIDS is quite hard to catch as the body secretions of an infected person have to enter a lesion in the surface of the recipient's skin – either through sexual activity, intravenous drug use or through transfusions of blood. On the other hand the speed at which the disease was spreading, its virulence and mounting number of cases attributed exclusively to heterosexual contact, were also stressed.

AIDS accelerated the discussion of sexual practice which now became common on prime-time on television. The new explicitness startled people. The pop star, Bob Geldof, famed for his fund raising for starving Ethiopians, appeared on the screen of cinemas in a government sponsored advertisement and said, fingering a condom, 'It's fucking serious. Stick one of these on your dick.' Sexual behaviour also changed – for a while. The *partouses* in Paris closed, and parties where everyone stripped off were no longer a feature of the scene. Homosexuals in particular began to take precautions that they would never once have contemplated. The doctrine of self-realization, so beloved by T.H. Green and those sober idealists at Balliol, had become during the twentieth century a gospel of doing one's own thing and seeing how far the body, stimulated by drugs, could act out whatever desires the mind could dream up. Now weight-watching, jogging, limitations on smoking and drinking became popular. The new puritanism took the form of high-minded campaigns against not just AIDS but other forms of pollution – acid rain, nuclear waste, insecticides, rain forest erosion, aerosol sprays – all designed to promote virtue and curb the selfish desires of thoughtless men and women.

5

OUR GENERATION WAS, of course, divided when they looked back on the change in manners and morals. Some – thoughtful, doubting, sensitive, who heard themselves scolded for the growth of crime, violence, drugs or promiscuity – were much disturbed by the consequences: from the passing of virginity as an ideal to the marketing of pornography. Had they passed their lives so that Molly Parkin or Julie Burchill might write novels that were intended to show how far women were unshockable? The rise in the numbers of divorces was alarming when everyone acknowledged the bad effect upon children when their parents part. How much of juvenile delinquency, insecurity and bitter unhappiness among children sprang from the day their father disappeared from their lives? Many of us had mixed feelings about the change in conventional manners. Every generation winces as they hear the pronunciation of English change and is apt to think the mode of manners that ruled when they were young (and which they then regarded as stuffy) has become vulgarized. Every generation finds their own wit suddenly out of fashion and replaced by a society that seems coarser. Worse still Our Age saw the very virtues they had valued above all others vulgarized. Every generation finds difficulty in comparing society as it now is with the society of their youth.

Some would say we had achieved very little. The most common offence to land homosexuals in disgrace had been acts of gross indecency often committed in public lavatories. That was still a crime. The age of majority was reduced to eighteen, but the age of consent for homosexuals remained twenty-one. Moreover, the police still found the pursuit of homosexuals an easier way of obtaining convictions than bringing professional criminals to trial. In the eighties a Conservative MP had his career blasted by being accused of groping in a club a police officer who had brought with him a policewoman to corroborate his evidence. What the police were doing in a private club, other than to act as *agents provocateurs*, remained obscure and the prosecution failed.

Social investigators took particular pains to establish how little had changed. They claimed that divorce had not changed the institution of marriage, which remained as strong as ever. If the young made love earlier it was because they were capable of orgasm and menstruation at an earlier age. In the sixties a survey revealed most boys still wanted to marry virgins, but in the eighties John Gill argued marriages now resembled the practice of the sixteenth century when a 'little marriage' or cohabitation preceded the formal wedding. When in the seventies the age of marriage rose for the first time in fifty years, it was to be understood as a postponement not a rejection of marriage. The Values Survey for Great Britain (1985) declared that couples divorced not because they despised marriage but because they prized it so highly that nothing but a perfect union was acceptable. Alan Sked concluded that so far from there being a moral collapse in Britain 'the permissiveness of the 1960s represented only a small increase in individual freedom and that in this important area a great deal more remains to be done'.

And yet, despite these equivocal platitudes, there had been a remarkable change in sexual attitudes and practice throughout society. The tolerance of homosexuality and the change in the status of women had one curious by-product. Men and women became more androgynous. Edward Carpenter's prediction was not as fanciful as it once must have seemed. Men and women often wore the same sort of clothes, did the same sort of jobs and some were bisexual. Men in the educated classes became gentler, women tougher and more independent. In the twenties efficient contraceptives severed the bonds that bound sexual act to reproduction in the educated classes, and in the seventies sexual acts were severed from courtship and marriage. Many people were freer to do what they wished and used that freedom wisely or foolishly according to their disposition. People knew far more about sexual behaviour and were less ready to pontificate about the normal and the desirable. But nothing will ever soften the agonies of rejection young men and women suffer, or the regret old men and women feel that the most poignant experiences in life have eluded them.

Our Age heard the sixties derided as a cock-eyed society that lived for folly and futility. In fact it was a time of unparalleled vitality in the universities and colleges and the arts. The excitement of liberation made the country fizz. The Royal Opera was at its height, the Royal Ballet twinkled with stars and was fêted abroad, the English National Opera, given a home at the Coliseum by Arnold Goodman, brought out new singers and, more important still, new composers. The Arts Council and the Gulbenkian Foundation promoted the arts in the provinces. The theatres hummed. British actors and actresses had no rivals in Europe or America. New plays frisked like lambs, some weird, some sharp, many funny, all different from the staid old sheep they were displacing. Even that habitually ailing concern the British film industry perked up. Television threw off its old clothes and did indeed then become the best in the world. Galleries opened up not only in London but in provincial cities where painters could exhibit – the generation that had benefited in schools by art teaching that was the best in Europe. The number of book titles published rose each year.

Clothes dazzled. British designers became masters of zany, fetching, seductive fashion: the cooky look made life that more gay. People began to dine out in the restaurants where the boys and girls who waited wore jeans and Elizabeth David wrote the menu. New magazines caught on, newspapers woke up and produced colour supplements and features, the arts became a feature and not a pimple on society's face. London became one of the world's musical centres in more ways than one. British pop music swept the world and English footballers regained their supremacy in the World Cup. It was a time when manual workers began to take holidays abroad. Whatever the disappointments in politics, it was a time of great happiness. People felt it was good to be alive and at the same time learnt concern for the unfortunate and dispossessed. They had had a taste of honey.

CHAPTER 11

The Deviants – Evelyn Waugh

THE WRITER WHO despised the values of his generation most savagely was the one who at first sight seemed most to belong to it. Evelyn Waugh was one of the Oxford Wits and perhaps for that reason it took long for him to be recognized as the greatest novelist of his time. In Britain the pundits wrote him off as a minor talent, a comic novelist. Graham Greene, Henry Yorke and Angus Wilson have said he was the master of them all, but it was Graham Greene and J. B. Priestley who won the Order of Merit and honorary degrees at universities and Angus Wilson who was knighted. Waugh, who would dearly have liked to be a knight, was offered a CBE. He refused it, saying that he would wait until Her Majesty considered he had won his spurs. He waited in vain. American intellectuals never put him beside Faulkner, Hemingway or Scott Fitzgerald; Edmund Wilson, who admired his early novels, was revolted by *Brideshead Revisited.* Americans thought him a cad and a snob. On the Continent intellectuals thought him to be excessively insular: there is no translation of Waugh as daring as *Avanti Jeeves.*

Perhaps it was because he did not criticize the culture of his country in the acceptable way. No one could have been more severe than Angus Wilson on the morality of the educated classes or on Britain's Establishment politics than Graham Greene. Anthony Burgess and Iris Murdoch were as aware of evil as Waugh. But novelists who win a reputation as pungent critics of their country's culture often single out the virtues and vices that intellectuals of their generation already stress. Graham Greene, for example, seems to be the most unorthodox of Catholics, teetering on the verge of infidelity. But by the standards of his generation he was the soul of orthodoxy. The virtue he put first was compassion. So did they. In his novels he wants to show that compassion, God's mercy, operates far further than the theologians allow. It flows towards 'the edge of things: the honest thief, the tender murderer'. It is there waiting for that figure which Walter Allen saw recur in his novels – the man on the run from the police, from belief in Catholicism or communism or western democracy, from God himself. Greene was orthodox in hating hypocrisy. He was orthodox in playing the political game of *tu quoque*: what difference is there between American aggression in Vietnam or Central America and Soviet intervention in Eastern Europe or Afghanistan? He played John the Baptist to the sixties praising those who did their own thing, took a chance and sympathized with terrorists. He satirized the soulless bureaucratic counter-intelligence men who were after them. Graham Greene was Catholicism's double agent, one of God's spies, taking upon himself the mystery of things, with pity for worker priests, whisky priests; a One World man opposed to Popes who preached anti-communism, aware that pity can lead the Scobies of this world into mortal sin but the friend of those who suffer, the enemy of governments, institutions, and phoney organizations like secret services. The paradoxes of the faith, Catholic or Communist, intrigued but did not trouble him. He was an orthodox *gauchiste.*

Evelyn Waugh was the real deviant of my generation. He went against the grain of decent opinion, he deviated from the values we esteemed. Even those who praise him dissociate themselves from his infatuation with the English aristocracy and his contempt for all other classes. They lament that he was a reactionary. They deplore his cruelty as much as his snobbery. In order to explain these aberrations they declare Waugh was a disillusioned romantic. Graham Greene wrote, 'He is a romantic in the sense of having a dream which failed him.' His first marriage, the Second World War, even in the end his church, turn out to be illusions; but instead of becoming an English Montherlant he falls in love with the aristocrats he formerly satirized and is so bigoted a Catholic that an Irishman, Conor Cruise O'Brien, denounces him.

Indeed the whole of his oeuvre has been read as an attempt to bolster his self-confidence. His critics declare he wanted to be sure that he really was in with the upper classes and would not, like Paul Pennyfeather at the end of *Decline and Fall*, find himself once more drinking cocoa with Stubbs and listening to a paper on the Polish plebiscite. He wanted to be told everyone had stopped mocking him as a cuckold after his first wife had left him. He was determined to be not, like so many of his fellow writers, an *embusqué* in some ministry or editing some magazine, but an officer and a hero. Yet by the end of the war he knew he was not. 'It is pleasant,' he wrote in 1945, 'to end the war in plain clothes writing. I remember at the start of it writing to Frank Pakenham that its value to us would be to show us finally that we were not men of action. I took longer than he to learn it.' Was this what led him to romanticize failure – the failure of Charles Ryder to get religion or to get Julia, the failure of Guy Crouchback to make his fellow officers see what the war was really about?

What is it then that makes Waugh a deviant in the history of our culture? Not surely that he was a man of the right, an apologist for Mussolini and Franco, who despised parliamentary politics. After all, the generation before his, Proust, Mann, Joyce, Lawrence, Yeats, Shaw and T.S.Eliot, despised democracy. Nor was Catholicism the mark of a deviant at a time when Belloc urged with some success that it was *fashionable* to convert to Rome. What made Waugh a deviant was not that he became a Catholic but that he became an Augustinian Catholic.

Orthodox Catholics by definition receive all the tenets of their faith, but even the saints betray their predilection for one part of it which each according to his temperament emphasizes as supremely important. The clue to Waugh's predilection is to be found in *Decline and Fall* written before his conversion, where Mr Prendergast confesses to a very special doubt.

> You see, it wasn't the ordinary sort of doubt about Cain's wife, or the Old Testament miracles or the Consecration of Archbishop Parker ... no, it was something deeper than that. *I couldn't understand why God had made the world at all.*

Catholicism explained to Waugh why the world was as evil and horrible as it was. Catholicism explained the vile bodies in it. It also explained to him why *he* was evil and so often cruel and odious. Such questions still trouble us today. We have no difficulty in finding explanations why the world is so full of evil. We are less ready to find reasons why we ourselves are so disagreeable, so prone to rage, so full of conceit and self-gratification, so envious of other people's success and happiness, so willing to cause others unhappiness in order to give ourselves pleasure. Still, we manage to find reasons, and when things get bad the analyst is at hand. Most of us admit that, though we do not always act as we should, we have nevertheless a free will and by exercising it we can and should behave better, or, if that sounds too parsonical, live a more fulfilled or rewarding life.

Of course we know that there are limits to our powers. We are born with a certain temperament and that temperament in turn is modified, by no means always for the better, by our upbringing and circumstances. If we try to change ourselves and bring our worst defects more under control, retribution follows. We lose some of our more attractive attributes such as spontaneity, gaiety, generosity. Our generation comforted itself by discovering behavioural laws which explained the personality in terms of the unconscious. These instinctual drives and social determinants were reassuring because they diminished personal responsibility, always so disagreeable and embarrassing. And yet human behaviour cannot be described solely in terms of impulses, drives and delusions. Some people believe that mankind is powerless and held in the remorseless grasp of the impersonal forces of history, economics and geography. But even they accept some personal responsibility in day-to-day life. We know we can to some extent control our actions. Infants learn to control the most primary actions of weeping, drinking and excretion and in so doing the will plays its part. But why, if we are free, do we so often choose evil?

From earliest times men have tried to explain why this was so. One explanation is perennial. The Psalmist was among the first to use it. 'It is he that hath made us and not we ourselves' runs part of a verse of the Old Hundredth (the name Waugh gave to one of his fictional nightclubs). Edward Fitzgerald, the translator of the *Rubaiyat of Omar Khayyam*, chose that verse for his tombstone, well remembering the twelfth-century poem he had translated from the Persian: 'We are helpless: thou hast made us what we are.' Henry VI wrote a prayer which runs: '*Domine Jesu, qui me creasti, redemisti et preordinasti ad hoc quod sum: fac de me secundum voluntatem tuam* ...' Why, if God creates us and does with us what he will, that is to say predestines us to be what we are, why are we so evil?

No doctor of the church gave a more authoritative and exhaustive answer to that question than St Augustine. In his great dispute with Pelagius he argued that the Pelagian doctrine of free will was just such as might be expected to have come from a monk ill-acquainted with the world. Pelagius put forward a liberal, common-sense view of free will. To Pelagius the world of nature was good because God had created it. Children were born good though generations of sinful parents made it very difficult for them not to sin. Yet anyone could, if he only made use of the free will God had given him, do good rather than evil.

Augustine was convinced by his own experience that this was wrong. Anyone will understand his quandary who has enjoyed being young and wanting to get on in the world as much as Augustine did, when he was making his name as a dazzling rhetorician and keeping an attractive mistress. Anyone who has known temptation knows that the will is not the simple faculty Pelagius thought it was. It can hold contradictory impulses simultaneously. The mind, said Augustine, commands the body and the body obeys. But when the mind tries to command itself it often meets with resistance or open rebellion. In that famous sentence in the confessions, Augustine recalled his youth and his prayer to God. 'But I was very miserable when I was young, miserable in the early days of my youth, and I asked you to make me chaste and I said: give me chastity and continence but don't give me them yet.' So Augustine concluded that no one can stop sinning simply because he wants to do so. It is only God's grace, and his grace alone, which prevents a man from sinning. Nothing he did himself could help. His will alone was powerless, and hence he could not claim any merit if he did not sin. This was the real meaning of original sin.

Augustine lived in an age which had seen the collapse of civilization as men had known it for four centuries. Surely it must have been caused by the triumph of evil. Intellectuals buzzed with explanations. The neo-platonists produced the ingenious but unconvincing explanation that evil belonged to the world of non-being. The Manichees declared that there were two worlds, the world of light created by God and the world of darkness created by the devil. Augustine himself became a Manichee for eleven years because he was bewildered by the existence of evil in a world made by God. Only gradually did he come to believe that God created everything, and it was sin which brought about evil. Evil meant the deprivation of God and the Good. That is why the world was infected throughout with evil.

Augustine then went on to explain man's relation to society and the state. There were two cities, he said, the city of this world and the city of God. The city of man was not wholly evil. After all, God had created it. The church was of it, Christian emperors ruled it and men had duties of civil obedience to the emperor. But it was not the business of the state to realize justice. Only the city of God can be a just state. A Christian state was better than a pagan state, and only the church could unite true believers: *salus extra ecclesiam non est.* But both were founded on aggression, oppression and greed. Power on earth changes hands. So far from the sack of Rome by Alaric being a portent, so far from it being a punishment on the empire for becoming Christian, it was merely one of hundreds of examples of changes in fortune which seem momentous to those alive but are insignificant in the eyes of God or when set against the history of the world.

There is a terrible chapter (VI in Book XIX of *The City of God*) where Augustine considers the plight of a judge. A judge in attempting to discover the truth of a crime may put a man to torture. What if the man dies under torture; or, unable to bear the pain, confesses to the crime though he is innocent? And what of his accusers? They may have sincerely wished to bring criminals to justice, yet if they cannot prove the truth of their accusations the judge will feel himself compelled to put them to torture for bearing false witness. In doing these acts does the judge commit a sin? Not unless he acts through malice. He does these things because 'his ignorance compels him'. He should recognize 'the misery of these necessities'; all he can do is to plead with God to deliver him from such dilemmas. Like the judge we must do the best we can, but no one should for an instant delude himself that he can execute justice or understand the depths of human responsibility or action.

Waugh dismissed politics no less equivocally:

> I believe that man is, by nature, an exile ... that his chances of happiness and virtue ... generally speaking, are not much affected by the political and economic conditions in which he lives; I believe ... that there is no form of government ordained from God as being better than any other; that the anarchic elements in society are so strong that it is a whole-time task to keep the peace. I believe the inequalities of wealth and position are inevitable and that it is therefore meaningless to discuss the advantages of their elimination; that men naturally arrange themselves in a system of classes; that such a system is necessary for any form of co-operative work ... I believe that Art is a natural function of man; it so happens that most of the greatest art has appeared under systems of tyranny, but I do not think it has a connection with any particular system, least of all with representative government, as nowadays in England, America and France it seems popular to believe.

St Augustine explained the decline of Britain and the decay of her empire. The whole world was so sunk in original sin that by no act of their own will could men change things for the better. Progressives, reformers, liberals and socialists were particularly impious because they were attempting to realize the city of God on earth. Even righteous wars were futile: Augustine said that victories bring death with them or are doomed to death. That is why Waugh's trilogy, *Sword of Honour*, proclaims the triumph of dishonour and the betrayal of such ideals as its hero had when he joined the army.

When Waugh in his novels creates virtuous simple heroes like Tony Last and Guy Crouchback they are doomed to be victims. When he creates rogues and scoundrels they hit the jackpot. No wonder: for Satan is a prince in this world and Augustine taught us that man should not put his faith in governments, soldiers or judges. He should welcome calamity as a reminder to keep his eyes fixed on the eternal city of God. Opt out is the moral. 'These characters,' Waugh wrote in the dedication of *Put Out More Flags*, 'lived delightfully in holes and corners and have been disturbed in their habits by the rough intrusion of history.' The quietist and cynic will make more of life and do less harm than the progressive who fabricates futile plans for international peace and the elimination of poverty. Of course there must be no truck with pagan religions such as communism, but Catholics should not delude themselves that the spread of communism is worth a crusade. In the eyes of God it was a temporary aberration, like Nazism, or the Reformation, another instance of man's perennial iniquity and God's amazing grace.

As an Augustinian Waugh was a contrast to the previous generation of Catholic apologists. The neo-Thomists had wanted to show how rational Catholicism was. The modernists such as Von Hugel or Loisy wanted to show how humane and in tune with historical scholarship it was. Per contra Waugh thought how sensible St Bernard had been in dealing with presumptuous intellectuals such as Abelard. In the last sentences of *Decline and Fall* there is a reference to the Ebionites. (The Ebionites were a sect of poor Jewish-Christians who rejected the Pauline Epistles and thought that Jesus was the human son of Joseph and Mary until his baptism when the Holy Spirit lighted on him.) The passage reads: 'So the ascetic Ebionites used to turn towards Jerusalem when they prayed. Paul made a note of it. Quite right to suppress them.'

He had even less use for Chesterton's eccentric socialism and empathy with the poor. Catholicism was not vinous and beery good cheer nor a religion of joy and ebullience encompassing all man's activities, the tavern and the country fair. He had more in common with Belloc: the same delight in bigotry and, towards the end of his life, the same misanthropy. His anti-semitism was not as disgusting as Belloc's but that was because in the company of friends like Diana Cooper he had to moderate it. But Belloc's curious republicanism, Belloc's delight in Danton and the French Revolution and his assumption that France was the centre of civilization, were as strange to Waugh as Belloc's lack of interest in Catholic theology. The four last things and the most terrible images of the Christian faith were constantly before his eyes: he refers to them and the liturgy time and again in his letters. Christopher Sykes teased Waugh once by suggesting that hell must be his favourite dogma. 'If,' he replied, 'we were allowed "favourite dogmas" it might be. If you mean I see nothing to doubt in it and no cause for "modernist" squeamish revulsion, you are quite right.'

Someone may wonder why so strong an Augustinian did not remain a Protestant. Did not Luther appeal to Augustine's authority? But one has only to think of the French Catholic tradition to see how ascetic and puritanical it is. Armand de Rance founded the Trappists; the Jansenists were strict and straight; St Bernard imposed severities upon the Cistercians, and the twelfth-century Carthusian, Prior Gigue, justified ascetic practices with rare logic. Indeed, Waugh's analogue in France was Mauriac whose remorseless analyses of the depravity of the human heart are matched by his power to depict the love of a married woman for a young man, by his delight in sensuous beauty and in the charm of youth's high spirits.

There was, however, a particular reason why Waugh could not endorse Protestantism. Although Protestants make allowances for backsliders they have always been inclined to believe that the converted should lead a changed life: the change was evidence for the conversion. Waugh never expected to change his nature. He needed to be convinced that if he continued to commit the seven deadly sins he would be saved so long as he submitted to the Roman Church, confessed and was sustained by her sacraments. Commit the seven deadly sins after conversion he certainly did: most prone to envy, gluttony and anger, far from sound on pride and covetousness, and at the end of his life more and more a prey to accidie or the melancholy that springs from boredom and dissatisfaction with life. The one sin he mastered was lust. When Nancy Mitford upbraided him for his cruelty to some young man who had tried only to express his admiration, he replied: 'You have no idea how much nastier I would be if I was not a Catholic. Without supernatural aid I would hardly be a human being.' He asked Cyril Connolly never again to invite him to meet Dylan Thomas. 'He's exactly what I would have been if I had not been a Catholic.' He would ask his friends how it was possible for him to deny the existence of evil in the world when there was so much evil in himself. His self-hatred was deadly. He never once hinted that he was brave, generous in private and loyal to his friends. What more disobliging self-portrait has any writer left than that in the first chapter of *The Ordeal of Gilbert Pinfold*?

In fact his generation treated him as a deviant. Most of them considered class divisions to be a blot on our national life and consequently resented those who used the old social barriers as a fortress from which to attack the new enemy of Hoopers and do-gooders. Nor were they wrong about Waugh's relations with his social inferiors. The bullying, sardonic, insulting manner he adopted was appalling. It was this that made his commanding officer Bob Laycock regard him as 'so unpopular as to be unemployable'. He bullied with diabolic cleverness, so his biographer said, picking on the weak and defenceless, putting those ill at ease ever iller, probing for the social failing or lack of security. When Laycock decided to risk taking him with his commando for the landings in Sicily, his brigade major said to him: 'You will regret it, Brigadier. Evelyn's appointment will weaken the brigade as a coherent fighting-force. And apart from anything else, Evelyn will probably get shot.' 'That's a chance we all have to take.' 'Oh, I don't mean by the enemy.'

What intellectuals resented, however, was not Waugh's portrayal of the Hoopers and Trimmers. They resented his infatuation with the upper classes. Ever since J.B.Priestley apropos *A Handful of Dust* gave him the patronizing advice to 'leave the world of society light-weights', critics lamented his snobbery. Wodehouse never asked us to take the Drone's Club seriously. Why then should we admire the members of Brats'? Did Waugh admire them? During the war, it is true, he let his guard drop. The closing sentences of *Put Out More Flags* refer to the time when in 1940 Britain alone was left opposing Nazi Germany and her accomplice in the partition of Poland, Soviet Russia. It is then that the old buffer Sir Joseph Mainwaring said: 'There's a new spirit abroad. I see it on every side.' 'And, poor booby, he was bang right,' added Waugh. Then in 1941 – he found to his fury that we were fighting on the same side as Stalin and his commissars. In *Brideshead Revisited* he romanticized the Flyte family – though, it is worth pointing out, none of the individual Flytes. But he does not ask himself why he was dazzled by them. Pansy Lamb told Waugh that when she looked back on her debutante days of going to balls in historic houses, she recollected that:

> Most of the girls were drab and dowdy and the men even more so . . . Nobody was brilliant, beautiful . . . most were respectable, well-to-do, narrow-minded with ideals in no way differing from Hooper's except that their basic ration was larger. Hooperism is only the transcription in cheaper terms of the upper class outlook of the 1920s and like most mass productions is not flattering to its originators.

Yet in fact Waugh understood these matters all too well. He simply didn't have the stamina of the dedicated sycophantic snob. 'Yes,' he said of one aristocrat of the highest lineage. 'Yes, I used to know him with the Lygons. But he's dull, so dull. And you can imagine how much I wanted to like him.' As Christopher Sykes said, true snobbery is made of sterner stuff. Indeed it is the ancient aristocracy themselves who are the most hardened snobs. Their favourite topic of conversation is kinship in its most simple anthropological form of who married whom. Waugh was in fact not quite at his ease with the old straightforward nobility. Nor they with him. They summed him up accurately as a dangerous arriviste. His clothes were sometimes a comical caricature of what a country gentleman and a former officer of the Blues would wear. He was not invited to Hatfield, Houghton, Hardwick or Holkham. His intimate friends were declassé aristocrats: Diana Cooper, Nancy Mitford, Ann Fleming, spirited women who had broken out of the suffocating embrace of eligible matches and estates.

The Augustinian conception of grace shone through his writings. If a man was brave, spontaneous, generous and ardent, if he was open and ready to accept life, or held charitable views about others, or if he did good to others, especially to the poor or to those ill at ease, there was no merit in it. Whatever good he did was alone due to God's grace and it was presumptuous to praise him at all. Someone suggested that his friends, who were so agreeable, loyal and charming, needed only a divine spark to perfect them. The old Augustinian spoke: 'They were aboriginally corrupt. Their tiny relative advantages of intelligence, taste, good looks and good manners are quite insignificant.'

At the end of *Decline and Fall* Peter Beste-Chetwynde staggers into Paul's rooms at Scone College, tipsy after the frolics of the Bollinger. 'You know, Paul, I think it was a mistake you ever got mixed up with us, don't you? We're different somehow. Don't quite know how. Don't think that's rude, do you, Paul?' Waugh knew in his heart he was different. When the muse spoke to him in 1943 and he knew he must get *Brideshead* down on paper, he did not hesitate to pull every string to get three months' leave. One of those strings was pulled by Brendan Bracken. That did not inhibit Waugh from caricaturing him as Rex Mottram, an adventurer with all the smooth techniques of power learnt in Fleet Street and all the worship of success learnt in the City.

He might, however, have been expected to get on with Duff Cooper. But no; at the embassy in Paris he needled him by insisting that when Duff Cooper had been minister of information at the time when Hitler invaded Soviet Russia, his indiscriminate praise of the Soviet Union had been one of the factors which had led to the return of the Labour government in 1945. Suddenly Duff Cooper turned purple and yelled at him, 'It's rotten little rats like you who have brought about the downfall of the country' – and then accused him of homosexuality, cowardice and pacifism. And yet, ludicrous as the charges were, Duff Cooper sensed that Waugh was a *déraciné* of the twenties and not, like himself, a guardee of the Great War who had fought in the trenches. Waugh was a malignant tease. Unlike others who had commanded troops, he refused to become a responsible leader taking his place in the Establishment. To Duff Cooper, Churchill had been the architect of victory, to Waugh – who never allowed awkward facts such as the decline of British military and political power in relation to America and Russia to affect his views – Churchill, with his deluded tolerance of Uncle Joe, and of anti-Catholic totalitarians such as Tito, betrayed all that the war should have been fought for.

He admired the self-assurance of the upper classes. All his most lively characters glow with self-assurance: among them the slum evacuees, the terrible Connolly children. But he himself did not always have self-assurance. Cyril Connolly found him when they were undergraduates roaring drunk outside Balliol and asked him why he was making such a noise. 'I have to make a noise because I am poor,' he said. Self-assurance came with the success of his books and the entrée to London Society. But he remained different. Anyone as aware of his own failings could hardly be expected to be indulgent to the failings of others. He had only to glance at someone and his eyes travelled down to that person's feet of clay. We all have feet of clay. Yet part of the agreeable hypocrisy of life, indeed what makes social gatherings supportable, is that we glance away when we see our friend's feet of clay. Waugh would not join in the hypocrisy.

Waugh was not the only Augustinian among his generation, and perhaps it is worth while making a short detour to examine another. One of the most successful publicists of Our Age, Malcolm Muggeridge, ended his days as a supralapsarian. A sublapsarian at the time of the Synod of Dort in 1618 believed that man was created naturally good until Adam and Eve disobeyed God, and ever since their descendants had been conceived in original sin. A supralapsarian held a more heroic and satisfying view of the matter. Being omniscient and omnipotent God must have determined *before* the Fall of Man which few of his created creatures he would elect to salvation and exactly how numerous the large majority of the damned would be.

Muggeridge was brought up to believe exactly the opposite. His father was a primitive socialist. He thought that man, being naturally good, need only change his economic and social relationships to create a better world. Secure in this faith Muggeridge married a niece of Beatrice Webb and was sent by the *Manchester Guardian* in its most high-minded and progressive days as its correspondent to Russia. Within two months the scales fell from his eyes. When he found that his own editor suppressed his reports on conditions in the Soviet Union, he wrote a novel to expose the hypocrisy of his newspaper's liberal tradition and its so-called fearless exposure of tyranny and oppression. The *Manchester Guardian* then sued him. As usual penniless, he had to settle out of court and found himself a pariah in the best progressive circles. So he left to work in India and there had an intimation that the collapse of religion was the prefigurement of the collapse of the world.

At this point one can only suppose that he decided to follow Luther's advice, 'Be a sinner and sin strongly', since on his return to England he agreed to write a gossip column for Beaverbrook, the most shameless of the great whoremasters of Fleet Street. During the war he was a natural recruit for the Secret Service and was sent to Lourenço Marques, which buzzed with agents of all the combatant countries. Like Graham Greene he learnt to despise clandestine agencies and after the war came into his own as a journalist on the *Daily Telegraph.* Then he became editor of *Punch* which he transformed from the moribund weekly of the aged middle classes into a satirical magazine, losing considerable numbers of its old readers and winning a lot of new ones, until he made it so biting that the proprietors and he decided to part. Then came his greatest hour and most audacious sin. For over ten years he became a celebrity on British television, known to so many millions that he received the ultimate accolade. A waxwork was made of him at Madame Tussaud's.

How did a supralapsarian become a TV celebrity? Muggeridge was a man who could charm birds off trees: animated, affable, amusing and incapable of losing his temper. Gossip, he believed, was one of the few subjects that was still worth discussing, though for one so keen to spot portentousness in others he oddly enough dignified gossip by calling it 'interaction of human beings'. Unlike Waugh he could hardly bear to say a harsh word to anyone however much he disapproved of them. He despised Somerset Maugham as a homosexual who could know nothing about women and therefore ignored how great a part procreation and affection played in their relations with men. 'It is this preoccupation with physical appetite, which he doesn't feel, that makes Maugham's work so intensely vulgar – rather like Balzac's to the rich, or Evelyn Waugh's to the highly born, or like Graham Greene's to the good.' Yet twenty years later, hearing Maugham dither whether or not to move his paintings to Switzerland, he burst out, '"We don't care about your pictures or anything. We just want you to be happy and serene!" I think he was pleased.' Amiable; but sincere?

To some predestination may seem a dispiriting doctrine. To the faithful it abolishes all doubts and answers all questions. All the nuances, the hesitations, the discriminations, which some think make life intelligible and give it meaning, are ironed out. Whatever human beings do to right injustice is futile. For Muggeridge, everything was done under the Great Taskmaster's eye. 'Everything we do, say, wear, think, set of a hat, drop of a trouser-leg, expresses us.' To wear peep-toe shoes revealed a trivial and corrupt heart. But it was not his puritanism but his supralapsarianism that irritated his contemporaries. He related in his diary how the senior officer in the mess, to which he had been assigned in the army corps Montgomery commanded in 1942, took him aside and asked him to find another mess. 'It was my talk, he said, which had caused the trouble ... People couldn't stand it ... I have never found any difficulty in understanding how irritating I can be to other people; perhaps because I do so often irritate myself.' What the other officers probably could not stand was his smiling ridicule of the generals and politicians and of those military routines necessary for an efficient army. He sapped the morale of his brother officers. Did Muggeridge say to them as well as to his diary that while the defeat of the French 'is at least outward and visible', his own country's defeat, no less inevitable, would be 'inward and invisible'? He resembled Waugh who had sneered at Churchill's war-time oratory which, he said, had never touched ordinary people. Perhaps he forgot that oratory was practically the only weapon the army then had.

His fellow journalists, who knew that few among them had enjoyed more than Muggeridge the pleasures of the flesh, sneered at his conversion and dubbed him St Mugg. His old friends such as Anthony Powell dropped him. But they had forgotten – as indeed at times the churches seemed to have forgotten – that what distinguished Christianity from humanism was that Christians were commanded first to love God and discover their relation to him, and only second to love their neighbour. Nor did the media men understand Muggeridge's Augustinian belief that one is justified by faith not works. He complained that they were 'caught up in the almost universal fallacy that the good Christian is one who tries to behave in what he supposes to be a Christian way, and not the "changed" man, the man who's put away the old Adam and tried in the flesh to be reborn in the spirit.' But his world was one in which vice alone existed and virtue had no place. Whether or not he had ever heard of the existence of the Seven Gifts of the Holy Ghost (wisdom, fortitude, etc.) remains obscure. Or perhaps he thought the Holy Ghost had been somewhat stingy in distributing them.

On one count neither Muggeridge nor Waugh was deviant. They shared the assumption, common to many of Our Age, that no one of taste or discrimination should pursue a business primarily to make money and make it more efficient. It was an assumption made by the Oxford Wits, by Leavis and by the descendants of Bloomsbury. Charles Ryder earned his living by painting, Rex Mottram by shady finance. 'Only war could put Rex's fortunes right and carry him into power.' No gentleman would become one of Lord Copper's 'sad-eyed, smiling hangers-on', who in return for an income were at his mercy – trinkets, like writers in Hollywood, who are picked up and dropped as if they were call girls. The only way of retaining one's self-respect and one's innocence is to have a private income. On another count, too, Waugh was of his generation. He lamented the pillage of the countryside. Like Lawrence he wrote unforgettable passages protesting against the transformation of rural England into ribbon development, arterial roads, factories, disused canals and bungalows. As Forster used Howard's End Waugh used old houses, King's Thursday, Anchorage House, Hetton and Brideshead, as symbols of England's beauty. (The word beauty is appropriate. Waugh was an old-fashioned aesthete in art: he regarded Picasso as a menace and modernism in painting a gigantic hoax imposed upon gullible art lovers.)

Waugh was a deadly controversialist and he unhorsed his enemies in the lists with insolent ease. But there was one enemy whom Waugh did not defeat, though he used all his weapons; ridicule, jeering and the cutting edge of his faith. In *Helena* he pictured the Christian apologist of Constantine's day saying:

> 'Suppose that in years to come when the Church's troubles seem to be over, there should come an apostate of my own trade, a false historian, with the mind of Cicero or Tacitus, and the soul of an animal,' he nodded towards the gibbon who fretted his gold chain and chattered for fruit ... 'He might be refuted again and again, but what he wrote would remain in people's minds when the refutations were quite forgotten. This is what style does – it has the Egyptian secret of the embalmers. It is not to be despised.'

Waugh was too honest to deny that Edward Gibbon had won immortality and that his urbane ridicule was likely to continue to unsettle men's faith. Gibbon had denounced the persecuting spirit in Christians and of deists like Voltaire. His view of history was neither superficial nor optimistic and he was as aware as any theologian of evil. Since he could not fight Gibbon, Waugh turned on his reincarnation in Hugh Trevor-Roper, who – though no foe to rational religion – was the anti-clerical, anti-Catholic hammer of mumpishness in all its forms. Their encounters were severe, and for the only time in his life Waugh met an adversary whom he failed to destroy and gave as good as he got. Trevor-Roper had no sympathy for morbid Augustinianism. He thought Gibbon was right to censure the early Christians for opting out when the Roman Empire began to crumble under barbarian assaults. Gibbon believed that men have civic duties and a decent society depends on their observance of these duties. Gibbon was at one with Celsus, the earliest pagan critic of Christianity, who objected to the Christians refusing to declare their loyalty to the state; and like Lucian of Samosata mocked the fate of the bizarre convert and apostate Peregrinus who burnt himself at a stake in public at the Olympic games to crown, as he said, an exemplary life with an exemplary death. So far from being irreligious Gibbon was converted to Catholicism at Oxford, returned to Anglicanism at Lausanne and died a deist convinced that 'religion was the best guide of youth and the best support of old age'. Trevor-Roper followed Gibbon in commending sensible tolerant churchmen and in hating what gave Waugh pleasure: bigotry. Those who are diverted by Waugh's misanthropy have to face the challenge of the eighteenth-century enlightenment. These rationalists insisted that private virtue cannot exclude civic virtue. Morality cannot be reduced solely to the salvation of one's soul. Politics demand to be considered and destroy all claims that there is a general ethical rule by which all conduct is to be judged. In political life man is faced not by one set of duties but by many: his duty to his family, the institutions and groups and calling to which he belongs, some of which are voluntary and others involuntary. In politics no one speaks for himself; he represents his friends and the conflicting interests of numbers of groups. To love one's neighbour may be a great commandment but love is different from cooperation, trust and goodwill, which are its equivalent in politics. Man the political animal operating in social groups is confronted with a different moral situation from that in face-to-face relationships.

Nevertheless, Waugh threw down the gauntlet, and as one reads him one is not all that ready to pick it up. His prejudices may be absurd, his ideals archaic, his snobbery irritating and his cruelty revolting, but the Augustinian view of life explains through its integrity and coherence why our society takes the course it does and why people still behave in ways which are either disgusting or calamitous. Waugh was saved from hatred by his humour and Rupert Christiansen used two participles to describe it: blistering and terrifying. Infidels, heretics and schismatics, as well as the orthodox, can pick up his books and rock with laughter. They do so at their peril. In ghost stories the teller of the tale is sometimes described as becoming aware that he is being observed by an invisible but hostile presence. So the reader of Waugh's novels, as the smile fades from his face, may well be unable to control a shudder. No wonder Hilaire Belloc, when he first met this new young Catholic writer and looked at those blazing eyes, arched eyebrows and pitiless gaze, muttered to himself: 'He is possessed.'

PART II

CHAPTER 12

Our Age Forms Political Loyalties

1

IN 1936 TWO hundred men set out to march to London from Jarrow. In London the infant mortality rate was fifty-one per thousand live births, in Jarrow it was 114. In London about ten per cent of insured workers were unemployed, in Jarrow sixty-eight per cent were unemployed. The march was different from the run of demonstrations at that time: both Conservative and Labour party officials helped to organize it. William Deedes recalled being sent as a young journalist on the *Morning Post* to report on it. He drew the obvious contrast between the marchers, thin, silent and dignified, and the slogan-shouting students who escorted them. These were men whose wives sent their children to school on an empty stomach and, when the children returned, had only a slice of bread and a thin spread of jam to give them for their tea. Some areas such as the Midlands, some cities such as Leicester, had hardly been affected. But in the black areas the number out of work with minimal relief, and that harshly administered, was terrible. So too was the length of time they were out of work. If the heart of a hard-headed journalist of the right could be so moved, what of the hearts of the students, most of whom for the first time came into contact with the unemployed?

The plight of the unemployed was never far from the minds of those of my generation who went into politics. I remember when I was fourteen asking my father what could be done to find work for the unemployed. He said nothing could be done. I knew him to be a kind and generous man, but I could not believe him; and like my contemporaries, Conservative and Labour alike, believed that the state could engineer employment. How else was it to be done? And thus came the swing to collectivism from which hardly any of us dissented. But the metaphor of a pendulum is misleading. It resembled more a car being driven with the hand brake on. Each party, as W.H. Greenleaf put it, was a living oxymoron, reflecting one day libertarian principles and the next day collectivist attitudes. Lloyd George led the party of individualism and free trade but he had introduced insurance relief for the sick and old and unemployment benefit. Labour was the party of trade unions but also of nationalized industries, run by technocrats and guided by research. Conservatives defended the acquisition of wealth and property, but it was Joseph Chamberlain who asked, 'What ransom will property pay for the security it enjoys?'; and his son Neville, a most able minister of health, cleared slums, stopped ribbon development and laid down national policies which were to be locally administered. What image then did the three parties assume for us as we grew up?

It is part of the mythology created by the left, and especially by the marxists of those days, that virtually all intelligent young men and women were of the left and as often as not communists. This was the excuse Anthony Blunt gave, and Eric Hobsbawm said of his contemporaries that 'if they had any kind of political consciousness the odds were that they were very left wing'. Hugh Gaitskell and the LSE students passed into folk history as the minority during the General Strike who sided with the strikers: but not all the undergraduates who drove buses and humped sacks of food during the General Strike were bone-headed athletes. As in the 1985 Scargill coal strike, most thought that faced with such a challenge the government must win the day if there was to be government. The vaguely Liberal, faintly Labour, the unpolitical yet opposed to Hitler, have been forgotten and the strength of Conservatism among the young has been underestimated. The last election in which any British government was returned by more than fifty per cent of those voting was in 1935. In 1940, after years of unemployment and the humiliations inflicted by Hitler, fifty-one per cent in a national poll said they would vote Conservative and a bare twenty-seven per cent favoured the opposition parties. Not all of that fifty-one per cent were elderly or unenlightened. Geoffrey de Freitas, a future Labour minister, recalled that when he was president of the Cambridge Union in the post-Depression years the Conservatives never lost the customary motion of confidence in His Majesty's Government. Young Conservatives did not concern themselves with the platitudes of Lord Eustace Percy and the eccentricities of Lord Hugh Cecil. Quite a number ran up ideas like those being put forward by the neglected Harold Macmillan or the irrepressible Keynesian Conservative of our generation Bob Boothby.

Establishment conservatism made an appeal of a different kind. The Empire was given great prominence and the Ottawa agreements gave it even more importance. But the appeal to the young was more subtle than flag-waving. To be a Tory was to be sophisticated, it was to take pride in never being taken in. At Stowe I was taught history in the sixth form by William McElwee. On going down from Christ Church he had studied under Namier at Manchester and he gave us Namier's books on politics in the reign of George II and III. Interest, not ideas, governs men's political action and allegiance, McElwee would tell us: what mattered in politics was the power to win victory over one's enemies, what needed to be exposed was the claptrap of abstract ideas, sentimental schemes for world government and absurd pretensions to rights.

The most ridiculous of all quotations, he would say, was 'Where Freedom slowly broadens down from precedent to precedent'. We also read the now forgotten F.S. Oliver, who used Lenin to illuminate Robert Walpole's career in *The Endless Adventure* and began his chapter headings with such maxims as 'Idols and Ideals are not always derived from Morals', or 'How a politician will use Idols and Ideals to help him gain power and keep it'. The old ruling class did not consider that politics were about ideas. They were about people. You often have to take sides, and in order to explain why you trot out reasons and sometimes even invoke principles. But these are of no importance. Politics are a matter of luck: you can easily be caught on the wrong side. If your ancestors lost their lands or their heads on the scaffold, or if you were disgraced, or quarrelled violently with the leaders of your own party, you are not much disposed to see the political world in black and white. You convicted yourself of being historically illiterate if you said that Gladstone was 'right' over Home Rule for Ireland. When, except possibly between 1937 and 1940, was Winston Churchill 'right'? As late as 1937 he said he hoped Hitler, despite his methods, might turn out to be a great figure whose life could enrich mankind. Never trust a reformer when he promises a happier future. Reformers discover that the consequences of their reforms are always remote from what they intended. Conservatives impressed the unimpressionable who disliked being fooled or taken in by theories.

And what did the Liberals look like? Some of us found ourselves agreeing with Keynes when he said that Conservatism offered him 'neither intellectual nor spiritual consolation'. It did not appeal to his self-interest nor promote the public good. Nor, he said, did Labour. Labour was a class party and 'their class is not my class. The class war will find me on the side of the educated bourgeoisie'. In the twenties Liberalism still made an appeal to the first cohorts of our generation. Beverley Nichols, that ready guide to chic, made his Oxford undergraduate hero in *Patchwork* stand as a Liberal candidate for the presidency of the Union; it was unthinkable that he should have been a socialist. In their prime the Liberals had a more imposing array of intellectuals than Labour. Keynes, Hubert Henderson and Walter Layton from Cambridge, Ramsay Muir and Ernest Simon from Manchester, Gilbert Murray and the young Roy Harrod from Oxford. Beveridge at LSE argued that judicious controls over monopolies, public works to reduce unemployment, town and countryside planning to eliminate ribbon development could reduce the squalor of life and reform capitalism.

They did not leave research to the Fabians alone. Israel Sieff, Leonard Elmhirst, Julian Huxley and others, all men of the centre, set up a research institute, Political and Economic Planning. A new set of public figures began to study reform in education, town planning, health and poverty: Boyd Orr, Eleanor Rathbone and Montague Barlow. They came up against the orthodoxy of the mandarins. Between the wars the Treasury was willing to sanction a little expenditure here and there rationed equally between departments; but not a bonanza, not a plan to reflate the economy – where was the staff to see the money was spent with propriety? The argument ran then – and it is familiar today – that if the government sells bonds to finance the deficit caused by spending money on public works, it will stop businessmen financing new industry because interest rates will have been forced up. This was the line Churchill took as chancellor of the exchequer in 1929. He was speaking with the tongue of the Treasury mandarin Richard Hopkins; and Hopkins took a similar line when he fenced with Keynes in 1930 before the Macmillan Committee.

But a revolution was germinating. Until 1929 Keynes had argued that specific difficulties in world trade and finance prevented Britain adjusting to market forces. After 1931 Keynes argued that the world slump showed Britain was not suffering from a particular malaise of her own. The whole of capitalism had caught an infection. *The General Theory* did not appear until 1936 but its conclusions were to take shape five years before it was published. The remedies Keynes suggested were all the more convincing since in 1937 rearmament began to produce the very results Keynes had predicted. A.V. Alexander on the Labour benches picked up the point: if extraordinary expenditure on rearmament could reduce unemployment why could not extraordinary expenditure on other public works produce the same result? By the end of the war Richard Hopkins was enduring the pains of conversion. He became a Keynesian even in investment policy; and by advising the Church of England to switch from gilt-edged to equities he saved the livelihoods of the Anglican clergy.

Thus began a fable that sustained Our Age. The fable ran like this. If only Lloyd George and Keynes had had their way and the government had reflated rather than deflated the economy in 1929, still more so in 1931, full employment would have replaced unemployment. If only Hopkins and the Treasury had been defeated, the years which rotted the soul of the nation would have been a golden memory. Were the mandarins mistaken? Possibly; but not certainly. In recent years scholars have argued that Lloyd George's programme of public works in 1929 was too small to make any difference, and in the early thirties expenditure would have had to be so vast to produce full employment that it was not practicable politics. In any case the legend came too late to sustain the Liberal Party. Shattered in the 1931 election, Liberal causes and interest groups no longer inspired Our Age. It became the party of the discontented and of the children of the great Liberals of the past, Laytons, Bretts and the Asquith clan. Some of them, such as Spender and Simon, became exasperated with their heritage. The formidable Liberals at LSE – Robbins, Arnold Plant, Cannan and John Hicks – became the allies of conservatism just as after the war the dead Keynes was body-snatched by Labour.

Labour's appeal to Our Age was muted unless you came from a home where no one would have considered voting for any other party. The defeat of 1931 left Labour intellectually bankrupt. For instance Dalton, at that time teaching at LSE, heard Robbins dismiss the report of Labour's economic advisory council that Keynes had drafted. He brought Robbins's views to the attention of Snowden at the Treasury; but when Snowden adopted Robbins's policy, Dalton refused to follow him into the National Government, even though Snowden was taking the very course Dalton had recommended.

Nevertheless, Labour had a deposit account that saved it from bankruptcy. Tawney opened the account by suggesting that you did not have to be a marxist to explain injustice. Max Weber had provided an alternative explanation of history. Protestantism was the religion of capitalists and its ethic of hard work, abstinence and the righteous pursuit of wealth absolved the capitalist from the old medieval duties of a lord to feed the poor and do well by his tenants. Men forgot that property contains a function. The church, which should have been the first to preach social responsibilities, failed to remind men that they are their brothers' keepers, and acquiesced in the new acquisitive society. What then is to be done? Capitalists seldom consider anyone but themselves; and therefore when concentrations of property become too large they should be transferred to public ownership. Property which comes from profits made by luck, or from a monopoly or from urban ground rents or from royalties should be expropriated or nationalized: particularly property which enables the owners to control the lives of those who work for them. Tawney applied Weber's analysis of capitalism to explain the origins of the Civil War. He told you it was a matter of decency as well as economic sense to be a socialist.

To Tawney socialism was about equality or nothing. Nothing would do but the removal of inequalities in public life whether it was the public schools, or the grotesque honours list rewarding Labour leaders with knighthoods. Tawney's reply to Ramsay MacDonald, who offered him a peerage, was a classic: 'What harm did I ever do to the Labour Party?' He hated snobbery, he hated money, he despised the ruling class: and that included the intellectual elite, living off their rents and lamenting the failings of their servants. He despised Clive Bell's *Civilization* as exhibiting a different kind of snobbery. He lived his life in conformity with his creed. He had refused during the war to accept a commission and remained in the rank of sergeant. In old age he was always on the verge of bankruptcy – anything he earned he gave away – though part of his poverty was the fault of his wife, William Beveridge's sister. Kingsley Martin said that Tawney wrote *The Acquisitive Society* and his wife illustrated it.

Tawney was a sage, Harold Laski a guru. Laski's writings can have convinced few first-class minds – Ralph Milliband perhaps excepted. But every student memoir recalls his personal kindness, his dedication to his students irrespective of whether they agreed with him, his power to magnetize his audience. He was a guru particularly to his Indian students whom he treated with special friendliness. At LSE the powerful classical economists met their match on the left in Lance Beales, Nicholas Kaldor and Willie Robson. Abba Lerner at that time was a Trotskyist and there were others further to the left like Bernard Floud and David Glass. The only figure to rival these at Oxford was Douglas Cole. But Oxford too could muster a formidable number of young dons on the left: Bruce Macfarlane, A.J.P.Taylor, Hugh Jones, Richard Pares, Frank Pakenham, Freddie Ayer, John Fulton, Dick Crossman, A.L.Rowse, Patrick Gordon Walker, Stuart Hampshire among them.

The biographies of those on the left tell of the influences that led to their conversion. Socialist politics is an endless tale of manifestoes, little magazines, committees and societies. 'Agitate by day and propagate by night' as Ramsay MacDonald said in an unguarded moment. The Fabian Society and the *New Statesman* had longer lives than most, and a schoolboy might begin to have subversive thoughts after reading Chesterton at thirteen, Wells at fourteen, Shaw at fifteen. But nearly all at some time, if they were to form a loyalty to Labour, came up against that ancient institution, the Webbs.

Today the Webbs appear so workaday, so monochrome, so joyless – he so drab and she so censorious – that the thousands of hours of labour on which their achievements were built and their influence over two generations of Labour Party activists are swept aside by those who see only the shores on which their industry ran into the sands and forget how enormous and lasting a change they made in the expectations we have from government. They were nearer to the dogged individualism of the British working-class family than those who tried to convert such families to syndicalism and workers' control. Perhaps through vanity, certainly through exasperation with the events of 1931, which seemed to them to be the death knell of capitalism, the Webbs went overboard at the end of their lives for the planned economy of Stalin's Soviet Union; but it was they who popularized the notion, so crucial a belief to us, that by using rigorous methods of examining evidence men could discover how to construct a society that would be both more efficient and more just to replace the present muddle of booms and slumps – of coffee being burnt as fuel in Brazil when it could have been drunk in Europe.

There was one further reason why people came to believe that capitalism was irrevocably sick. The collapse of currencies and businesses all over Europe had been seen before, but the Depression of 1931 had begun in the citadel of capitalism, in America. There was a scientific explanation of the illness. It had been diagnosed by Marx.

2

FEW OF THE earliest communists and fellow travellers among us taught in the universities: like Palme Dutt they were active in politics, or they became journalists like W.N.Ewer or Raymond Postgate. At first the only prominent marxist don was Maurice Dobb at Cambridge. But in the late twenties after the failure of the General Strike a group of scientists came together there attracted by the charisma of J.D.Bernal. 'Sage' Bernal was as literate as he was numerate, almost as expert on Dostoevsky as on crystallography. The young C.P.Snow and Nunn May sat at his feet. So did Alister Watson, the best marxist theoretician in the circle, from whom Anthony Blunt learnt his marxism. Watson also belonged to another scientific group in the Cavendish run by Peter Kapitza who had been allowed by the Soviets to research under Rutherford. This was the heroic age of nuclear physics and in the lab were a number of marxist sympathizers: Blackett, Powell, Schoenberg and later Burhop. At that time John Cockroft was close to them.

These scientists, gripped perhaps by that passion for efficiency that inspired Edwardian reformers, staked out a claim that scientists should replace politicians as the effective rulers of the country. Architecture, planning, economics, social administration and transport systems could all be conducted on scientific principles. The founder of biochemistry at Cambridge, Gowland Hopkins, had a vision of what he called Solomon's House where a body of scientists would sift scientific papers to see which would be used to solve social problems. Ritchie Calder wanted the House of Lords replaced by a senate of scientists. Why stop at the House of Lords? asked Frederick Soddy. Julian Huxley wanted polls and sampling to do the work of elections and the unscientific talking-shop of Parliament replaced by a central planning council. Joseph Needham praised Herbert Spencer in the lecture established in his honour but argued Spencer had got it wrong. Capitalism and individual freedom were not the end but a stage in evolution. Collectivism would replace them. It was an article of faith for C.H.Waddington and Julian Huxley that as science progressed so did the good. Evolution was the process of the good replacing the bad and we must go along with the cosmic progress. This was the very reverse of T.H.Huxley's contention that nature was red in tooth and claw and morality consisted in 'combating the cosmic progress'. But then, Stephen Toulmin once noted, you have only to compare a photograph of T.H.Huxley with that of his grandson Julian to observe the difference between the granite jaw and beetling brow of Darwin's bulldog and Julian's mild inoffensive gaze.

The supreme offering came from Bernal. Russell, Aldous Huxley and Orwell were appalled by their brave new worlds. Bernal was entranced by his. He started from the premise that politics in a democracy destroyed efficiency. Men's wishes fluctuate and retard progress. Those fluctuating desires must be brought under control. Man's will must be made to conform to the external world of scientific necessity; and this could be done by biological engineering. Bernal appealed to the scientists' desire for power and influence. To some communist intellectuals the future alone had meaning. When Stephen Spender pleaded with Edward Upward, Isherwood's contemporary at school and Cambridge, that, though he welcomed the revolution, self-expression and the liberty of the individual mattered, Upward took the pipe out of his mouth and murmured, 'Gandhi'. Upward was indifferent to the present. It had no interest or meaning except as a pre-revolutionary past.

It was part of communist tactics to capture groups and societies. In the late thirties they had captured most of the Labour and socialist societies in universities just as in the twenties they captured the Labour Party's research department. At Cambridge the Majlis, the society for Asian students, became their main anti-imperialist platform. They also captured the oldest of all undergraduate discussion groups, the Apostles. When Keynes said to Kingsley Martin that, outside the ranks of Liberals, no one was worth sixpence in politics except the post-war generation of intellectual communists under thirty-five, it was those among the Apostles he had in mind. What captivated them and their contemporaries? Why did so many marxists come from prominent Liberal families? Was it the reputation Trinity had as the greatest scientific college, and the presence of Dobb and Blunt there, that made it the centre of communist agitprop? Why did communism become the new religion?

Marxism explained everything. It explained how the past becomes the present and what the future would be. A former Ullstein journalist, Arthur Koestler, recalled the impact of marxism upon him.

> I began to read Marx, Engels and Lenin in earnest. By the time I had finished with *Feuerbach* and *State and Revolution*, something had clicked in my brain which shook me like a mental explosion. To say that one had 'seen the light' is a poor description of the mental rapture which only the convert knows ... the new light seems to pour from all directions across the skull: the whole universe falls into pattern like the stray pieces of a jig-saw puzzle assembled by magic in one stroke. There is now an answer to every question: doubts and conflicts are a matter of the tortured past.

For Koestler the events in Marx's apocalypse seemed to be taking place before his astonished eyes. The Depression was the final stage of capitalism destroying itself through its own contradictions as dog eats dog, and the proletariat, steeled by hunger or unemployment, was at last acquiring class-consciousness. Through the leadership of the party the working class bursts its bonds and overthrows the cowering bourgeoisie. Disintegrating and sullen, unable any longer to behave 'rationally' as the false economics by which it conducts its affairs no longer give answers, the bourgeoisie lashes back in a last ineffectual effort to survive and spawns a hideous child with the face of the petty bourgeoisie and the body of the lumpenproletariat. The child is called fascism. For a time it may gain strength, aided as it will be by so-called social democrats who should at once be seen for what they are: social fascists. The army and the police, the lackeys of the ruling class, may provoke violence. But the day is at hand when the revolution, violent if need be, but more likely in Britain to come about by the crumbling of institutions, brings the people to power inspired by the leadership of the Communist Party. 'The expropriators will be expropriated.'

Such was the rhetoric; but there was also the dialectic. Marxism seemed to possess a method that solved intellectual as well as social problems. Common-sense says there must be a number of social classes but marxism demonstrated that in the last analysis there could be only two. If some fool objected that this was not so, you applied the heuristic method. Even if at this minute there are more than two classes you must act as if there are only two, and persuade others of this objective truth and thus bring about the revolutionary situation that will crystallize two classes, those for the revolution and those against it. The class struggle itself produces the two classes; and as the struggle is an historical fact, as true for the present as the past, how can anyone deny that society is divided into two – or at least that it will be so very shortly – and if so why not accept for all intents and purposes that it has happened now? The Italian sociologist Mosca once observed, 'The strength of socialist and anarchist doctrines lies not so much in their positive as in their negative aspects – in their minute, pointed, merciless criticism of the present organization of society.' That accomplished Keynesian, Joan Robinson, said much the same when she wrote, 'Voltaire remarked that it is possible to kill a flock of sheep by witchcraft if you give them plenty of arsenic at the same time. The sheep in this figure may well stand for complacent apologists of capitalism, Marx's penetrating bitter hatred of oppression supplies the arsenic while the labour theory of value provides the incantations.' So communists did not reply to criticisms of the Soviet Union. They simply cited the victims of capitalism, the millions of unemployed, the millions killed in imperialist wars and the brutality of competition which could be replaced by planned cooperation.

Marxism also performs the office of the priest of Nemi. Every generation nurses the secret wish to kill its predecessor, the priest who is in possession of the temple. Even when they acknowledge, say, in literature that their fathers brought some art form to perfection, like the sonnet in the sixteenth century or the rhymed couplet of Boileau and Pope, it has to be proscribed because no advance in that direction is possible any longer. Revolting against the sham of life under their parents' roof, a few of the young left home, sometimes school, and set up on their own in cheap flats plotting to overthrow their fathers' generation. Esmond Romilly became a brigand pillaging the houses of the respectable and Philip Toynbee the Pantaloon of student communism. Marxism legitimized the condemnation of the old. The editors of the *Spectator*, *Punch*, and the *Westminster Review* found their kinsmen, John Strachey, John Lehmann and Stephen Spender, disavowing them. For many more people than we care to admit moral indignation is the supreme joy in life; and it takes hold of us all the easier when we are young because we have little power to impose our will on events.

When people recall the names of the communist sympathizers among Our Age in the thirties, they think of the poets and writers; but the more lasting converts to marxism were the young historians. Graduates of Oxford and Cambridge they came from grammar schools and often from nonconformist families – Methodists such as Christopher Hill, E.P. Thompson, Ralph Fox and Sheila Rowbotham. After the war they helped to found *Past and Present*, a journal open to historians of any persuasion but sub-titled (until 1958) as a 'journal of scientific history'. It was an offshoot of the party's Historians Group and Eric Hobsbawm was its first assistant editor, Gordon Childe, Maurice Dobb, Christopher Hill, Rodney Hilton and Hugh Jones being on the board. This was the nucleus of a body of marxist historians of distinction who were influenced by the French historian and lifelong Jacobin Lucien Febvre. Some seized on the Civil War, others on radicalism in the past, or early revolts by working-class groups, or, as Hobsbawm did, primitive rebels. Raymond Postgate urged Our Age to write 'people's history', untainted by battles in war or in Parliament; and during the war ABCA sessions introduced dozens of thoughtful soldiers to a new way of looking at history. They were more important than the public school rebels who basked in the limelight.

The book that anyone concerned with politics among us was expected to read was John Strachey's *The Coming Struggle for Power*. (Cosmopolitans also read Malraux's *La Condition Humaine*.) Strachey's scenario was simple. The Great War had been an imperialist struggle for markets, but the workers would be duped no longer and would choose communism. And yet perhaps Harold Laski was an even more telling catechist. Laski had come to believe that socialism could not be brought about in a parliamentary democracy. While still retaining some faith in constitutional and legal forms he became an advocate of revolutionary change. That was to be brought about, not by violence – that being too strong for Laski's stomach – but by a convergence of interests among the dispossessed. Laski persuaded himself that he could continue to correspond with Mr Justice Holmes of the Supreme Court wearing the sober suit of a constitutionalist and believing in the separation of powers, and at the same time change into the tweed coat and flannel bags of the ardent revolutionary and use the language of class warfare. He was made to face the contradiction after the war. The *Express* declared he had advocated change by revolutionary means in a speech made in the 1945 election. Laski sued for libel. He was annihilated in the witness box, suffered swingeing costs and died two years later. Seldom has illogicality in the writings of a political scientist met with such dire punishment.

Events abroad drove intellectuals to communism. If you were a marxist, you were almost certain to belong to the Communist Party and that meant being loyal to the Soviet Union. Returning in 1930 from seeing street fighting, provoked by the Nazis in Berlin, David Guest and Humphrey Slater became convinced that communism alone could resist fascist violence. Events at home were almost as convincing. The educated classes themselves faced unemployment: between three and four hundred thousand out of two million white-collar jobs had disappeared. The left-wing journalist writing for Beaverbrook became a common phenomenon. Many of Our Age became schoolmasters for want of anything better during the Depression: Day Lewis, Calder-Marshall, MacNeice, Driberg, Upward, Michael Roberts, T.H.White, J.C.Powys; and we who were schoolboys admitted Auden to join our pantheon. (I remember construing at school in 1934 Auden's sonnet, 'Sir, No Man's Enemy Forgiving All' as if it were Vergil with a much cleverer contemporary who later joined the Party and, adopting a new accent and speech, became a professional trade unionist.)

By then Geoffrey Grigson, Michael Roberts and John Hayward had acclaimed Auden, and the other poets in the famous Quartet acknowledged him as their leader. Empson described one of Auden's early works as having 'the sort of completeness that makes a work seem to define the attitude of a generation'. That was not Leavis's view of Auden. To Leavis that poem 'in its combination of seriousness and flippancy presents in the form of a feud between two hostile parties the stultifying division in his own consciousness'. Was Auden expressing *saeva indignatio* or amusing himself and his friends? Both Leavis and Empson were right. The very defect that Leavis diagnosed in Auden – his inability to repress his public school humour – made him the poet who represented his generation. Auden's gifts, his lyricism, his mastery of metre and that colloquial tone of voice carried all before them. He spoke to the young. 'Here I am, here are you: But what does it mean? What are we going to do?' For every botched satire such as 'The Dance of Death' or 'The Dog Beneath the Skin' there were poems in which the direction was certain. Never more so than in 'Spain'.

No one can have a glimmering of the feelings of the intelligentsia of the left in the pre-war years who does not recognize that the Spanish Civil War obsessed them. For that generation Guadalajara and Teruel sounded as mournful as the Somme and Ypres to their fathers. They thought no one could dispute that it was a war in which justice was solely on one side, perhaps the only such war ever known in history. Was it not an *authentic* war, in which the forces for good were ranged against the forces of evil, a war in which a pacifist such as Julian Bell, fresh from watching Japanese aggression in China, could drive an ambulance conscience-clear and meet his death? Perspective played no part in this vision and the most vehement knew nothing of Spanish history. They did not see the war as the culmination of a hundred and fifty years of civil strife. They ignored the mortal weakness of the government and the splintering of the nation as chunks of the left, as well as the right, fell away and rejected the government's authority. They hated to be reminded that murders by one side were the revenge for murders by the other. Yet the fact remained that a legitimate Republican government, supported by the professional classes, the intelligentsia and a poverty-stricken working class, was facing an armed insurrection led by generals who gloried in being fascists, and were backed by industrialists and the business community. All over Europe men took sides, Germany and Italy sending troops and arms to Franco and using Spain as the testing ground for their armaments and tactics, the Soviet Union too in the end shamed into sending tanks, aircraft and commissars. In England the liberal left intellectuals were almost to a man and woman supporters of the Republic. They moved in a fine frenzy of mass meetings, demos, lectures, pamphlets, articles and fund raising. Little magazines and societies sprouted. Gollancz founded the Left Book Club. Within months it enrolled fifty thousand members. Claud Cockburn obliged by regaling the readers of *The Week* with the scandals of capitalism. (It made its name with inspired stories of the Stavisky scandal in 1934 in which such figures as the sinister Chiappe, the brutal head of the Parisian police, and an engaging figure called Jo-Jo le Terreur played their part.) A visit to Spain became obligatory for activists. In 1935 Anthony Blunt and Louis MacNeice went there, the next year Auden and Isherwood, Stephen Spender and Cyril Connolly. Auden went for a few days to the Aragon Front where Orwell was serving; through no fault of his hardly a shot was fired. But they were not there to fight. They went intending to change public opinion in Britain and to 'see the truth'; and when they had seen it, more often than not they returned disillusioned, as those who live by ideas often are.

The disillusion did not surface at once. Auden spoke hardly at all to his friends about his experiences of seeing churches burnt and priests murdered. When Nancy Cunard polled intellectuals, he replied, as Spender and MacNeice did, giving honourable reasons why he wanted the Republic to win without praising the communist or anarchist rule. None of these reservations were apparent when he published 'Spain'. The poem is in fact a disquisition on the workings of history and disappointed the communists who cast him in the role of recruiting sergeant. Yet it read to his contemporaries as a call to action because 'I am your choice, your decision. Yes, I am Spain.' They had to decide because 'We are left alone with our day, and the time is short, and/History to the defeated/May say Alas but cannot help or pardon.' The refrain, 'But today the struggle', was as orthodox as a party pamphlet and students felt the poet speaking to them personally when they read:

> To-morrow for the young the poets exploding like bombs,
> The walks by the lake, the weeks of perfect communion;
> To-morrow the bicycle races
> Through the suburbs on summer evenings. But to-day the struggle.

Even more dramatic to the young was the line which Auden was later to repudiate, 'The conscious acceptance of guilt in the necessary murder'. Orwell took that line to mean acceptance of the marxist doctrine of 'objectivity' – a murder is not a murder if objectively it can be shown to be a necessary act in the struggle to establish the dictatorship of the proletariat. Auden was not eccentric. The poets of the thirties were intoxicated with the idea of violence. You could not be sincere unless you were prepared to have blood on your hands. For Day Lewis it was the hour of the knife, for Spender light was to be brought to life by bringing death to the age-long exploiters. 'We're much ruder,' boasted Day Lewis writing to his scavenger press baron, 'and we're learning to shoot.' When eventually war came none of them chose to shoot.

That was natural enough. The poets saw themselves as bards, harp in hand, singing their epic as the warriors streamed past them. In this they were no different from the ardent intellectuals of the left. 'Stanley Baldwin must be sacked, Eden must be made to act, join the Franco-Soviet Pact,' they chanted on the demos. Collective security would do the trick. Send arms to Spain: there was no need for Britain to arm; there was no need for them to fight. That was how the Popular Front of communists, socialists and pacifists could hold together. But a younger poet thought differently. John Cornford accepted the necessary murder. Victor Kiernan remembered him telling 'with peculiar relish a story of Bela Kun machine-gunning five thousand prisoners ... he told it not in a spirit of sadism but of appreciation of the act of political necessity'. He was not there to read 'Spain'. He was already dead, killed on the English Crest at Boadilla on his twenty-first birthday.

Cornford became the symbol of sacrifice for the ideals of the Party. When I became a history specialist at Stowe I remember him sitting in the classroom slumped at his desk, contemptuous of the level of discussion, waiting only for the end of term when he could win a major scholarship to Trinity. Three years later I saw again his handsome Moorish face, a cigarette hanging from his lip, his shoulders hunched, as he slouched past marshalling the ranks of a demo at Cambridge. He emitted power, energy and conviction. He did not set out to charm: his mission was to convince. Other members of the

Party became mawkish when they tried to express their loyalty to it: how many novels did one read in those days in which hero and heroine came together only because they learnt to realize that the Party came first?

But when Cornford wrote to Margot Heinemann, 'I love you with all my strength and all my will and my whole body. Loving you has been the most perfect experience, and in a way, the biggest achievement of my life. The Party was my only other love ... I worked for it with all my strength and loved you as much as I was capable of.' When Cornford wrote that, it was not rhetoric. He believed in the Communist Party with all the ardour a young priest feels for the church on being ordained and able to say mass. He felt as he did because he worked fourteen hours a day orchestrating propaganda and converting erring comrades who strayed from the party line. He found no difficulty in 'the expending of powers on the flat ephemeral pamphlet and the boring meeting'. He did not, like other poets, examine how he felt confronted with war and fascism. Harsh as always, he dismissed Spender's poetry as 'a literary fashion not a historic reality'. Cornford had experienced what it was to be shelled and his verse shows it. You feel that Rupert Brooke in his famous sonnet is looking about for sentiments appropriate to the moment. You feel Owen and Sassoon are choked with pity and rage at the meaningless slaughter. But nothing shook Cornford's conviction that the misery and the ugliness of the war were necessary.

> We buried Ruiz in a new pine coffin,
> But his shroud was too small and his washed feet stuck out.
> The stink of his corpse came through the clean pine boards
> And some of the bearers wrapped handkerchiefs round their faces.
> Death was not dignified.
> We hacked a ragged grave in the unfriendly earth
> And fired a ragged volley over the grave.

Cornford became the poet-intellectual of the war against fascism and a celebrated photograph of him and his wife in profile was stuck on the walls of many left-wing undergraduates' lodgings. In fact eighty per cent of the two thousand or more British volunteers who joined the International Brigade were working class and a high percentage of them were killed or wounded. But the legend of intellectuals and workers marching together had been created; and with it that climate of opinion in which the young saw their country as being governed by a clique of men, as incompetent as they were misguided, who were determined to put the interests of their class, their inherited wealth, their way of life before the interests of humanity, justice or indeed of Britain itself. In the universities Spain swelled the membership of the marxist-dominated socialist societies. Brian Simon, a lifelong communist, claimed that at Cambridge a thousand out of some eight thousand under-graduates belonged. At LSE the numbers trebled.

In France the intelligentsia were divided – Mauriac at one time supported Catholicism and Franco. In Britain Robert Graves, Roy Campbell and Wyndham Lewis came out for Franco; Evelyn Waugh said that had he been a Spaniard he would have fought with Franco but as an Englishman saw no need to choose. Eliot and Maugham joined the old buffers who agreed with Bernard Partridge's cartoon in *Punch* of the damsel Spain being fought over by two bandits. Conservatives such as Rab Butler and Alan Lennox Boyd were distressed (as Auden was) by the sight of churches burnt to the ground. Quite a number of Conservatives preferred Franco's cause. Stephen Spender was indignant to find the British minister of the international commission in Tangier lamenting that his Spanish colleague, poor old Prieto, should have chosen the wrong side; and in Gibraltar he was told without a shadow of irony by a retired British official why the Spanish workers all supported the Republic: 'It isn't the British conception of democracy at all. It's what ninety per cent of the people want.' That was enough to make Spender join the Communist Party for a few months when Pollitt suggested he should help the Republican cause. It needed Churchill's son-in-law Duncan Sandys to make Churchill overcome his prejudices and regain his fine sense of *realpolitik* to come into line with Harold Macmillan and Bob Boothby. 'Franco,' he told an Argentinian newspaper, 'has all the right on his side because he loves his country and is defending Europe against the communist danger. But I – I am English and I prefer the triumph of the wrong cause. I prefer that the other side wins because Franco could be an upset to British interests.'

Our Age were overwhelmingly on the side of the Republic and, as its plight became more desperate, the left convinced themselves that Chamberlain's indifference to German and Italian aid to Franco was part of a plot to sell the pass in Europe as the Conservative government had done in Ethiopia. For all their fine words about collective security were they not by nods and winks encouraging Hitler to turn against the Soviet Union, the one ally the working class possessed? And so it came about that the spellbinders of the left – Laski, Cripps, Kingsley Martin, Bevan, Michael Foot, the great cartoonist Low – declared that the British capitalist government was more to be feared than Hitler. Rearmament must be opposed. The arms would be used to shoot trade unionists who would be organizing the great General Strike that was to stop the government waging a war of aggression against the anti-fascist front. In days gone by Shelley, enraged by the massacre of Peterloo, wrote *The Mask of Anarchy* in the same state of exalted innocence, preached passive resistance and had his vision of the sons of liberty rising like lions after slumber, in unvanquishable number shaking their chains to earth like dew, 'Ye are many – they are few.'

3

NOT ALL OF us lived on these high peaks. It is an error to think that the young must be interested in politics. Not all that many are. I cannot remember reading either *The Times* or the *Manchester Guardian* day in day out until the war. To spend one's time agonizing and agitating about matters over which one had not the faintest power to influence when there were so many other interesting things to do seemed to me and many others absurd. Politics did not interest, for instance, the future professor of archaeology Glyn Daniel: the nature of God, sex, films and music were, so he recollected, what he and his friends discussed. Most clever students are interested in their own concerns, the general ideas generated by the subject they study and their own special delights, travel, music, sport, games or acting. Some of the most brilliant rarely emerge from the library or the lab. Above all they enjoy gossip: about their friends, their teachers and the self-advertisers among their contemporaries fluttering on their way from the Union to worldly perches. They listen with particular pleasure to those dons who are sceptics or iconoclasts; or who pursue a subject with such open-mindedness that the lecturer seems to be groping only a few steps in front of his audience. They are liberal in the sense that they dislike rules, regulations, prigs and proselytizers. Some fall in love. What the world calls burning issues to them resemble a smoking rubbish heap, insignificant when set against the all-consuming obsession they feel. They read poetry and novels: sometimes they live vicariously through literature and imagine that they too are suffering the torments of Catullus. Keats wrote some sharp words about such 'yawning and doting a whole summer long, Till Miss's comb is made a pearl tiara, And common Wellingtons turn Romeo boots'. It is no reason, he added, why 'such agonies should be more common than the growth of weeds'.

When I went up to King's in 1935 it was a liberal college, not much concerned with party politics. The peace movement, however, flourished. It was only three years since Lowes Dickinson had died. As one of the first protagonists for the League of Nations he wrote his own polemic, *The International Anarchy*, against the Great War and Versailles. But he had not been a pacifist in the Great War and was more of a realist than appeared. When Japan invaded Manchuria and he saw no action would be taken against her, he exclaimed, 'Then it's all up with us.' When he died in that year a society was formed and called after him to discuss how war could best be outlawed. The president was Gerald Shove, an intimate of old Bloomsbury, an austere man of great purity. Shove annoyed the marxists by arguing that if war between nations was folly, civil war was no less barbaric; and both fascism and communism had led to civil war. Shove was a pacifist as was one of my directors of studies Christopher Morris, who during the war joined the cryptographers at Bletchley. I was fortified, however, in my detachment from politics by my other director of studies in history Ronald Balfour who was to be killed in the last weeks of the war when the Germans were shelling Cleves and Balfour was trying to save the city's archives. He used to say, 'We knew politicians were stupid but we did not believe they would be that stupid so soon.' Few of the dons at King's were much concerned with politics, though there was one exception: the English literature don, Peter (F.L.) Lucas, who had fought in the Great War and wrote many articles and letters to the press opposing appeasement, urging rearmament and denouncing the left for being double-faced.

For all their ardour the left did not capture my generation – even though for a time they captured the history of the thirties. They were too innocent, unsophisticated and puritanical. My friends and I collected examples of communist puritanism. 'I dislike "The Ode to a Nightingale", it's a status symbol' was the kind of comment we treasured. But there were two formidable marxists among my contemporaries at King's. One was an Etonian Indian, Mohan Kumaramangulam, later killed in an air crash while a minister under Indira Gandhi; the other was Eric Hobsbawm, a year junior to me, astonishingly mature, armed cap-a-pie with the Party's interpretation of current politics, as erudite as he was fluent, and equipped to have a view on whatever obscure topic one of his contemporaries might have chosen to write a paper. Those who take no part in political activities often harbour strong political views when roused, and it was Hobsbawm who provoked me to break my rule and speak at the Lowes Dickinson Society. He defended the proposition that, given certain circumstances (which to me seemed both improbable and undesirable), the next war could be fought to save democracy. I took the line – so my commonplace book tells me – that to talk of fighting for democracy was hypocrisy. It would be a war between fascism and Chamberlain's capitalism, and we would fight for that capitalism to survive as a nation. I was quite wrong. But then so, perhaps, was he.

CHAPTER 13

The Obsession with Munich

1

THE EVENTS THAT led to Munich left scars that never healed upon the minds of our generation. The 'lessons' of Munich misled politicians and the public for years to come. It led the Labour government to incur expenditure the country could not afford at the time of the Korean war – expenditure that was to split the party. It so obsessed Eden and Macmillan that over Suez they convinced themselves that Nasser was Hitler. Munich was used to justify the Falklands war. It became a symbol of political misjudgement. Its history was distorted with verve by Michael Foot and Frank Owen when they wrote *Guilty Men*, as influential a pamphlet as the letters of Junius. The left captured those days and indicted Conservatives in the eyes of a generation.

Yet the real culprit was the second of those formative movements of my generation – pacifism. Years later my schoolfellow, Robert Kee, was studying the Foreign Office archives and he judged the crucial year to be 1932. That was the year the Disarmament Conference met. In the twenties the doctrine of the balance of power was regarded as a wicked delusion responsible for 1914. It had been replaced by the doctrine of collective security under the Covenant of the League of Nations. The Locarno Pact set out the terms which bound Britain to come to France's aid. The covenant and the pact stood like Arthur and Gawain guarding the citadel of civilization. But a seductive figure, Morgan le Fay, materialized, determined to take Excalibur from them. This was the spirit of disarmament; and when they sat down at the table noble Arthur of Britain was under her spell. The conference ran aground on the rock of Versailles. France wanted to preserve Versailles because it set limits to German rearmament. Germany, now once again in the comity of nations, wanted those limits revised upwards and demanded to be treated as an equal. Britain saw herself as an honest broker between France and Germany: there would never be lasting peace until the wrongs of Versailles had been righted. While the conference was sitting Hitler came to power. Within a few months he walked out of it and gave notice of Germany's withdrawal from the League.

Such, however, was the force of the peace movement that so far from being alarmed by the advent of a nationalist anti-parliamentary government in Germany, the British government became ever more anxious to dispel what was called Germany's inferiority complex. Anthony Eden (a contemporary of Maurice Bowra at Oxford) was the first to utter in 1934 the fatal word 'appeasement'. That pseudo-elder statesman Jan Smuts pleaded that 'fair play and sportsmanship call for a frank revision of Versailles'. Hitler then announced an expansion of the German army in defiance of Versailles. The French were angry, Mussolini was appalled; but they got no support in London. British diplomacy proceeded by hints. John Simon assured the Nazi government that Britain had not the same interest in Austria as in Belgium. The French were told that the British could not regard Hitler's claim to the Sudeten Germans in Czechoslovakia as a cause for war. They were also told that Britain would not intervene if the French opposed Hitler marching into the Rhineland – what was it but his own back garden? When in 1936 Hitler did so and broke Locarno as well as Versailles, the French were so demoralized that all the French generals did was to cancel army leave. Eden once again spoke of appeasement. The post-war belief that Hitler could have been stopped in 1936 was a delusion. There was no possibility of the French or the British opposing the Rhineland occupation.

This was to have a sad consequence after the war for us. The British thought de Gaulle's touchiness and his later intransigence over Britain joining the European Community sprang from France's humiliation in 1940. The French saw it differently. Why should the British preen themselves on their lone resistance to Hitler when they had sacrificed, in turn, Austria, Czechoslovakia, Poland and France in pursuing their own foreign policy? Perfidious Albion had played its part in rotting French resolution when every time France wanted to stand on Versailles Britain betrayed her. A defence of a kind can be made for Chamberlain by arguing that when he became prime minister he simply followed the policy of the government in which he had been a minister. Only now he followed it with decision instead of vacillation. Yet if Hitler had not invaded Czechoslovakia in 1939, would not Chamberlain have given him Danzig and Halifax done a deal over the colonies?

No one who reads Chamberlain's papers can doubt how much he was haunted by the spectre of war. Grey with remorse the Old Men were determined not to lead Our Age into another war. No doubt Chamberlain thought another war would end 'his' kind of civilization. No doubt he thought the Empire would not survive another strain on its loyalty. The peace movement expressed in another form his own emotions. The Old Men could comfort themselves that they were at least in line with public opinion. In 1933 at a by-election a Labour candidate argued that the League should preserve peace and rearmament should be opposed: he converted a fourteen thousand Conservative majority into a majority of five thousand for himself. The swing in seven other by-elections within the next few months was comparable. In 1934 Ponsonby, Donald Soper and Bertrand Russell formed the Peace Pledge

Union and Robert Cecil launched the Peace Ballot. Attacked for war-mongering, the government was informed a year later by Cecil that eleven and a half million people had answered the five questions on the ballot paper and of those three million were opposed to military sanctions against an aggressor.*

Those who voted for the Oxford motion not to fight for King and Country were following the trend as the Union usually does. Hitler did not weaken the peace movement. On the contrary the smell of danger strengthened it. Russell argued that if the Nazis invaded Britain we should treat them as friends and coerce them if necessary by civil disobedience. They would be too embarrassed to retaliate. Alan Ryan tells us that almost at once Russell knew what he had written was rubbish. But Russell had immense influence among progressives. He published his version of the horrors of technological society and was somewhat put out by the similarity of Aldous Huxley's *Brave New World.* When Huxley and Gerald Heard left for America they were understood to be turning their backs on the old corrupt civilization of Europe that was tearing itself apart. As late as 1939 that homespun philosopher and indefatigable womanizer at Fabian summer schools, C.E.M.Joad, argued that the League of Nations should be replaced by a federal parliament with an armed police force since the League was a mere gang of burglars who had grown to look respectable but were not to be trusted. (The burglar was in fact Joad who had stolen the image from a 1935 speech made by Stafford Cripps.)

The left among us were in the grip of an obsession that they would be tricked into another war. They wanted it both ways. They wanted to stop aggressors but not by fighting or rearming. They had not the faintest understanding of how long it takes to train and equip armed forces in order to make resistance effective. They wanted somehow to reconcile their decent instincts and their explanation of events with a policy that would not outrage them. They found in Kingsley Martin of the *New Statesman* the man who could square their determination never to fight again with their desire to 'stand up to Hitler'. Martin was the most brilliant editor of his day whose success depended on knowing by instinct what progressives in politics would be arguing and agonizing about in their country cottages each weekend. We do not demand consistency in our favourite periodicals. We want reassurance; and the best editors are casuists.

Consider Kingsley Martin's performance at the time of Munich. On 23 July he urged that reasonable concessions should be made by Czechoslovakia; but that Britain should not become a willing partner to its destruction. On 30 July he approved the Runciman mission. On 6 August he referred to

* When Baldwin said he would have lost 'the election' had he come out in favour of rearmament, his opponents seized on the phrase in an allusion to the General Election of 1935 and accused him of deceit and double-dealing. R.J.Basset later showed that Baldwin's speech made it clear that he was alluding to a hypothetical election in the years 1935–6 when he had no mandate to rearm. But leaders should not wait for mandates in an emergency and his apologists overlook his inertia.

'the old illusion that strong arms and collective opposition meant peace'. On 20 August he considered Germany should be warned not to become an aggressor. On 27 August, anticipating *The Times* by ten days, he supported a policy of appeasement. If Runciman judged no internal solution was possible, Czechoslovakia's frontiers should be revised. Russia was too distant, France would not honour her pledges – and therefore we should recognize (the logic of the argument is obscure) that Spain was the real issue and arms should be sent to the Republicans by Britain since that would 'strengthen hopes of peace in Central Europe'. On 17 September he welcomed the Berchtesgaden meeting. On 24 September the Anglo-French plan for a settlement was said to have been betrayed by Chamberlain. But on 1 October Chamberlain was no longer the villain. Everybody knew that a war would resolve nothing; and people in Britain contemplated the prospect of war with nausea. After the Munich Agreement on 8 October, however, he declared that since the British public had after all been willing to go to war, war could have been averted with less devastating consequences if only Chamberlain had been firmer.

Kingsley Martin was not alone in taking this line in the *New Statesman*. That eminent member of its board, Maynard Keynes, opposed any commitment to Republican Spain and hoped, so he told Martin, that Chamberlain's policy of appeasement would succeed. He favoured the revision of Czechoslovakia's frontiers and his memories of the Great War made him oppose 'sending the average man to fight ... for reasons which appeal only to a minority'. When war came, however, their views diverged. After Poland's defeat Martin changed tack again and suggested that perhaps now was the time to make an approach to Hitler. If only Hitler would speak all would be well. This, as Gerald Berners observed, was said after a four-hour speech by the Fuehrer and all was not well. It brought down upon Martin Keynes's well-known rebuke that he had left the defence of the country to Colonel Blimp for whom three cheers.

The Labour Party was haunted and hamstrung by its pacifist past. Bevin's famous humiliation of Lansbury at Conference converted Labour from multilateral disarmament, but the conversion was only to armed deterrence. The party still opposed rearmament and argued that a mere declaration of collective security was sufficient to deter aggressors. In 1937 Dalton got his party to commit itself to rearmament, but in 1939 Labour voted against conscription. Although Dalton had his young Fabian protégés behind him, his loud mouth and dishonest face did not endear him to the educated classes. Nor were the Liberals better. When Hitler began to rearm, Lloyd George was another who called for fair play towards the sixty thousand Jews in Germany, yes, but also to the sixty million Germans who were tearing up Versailles

– on the ground that other countries, with the exception of Britain, had rearmed instead of disarmed: so why not let Germany do the same?

Stafford Cripps was, perhaps, the most fascinating example of the intellectual who could not bring himself to reject all wars but was prepared to support only 'one worth fighting for'. Not a war in defence of the League or to restrain Mussolini, or to defend an imperialist Britain; indeed not until a workers' government could be formed in Britain would it be safe to rearm. Cripps convinced himself that capitalism, now in its death throes, would twist in its agony before expiring and try to destroy the working-class movement. The rulers would start an arms race or seize arbitrary power. Had not the workers been somehow tricked out of power in 1931 – by a banker's ramp, by MacDonald's treachery, by the King himself – and power usurped by a government who had cut the workers' living standards and thrown millions out of work? He even went so far as to say that on the analogy of 1917 the defeat of Britain by Germany would enable a workers' state to be created. When Cripps called for a popular front with the Communist Party it was on the communist terms that rearmament must at all costs be stopped.

Writing to his brother after Munich, C.P.Snow forecast that within three years fascism would spread 'quickly and fairly quietly over France and England beginning with an increase in censorship and ending with anti-semitism and will last our life-times. There is no one to fight against it.' Even Orwell, returning disillusioned from fighting in Spain, continued to nurse most of the illusions of the left. 'I do not see how we can oppose fascism,' he wrote to Geoffrey Gorer, 'except by working for the overthrow of capitalism starting, of course, in one's own country. To collaborate with a capitalist-imperialist government against fascism would be to let fascism in by the back door.' And so it came to be argued that a British government had to satisfy rigorous moral criteria before its foreign policy – let alone its decision to declare war – could be endorsed. A war had to be 'authentic'. Looking back on his feelings as a schoolboy at Westminster in the thirties Richard Wollheim defended his practice of advocating at the same time two conflicting policies – opposition to Hitler and opposition to rearmament – and denying that they conflicted. He explained that

> Communism was an indispensable ally in the fight against fascism. It gave the fight authenticity. Without Communism on our side Fascism would either be left intact or be replaced by something insufficiently distinguishable from Fascism ... I did not think of myself as prepared to join up until the German invasion forced Russia into the war. Then it gradually gained authenticity for me.

Authenticity is a shady customer. For a state of affairs to be 'authentic' it must correspond to what life *ought* to be like. To the left the Spanish Republic ought to have won and the Soviet Union ought to have declared war on

Hitler to preserve Poland's independence in 1939. When reality did not match the picture book illustration of the world you withheld your approval. In a sense this was what the left had been doing for years – withholding support for rearmament on the grounds that there could not be an 'authentic' armed state unless the elected government resigned and was succeeded by a people's democracy.

Those who believed in authenticity were in for another shock. The old buffer in Gibraltar who angered Spender had more of a point than Spender allowed. Republican Spain became a people's democracy, its various provinces ruled sometimes by the legitimate government, often by committees of the Communist Party or by anarchist groups. The policy of the communists turned two of those who had fought in Spain into the most famous anti-communists in Britain. Arthur Koestler still imagined he was a communist when he was released from Franco's gaol. But not only had he seen how the Communist Party put Russian interests before the Spanish Republican cause, he now heard of the arrests and trumped-up charges levelled by the Party against Central European comrades who he knew would never have betrayed it; and the Nazi-Soviet Pact destroyed whatever loyalty he still had left. In 1940 he published *Darkness at Noon*, perhaps the finest work of imagination ever to illuminate communist mentality.

The second was George Orwell. His two famous satires on totalitarianism did not appear until after the war but since 1935 he had shown his contempt for communist tactics. That was why he went to Spain under the auspices of the Independent Labour Party and joined the POUM Trotskyist militia under Maurin and Gorkin. (The anarchists under Durruti formed a different faction.) Orwell had plenty of experience of communist tactics abroad. He was now to experience them at home. Taking advantage of Orwell's absence in Spain, Victor Gollancz issued a new edition of *The Road to Wigan Pier* omitting the second part which contained some home truths about communism. He did so even though Orwell had refused to allow the book to be bowdlerized in this way when it was selected by the Left Book Club and Gollancz had written a fellow-travelling introduction to it. When Orwell returned from Spain Kingsley Martin spiked his review of Franz Borkenau's book on the Spanish war on the grounds that it contradicted the *New Statesman*'s line on the war; and only the threat of libel stopped Harry Pollitt from repeating that Orwell's chief worry was that the working class smelt. (Orwell had in fact written that middle-class people were brought up to *believe* the working class smelt.) Anyone on the left who pilloried communist double-speak as Orwell did was worked over.

People today censure the left of those days for their credulity and self-deception. How could they believe in the Zinoviev trials and the grotesque confessions of the guilty? Gide had repudiated his former endorsement of Stalin's regime. Why did no one ignite the vapourings of the Webbs? Did the reports in the *Manchester Guardian* count for nothing? Bertrand Russell said the left refused to face the truth because intellectuals too often became besotted by power and wanted to keep in with those who wield it.

In recent years those British intellectuals have come under attack from their confrères in New York where ideas are taken more seriously than in London. The Calvinists taught that man is accountable to God for every deed and every utterance because there is a direct causal chain linking evil to evil. Utter a careless word and, as a consequence, some brother or sister enters into a life of sin. That is why discrimination is a peremptory duty, and to identify error in others a positive injunction. In New York that strain of rabbinical Calvinism lived on. The stand you took on Stalin's purges and Trotsky's theory of revolution, or on the tactics employed by a local on strike, was regarded as evidence that you were or were not of the devil's party. This ruthless search for political exactitude continued long after the war so that the precise date on which one left the Communist Party, opposed the loyalty oath or opposed the Vietnam War, was a matter which divided friends and dissolved alliances. By 1934 the communist intellectuals in New York had split into Stalinists and their Trotskyist opponents who founded their own little magazine, the *Partisan Review*. Why were those intellectuals in England who had similar doubts so unwilling to speak out?

The poets and pamphleteers took this criticism to heart, and after the war tried to make amends. Some like Day Lewis and Rex Warner renounced politics, others were appalled they had been gulled. Auden first altered the line about the 'necessary murder' and then would not allow 'Spain' to be reprinted in his collected poems. Any poem he considered marred by revolutionary gush he censored; God was no longer to look smilingly on new styles of architecture and a change of heart. Spender, the most troubled of all, had the courage to describe his declaration of faith in the Party as abject and shameful. He spent a decade, as did Koestler, exposing and opposing the communist line and became co-editor of *Encounter*. Orwell was as effective an anti-communist as Koestler. He knew politics were partly about ideas; but he rarely asked himself where his ideas were going and whether one of them found across its path a No Trespassers sign that another idea had planted there. On the other hand Koestler had the same cast of mind as the Central European refugee in New York, sharp, penetrating – and unforgiving.

Yet the poets and pamphleteers had an excuse which was better than their critics writing with hindsight allow. The Soviet Union appeared in the thirties to be the only country that would oppose fascism with arms if necessary. In a war you should not look too nicely at your ally's failings. Exactly the same criticism was to be levelled at Churchill and Roosevelt during the war for their genial acceptance of Uncle Joe. The New York intellectuals could afford to dispute among themselves: truth is easier to pursue when you do not have to face the political consequences of your purity of heart. They and America could stay neutral. The English fellow travellers realized that the one hope of halting the fascist powers was for France, Britain and the Soviet Union to combine. Yes, they were wrong to blind themselves to Stalin's tyrannies. But their real sin was to fall for the Communist Party line that to rearm and enforce compulsory military service was to betray the working class. How was Hitler ever to be stopped except by force of arms?

2

NO EVENT IN our lifetime so divided the country as Munich. Families were divided, friendships were severed and shame vied with relief as the ruling emotion. But we were not divided. A few pacifists hoped for the best but were ashamed of the betrayal of Czechoslovakia. Most of us were indignant. Even in old age the fire of resentment can still flare up when some book or performance makes me remember how month by month my contemporaries and I watched our country slide down the slope that must lead to war and heard our elders and our rulers applaud each new disaster as a step towards lasting peace. It had been difficult to hate Baldwin, he was too decent a man and some of his enemies, such as the press barons, were one's own black beasts. But Chamberlain was different. Here was a premier well read in English and French literature, founder of his city's orchestra, a botanist, a traveller, and an exceptionally able administrator both as mayor of Birmingham and at the ministry of health. He was a real leader, a dangerous opponent using every weapon to maim dissenters in his party and to express his contempt for those outside it. He had neither humour nor imagination – sad deficiencies in a prime minister. His supporters behaved like John Buchan's heroes. 'We decide what to do,' Philip Lothian told Geoffrey Cox, the perceptive cub reporter from New Zealand, 'and then send for the newspapers and tell them to sell it to the public.'

Claud Cockburn, who invented communist myths with an ingenuity that rivalled Willi Muenzenberg, concocted the story of an upper-class conspiracy of appeasers, which he called the Cliveden set. In fact the visitors to Cliveden were pretty equally divided. Philip Lothian, Lionel Curtis and Geoffrey Dawson were appeasers; Lionel Hichens, Bob Brand and Edward Grigg opposed their policy. Indeed Cranborne and Macmillan were also often there. But in some of Nancy Astor's guests the spirit of Milner's kindergarten was at work. They held the view that the world is ruled by a few men of power and to catch their eye is the surest way to mould events. Self-satisfaction and a refusal to believe that evil existed was to make Lothian and his co-religionist the Christian Scientist Nancy Astor such indignant supporters of Chamberlain.

Nancy Astor was a character straight from the pages of Shaw or Forster, determined to impose her will, contradicting anyone with whom she disagreed. Nothing pleased her more than a punch-up. She bored in, flinging jabs and combination punches, got hit but never threw in the towel. She was never soft on Hitler; but she was gripped by an invincible conviction that there would be no war and anyone who doubted Chamberlain's policy should be put down. When Churchill rose to deliver his memorable speech on Munich, she tried to put him down. She liked putting people down. She had a streak of cruelty that nearly estranged her affectionate sons who took hard knocks from her; yet unique as she was our generation thought her typical of the ruling class: numbed by the fear of communism and hypnotized like rabbits by the fascist stoat. For that was what Halifax appeared to be to the young — not a noble stag at bay but a bewildered, timorous rabbit. There is no better way to penetrate the mind of the rulers of that time than to read Halifax's memoirs – the very title tells the tale – *Fullness of Days*. He said he was puzzled why after the war British governments still thought so ill of Franco. But insight was not Halifax's strongest suit. When Churchill felt secure enough to sack him as foreign secretary and persuade him to become ambassador in Washington, Halifax recorded his 'lively feeling of gratitude to Providence, operating through Churchill, for having put it in my way to have an experience that has been and will remain quite unforgettable'. His wife, far more fly, knew exactly why Churchill offered him the job.

Were those on the left among Our Age justified in thinking that Chamberlain was at heart determined to sell out to Hitler by persuading him to turn on Soviet Russia and not the West? Even such mild equivocators as Baldwin hoped Hitler could be persuaded to turn to the East; and Hitler himself kept hinting he would guarantee the integrity of the British Empire in return for a free hand in Eastern Europe. Was it not significant that Chamberlain preferred Mussolini as an ally to the Soviet Union? No wonder they suspected Chamberlain had not forgotten how the Soviet Union financed the spread of sedition and militant unionism in the twenties and menaced the social system he and his class wanted to preserve; and this may account for the feeble way he pursued an alliance in 1939 with Soviet Russia. But the suspicion proved later to be unfair. Chamberlain faced a moral dilemma. An alliance with Stalin was to be had only at a price: the annexation of the Baltic States and revision of the Brest-Litovsk frontier. If Germany was wrong to annex Czechoslovakia, how could Chamberlain connive at Russia swallowing these little states created by the Versailles Treaty? But those in search of allies have often to swallow their principles as Grey did in 1914 when the Liberals found themselves allies of the Tsar.

The trauma of Munich split the young Conservatives as well as their elders. During the by-election at Oxford, Quintin Hogg's opponent, Sandie Lindsay, was supported by dissident Conservative undergraduates: most returned to the fold, some did not. Those who defended Munich at the time found they had to defend themselves often later in life. Quintin Hailsham, as he had now become, and Alec Home both spoke of the strength of the peace movement and the numbers of people who thought Hitler had a good case for incorporating the Sudeten Germans. At any rate when war came, they said, the country and the Empire were united. And were not our military preparations so deplorable that we would have lost a war in 1938? Hailsham used the curious argument that Chamberlain appointed Inskip to coordinate defence after Munich on the grounds that to appoint anyone more vigorous would have offended Hitler – hardly an argument to support another used by the Municheers: that Chamberlain signed to gain time to rearm. The fact is that Chamberlain and the appeasers believed that they really had done a deal with Hitler and peace was assured.

Chamberlain's conceit was iron-cast. Intellectuals who had seen Hitler's rise to power at first hand – Isherwood, Spender, Lehmann, Naomi Mitchison – or the American correspondents, Gunther, Shirer and Knickerbocker, knew what the Nazis were like and how they operated. But Chamberlain saw foreign affairs as a matter of getting on personal terms with his equals. He would listen to no one, not even his own brother, who warned him what kind of a man Hitler was. In May 1933 Austen Chamberlain had said that anyone who proscribed a whole race, the Jews, within the borders of his country would be a menace to the world. In 1935 Austen begged the government to make it plain that Britain would not stand for the re-militarization of the Rhineland. But no; Jock Colville, Neville Chamberlain's private secretary, who was devoted to him, thought in May 1940 that he 'suffers from a curious vanity and self-esteem which were born at Munich and have flourished ever since'. Even today I cannot think of him without recalling the hatred which my contemporaries and I felt for him – for his insolent self-righteousness and for clinging to office after Czechoslovakia was destroyed by Hitler; after the war began; even after Norway was invaded. Will history think more kindly of him than Our Age did?

History has already begun to do so. Chamberlain was typical of that generation who thought the preservation of the Empire was the most important cultural goal as well as being the key to Britain's security. The one eventuality that might destroy the Empire was war: the dominions' prime ministers told Chamberlain at Munich that their peoples were as unenthusiastic for a war over Czechoslovakia's frontiers as he was. The Foreign Office itself sympathized with John Simon's desire to keep out of the quagmire of Central European politics: it was an attitude that went back to Robert Walpole. It was his opponent Carteret who thought it was the duty of our diplomats to 'knock the crowned heads of Europe together and jumble something out that may be of interest to our country'. Walpole always defeated Carteret. To rearm, it was argued, would weaken the pound on the exchanges: and in any case Britain's only hope was for a short war – unless of course her sole contribution was to institute a naval blockade, in which case her only hope was for a long war.

But what could Britain offer her enemies or her allies? Stalin had far more to gain from Germany than from Britain who impressed him neither as a military power nor as a diplomatist – Britain in his eyes was unrealistic in not giving him a free hand in the Baltic States. How could the Red Army help Poland if the Poles refused to permit it to march into their country to engage Hitler's forces? It was the same with Mussolini. Richard Overy and Andrew Wheatcroft remarked, when they considered how each country reacted as war approached, that statesmen as well as the populace thought of other countries in stereotypes. The West regarded the Japanese as bow-legged and short-sighted, improbable soldiers; the Japanese regarded the West as racially inferior and decadent.

In the days before air travel statesmen were more isolated. After the Bolshevik revolution, as they called it, the ruling class in every western country was haunted by fear of their left-wing parties, exacerbated by the Depression. It was in Britain's best interests to preserve peace as long as possible, and that chimed with the pacifist mood of the country. It was in Stalin's best interests to preserve peace as long as possible to rearm and train replacements for his generals and senior officers whom he had executed believing them to be in Hitler's pay. It was also in his interests to ally himself with a power that was not too mealy-mouthed to give him the technological aid and territory he needed. It was in Roosevelt's interest to preserve the peace Americans were determined to enjoy and not once again to be fooled into interfering in Europe. Why should we be surprised, therefore, that Chamberlain acted as he did playing from such a weak hand?

But there was a historian of Our Age whose revision of the history of Munich went further. At the time A.J.P.Taylor had been a bitter critic of Munich, and after the war he wrote a short book to explain why Germany five times in seventy-five years had broken the peace of Europe. Alan Taylor was a master of the documents and literature on the origins of the First World War: now he would master those of the Second. He also, as we shall see, took a delight in paradox and shocking the benighted. Now was his chance to shock them rigid. He argued that Hitler was a German statesman in the traditional mould, a Stresemann or Rathenau, in policy no different from them. Like them he wanted to undo Versailles and recover influence in Central Europe. But not by war, still less by annexation of Bohemia or Austria. He had no deep-laid plans. He reacted to the follies of others such as Schuschnigg who provoked him to march into Austria. He merely took advantage of the Sudentenland tension: he did not create it. Admittedly he always doubted whether the Munich settlement would work and when it didn't he tore it up. But there was nothing 'sinister or premeditated' about it. Nor did he wish to destroy Poland: only to get Danzig. And when he signed the Nazi-Soviet Pact he believed he had averted war. True, Hitler miscalculated 'through launching on August 29th a diplomatic manoeuvre which he ought to have launched on August 28th'. But the blunders of the West were less venial. 'The House of Commons forced war on a reluctant British government, and that government dragged an even more reluctant French government in their train.' How much wiser Chamberlain had been at Munich which was 'a triumph for all that was best and most enlightened in British life: a triumph for those who had courageously denounced the harshness and short-sightedness of Versailles'.

Taylor raised a question fundamental in political history. Is any war ever justifiable? Would not every nation be better off if it refused ever to go to war? Taylor believed his countrymen, unbalanced by the heroics that the word Munich aroused, should ask themselves whether the declaration of war in September 1939 that led to the death of six million Poles had been too high a price to pay for their heroics. How much more fortunate Czechoslovakia, preserved by Munich, had been!

It was hardly surprising that the investigator of Hitler's last days in the bunker (an account that still stands despite the mountains of material that later became available) reached for his stiletto. Trevor-Roper was Taylor's antithesis: Taylor from a Quaker school priding himself on having democratized Magdalen's undergraduate entry, Trevor-Roper a Carthusian at his ease among the bloods of Christ Church, a rider in point-to-points. Taylor writing in short staccato sentences snapping out his paradoxes, Trevor-Roper the master of a sinuous, graceful ironic prose that descended from Gibbon. He wrote at his best when he smelled humbug or falsehood, and few things pleased him more than to unmask a charlatan. The skill with which he depicted the manoeuvres of Laudian Arminians against Puritans in the cloisters of Oxford and Cambridge long ago made one feel that he had acquired it steering between the whirlpools of intrigue in Oxford common rooms. The contests for the professorship of poetry which so beguiled the media in the fifties were beneath him; but the contest for Chancellor of Oxford was another matter and he deployed every art to bring Harold Macmillan home.

He too was a master in handling evidence. But whereas Taylor gave the impression that all the evidence lay in the documents, Trevor-Roper believed the documents needed to be set against what men and women believed to be true at the time. Men and women at the time saw Hitler as a fanatic who had planned to conquer Europe. How was it Taylor saw him as 'just a more violent Micawber waiting for something to turn up'? Was it not because Taylor believed statesmen never made history? And yet before our eyes there were scores of men such as Bismarck and Lenin who changed the face of Europe. Or was it because Taylor believed himself to be, unlike his academic colleagues, a tough realist who accepted the realities of power: and that meant accepting Germany's ability and right to overthrow Versailles? Now in fact that was what Chamberlain and perhaps the majority of the British people as a whole were willing to accept. Yet they changed their minds. Passionate for peace they became determined to fight. Why? The reason, of course, was that they became convinced Hitler was after world conquest.

Nothing odd about that. Had he not told anyone who cared to listen what his plans were? There they were in *Mein Kampf*; and in the Hossbach Memorandum (an account of his speech to his war leaders in November 1937). Yet whenever Hitler said what his intentions were, Taylor declared he was only talking for effect. Despite the fact Hitler had always said he wanted to settle a hundred million Germans in the Ukraine, why did Taylor say there was no evidence that he proposed to exploit or exterminate Ukrainians? 'Apparently he never considered the question.' The acid rose in Trevor-Roper's gorge. 'As if Hitler had not made his answer perfectly plain! As if he had any scruples about transporting or even exterminating populations!'

So Taylor reached the preposterous conclusion that those who forecast correctly from the evidence in the thirties what Hitler would do were wrong and the appeasers like Chamberlain – and Beaverbrook – were right. Whenever Taylor came across a document inconvenient to this thesis he explained that the duty of the historian was to push through the cloud of phrases to the 'realities beneath'. What in effect that meant was that the British should accept the diktat of whoever was the most powerful nation in Europe. In 1939 it meant accepting Hitler's word that he wanted nothing more than Danzig – though we now know he was set on the destruction of Poland.

The controversy was in no way historiographical. It was not a dispute between rival schools of history and only marginally about the interpretation of documents. It was a moral argument and inevitable because Hitler, the Nazi conquest of Europe and the extermination of the Jews, was the most cataclysmic historical experience in the lifetime of Our Age. The good-hearted David Astor spent time and money searching for an explanation. He had become a friend of Adam von Trott, hanged for his part in the 20 July plot to assassinate Hitler, and was tormented by the fact that a civilized people had turned a blind eye to gas ovens and camps. George Steiner, musing as he often did on the Holocaust, would fall into a parody of his normal prose style of piling clause upon clause, concept upon concept, reference upon reference to a dozen or so cultures, languages and disciplines, so as to construct sentences so dense as to be almost indissoluble. Hitler's ghost haunted Germany as in the decades after the war Germans tried to come to terms with their past; and in the mid-eighties a dispute of astonishing acrimony, the so-called *Historikerstreit*, broke out in Germany on whether Hitler and the Holocaust was a unique act unparalleled in modern times, or whether, terrible though it was, it was not different in kind from Stalin's policies and actions before and during the war.

Taylor used to boast that his interpretation of these events was accepted by all serious historians of the period. He deluded himself. By the eighties, despite the attempt of David Irving and others to replace Hitler by Stalin as the villain of Europe, we remained convinced that however fatal the errors of the rulers of the West had been Hitler was the only man in Europe who was willing to move his troops across a hostile frontier defended by specific guarantees and therefore risk a European war. No one else was.

3

FASCISM DID NOT make much headway in Britain, certainly not among us. Very few of the appeasers actually liked the Nazis or wanted to imitate them. They could not believe that anyone could take such an ideology seriously. The Establishment belief that in high politics statesmen all talk the same language made the Conservative leaders insensitive to fascist ideology. They thought Hitler's ideas nasty but irrelevant. As for the little local outburst in England of this disease, it was no more than a nuisance. To them Mosley's anti-semitism was more ill-judged than dangerous. Churchill once asked Putzi Hanfstaengel to 'tell your boss from me that anti-semitism may be a good starter but it's a bad sticker'. There was a fine side to this belief. When war came Mosley and his wife were imprisoned, but before it ended were set free. For Churchill Mosley had broken no law, had certainly not committed treason. He had merely preached a lot of nonsense and must be allowed to go free as soon as the threat of Nazi invasion had receded. The cause of legality and liberty triumphed over ideology.

But there were, of course, Nazi sympathizers and Hitler's British supporters were as much in earnest as Stalin's. Years later when right-wing journalists exploded in righteous indignation about the Cambridge spies and fellow travellers, it slipped their minds that a few dukes and sundry other peers were open Nazi supporters; that a former director of naval intelligence had to be held in detention along with Oswald Mosley; and that the fashionable hostesses Lady Cunard, Mrs Ronnie Greville and Lady Londonderry were open in their admiration for Hitler. Still, a distinction should be drawn between spies and those who sympathized with foreign tyrants. Few among the Conservatives who backed the wrong horse suffered much.

But one did. The Mitford girls enjoyed shocking the elder generation and their contemporaries. Decca, who married Esmond Romilly, became a communist; Diana married Mosley; and Nancy teased Evelyn Waugh by declaring she was a socialist and told the authorities in 1939 that they ought to detain her own sister. This was Unity, the most high-spirited of the lot, the favourite daughter. By no means a dumb blonde, an art student who had charmed Carrington (so wrote Lytton Strachey) with a mind unblemished by formal education, Unity too determined to shock the world. Her elder sister was married to the leader of the British fascists. Very well, she would go one better and embrace the principles of the most baleful fascist of them all.

Hitler recognized her devotion and flattered her. She fell. Who in her class and at her age would not have enjoyed being joined at table by the most talked of statesman in Europe? She idolized the man who – as she saw it – had given Germans back their self-respect, had given the unemployed work and circuses. And what was the price? He had detained his political opponents and encouraged some enthusiasts to smash a lot of glass. Not that the broken glass gave her a qualm. Hitler offered her a choice of apartments from those requisitioned from Jews after the *Kristallnacht* and she inspected them while the Jewish families watched her. 'I want everyone to know, I am a Jew-hater,' was her contribution to *Der Stürmer*; and when, after the occupation of Austria, five thousand Jews were left to float downstream on the Danube with no hope of refuge, she rejoiced. 'That is the way to treat them, I wish we could do that in England to our Jews.'

To speak in this evil way was to break with the ruling-class notion of politics: *Surtout, Messieurs, point de zèle.* What distinguishes this code from that of the Mafia is that honour is not interpreted as *omertà*. Why in England was Jew-baiting rejected as disgusting? Of course anti-semitic remarks or subtle exclusions were made, but virulent ideological anti-semitism broke the code of amused tolerance towards odd religions and sects. With her brother-in-law sending telegrams of congratulations to Streicher and her father a Nazi sympathizer Unity bubbled over with received ideas, for she had none of her own. Alastair Forbes, the best English expert on the personalities of the European upper classes, doubted whether she would ever have harmed a fly. Her infatuation was part of what he called her *Schwärm und Drang.* Certainly she never denounced a Jew or Gentile. Perhaps, as he argued, all her professed hatred of Jews was part of that desire to shock – like Ben Hecht saying he felt 'a song in his heart' every time the Irgun Zvai Leumi strung up or shot a British soldier. Such bad talk has become the commonplace of our times. Yet can one believe, had she continued to live in Germany, she would have raised her voice against the Nazi treatment of the Jews?

The question never arose. For in one sense Unity Mitford remained true to the upper-class notion of politics. She did not defect. She shot herself in Germany when war came; and was brought back to her parents to die a few years later crippled and spurned. She was in her early twenties. Which of our early follies are punished with such terrible severity?

CHAPTER 14

The Roaring Forties

1

IN THE SECOND World War Our Age won their spurs and their ideas and experiences of their youth came together to form their *mentalités*. Remembering the battue of skilled minds in the trenches, the authorities treated intellectuals as a species to be preserved to do the jobs intellectuals can do. Scientists were offered jobs in secret laboratories, mathematicians and classical scholars were recruited as cryptographers, poets and novelists joined the fire service, economists and historians became civil servants. The War Office Selection Board employed psychologists, the Political Warfare Executive dons and the Ministry of Information and the BBC men of letters. Even in the armed forces intellectuals, who would have struck terror into the hearts of their men if they had been commanding a platoon, were slotted into jobs where they could use their talents. They were moved, sometimes against their wishes, into research and development, or the administrative, judicial or quartermaster branches of the staff. Cruel observers described the cap badge of the Intelligence Corps as a pansy resting on its laurels. There was no rubbish of turning down as officers those who spoke with accents. The authorities responded to the demand for fair and tolerant treatment. Conscientious objectors were dealt with humanely; and as a result some who had been exempted from service in the armed forces joined up after the Battle of Britain.

We were, however, by no means all *embusqués*. Bill Williams, later to be Montgomery's intelligence chief and warden of Rhodes House, had joined the Territorial Army. Monty Woodhouse, Patrick Leigh Fermor, Xan Fielding, Nigel Clive were later parachuted into Greece, Bill Deakin into Yugoslavia and Francis Cammaerts into France; bomber pilots such as my school fellow Leonard Cheshire and numbers of others did brave individual feats whether or not in uniform. Nigel Balchin's gammy-legged Sammy, the frustrated scientist at war in *The Small Back Room*, was somewhat different in real life. Victor Rothschild worked on anti-sabotage in MI5 and dismantled booby-traps.

Nevertheless the mood of the younger members of Our Age in the armed forces was not heroic. It was wary and mocking. They were determined not to be fooled by propaganda and militarism. Their mood was: if I am to take part in this war, I will do so on my own terms. They prided themselves on sending up the elderly dug-outs who were outraged by their conduct and ridicule of square-bashing. Training to be a pilot Richard Hillary was amused to see Nigel Bicknell pinning red tape round the orders of the day. The young baronet, Martyn Beckett, before the war had joined the special reserve in the Coldstream. He came on parade late wearing the patent leather shoes in which he had danced all night and had to resign his commission. 'I never did think much of the Coldstream,' said the colonel of the Welsh Guards when he applied for a commission after serving in the ranks: four years later his squadron was the first in the Guards Armoured Division to enter Brussels.

A few, however, were incorrigible. Philip Toynbee, a master of self-destruction and abasement, somehow survived training at the Guards depot at Caterham. At Sandhurst as an officer cadet he returned one night in a three-tonner, apparently incapably drunk, but managed to outwit his friends as the vehicle swung past the sentries at the entrance: in a twinkling he removed all his clothes. The army persevered; but though he said he yearned to face danger, no officer can have had a longer list of postings or more extended leave as he was moved on by one exasperated commanding officer after another. By 1945, military patience having expired, he had ended up in the Ministry of Economic Warfare, where Harold Nicolson had twice to intervene to prevent him from being sacked. Sent to Brussels, he dressed up as a padre in battle dress and dog collar, and went to the railway station to greet war-weary troops from the front and ask them if they were saved. On this occasion it was he who was saved from the well-deserved justice of a court martial by Bill Williams, who said, 'We sent him to London on a very slow train.' Only Guy Burgess and Captain Grimes were saved more often.

Our Age were hedonists determined to enjoy themselves. 'Most of the war seemed to consist of hanging about,' said Evelyn Waugh's Peter Pastmaster. 'Let's at least hang about with our friends.' This was the spirit which led to the multiplicity of small private armies, commandos and special units depleting the routine units of armoured and infantry divisions of their best potential leaders. And so arose one of the paradoxes of the army during the war. Intellectuals satirized the inefficiency of the army and its outdated training programmes but they also denigrated the general who recognized the fact. They did not warm to Montgomery's personality. But Montgomery knew too well that he had no cadre of trained commanders and staff officers to draw upon, few potential army or corps commanders and not all that number fit to command divisions: such is the inevitable fate of a country with only a small professional army. That was why he was fanatical about training. Montgomery knew that he was commanding a citizen army which had been brought up on the story of Passchendaele. They did not want to be killed. Even so mild a commentator on his times as the diplomat William Strang noted that the troops in the Second World War were less brave and less prepared to sacrifice their lives than those in the First.

Of course, there were crack units such as Lovat's and Laycock's commandos, individual regiments such as the Guards and heroic individuals in the battalions and regiments of the line, but Montgomery recognized his first task was to persuade his troops that, although some of them would die in battle, as few as possible would do so since he had deployed immense superiority in aircraft and artillery and had made a foolproof plan. Montgomery was accused of being slow and unadventurous as a commander, unwilling to move until everything was, as he would say, properly tee-ed up. His commanders too, more concerned and humane than their predecessors in the Great War, were reluctant to incur heavy casualties. Nor was it all that different in the American Army. Patton had a fine reputation for moving fast not only in Sicily and France but in the Ardennes; but most of the American formations were no faster or more professional than the British.

The incomparable professionals were the Germans, amazed by the slowness of the Anglo-Americans to exploit success. They clung on when reason would have dictated retreat against an annihilating superiority in aircraft and fire power. They were better trained, more resourceful and braver than their enemies. They had learnt that the best way of saving casualties in battle is to react fast and take risks rather than wait and mount a meticulous planned attack. They were also better armed. The famous 88 mm dual purpose anti-aircraft and anti-tank gun, the PZIV and Panther and Tiger tanks, the Stukas and later the Focke-Wulf 190 were all superior to their British counterparts. Indeed it was scarcely fair to blame too much the troops or their commanders in the Eighth Army in North Africa for their defeats until Alamein: their tanks and guns were so inferior to those Rommel employed. The painful paradox, however, remains. The morale of the German armed forces, right until the final three weeks of the war, remained unbroken and they continued to fight with unparalleled discipline and skill. Only on the Russian front was their bravery and, in the end, their skill in battle matched; and there they were outnumbered and also out-gunned. Some of Our Age became obsessed for a time after the war by the conundrums of Nazi power: how this loathsome tyranny had gulled the Germans into accepting the destruction of human rights, the concentration camps and massacres on the Russian front, and the Holocaust. But we flinched from the even more bewildering question: how did this squalid regime command the loyalty of their troops who were readier to die than our own?

The end of the war marked a change of manners concerning one topic. The revelation of the Holocaust in the concentration camps altered the way the educated classes spoke and felt about the Jews. Anti-semitism never dies;

like other forms of xenophobia it festers and erupts on strange issues. But at any rate after 1945 it became bad form and was regarded as disgusting to talk in a derogatory way about Jews, still less discriminate in public against them. No doubt some clubs and public schools still operated a ban or a quota. During the war Claude Elliott, the headmaster of Eton, got the fellows to pass an amendment to the statutes, excluding from entry to College, i.e. through open scholarship, any son of a naturalized subject. He intended to exclude the children of Jewish refugees. When in the sixties Freddie Ayer challenged this exclusion and pointed out that he had been just such a boy when elected to College, Macmillan (who had been himself in College) advised Elliott, by that time provost, that the statute should be amended and the boy in question admitted. The kind of anti-semitic remarks common enough among Keynes's and Harold Nicolson's circles disappeared. Underground, perhaps: but Jews were now wholly accepted in public life.

It followed too that among the educated classes there was great sympathy for the state of Israel. The politics of oil had always made the Foreign Office favour the Arabs and the plight of the Palestinian refugees reinforced this bias. But it was no longer unchallengeable. The victories of the army of this minute state against simultaneous attacks by Egypt, Jordan and Syria astonished and delighted Our Age. They saw with sadness support for Israel melt when the policies of Begin and Shamir, and the stranglehold over the Knesset exercised by the ultra-orthodox parties, changed Israeli politics and nullified the attempts of men such as the Mayor of Jerusalem, Teddy Kollek, to reconcile Arabs within the city.

The fact that there had been no butchery (comparable to the Somme) in the battles of the Second World War helped to reconcile intellectuals to the state. The state too was becoming reconciled to the intellectuals. The planning of the Home Front by the civil servants, many of whom were temporary, was a triumph. The scientists made a spectacular contribution to winning the war. The development of radar as a means of defence and of attack against U-boats, the device to neutralize German radar, the artificial harbour, the dam-busting bombs, and a host of other inventions made the Establishment realize how important scientists were in war.

This strengthened the belief both by scientists and engineers in technocracy and of the ruling class in the virtues of a planned economy. If it was possible to organize production and distribution so efficiently in war, why could it not be done in peace? Oliver MacDonagh maintained that it was administrative need rather than Benthamite or collectivist ideology that drove politicians to use the machinery of state to remedy some abuse or shameful iniquity in Victorian times. Similarly Paul Addison showed how the rationing and regulations enforcing equality of sacrifice converted people to think that these were virtues not misfortunes. The symbol of England became the queue.

When the civil servants urged adding petrol and clothing to the list of rationed items to free for military supplies freighters and tankers, which were being sunk at an alarming rate, Churchill growled. He thought it would lower morale. He misjudged the mood. People welcomed the extension of rationing. For them it was a way to dish the rich for eating in restaurants and getting preference in shops.

J. B. Priestley, Archbishop Temple, Arnold Toynbee, Beveridge, all preached that after the war society should be animated by the ideals that sustained the nation through it. Everyone should make sacrifices to benefit the community not the owners of property. Plan consumption as well as production and thus abolish unemployment, see that the distribution of goods is equitable, demolish privilege. Addison did not claim that Colonel Blimp, *Picture Post*, the discussions by soldiers in ABCA sessions and reformist propaganda in themselves converted the country to socialism. The higher wages of workers, the mobility of labour (sixty million changes of address), the erosion of class barriers and the Russian alliance were as important. If industry was nationalized in Russia and their armies were winning, why not nationalize ours?

So blueprints for a better world were the rage and independent bodies like the 1941 Committee were set up with David Astor, Thomas Balogh, Ritchie Calder, Douglas Jay, Christopher Mayhew, Peter Thorneycroft and Richard Titmuss among the representatives of Our Age. When the party truce threatened to make by-elections a formality, Acland formed the Commonwealth Party and won four seats from the Tories. And then during the war Beveridge published his Report; and in 1945 to the astonishment of the world the British electorate turned Churchill out of power and replaced him with a Labour government that for the first time had an unassailable majority. There were some among us who voted for Churchill who were disenchanted by what they took to be Attlee's dimness; but the majority, I suspect, voted for Labour even if some never voted that way again. It was a vote for fair shares against grandiloquence in foreign policy, for reconstruction, a planned economy, technocracy and also (for voting is always self-contradictory) for greater personal freedom and less respect for authority. The vote found its expression, bewilderingly enough, in the utterances of two Etonians, exact contemporaries, one exhibiting the spirit of the twenties, the other of the thirties. They were Cyril Connolly and George Orwell.

2

GEORGE ORWELL'S POPULAR satires on totalitarian communism were seized on by the Cold War warriors who tried to dress him up in their uniform: a man who wrote with contempt about the pansy left must have enlisted in the heavenly host and somehow forgotten it. In fact Orwell continued to wear the grey flannel bags and grimy shirt of the dedicated socialist. He remained a biting, bleak, self-critical, self-denying man of the idealist left. If he despised the intelligentsia of the left for deceiving themselves, he hated still more the clubmen of the right. He could even slip into marxist categories of thought. Writing during the war for *Partisan Review* he reported that the railings of London squares in the West End were spared when those in working class districts were torn down to provide scrap metal. Mark Benney, a social analyst born in the working class, told him that he must know that to be untrue. 'Anyway, it is essentially true,' Orwell replied.

A denouncer of lies, he did not hesitate to make the effect he wanted by distorting events in his own life. His friends in the ILP found him a typical Wigan lodging, his host unemployed, cold water only, outside lavatory, but with working-class pride kept clean and tidy. He left to find something worse and dirtier and his host concluded that all he wanted was to make the working class out to be feckless and squalid. In that his host was wrong. He wanted to find out what it was like to be unemployed and under the thumbscrew of the Means Test that permitted officials to peer into every corner of the lives of the poor; and he praised the warmth and homeliness of the families he lived with and contrasted their lives with the acquisitiveness of the entrepreneurs and the arrogance of his fellow intellectuals. In common with Tawney, Orwell made the young feel ashamed to belong to a society that cared so little for the dignity and health of their fellow citizens.

He had a simple explanation for England's decline. The ruling class were not, as in France, treacherous. They were invincibly stupid. 'Even at this moment (in 1940) hundreds of thousands of men in England are being trained with the bayonet, a weapon entirely useless except for opening tins.' Since socialism threatened their income, the rulers sided with fascists. Generals and admirals who had given their lives to the study of war were unable to grasp that a hostile Spain was a threat to Britain. Vast social changes were needed and the bombing of London might convince people that 'a planned economy might be better than a free-for-all in which the worst men win'. As for the intellectuals, first they were anti-British and praised America as being more democratic, next they denounced America as an imperialist power. They could be relied on to collapse when the going got tough.

Orwell believed in the brotherhood of man and did not take to Belloc or Malcolm Muggeridge whom he thought too cynical and small-minded. But neither did he share H.G.Wells's version of the brotherhood: Orwell had no use for the man of science working towards a World State. The trade unions? Orwell dismissed them as anti-semitic for preventing Jews in large numbers finding refuge from Hitler in England. And yet, like Forster, he took pride and delight in the pluckiness and irreverence of the English working class. He shared their hatred of nosy parkers and their love of liberty. They believed in the law, 'they can't run me in, I haven't done any wrong'. 'They can't do that, it's against the law.' You could not bribe newspapers in England.

The English still believed in justice and objective truth, their patriotism was stronger than their class hatred.

Orwell spoke with the voice of ethical socialism – that long tradition which some like to take back to Thomas More and which includes the Tory radical Cobbett, the tradition of putting the interests of the poor and of those who earned wages before those who earned salaries or belonged to the governing class. While socialists and social democrats disagree about how equality of incomes or status is to be brought about, they are united in believing that equality means treating people as equals. Great differences of income exist in Greece as in Italy, but the Greeks treat each other as equals. So do most Americans, and those that do not run the risk of being pelted with mud if things go against them.

Orwell hated to see men touch their forelock or women defer to those who considered themselves their betters. The petty snobbery of gentility was even more galling than the rulers' insolence to the mass of people they considered below them. It was not enough to want to improve the lot of the poor. You must always take their side on the innumerable occasions when ordinary people are elbowed aside by the great, or knocked over by the governmental machine, or snubbed, or ignored or slighted. But Orwell and the British socialists differed from Sartre and the French *gauchistes*. Flaubert declared war on the bourgeoisie and from then on French intellectuals condemned middle-class culture in all its particulars. Orwell too had his inexpugnable aversions, but British socialists did not regard their adversaries as incapable of conversion and severed for ever from the elect. Orwell was far fiercer than Tawney but he spoke to the decent feelings of his own class in the hope of shaming them to follow him. Some did. He was the first saint of Our Age, quirky, fierce, independent and beholden to none.

His fellow Etonian was no saint. If Orwell resembled Evangelist in *Pilgrim's Progress*, full of rebuke and admonition, Cyril Connolly cut a poor figure as Christian. He was all for a wallow in the Slough of Despond (which for him was called angst), and so far from putting his fingers in his ears at Vanity Fair, he indulged in a prolonged shopping spree there. No cage or pillory for him. Accidie was his besetting sin. And yet in a tired and tattered way he was a pilgrim and journeyed on, sending at intervals ironical messages of encouragement to his fellow pilgrims, hooted at by the upper class philistines, savaged by his malevolent friend Evelyn Waugh and rejected as affected by the earnest left. He did not inhabit the parish of Bloomsbury. In Bloomsbury a party or frolic was earned, so to speak, by weeks of dutiful devotion to art, to the cultivation of the mind or the opening of the heart. Frugality and austerity were to Connolly the most repugnant words in the language. He lived on unearned pleasure. As an Oxford Wit who conveyed, like a drawing by Constantin Guys of the *belle époque*, the spirit of Oxford in the twenties – the discovery of travel, waisted suits, monogrammed silk shirts, Oxford bags, foie gras and Yquem, nightclubs — that combination of hope, cosmopolitanism, bitterness, pessimism and, inevitably, debts. Waugh thought him 'the most typical man of my generation ... He has the authentic lack of scholarship ... the authentic love of leisure and liberty and good living, the authentic romantic snobbery, the authentic waste-land despair, the authentic high gift of expression'. Waugh naturally deplored the fact that he did not believe in hell and did believe in America, practised weekly journalism (from which Waugh had emancipated himself), and made obeisance to psychoanalysis.

Very fittingly as the evangelist of modernism he reminds one of Wilde. Like Wilde he made lists: not those tiresome lists of semi-precious stones, but lists of nostalgic memories of pleasure. He had similar spasms of silliness. 'It is a suggestion of the primitive that I crave. Hence the appeal of sandals for they alone permit human beings to hold themselves naturally.' Wilde thought that in his day the only way that an artist could make himself heard was to be a popularizer. He wanted, John Stevenson once said, to fuse the classical and romantic traditions as Keats had done. But he wanted something more: to fuse religion, aesthetics and ethics. He knew he would be called frivolous but was aware that those who try to avoid that charge too often fall into the ditch of earnestness where creativity perishes. So Wilde popularized, and the product of the fusion was the more saleable commodity of aestheticism. Connolly realized that by his day the popularizer had displaced the artist, and like Wilde he abandoned the struggle and became an impresario. Both he and Wilde knew they had sold out but both retained a core of seriousness their critics failed to recognize.

Yet even Waugh conceded that Connolly was clever. 'Imprisoned in every fat man a thin one is wildly signalling to be let out' won grudging approval. He was the most overeducated boy that Eton produced in this century, reading Petronius in chapel and Aristippus of Cyrene in class. He overcame every obstacle at school. The magical personality, the intelligence, the speed of his cleverness, the inventiveness of his mimicry were always to win him a special devotion among his circle of admirers. He invented a shorthand prose, sharp and quick, the antithesis to the shapely sentences of Strachey or Logan Pearsall Smith. He never lost the art he learnt at school of making people laugh; his satires on Huxley and James Bond and the evocation of Brian Howard in *Where Engels Fear to Tread* were genuine achievements in fantasy. But he was to renounce at every stage of his life the success his gifts brought him at Eton. He sanctified failure. He practised the cult of striving with none for none was worth his strife. Forster said of himself that he warmed both hands before the fire of life – and put it out. Connolly made it blaze up, fired by the Mediterranean sun and food that he adored. But he was not merely suspicious of worldly success, he declared there was no point in writing books unless each was a masterpiece.

In *Enemies of Promise* he explained why English writers in general and he in particular did not write one. Nothing dissipated a writer's talent more, he said, than reviewing. Yet, rather like Ben Gunn who spent his share of the doubloons from Treasure Island in under three weeks and found himself as he feared keeping a lodge, Connolly settled for the last twenty-odd years of his life as the lead reviewer of *The Sunday Times*. He made a second attempt to explain the block in *The Unquiet Grave* and put the blame on 'slums, great cities, proletarian poverty and bourgeois boredom, tyrannies and family and herd ... we are in fact within sight of achieving a world neurosis, a world in which atrophy of the instincts ... abuse of the intellect and perversion of the heart will obliterate our knowledge of the purpose of life: humanity will choke on its own bile'. No wonder the last sentence of the last editorial he wrote for *Horizon* ran, 'It is closing time in the gardens of the West ...' And yet he continued to see himself as an observer caught in the conspiracy of life, at once a member of the junta and a spy within it, already judged and condemned. The very titles of his volumes of essays – *The Condemned Playground* and *Previous Convictions* – expressed his belief that he was a character in Kafka.

He saw his generation as epitomized by another fellow Etonian, Anthony Knebworth, who had died in the thirties in an air accident. Knebworth's father, Lord Lytton, wrote a memoir mourning the early promise cut off in its prime, but for Connolly that early promise in Baldwin's England had already gone sour and was curdling into fascism 'oblivious of the two great conceptions of our day: that of artistic integrity, the life of the spirit and that of social justice, the palpable and obvious love of man for man'. He thought the myth of Palinurus mirrored himself: he was a pilot who fell asleep at the helm, slipped into the sea and drifted ashore only to be murdered by the savage inhabitants. Citing the writers he loved from Horace to Rimbaud he found in them what he searched for: 'Love of life and nature, lack of belief in the idea of progress; interest is mingled with contempt for humanity. These masterpieces (mostly high peaks of the secondary range) reflect either what Palinurus would like to be or a self to which he is afraid of confessing.' Confession opened the road to salvation, salvation was won by recognizing what a masterpiece is and why one is incapable of writing one. But above all salvation consists in genuflecting before the shrines of dead artists and recollecting the anguish, poverty and humiliation they suffered. *The Unquiet Grave* was Connolly's masterpiece, the virtuosity of the writing transforming it into a prose poem to luxury and nostalgia. It is the tombstone of the Oxford Wits.

Many thought his best achievement was to edit the wartime *Horizon*. He became for a decade the circus master of London literary life. Round the ring pranced his young horses and a succession of young women answered with varying degrees of compliance the crack of the whip. There was a sado-masochistic atmosphere in the *Horizon* office. He put on the rack the sweet-natured Lys Lubbock, described by Bowra as a mouse at bay, by promising marriage and refusing to marry her, and then as soon as he was married to Barbara Skelton badgering her to return. Connolly could not stop torturing women any more than his other assistant, Sonia Brownell, could stop torturing men. Like other little magazines *Horizon* could count numbers of writers, Angus Wilson and Dylan Thomas among them, who were first published in its pages. But the reason it spoke to the literati of Our Age was its contempt for politics and refusal to add to the edifying unction of the justice of the allied cause.

It was the enemy of insularity, publishing disquisitions on French, Russian, German and, above all, American literature. Connolly believed that English novelists were becoming anaemic. He looked to America to give a blood transfusion to the English language. He admired Faulkner and the early Hemingway and was dog-like in his devotion to Edmund Wilson, the greatest man of letters of the thirties and forties. Peter Watson, who financed the magazine, also made it unique for its articles on the new generation of painters. The Euston Road school, Colquhoun and MacBryde, Johnny Craxton and Lucian Freud as well as Moore and Sutherland, became known to intellectuals. People spoke of the magazine as in the same class as Eliot's *Criterion* or the American *Dial. Horizon* is a mirror of the culture of the forties, an extension of Bloomsbury criticism. It said, 'Look, this is what is going on,' and Connolly gave no reason for his choice of exhibits. It did not set out to convert and mould the judgement of the next generation as *Scrutiny* did. It was a mood not a programme. Frank Kermode chided him for his slipshod work on modernism. Indeed academic critics treated Connolly as if he was a hunting parson who had blundered into the Oriel Common Room when Newman and Keble were discussing the illapse of the Holy Ghost at Pentecost. But Connolly made his readers feel that he loved literature. How many critics do?

Connolly professed to be a kind of socialist. He hated intolerance, dragooning, organization, discipline, adherence. After the defeat of Republican Spain he turned against politics, and when the war came was not going to join what the worthy called 'the war effort'. Sitting in the Gargoyle he and Philip Toynbee would chant, 'We hate the war. We hate the class war, we hate the sex war, we hate the war.' He shared the view of Cocteau who said to a young poet about to join the Resistance, '*Vous avez tort. La vie est plus grave que ça.*' And yet he left in the midsummer number of *Horizon* in 1946 what amounted to a political testament and set out the reforms he thought desirable.

Paul Johnson in his diatribe against intellectuals spotted that Our Age put most of them into effect: the abolition of capital punishment; penal reform;

new towns; preservation of old buildings; limitations of the powers of landlords; subsidies for light and heating; subsidies for the arts; subsidies for food and clothes; free medical treatment; abolition of censorship; abolition of MI5's dossiers and telephone bugging; reform of the laws on homosexuality, abortion and divorce; recognition of rights for children; laws against racial and religious discrimination. To Johnson, a paladin of the crusading knights of the right in the eighties, such hedonism undermined social controls and discipline. Our Age was disposed to agree with Connolly that social controls should be undermined.

In the late forties we began to move into positions of authority and influence. Rab Butler was re-educating the Conservative Party and in his research group were the ministers in future Conservative governments. Gaitskell became chancellor of the exchequer. The public school socialists, Dick Crossman, Kenneth Younger and Geoffrey de Freitas, were to become prominent in opposition. Some wartime civil servants returned to become dons or manage nationalized industries, but numbers of the most brilliant such as Eric Roll remained in post. In 1948 Alan Pryce-Jones became editor of *The Times Literary Supplement*, and in that year David Astor took over the editorship of the *Observer*. Solly Zuckerman had returned to academic life but kept a base in Whitehall; and when Tizard retired, Eddie Playfair, by then permanent secretary at the War Office, inserted Zuckerman's name on the shortlist for the post of scientific adviser to the Ministry of Defence. Zuckerman was to become the most influential scientist in public affairs during the next twenty-five years. Maurice Bowra became vice chancellor of Oxford. Kenneth Clark, who had disentangled himself from public posts and begun to write a series of books on painting, accepted in 1954 a new post that was significant as a clue to the achievements of my generation: he became the first chairman of the authority set up to control commercial television.

Broadcasting gave us the opportunity to popularize our views on a scale hitherto unknown to intellectuals. In 1945 the BBC broadcast its Third Programme. Its first head was George Barnes, a liberal Conservative by temperament and masterly in manoeuvre within the multiplying echelons of the BBC. Barnes belonged to the intellectual aristocracy (his half-sister was Mary Hutchinson) and married within it. The first evening's programme included the Goldberg Variations, Britten's Festival Overture, Joyce Grenfell and Stephen Potter for humour; and in the first week the audience, which settled down to between one and two and a half million, heard *Man and Superman* in its entirety, *Huis Clos* and *Don Pasquale*. In 1947 fifty talks were given in a series on the ideas and beliefs of the Victorians. The queen of the Third Programme was Anna Kallin, a Russian émigré, a highbrow of uncompromising standards and an irrepressible sense of humour, prodigiously *au fait* with European culture past and present. Her room in Broadcasting

House resembled Madame du Deffand's salon. The Third became the patron of dons and sometimes appeared to be broadcasting solely to them.

Nor was the Third Programme the only institution to give employment to intellectuals. The British Council and Arts Council began to grow in size; the Sunday newspapers offered more jobs to reviewers – Raymond Mortimer and the music critic Desmond Shawe-Taylor left the *New Statesman* for *The Sunday Times* and Cyril Connolly was for a time the lead reviewer for the *Observer*. Publishing houses multiplied and another business began to grow offering as good opportunities to the clever – and to women as well as men. This, as Dorothy Sayers had recognized in her best detective story, was advertising. Among the partners of Mather and Crowther were the former communist, Francis Meynell, and Francis Ogilvy, a first in classics, and his even more successful brother. Advertising – spoken of with horror by I. A. Richards and Leavis – appeared to be more entertaining and with greater opportunities than merchant banking for helping to improve other people's businesses. Our Age watched with mild surprise the apotheosis of the dissidents of the previous generation. Bloomsbury shook their heads as Keynes accepted a peerage and took a box to see *Iolanthe*; and the anarchist Herbert Read was dubbed a knight.

The last cohorts of Our Age appeared in the universities in the late forties. At LSE it was the era of Bernard Levin and of practically all those who were to make their name as sociologists. At Cambridge it was the era of Norman St John Stevas and Percy Cradock. But it was at Oxford that the galaxy shone at its brightest. Edward Boyle, Ian Gilmour, John Grigg, William Rees-Mogg among the Conservatives; Mark Bonham-Carter, Tony Benn, and Peter Parker on the left; the philosophers David Pears, Tony Quinton, Richard Wollheim; the writers Kingsley Amis, John Wain, Robin Day, Alan Brien and Ken Tynan. Did they all share the ideas of Our Age? Ken Tynan did. He broke the mould of theatrical criticism. By then the ageing doyens of theatre critics, James Agate and William Darlington, who revelled in the mysteries of the green room and the art of timing and gesture in a well-turned play by Terence Rattigan, did not speak to younger intellectuals. When Tynan praised Brecht, Ionesco and Beckett, he spoke the language of modernism and cosmopolitanism. The king of his theatre was Olivier not Gielgud. He belonged to the new generation of grammar schoolboys but (unlike the next generation of the fifties) he assimilated the manners of his public school contemporaries. Ronald Bryden noticed how compulsively competitive his early reviews were. His use of rare words such as *cicisbeism* and *erethism* were challenges in literacy, 'the game of vocabulary flashing and cultural reference pinned down by Harold Pinter and Joe Orton as Britain's national sport'.

But one among Tynan's cohorts spoke a different language. Kingsley Amis was greeted with offended chirrupings by the cultivated literati for celebrating in his first novel a rogue who exploited their genteel culture and referred to bloody Mozart. Somerset Maugham had to swallow his bile when *Lucky Jim* won Amis the prize Maugham had founded to enable a young novelist to travel the world. Both Amis and Larkin loathed what Raymond Mortimer called 'Dear Abroad'. They had no wish to meet foreigners, stare at cathedrals or shuffle around galleries. They hated intellectual snobbery as much as social snobbery. They despised dilettantes who were not professionals – and this professionalism marked them more as the leaders of the fifties than as of my generation. Like Auden, Amis and Larkin were masters of prosody. Unlike him they despised the experimental and the obscure. It is true that Amis bore one hallmark of Our Age. His sense of humour was prodigious and, like Waugh's, macabre and fantastic: Betjeman found him uproarious.

From the start Amis mocked Our Age for allowing their ideals to degenerate into pieties. He shifted the class barrier and moved it further down the road as the young H.G.Wells had done. Amis sent up sniffy public school culture and put in its place the life of the uninhibited grammar-school boy who knew how to make girls and put away the booze. That was the relaxation a young lecturer at a civic university needed; and if, in addition, he was a professional poet and novelist he would learn more from such a life than lecturers who cared about their students. Amis was not all that different from his contemporaries who became dons at Oxford. Maurice Bowra regarded Marcus Dick at Balliol as a new phenomenon – 'Gives a tutorial with a bottle of whisky on the table and a girl stashed in the bedroom.' Hidden by the splendour of that galaxy at Oxford in the late forties was a girl who was not stashed in any don's bedroom. Her name was Margaret Roberts. In a few years she would marry a businessman called Denis Thatcher; and forty years on Kingsley Amis would cheer her iconoclasm.

3

THE TWO PRINCIPLES of Orwellian austerity and Connollesque hedonism were exemplified in national politics. Austere the Labour government could not help being. They were beset by calamities not of their making, the legacy of the devastation caused by the war and the gargantuan obligations Britain still held. But for my generation the Labour government of 1945 was the great landmark of their times that had introduced an irreversible revolution into British life, greater than the Liberal governments after 1906. Not many believed that the nationalization of the Bank of England, of coal, electricity, gas, the railways and finally steel transferred power out of the hands of the workers. But they did believe the state would now make the long overdue investment in new plant in basic industries which for so long their capitalist owners had neglected. They believed that landlords would be checked both in the way they used their land and in the rents they extracted from their tenants. All land fell under planning controls and was subject to a development charge. Haphazard ribbon development would be stopped and the countryside cared for. They believed that the welfare services and supplementary benefits would lift hundreds of thousands out of the anguish of extreme poverty and calm the anxieties of millions more. Beveridge's national insurance scheme was virtually enacted; and most remarkable of all achievements was Bevan's creation of a health service which owed little to the wartime White Paper. We now had a society, wrote Addison, 'where the welfare of every citizen was a precious natural asset'. The new ideal was not just to spread a trapeze net to provide minimum subsistence for the poor and afflicted. The children of the slums, the evacuees in 1939–40, their heads covered in lice, who appalled hosts in comfortable country homes and struck at their conscience, were to be treated too as war casualties. People, as well as plant, were investments. And yet every item in the Labour legislation had been proposed before 1945 by men who were not socialists. Even nationalization was an extension of the model of a public corporation.

During the war people had observed the decencies of equal treatment. They disliked the rich for jumping queues, and buying special privileges and boasting of their *tuyaux* and inside edge which got them delicacies and scarcities. The wretched refugees of Mitteleuropa might tip the grocer and butcher, as was the custom in their country, but they met with black looks. Decent people accepted the need for fair shares. That was the spirit which animated Bevan's National Health Service. It left a loophole for the queue-jumper by sanctioning private practice; but it expected decent people to join the queue. It was the same with education. The direct grant and maintained grammar school were there for decent people: if you insisted on buying a special education for your child there were the independent public schools. Cash was knocked off its throne. You took pride in the fact that you did not slip guineas into the hand of the doctor, that you paid nothing for your library, art gallery and social benefits. They were public goods for which there was no means test. To spread this system of free public goods (free travel for the child to go to another school to learn the violin or get remedial treatment for dyslexia) became an ambition. But to pay for this you should keep to the rules. As in war, no queue-jumping. Accept your rations.

You did not have to look far to find the antithesis to this high-mindedness. The Black Market, the world of Sydney Stanley and Rachman. Nor by any means were all Our Age animated by this austere and noble spirit. Elizabeth Bowen became rancid in her dislike of the welfare state. The war stirred her Irish blood and she preferred to live in Ireland. They chose cultural symbols to distance themselves from the new egalitarian society by jeering at progressive puritans such as Cripps or Edith Summerskill. They rejoiced each time there was an opportunity to differentiate themselves from the rest of their countrymen and women and reject austerity and economy clothing. They cheered Dior's New Look with the sense of having won a battle. Others among Our Age groaned at having lost a battle when the Royal Family appeared once again in white tie and tails or morning coat, those symbols of class superiority. A black tie, yes; but why these relics of discomfort and snobbery?

Just as Butler acknowledged the ideals of the welfare state so the new generation of socialists among Our Age were not ashamed to welcome Connolly's hedonism. Not for them the bleak vegetarianism of Cripps. Gaitskell was a true child of the twenties: he loved dancing. Bevan had no shame in being a champagne socialist, Roy Jenkins liked good company and good wine and Tony Crosland produced a theoretical justification for pleasure. In *The Future of Socialism* he declared that socialism was also about enjoyment, gaiety and consumption. We should want economic growth not for its own sake but because it gave us greater opportunity to enjoy the good things of life, always accepting that by pursuing the goal of equality these good things were enjoyed by the many and not the few. Socialists should not dream in sackcloth. Socialism meant enjoyment.

So the tide turned in disciplined Britain against controls. The most irksome had been the direction of labour, although without it a full socialist economy could not operate. When that went, a lot of other controls were bound to go too. It was not Conservatives but Harold Wilson in 1948 who announced on Guy Fawkes Day that the Board of Trade was making a bonfire of controls. In future the economy was to be managed through Keynesian budgets; and this again was what businessmen and the trade unions as well as ordinary people wanted, while at the same time they wanted fair shares for all.

Full employment meant more than a Keynesian statistic to us. It embodied all their hopes for a more decent life for the working class, those great armies of cloth caps that moved en masse to the terraces of the football grounds on Saturday afternoons. We were the first generation to recognize the importance of trade unions and to sympathize with their aims. The war and full employment had returned bargaining power to them. We believed that they were the key to ending the appalling relations between management and labour. The capitalists of 1800 had at their disposal a limitless supply of labour but their businesses were often under-capitalized and they needed quick returns. So they cared nothing for housing, drainage or safety and paid their workers minimum wages for maximum hours. By these means Britain had dominated the industrial world. But the price of domination was the undying hatred of the workers for their bosses. The odd paternal industrialist like Baldwin knew and cared for the men and women who worked for them. But the workers organized in self-defence against their taskmasters and sent their representatives to negotiate or to call a strike. And so the terrible succession of strikes and lock-outs continued, culminating in the syndicalism of the pre-1914 years that led to the General Strike.

This story ate into our consciousness; and indeed the generation before ours produced idealists such as the holder of the Victoria Cross, Geoffrey Vickers, a company solicitor who devoted his life to drafting proposals for improving industrial relations. Nowhere was this desire to conciliate the unions more evident than in the Conservative leadership. The new men of Our Age, Butler, Macleod and above all the Great War veteran Harold Macmillan thought that the greatest error of the pre-war Conservative party had been to become identified as the opponent of the trade unions. It is instructive to see how in responding to this challenge we displayed weakness as well as sagacity. Industrialists were persuaded to set up university posts in industrial relations, but no one asked how, if at all, the knowledge generated could be applied to the shopfloor. What was more the holders of these posts studied industrial relations with the needs and practices of the trade unions in mind. Only rarely did they consider why differences between the unions and management were irreconcilable. It came to be assumed that, harmony being the goal, there must always be a predilection in favour of compromise, splitting the difference between what the unions demanded in wages and conditions of work and what management declared they could afford to offer.

Soon dons, economists and others in social studies, were called upon to adjudicate in a national stoppage. It was one of the misjudgements of the dons to imagine that one had but to analyse a problem and come to conclusions and the problem was solved. The *implementation* of policy did not concern them: how admirable sentiments were to be translated into action was not their business. Just as scientists would gesture towards instances of 'spin-off' on to industry to justify fundamental research, so social scientists argued that the accumulation of knowledge by itself or the creation of economic models was a sufficient reason for investing more public funds in research. Sometimes, as with Richard Titmuss, such research affected policy and the workings of the welfare state. Do this, said the social scientists and turned away. Had they seen why their proposals were inept or unacceptable, or required a degree of political will that was lacking, they might have thought again. They were strong on what, weak on how.

The marxists? They did not disappear even though the last cohorts of our generation became orthodox Labour or Conservative supporters. But a minority among us rejected the line taken by Bevin and the Foreign Office. They believed Europe to be on the verge of a people's revolution. The corrupt regimes in the Balkans, Hitler's willing accomplices, had been overthrown. Why then did a Labour government prevent the communist-led resistance in Greece taking over and allow a plebiscite to enable the king to return?

Why did it concern itself with the rights of the reactionary London Poles? Why did the government slaver over capitalist America and reject Britain's natural ally Soviet Russia? And at home why did the government listen to the voice of sound finance in 1947 and rein in the housing programme? Was the Labour movement once again being betrayed by a Labour government? Meeting Kingsley Martin on my return from Germany at the end of 1946 I discovered him to believe that but for the presence of Anglo-American armies all Europe would have been governed by socialist regimes installed by popular acclamation. Dick Crossman and Barbara Castle, as well as fellow travellers like Zilliacus, took this line. In 1945 Major Denis Healey urged at the party conference that Labour should dissociate itself from Tory foreign policy and 'assist the socialist revolution wherever it appears'. Labour should not be 'too pious and self-righteous when occasionally facts are brought to one's notice that our comrades on the Continent are being extremist'. These comrades were right to use their police to punish the 'depraved, dissolute and decadent upper classes'. Thomas Balogh, who was to have considerable influence with Harold Wilson, declared that the dynamism of the Soviet economy would give the USSR in ten years 'an absolute preponderance economically over Western Europe'.

The war years conditioned the young to see politics in black and white and to expect that anyone, for instance in communication with Pétain, should be humbled. My simple faith was shaken on landing in France in 1944. Simone de Vogüé, alone with small children as her husband had been taken hostage on D-Day and sent to a concentration camp, invited me to billet myself in her house. I discovered that her brother-in-law too was a prisoner and had been condemned to death for his work in the Resistance. How was it that his sentence had been commuted? 'We naturally implored le Maréchal to appeal for clemency.' One began to learn that all was not black and white in occupied Europe. One began also to learn about communist tactics in the Resistance. They had done their best to rot morale in the months when the Soviet Union was bound to Hitler by the Nazi-Soviet pact. Now they had the ultimate objective of seizing power after the German armies had been driven out. On the War Cabinet intelligence staff I had seen how in Greece Elas husbanded its strength not to fight Germans but to eliminate rival resistance groups. Elas later marched on Athens.

In fact the vision of Labour's left and the fellow travellers bore no relation to the simple desires of human beings all over Europe. All they wanted was food and shelter and freedom from the authorities. This was what I observed among the millions of refugees in Germany where until the autumn of 1946 I had been supervising the rebirth of political parties and helping to stop the communists taking over the Social Democratic Party, the SDP, in Berlin. The majority of Our Age saw the Cold War as the consequence of the determination of the Soviet Union, before the war had ended, to impose unpopular communist regimes on their neighbouring states and to crush resistance in them. When Crossman and others published in 1947 a pamphlet called *Keep Left* Denis Healey, who had discarded his wartime illusions, replied with *Cards on the Table*, a tough defence of Bevin's foreign policy. Healey slated the Soviet Union for its propaganda offensive that depicted Britain as a 'decadent reactionary power'. He saw that America was no longer following Roosevelt's line of dividing the world with Soviet Russia. America recognized where her interests and allies lay.

By 1948 Healey accepted the western alliance under America and nuclear deterrence and defended it for over thirty years, losing any chance he ever had of the party leadership. The humiliating terms of the loan America imposed upon Britain, and the abrupt end to lend-lease which broke British power, were replaced by Marshall Aid. America saw that the British, so far from trying to get America to underwrite the British Empire, were leaving India and, under economic necessity, Greece too. Britain had become an American client state but a client state that had her uses in helping to police the danger zones. That was resented by the old guard Tories who sneered at American misjudgements: they made their own misjudgement on Suez. But it infuriated even more the extreme left to whom Marshall Aid was an American attempt to impose an economic hegemony upon the world.

At what point did allegiance to the Soviet Union snap? Over Poland or the takeover of Czechoslovakia and Masaryk's suicide? Over Hungary? Over Khrushchev's revelations of Stalin's rule? For a gifted undergraduate whom I taught at King's and who became a professor of medieval history, it was Stalin's reconciliation with Tito. The reconciliation? He explained: 'I had spent months defending the communist line that Tito, when he stood up to Stalin, was a counter-revolutionary. When the line changed overnight, I felt emotionally bankrupt.' The crushing of the revolt in Hungary and the execution of its leaders led to mass secessions from the party, and allegiance to the policies of the Soviet Union began to be regarded as no longer a necessary article of faith for marxists.

Many of Our Age who had been communists or fellow travellers in the thirties sloughed off their skin. Some who were bitter at being duped became professional anti-communists: a debilitating faith which skewed the vision of life almost as much as the professional marxists. One of the earliest brains to drain before the war to America was a clever grammar-school boy who was sickened by the C.S.Lewis approach to English at Oxford. He purged himself by writing a dazzling defence of those whom it was fashionable to portray as proto-fascists – Carlyle, Nietzsche, Wagner, Stefan George and D.H.Lawrence. Eric Bentley then turned to drama and was one of the first to praise Brecht's plays. But he was not fooled by Brecht who, he thought, wanted the theatre to be as much the temple of logic as a laboratory determined to take art down a peg. 'These are the facts, face the consequences,' said Brecht: but he never allowed one to question whether the facts were facts. Nevertheless Brecht's theatrical sense triumphed over his ideas. Bentley thought his generation, so intent on changing the world, were too ready to despise those who put individuals first. Their zeal for the Party concealed their fear of the self. His sense of equilibrium was admirable.

Other dons remained true to the faith, Victor Kiernan and John Saville among them. Some still wanted to show why Soviet communism was to be preferred to American capitalism. These men and women still believed they had made the correct choice in the great historical division of their times. Among them were the Cambridge spies.

CHAPTER 15

The Cambridge Spies

1

THE SAGA OF the Cambridge spies was more than a hunt for a Third or Fourth man. The discovery that young men of the upper middle class had become Soviet spies turned into a long-running inquest upon the culture, morality and patriotism of intellectuals of my generation that the coroner kept on adjourning as spy after spy fell out of the cupboard. We had put their elders in the dock for sanctioning the slaughter of the First World War. Now we found ourselves charged with aiding and abetting totalitarianism which our country had fought to destroy in the Second.

When Rebecca West published her book on the meaning of treason in 1949 she was more concerned with those who had gone over to the Nazis than with the scientists who gave the secrets of the atom bomb to the Soviets. No one identified with foreigners such as Fuchs or Pontecorvo, and Alan Nunn May was such an obscure figure that only later did it become significant that he had been at the same college at Cambridge as Philby. Some scientists tried to get his sentence reduced on the ground that he was a lone idealist. And did not the Red Army deserve all the help it could get as it fought its way to Berlin? The protests faded when some months later it became clear that Nunn May was part of a ring of Soviet spies and had passed his information after the war and not during it.

The flight of Burgess and Maclean was a very different matter. They were not obscure and they came from the upper middle class. Donald Maclean's father had been a cabinet minister and Donald went to the public school that educated Auden and other revoltés. Born into the inner circle of the Liberal Party he had been one of the many beaux who courted Laura Bonham-Carter, who was to marry Jo Grimond. Her mother Lady Violet – she was later to defend Melinda Maclean when the press pack were after her – had been a member of the selection board for the diplomatic service when Donald was interviewed. His communist past at Cambridge was known and he was asked about it. He replied that he had held such views and had not entirely shaken them off. The candour of his reply impressed the board. So did his appearance. He was not unlike Rupert Brooke, as moody as he was handsome.

In Washington during the beginning of the Cold War his capacity for hard work opened secret doors for him in the Pentagon so that the shock of his exposure was all the greater among his American colleagues. He was the most dedicated communist of the lot and his puritan, teetotal, blinds-drawn-on-Sunday upbringing gave him the inner conviction of James Hogg's Justified Sinner, that what was sin to others was to the elect righteousness. He was the only one of the Cambridge spies who disliked the life of deception and he began, as the strain told, to drink more heavily and got involved in fracas. He was promoted to counsellor and posted to Cairo, and it was there that the worst incidents occurred. He and Philip Toynbee broke up the apartment of a girl in the American Embassy and he was sent on sickleave to London for psychiatric treatment. There the outbursts continued, and this time he broke up Toynbee. By now Toynbee had become a fervent anti-communist, and when he abused Alger Hiss Maclean knocked him down saying, 'You are Whittaker Chambers.' But the inference that Maclean saw himself as Hiss was lost on Toynbee. None of his colleagues had any suspicions. When William Strang, the head of the Foreign Office, gave permission for Maclean to be put under surveillance, he was incredulous that this good-looking scion of the Great and the Good should be suspected.

If Maclean looked too much like the model young diplomat to be a spy, Guy Burgess's indiscretions were such as to defy any secret service to employ him. But there are as many erratic and self-indulgent spies as there are faceless automata. Burgess knew how to open doors not through hard work but by effrontery and the charm of his vitality. He had the good looks of a boy, and resembled the drawings of Harry Wharton of Greyfriars in the Billy Bunter stories. He was merry, with a mind like quicksilver, ready to be amused and to amuse. His marxism was not a lesson learned and regurgitated, it emerged as a genuine vision of life; he never talked or thought in the jargon. He had a real delight in general ideas and understood the springs of political action in a way that gave politics a dimension which his listeners had not grasped until then. In the thirties his judgements went against the grain. He thought George Eliot the greatest of English novelists, *The Marriage of Figaro* the most important opera, and at the height of Lytton Strachey's fame he pronounced him inferior to the eminent Victorians he pilloried. To him Britain's imperial past and the Royal Navy were being betrayed by feeble aristocrats like Halifax, and the ruling class behaving with all the folly born of the contradictions in capitalism as Marx had predicted. He was a true Stalinist in hating liberals more than imperialists. Whereas to Blunt patriotism was a meaningless concept, Burgess in a dotty, quixotic way retained a romantic notion of his country. He simply believed that Britain's future lay with Russia not America.

In one sense Burgess remained an undergraduate all his days, reading the same books, listening to the same music, repeating the same themes. He was not a rebel nor an idealist, still less a misfit. At Cambridge he was a liberator – one of those students who appear to their contemporaries to be more assured, more able to liberate them from the conventions of family, school or class. Burgess could bully as well as charm: he could make an acquaintance feel small by a sneer and at the next moment laugh the matter off with a smile. He was a scamp who became a scoundrel, but there was something memorable in the effrontery of one who, having a copy of the Kinsey Report at that time unobtainable in England, kept it in the most secure place he could find – the private safe in Ernest Bevin's room in the Foreign Office. He could get a trade unionist to give a talk on the BBC worth listening to – and persuade his superiors that it was time the BBC did so. Churchill gave him a copy of his speeches and wrote on the flyleaf praise for 'his admirable sentiments'.

The time would come when his elders and contemporaries would say how they had seen through him at once and express surprise that one so unreliable could have been taken on by Hector Macneil as his personal assistant in the Foreign Office and then become established. But Isaiah Berlin (who Burgess suggested should accompany him to Moscow in 1940) spoke of him in public as a friend and was not ashamed to acknowledge him. I met him often in London, particularly at the Reform Club to which numbers of my friends belonged: he always ordered a double port so that the waiters used to call it a double Burgess. In 1949, when he was to preside at the annual dinner of the Apostles in London, he visited Cambridge to meet the secretary of the society and then called on me. He walked me up and down King's Parade, as if he was trying to square me and win my vote on some academic matter. In fact he was insisting that I must realize that Stalin held the most enlightened views on homosexuality: the stories that homosexuals were sent to camps in Siberia were American propaganda. Did he wish to impress me that he had a secret line to the Kremlin? It never crossed my mind that he had.

Nor anyone else's. For when acquaintances were asked whether Burgess had ever tried to recruit them, they recalled not the engaging young man of the thirties but the prince in Bohemia he became during the war. He used to cook, his friend Goronwy Rees recalled, in a heavy iron saucepan 'a thick grey gruel compounded of porridge, kippers, bacon, garlic, onions and anything else that may have been lying about in the kitchen', a dish which sustained him over each weekend. Chewing raw garlic was only one of his minor social disabilities: in his Foreign Office days a minute was circulated requiring him to desist. He kept in the shambles of his Bond Street flat a flitch of bacon hanging on a string outside the window which was hauled up when he needed to hack off a slice, and was then consigned again to outer space.

Grime covered everything. Every table, lampshade, sheet and blanket was scarred with burns, the stigmata of so many drunken evenings. The bath had no plug; in its place was a sock once white but by now dark grey with dirt into which a squash ball had been thrust. Screams rent the air at night in the building because his flat was sandwiched between two others inhabited by prostitutes, but it was a moot point whether the traffic in and out of their rooms was any heavier than that in and out of his. His habits were filthy, going far beyond those of negligent bachelors; in his Foreign Office days he was often sodden and sweaty. He had the appearance of a man who had just stepped off the Golden Arrow after a night in the Rue de Lappe. Maurice Bowra in a characteristically vigorous phrase used to complain that he had shit in his fingernails and cock-cheese behind the ears. Even Evelyn Waugh's imagination did not dare create such a monster of improbability. How was it possible to suspect that his boasting of being in the know and his mysterious yet impressive contacts were not clouds in the dream world he inhabited? And yet he was a spy.

At first when the two men went missing, officialdom decided to stick to the bare truth that no one knew where they were and therefore nothing could be said. From then until Peter Wright's book on his time in MI5 appeared, the press and the Establishment skirmished. Beaverbrook did not miss his chance. His newspapers took the lead in pursuing anyone who knew the two men. Clearly they had been protected by the Establishment. How could these two drunkards have kept their posts in the Foreign Office, how could they ever have been recommended to join it? Were they not typical members of a decadent and mealy-mouthed intelligentsia? The press trumpeted its indignation. Heads must roll. Mr Big who protected the two must be unmasked.

The result was predictable. The Establishment closed its ranks. The security services had to be cleared of the charge of incompetence and the Foreign Office of negligence. The Establishment were determined not to allow Beaverbrook to play the role of Senator McCarthy and cause droves of innocent men and women to lose their jobs through guilt by association. The Conservatives remembered what *épuration* had been like in France; and the Labour government saw how damaging such a witch-hunt could be to their party when some of its best ministers and young aspirants from Aneurin Bevan to Denis Healey had been advocates of the Popular Front or members of the Communist Party in the thirties.

Intellectuals were in no doubt where they stood. They were up in arms at the behaviour of one of their number. In 1956 Burgess and Maclean ended speculation by appearing at a press conference in Moscow, and one of Burgess's friends panicked. This was Goronwy Rees. One evening at the Gargoyle before the two men vanished, Maclean had lurched over to Rees's table and said, 'You were once one of us but you ratted', before collapsing insensible with drink. Rees probably was one of Burgess's sources. Then the Nazi-Soviet Pact disgusted him and he cut adrift to join the army. He had remained, however, a close friend of Burgess who was godfather to one of his children, and the press blackguarded him and his wife when they discovered that one of the last telephone calls Burgess had made was to say goodbye to Rees.

Rees was alarmed that Burgess would implicate him in public and determined to get his blow in first. He was by now principal of one of the colleges of the University of Wales but in a moment of madness he sat down and wrote an indictment not only of Burgess but of his friends, and in particular of those friends who were in high places or had been in the security service during the war. His literary agent did what agents are supposed to do: he got the best price he could for the articles from a popular Sunday newspaper, part of the contract being the horrifying stipulation that the newspaper should be entitled to rewrite the articles. In them Rees maintained that Burgess had blackmailed people to obtain secrets; that he was protected by his homosexual friends in MI5; and that he should have been expelled from the service on several occasions. Some people were mentioned by name as associates of Burgess, others were identifiable, and the last article closed with a plea to root out the traitors in our midst.

The explosion detonated by these articles was atomic. But the blast walls of the Establishment are so cunningly constructed that the person most hideously wounded was Goronwy Rees himself. The Welsh nonconformist conscience, preened with self-righteousness, took him to task. A public inquiry was set up at Aberystwyth to investigate whether Welsh students were at risk under a principal who admitted in public to have known such a lascivious man as Burgess. Every detail of Rees's private life was twisted to discredit him. Had he not given students a glass of sherry? And was it proper to be so friendly with them? Even the puritans on the inquiry could not fault him; but they characterized the articles as a 'lewd document' and so poisoned his relations with his staff that he had to resign. Not only from Aberystwyth. When a London literary hostess wrote to cancel an invitation to dinner he realized, as he put it, that he was no longer *salonfähig.* Maurice Bowra wrote to suggest he plant a Judas tree in the college grounds and other friends took the line that to start a witch-hunt was inexcusable. Much sympathy was expressed for Anthony Blunt who once again became the subject of rumour. Rees was accused of joining the press hounds in their pursuit of his former friends.

In a sense he had. Goronwy Rees was the son of a well-known Calvinist Methodist minister and had won a scholarship to Oxford which welcomed and wooed him offering him friends, prizes and a fellowship to All Souls'. But he was never won over. He believed, as many of his generation did, that the Establishment, of which Oxford was a part, was responsible for Britain's decline and was concealing the truth. According to his own account, when he braced himself to go to MI5 and denounce Burgess as a spy, only to be told that the bird had flown, he was given a hard time by two senior officers, Guy Liddell and Dick White. To him this was proof that they were covering up. To them Rees's sudden conversion, conveniently late, suggested he was trying to conceal his own pre-war past. He was, in fact, a clever man and an excellent journalist. Staunchly heterosexual he had had a number of affairs. But he was a rogue. Rosamond Lehmann knew that they were to part only when she read the notice of his engagement to be married. But then she had in her turn snatched him away from Elizabeth Bowen when they were both staying as her guests in Ireland. In one of her best novels, *The Death of the Heart,* Elizabeth Bowen took her revenge by creating a character modelled on this

> ... bright little cracker that, pulled hard enough, goes off with a loud bang. He had come up to Oxford ready to have his head turned. There he was taken up, played up, played about with, taken down, let down, finally sent down for one idiotic act. His appearance was charming; he had a proletarian, animal quick grace. His manner, after a year of trying to get the pitch, had become bold, vivid and intimate. He became a frank *arriviste.* His apparent rushes of Russian frankness proved, when you came to look back at them later, to have been more carefully edited than you had known at the time.

Malice, as so often, contains some truth in it.

There was a particularly unfortunate sequel to Rees's articles. When Burgess and Maclean fled, one of the ablest American counter-intelligence officers, Jim Angleton, suspected Philby of being a Soviet agent within the British Embassy. His chief, General Bedell Smith, insisted that Philby should leave Washington but he refused to pass on Angleton's evidence for fear that that, too, would be leaked to the Soviets by another British spy. Philby was forced to resign from the service to the chagrin of his friends in MI6 (the secret intelligence service) who believed him to be innocent. His chief Stewart Menzies was among them; but Dick White, by now head of MI5 (the security service), was frustrated by Anthony Eden's refusal to pull Philby in for further investigation. Later a blundering MP heard rumours and accused Philby under privilege in the House of Commons. Harold Macmillan was forced to exonerate him. What was worse Philby's friends in MI6 re-employed him in Beirut where he lived as a newspaper correspondent so that at one time he was being paid by the KGB, MI6 and the *Observer* – which had been assured by the Foreign Office that Philby was no longer in the intelligence service.

Philby was the most professional spy of the quartet: skilful, dedicated and ruthless. He also did the most damage. Menzies liked him because he was not an intellectual and saw him as the next head of the service but one. Nothing odd about this fellow: a straightforward man not obsessed with theories or doubts. Philby was uninterested in marxism. He was a true organization man, and his sole object in life was to serve the organization for which he was working – the KGB. His colleagues admired him as a workaholic, but one who was able to relax and at times resemble an alcoholic. All four of the Cambridge spies managed to acquire positions of importance but Philby rose the highest, using the jealousies in the top echelon of MI6 to get rid of his one rival. He watched with relief the return to civilian life after the war of the few who might have rumbled him.

It was the fourth spy whose eventual exposure produced the greatest sense of outrage. Anthony Blunt's success as a scholar, as one of the mandarins of the art world, the admiration he won from friends and pupils, his distinction of mind and bearing in public, the fact that he was second in reputation only to Kenneth Clark among English-born art historians, and the irony of his position at court as surveyor of the Queen's pictures, combined to make people want to known about him. He had too much hauteur to be a charmer. He was a fascinator. He fascinated people with his quick, engaging, cool and assured talk. He baited his conversation with gossip, inside gossip, gossip to which only he had access. When he had gone, it dawned on you with what skill he had faintly denigrated those about whom he talked. They would be humbled by a flick of the whip here and a twist of the knife there.

He was not only a fascinator. He was a manipulator. He wanted more than most people in academic life to have his own way. Since the Courtauld Institute was for years the only major centre in Britain where the history of art was taught he nearly always did so. When at Cambridge we refused to toe the line and appoint one of his dim protégés, preferring first Michael Jaffe and then Francis Haskell, he got into a huff. But despite his public position he preserved the privacy and dislike of worldliness that was characteristic of his generation at Cambridge. Not for him the social life of the Kenneth Clarks. Many regarded Clark as a friend but Clark had no intimate friends. Intimacy was as natural to Blunt as privacy.

His work on Poussin was a major achievement and he had produced a catalogue of the French drawings at Windsor. He taught his students to interpret art through the society that gave it birth, though the crudity of his early marxist interpretation of art disappeared. A few of his students disliked him, disliked his autocracy, disliked the spite against those who offended him, disliked his habit of teaching from photographs and neglecting the need to look at the actual painting itself, the brushwork, the *pentimenti* and the way the painter achieved his effect. But most admired him, and to many and to younger colleagues he was unwearyingly kind. When he fell it was a far greater shock to Our Age than the exposure of the professional Philby or the unstable Maclean.

Despite his protestations when he was exposed, Blunt never repented or intended to keep his side of the bargain and help his interrogators. He had, one might say, an obsession that he should be seen to be right in all he did or said. Of the four Cambridge spies he was the least dedicated to the

Soviet cause and probably regarded what he did as justifiable at the time and a matter of no consequence afterwards. It fitted the atmosphere of intrigue and manipulation that he enjoyed in his personal and academic life. He was someone who early in his life lost touch with reality in personal relations as well as in political life. He was loyal not to his friends but to his own image of himself. That was always important to him. People were right to think him arrogant, but it was an arrogance that is well known in the academic world and is often inseparable from success in scholarship.

Over the years the spy fever had been mounting in Britain. Nor was this surprising. Shortly after Rees's articles had renewed the hunt for the third man, first George Blake and the third man himself, Philby, were exposed. Then followed Vassall and other small fry and the Lonsdale–Kroger ring. Was there not also a fourth man? Which sinister don at Cambridge had recruited Philby and Co? *The Times* ran a story that it was Donald Beves, the good-natured, old-style bachelor don at King's. When that was shown to be ludicrous another journalist pronounced that it was A.C.Pigou, the renowned welfare economist and also a fellow of King's, best known politically for joining the campaign for free trade in the general election of 1905. But by now a different class of sleuth was at work prepared to take his time and dig in the archives. By making use of the US Freedom of Information Act Andrew Boyle discovered numbers of leads that pointed to Blunt who, if rumour and hints became too positive, threatened authors with a libel action. When Blunt heard about Boyle's book he got his lawyers to make a discreet enquiry asking the publishers to allow him to see an advance copy. Lawyers are discreet but the recipients of their letters are often not. *Private Eye* heard of that approach and let fly – it retailed the case Boyle had constructed and for good measure added that Blunt lived with a former guardsman. A question was asked in the house, and the prime minster had to acknowledge that when MI5 had confronted Blunt in 1964 he had been promised immunity from prosecution if he would confess.

2

THE NOISE FROM the press disconcerted some of my generation. And yet it was natural enough. Immigrants and refugees may have divided loyalties, but if such a man as Blunt, cradled in the bosom of the social and intellectual Establishment, could have been treacherous and his treachery concealed for so long, then trust, on which democratic government rests, is undermined. Why had this arrogant intellectual been given immunity? Was it his social standing that enabled him to escape the prison sentence passed on smaller fry? Had he not been, wrote one correspondent, 'closely involved in the counsels of our Sovereign?' – which elicited the response that perhaps it should be assumed that the Queen was a patriot and unlikely to have been suborned. The journalists kept on repeating that he had been 'stripped of his knighthood by the Queen' – a trope that conjured up the spectacle of his Sovereign at Buckingham Palace ordering his sword to be snapped and his spurs bent double while personally divesting her errant courtier of articles of clothing.

His crime was the fault of the misplaced idealism of the thirties, it was the fault, said Correlli Barnett, of E.M.Forster's 'intellectual wetness', it was the fault of indolent prime ministers and lily-livered home secretaries who treated the security services with indifference or suspicion and reinforced their introversion, it was the fault of the services for employing double agents. *The Times* declared it was the fault of Bloomsbury, and that dismissive cult of the intellect exemplified by Keynes. Or perhaps it was the fault of logical positivism, the fault of the Cambridge philosophers who rejected the 'noble idealism' of Hegel. At that L.T.Hobhouse must have turned in his grave since after the First World War he had written a book to denounce Hegel as the progenitor of Prussian militarism and the apologist of the state. Had not Hegel argued that the state expressed the real will and then identified the real will with the general will of the people? But then no one any longer expected *The Times* to know the difference between Idealism and idealism.

The journalists had always seen the treatment of the Cambridge spies as a skirmish in the class war, and their indignation knew no bounds when Blunt gave an exclusive interview to *The Times* and a few quality papers, and the pack were denied being in at the kill and tearing the old dog fox to pieces. The press were right to roast Whitehall. The bachelor ambassador in Cairo where Maclean disgraced himself had too much of a fellow feeling for him and regarded any criticism of a member of his staff by anyone outside the service as beneath his notice. The ambassador in Ankara should have protected the defector Volkov whom Philby managed to betray to the KGB before he could escape; and when the venture failed he should have found out why. Had he done so Philby would have come under suspicion. The excessive secrecy surrounding the intelligence and security services time and again put the government on the wrong foot: how can one restore confidence in the service when the convention that MI6 did not exist still held good?

Nevertheless bureaucracy had some of the answers and they illuminate the nature of my generation. Why had these communists not been vetted? The truth was that in the hectic days after war was declared there was not much time to vet anyone – certainly not in 1940. I myself was compulsorily commissioned into the Intelligence Corps because I had admitted to knowing some French and German. A civilian friend of my father's, who advised Kenneth Strong, the colonel at the head of the German section of intelligence in the War Office, on railway capacities in Europe, recommended me to him as someone suitable to monitor German troop movements. No more bizarre recommendation could have been made, but all through the army in 1940 the ignorant were being told to learn. No one vetted me and within a week I was piecing together the reports of agents in the Balkans and the early stutterings of Ultra. Blunt was indeed rejected but in the confusion of 1940 got into MI5. Some of us knew that the intelligence services were staffed in peacetime with men who regarded Stalin as the first enemy, and Hitler a disagreeable fellow but a potential ally; and they rejoiced to see intelligent men of the left being recruited to redress the balance. The scandal of Philby's recruitment was not that he had been a communist in Cambridge. It was that he had been a correspondent on Franco's side in Spain and a member of the Anglo-German Fellowship (which he joined to cover his communist past). Philby was first recruited to SOE to organize sabotage in Europe and only later wormed his way into MI6.

How was it possible, the journalists asked, that the escapades of Burgess and Maclean did not lead to their dismissal? No captain of industry or entrepreneur would tolerate such fellows for five minutes. But bureaucracies have to be more circumspect. The small print of Estacode, the civil service bible on conditions of employment, provides protection for mandarins against the prejudices of their superiors – or their political masters. No one could deny that Maclean was a meticulous worker. (Indeed, if Fleet Street sacked its lushes some of its best correspondents would disappear.) In his book on Maclean Robert Cecil admits that British diplomats were slow to adjust to the internal pressures of the Cold War, to suspect and then to report suspicions of devious behaviour. But security conflicts with another need, the need for *esprit de corps* which forms only when the men and women in the service trust each other, will cover for each other's mistakes and not be in fear – as every Soviet official is – that a colleague will denounce him or her to the KGB. The Foreign Office may be too clubbable; and because its business is to reduce tension between governments, it did at times thwart MI5 in its moves against spies. But when Alec Home on MI5's advice decided to expel 105 members of the KGB, it was Denis Greenhill, the head of the Foreign Office, who urged Home to ignore Gromyko's threats and Reggie Maudling, the home secretary, who opposed the move on the grounds that it would make Britain a laughing stock.

But surely the immunity promised to Blunt was the Establishment's attempt to sweep his treachery under the carpet? Spies in Britain have a far more effective protection than the machinations of officialdom. The rule of law protects them. So does the British adversarial system of justice. Even with Michael Straight's evidence – which was no more than a recollection of conversations in Cambridge thirty years previously – the case against Blunt would never have stood up in court. Can one imagine what a Queen's Counsel would have done to Golitsyn in the witness box? Blunt knew this. So did his interrogators. MI5 was to be humiliated in the courts when Giuseppe Martelli of the Atomic Energy Authority was acquitted after being defended by Jeremy Hutchinson. The jury took the curious view that to own spy equipment and be in contact with the KGB was insufficient evidence of spying. In other cases British juries declined to believe double agents. Blunt was in such a commanding position that he never kept his side of the bargain. He volunteered the minimum: information had to be dragged out of him bit by bit.

The journalists, however, were out for the intellectuals as well as the Establishment: in fact, part of their case was that the two were intertwined. They probed for wicked dons or some clandestine organization spreading corruption. In this they were assisted by that quintessential Oxonian, Hugh Trevor-Roper. Trevor-Roper relished the thought that Cambridge bred spies whereas not one came from Oxford. But then Cambridge had always been disloyal, puritanical in the seventeenth and Whiggish in the eighteenth century – had always been intense, insular and over-serious, a university dominated by its scientists with their narrow conception of what was 'true'; so unlike Oxford with its worldly acceptance of the nature of politics in which truth plays a small part but sagacity, judgement, courage and pliability a great deal. Had not Cambridge between the wars become subservient to its gurus – Russell, Moore, Forster, Bernal and unsmiling sectarians like Leavis? Even its Conservatives were grim doctrinaires like Enoch Powell. Small wonder that Cambridge communists carried their disloyalty to such lengths and displayed such intellectual arrogance.

Perhaps Trevor-Roper had forgotten the long line of Oxford prophets in the nineteenth century who inspired such passionate loyalty – Keble, Newman, the Arnolds, father and son, Jowett, Ruskin, Pater and Green. Perhaps he had also overlooked an authentic Oxford spy, Michael Carritt, who in the 1920s joined the Indian civil service and passed secrets to P.C. Joshi, the general secretary of the Indian Communist Party. Taking early retirement Carritt enjoyed his pension until 1940 when his activities were discovered. He lost his pension but was not prosecuted. He lived to publish privately in 1985 an account of his work with the communist underground which displayed the same belief in his own rectitude as Maclean.

But Trevor-Roper found another nefarious Cambridge influence. Both the American Michael Straight and Leo Long, a working-class student at Trinity, were protégés of Blunt and both were members of the very society to which Blunt and Burgess belonged. This was the Apostles. To Trevor-Roper this 'egregious secret society of self-perpetuating, self-admiring narcissi' had in Blunt's time become 'purely social'. Was not the apostolic rule of secrecy the drug that induced some Apostles to choose as their double life the most secret of all professions, the spy? The Apostles lived by the rule of the sanctimonious Forster and the complacent Moore. Trevor-Roper caught to perfection the unctuous tones of Blunt's relationship with Michael Straight. Distraught after John Cornford's death in Spain, Straight told Blunt he had decided to stay in England. 'Some of your friends have other ideas for you,' said Blunt as he laid his hand on Straight's shoulder, and informed him he was to return to New York, go into Wall Street and become a spy for the Comintern. 'So might St Paul,' wrote Trevor-Roper, 'have sent Timothy to the Christian cells in Greece or the Jesuit general a doomed missionary to the secret priest hole of Elizabethan England.' Such a society as the Apostles, he continued, could never have existed at Oxford where 'it would have been blown up from within or laughed out of existence'.

It may well be that at Oxford the main point of belonging to a club is to advertise that you belong to it and give pain to those who don't. Why the Apostles kept its membership and affairs secret was simple. In the 1850s a tuft-hunter had sucked up to its members, got himself elected and then at once resigned with the feather in his hat. So the society, disliking those on the make, became anonymous. A club that had so few members and did not promote itself can hardly be called very social. The sole purpose of the Apostles was to discuss general ideas – as true in Blunt's day as in Henry Sidgwick's. Speaking of his time in the 1860s as an Apostle Sidgwick said:

> I can only describe the spirit of the Apostles as the spirit of the pursuit of truth with absolute devotion and unreserve by a group of intimate friends, who were perfectly frank with each other ... Absolute candour was the only duty that the tradition of the society enforced ... There were no propositions so well established that an Apostle had not the right to deny or question, if he did so sincerely and not from mere love of paradox. The gravest subjects were continually debated, but gravity of treatment ... was not imposed, though sincerity was ... No part of my life at Cambridge was so real to me as the Saturday evenings on which the apostolic debates were held; and the tie of attachment to the society is much the strongest corporate bond which I have known in life.

Burgess could have written those words. The Apostles were devoted to each other because they felt they were discovering truths hitherto unknown. They were not unique. Young intellectuals often feel that. When, thirty years later, Peter Wright was interrogating the circle of friends Blunt and Burgess belonged to in the Apostles he was amazed by the intensity that held them together. Aesthetes and intellectuals still felt beleaguered in the inter-war years and they knew the joy of discussing general ideas without straining for effect. It is not only roisterers who recall they have heard the chimes of midnight together.

But was not the secrecy of the society reinforced by another secrecy – the secrecy that homosexuals then practised? In Keynes's and Strachey's day this was so. But during the years between the wars only three of the forty-four members in addition to Blunt and Burgess could be called lifelong homosexuals. There was a certain spice in belonging to an in-group with its own semi-secret language and haunts. But it was not the secrecy of the homosexual mafia that mirrored the life of the spy: it was the danger. To be convicted then of picking up rough trade in pubs or public lavatories spelled social ruin and dismissal from one's job. The danger was mitigated only by the fact that the Homintern looked after its friends. The spies could rely on support from a community ready to make excuses for deviant behaviour.

At the time when Blunt, Burgess and Leo Long were members of the Apostles, the society was certainly marxist. It would have been odd had they not responded to the movement in ideas of their time. Tennyson, Sterling, Kemble and Trench responded so strongly to the liberalism of the 1830s that they became involved in a disastrous Liberal insurrection in Spain. In G.M.Trevelyan's time the discussions were again political about imperialism and radicalism. In 1900 Keynes, Strachey and Woolf responded to the philosophy of Russell and Moore. Then in the mid-twenties the mood again changed. The earliest marxist members were elected before the days of the Depression. To 'capture' societies which communist students identified as significant became party policy. Blunt and Burgess successfully infiltrated the Apostles, and Victor Rothschild complained to Keynes about the endless analysis of marxism. But even so, of the thirty-one members elected to the society between 1927 and 1939, fifteen were communist or *marxisant*. Then after the war the intellectual climate changed and there was not a marxist to be seen among the Apostles apart from Eric Hobsbawm. Peter Wright managed in his memoirs to suggest that most of them were spies. In fact he never obtained a confession or evidence that any of them were, not even from Alister Watson who was moved from a sensitive government post. Two notable public servants, Andrew Cohen and Dennis Proctor, certainly were not spies; and neither Philby nor Maclean were members.

Yet Hugh Trevor-Roper was right to sense something in the Cambridge air different from clubbable Oxford, something nonconformist and therefore likely to treat the judgements of the great world with disrespect. The scientism of Bernal and Haldane ran through the veins of the spies. But here again came a paradox. Science and mathematics were to speak with another voice, and the very influences which, according to the Oxford critics, led to the corruption of youth in Cambridge created the intelligence agency that was the most successful of any nation during the war. Many of the cryptographers who produced Ultra were agnostic, heterodox dons who did not set much store by the normal interpretation of patriotism or democracy. The nucleus came from King's, in the early years the majority from Cambridge. The most remarkable of the cryptographers was a young don from King's, Alan Turing. In 1937 he had challenged Gödel when he wrote a paper called 'Computable Numbers' that so impressed John von Neumann, famous for his theory of games, that he invited Turing to Princeton. For what Turing had done was to rehabilitate Hilbert. Hilbert argued in the classic tradition that all the formal procedures of mathematics and logic were contained within a self-contained system. You asked three questions of the system. Is it complete, is it consistent and is it decidable? Gödel said that was a dream. No mathematical system could be *both* complete *and* consistent. Turing saw Gödel had left one question unanswered. Could one decide whether any mathematical statement was true or false? Turing thought there might be some systems that were 'decidable'. Suppose one imagined a machine that could repeat its numerical operations indefinitely?

Turing would not stay in Princeton and returned to King's. In the war at Bletchley he built a machine, not the machine of his imagination but one that could keep ahead of the changes of key on the German Enigma machine and thus read all enciphered messages of the German armed forces that were sent by radio. The cryptographers and their auxiliaries (who made what was deciphered intelligible) did not win the war, but they stopped Britain losing it: they just managed in the nick of time to win the battle of the Atlantic by deciphering the U-boat traffic. They also enabled commanders to save the lives of their troops by telling them where the enemy was and sometimes what he would do next.

It so happened that when I returned to King's after the war I had rooms beneath Turing, both of us living as bachelors, and he helped me to understand what some of the great mathematicians were at whom I was studying as I worked on the history of ideas. I liked his sly, secret humour. Turing was all that the journalist spy-hunters hated most. His inner life was more real to him than actuality. He disliked authority wherever he was. (There was none at King's, and not much at Bletchley, but what there was he evaded and went behind the backs of the authorities straight to Churchill to get what he wanted.) Sceptical of politics and schemes for reforming the world, he was not likely to be elected to the Apostles in its marxist days. But then he was not a typical public school rebel. He was a cross-country runner of international stature and enjoyed games and treasure hunts and silliness. He poked fun at conventional people, enjoyed teasing the humanists by arguing that thought was made up of inputs and outputs and of storage capacity. If a machine could solve problems, could it not also think? Could it not write a sonnet? (Leavis exploded.)

Turing was the purest type of homosexual longing for affection and love that lasted. He was so remote from the wisdom of the streets that when he was a professor at Manchester, where he had found a working-class lover, he went straight to the police when the boy stole some of his things. They were astonished that Turing showed no sign of shame and thought he had done the right thing to expose dishonesty and the betrayal of trust that goes with love. The laws of his country which he had served so well closed in on him. He was sentenced to psychiatric treatment, given hormones and to his disgust grew breasts. He killed himself. Stephen Toulmin saw him as the product and victim of his social class: it gave him the freedom to be eccentric but destroyed him when he ignored the conventions. But there was one convention which he and the sloppy, free-wheeling community of intellectuals at Bletchley did not forget. They did not betray their obligation not to reveal what they had been doing and kept their secret for thirty years after the war. The spy-catching journalists, who fingered the Cambridge intellectuals of the thirties with such scorn, forgot to look at Bletchley.

The exposure of Blunt showed how ambivalent the reactions of the educated classes were towards the spies. Blunt might have shown his regret for the past by resigning from institutions to which he had been elected to spare them embarrassment. But at first he did not, and Jack Plumb led a caucus to expel him from the British Academy. After some discussion a masterly motion was proposed 'to move to the next business', and carried with much relief. Blunt in the end resigned and Alan Taylor had the satisfaction of resigning in sympathy. In my judgement the Academy was right. As vice chancellor of the University of London I was asked to move that Blunt be deprived of the title of Emeritus Professor. The title is not an honour: it is recognition that a scholar has served the university well. I refused on the ground that to do so would make Blunt into the kind of non-person that the old guard communists in the Soviet Union became after Stalin liquidated them. I felt much the same when the press pack demanded to know why I had allowed Maclean's son to read history at University College when he decided to leave the Soviet Union and live in Britain. What distinguished the West from the Soviet bloc, I said, was that we did not punish children for the crimes of their fathers.

The intellectuals did not come out well from the inquest on the spies. For nine days *The Times* printed letters on Blunt's exposure, many of which sympathized with him. This astonished Americans as well as the British press. Robin Winks, an historian who had been studying the record of Yale men in the American intelligence services, recorded that although Americans were outraged by Blunt's treachery, 'there were many in Britain who thought that Blunt had suffered enough for the indignities of his loss [of his knighthood]. One might conclude that the two nations simply thought about treason somewhat differently.'* Was Robin Winks right to be disturbed by the reaction to Blunt's treachery? What defence was made for the Cambridge spies?

* To an Englishman this sounded odd. Would not Dwight Macdonald have taken a different view from Sidney Hook, or Fred Dupee from William Phillips, or C. Wright Mills from Irving Kristol? The celebrated duels between Trotskyists and Stalinists among the New York intellectuals in the thirties would surely have been staged over Blunt: as indeed they were over Hiss.

3

THE FIRST TO defend them was the most renowned novelist of Our Age throughout the world. Graham Greene was a virtuoso composer of variations on the theme of betrayal. He exonerated his old friend Philby by comparing him to one of those heroic Jesuit priests who returned from their seminary on the Continent to subvert the England of Elizabeth I. He went even further in a lecture he gave in Hamburg on 'The Virtue of Disloyalty' in which he regaled the students by attacking that bourgeois poet Shakespeare winging his way to a house and a coat of arms at Stratford, a Catholic apostate, the apologist of the existing order, out of tune with all those in his time and in ours who have stood up in protest against authority. What a contrast Shakespeare was to his fellow poet the Jesuit Southwell, who died in torment on the scaffold executed for 'disloyalty'. The writer, said Greene, must always stand for the victims and be ready to change sides at the drop of a hat. In our times the writer in the West must be disloyal to capitalism and the writer behind the Iron Curtain must be disloyal to communism.

There was another novelist who soliloquized after Greene's throwaway line. John le Carré became the master of the spy story and head executive of the corporation he took over from Buchan, Maugham and Dornford Yates. He realized that it was no longer possible to sell the old vehicle in which our men were heroes and their spies were villains. Sandy Arbuthnot, Ashenden and Jonah Mansel were as obsolete as Sunbeams or Hispano-Suizas. There was a souped-up model with a sexy Italian body built by Ian Fleming, but its designer cared only that people should know martinis should be stirred not bruised. Le Carré's new model had every gadget: he was a master of the jargon – skip distances, Joes, Gees, nose-cones and burn boxes. How should he not be since he himself had once been a member of the firm? He wanted his readers to brood on the psychology of the spycatcher, the spy-runner and the spy. All three betrayed each other day in day out as if they were in a circle of the inferno. What then was the moral difference between spying for the Soviets and spying for the West? In his novel le Carré's 'perfect spy', Magnus Pym, betrays whomever he loved: at school an upper-class boy who befriended him to the headmaster; a Czech refugee to the MI6 officer who recruits Pym; the officer and MI6 by becoming a spy; his wife and children by running out on them. The East may be worse than the West but not by much.

Brecht used to say, 'The East and the West are both whores. But my whore is pregnant.' Le Carré epitomized the despair of the left at the end of the seventies. He saw the firm as the symbol of Britain's decline, a country where 'failed socialism is being replaced by failed capitalism'. The old ruling class that in its incompetence recruited the Cambridge spies and then bungled their arrest was finished; but what was the alternative? On the one hand a party whose leaders spent their time running away from the country's problems, abdicating power to pressure groups and knifing their two best men so that neither should lead the party. On the other a party with a spiv philosophy in which the consumption of goods and money, preferably gained by dubious means, were the ultimate values. Perhaps it was all at one with this obsession about identity that Karl Miller published his book *Doubles* which explored our need to explain why each of us is more than one person playing different roles in the street, the office and in bed.

The American philosopher Judith Sklar raised another paradox. Character, she argued, is what saves the reputation of those who betray their trust. She cited the extraordinary case of Robert E. Lee. Here was the most respected general in the US army who was offered command of the Union forces, who thought slavery wrong and the Union indissoluble but who put kith and kin and Virginia before his duty to his country. That led to a civil war in which the South was ruined and the dead on both sides lay in heaps. And yet such was his character that he became 'one of America's classical heroes'.

That great historian Thucydides condemned Pausanias but excused Themistocles for going over to the Persians. Why? He could not withhold his respect for Themistocles's intelligence and character. On the other hand Thucydides declined to accept Alcibiades's excuses for throwing in his lot with Sparta. Why? Back again came the public school answer: flawed character. If one takes Sklar's argument further one can hardly argue that the Cambridge spies were of the same mettle as Lee or Themistocles; but they were not nonentities. None lost his nerve, none behaved abjectly. Rebecca West failed to show that their characters were twisted or distorted beyond the twists and distortions in our own lives. They had faith in their cause and they had hope for the future. They could argue they were living in a world in which betrayal was becoming a norm as secret police forces multiplied, fierce political divisions bred terrorist groups, and immigration made loyalty to one's national or racial entity more real than loyalty to the state to which one had migrated.

These arguments are not convincing. Graham Greene's pretty little trope about disloyalty rests on the premise that there is not a penny to choose between the culture of totalitarianism and the culture of western democracy – and not American capitalist democracy but British democracy. To pretend that these differences do not exist is dishonourable. Somehow the image of Philby as the fearless Jesuit in Elizabethan times seems a bit shop-soiled. Unwise, too. One does not have to be Macaulay or Froude or Kingsley to prefer Tudor rule to the gloomy repression of the Inquisition in Philip II's Spain. It was not as if there had once been a communist regime in England, as there had been a Catholic church celebrating mass according to the Roman rite. Nor were the laws concerning treason and the duties of servants of the state changing every few years, as they were in Tudor times, and great men, trapped by the new laws, were being beheaded on Tower Hill.

Similarly, to an historian le Carré appears as a child of the sixties who had accepted the mode of thought propagated by the Frankfurt School. He is playing the game of *Sein und Schein*. What seems to be true is not true. The very improbability of the confessions of Bukharin and the old Bolsheviks in the Moscow trials proved they were guilty. If there were any waverers who kept on producing unwelcome facts they must be dismissed and told that facts which contradict social analysis were irrelevant. Facts were delusions, *Facktenmull* as the student activists of the sixties called them, the bric-à-brac of positivism.

Many of the letters from intellectuals sympathizing with Blunt welcomed his excuse that 'almost all the intelligent and bright young undergraduates had become marxist under the impact of Hitler's coming to power', and were inclined to argue as Victor Kiernan, a veteran communist, was to argue some years later, that the thirties justified any action. For Kiernan the left were then fighting 'absolute evil'. How should they not believe their cause was 'absolutely good' even if 'painful experience showed that the second of these beliefs was in part illusion'? Loyalty to the dying past was as archaic as drawing-room table manners. The spies did what their consciences told them to do and they should be honoured.

But there were plenty of intelligent and bright Cambridge undergraduates who did not so despair of the policies of the Conservative and Labour parties that they signed up with the communists: still less transfer their allegiance to the Soviet Union. There were others who knew what the thirties were from experience, not ideology. Blunt used to tell Peter Wright during interrogation that he did not understand the thirties. Wright replied that he understood them only too well. That was when his father, sacked from the Marconi Company, took his son away from his school unable to pay the fees and took to the bottle. Wright did not think this gave him the right to sign up with a foreign power and take orders from its agents. Even if one stretches charity far and allows that an assured young communist, convinced that Conservative governments would always kowtow to fascism, could be excused making the dramatic gesture of becoming a Comintern agent and fall for the flattery that Stalin himself saw your reports and had you in mind. That was no reason in 1940 to lose faith in your country's government. None of Churchill's countrymen doubted Churchill's resolve to fight Hitler and Mussolini. The Nazi-Soviet Pact should have made all the spies reconsider their allegiance as Goronwy Rees did. For after the pact their reports could have been passed from the Soviets to their Nazi allies.

Then there was the reproof Blunt flung at Rees when he said he was going to denounce Burgess to MI5: Forster had said that if he had to choose between betraying his country or betraying his friend he hoped he would have the guts to betray his country. Rees had replied that the antithesis was false –

one's country was a dense network of individual and social relationships in which loyalty to one particular person formed only a single strand. It was a put-down both of Blunt and Forster. Justified, too. Forster had gone on to say, 'Love and loyalty to an individual can run counter to the claims of the state. When they do – down with the state, say I, which means that the state would down me.' But what state? The state which he had just given two cheers for because it was a democracy? To the England, the countryside which he loved, to its ordinary, irreverent, independent citizens? Everyone who reads Forster's essay can see what he detested: states where the supporters of the regime wore brown, black or red shirts. But what of the states where they did not? To suggest that the choice was so simple neglected the cases of hundreds of men and women whose loyalties were torn, and some of the most moving plays from *Antigone* to *Don Carlos.*

Some members of our generation as they grew up and became bankers, executives or civil servants were fond of saying that the root of the trouble was 'logical positivism'. If Frank Ramsey was concluding at Cambridge that there was nothing left to discuss, because, when we did, all we were doing was comparing notes, or when later Freddie Ayer was teaching the young that ethics was technically nonsense, was it any wonder that morality was undermined? Yet in fact when the spies were recruited utilitarian ethics was going strong at Cambridge and Kantian ethics at Oxford. After the war, so far from ethics withering away, books on it fell one after another from the press – by Toulmin, Nowell-Smith and Richard Hare. After the war versions of utilitarian ethics came to be used in discussing the moral problems with collectivism and the welfare state. So when one don declared that Blunt's work on art history should be weighed against the 'minor and ultimately irrelevant part of his life', he was in effect arguing that Blunt's contribution to scholarship and his academic career were so distinguished that their contribution to the sum of human happiness was far greater than any diminution of that happiness his spying could have brought about. The insensitivity of this kind of moral reasoning reminded me of a course of lectures I attended as an undergraduate on theories of the modern state – the very same Burgess should have attended six years previously – given by the eccentric clergyman fellow of Trinity, F.A. Simpson. Simpson allowed that both utilitarianism and Hegelianism gave remarkable insights into political life. But as ethical systems neither could account for the conduct of the Good Samaritan.

That parable may not have been uppermost in Bernard Williams's mind when he began to write his important treatise on moral philosophy, *Ethics and the Limits of Philosophy,* but he had for long been dissatisfied with utilitarianism. He had found it unsatisfactory when he wrote the report of his committee on obscenity and pornography. Williams did not give ground to that middlebrow clamour for a doctrine of 'absolute' ethics. No system of ethics holds water; they all spring leaks when tested. But when he asked himself which of these systems came nearest to giving us criteria for leading a moral life, he discarded the utilitarian ethics elaborated by Richard Hare or the contractual ethics of John Rawls. Nor did the moral imperative in Kant's practical reason seem any better.

Williams went back to Aristotle. Aristotle may look to us too much of an optimist; and the habits of the society in which his ideas grew are foreign to ours. But Aristotle was right to perceive that ethics are grounded in character and human nature: not in method, not in giving reasons for behaving in this way rather than that. The magnanimous Man of the Nicomachaean Ethics scorned to be fearful or dishonest because he recognized honour as a good and because he would not debase himself to the level of the cowards and crooks. Williams came to the conclusion that there were 'thick concepts' in ethics – honour, mercy, scrupulousness – which derive from actual moral situations that occur in the world. He maintained that knowledge of these rather than belief in God's will, or the principle of the greatest happiness of the greatest number, or the categorical imperative were more likely to make us behave decently.

Honour was not a virtue that played much part in the moral discourse of Our Age. It was one of the words which Paul Fussell identified as debased by the language of the First World War where men died 'honourably' on the fields of Flanders when in fact they died drowning in mud or frothing at the lips, gassed in a crater. Bentham had removed honour from ethics because it threw no light on whether an action was one which would promote individual happiness or the greatest happiness of the greatest number. So the apologists for the spies were content to quote Sir John Harrington's explanation why treason never prospers: 'For if it prospers none dare call it treason.'

But did not Harringon's contemporary suggest there was another matter to be considered before one betrays one's friends and the state? 'Well, honour is the subject of my story,' said Cassius when he set out to recruit Brutus, because he knew that unless he could convince Brutus that it was honourable to kill Caesar he could not win him over. Mark Antony's irony about the honourable men who killed Caesar rings true. All the conspirators, he said, did what they did in envy of great Caesar, save only Brutus; and Octavius ordered that Brutus's 'bones tonight shall lie, / Most like a soldier, ordered honourably'. Was there a single one of the Cambridge spies who acted honourably?

Although technically the spies never committed treason as the Soviet Union was never at war with Britain, how do they compare with Roger Casement who did commit treason in the First World War when he ran arms to Ireland to use against the British? Like other Irish patriots Casement lost faith in Britain's promise to grant Home Rule, and the die-hard defiance by Carson and his associates in the summer of 1914 gave him good cause to doubt it. As an Irish patriot he declared he owed allegiance to Ireland rather than to Britain – even though in international law Ireland then did not exist. But Casement betrayed no one. Philby and the rest did not have Casement's justification. No part of the Soviet Union languished in British hands. Nor by 1940 could there any longer be doubt what Stalin's regime was like. Were the iniquities in British life so acute that Philby had to do cruel deeds for Stalin's inhuman secret police? Stauffenberg, Trott and the July 1944 plotters felt their government had betrayed them by standing for hideous ideals and putting those ideals into practice; and therefore their conspiracy was justified. Had the Cambridge spies any such justification? They may have been as dedicated as the German plotters. But honourable?

Some excused Philby on the grounds that as a professional he could hardly be blamed for betraying would-be Soviet defectors: that was part of his business. But he not only sent Soviet defectors to their death but anyone in Europe who had worked for the British during the war against Hitler. The railwaymen in Hungary and Rumania who had reported the train-loads of German troops on the move to Greece were marked down by Philby as capitalist agents and were liquidated after the war. Blunt, too, had blood on his hands. The don who referred to his spying as a 'minor and irrelevant part of his life,' had curious standards of irrelevance. Blunt informed his Soviet control of a British agent in Moscow who provided MI6 with Politburo documents. The man disappeared. And in the course of rifling diplomatic bags Blunt passed on to the Soviet Union information about agents and other individuals hostile to communism.

Philby admitted no duties to his wives, his women or his colleagues. He regarded them as walk-on parts in the drama he was playing. After he fled to Moscow he took Melinda Maclean away from her husband; and then realizing that advancement in the KGB would be more likely to come if he became a Soviet citizen, he ditched her. Blunt was certainly loyal to his fellow conspirators. He cleared evidence incriminating Philby from Guy Burgess's flat. But what of his other friends? He and Burgess never stopped saying how much friendship meant to them and how devoted they were to their friends. When MI5 told Victor Rothschild of Blunt's guilt he could hardly believe that someone he had admired as much for his moral principles as for his intellect had been a Soviet agent. 'You never get over a blow of that sort!' Ill-judged as Forster's aphorism was, it is clear what he meant by writing: 'Personal relations are despised today ... and we are invited to get rid of them and to dedicate ourselves to some movement or cause instead. I hate the idea of causes.'

The Cambridge spies betrayed their friends as effectively as their country. They believed in a cause. Love of one's country is not a cause. But perhaps philosophers will allow that it is a thick concept.

PART III

CHAPTER 16

The Impact of the German Renaissance

1

FEW INTELLECTUALS REMAIN immobile, trapped for ever in the assumptions they formed in their youth. They react to their contemporaries abroad and later to their successors who are modifying or revolting against their vision of life. By the 1950s the first cohorts of our generation were moving into the seats of authority and the next cohort of the thirties was experiencing a cultural shift. They no longer looked across the Channel, they looked across the Atlantic. 'Sent by America' was the title of an article Charles Fletcher-Cooke wrote during the last year of the war, returning after a visit there enchanted by the vitality of American culture.

Americans did not always reciprocate the enthusiasm. Edmund Wilson's visit to England after the war was not a success. His sour observations could be written off as the belch of a grouch, but in 1955 the American sociologist, Edward Shils, who had been teaching at LSE and moved between Chicago and London, gave British intellectuals a lecture. He told them they were self-satisfied, insular and genteel, too addicted to wine and food, wild flowers and birds, too amused by eccentricity. Oxbridge and London exuded a cosy culture and slighted the civic universities and provinces. The fashionable authors of the day – Powell, Plomer, Antonia White, Elizabeth Bowen – barely recognized the existence of the working class or businessmen; and even those who knew and appreciated provincial life like Cooper, Amis, Braine and Wain, gravitated to London. When Amis left Swansea to become a don at Peterhouse it was in its way as much a shock as Auden and Isherwood going to America. There was a middle-class culture, the culture of provincial businessmen who had founded Britain's civic universities, a puritanical and pharisaical culture but proud and self-reliant. But the civic universities found that the best local talent in their schools opted for Oxford and Cambridge whose dons seemed to take a particular pleasure in slighting their provincial colleagues. They did not confine their slights to Britain. Shils detected a nasty resentment of America. There was never a word of praise for the achievements of American academics and artists. Nor for their independence of mind. Americans were the true freewheelers, not the British dons and writers who remained creatures of the Establishment.

Twenty-five years later Arthur Marwick endorsed Shils's verdict. British culture after the war he maintained was class-ridden and insular. Philosophers ignored existentialism and, although artists, architects and designers flourished, much of their work was derivative. Marwick impaled my generation upon Morton's fork. If philosophers worked within their own empirical tradition that stretched back to Hume and beyond and treated existentialism as fashionable rubbish, they were insular: if architects looked abroad to the Bauhaus for inspiration they were derivative. But this much is true. Whereas in France intellectuals after the war were ebullient and inspired by ideas that had germinated during France's political decay and defeat, British creative writers were exhausted by the war and dispirited when it was succeeded by the harsher privations and more deadening squalor of the peace: the enthusiasm of *Horizon* and Lehmann's *New Writing* evaporated. The Second World War had cut Britain off from continental experience – the experience of being occupied by the Nazis. Trying to come to terms with this paradox British intellectuals became obsessed by Hitler's success. How was it that the Germany of Goethe and Beethoven had become the Germany of Bismarck and Hitler? The question was too narrow. They forgot to look at the long perspective of German genius. The intellectual challenge we faced did not come from America and only secondarily from France. The way we had looked at our society and explained how it operated was challenged by a movement of ideas that had been gathering strength for years and with which Our Age now had to come to terms. They were the ideas of the German Renaissance.

To this day we hardly recognize that a phenomenon occurred in the eighteenth and nineteenth centuries that was as remarkable as that outburst of creativity we call the Renaissance in Italy. It was the German Renaissance – the renaissance of a culture mutilated by the Thirty Years War. It transformed European culture and, like a star exploding, it continued to hurl radioactive particles into space well into the twentieth century. The German genius – in Austria, Bavaria, and North Germany – did not express itself through the visual arts, noble as are the grave simplicities of Schinkel's architecture and ravishing the extravagances of Zimmermann, Neumann and the brothers Asam in the baroque churches they built and decorated. It expressed itself through music, and from the end of the seventeenth century their composers began to dominate Europe. Some were pure musicians like Bach, Telemann and Schubert; but others were self-conscious artists burning to express ideas, such as Beethoven or Wagner or even that seemingly purest of all Mozart.

Ideas . . . The German philosophers were perhaps even more influential than the Italian humanists had been in making men see the world through different eyes. Men had always understood there were impersonal forces beyond their control that governed their fate. The German thinkers made this idea live. They thought the French and English rationalists presumptuous to impose new constitutions and legal systems upon nations in order to promote the happiness of mankind. Reality was different. Men were in the grip of historical forces, prisoners in the war between nations or classes: their institutions, their customs, their laws were the product not of human reason but of the community and corporation. Men had to discover their identity before they could express themselves. The German thinkers recognized that nationalism was a far more deep-seated emotion than the religion of humanity. They rejoiced in the conflicts between irreconcilable principles, Apollonian against Dionysian, *naiv* against *sentimentalisch*, reason against understanding, the will to power against the renunciation of will. They denied that human nature was everywhere and at all times the same. They stressed that men lived in different towns, joined different guilds or societies, and therefore belonged to different cultures. Each culture had its own language, each was inspired by its own history, each developed a lifestyle moulded by its system of law, land tenure and local government. The strength or weakness of its communities and corporations was more important to the understanding of a nation's history than the story of its kings or rulers. Discover what those strengths and weaknesses were and you could write a nation's history.

Few English thinkers considered what nationalism meant. To them it was obvious. Conservatives saw it in terms of the heritage of Drake, of Trafalgar and Waterloo, culminating in the British Empire; Liberals saw it as a noble movement in Europe, which was to unite Italy and expel the Turks from Greece and the Balkans, though they also spoke of the dangers of jingoism. The English had no notion how much their patronizing bonhomie wounded the feelings of their subject peoples from the Irish to the inhabitants in their latest colony. But the Germans could. They had known what it was to be despised as ineffectual bumblers, to be citizens of a multitude of small states, humiliated by their worldly political neighbours the French, and treated as a laughable collection of pedants and theorists by their elemental neighbours, the Russians. That was why Germans were such eloquent champions of nationalism and why the marxists of the Frankfurt Institute of Social Research were to make such use of the notion of alienation.

The German thinkers, then, confronted Europeans with the notion that events are determined not by individuals but by an impersonal process. On what the process was or how one unravelled it they differed. That impersonal forces were at work in the world was not news. The ancient Greeks called them fate, Machiavelli called them fortune. The Germans went further in thinking that impersonal forces, far more than individuals, governed events; and that the best hope for individuals was to jump on to the bandwagon of, some said the nation-state, others the class struggle, and roll along with it. Nor was this degrading because an individual could use his influence to make the cosmic process work less harshly.

The English did not understand that German historians and sages were looking at society in a new way. It was true that the Victorians were well acquainted with German thought. Did not Coleridge read Schelling, Carlyle Fichte and Jowett introduce Hegel to Oxford? Did not George Eliot translate Feuerbach and Strauss? So they did; but they domesticated these tomcats by neutering them. When Nietzsche declared that morality itself was immoral, or Hegel and Marx argued that the only freedom of choice open to you was to identify yourself with the historical movement, they averted their eyes. As a result when in the 1960s the American scholar Stuart Hughes examined the influential social theorists of the turn of the century, men who had revolted alike against classic positivism, he mentioned in Italy Pareto and Mosca, the Idealist Croce – and the marxist Gramsci; he mentioned in France Durkheim, Sorel, Benda and Alain; he mentioned among Germans Dilthey and Meinecke, he spoke of Michels and, above all, he spoke of Freud and Max Weber. In Britain he mentioned no one. He might have glanced at Frederick Maitland, but that historian's historian was too imprisoned in medieval archives to write a treatise about German historiography. He might have mentioned Kipling. Like Weber Kipling did not consider whether religion was true or good. He accepted it as a social fact and understood that different religions produced different codes of conduct. But who else was there?

English thinkers still interpreted society in terms of the individual. In Germany self-realization was an explosive, revolutionary idea, subversive of current ideas about international relations, duties to our fellow citizens and one's soul. The English turned self-realization into a sensible, limited way of taking Mill a stage further. In Mill's unheroic universe, so that argument ran, we are free to go to the devil unless it can be shown beyond reasonable doubt we will harm our neighbours. His critics demurred: surely man was made for better things. We will be more free if we have laws to restrain us from doing what in our better moods we would always want to do: who would want to pollute the air with his smoking factory chimney? So the English used self-realization as a prop for collectivism. It had none of the terrible overtones of Alva's response to Egmont's question: '*Was ist Freiheit?*' '*Recht zu tun.*' The English, having extracted the liver of self-realization from the German goose, made it into a pâté of positive freedom and threw away the carcass.

The German philosophers challenged the English empirical tradition. By drawing a distinction between pure and practical reason Kant made it seem self-evident that a serious man had to go behind the appearance of that system of thought which for Englishmen was second nature. So-called rational induction from facts to hypotheses was useful only for understanding the natural sciences. If he was to talk sense about social and moral subjects, he must use a different kind of reason. Hegel and Marx argued that men realize themselves by understanding and identifying with the historical process. History is the way in which reason unfolds itself: history is no longer the record of God's will or Nature's laws being fulfilled. However varied all the cultures and different societies are, there is an end to which the whole of history is working. How does one discover this end, how does one decode the historical process? Not through British empiricism. The picture of the scientific historian piecing together the facts from evidence is a distortion. How can one observe dispassionately when one is part of the historical process oneself? 'Scientific' deduction is biased deduction – biased by the ideology of the historian himself. So one did not discover the historical process by amassing facts and making deductions from them. No, there must be a new method – for instance, the dialectic – but, whatever the method, facts were irrelevant and misleading. If someone objected that the process was contradicted by certain facts, either the facts were false or they would become irrelevant as the process unfolded. Perhaps the most disquieting claim of all was that empiricists were deluded in imagining that their conclusions were objective.

It is of course true that there were other philosophical strains in the German Renaissance which the British found more acceptable. Scientific materialism, the natural child of triumphant German scientists, was as much a part of it as music or romanticism; and did not Ayer develop his version of logical positivism from Carnap in Vienna, did not Wittgenstein come from that city? So did Freud; yet respected as Freud was among us for his clinical work, Freudian analysis did not permeate British culture as it did American culture. There by the 1960s no prestigious Hollywood movie was without Freudian credentials.

There was another reason for British indifference to the German Renaissance. In the first half of the twentieth century, when we were growing up, continental culture spelt France. You read Proust probably in the Scott-Moncrieff translation, as many volumes of Jules Romains' *Les Hommes de bonne volonté* as you could manage and Roger Martin du Gard. Valéry and Apollinaire were the admired poets and Paris the capital of Les Six, modern painting and the theatre of Giraudoux and Mauriac. We were bound to France by ties of emotion. When France fell, you were haunted by Aragon's poem 'Les Lilas et Les Roses', and when Paris was liberated you heard again the *chansonniers* Tino Rossi, Charles Trenet and Edith Piaf. The old snobbery returned. To be able to say that after the Liberation you had seen Marguerite Jamois at the Vieux Colombier in *Lorenzaccio* or Sartre's *Huis Clos* was to score points in the game of advertising you are around.

Immediately after the Liberation Sartre captured British intellectuals as well as his countrymen. There were the customary astonishing Gallic paradoxes ('We have never been more free than under the German occupation'); but soon the astonishment turned to bewilderment. Was this harsh morality the child of the agonizing conflicts of duty and honour that afflicted Frenchmen during the Resistance? The hero of *Les Mains Sales* says 'My hands are filthy. I've dipped them in blood and shit up to the elbows. Do you think you can govern and keep your spirit clean?' Gradually it dawned that Sartre was not talking of the Resistance but of the Revolution – that perpetual Revolution of 1789 whose conflicts are refought every generation in the Sorbonne.

For Sartre modern society resembled a queue – orderly at times, perhaps, but since each of us knows he may be the one who does not get a seat in the bus, the others in the queue threaten him. '*L'enfer, c'est les autres*' is the famous line in *Huis Clos*. It is 'the others' who rob us of our liberty, just as we rob them of theirs. It is the third person in our room who poisons love and makes a true relationship between lovers impossible. How can we escape from this nightmare? There is an answer. Don't form a queue or what Sartre called a series. Form a group. A group is held together by commitment. Each converts his individual praxis into a common praxis. The working class becomes a group when they commit themselves to socialism. What holds the group together? The oath. Each member of a group takes an oath.

Sartre makes one think of the painting in the Louvre by David, the artist of the Revolution, of the Horatii brothers taking the oath vowing loyalty to each other and their cause. What keeps men true to their oath? Terror alone prevents the group degenerating into a series. Terror is the licensed violence that eliminates serial violence. Everyone in the group knows his life will be forfeit if he betrays his brothers. The state is entitled to exercise terror provided that it identifies with the cause of the working class: for terror is legitimized when those who have vowed loyalty to the group authorize the state to command them. That is why Robespierre is the true hero of 1789. Terror is the sole guarantee of fraternity. And of liberty too. For when I surrender my liberty to the group I vow loyalty to the Revolutionary State.

Quite soon, despite our admiration for Sartre's novels and plays, we became repelled by his double-speak defence of Stalinism. Immediately after the war Sartre still numbered Koestler and Camus among his friends. By 1950 he was not on speaking terms with Koestler, by 1952 with Camus. For Sartre it was *mauvaise foi* to criticize the Soviet Union. 'An anti-communist is a cur. On that I shan't change my mind, and I never will.' For Sartre the Korean war and the McCarthyite era were decisive. He denounced America as a fascist state for executing the Rosenbergs but not the Soviet Union for executing Nagy. Nor would he plead for the political prisoners behind the Iron Curtain. For the next three decades no single intellectual had such influence on his generation and the young in France. He wrote millions of words, he edited, agitated, attended meetings, organized demonstrations, took decisions with calculated purpose – such as refusing the Nobel Prize – was at once philosopher, playwright, novelist, critic and letter-writer, and he politicized the young to burn with a hard gemlike flame of anti-Americanism. Charmed with his musical voice and gift for fantasy, strangers hung on his lips. He was followed to his grave by tens of thousands.

Gradually we began to realize that in the summer of 1940 the Germans had won two victories. They had conquered the French mind as well as the French state. Durkheim and Bergson had been displaced by the three Hs – Hegel, Husserl and Heidegger. Practically all the well-known intellectual contemporaries of Our Age from Raymond Queneau to Foucault had attended the courses on Hegel given by two remarkable teachers, Alexandre Kojève at the Ecole Pratique des Hautes Etudes and Jean Hypolite at the Collège de France. It was Kojève who introduced Sartre to the idea that 'success absolves the crime because success is a new reality that exists'. It was Kojève who taught Sartre that the philosopher cannot reproach the tyrant because the philosopher no less than the tyrant is determined to impose his vision of life upon society. How ironical it was that the two most original philosophers on either side of the English Channel – the Austrian Wittgenstein and the German Heidegger (Sartre's pastor) – both doubted whether philosophy was an academic subject: Wittgenstein because he found his fellow dons insufferable, Heidegger because he was expelled from Freiburg for a few years for being an active Nazi supporter and persecutor of fellow professors. Both treated philosophy as religious experience, both were tyrannical. British analytic philosophy absorbed Wittgenstein, French philosophy was overpowered by Heidegger and his forebears.

In the eighteenth century Frenchmen admired Newton and Locke, in the nineteenth Englishmen admired French *clarté* and *logique*; but now French discourse became obscure and opaque, and after 1945 philosophers on one side of the Channel could hardly speak to those on the other. Freddie Ayer was to pay a generous tribute to Merleau-Ponty, whose mentor was Husserl, but phenomenological philosophy made no impact whatsoever in England, until in the seventies the Radical Philosophy Group formed and welcomed in the new universities young rebels against analytic philosophy. But we considered that in France facts had become illusions and individuality irrelevant. What mattered there was to measure the impersonal forces that held men in their grasp and through discourse to penetrate their structure.

There was one French intellectual who tunnelled under the Channel. Raymond Aron, so Simone de Beauvoir recalled, was a barb in Sartre's side. Aron, a despised socialist, had the knack as early as the thirties of getting his opponent in the fork of a dilemma and then crushing him with one sharp hammer blow. 'There is a simple alternative, *mon petit camarade*, take your choice . . .' But by the end of the war Sartre's mastery of the arts of rhetoric and publicity overwhelmed Aron. 'Better to be wrong with Sartre than right with Aron,' jeered the left. However grotesque Sartre's sallies were (anti-semitism is purely a bourgeois vice, from which the working class is entirely free), he was all of a piece. Aron was not. He was complex and antithetical: a journalist writing a column for *Le Figaro* or *L'Express*; an academic holding his research seminar at the Ecole Pratique des Hautes Etudes; a follower of de Gaulle who broke with the Gaullists; an opponent of l'Algérie Française and of the 1968 student rebellion; a Jew devoted to Israel who refused to attack la Nouvelle Droite as being likely to have encouraged the bomb attacks on synagogues in the eighties. A man who died from a heart attack directly after giving evidence on behalf of his old friend Bertrand de Jouvenel who was suing an Israeli historian for denouncing him as anti-semitic, Aron had a real feeling for his generation, our French contemporaries. He accepted that some of them would have at some time kept strange company because the Third Republic was so feeble and corrupt. He accepted too that de Gaulle was right to destroy the Fourth Republic. He was very English in accepting that politics was the art of the possible.

In his memoirs he told how, when invited in 1932 by an under-secretary of state to give his views on Hitler, he delivered '*un laius, brillant, je suppose, dans le pur style normalien*'. The under-secretary then asked him on behalf of the minister, 'What would you do if you were in his place?' That was not a question a *normalien* would deign to answer, and it taught Aron that it is conceited and self-indulgent to deliver moral lectures to politicians unless they can be translated into political action. Aron lacked the imagination to transform his relentless common sense into the kind of paradox that would make his opponents look petty; and the cord that bound my generation to Paris snapped.

There was another reason for their defection. Paris was no longer the cultural capital of the West. If painting had a capital city it was New York. The experimental novel ran into the sands in England and the *nouvelle vague* did not wash the sands away. Ed Shils was a shade unfair to criticize us for ignoring American culture. They had already admitted Faulkner, Hemingway and Scott Fitzgerald to the canon; and they were devotees of the Marx brothers. The fellow travellers and the Nancy Mitford set might sneer at America and resent Britain becoming a client state of America, but the dons liked their ardent American graduate students studying under the GI bill of rights. Before the war Denis Brogan was almost alone as an interpreter of American politics; soon after the war chairs in American history and literature were set up. There was also a particular academic subject at which Americans excelled, for unlike nearly all British universities Americans recognized what the German Renaissance had bequeathed them. That was modern sociology.

2

THE WORD 'SOCIOLOGY' was uttered by members of my generation with terror or contempt or despair: terror at the barbarous language sociologists employed; contempt for a subject which was said not to exist or, if it did, which had produced, as Isaiah Berlin used to maintain to me, no single thinker of any significance – no, not even Weber; despair by those like myself who lamented that by dismissing sociology we showed deplorable insularity and impoverished numbers of kindred subjects such as history.

There are no posts in the history of ideas in British universities and I was lucky enough on my return after the War to be appointed to a lectureship in the economics faculty at Cambridge, where I was asked to lecture on modern English political thought. I could find practically no twentieth-century theorists worthy of the attention that one would pay to the utilitarians or to Hegel, or to Marx and his commentators. There was indeed Oakeshott: but should one spend hours poring over MacIver or Barker or Cole or Laski or Weldon? My economist colleagues were sceptical when I suggested they might establish at least a lectureship in sociology; but, kindly as ever, they set aside a sum for three years to invite an American sociologist who would convince them there was such a subject. Calamity followed. Munia Postan put forward the name of the high priest of theoretical sociology, Talcott Parsons, to be the first visiting professor. Parsons's impenetrable jargon and extreme abstraction did not impress the Keynesians; and it was only the sardonic, elegant and incisive George Homans rounding off the series who redeemed the experiment. So I offered some lectures on the early twentieth-century sociologists, and hoped the tide would turn.

Not that anyone would have dreamed of pursuing sociology at Oxford or Cambridge. Before the war LSE had been the one place where the social sciences were honoured as a way of analysing life. There were a few who taught the elements of sociology elsewhere, Sargent Florence at Birmingham and Simey at Liverpool, and that second generation adherent of Bloomsbury, Sebastian Sprott, at Nottingham. At LSE there was another with Bloomsbury connections, Tom Marshall, an unemphatic, open-minded social democrat who explored the class structure while the colourless Ginsberg expounded Hobhouse. But in the post-war years the department at LSE went into top gear under the influence of two inspired scholars, one caustic the other ferocious. David Glass, the outstanding British demographer, took the lead in empirical or statistical research; the other was Edward Shils, a master of theoretical sociology, not afraid to bludgeon with his erudition those who did not realize sociology was a subject that rested on a great European intellectual tradition.

The young lecturers and teachers at LSE – Jean Floud, Tom Burns, Donald Macrae among them – were to fill the top posts when universities recognized the subject, and they taught the last cohort of Our Age which included A. H. Halsey, Asher Tropp, David Lockwood and, from Germany, Ralf Dahrendorf. Most of them, Halsey remembered, came from working or lower-middle-class families in the provinces. Most had won scholarships to grammar schools, most were committed Labour supporters of Attlee's kind of democratic socialism and most determined to use what they learned about their own society to change it. They were sickened by the communist takeover of Czechoslovakia, the Soviet invasion of Hungary and by Suez. They were also sickened by academic, as well as social, snobbery – by the assumption outside LSE that their subject was bogus and attracted only second-rate minds.*

The sociologists of my generation suffered the same anxieties that troubled the engineers when confronted by the pure scientists. Some of the best work was done by applied sociologists such as Richard Titmuss. He told civil servants what was going on in the welfare state, what class of people benefited and who should have benefited but had not. The influence of this saintly man on social policy in the sixties can hardly be exaggerated. Ministers discovered that these outsiders rootling in Whitehall's back yard could help them and, as dons began to be seconded to the ministries, the civil servants became less suspicious of them: they saw that the lifestyle of the intruders resembled their own.

Titmuss justified the welfare state by showing that the health service, for instance, grew out of the necessities of the air raids during the war. Yet many of the best practitioners in Britain were sociologists without knowing it, discovering like Monsieur Jourdain that they had been speaking prose all their life. In 1970 the young sociologist, W.G.Runciman, reminded an American sociologist who thought the British contribution to the subject pedestrian that he should read not only the work of academic sociologists. Beveridge had been astonished to be told by Tom Marshall that his report was a sociological treatise. No one ever referred to Malthus as a sociologist; but what was he if not?

Britain had in fact a long history of sociological investigation marked by the founding of the Statistical Society and the census of 1851, the Blue Books, and the work of Mayhew, Booth and the Webbs in Victorian times. By 1970 this work was paralleled by the Social Survey, the work of the Oxford Institute of Statistics on the distribution of income and wealth, by the MRC on the families of schizophrenics, of the Institute of Child Health on the social behaviour of nursery school children and so on. What could be more unfair than to quote Peter Willmott on East London adolescents, and not the Opies on the language of schoolchildren and nursery rhymes; John Bonham on the middle-class voter and not David Butler on general elections; Elliot Jacques on industrial relations and not Alan Flanders or Hugh Clegg; and finally to cite Alasdair MacIntyre and Arthur Marwick as social historians

* Halsey recalled their sense of outrage when, in an attempt to seduce some of the brighter graduates at Cambridge to study the subject, I got King's to offer a fellowship in sociology to a graduate of Oxford or Cambridge. I had already persuaded Edward Shils to accept a senior research fellowship, and I had my sights on W.G.Runciman. But this was maladroit; and when Max Gluckman asked us not to exclude graduates from the few sociology departments in civic universities, we bowed to his protest and elected John Goldthorpe of LSE.

and not W.L.Burn, Asa Briggs, Eric Hobsbawn or Moses Finley? Could anyone maintain that Hugh Trevor-Roper's study of witchcraft was devoid of sociological insight? He might have added such books as Richard Hoggart's much read *Uses of Literacy* or Raymond Williams's work on culture and society or, even more to the point, Ian Watt's study of *Robinson Crusoe*.

The most original and influential sociologist of Our Age worked in this tradition. Michael Young resembled Cadmus. Whatever field he tilled, he sowed dragon's teeth and armed men seemed to spring from the soil to form an organization and correct the abuses or stimulate the virtues he had discovered. Were consumers conned by manufacturers and advertisers? Let them form an association to test the products and appraise their worth in the new periodical *Which?* Did studies of kinship and family reveal that few from East London would ever enter higher education? Let an Open University, teaching through correspondence and television, be set up to act as a trampoline which could bounce back into education those who had fallen off the trapeze at an early age. He became the first chairman of the Social Science Research Council, of research trusts, extension, health and visual arts colleges, mutual aid centres, councils for education and poverty, and organizations for the Third World. Each provoked or sprang out of a piece of research. Michael Young was a remarkable example of the merits of the education at Dartington Hall. He knew neither what a groove was nor the meaning of orthodoxy.

When Jean Floud emigrated from LSE to Oxford and met philosophers she realized at what a level of intellectual rigour they operated. Maybe she was over-impressed; but there were no British analogues to the heroes of American sociology – Riesman, Shils, Bendix, Merton, Lipset and Bell. The next generation, however, produced a notable theoretician. Garry Runciman's provenance was as remote as could be from that of the LSE sociologists. An Oppidan Scholar at Eton who had won a fellowship at Trinity on the strength of his dissertation on Plato's *Theatus* and *Sophist*, the grandson of a Girtonian who had got a first in history in 1890 and nephew of Steven Runciman, the renowned historian of Byzantium and the Crusades, he had studied sociology under Robert Merton at Columbia and was to combine the career of a Trinity research fellow with running his family shipping firm. But he was at one with the LSE group in wanting to transfer a higher proportion of wealth to the worse off from the better off without reducing the amount of wealth they both produced. He differed from his LSE colleagues in one respect. He doubted whether sociologists were better qualified than anyone else to tell government or industry what policies to pursue. When he came to write his major treatise on sociology after his work on relative deprivation, he argued that in principle the human and the natural sciences did not differ in the way they explained life. Both depend on the accuracy of their observations and the validity of the hypotheses that explain cause and effect. While incorporating the insights of the German revolution in thought, he remained true to the British empirical tradition. But there was a price to pay for his versatility. Since neither he nor Michael Young had the time or inclination to become heads of departments, they did not lead and mould a new generation of scholars.

In Britain much of the intellectual energy that might have animated sociology had gone into anthropology – not surprising in a great colonial power. Again it was at LSE that many of the anthropologists, Raymond Firth, Meyer Fortes and Edmund Leach, had worked. It was as if anthropologists felt they had to apologize for the bad behaviour of their grandfather James Frazer. *The Golden Bough*, that classic of the English positivist tradition, treated tribes as savages and magic as a primitive form of reason. Thereafter each anthropologist was out to show that primitive society was neither lower nor in essence different from our own because each was susceptible to the same kind of analysis. Malinowski showed that customs, technology, law and economics could all be explained in terms of the function they performed in helping the tribe to survive and reproduce itself. This did not satisfy Radcliffe-Brown. He said that Malinowski's argument was circular. To say that social institutions enabled a tribe to survive and procreate told one nothing; for if they did not the institutions would not exist. But was not functionalism of any kind inadequate? asked Fortes and Evans-Pritchard. Human societies have to be explained by showing how each exemplifies an ideal type. Contrast a state centralized under a ruler with a society that has no head, and you will find you have to concentrate on the kinship structure of those societies rather than on their economic predicament.

And then two waves of ideas from the Continent broke upon Our Age. The first came from France but not from Sartre. Lévi-Strauss had escaped from the persecution of the Jews to America where he met the master of phonetics Roman Jakobson. Working from his ideas and those of the Swiss linguist Saussure, Lévi-Strauss argued that it was an error to think that a tribe holds together because everyone descends from a common ancestor either in the male or female line. And it would be equally wrong to think that tribal solidarity could be produced by some kinship pattern, e.g. between in-laws. No: it was the structure of ideas in the mind about kinship, not the actual relationships, that held the tribe together. Using the methods of linguistics Lévi-Strauss interpreted society as a system of messages. The *facts* of exchanges between groups were irrelevant. Men may imagine that they observe rules and laws but in reality everything they do consists of signs and symbols.

Edmund Leach, the most original anthropologist of Our Age, had his differences with Lévi-Strauss but it was he who made structuralism the new popular concept. Kinship was no longer to be regarded as a single functional system. It expressed other social relationships that might be economic or military.

It was a series of cognitive patterns, expressed in language, logic and communication. Leach wanted to destroy the model of a primitive society being governed by a single code of behaviour. In his studies of the Burmese Highlanders he showed how two codes existed side by side and fought for mastery – and was not this like our own society? The most exuberant of theorists, Leach rejected any one theory. 'I'm a structuralist for one half of the week and a functionalist for the other,' one of his students recalled him saying, leaving one wondering what day of the week it was. Quirky, unpredictable, a believer that truth emerges from contradiction, a roughneck in argument, he was the most charismatic teacher in the subject and his reinterpretations of the injunctions in Leviticus and on myth and ritual dominated the study of the next generation. He echoed the German romantic thinkers in arguing that marriage, family and incest carried different meanings in different societies. He rejoiced that all universal systems of human behaviour such as capitalism or marxism had been contradicted by the existence of primitive tribes; and the same held true for advanced industrial societies.

Anthropology was not the only discipline affected by structuralism. In 1958 Yves Bonnefoy noticed the differences between literary studies in France and in England. Roland Barthes analysed first advertisements, next the media and then literature as sets of images, myths that it was the duty of the critic to reveal and expose as propaganda. Structuralism 'de-centred' the individual in the same way that Darwin had de-centred the human species by showing how it had evolved. All the French savants – Barthes, Braudel, de Man, Lacan, Foucault, Derrida – were relegating the individual human being to insignificance. Authors and books, events, and sexuality itself, disappeared beneath waves of abstraction. Our Age remained sceptical. Frank Kermode, as befitted an expert on modernism as well as Milton, mastered structuralists and their progeny and supported its practitioners in Cambridge. Indeed he resigned the Regius chair when he thought his colleagues too resistant to strengthening that side of literary studies. But in the end he retired disgusted by their pedantry.

Another don in the English faculty of Our Age, Graham Hough, saw the incursion as part of a conflict as old as the middle ages between those who want to recover the meaning of great literary texts and those who regard this as impossible and unrewarding, the text being an excuse for an infinite variety of reinterpretations since its original meaning is lost. He looked with some contempt on semiotics as an ingenious means of inventing problems to be clever about. They become more complex still when linguistics, psychoanalysis and marxism are brought in to solve them. But semiotics have nothing to do with what students, or indeed the literate public, want – which is to hear what authors had meant and why they were great. He summed up the opinion of most of his contemporaries when he called the later manifestations of French thought an exercise in skilful mystification. One might admire Lévi-Strauss and Barthes; but the complexity of the method and the obscurity of the language used by Lacan and Derrida brought returns so diminutive and diminishing as to bring speculation itself into contempt.

No sooner had this wave from the Continent broken than it was followed by a second wave. The second wave was caused by the explosion of another piece of fissile material from the German Renaissance. Both waves derived their force from the greatest of all German romantics – Marx. The second wave was in fact a reinterpretation of marxism by the German sociologists who lived in exile in New York during the war: Marcuse, Adorno, Horkheimer and the rest. Indeed Peter Dews of the *New Left Review* argued that had the French intellectuals read Adorno they would have found their own insights identical with his. The Frankfurt exiles had asked why it was that despite Marx's predictions capitalism still survived its internal contradictions. They concluded it was because mass culture had rotted the will of the proletariat. Alienated from their society, their minds blown by advertising, media manipulation and soap operas, the masses had become incapable of revolutionary action. Intellectuals must therefore initiate such action and set the pace by restructuring their own institutions. They will start with the university because it is an institution designed to coerce students into accepting the hypocrisies of liberalism by practising repressive tolerance.

The impact of these savants had an immediate effect. University after university in the sixties began to set up departments of sociology and linguistics. And now the fatal consequence of the dons' stiff-necked rejection of sociology in the past became apparent. The cadres of young staff were not there; the few institutions that taught the subject in the fifties could not produce them overnight. When other subjects in the expansion of higher education were scraping the barrel for staff, social studies had no barrel to scrape and lecturers of modest attainments got appointed to the retiring age. Some of these departments adopted marxist interpretations of society. Stuart Hall, fresh from editing the *New Left Review*, ran the Centre for Cultural Studies in Birmingham where the art of understanding politics was not the study of facts and opinion polls, psychology and other positivist devices; you could understand it best through analysing culture and applying the 'correct' ideology.

The *New Left Review* was taken over by Perry Anderson and Robin Blackburn of the hard left, and soon Anderson's voice was heard reproving the sociologists of Our Age for being wizened provincials who imagined the subject could be studied dispassionately. Then one heard Edmund Leach in his 1967 Reith Lectures reprimanding scientists for their cult of detachment: they should 'take a personal view of how things ought to be and then try to bring it about'. The ghost of Bernal spoke through him. Next one heard the contention that sociologists should promote the destruction of the capitalist structures. Departments of social administration such as Titmuss ran, which studied how to make capitalism less oppressive, should be subverted by ginger groups. You should not study the Health Service to discover ways of improving it. You should study it to illustrate the corrupt practices of capitalism. Next moralizing journalists, who as students had picked up this tone of voice, rebuked dons for 'promoting the cult of the fact' that sprang from 'the liberal ivory tower approach'. When dons protested against the methods used by the militants in disrupting institutions, the journalists told them they should have studied the deeper causes, the fundamental issues at stake, using the methodology of Habermas and the Frankfurt School instead of 'taking student propaganda too literally'. A new generation of marxist students appeared.

No wonder the liberals among Our Age, still more those who had renounced the marxism of their youth, rubbed their eyes. Had they not refuted for ever in the forties such theorizing? And here the heresies of marxism were appearing in brand new spring clothes as saucy as ever. No wonder in America William Phillips, the editor of *Partisan Review* and veteran of battles in the thirties with the Stalinists, said that the days when he had confronted the Stalinists were so long ago that he had forgotten how to answer such questions; and Nathan Glazer wrote a book against marxism called *Remembering The Answers*.

The word 'structure' began to be used as a talisman. What was wrong with local government? Its structure. And the National Health Service? Its structure. Is the educational system unsatisfactory? Change its structure. If British industrial companies are in decline, encourage mergers and change their structure. What indeed was wrong with Britain? The class structure. A new age of governmental enquiries dawned; royal commissions, national and departmental committees were set up, and individual institutions followed their lead. These committees commissioned research. Had not O.R.MacGregor, when he crucified the Morton Commission on divorce, pointed out that time and again government was taking decisions about social policy without any of the most elementary information, and what information they had they did not analyse? No student disturbance but the institution concerned set up an inquiry into its causes. Certainly research improved the quality of Command papers and other government documents; but the quality of their recommendations did not necessarily improve.

It was not only the structure of institutions that was being questioned. When the expectations of dozens of well-intentioned pressure groups failed to be realized, they became convinced that sinister and hidden forces must have been at work to thwart the reasonable remedies they put forward to help, say, single mothers or disabled pensioners. As Brian Abel Smith of Child Poverty Action said, 'Many of us thought that once you exposed a problem, a Labour government would react. And it reacted in only a very small way, which caused a great disappointment.' As a result during the sixties authority in all its forms – hospital boards, local government committees, management, vice-chancellors – found themselves under attack; and they heard a new disagreeable question. The question was phrased with simplicity: 'Why are you such a shit?' Here is a social problem, so the argument ran, which has been 'thoroughly researched'. Our research team has provided an unanswerable solution. The solution requires the expenditure of a few millions, a trifle compared with the cost of the latest defence weapon or prestige aircraft. It also requires the employment of numbers of bureaucrats and the establishment of supervisory or advisory boards who will tell the minister what should be done as the scheme evolves. What, then, prevents authority immediately fulfilling this programme? The economy? You must be joking – this social evil is so dire that any man or woman of good will must wish to eliminate it at once. It costs a fraction of a nuclear missile. You still say it is impossible? Then it is clear that you yourself are the stumbling block impeding the way of progress. Why are you such a shit?

CHAPTER 17

Historismus and History

1

THE BRANCH OF social studies that attracted the largest number of Our Age was history. Many of the cleverest sixth-formers in the schools studied it – a soft option said the slighted teachers of classics. British historians had for long been influenced by the ideas of the German Renaissance. At the end of the nineteenth century Maitland began to interpret English history through its legal and local institutions rather than through the personalities in the struggle between Crown and Parliament. Now the history of nation states began to be examined through their social structure, their economy, their geography and the balance of power between social classes and status groups. German historiography was volcanic. It fertilised the British way of writing history. But at times it resembled a stream of lava.

Immediately after the war the banner of this new version of *Historismus* was no longer carried by German historians. Struggling in desperation to find a way of coming to terms with the falsities of Nazi-inspired history, German historians became less ideological. They returned to Ranke, even to positivist history. Not until the sixties did Adorno, Horkheimer and other marxist exiles from Frankfurt breed a new school of marxist historians. The impetus for the new version of impersonal history came from France. The fashionable stance among French intellectuals was marxisant – though the nation that could boast of Montesquieu, Fustel de Coulanges and Durkheim had its own tradition of social theory. Marc Bloch had been shot by the Nazis, but his colleagues, Braudel and Febvre, were at the heart of the VI*me* section of the Ecôle Pratique des Hautes Etudes. Their periodical *Annales* was to have immense influence.

The Annalistes dismissed historians who wrote narrative or traced the evolution of an institution such as Parliament. When G.M.Trevelyan published his best-selling social history of England, which he described as the history of a people with the politics left out, *Annales* reviewed it under the title '*Tout va très bien, Madame Angleterre*'. History was not about events or concerned with statesmen, military commanders or thinkers who imagined they changed the course of history. Nor was it a set of facts discovered by the historian. The true historian recorded 'total social fact' and interpreted society through its geography, climate, agriculture, commerce and demography. He should interest himself in the movement of prices, the difference in lifestyles of marsh-dwellers and mountain shepherds, and in the beliefs and attitudes of these groups. In other words historians should work like anthropologists and describe the culture of the society they studied. They should ask what were the *mentalités*, the set of assumptions often subconscious and unspoken, that dominated men's minds.*

In 1935 Munia Postan moved from LSE to Cambridge and tried to interest his colleagues in Marc Bloch. There were few takers. He was appalled by the elderly dons. As he wrote to his former colleague, the anthropologist Raymond Firth, 'They read little, know less and are smug and conservative in the worst Edwardian manner . . . sneer at "fellows with ideas" or tell funny stories about Americans. It is all very painful and explains why so many of the younger scientists here turn communist.' Postan was to change this and create a school of economic historians. Two of our best historians became heroes of the Annalistes. In the thirties Moses Finley had been a Party functionary and, although he slipped away from the Party, he remained something of an old apparatchik in his manoeuvres – a brand plucked from the burning but with the smell of burning still strong upon him. Expelled from Rutgers in McCarthy's days, when he refused to testify before the Senate Committee, he emigrated to England and won the regard of Arnaldo Momigliano who believed that the future of history lay with the Annalistes. Finley asked questions about the ancient world that an anthropologist would have asked: what kind of society Homer was describing, what its economy was, why the heroes exchanged gifts and so on. *The World of Odysseus* was a work of great originality; and in 1963 Pierre Vidal-Naquet devoted a laudatory article to Finley in *Annales*. Finley went on to analyse Periclean Greece. He declared that British scholars had for long sentimentalized Athens. They attributed modern notions of liberty and democracy to a society that was imperialist and rested on slavery. We should accept that, far from handing down to us eternal truths, Greece and Rome were totally 'other' – as unlike our own culture as that of an African tribe or Polynesian islanders.

Like the Annalistes Finley would admit no other approach to history. He pulverized anyone who exhibited positivist tendencies and anathematized German historians for imagining they could write history that was factual and free from bias. He turned on the cliometricians, who might have thought

* Zoe Oldenbourg, a pupil of Marc Bloch, used to picture in her historical novels of medieval society men caught in the toils of conflicting value systems each competing for the individual's loyalties. How to reconcile Christ's message in the Gospels with the edicts of the Church, with orthodox Christian movements, such as crusading, and unorthodox movements called heresies, or indeed with the 'old religion' of magic and witchcraft still surviving underground? Worse still, how to reconcile these obligations with duty to one's family, obligations to one's lord, obligations to the King, duties inherent in different kinds of law and the customs of the province or locality, and with the ethic of one's calling?

Finley would have regarded them as allies, for claiming too high a degree of accuracy. What men intended to do was for Finley irrelevant. They did what they did because they were imprisoned within economic and social structures and their freedom was the freedom of the prison exercise yard. Of course the structures changed as technology, the terms of trade and other forces changed; but a historian cannot rely on common sense or assume that human beings act in much the same way over the ages. He has to construct a framework and he can hardly do better than ask Weber to give him one. What will not do is for historians to interpret the economic behaviour of the ancient Greeks by analysing them as if Adam Smith or Ricardo had been their contemporaries, or their social relationships and slavery by using marxist concepts of class.

Finley's analysis of the economy and customs of Homer's world was a revelation. But was it true? Positivist historians dubbed it 'the use and abuse of Homer'. For instance, Finley declared that in Homer there is only one word for woman and wife. That showed the ancient Greeks regarded women as chattels. But is this how Penelope appears in the *Odyssey*? And do not the French today make one word, *femme*, describe the two roles? When in the eighties the deconstructionists argued that the text of a document revealed nothing but the mind and social origins of its originator, and had no connection with what the benighted persisted in calling historical facts, the dangers of working from ideal types became apparent. One entered a world in which fair was foul and foul was fair, and the historian became a sorceress who turned facts into theories at the stroke of her wand.

The doyen of marxist historians was Christopher Hill and it was he who determined to do for the English revolution of the seventeenth century what the marxists in Paris had done for the French Revolution. Hill was perhaps the only historian among his generation to found a school – many had clusters of disciples but few were queen bees who kept the hive together and working as Hill did. When he became master of Balliol, he refused to live in the gloomy lodgings within the college, no doubt on aesthetic as well as on ideological grounds; and he had the happy experience of being as much honoured by the left in his old age as in youth. He became the recognized authority on the myriad of puritan sects and factions that formed among working men whose faith led them to become active in politics. But why had such revolutionary political consciousness not realized its potential either then or in the nineteenth and twentieth centuries?

Edward Thompson, and George Rudé in his studies of Captain Swing, therefore analysed the making of a working class that realized how much it was being exploited. Thompson broke with the old marxist dogma that the state was a mere reflection of the mode of production. He saw that, however much such institutions as the Church or the House of Lords are part of a facade, some aspects of governance such as the common law are autonomous and may at times even favour the working class. But it was Thompson also who revived interest in Cobbett and the system of 'Old Corruption', the power of patronage and bribery, the less overt means whereby the Establishment maintained its power: the subterranean power of police files, of extensions of criminal law and the growth of civil service powers that reach into our own times through MI5 and MI6. Part of this hegemony is higher education itself: Thompson became in the seventies something of a folk hero for resigning his chair at the University of Warwick on the ground that students were being trained to become good capitalists. The English marxist historians should not be underestimated; and in the seventies they were mentors of a new generation whose spokesman on television was Stuart Hall and whose periodical was the *New Left Review*.

The other charismatic figure on the left who drew large audiences was Raymond Williams. Williams drew his theories from his engagement with Eliot and Leavis rather than from marxism or the structuralists. Eliot's 'dissociation of sensibility' in seventeenth-century England was not to be understood by analysing metaphysical imagery: it occurred because politics was changing and language with it, and because the readers of poetry were multiplying. The revolution is indeed taking place, but it is a long revolution. As more and more people become truly literate, the old elites will be dispossessed and a new literature born. Williams liked to compare industrial society to traffic in a city. The flow of traffic is determined by rules but the driver himself is free to make his own car change direction; and it is this freedom that blinds people to the inexorable social forces that dictate the flow of events in their own lifetimes.

To the generation of the sixties with their concern for popular culture Williams was a sage. To me he seemed a nonconformist spellbinder, rhetorical, evasive and vacuous. He wrote in the rhetoric of the old left. There were 'breakthroughs in experience' and 'lively arguments and controversies extending and intensifying' a 'long crisis' that (of course) 'mounts' as we are 'caught in a tension'. We can, however, 'at the level of theory break the deadlock' so that 'the whole process resembles a cultural revolution'. The taste of the elite governed the study of English literature. He wanted to replace it by the study of culture and communications. Then in 1971 Williams declared that his long plod towards the revolution had been anticipated by the Frankfurt School and by Racine's new interpreter Lucien Goldmann, and the sociology of literature and culture fell out of his hands into those of the structuralists and the neo-marxists. You should no longer study a poem or novel as an autonomous work of art: it was determined by society. Lost in the maze of structuralism the young Turks found the way out through neo-marxism. Here was a system with preordained analytical priorities and its own delectable theology of orthodoxy and heresy.

Perhaps personal partiality disturbs my judgement but to me the most impressive of all the marxist historians was my contemporary as an undergraduate at King's, Eric Hobsbawm. A refugee from Hitler as a schoolboy, Hobsbawm remained a central European and a continental marxist at home in the labour movements of all countries, as much an expert on the Italian Communist Party as on the revolutionary folk heroes of Latin America. His marxism was always sophisticated, illustrated by reading in many languages and brilliant in its range of reference and sources. No one could accuse the author of *Primitive Heroes* or *Labouring Men* of ignoring individuals in history. But his three-volume synthesis of English society in the nineteenth century was regarded by the Annalistes – and not only by them – as a contribution to history fit to be mentioned in the same breath as Braudel's history of the Mediterranean. He was in the forefront of a controversy as classic as that of the rise of the gentry in seventeenth-century England, namely whether the industrial revolution had depressed real wages and lowered the standard of living of the working class as well as brutalizing them. His opponents countered his statistics by trying to demonstrate that between 1781 and 1851 living standards for the working population as a whole rose by 140 per cent; and they challenged the marxist contention that industrialization occurred because the owners 'forced savings' from the workers and lowered their living standards. (One fact was incontrovertible: industrialization saved the population which was growing at an immense rate from starvation and improved the condition of the working class every half-century. But many workers until recent times were lucky if they lived long enough to make that calculation.)

Success took some time coming to Hobsbawm.* This may have been because he never concealed his communist sympathies in public affairs. He was adept at trumping his opponents' aces in the game of *tu quoque* and never missed a trick in denigrating American policy. Good company and humorous, he was a natural Euro-communist: Gramsci and Berlinguer were more to his taste than the gloomy Stalinists of the French Communist Party. He accepted that the revolution, so feared in advanced industrial countries, was not a practical possibility. It was on the fringe of Europe, in Spain, the Balkans and Russia where it erupted – and in Mexico, Cuba and China. Similarly he admitted that it was in the nineteenth century that history was best interpreted through classic marxism because it was there that the workers formed parties and trade unions in self-defence against the capitalists who were driven

* Dons often whisper in private that marxists make devious colleagues: appoint one to a department and in ten years they will have taken it over. Liberals pride themselves on their dispassionate observance of merit, but they are often determined to keep a cuckoo out of the nest however fine his feathers are. Hobsbawm had been elected to a fellowship at King's after the war but had no chance of a lectureship at Cambridge so long as that refugee from the Bolsheviks, Munia Postan, had influence. Nor were matters different at London. After seven major publications, among them original studies of primitive rebels and bandits (but excluding an erudite work on classical jazz), he still had to wait for a chair until the colleague best placed to block his promotion retired. This professor maintained that there were at least two others in the department superior to Hobsbawm – though research has failed to identify them.

to new forms of exploitation such as imperialism and fascism though each contained the seeds of its destruction.

For him the Labour movement was an inspiring reality with a time-honoured past. Since the war it was in danger of disintegrating because the trade unions, each in its sectarian objective to obtain the maximum advantage for its members, had divided the movement and pitted one set of workers against another. Instead of standing by each other the proletariat had become corrupted by the consumer economy so that sections deserted to the enemy. Like Hoggart, Hobsbawm mourned the decline of the warm-hearted, loyal, working-class culture that still flourished at the end of the war. His heart was at one with his head. When the left foundered he was harrowed by depression. When its fortunes rose he revelled. (In 1968 he returned from the Left Bank bearing a stone of *pavé* uprooted by the students.) Nor was he insular in his suspicion of acquisitiveness. He maintained that the students in Beijing in 1989 were protesting against the deviation by the leaders of the Chinese Communist Party from Mao's ideals of self-sacrifice and fair shares. Revolted by Margaret Thatcher's success, whom he regarded as leading an exceptionally dangerous reactionary regime, Hobsbawm called for a coalition of all parties and groups on the left – in particular the liberal educated classes.

In the seventies the marxisant scholars, led by Hobsbawm, Thompson and Williams, succeeded in capturing the loyalty of some of the younger generations of intellectuals because they related the past so seductively to the present. But history is as subject to fashion as clothes. Betty Behrens noted how three successive holders of the chair of the French Revolution at the Sorbonne – Mattiez, Lefebvre and Soboul – were accused of popularizing a version of that great event by employing the methods of vulgar marxism. Certainly the histories of 1789 that appeared on the bicentenary were nearly all sceptical of the orthodox view, both of the *ancien régime* and of the groups and individuals who brought about its collapse. Similarly in England the historians of the Russian Revolution, E.H.Carr and Isaac Deutscher, were elbowed aside by Leonard Schapiro and Robert Conquest; and Soviet historians at last began under Gorbachev to revise their own history.

Even Christopher Hill was to be subjected to a devastating review by the American historian J.H.Hexter. Hexter had already acted as a referee between Trevor-Roper and Lawrence Stone in their encounter over the rise of the gentry. Now he put Hill's method of writing history under the microscope. Hill, said Hexter, was beyond doubt prolific – between 1961 and 1972 he had published seven books of 2500 pages. He was also enormously erudite – in twenty-one of these pages he referred to forty-seven secondary sources, thirty seventeenth-century pamphlets, twenty-four collections of sources, forty-two treatises, in all 150 works. But how did he use his material? Historians, Hexter continued, are either splitters or lumpers. Namier was an extreme splitter: he saw so many exceptions to any generalization that explanation became impossible. Hill was a classic lumper. He put the past into boxes, boxes cunningly fashioned to fit his own conception of the past. But Hill was not only a lumper: he was a source-miner. He threw up a mountain of spoil from the mines of his erudition. And then by his own admission he picked out from the spoil those examples that supported his case. To Hill this needed no apology: had he not made it clear he was advancing a theory? This was his way of advancing it.

2

HEXTER'S CRITICISM WAS only one example of our generation's response to the notion so central in the ideas of the German Renaissance, that history is the study of the impersonal forces at work in society. But it was the nature of history, rather than the structures of society, that exercised the minds of Our Age in the years immediately after the war. How should we write history, how do we reconstruct it, what part is played by impersonal forces and what by chance, contingency and people?* They thought their predecessors in the profession a dull lot. In pre-war days it had been dominated by Powicke. It used to be said that when elections to the British Academy were being considered Powicke would plead that this time it was the turn of the medievalists. If it was pointed out that the last five elected had been medievalists, Powicke at once agreed that the best man should be elected; and in his views the best man turned out to be – a medievalist. The work of the medievalists tended to be narrow; Trevor-Roper unkindly used to say that they had reduced history to the editing of the laundry lists of nunneries; and eventually the modern historians in the Academy struck and set up their own sections. Most historians of Our Age rejected all interpretations that saw the past as the story of progress or the evolution of cycles of change. The new ideal was to interpret the past for its own sake and in its own terms. This ideal was not necessarily hostile to the doctrine of impersonal forces. But it was as hostile to marxism as it was to a liberal version of progress.

The historian who more than any other preached this doctrine was Herbert Butterfield, whose denunciation of the Whig interpretation of history became famous. His work, *The Origins of Modern Science*, was even more striking because it showed how great scientists in the past, who were portrayed by liberals as martyrs vilified in their days by priests and obscurantists, in fact often gave explanations of their discoveries that their contemporaries regarded as inaccurate as we do today. Butterfield argued that Galileo's contemporaries

* Historiography concerned Isaiah Berlin, Herbert Butterfield, Geoffrey Barraclough, E.H. Carr, Michael Oakeshott, Karl Popper, Hugh Trevor-Roper, J.H. Plumb and Gordon Leff: and also philosophers such as Patrick Gardiner, W.B. Gallie, P.H. Nowell Smith and J.A. Passmore.

had good justification for believing him to be in error. Science was not the story of linear progress, but a series of starts and stops, many of them false starts, and affected almost as much as theology by the assumptions of the times.

Butterfield was characteristic of those who took what they needed from German historiography and turned it to serve their purposes. A Methodist with a twinkling eye, a fascinator whose chief pastime was academic intrigue, Butterfield scorned every orthodoxy. He became best known to the public for his books on Christianity and history which at times reached a point of such Delphic ambiguity that attentive readers were baffled. Some of his pupils felt baffled for another reason. Charles Fletcher-Cooke, a future Tory minister, said it was Butterfield's delight to show that nearly every reform produced results quite other than those the reformers intended. He organized in and from Peterhouse a kind of militant conservatism distinct from the Establishment conservatism of most Cambridge colleges. It was radical, reverent towards Christianity, irreverent towards liberals and scornful of socialists. His adjutant was Brian Wormald, his young lieutenant Maurice Cowling, a devoted tutor whose school of right wing iconoclasts was to make an impression in the eighties. In Oxford and LSE Butterfield made almost no impression.

To him Christianity gave meaning to history and he was as critical of those who saw no purpose in history as those who did. Namier's obsession with individuals manoeuvring for power, he thought, reduced history to a tale told by an idiot; and Butterfield claimed that Namierism was 'the most powerful organized squadron in our historical world'. On inspection the squadron turned out to consist of two junior historians. Butterfield's denunciation of Namier, however, won loud applause. Namier had put a time bomb under the Englishman's conception of his history. (He described Trevelyan as 'representative of all that is worthless in history'.) The prince of bores, rude, arrogant, venerating Britain as the land of liberty that had been won by its aristocracy, Namier obsessed us even after his death. But there was another reason why Namier irritated us. Namier believed that politics was solely about power, and that ideas, religion, law were mere superstructure. Our Age was suspicious of anyone who claimed to have discovered one infallible method of unravelling the past.

Even more were they on their guard against teleologists such as E.H. Carr. Carr denied that historians could be objective and urged them to identify with the march of progress. His voluminous history of the Soviet Union always praised Stalin's victories over his rivals who had backed the wrong horse, and presented these victories as wise and inevitable. Carr did not escape lightly. Isaiah Berlin declared that Carr presented 'the most monumental challenge of our time to that ideal of impartiality and objective truth and even-handed justice in the writing of history which is most deeply embedded in the European liberal tradition'. For Trevor-Roper Carr was a reincarnation of all that was displeasing in Whig historians. Why did Macaulay, great historian though he was, seem vulgar? Was it not because 'persons and societies which did not accept his ideas of progress were caricatured, their ideas travestied or ignored'? Carr considered Trotsky, Bukharin and the rest had been proved wrong by history, and no historian since the days when men wrote Catholic or Protestant history treated evidence with such dogmatic ruthlessness as Carr did. It is not wrong to see progress in history; but history does not *consist* of progress.

Hugh Trevor-Roper perfected the historical essay as the most beguiling form of enlightening his readers about the past. He was the most eloquent, sophisticated and assured historian of Our Age, and never wrote an inelegant sentence or produced an incoherent argument. Trevor-Roper was not a man to take a lead from Cambridge. If Bertrand Russell regarded Oxford with suspicion and treated no one as wholly serious unless he had been exposed to the cool reason of Cambridge, Trevor-Roper regarded Cambridge as a gloomy backwater, the kingdom of Pope's Dulness where 'Laborious, heavy, busy, bold and blind,/She rul'd in native anarchy the mind.' Butterfield was right to ask us to study the past for its own sake, i.e. in its own terms, but puritanical in refusing to acknowledge that this was the best way to understand our own predicament. Of course we must not write history as it might have been: history is what happened. But we must ask ourselves what other options were open to men at a particular moment in time. There are never only two options – Kerensky or Lenin. There was nothing inevitable about the acceptance of Christianity as the religion of Europe – it could have been Mithraism, also adopted by a Roman emperor as the imperial religion; or Egyptian Syncretism; or even, had paganism still held out for two more centuries, Islam. How intriguing to think of the British, who are natural Protestants, embracing the Shi'ite faith and trembling before the edicts of an ayatollah of Lambeth. States may be created to express a culture – nineteenth-century Germany, twentieth-century Czechoslovakia or Israel: but the virtue they exemplify will be perverted by the imperative demands of power. Which of the early Zionists foresaw Israel as the miniature Prussia of the Mediterranean?

Trevor-Roper paid a handsome tribute to the Annalistes. Braudel was right to establish in over four hundred pages the impersonal constraints that limited the power of Philip II before introducing him to the scene. He was right to contradict Marx and assert that ideas – *mentalités* – were not mere epiphenomena but independent systems of thought as coercive as geographical and economic factors. Witchcraft was just such a *mentalité* – and so far from reason dispelling belief in it, reason reinforced belief in it. Indeed Trevor-Roper seemed to endorse the Annalistes' belief in *conjonctures* – those moments of crisis or achievement that resemble the confluence of two majestic rivers or a disastrous flood. He chose two lost moments in history as examples of what might have been. The Pacification of Ghent in 1576 might have preserved the Netherlands as one state, when it was the economic and cultural heart of Europe. Had Englishmen recollected in 1641 the advice Francis Bacon gave to James I England might have been saved from a revolution and Ulster from Scottish settlers who turned the province into a fortress. Where Trevor-Roper parted company from the Annalistes was on their scholarly politics. He did not fume like Geoffrey Elton at their contempt for events and their love of structures and *conjonctures*. But he too thought history moved and was not a series of snapshots; and he too opposed those who claimed to have discovered one infallible method of interpreting history and then, like the Annalistes, despatched to the guillotine those who did not join them.

Trevor-Roper showed how much historians of Our Age could absorb the lessons of the German Renaissance while retaining the virtues of traditional British historiography. There were, of course, historians such as Keith Thomas or Peter Laslett's group studying the institution of marriage and fertility rate and applying demography to history, or historians of the family such as Lawrence Stone, or Asa Briggs challenging the metropolitan account of politics and culture and revealing the richness of urban and regional England. We learnt to study the artefacts of the past, the pace of technological change. But how much did any of the following owe either to the Annalistes or to the neo-marxism of the Frankfurt School? – Steven Runciman who saw the Crusades as the last of the barbarian invasions; David Knowles putting an end to fifty years of controversy about the dissolution of the monasteries; John Elliott reminding us of the tribulations another great imperialist power in Europe, Spain, had endured when its supremacy faded; Victorian scholars such as Lance Beales; Denis Mack Smith dismissing the Liberal interpretation of the Risorgimento; John Habbakuk and Peter Mathias in economic history; Owen Chadwick in religious history; Oliver MacDonagh and Sammy Finer in administrative history; James Joll in international relations; and in the history of art John Pope-Hennessy and Francis Haskell who created a new branch through his work on patronage. The many professional historians who used biography as the medium of examining the past was an overt rebuke to the pretensions of the Annalistes.

Indeed Richard Cobb was an open opponent of the methods of the Annalistes. If Theodore Zeldin analysed France in their fashion, Cobb regarded sociology as 'a detestable and deplorable subject that will destroy any historian who gets involved with it'. Sceptical of quantification, uninterested in the rise or fall of the gentry, Cobb thought history was about the individual lives of people. His book on the revolutionary armies and his accounts of the sans-culottes, bandits and suicides made him the best-known historian of revolutionary France at a time when the methods of the Annalistes had so depersonalized history that French schoolboys could no longer distinguish between an *hebertist* and an *indulgent* or between 9 Thermidor (the fall of

Robespierre) and 16 Thermidor (the vote to make Napoleon first consul for life). For Cobb history was about the odd ways in which people lived or the places where they died.

Perhaps the most extreme example of history written without reference to German historiography and its evolution in *Annales* was A.J.P.Taylor. Known to an enormous public, first as a political commentator on television and next as an incomparable lecturer holding his audience for an hour without notes or teleprompter, Taylor called himself a radical. He was really a populist, a type known better in America than in England. He was at odds with his country's culture. He disliked Britain's cosy, cohesive political life in which positions of importance were filled by public school men or by those who had learnt to conform to their manners. Taylor's hero was the people of England. They were not the equals of their rulers, they were superior to them. The people know what makes them happy, but their rulers whore after other ends – wars, prestige public buildings and works of art by which they will be remembered. The people's enemies are the civil servants, sophisticated intellectuals and business men, who use the rule of law and convention to defeat popular control. Lloyd George and Beaverbrook were his heroes because they too loathed the Establishment, and welcomed the brash, the unscrupulous, the nonconformers. They often won by appealing to the people direct over the heads of the ruling class.

Taylor had been one of Namier's graduate students. For him the key to history was power: who took the decisions? Why this rather than that? Or had the politician in reality no choice? In either case did it really matter? Taylor thought it rarely did. Ministers take decisions against their principles and produce results the opposite of what they intend. His volume in the *Oxford History of England 1914–45* was a tour de force. He revelled in the unforeseen connection, or the paradox that unemployment in the thirties created a higher standard of living for the majority, i.e. for those workers who were employed. Ideas, intellectual movements, were of no importance. For him (as for Hobsbawm) high art was an irrelevance because it had ceased to be popular. He declared that Charlie Chaplin, not Virginia Woolf, was the most important artist of the first half of the century. Nor did he mention the triumphs of the scientists and technologists. But Taylor paid a price. The left to which he was devoted considered he had sold out to Beaverbrook: no honours fell upon him in Wilsonian times. And Oxford never gave him the professorship he deserved. The suspicion hung about him that he prized shocking his sober colleagues more than telling them the truth – although his accuracy on matters of fact and scholarship in modern diplomatic history was legendary. Taylor's last chance of preferment vanished when Harold Macmillan as prime minister wafted Trevor-Roper, a true son of Tory Christ Church, into the Regius chair, an act for which Trevor-Roper displayed his gratitude when he became Macmillan's campaign manager in the contest for the Chancellorship of Oxford and brought his man in with a handsome majority.

For all François Crouzet's mild amusement at Trevelyan's notion of social history there was one historian who took the unfashionable line of praising him. This was Jack Plumb, a formidable scholar, generous teacher and indefatigable entrepreneur. But he warned that the star of history was setting. Schoolchildren no longer pictured their country's history as the unfolding of its destiny nor, as the ideas of the German Renaissance gained currency, as the story of its heroes and *fainéants*. If people sought an explanation of the present, they expected to be given a theory of society and of the way it changes. In the schools history had become subsumed under social studies and the history of England regarded as lamentably chauvinistic and narrow. There were pitifully few historians among the next generation, he considered, who understood men and women as Gibbon, Macaulay and Trevelyan knew them. No one in a modern British university any longer had the leisure to spend decades on the research needed to produce works of magnitude and profundity. We had become men and women of one book or one theme. Plumb himself was excellent evidence that the past was not dead, but he was right in thinking that his generation was the last in which clever sixth-formers believed history explained the present. And in some universities students could graduate in history without ever having had to make the effort in imagination by studying medieval history to understand a culture remote from their own.

Among my generation was a scholar who began his academic career as a philosopher at Oxford and found his metier in a nook of history hardly recognized in England, the history of ideas. This was Isaiah Berlin.

3

NO ONE AMONG Our Age wrote with greater originality about the philosophers who were at the heart of the German Renaissance than Isaiah Berlin. He begged his contemporaries to stop regarding them – and indeed their analogues in Russia – as benighted romantics who were of no value to Englishmen reared in the tradition of Hume, Mill and Russell. He praised them for recognizing the passion men and women feel for their homeland, their own specific culture, for their nation or for their community – say, a mining village. These were what gave them their sense of identity. Marx ignored this. Berlin knew how Jews in Eastern Europe felt alienated from the society in which they lived; and from this understanding he perceived how Germans in the nineteenth century felt alienated from a Europe dominated by French culture and sophistication – just as in our times Third World countries are alienated by the western sense of superiority. Berlin understood, indeed sympathized with, the German revolt against the soulless mechanical rationalists of the

French Enlightenment. Rooted though he was in the English philosophical tradition, he declined to take sides because he recognized how the vision of life of the German thinkers contained insights that were invaluable. He was not a deviant like Waugh or Leavis, but he often held unfashionable views.

Unfashionable? How could this be? Was not Berlin a member of the Order of Merit, a knight, elected president of the British Academy; had he not been a fellow of All Souls' for most of his life except for the years when, to honour his debt to Oxford, he agreed to become the first head of the new graduate college founded by the Wolfson and Ford Foundations? Here was a man who won prestigious prizes and doctorates, who was fêted from New York to Jerusalem, the cynosure of people who had nothing in common with each other – millionaires, obscure scholars, secretaries and celebrated musicians. They were enchanted by his talk, his allusions, his delight in comedy and his affection for incongruous people. They did their best to keep up with his phenomenal speed of speech. When he talked his tongue had to sprint in order to keep up with his thoughts. His lectures were unforgettable. Appearing with a sheaf of notes he rarely looked at them and spoke in long sentences, clause falling after clause, each filled with epithets and metaphors in order to convey the exact shades of meaning he had in mind. Occasionally he would pause and look at the ceiling as if to pick out of the air the only phrase that would transfix the butterfly of the idea fluttering in his mind.

And yet, though he materialized in the beau monde and graced official gatherings, he defied categories. He was neither a socialite nor a socialist. Not an unworldly philosopher like Moore, nor a moralist of uncompromising views like Leavis or C.S.Lewis, nor a man identified with a movement like Laski or Cole, nor a public figure like Kenneth Clark or A.J.P.Taylor. He did not pronounce on public issues. No one could say what his views were on trade union reform, the balance of payments, university entrance or the poverty trap. He remained marginal to the central issues of any region of national life. Only in his commitment to Zionism and in his concern for certain cases of personal liberty or injustice was he likely to take a stand in public. He was not a guru like Forster or the other Edwardian sages. He did in fact hold unmistakable views about human beings and was quick to detect feet of clay in friends as well as acquaintances. He disliked, though he did not censure, ungentle behaviour or sexual exhibitionism. People who prided themselves on being tough realists, or fancied themselves as technocrats, were not to his taste: such men had to exist, but he saw no reason to applaud them.

Why did his editors see him swimming against the current of his times? Berlin challenged the prevailing clichés about liberty. For him the classic English interpretation of liberty was correct. It meant not being coerced, not being imprisoned or terrorized. When he wrote, the conception of freedom that emerged from the German Renaissance was in vogue. The young were taught in sixth form and university all the fallacies in John Stuart Mill's *Essay on Liberty* and were encouraged to believe that T.H.Green's definition of positive freedom was superior. Gladstonian liberals declared that socialist plans to nationalize industry and control production infringed personal freedom. But Green argued that so far from diminishing freedom such measures could increase it. A few people's freedom would be curtailed but vastly more people would now be made free to do things that hitherto they had been unable to do. The sum of freedom would increase. 'Freedom for an Oxford don,' it was said, 'is a very different thing from freedom for an Egyptian peasant.'

Berlin said this view was claptrap. Yes, the peasant needs food and medicine but the minimum freedom he needs today, and the greater freedom he may need tomorrow, is not 'some species of freedom peculiar to him, but identical with that of professors, artists and millionaires'. It may well be necessary to sacrifice freedom to prevent misery. But it *is* a sacrifice; and to declare that I am really more free is a perversion of words. It may be that society is more just or prosperous and all sorts of poor people are now able to enjoy holidays abroad or have a decent home. They were free before to enjoy these things but they did not have the money. It was a perversion of language to say that now for the first time they were free.

Perversion of language is not a philosopher's fad. It matters. It matters if we say we are more free when new laws are passed to compel us to wear seat belts in cars. We may be safer and the law may be admirable, but we are less free. Suppose we follow Rousseau and argue that no one in his right mind would wish to be a slave of ignoble passions. Suppose I am an alcoholic, a slave to the bottle? Would I not welcome being freed from that slavery? Surely my enlightened self would wish to renounce that part of my liberty that enslaves me to the bottle. Few of us are saints. Saints declare, 'In thy service is perfect freedom, renounce worldly vices and live according to a spiritual rule.' But what are we to do with the majority of mankind who are unable to master their sinful passions? Here, said Berlin, the real horror of a purely rational view of life unfolds. For if it can be shown that there is only one correct view of life, people who fail to follow it must be forced to do so. Positive freedom is the road to serfdom.

Berlin's defence of negative freedom dismayed the left. The extreme left in the person of Anthony Arblaster denounced him; the moderate left such as Charles Taylor argued that many people don't know what's best for them because they are ignorant or because their judgement is distorted by spite. But Berlin was not an apostle of the new right. He did not beat a drum-roll for Hayek. Liberty was only one of the good things in life for which he cared. For him equality was also a sacred value, and those who rejected equality as a bad dream were unsympathetic to him. He acknowledged that if liberty for the powerful and intelligent meant the exploitation of the weak and less gifted, the liberty of the powerful and intelligent should be curtailed. To publish a book in England, however offensive to Moslems, was one thing. But to sell the same book in the old city in Jerusalem with maximum publicity and invite riots and death was another. To make distinctions of this kind was the justification of pluralism.

Pluralism is a dingy word. Most people accept that there are many groups and interests in society and a good society arranges for them to tolerate each other's existence: indeed the most powerful of all institutions in society, the state, should make a special effort to give these minority interests as much scope as possible. Most people think pluralism is a pragmatic compromise. It does not compel us to abandon our belief in socialism, or in the beneficence of the inequality produced by the market economy, or our belief that there is a rule, could we but act upon it, that should govern all our lives. But Berlin meant something much more disturbing. He took the unfashionable view that good ends conflict. Equality and freedom frequently conflict; and to get more of one you have to surrender some part of the other. Consider the plight of Antigone. Sophocles thought she was right to put respect for the corpses of her beloved brothers before her obligation to the law. ('My nature is to love not to hate.') Sartre took the opposite view. Or consider spontaneity. It is a virtue: but we should not expect to find it uppermost in the abilities of the secretary to the cabinet. Indeed one could argue that spontaneity is the last quality one wants such a high bureaucrat to exhibit. Values collide and often cannot be made to run in parallel. And not only values. Propositions too. Truth is not a unity.

It was on this matter that Berlin dissented from the English analytic philosophers. The summit of his ambition as a young man had been to get the group that centred upon Austin and Ayer to accept some point which he regarded as original or important. To have done that would have been to establish something that was true. True, because the circle's discussions – though most of the points made were minute distinctions in logic or perception – were sustained by a great unspoken assumption. The assumption was that all solutions to all major problems can be found if we try hard enough. Philosophers accepted as axiomatic that there could be only one true answer to a question: other answers were errors. Moreover, all true answers must be compatible with other true answers. Truth is a unity. The good life must conform to these truths which philosophers discovered: otherwise it would not be good. In the end either we or our successors will discover these truths. And when we do we shall be able to reorganize society on rational lines free from superstition, dogma and oppression.

Berlin came to disagree with the most powerful voices in philosophy because he did something not all that common among philosophers immediately before and after the war. He read the works of philosophers long dead, indeed of some who would not in Oxford have been called philosophers – weird German romantics or Russian revolutionaries, Herder and Hamann, Belinsky and Herzen. He read them not to convict them of error and contrast them with the truth as we know it today. He did not use them to illustrate the climate of opinion of a past age. Nor did he divide them into those who point the way to saner times and those whom tyrants have used to justify their cruelty. What he did was to evoke their vision of life and contrast it with other visions of life. That was not all. He denied that there was any way of proving that one vision was more valid or more justifiable than any other. One might find Joseph de Maistre's analysis of society hateful, but we would be wrong not to realize that it contained some terrible truths however much liberals might shudder at the conclusions de Maistre drew from them. Consider Nietzsche. In his works are conclusions which the Nazis tried to translate into political action. But we would be amputating part of our sensibility if we failed to receive Nietzsche's astonishing understanding of a world no longer willing to accept the sanctions of religion as valid. Or consider Carlyle. Set beside his contemporaries, Marx and Tolstoy, he cuts a very poor figure. But he was nearer the truth than Marx and Tolstoy in reminding us that nations and societies need leaders. We do not have to agree with Carlyle when he praises Frederick the Great and Cromwell for the harshness and inhumanity of their decisions. But Marx and Tolstoy were wrong to declare that statesmen are so insignificant that they do not influence events. Churchill, Roosevelt and Ben-Gurion had a crucial influence upon the destiny of their countries.

Was Berlin a relativist – was he saying that there is no disputing about tastes, or that we can never understand another culture because we cannot get inside it? Certainly not. However different we were from Polynesian islanders or ancient Athenians, the very fact that we could imagine what it would be like to be one meant that comparisons between cultures were possible. Our ability to recognize virtually universal values informs every discussion we have about the nature of man, about sanity, about reason. Was he then an anti-rationalist? Impossible for one of his training at Oxford. He was opposed to Oakeshott because he believed reason could be applied to numbers of social problems and produce results. Reason may diminish the bruising conflicts between good ends. Peaceful trade-offs are possible, nor are they always fudges. Reason is needed to sort out the conflicting claims of justice, mercy, privation and personal freedom. It is true that every solution creates a new problem, new needs and demands. If children have got greater freedom because their parents fought for it, the children may make such importunate demands for a juster society that they threaten the very freedom their parents fought for. The ideas that liberated one generation become the shackles of the next. In saying this Berlin was reminding us that philosophers alone cannot explain the nature of being: the historian too can enlighten us. The history of ideas is the gateway to self-knowledge. We need it to remind us that people are not an undifferentiated mass to be organized as efficiently as possible. Efficiency and organization should not be regarded as the ultimate goals in life. They are means, limited means, to enable men and women to live better and happier lives.

Berlin, then, was hostile to the pretensions of technocrats and revolutionaries. The technocrats driving through their plans against opposition, sublime in their indifference to the ignorant opposition of those for whom they are certain a better future exists, appalled him by their lack of humility. The revolutionaries, oblivious to suffering, equally appalled him. Sometimes it maybe necessary to go to war, assassinate a tyrant, overthrow law and order. But there is an even chance that no improvement will result. One of his favourite quotations, which he used time and again, was from Kant. 'Out of the crooked timber of humanity no straight thing was ever made.' He recognized that his beliefs were not those to enthuse youth. The young so often want to fight and suffer to create a nobler society. But, even when set against the most dedicated and pure socialists of Our Age, he seems to me to have written the truest and the most moving of all interpretations of life that my own generation made.

CHAPTER 18

Science, Art and Wealth

1

THE GREATEST INTELLECTUAL triumphs of my generation were won by the scientists and mathematicians. Unlike our philosophers or economists our scientists surpassed the achievements of their predecessors. For the next twenty-five years their work won the admiration of their contemporaries just as painters were admired in fifteenth-century Florence or poets in Victorian times. Between 1945 and 1988 British scientists won forty Nobel Prizes; one of them, Fred Sanger, won the Nobel twice; and until the eighties it was odd not to find a British scientist in the list. Some became the statesmen of science, like Patrick Blackett, John Cockcroft and Alex Todd. Others like Peter Medawar the public, intelligible and enlightened face of science. Others, like Andrew Huxley, became renowned for their critical power to appreciate at an international gathering just how important or just how tenuous the inferences were in the paper being discussed. The older physicists of our generation who had worked under Rutherford – Blackett, Chadwick, Cockcroft, Walton and Aston – found successors in the labs run by Harrie Massey, Powell and Flowers. Nevill Mott, who transformed the Cavendish from Rutherford's famous centre of nuclear research into a lab no less famous for solid state physics, won his Nobel for work done in his sixties. New branches of subjects sprouted: topology, fluid mechanics, electronics, radio astronomy under Ryle, and biophysics under Katz. Alan Hodgkin and a dozen others developed Adrian's work on nerve physiology and Florey and Chain made penicillin a marketable drug. Perhaps the most astonishing achievement was the work done in molecular biology in the lab where Perutz, Crick, Kendrew, Brenner and Klug worked. They revolutionized genetics. It was a lab in which the leaders encouraged their juniors to contradict them if they thought they were wrong and discouraged secrecy, envy and rubbish about stealing ideas. It was a lab where the leaders knew what every scientist in it was working on and spent the minimum of time on paper work or travelling to international conferences.

Cambridge was the capital of British science. At one time Oxford humanists would plead that Lindemann was not their only scientist of note: was not Florey also at Oxford? After the war that changed. Imperial and University

College London and Oxford were as much centres of scientific excellence as Cambridge. Edinburgh, Manchester, Bristol and half a dozen institutions such as the Medical Research Council unit at Mill Hill became places with an international reputation. Many civic universities as the years passed could boast of departments attracting research grants from industry and government. The labs captured the best brains graduating in science and engineering: graduate students from home and abroad flocked to professors who may not have won a Nobel Prize but who were, like J.Z. Young, luminaries, *grands patrons*. Whenever you talked to university scientists, you could sense the excitement and the pride they took in their calling.

Britain could not rival America. The scale of American science, the almost limitless funds for research often in institutes free from the duties of first degree teaching, were beyond anything this country could offer. Still, Linus Pauling could recognize a skilful operator, and when he looked at the size of Todd's new chemistry building at Cambridge he murmured, 'Well, Alex, you sure got under the wire that time.' American-born scientists excelled in every field but they received a remarkable reinforcement. Hitler's persecution of the Jews caused the migration of the greatest concentration of talented scientists in the world. Like humanists from Byzantium or the Huguenots from France, German scientists enriched the land they fled to. Few of them were to stay in Britain. Nineteen of the twenty-one major figures who fled here left for America. The tiny number and size of British university scientific departments; the concern lest all vacant posts should go to the refugees leaving none for promising British scientists; the preference for giving permanent posts to younger men from Australia and New Zealand (who had given Britain Rutherford, Bragg and Massey); and the resentment felt by the refugees at being interned in the Isle of Man when in 1940 Britain was threatened by invasion, discouraged the refugees from staying. The Academic Assistance Council itself discouraged the refugees from applying for junior posts for fear of antagonizing opinion. It was not that they encountered anti-semitism or xenophobia. It was just that the tidy, bureaucratized culture of the country, in which every consideration was weighed against another, poulticed British magnaminity. An ICI scheme under Lindemann to integrate some into industry failed: one industrialist wrote to Bragg, 'We do not regard these Central Europeans as entirely reliable from the national point of view.'

The refugees soon realized that America was the better bet: more posts, more universities, and more industrialists who saw the value of research. As Hans Bethe said, 'America had been a country of refugees from the beginning.' Some such as Max Perutz or Bernard Katz stayed, but the names of those who left for America is a roll-call of famous scientists of the forties and fifties: Max Born, Fritz Loudon, Max Delbruck, Erwin Schrödinger, Leo Szilard, Edward Teller, Victor Weisskopf and Einstein himself. The humanities fared better and kept art historians or classicists such as Eduard

Fraenkel and Otto Skutsch. The Central European refugee became part of British intellectual life, leavening our insularity and enriching our culture.

The scientific adviser to government became a familiar figure. Patrick Blackett and Solly Zuckerman were the best known among the scientists after the war. During it Blackett's record of advice was admirable: he and Tizard were right about bombing policy though Lindemann defeated them; and it was Blackett, appalled by the fact that only twelve thousand qualified scientists and engineers were engaged in civil research at industry's expense, who persuaded Harold Wilson to set up a ministry of technology. But Blackett failed to appreciate the difference between wartime when the state was the customer and peacetime when the individual buyer was the customer. He thought there were too many small industries and he was at sea in Whitehall. Frank Cousins was his minister, and that finally sank him when the former trade union chief of the dockers did nothing to overcome the dockers' resistance to container ships. Zuckerman was far more successful.

During the fifties and sixties the educated public became better informed about scientific research. The publication of *New Scientist* and paperbacks meant that literate people were no longer dependent solely on *Nature* and *Proc. Roy. Soc.*, and masters of *haute vulgarisation* like 'Bruno' Bronowski performed on television and radio. Bronowski was well read in literature. A devotee of Blake, he became one of a number of writers – the English don Tom Henn was another – who enjoyed contrasting the scientific with the humanist mind. The war, however, had made people apprehensive as well as appreciative about science. War usually does. People try to wash away their guilt by paying professors to save them from making the same error again and landing themselves in another war. After the Great War it seemed to high-minded men that the nations had forgotten they were bound by law. So posts were established in public international law. After the Second World War and the atom bomb, departments in the history and philosophy of science sprang into being in the belief that laymen should understand what science was about and the scientists should understand what they were doing to civilization. Irritated by the superciliousness of the humanities, a scientist turned publicist decided to enlighten the public. This was C.P.Snow.

Charles Snow had suffered one of the worst misfortunes that can overtake a young scientist. His line of research was infra-red spectroscopy. He published a paper announcing he had made a discovery of importance and then had to acknowledge that further experiments showed his theory was false. During the war he became a scientific administrator in Whitehall and continued after it to recruit scientists to the civil service. He began to write novels, and became a pundit, broadcasting and lecturing. His novels about academic and political life were hardly up to Trollope since his characters were wooden and his prose banal, but they were about civil servants and dons in the corridors of power, in themselves a rebuke to the experimental novel and the concerns of Bloomsbury. He had grown up in a great period of Cambridge mathematics and science – he used to watch cricket with G.H.Hardy – and thought the professional academic critics of literature insular: how often did they refer to Russian and French novelists? He was a man of the left but a technocrat. He believed in centres of excellence in education – British grammar schools, Soviet specialist schools and the Grandes Ecoles. Invited to give a public lecture at Cambridge, Snow determined to strike a blow for science and put the narrow humanists in their place. In 'The Two Cultures' he lamented the fact that so few scientists read literature and scarcely a humanist knew the second law of thermodynamics. But he left his listeners in no doubt which of the two cultures was the more important. The scientists, he said, had the future in their bones.

Had Snow shown how early specialization in the schools inhibited humanists from understanding science or scientists' literature; had he contrasted our system geared to educating an elite with the Soviet system tuned to the production of cadres of middle-grade technicians; had he argued that the industrial revolution had increased the real wages and standard of living of the working class, his lecture would have been worthy instead of notorious – and forgotten within a week. But no. Snow was a kindly man and generous to the young, but of a stark insensibility. He spoke with the geniality of a man of the world, he took you by the elbow to explain what ignorant Luddites the modernists were to bewail the squalor and misery caused by industrialization – how 'nine out of ten of those who dominated literary sensibility (like Yeats or Pound) were not only politically silly but politically wicked', men or women who had brought Auschwitz that much nearer. Gripping the lapel of your coat and sticking his great face into yours, he told you that Ibsen was one of the few writers who understood the industrial revolution 'and there wasn't much that old man didn't understand'.

F.R.Leavis was then at the height of his fame at Cambridge, and he considered Snow's lecture to be a personal challenge. He too chose a public lecture as his weapon for the duel. Only genius, said Leavis, could justify the tone of Snow's remark about Ibsen and 'one cannot readily think of genius adopting it'. He then proceeded to deliver an onslaught that was of such unparalleled ferocity that Lionel Trilling rebuked Leavis for adopting a 'bad tone, an impermissible tone'. But Trilling had no doubt that Snow was wrong. There is no such thing, he said, as a scientific culture that tells us what is valuable or worthless. Snow should never have dismissed in his jaunty way the writers who were sickened by the effects of industrialism. The standard of living matters but no civilized person accepts that the quality of life can be measured in terms of real wages alone. Literature, said Trilling, not science, helps us to understand the meaning of life. It helps to create our culture and to criticize it. Every great writer in modern times, with varying degrees of passion, has expressed his resentment at our civilization and his bitterness that the generous desires we as individuals entertain cannot be fulfilled.

Some intellectuals, when they looked back on that debate, thought how alike Snow and Leavis were. Both were provincials who detested metropolitan culture, both were educated at grammar schools, both stood for the simple decencies of hearth and home. Both by this time detested modernism, but were monists who saw life as a single block of experience. Neither understood that not all men of good will can accept a single cultural ideal. Of course Snow was wrong to imply that the most gifted and motivated people become scientists and only sad-sacks devote themselves to literature and the humanities. Equally Leavis was wrong to evade Snow's charge that the modernists were pessimists: he would never acknowledge the existence of the apocalyptic Lawrence, the Lawrence of *Kangaroo* and *The Plumed Serpent*, the Lawrence who searched for an anti-democratic religion.

The response to Leavis's lecture was electrifying. The *Spectator* was deluged with letters; John Maddox wrote an exposition in the *Guardian* of the second law of thermodynamics; and there was a considerable increase in the entropy of the educated classes. Of the first thirty-two letters only five favoured Leavis, though later the balance was more even. That confirmed Leavis in his view that those who wrote to such periodicals were 'flank-rubbers' – and there flashed across the mind's eye the image of a herd of literary beasts, led by Dame Edith Sitwell, lowing as they chomped their way across the meadows. At the end of the affair it was clear that Leavis had not only destroyed Snow's case, he had destroyed Snow. From that time middlebrow opinion, which had been prepared to endorse Snow's belief that his novels were a literary landmark, wavered and deserted him. Snow's standing in politics, however, was unaffected. He got the Labour Party to accept that science was part of the socialist conception of life and was behind Harold Wilson's promise in 1964 to 'build socialism in the white-heat of the scientific and technological revolution'. He became junior minister to Frank Cousins and had as little success as Blackett. The impact on science of the debate with Leavis was negligible.

Nevertheless Our Age heard the rumble of discontent. They believed scientists improved the quality of life, but their successors were at first sceptical and then hostile. The *New Left Review* considered Althusser's scientism more important than science. Perry Anderson never mentioned science in his essay on the nation's culture. Then in the seventies ominous signs appeared. Those in CND who wanted to ban the bomb now wanted to dismantle all nuclear power stations. Physics was no longer a neutral subject and physicists could no longer plead that they were the dispassionate discoverers of a power whose use for good or evil depended on politicians. For the left science became an aspect of American imperialism. Animal lovers raided laboratories to release cats and mice, biologists were castigated for considering research on embryos *in vitro*, the molecular biologists reprimanded for genetical engineering. As snooker players took beta blockers and weight-lifters steroids, pharmacologists – who by the eighties had overtaken the physiologists as the trendiest medical scientists – were supposed to feel responsible. Ian Kennedy made his name in legal research as an authority on medical ethics. Some feminists declared science to be a symptom of man's aggressiveness, the lust to dominate nature. Science was said to devalue the passive, contemplative, harmonious side of nature.

As the years passed, Westminster, Whitehall and industry began to ask not whether fundamental research was valuable – none but an ignoramus could doubt that – but how many labs should be engaged upon it. When Victor Rothschild was chairman of the Agricultural Research Council in the fifties, he made sure that the Lord President of the Council (who was responsible for the research councils) understood the necessity for fundamental research. When fifteen years later he became head of Royal Dutch Shell's research, he wondered whether he had been right. Should the laboratories of the Agricultural Research Council, such as that at Babraham, be engaged in open-ended research? One can research for ever on the physiology of the cow: should not such a laboratory concentrate on project research, with a limited objective and of immediate concern to agriculturalists? Rothschild recommended government to place part of the funds of the research councils in the hands of the consumers of research: they rather than the lab should decide what research was to their best advantage. Some said he was up against the professional snobbery of scientists. If prestige and fellowship of the Royal Society depends on your success in fundamental research, and if most applied research is regarded as less important and mind stretching, you will opt for fundamental research. The esteem of your peers and your chance of advancement depend upon it. With some reluctance the Royal Society began to elect a higher proportion of engineers in the seventies and the Scientific Research Council incorporated the word engineering in its title.

2

IT BECAME A game for intellectuals to discover connections between science and its apparent opposite, art. Did not Racine reflect Cartesian science, or Pope and the Augustans Newton? After all, Goethe called his most profound novel by a term then current in chemistry, 'elective affinities'. From these analyses rolled vast speculations. George Steiner argued that when structuralists and deconstructionalists denied a poem had anything to do with what the poet felt and intended to convey, and when they turned poems into symbols of communication, they were in some fashion speaking the same language as cosmologists who talk of black holes and physicists who use the principles of indeterminacy and undecidability. Intuitive art, uncontrolled by laws learnt in the atelier, was all of a piece with an irrational universe. But how seriously should one take the metaphors scientists use – that God is left-handed or does not play with dice? Are they really analogues, do they really have any logical connection to the rational activity of experiment and verification that occupies scientists?

Our Age lived under the shadow of modernism but after the Second World War the tension between traditionalists and modernists diminished. Particularly in music. The market created by broadcasting on radio and then on television, by the cassette and by the long-playing and later the compact disc, gave composers and performers undreamt-of opportunities. The BBC supported no fewer than thirteen musical orchestras and enterprises. Millions watched opera on television. The influence of impresarios at the BBC – Walter Legge, William Glock and Hans Keller – was incalculable, and the appetite of the producers to fill the hours on Radio Three was so prodigious that first Monteverdi and then the work of long-forgotten baroque and romantic composers was revived. Ensembles resurrected crumhorns and other medieval instruments as taste moved backwards as well as forwards; groups of singers, small orchestras that in the past would have been amateurs now earned a living as professionals. Then came the demand that music should be played on instruments of the period in which it was composed, to reproduce an 'authentic' sound. Meanwhile every nuance of nostalgia for the music of their youth was available to Our Age. A diminishing but loyal band followed the developments in jazz; the French and the Berlin *chansonniers* had their devotees; so did ragtime. Whatever form music took, rhythm began to overwhelm melody. One genre moved irrevocably into the past. The tunes of Irving Berlin, Gershwin, Kern, Hart, Coward and Gay came to be listed in the catalogues of nostalgia. The vapid three stanza and reprise melodies of English musical comedy died away at the sound of rock and the relentless beat of the Beatles.

The composers of our own generation, Benjamin Britten and Michael Tippett, won a vast following and the composers whom Constant Lambert had celebrated as the great figures of modernism – Stravinsky and Schoenberg – were now part of the repertoire. Mahler became the third most performed and recorded composer. *Wozzek* joined the repertory of opera houses and the English National Opera performed operas by living composers: even the Royal Opera House staged Stockhausen's *Donnerstag auf Licht.* Atonal and serial music were not neglected; and Harrison Birtwistle was accepted by Our Age as much as by the young. Peter Heyworth, an exacting critic and an enthusiast for the most austere and the most adventurous composers, thought that impresarios were too timid and British composers still too tame; but taste had in fact changed.

Among the great classics, too, the Three Bs no longer sat in lofty eminence: indeed Brahms fell into some disrepute as Britten loathed him. Mozart now sat on a throne beside them. There had never been a time when Mozart was not admired, particularly by composers, but Our Age found his music as profound and moving as that of Bach and Beethoven. They put his operas and those of Verdi on a par with Wagner, a judgement that would have shocked Ernest Newman, the pundit to whom our generation listened as adolescents. The change in sensibility which deified Mozart is a key to the understanding of Our Age.

Modernism created an insoluble puzzle in art. It came to encompass so many styles and movements that it ceased to have meaning. Magritte and Max Ernst had applied paint so as to conceal brushstrokes. What had this to do with the impasto and brushwork of artists after the war who made their statement through them? Ernst Gombrich's Romanes Lecture led to a sprightly exchange of letters between him and Quentin Bell. In that lecture, given in the Sheldonian Theatre at Oxford whose ceiling was painted by Streeter, Gombrich had asked how it was possible to refute the claim made, when Streeter was alive, that 'future ages must confess that they owe more to Streeter than Michelangelo'. It was a claim that implicitly accepted the notion of a canon of excellence and it could be refuted only by consulting and defining that canon. Quentin Bell, brought up in Bloomsbury, was sceptical of canons. For three centuries Botticelli had been ignored. At the beginning of the twentieth century educated taste considered Van Dyck superior to Rubens: neither Piero della Francesca nor Cézanne would have been included in the canon. To this Gombrich replied that the canon is not a ranking order. But, though taste is bound to change, we cannot ignore the judgement of the past. No judgement can be solely ours, no critic starts from scratch. Yet whatever we may say about the past it was certainly clear that there was no canon governing contemporary art. Bell was perturbed that the bad art of the salon in which painters guessed all too well what the public thought was a good painting and, in satisfying the market's taste, painted dreadful paintings, had now been replaced by conformity to nonconformity. Once a style, or a movement, was identified, the chase was on to catch it. Was it not absurd that incomprehensibility had become a requirement for good art?

There had been a revolt against the triviality of Parisian art in the thirties. The surrealists were amusing and tried to be shocking. The Euston Road school did not think painting was amusing. They proclaimed the importance of drawing and tonal values, and above all of seriousness and devotion to nature. William Coldstream, Claude Rogers, Rodrigo Moynihan and Victor Pasmore were not doctrinaire; one or other might enter an abstractionist phase and then return to the old ways. But as the years passed we saw hundreds of thousands of people come to exhibitions of abstract art, and the literature to explain it grew ever vaster. By the eighties abstract and distortionist painters won the new prize competitions that business sponsors had established. Francis Bacon was recognized as Britain's most famous international artist and Howard Hodgkin his most likely successor. Brigid Riley's paintings were exhibited in Japan, and dozens of British abstract artists had shows in New York. The artists themselves talked in terms of spatial relationships, texture and surface tension. In fact the splashes and drips of colour, the splodges on the canvas, the structures of wire, bronze or stone at most created associations in the mind with objects – or with dreams. It was Henry Moore's gift of relating his most abstract works to Nature – to plants and human beings – that made Kenneth Clark, his powerful patron, write that his figures 'are not merely pleasing examples of design, but seem to be part of nature rolled round in Earth's diurnal course with rocks and stones and trees'. Yet a younger generation was to find the post-war output from Moore's Much Hadham workshop repetitive, mannered and devoid of the tension that great sculpture should exhibit. To our indignation they thought Moore to be the victim of Clark's patronage and his own success. To us Moore was the artist of international fame. And yet to me the artist with the most piercing and disturbing eye was Lucian Freud. Whenever I went to an exhibition of his paintings I thought of Rembrandt's Dr Nicholas Tulp in the Mauritzhuis at the Hague explaining the anatomy of the arm, so meticulous and merciless was Freud's exposure of life.

What will survive and take its place in the canon has always been a puzzle even in literature. A high-minded Victorian intellectual in, say, 1880 would have thought Browning and Meredith marked for lasting fame. Yet less than ten years later Wilde was to say 'Meredith is a prose Browning and so is Browning', and their reputations as profound sages never recovered. But Browning survived as a poet; was indeed hailed by Graham Greene as his favourite poet. Who could say what would survive from among those honoured by major exhibitions at great galleries? To see the critics salute a charlatan such as Andy Warhol was sobering: would celebrities be hailed in the next century as the creators of masterpieces? No wonder collectors bought the modern art of the day before yesterday. Only a few private patrons, such as Charles Saatchi, followed the example of the young Stephen Spender or Jim Ede who, in the thirties and forties, though far from well off themselves, had bought the work of their contemporaries. Most artists relied for a living on part-time employment in art schools and on public galleries and foundations and enlightened corporations purchasing their works.

The artists of our generation became unsettled by the demands of modernism. The enchanting Bill Coldstream, a life enhancer and one of the few artists who could hold his own on committees, had been made chairman of a committee on art schools. He was mortified when his report was execrated by young artists then riding on the tide of the iconoclasm of the sixties. He came to share Victor Pasmore's despair that art schools had nothing to teach except mechanical techniques such as welding: which is as much as to say that techniques had nothing to do with the decision the artist makes about the painting or sculpture he is creating. Few art schools in the sixties and seventies made drawing from the nude compulsory. Art became equated with fashion. The optimism and self-confidence of the artists disintegrated as they saw their pupils aping American performers who amused themselves by exploiting gullible entrepreneurs on the qui vive for an artist whose works would prove to be an investment.

It is perhaps a judgement upon them that they left others to protest. Lawrence Gowing did in fact restore a curriculum to the Slade School when he succeeded Coldstream and, in despair at the anarchy at the Royal College of Art, its governors appointed Jocelyn Stevens, the well-to-do magazine tycoon, to be its director: many of the staff left and the college was restored to its original purpose of training students in design. People began to ask what art schools were for. Had they a vocational purpose, such as training students to design better graphics, clothes, furniture, packaging consumer goods of every size and value etc., at which Britain was conspicuously weak? Or were they simply to multiply the numbers of painters and sculptors? Or was it true that you could not do the first without doing the second?

It was left in the eighties to a pupil of Maurice Cowling at Peterhouse, Peter Fuller, to launch a counter-attack upon modernism in his quarterly *Modern Painters*. Fuller had once been beguiled by the marxist art criticism of John Berger. So he wrote a book called *Seeing Through Berger.* Like the distinguished Australian critic Robert Hughes, Fuller believed that the modernist tradition was disintegrating. It should be replaced, said Fuller, with a fine display of Leavis-like chauvinism, by the British tradition in art. To us this seemed problematical.

The aesthetes of the oldest cohort of our generation considered that the novel had been finished off by Proust, Joyce and Virginia Woolf and would have to be re-invented. They waited in vain for some new advance. English novelists returned to Fielding and Smollett. British novelists did not export easily. Graham Greene was indeed a hero on the Continent; but it became a black joke that he was always rejected by the judges for the Nobel Prize. (They at last awarded it to William Golding.) Arthur Marwick expressed the horror high-minded intellectuals at home and abroad felt for Waugh: 'still fawning on a particular social class' was his verdict and – bizarre judgement – thought him inferior to Ford Madox Ford.

We expanded the scope, the range, the styles of the novel. Sometimes surreal, often fantasist, but also dealing from the inside with working-class and lower-middle-class life. The scene shifted from the sensitive young man struggling with public school hang-ups to scenes from provincial life by

William Cowper, the forerunner of John Wain, John Braine and Alan Sillitoe. Kingsley Amis opened a door on to a world which to the elderly aesthetes smelt of stale beer and vomit, and to some of us was fresh air. Angus Wilson, in common with Waugh, punctured the ethos of his own world: the sensitive, homosexual intellectual. But many of the most interesting novelists of our generation were women: Ivy Compton-Burnett, Rosamond Lehmann, Iris Murdoch, Jean Rhys, Stevie Smith and Muriel Spark. One of the most original publishers, Carmen Callil, made her name publishing only women writers and in the process reviving those taken for dead and revealing others whom the run of publishers did not recognize were alive. As the circulating library was replaced by the paperback, the number of imprints going far beyond the scope of travel and cookery books multiplied exponentially. Vast new pastures opened before the educated classes.

On the other hand most of our poets remained faithful to modernism, cerebral in diction and wit, the heirs of Eliot and Graves; they wrote for each other, the avant-garde, the critics and the campus. The famous four poets of the thirties went their ways after the war. Auden was never to write as well as he had when he lived in England. He felt suffocated there; but cut off from the associations of his youth, spontaneity and depth of emotion were impaired – or so it seemed to English intellectuals. Day Lewis turned back to Hardy, MacNeice (whose verse in the eighties had worn well) became a BBC impresario, Spender became an ambassador for English poetry, the visiting professor on many an American campus, no conference without him. Poets spoke from the confessional explaining their psychoses. Often the violence of their language defeated its purpose: it neither induced catharsis nor shocked. Deft anthologizers picked their favourites. Yeats had chosen for his edition of the *Oxford Book of Modern Verse* Roy Campbell, William Plomer and George Barker. Kingsley Amis, publishing in 1988 his anthology of two hundred English poems chose, apart from the obvious moderns, Kenneth Allott, Roy Fuller, Lawrence Durrell, Elizabeth Jennings, Roger Woodis, Donald Davie, far more R.S. Thomas than Dylan Thomas; and naturally for him Betjeman and Larkin.

The common reader did not doubt whom he preferred. John Betjeman wrote lines as memorable as those of Kipling and Browning and was the best known Poet Laureate since Tennyson. Even more insular was the most considerable of the post-war poets among us, the withdrawn Philip Larkin. As hostile to progressive intellectuals as his friend Kingsley Amis, he may have been a university librarian but he did not write university poetry. He was the poet of common sense, dead-pan humour, never reading his poetry in public or lecturing, contemptuous of modernism, an English poet as unlike Lowell or Ginsberg or Ashbery as it was possible to be. Sceptical of modern poetic rhetoric, bleak, witty, he told us of fear, loneliness and the finality of death.

To modernists Betjeman represented all they feared most in British life: the inveterate British preference for nostalgia and charm – the charm Anthony Blanche warned Charles Ryder in *Brideshead* was the English vice. But it was not in poetry that Betjeman's delight in nostalgia affected public taste.

Perhaps no profession faced the future with such confidence as did the architects. The destruction by wartime bombing and the determination of their contemporaries to improve the deplorable record of British architecture between the wars gave them their chance. In the post-war Festival of Britain they took it. The modernists captured one after the other the university architectural schools: Matthew at Edinburgh, Gardner-Medwin at Liverpool, Martin at Cambridge and Llewelyn-Davies at London. The Oxbridge colleges became their patrons. Practically all the leading firms were commissioned to embellish these universities in the greatest building spree since Victorian times. The new universities each commissioned an architect to plan their campus and design their buildings.

Yet it was among our generation itself that the movement emerged that was to undermine the reputation of their contemporaries, the leading architects. Betjeman evoked on television the beauties of Victorian churches and commercial exchanges and denounced the vandalism of planners and property developers who blithely demolished them and moved on to desecrate the countryside. Not for nothing had he and Harold Acton among the Oxford Wits collected Victorian bric-à-brac. Betjeman changed public taste by being funny and passionate about the past. So did Osbert Lancaster whose short books on architecture were exceptionally perceptive and amusing. The conservationists, led by Hugh Grafton, hunted the modernists in full cry, demanding an end to concrete fortresses, glass boxes and tower blocks approached by windswept walkways, an arena for prowlers and muggers. Why design buildings of elephantine dimensions that neglected their unobtrusive neighbours? Why did so many buildings, specifically designed to meet the functions which those who were to use them were going to perform, end by being inhuman? Was it right to refer with contempt to the arch of Euston station as a 'piece of the vernacular' and refuse to move and preserve it? I lived to see monuments and buildings that were execrated by enlightened opinion when I was a boy praised and petted like delightful old doggies.

But good architecture costs money and neither the state, and seldom private enterprise, were willing to pay the price. So often the client overloaded his brief or told the architect to design to a figure of cost per cubic foot which put a premium on low ceilings, narrow passages and minimal public space. Developers wanted a quick return on their money. Richard Rogers told his critics that because developers and their clients, haunted by escalating costs due to inflation, demanded the maximum square footage on a site for the minimum cost, an up-ended glass matchbox was the inevitable result. Abide by the laws of the market economy and that was what the public would get. Business firms had set the worst of examples after the war erecting mean and despicable offices in the bombed area round St Paul's.

In the public sector there was no time for second thoughts. You accepted the first design submitted; for if you did not you would lose your place in the queue of those wanting new buildings. Even when the contract was signed inflation would then force you to cut costs yet again, so that finishes were inferior and maintenance costs high. When Denys Lasdun at the University of East Anglia was told that he must abandon his ziggurat design and build more cheaply to UGC norms, he threw in his hand. Yet so powerful was the conservationist rhetoric that it was difficult to find a single major building created since the war which all sides agreed was a fine addition to the nation's heritage. In the eighties the Prince of Wales intervened. He was pained by what he regarded as the inhuman scale of much modern architecture and the egoism of architects who ignored the style of the surrounding buildings. He denounced with justification a proposed extension to the National Gallery as a monstrous carbuncle on the face of a much loved friend, and with no justification at all compared Lasdun's National Theatre to a power station.

But the battle of the styles is nothing new in the history of architecture: the Gothic revivalists dismissed Georgian architecture as soulless, the Queen Anne revivalists dismissed the Gothic enthusiasts for neglecting sweetness and light, Osbert Lancaster dismissed the Queen Anne inglenooks and gables as Pont Street Dutch. What will the verdict of the twenty-first century be on neo-classicism and toy-town architecture?

We took pride that they found Britain a country of philistines and left it respecting the arts. The open contempt for painting and music current before and after 1914 at the court and in the upper classes dissolved. Attendance at concerts, theatres, museums and galleries rose year by year. The Royal Ballet became in the fifties and sixties the greatest dance company in the western world. Margot Fonteyn was an incomparable ballerina and Frederick Ashton, a child of the twenties, a choreographer of genius. At last Britain had a state theatre in the Royal Shakespeare Company and later the National Theatre to rival the state-subsidized companies in Paris and Berlin. Never had there been such a cluster of star actors and actresses: Gielgud, Olivier, Richardson and Guinness, Edith Evans and Peggy Ashcroft. There were even playwrights among us who transformed the London theatre – Beckett, Osborne and Pinter. And the British cinema industry spluttered into prominence.

Yet as they grew older we shuddered. Tourism was destroying the sights, the landscape and the cities that they in their youth as travellers had known. Their mission to tell more people how the arts can delight and save was ending in their commercialization by promoters, sponsors and the market. The American syndrome crossed the Atlantic: to succeed painters and writers had to become celebrities and celebrity destroyed them as artists. Pessimism about the future settled like a cloud and seemed to inhibit, or at least darken, the imagination of the creators. It was different from the sulphurous cloud of rebellion against the present out of which came the iconoclasm of the pre-1914 modernist revolt with all the hope of building a new world. Perhaps future generations, viewing the second half of the twentieth century as a time of unparalleled wealth and peace for the western world, will wonder whether the pessimism was inspired by genuine concern for the luckless or by self-indulgence.

3

SCIENCE AND ART require money; and it was a matter of pride to Our Age that the budgets of the research councils and Keynes's brainchild the Arts Council increased in real terms under their influence. In order to do so the gross national product had to grow. Unfortunately we were more concerned with how wealth should be shared than produced.

Keynes had made a real revolution in the subject. He destroyed Say's law. Until then all economists had accepted what the great French eighteenth-century economist had expounded, namely that production always creates income which in turn creates demand. So total production and total demand must create maximum employment and hence there could never be persistent unemployment. Nor, given stable prices, could there be continuous inflation. Keynes said there could. He said that the national income had an equilibrium which was just as likely to be below full employment as to be equal to it. There could also be an equilibrium that came about through excess demand; and then there would be persistent inflation. That was why the state had to intervene to enable people to buy more goods and services: so the state spent more than it took in. Do that and full employment would follow. Conversely if people spent too much, the state would intervene to reduce their income. It would do this by raising taxes and reducing public expenditure so that inflation could be controlled.

Keynes convinced the economists of our generation that the government could manipulate the economy to control total demand – both current consumption and future investment. This was in effect what the government had done during the war. Governments liked to be told that it was good economic sense to spend more on welfare services as well as on defence; to lower taxes; to lower interest rates. The trouble was that governments did not like to be told that tax increases and cuts in public expenditure were needed to lower inflation: though that too was orthodox Keynesian economics. Nevertheless for twenty-five years some of his insights were applied; and maintained employment and a reasonably efficient welfare state.

Economics was a subject in which we considered we had no debts to pay to the Continent – or to America. No country held economists in higher esteem than Britain after the war, and our cohorts bristled with economists who advised the Treasury and individual ministries; were appointed to special agencies; and advised merchant banks and businesses. The post-war years came to be called the Keynesian era, but many who advised the Conservative governments in the fifties and early sixties were known for their differences with the left-wing Keynesians at Cambridge. John Hicks, Claud Guillebaud, Stanley Dennison and Dennis Robertson, who was a member of the royal commission on equal pay and on the council for prices, productivity and incomes (which in effect was devising an incomes policy), were regarded as the soul of orthodoxy.

By any standard our economists were formidable. Dick Stone, who devised the method for computing a nation's income and productivity, set up after the war a separate centre to teach the bureaucrats and students of other countries. Both he and James Meade won the Nobel Prize. Nicholas Kaldor should have won another for the work he did before the war at LSE; and Piero Sraffa, a refugee from Mussolini's fascist state, discarded the labour theory of value from Marx's criticism of capital and worked out his own growth model based on the production of commodities. Yet Keynesians would award the palm for originality to one who made his most pregnant contributions in seminar to the work of others rather than in his publications. Richard Kahn was called by Schumpeter the co-author of the *General Theory*. His manifesto of April 1932 six months later converted Keynes to Keynesianism, and he provided Keynes with the multiplier, the crucial concept in equilibrium theory. In the eighties some Italian economists dug up and published the dissertation which won him his fellowship at King's in 1929. Robin Marris declared that it contained the foundations of the theory of imperfect competition for which Kahn's close friend Joan Robinson was later to get the credit; and, even more important, it contained the foundations of the micro-economics that is missing from the *General Theory*. That omission was to weaken Keynes's reputation in the eighties.

The triumph of the Keynesians contained the seeds of their deterioration and indeed of economics in Britain. Both they and the orthodox often entangled themselves in advising Whitehall and international agencies. No wonder. Many had been civil servants during the war and emerged from Whitehall convinced *dirigistes*. A prolonged spell of bureaucratic life takes the edge off the intellect. Men and women emerge from it wiser, more adaptable and less hermetic, but not quite as sharp, not quite so *un*reasonable and therefore less disposed to question received wisdom, especially the received wisdom of their own group or of their contemporaries. The Cambridge Keynesians for the most part supported the Labour Party and were reluctant to question the party's policy. Joan Robinson and Nicholas Kaldor politicized the Cambridge faculty and it deteriorated. Keynesianism too deteriorated and was used to endorse a consensus formed by economists, journalists and intelligent politicians. As a result few of them protested in public against Labour's policy not to devalue in 1964 and 1966 despite the fact that practically all economists favoured that course. Nor did they challenge the received wisdom that to provide below-cost council houses was the best way of giving the poor homes. To argue that unemployment might enable the country to adjust to economic change, or encourage labour to become more mobile, or break the boredom of doing the same work, was regarded as obscurantist.

How high did inflation have to rise before it was thought too high a price to pay for full employment? If inflation wrecked the balance of payments, how high a price should be paid by interfering with international monetary levels in order to control the balance? The Keynesians became disillusioned when they saw the unions reject the incomes policy which the Keynesians believed to be in the long-term interests of organized labour. Richard Kahn said that in destroying incomes policy the unions had destroyed social democracy. British economists convinced themselves that the economy would grow so long as demand expanded and investors were given incentives. They forgot to investigate how far other factors – tariffs, progressive income taxation, regional economic development plans – hindered growth. British economists despised sociology. Had they been less insular and read Max Weber they would have learnt that it is not only the state and its welfare organizations that stagnate as they grow larger. Industry suffered the same paralysis as each executive hired a clever junior to do his thinking for him. Bureaucratization, no less than militant trade unionism, in the motor car industry nearly extinguished the Austin-Morris-Leyland-Jaguar conglomerate.

There was also a psychological reason why Keynes's very success undermined his theory. It was too attractive. The old orthodoxy descending from Alfred Marshall could not explain why investment in British industry was so low and unemployment between the wars so persistent. Keynes produced a new explanation, sufficiently difficult to baffle the old guard but sufficiently challenging to the young thrusters ready to convict their elders of senility. Paul Samuelson in America recalled how comforting it was for the young to know that they need no longer read the literature in the hope of giving a twist to some part of the orthodox theory. They revelled in disentangling savings and investments and relegating the ratio of money to income (the Marshallian *k*) to a minor part of liquidity preference. Keynes's ghost stood behind those who mocked the old guard. Had he not mocked the twitterings of the bankers and the City establishment, had he not besought us to trust in the superiority of reason over convention, had he not made Bloomsbury irreverence a mark of that superiority?

To be sniffy about Keynes's delight in his own brilliance and originality is to be mean-minded. He may have exaggerated the conflict between himself and the old orthodoxy: his one-time ally, Dennis Robertson, thought so.

But the conflict was genuine; and when his supporters – Roy Harrod at Oxford, Kahn and Kaldor at Cambridge – won the battle they were exultant. They established a new orthodoxy, and the next generation of young British economists realized that their careers depended on adhering to the theology. Some discovered a delightful dell impenetrable to most animals, the dell of model building. Watching Kaldor applying models for growth, Mark I with an engine designed by Pasinetti, Mark II with one designed by Mirlees, they turned from applying Keynesian remedies to the study of econometrics. Others, following their elders in imitating Keynes's manner, were too adept at caricaturing their opponents, too intent on producing brilliant solutions to problems of the kind that lent themselves to Keynesian solutions, to return to the intractable material of economic concepts. They forgot that for most of his life Keynes had been the leading theorist of money, and they wrote off their more pedestrian colleagues who were coming to disturbing conclusions.

These conclusions were in part, but by no means all, the work of the monetarists. Some members of the old guard, such as Devons at Manchester, had been disillusioned by their experience in the civil service of planning. But the most impressive critic of Keynes was the outstanding theoretical economist of Our Age. At Oxford John Hicks (with the Israeli professor Don Patinkin) was a seminal figure in the neo-classical movement that made fearful inroads into Keynes's view of the economy's equilibrium. He was regarded as a formidable foe by the Keynesians. ('I am turning in my grave,' said Joan Robinson, on hearing that Hicks had won the Nobel Prize.) There was, of course, also Lionel Robbins who was regarded as the leader of the old orthodoxy; but Robbins regarded his pre-war rejection of Keynes as one of the major errors of his life and he spent some time trying to build bridges between classical and Keynesian economics. Nevertheless it was in LSE that the opposition formed. Hayek had left it for Chicago soon after the war where he was joined in 1959 by the Canadian economist, Harry Johnson, who had been a fellow of King's but had left Cambridge tired of polemics. In 1966 he came back to LSE where he was a formidable opponent of the Cambridge Keynesians until he returned for good to Chicago and an early death. Another economist made his name as a sceptic of the planned economy and of the wisdom of giving aid to the Third World. This was Peter Bauer, as if to prove that not all refugees from Hungary were socialists like Balogh and Kaldor. There were Alan Prest and Alan Day; the economic historian and graduate of Chicago Bill Letwin; the political analyst Elie Kedourie; and, of a later generation, Kenneth Minogue. There is some competition for the credit of converting Keith Joseph to monetarism. One candidate was Alan Walters who predicted that Barber's budgets would bring hyper-inflation and was chief witness at the Conservative inquest on Heath's U-turn. Another, Ralph Harris, had learnt his economics at Cambridge not from the Keynesians but from their opponents, and was later to be chairman of the Institute for Economic Affairs. He was a tireless pamphleteer against the welfare state. There were others, too, who convinced Joseph and he in turn spoke to Margaret Thatcher's deepest instincts.

The essence of the monetarist reply was to restate quantity theory as a counter-concept to the multiplier. For long monetarism failed to convince politicians or civil servants because what it set out to cure – inflation – seemed so much less important than unemployment. It became a challenge to Keynesian policies when inflation reached double figures. Yet oddly enough it was their approach to the theory of money that confounded the monetarists. The new quantity theory of money ought to have provided a means for determining prices and output. It did not. It ought to have analysed how the supply side in economics responds to monetary fluctuations. It did not. It ought to have shown how monetary changes affected prices and quantities. In this it was only partially successful. Nicholas Kaldor himself used to joke that every time he was called by a foreign country to advise what changes should be made in its system of taxation, a revolution followed within a year or two. Much the same came to be true of Milton Friedman's advice except that in his case it was said that the government of the country he advised forestalled revolution by shooting or imprisoning its political opponents. Almost certainly the monetarist policies of Geoffrey Howe in 1981 exacerbated the trade recession and created a million more unemployed and more bankruptcies of industrial firms than would have been caused by the recession itself; and his successor at the Treasury no longer relied so heavily on the control of interest rates, bank deposits and money supply.

It will be long before economic historians are able to judge the issues between Keynes, Keynes's successors and Keynes's opponents. Kenneth Galbraith was convinced that Keynesian economics had not failed in Britain. What had failed was political will, political maturity. The trade unions would not practise restraint because government could not restrain prices. How was it that in Sweden, Switzerland, Austria and, more important still, in Germany and Japan, labour and capital managed to reach compromises and limited confrontation? Economists began, however, to recognize that the macro-economics debate was not the only one worth pursuing. Micro-economics was still important. As the economists of my generation retired the great visions of the past dissolved and were replaced by a myriad of models. Problem-model-solution became the new game; a games theory was used in these models to predict how management, labour and tax incentives would react in a given set of circumstances. Economics began at last to find competition in universities from hitherto rare departments of accountancy and business studies.

Nevertheless, as our economists retired, they faced a displeasing paradox. Why had Britain, famous for the fertility and energy of her theoretical economists, fared so badly in taking their advice when on the Continent where economists won little renown affairs prospered? Were economists, acting as consultants, less effective than entrepreneurs acting on a hunch? Both the Keynesians and the monetarists committed the same folly. They believed that their ideology revealed the truth instead of recognizing that no single set of economic propositions can encompass actuality. The Keynesians piled on controls; the monetarists rejoiced that non-intervention enabled them to avoid taking disagreeable decisions. Both forgot that Keynes was eclectic in policy, quite willing to change tack as the wind went round, both maddening and delightful in persuading you that the answer he gave yesterday was inapplicable to the conditions of today.

CHAPTER 19

How Our Age Discussed Morality

1

IN 1956 COLIN Wilson published a book called *The Outsider.* He had left school at sixteen and was a casual labourer, at times sleeping rough on Hampstead Heath. He wanted to illustrate the varieties of people who cannot endure the world as it is. Wilson called as witnesses Barbusse, Dostoevsky, Nietzsche, Wells, Kierkegaard, T.E. and D.H. Lawrence, Nijinsky, Berdyaev, Gurdjiev, Radakrishna and Ouspensky – but then whom did he not call? His book won a rapturous reception from the Sunday reviewers, Cyril Connolly leading the applause. There was an ominous silence in the academic world; and none of the sixty-two books Wilson published in the next thirty-odd years was ever reviewed in this way. Why was it such a popular success?

Nothing will ever stop people demanding large-scale explanations of the world. Religion supplied some of them: MacNeile Dixon's Gifford lectures *The Human Condition,* Reinhold Niebuhr's *Moral Man and Immoral Society,* C.S.Lewis's *Screwtape Letters.* There were interesting theological disquisitions from Ian Ramsay, reminders abroad from Barth of the terrible images of the Christian faith, billowing clouds of transcendental philosophy from Tillich in America who assured us that it was as atheistic to affirm the existence of God as to deny it. If God is so difficult to know and hence to love, should we not obey the second commandment at Holy Communion which is at least clear – to love one's neighbour as oneself?

Thus began a transformation of the Christian message. The liver and lungs were torn out of the old theology leaving the heart still beating. Compassion came from the heart, judgement disappeared. Personal evil and wickedness were no longer so sinful. Iago became a regimental sergeant major, sickened by drunken officers and a posturing general, who went rather too far in his plans to take both down a peg or two; Goneril and Regan, daughters driven beyond endurance by the extravagance of their mad old father and his yobbo knights. If each of us is the child of our genes, neuroses and repressions, is it not both selfish and otiose to concern ourselves with our own personal salvation – in any case a problematical affair since belief in a corporeal resurrection seems to have fallen on evil days? We should therefore concern ourselves with the poor at home and the plight of the Third World abroad. Compassion demands that we do not judge others as individuals. But we do and should judge others when they act as part of authority.

All the churches, Rome as well as the Protestant communities, heard this call and we witnessed the reorientation of Christian faith. Pope John's Vatican Council was as astonishing a phenomenon as Gorbachev's pronouncement that the Soviet state must be restructured; and the speed at which subsequent popes and the curia worked to contain the turbulence suggested that the guardians of the faith in the Soviet Union would also try to minimize the consequences. But the clergy, Catholic and Protestant alike, were transformed. In England the Conservative party could hardly believe their eyes when their oldest ally, with whom they had worked as partners since the Restoration of Charles II, could no longer be relied on. Salisbury sat in amazement when the bishops voted for sanctions against Rhodesia, Margaret Thatcher in cold rage when archbishops rebuked her for cutting subsidies to the poor and aid to the Third World.

Religion no longer gave us a large-scale explanation of life. Did philosophy? Was this the reason why Colin Wilson delved among speculative minds and why his public responded? The philosophers of Our Age were fortunate to inherit an urban estate which their predecessors had been clearing. At the turn of the century there had been considerable speculation on the site. There were some long-established families in possession of some of the apartments. Some were old, tottering intuitionists of the Church of England, though the more spry theologians had bought lodgings from the proceeds of their investment in Kant; and a few daring agnostics were trading under the name of Hegel. There was keen popular interest in the speculators. A liberal cabinet minister, Haldane, was known to be an Hegelian, a man who kept up with the new physics and urged his countrymen to research into atomic energy. The recent Conservative prime minister, Balfour, had written a work on the foundations of belief. One speculator, T.H.Green, had been portrayed in *Robert Elsmere* and another, F.C.S.Schiller, was to appear in *Sinister Street.* Philosophy gave answers to great questions. Had God finally been slain? Had the Absolute replaced him? What picture of the universe had the physicists painted?

And then Bertrand Russell redefined logic. The greatest logician since Occam, the most original British philosopher and finest writer of abstract prose since Hume, Russell transformed philosophy by a series of contributions of which the most decisive perhaps was his great paper in 1908 on descriptive functions. His little gem, a Home University Library book *The Problems of Philosophy* (1912), made his work accessible to the layman who now learnt that the object of philosophy was to ask questions rather than supply answers: questions that discredited authoritarians and suggested new possibilities in life. We must get rid of accepted opinions unless we can show that they are founded in logic or in empirical evidence. The urban estate soon presented a sorry spectacle. Outside their apartments sat former tenants – clergymen, metaphysicians, sages and political theorists – whom Russell, the bailiff, had evicted on the ground they were in illegal possession. Naturally the evictions took time. At Cambridge the Hegelian John M'Taggart was soon out on the pavement; and when the Wittgenstein of the *Tractatus* returned to Cambridge after the Great War philosophy was on the way to becoming an activity not an explanation of life. The search for clarity and truth was so severe and so much was discarded that one of the earliest philosophers of Our Age, Frank Ramsey, the brother of the future archbishop – he died at the age of twenty-six – wrote a paper entitled 'Is There Anything to Discuss?'

Wittgenstein towered over the other philosophers at Cambridge. He magnetized his listeners. He shut out every person or thing when he tried to turn his rumination into utterance, and his agony at the inadequacy of his utterance was painful to watch. For him philosophy was not a profession or an academic job. It resembled a familiar who wrestled with him, tripped him up, mocked him and never left his side. 'Of one thing I am certain,' he once said. 'We are not here in order to have a good time.' His silences and fits and starts of speech as he struggled to weld his thoughts together defied anyone to scoff, and such was his charisma that his gestures – the same groping for words and the same stammer – were copied by his pupils.

His philosophy rejected assurance: it consisted of endless self-rejection, endless heuristic enquiry, endless search which ended in blind alleys. He was still the man who made inexhaustible and exhausting demands on his colleagues: before the Great War he had demanded that the regulations for a Cambridge doctorate must be changed at once for him and believed Moore and Russell were prevaricating when they said they could not change them. I once saw him seize a poker and thought he would strike Richard Braithwaite with it when convicting him of error. When he left a room he continued to haunt it. He had already begun in the thirties to move away from the position he held in the *Tractatus.* He no longer saw propositions as pictures and philosophy consisting of the analysis of these pictures. He now saw propositions as instruments which could be put to different use. Their use was governed by rules just as games were defined by their rules. Different games had different rules; and that was why we had to discover what the rules were when we used words. What are the rules, for example, for praying? Philosophy was no longer concerned with proof of argument. Russell's search for the limits of human knowledge was futile. Knowledge sprawled and could not be made to stand to attention. There was no such thing as a 'correct' or scientific language or a 'rational' way of ordering things.

Wittgenstein said of himself 'I am not a religious man, but I cannot help seeing every problem from a religious point of view.' He admired St Augustine's *Confessions,* he admired Cowper and Blake. (In that he resembled Leavis; but unlike Leavis he enjoyed *Tristram Shandy*.) To him prayer, dogma, even the conception of an all-powerful God ('It would be my duty to defy him') were not at the heart of religion. At its heart was the commandment to live a better life. He was the finest kind of puritan and his fierceness echoed through Cambridge lecture rooms. It upset an unworthy Kantian, imported by error to Cambridge, who referred while lecturing to the writings of Dawes Hickes. 'We don't want to know what Dawes Hickes said,' came a voice from the audience. 'We want the truth.' Wittgenstein cared so much for the truth that towards the end of his life he would not write down what he thought it might be. So his ideas were circulated by his disciples in *samizdat* form, and it was not until after his death in 1951 that his *Philosophical Investigations* were published.

It took longer to evict the old guard at Oxford, and all through the time our generation went to university the battle there raged. A few dons remained Idealists, others called themselves realists and fell back once again on intuition – we know that God exists as we know two and two make four. The redoubtable H.W.B. Joseph questioned Russell's mathematical logic and made a fool of himself trying to refute Einstein's theory of relativity. There was more at stake in Oxford. Philosophy was at the heart of the most famous of all Oxford schools, Lit. Hum. or Greats. It was also integral to PPE or Modern Greats: in the eyes of Sandie Lindsay and others who had founded this school philosophy existed to tell us what good ends we should try to attain in politics, just as economics existed to explain what political decisions had to be taken to maximize wealth and distribute it fairly.*

But philosophy at Oxford was also about to experience a revolution. In 1867 Daniel Masson wrote: 'It is Mill that our young thinkers at the universities, our young shepherds on the mountains, consult, and quote and swear by.' Eighty years later the young shepherds were to quote and swear by A.J. Ayer. Russell had his differences with Ayer whose logical positivism was inspired by Carnap and the Vienna Circle. He had his doubts about Ayer's famous verification principle, but he regarded Ayer as an ally and angel of light; and Ayer revered Russell. Ayer was not an original philosopher, but he was an indefatigable advocate and controversialist of exceptional lucidity. Ayer did not make philosophy a religious experience like Wittgenstein. He made it fun. Wittgenstein had said in the *Tractatus*, 'the right method in philosophy is to wait until someone says something metaphysical, then show them it's nonsense', and similarly Ayer invited the young to do so. What could be more enjoyable than to astonish the unenlightened by showing them

* At Cambridge an embryo Modern Greats called moral science had formed in the nineteenth century but Alfred Marshall broke it up when he got economics set up as a separate technical subject, and the moral sciences dwindled into the pursuit of pure philosophy. Oxford had shown its true colours when Lindsay opposed a proposal to establish a Science Greats combining philosophy with science. The defeat of this proposal led Sidgwick at Cambridge (whom Lindsay despised as an arid utilitarian) to say, 'Philosophy in Oxford on which more intellect, time and money are spent than in any other university, with less result, will remain uncontaminated by any contact with reality, and will continue to interpret the facts of nature not as they are, but as they were believed to be a century ago.' The difference between the two universities in pre-1914 days could not have been better illustrated.

that the sentences they used were meaningless? To be a philosopher, Ayer suggested, was important – and not only philosophers enjoy being told that. The young felt they had clawed their way through woolly curtains and now saw Shelley plain. Philosophy, as Gilbert Ryle said, was to be 'talk about talk'. Language was no longer something you used without thinking about it. What impressed the young was Ayer's candour. If someone found defects in his model – and all philosophers use models and defend them – he would rejig it instead of prevaricating. He came to admit that he had never quite found the right form for his verification principle or met the criticisms Wisdom and others made of his analysis about how much we could know of other people's minds. The young also admired him for being an uninhibited Labour supporter who liked parties, girls, good company and disliked old boys, good form and priests.

The young philosophers at Oxford before the war – Austin, Ayer, Gilbert Ryle (Ayer's tutor), Stuart Hampshire, Peter Strawson, Herbert Hart and Isaiah Berlin – were to carry all before them. Lindsay's departure from Oxford shortly after the war to found the new University of Keele was symbolic. And so there began to form at Oxford a singular concatenation of talent among the younger members of Our Age: Dummett, Gardiner, Hare, Pears, Quinton, Strawson, Urmson, Warnock, Wiggins and Williams. The centre of analytic philosophy moved from Cambridge to Oxford.

But there was another move which was also symbolic. It symbolized a rift in the camp of the analytic philosophers. Ayer left Oxford to go to the chair at University College London taking Richard Wollheim with him. There he was to complement Karl Popper at LSE, the hammer of scientism and historicism who had arrived via New Zealand on his pilgrimage from Vienna. The rift was caused by John Austin who in pre-war days had been Ayer's rival at Oxford. During the war Austin had been Eisenhower's expert on the German order of battle. He liked to play Bach's unaccompanied violin partitas at home and resembled in appearance an inscrutable crane, bald-headed and angular. Like Moore he was a performer, unsparing in debate, austere. Whereas the positivists thought the most meaningful kind of discourse was scientific, Austin and the linguistic philosophers thought there were many kinds of discourse, and the business of a philosopher was to explain how they worked. Once you had analysed what the problem was that made a particular kind of discourse necessary – for instance, why do people need religion? – the problem, so it became fashionable to say, was not 'solved but dissolved'. When you discovered how language worked, when you disentangled one question from another, you found that many of the traditional questions in philosophy had disappeared. Unlike Ayer Austin did not argue from fixed principles such as the verification principle or sense-datum language. He would have nothing to do with the attempt to create a logically perfect language that reflected reality. Isaiah Berlin gave an instance of his approach – and he caught the tone of Austin's voice to perfection – when he asked Austin what he should do when arguing with a child who wanted to meet Napoleon. What if the child, answering all Berlin's explanations that it was impossible, kept on saying 'Why not?' Should one then say to the child that it had confused the material and formal modes in our language usage? Austin replied, 'Do not speak so. Tell the child to try to go back into the past. Tell it there is no law against it. Let it try. Let it try and see what happens then.'

If anyone thinks philosophy had got lost in a wilderness of pedantry, he should read Berlin's incomparable essay on what it was like to listen before the war to Ayer and Austin in discussion – 'Ayer like an irresistible missile, Austin like an immovable object' – Ayer advancing under the shield of his sense-data terminology, Austin peppering it with objections – Ayer changing his premises under these arrows and buckling on a new shield, only once again to be met with slashes and thrusts until he turned on Austin and said, 'You are like a greyhound who doesn't want to run himself, and bites the other greyhounds so they cannot run either.' Yet Berlin admitted that the Oxford philosophers were, perhaps, excessively self-centred, believing that no one outside the magic circle of Oxford, Cambridge and Vienna had much to teach them. The linguistic philosophers delighted in making distinctions but it was not all that clear why these distinctions were of interest or importance. You did not have to know anything now to be a philosopher; you had only to be clever and sincere. Naturally this appealed to the post-war generation who had to catch up for the years they had lost. Observers joked about a new age of scholasticism and recalled the days when monks calculated how many angels could stand on the point of a pin. (In fact they never did: any more than any medieval scholastic held that the earth was flat though they did believe it was the fixed centre of the universe.)

Austin and the linguistic philosophers at Oxford were to be taken to task by the man who began it all. At a great age Russell in 1959 denounced Oxford as the home of triviality and – like Sidgwick long ago – as a place where science and thinking scientifically was treated with contempt. He supported Ayer in regarding positivism as central to philosophy. But he went further. He wrote an introduction to a book by Ernest Gellner at the LSE who spoke of the 'mincing affectations' and 'donnish artificiality' of Ryle and Wittgenstein. *Words and Things* caused great offence and the air resounded to cries of 'Gellner, leave the house'. He did, in fact, leave it for anthropology. And yet there was something prophetic about Gellner's intervention. When we came to retire the subject was not in the same flourishing state as it was when Ayer first wrote. The impetus had gone.

Our generation had made philosophy popular in the fifties and sixties as it certainly is not today. Richard Wollheim recalled the continual discussion on the Third Programme of philosophical issues that Niouta Kallin and T.G.Gregory initiated. This was the philosophy which on Ayer's death was denounced as superficial, sterile and paltry. When Stuart Hampshire wrote his paperback in 1951 on Spinoza it sold forty thousand copies in three months. As our philosophers grew older they were more willing to follow Hampshire's lead and began again to study Kant, Plato, Aristotle and even Hegel through his English disciple F.H. Bradley. They studied the concepts of the classic philosophers – how they had approached the perennial problems, such as that of 'other minds'. They did not defect and become Kantians or Hegelians. Only a few months before he died Ayer asked someone who had quoted a sentence of Heidegger what it meant. Like a destroyer that had sailed within range of a battleship, the fellow turned away making smoke. The ideas of the German Renaissance pounded in vain on the sea wall of analytic philosophy. Marxists re-examined certain dogmas in their theology; Nietzsche in particular concerned historians of ideas; but the analytic philosophers considered the rigour of their own enquiries a better education than the dubious word-multiplication of the phenomenologists.

2

AS THEY LOOKED back at their youth a few among us – men of affairs no longer much given to the delights of pure speculation – blamed the logical positivists for dismissing ethics as nonsense: had this not led to the decline – well, not of the British Empire, but of respect for decency, duty, authority etc.? Nothing could be less true. We discussed ethics throughout our life with singular vigour. Nearly all the moral philosophers were utilitarians in the English tradition; and no wonder for the welfare state was itself an essay in utilitarianism. The dilemma over a century old still remained. How do we persuade people that the greatest happiness of the greatest number is identical with their own happiness? Or, alternatively, how do we persuade individuals that their own self-interest lies in agreeing to do things which at first sight may appear to be against their own desires? Richard Hare began by arguing that most of the objections to utilitarianism sprang from hard cases (which make bad law) or from attempts to show the greatest happiness principle does not work in every possible situation. And what alternative was there? Did you really want to surrender your critical judgement on what was right or wrong to the metaphysicians or to Sartrean confusions? Accept Marx's objectives if you wish; after all, he too accepted the greatest happiness principle. But if you do, you must understand that the marxists decline to discuss concepts or arguments and are more dogmatic than the metaphysicians. So why not call in the analytical philosophers? They resemble plumbers. The difference between the plumber and the person whose plumbing he had come to mend was that he had a bag of tools. But for these tools he would probably be worse at the job than the politician or civil servant who was having to deal with such problems most days of the week.

Hare was echoing Moore: get rid of the confusions, misconceptions and contradictions of previous philosophers and you are on your way to wisdom. Unfortunately there are few analyses of problems that are so simple and clear that either the problems disappear or can be said to be incapable of further definition. So instead of asking, 'What do you exactly mean . . . ?' the utilitarians became more sophisticated. The pursuit of pleasure was surely a very vulgar ideal. No theory of personal morality could be based on that. So one no longer talked of pleasure and pain or even good states of mind. One asked how we fulfil our desires, those that are personal to us as well as those that are altruistic. How can we enable people to get what they prefer and how do we judge what the consequences of our actions will be? But almost before they began to revise utilitarianism they faced a new set of clients, a horde of dissatisfied groups – women, black citizens, late developers, the mentally handicapped and the disadvantaged of all kinds.

The spokesmen for these groups looked across the Atlantic. They found in the American Constitution a justification for taking action on behalf of the disadvantaged. The Constitution spoke of rights. Two political theorists in America, Robert Nozick and John Rawls, both appealed to rights. Nozick spoke up for freedom. He said we had the right to be free to exchange our goods with other people until this created such enormous inequities that the state, as with anti-trust laws, was obliged to intervene. Rawls spoke up for fairness. He said the freedom to exchange goods had to be limited to the point where the least advantaged were given most. To orthodox utilitarians there was not a penny to choose between them in logic. Had not Bentham said rights were nonsense 'and natural rights nonsense on stilts'? What were rights but the age-old intuitions of the metaphysicians? What these modern seducers were doing was to make noble statements pleasing to right-thinking men but unsupported by evidence.

Nevertheless rights all the time gained ground as the primary concept in politics. It was bound to do so as people became more conscious of belonging to ethnic groups or pressure groups. Rights were a weapon against central government exercised by a political party acting as an 'elected dictatorship'. Rights reared their head in law, a subject which Our Age scarcely recognized since its practitioners were so uninterested in general ideas. No one who read law ever doubted the subtlety of English lawyers. But the common law, the entrancing task of citing case against case and countering an obiter by a chief justice against a judgement by a law lord, had not given much of a welcome to jurisprudence. It was a philosopher of our generation who changed this. Herbert Hart had the impertinence to bring moral concepts into play with legal concepts, and his encounter with the Roman Catholic law lord, Patrick Devlin, revived jurisprudence – until that time moribund in England. His successor in the Oxford chair took matters far further and indeed repudiated Hart's positivist jurisprudence. Ronald Dworkin came from

America where the Supreme Court can overrule President and Congress, where gradu- ate law schools are real centres of disputation, and where – as in the title of one of Dworkin's books – they take rights seriously. Dworkin considered the individual owes moral duties to others. He in turn is endowed with certain rights and has rights against the state. Not only must he be given a fair hearing, but the law must be interpreted to enforce moral principles. The judge must accept the existence of rights. That does not mean that judges can make what decisions seem to them fit about welfare, i.e. public policy. But they should make such decisions on matters of principle, i.e. the moral rights of individuals. The women who protested at Greenham Common against nuclear missiles had no case: whether nuclear weapons should or should not be deployed is a matter of policy. But to disrupt any institution that allows racial or sexual discrimination can be justified because the policy of segregation infringes the rights of others.

This reopened a familiar controversy. Did you favour before the war the liberal, if erratic, Mr Justice McCardie or the judge who time and again overruled him, Lord Justice Scrutton? Did you sympathize after the war with Denning or Simonds? Should a judge ever interpret the law to bring it into accord with modern practice and *mentalités*. Or must a judge state what the law is, even though he may think it unjust and outdated? Dworkin argued that a judge cannot interpret law without making a political decision however hard he must try to be neutral: there is no distinction between 'is' and 'ought'. A judge cannot guess what those who made a law intended: law cannot be discovered, it can only be invented. That was what outraged his critics. They maintained that the judge had to decide what the law is, not what it ought to be, just as an umpire has to enforce the rules and cannot alter them. It is this that protects the citizen against arbitrary government, it is this which enables him to know what the law is and safeguards his rights. It distinguishes authority from power.

Dworkin intended that his theory of law should benefit minorities and the disadvantaged. Indeed he argued that the rights of minorities should prevail against the goals of the majority. Homosexuals may be detested but their rights are as valid as anyone else's. Pornography must not be banned: to do so violates moral independence. Since a judge must, whether he likes it or not, be interpreting the law according to a theory of politics, it is essential that that theory is one which puts the highest priority on giving validity to rights and treating human beings as equals. He should therefore be suspicious of appeals to the law as the guarantor of private property or freedom of contract in a market economy.

What made his opponents chatter with rage was his contention that the law stood on one side and morality on the other. They replied that there was indeed a dichotomy. But the dichotomy was between what Dworkin thought was moral and the morality of the rule of law, which is the best barrier an individual has to protect himself against tyranny. When in opposition, Quintin Hailsham had called the astonishing constitutional power of Parliament and the executive an elective dictatorship. When he became lord chancellor he served in a government which many of Our Age considered was an excellent example of what he had feared. The most splendid and notorious Liberal among the law lords, Leslie Scarman, urged the passage through Parliament of a bill of rights. Many of his generation agreed with him. A few, like myself, regarded his remedy for a legitimate concern as likely to provide a paradise for lawyers under a system of common law.

But those who were sceptical of the argument from rights found utilitarianism, the other theoretical defence against arbitrary government, in no better shape. Just how sick utilitarianism as a moral theory had become was evident when a young philosopher at All Souls' came up with an ingenious explanation why we should not mind sacrificing our own interests for others. We don't exist. Human beings had no individual identity – they consist of a series of experiences. Why blame a person for breaking a promise when he is not really the same person as the one who made it? The fertility of Derek Parfitt's examples, the recklessness of his attack on common-sense views about human personality (on which traditional morality is based), won high praise from some philosophers of Our Age. Philosophy now began to resemble the French novel after Robbe-Grillet had abolished the identity of characters, authors and readers. Had not Diderot argued that the self is divided and drawn his portrait of Rameau's nephew whose self spoke with two voices? Since each of us plays many roles, how can we argue that there is one authentic self? Daniel Bell reminded us that modernism, which Hegel foresaw, sunders ethics and politics, law and morality, and proclaimed that art and morality are not constants governed by laws but explorations in which the sole duty is always to go on, go further. Parfitt was certainly dutiful.

Parfitt put altruism first. The subtlest and most subversive philosopher of Our Age put egoism first. Richard Wollheim rejected Parfitt's contention that a person is a bundle of mental and bodily states. When I want to achieve this or that, I think of myself and my life as a unity. Wollheim started from the familiar revisionist standpoint that the pursuit of pleasure in itself was trivial and dispiriting. Utilitarianism would never be reputable to those who care for the finer qualities in life unless individual utility takes precedence over the utility of others. People imagine if we follow our own self-interest we shall hurt others; and therefore they bring in a code of morality (whether or not disguised under the pretence that it is promoting the greatest happiness of the greatest number) to restrain our mistaken or selfish actions. But long ago Saint Augustine told us it was futile to imagine that by an act of will alone we could discipline ourselves: the sanctions of church and state were needed to force men to control their passions – particularly their sexual passions. And did not Freud too deny that will and passion, morality and instinct, are separate entities? The only energy available to the will is the energy of the passions. So morality narrowly conceived is entwined with another process, hostile to it – the cultivation of our individuality. If morality tries to act like a policeman or a priest, it impoverishes, enfeebles and destroys individuality. To judge others is arrogant and presumptuous: the only person a man can judge is himself; and even so he is better employed in 'self-concern' or living for the future. Moral obligation is a form of persecution anxiety, and concern for good or evil a form of depressive anxiety. Follow your instincts, then, before you consult the utility of others. As a version of utilitarianism for the permissive society it could not be bettered: but consideration for the utility of others, for even another solitary individual, seems to have vanished. Wollheim seemed to be leading a private crusade to abolish morality from personal relations while retaining the right to be as censorious as he pleased about political matters.

Richard Wollheim's critique was in fact a plan to incorporate within utilitarianism the kind of moral insight that is part and parcel of the novel. He cited the *Princesse de Clèves* as a reverie on the theme of truth-telling. The princess's devotion to truth that made her confess to her husband her love for the Duc de Nemours destroys her. For now that her husband is dead it makes her tell Nemours that their love, and indeed her life, is at an end. Her seeming faithfulness to her husband's memory and the guilt she feels for his death are not the sole explanations of her conduct. Her truthfulness was a device for placing a bad part of herself within him and, now that he is buried, she can reincorporate that bit of herself only by joining him in death. By bringing in Freud Wollheim reiterated his belief that old-fashioned judgements about conduct were simply out of date.

Bernard Williams too warned us to be cautious of judging others and not to trust a single technique in weighing morality. Williams welcomed people who were impulsive and by their very lack of balance and forethought enriched the lives of those about them. But how fearful it would be if everyone acted in this fashion. Some people, Williams wrote, have moral luck. The more we observe people the more we see that some who are weak and evil are not all that far removed from those who are weak and virtuous – and unimaginative. But evil is not always banal. Bureaucrats may fail to realize the evil they are inflicting but there are other officials who torture people for pleasure, not merely to keep their foot on the ladder to promotion. And we have seen how Bernard Williams turned against utilitarianism and appealed to Aristotle to restore some of the moral concepts, such as honour and mercy, that had been banished by the utilitarians.

The efforts of economists and social investigators as well as philosophers to rarefy and purify the philosophy they had inherited from Bentham, Mill and Sidgwick remind one of the efforts of the schoolmen in the fourteenth century. Aquinas had reconciled faith with reason, but Duns Scotus, Thomas

Bradwardine and Occam, in magnificent displays of reasoning within the confines of their *mentalité*, drove reason and faith apart again and made men despair that any advance would be made by using the methods and categories of the schoolmen.

The moral philosophers, who had evicted the metaphysicians and other impostors from the apartments allotted to them on the urban estate, settled down in one of them for a prolonged seminar on their use. At the end of it they found the rest of the apartments occupied by a new set of intruders. These were the literary critics. The critics belonged to the one original movement in the humanities which we invented. For utilitarians the primary ethical concept was the goodness of a state of affairs and the rightness of actions was secondary. The literary critics reverted to a religious view of ethics in which the primary question was 'What is it my duty to do, how should we live?' The answers to these questions, they said, were to be found in literature.

3

IN 1927 FORSTER delivered the Clark Lectures in Cambridge on 'Aspects of the Novel'. It was not the first occasion that Bloomsbury showed what they took to be the function of criticism. Strachey and Virginia Woolf had been contributing articles and reviews for long to the periodicals and in 1914 Strachey had written a revealing piece on Arnold. There was much in Arnold that Bloomsbury might have admired. Like Arnold, Bloomsbury enjoyed shocking received opinion. Like Arnold, they saw themselves as an elite, standing as a counter-balance to the country's political rules; and from this sprang such institutions as the BBC that were effective barriers to populism. Like Arnold, they believed in spreading sweetness and light as Keynes did when he laid the foundations of the Arts Council. But they rejected Arnold's theory of criticism. They rejected his contention that the supreme duty of the critic was to discriminate and judge. Victorian criticism, wrote Strachey, seemed to be concerned with anything but literature. What are we to make of Leslie Stephen's cool observation that, as he was uninterested in Donne's poetry, he would write about his life? And then there was Arnold saying that poetry was a criticism of life, and praising the criticism of life made by Dante and Milton. But what about Sappho, Catullus and Pope (who certainly gave us a criticism of life)? Arnold ignored them. In Bloomsbury's view criticism consisted in seeing what made the author tick, what distinguished his work from other work and gave it singularity. Judgement entered in only so far as the critic might be expected to set the work in question against his own urbane rationalism. If Bloomsbury can be said to have had a theory of criticism, it was deference to the artist coupled with an amused appreciation of the infinite peculiarities of human behaviour which defied the attempts of moralists to tape it and square it and tie it neatly into bundles with bows and labels.

It was not surprising that Bloomsbury held such a theory of criticism. It sprang directly from the manifestoes of modernism. Bloomsbury had no love for conservatoires or salons or academies. Arnold had a profound reverence for the French Academy, a body, said Strachey, 'which has consistently ignored every manifestation of genius'; and no doubt the annual exhibitions at the Royal Academy gave him exquisite satisfaction. But were not the worst enemies of literature the so-called scholars of literature at the universities, men who spent years of work trying to prove Racine inferior to Shakespeare or, more likely, avoiding any discussion of their poetry as such and taking refuge in philology or, like Cazamian, in historical exegesis? Certainly this was true in Britain. The departments of English at British universities before the Great War studied philology, Anglo-Saxon and the history of literature and language. At Oxford the decision not to include any author later than the early Romantics in the examination syllabus was perhaps a mark of respect for the views of the Victorian professor of history, Freeman, who said he did not want undergraduates to study 'chatter about Shelley'. W.P.Ker and R.W.Chambers at University College London used Freeman's very words to defend the syllabus there.

But in the 1920s a new faculty of English at Cambridge was established with a syllabus which did not compel students to learn Anglo-Saxon or to study genres and influences. It ranged over the whole of English literature to the present day and related it to the literature of Greece and Rome and to the English Moralists. It enabled a student to consider the theory of criticism from Aristotle to Eliot. The dons were determined from the first to meet the gibes of Bloomsbury that the last thing professors of literature ever asked themselves was why poetry and novels touch the heart. One or two of the faculty were genuine eccentrics, such as Chadwick and Manny Forbes, idiosyncratic and unpredictable in the way they taught. In 1922 the most original mind among them, I.A.Richards, published the first of his works on literary criticism. Richards has been guyed for wanting to turn criticism into a science by measuring poems by the number of 'appetencies' they satisfied. In fact he soon gave that up. He handed those attending his lectures a sheet of a dozen poems and asked them to say who they thought the poet was and what the poem meant. The results were startling. There was not the faintest agreement about the meaning of any poem. A greeting to Meredith on his birthday was confidently asserted to be a Cavalier drinking song. Most people, he concluded, could not construe their own language because their minds were filled with preconceptions and what he called stock responses. The close reading of the text Richards demanded he called Practical Criticism, better known in America as the New Criticism.

Richards was not alone in reinterpreting criticism. In 1920 he had sought out a poet whose verse had excited him and suggested he join the faculty at Cambridge. T.S.Eliot declined, and in that year brought out his own work of literary criticism. From then on in almost every year during the twenties a work of criticism from either Eliot or Richards appeared. *The Sacred Wood* introduced a new tone and new judgements into criticism. Many young intellectuals were hypnotized by the arcane references; the high manner Eliot had learnt from F.H.Bradley; the immediate judgement offered as a truth beyond question; the scattering of obiter dicta without much concern whether the reader picked them up or not; the new concepts of 'objective correlative' and 'dissociation of sensibility'; and, above all, the seriousness and concern for poetry by the finest of the modernists.

Eliot and Richards were to change the reading public's taste in poetry. They put the ambiguous, complex, intellectual, ironic poem above simple lyrics. Such poetry meant more than it said on the surface. Poetry was not magic and beyond analysis; it was only through analysis that one could respond to it sincerely. 'Sincerity' and 'honesty' were two words that were often on Richards's lips. He condemned the preciousness of the nineties and the bookmen: Pater was wrong to rhapsodize about the moments of ecstasy that art can induce. Richards hated pedantry as much as preciousness – literary history, the work of grammarians – and late in life Chomsky's linguistics. To read poetry should be to form lasting habits and dispositions in the way we feel.

Is poetry magic? Richards did not pass unchallenged. In 1933 A.E.Housman delivered in Cambridge a lecture on 'The Name and Nature of Poetry.' For the first time the austere classical scholar and poet was going to speak about a subject on which he had always refused to say a word and the Senate House was packed to the gallery. Housman did not bother to refute the new literary criticism. He simply pronounced that poetry could not be analysed. He had a test for a poetic line: if such a line strayed into his mind while shaving his beard bristled and blunted the blade. As the audience dispersed Ivor Richards was heard to say, 'It will take us experts ten years to undo the damage he's done.' But there were some who agreed with Housman. In 1928 George Rylands published a commentary on Mallarmé's answer to Degas. Degas had complained that his sonnets would not come out right, yet he was full of excellent ideas. 'My dear Degas, poetry is not written with ideas, it is written with words.' It was the exact choice of words, Rylands said, with their echoes, ambiguities, associations, harmonies, cadences and sometimes their magic, that distinguished the poetic from the banal. For if not – if content is the criterion – how is it that poets centuries later still move our hearts when they repeat the ideas, yes the platitudes, about life and death, existence and destiny that were uttered by the poets of ancient Greece and Rome?

Some of the thoroughfares that the dons chose turned out to be blind alleys, like Eustace Tillyard's division of poetry into direct and oblique. But the dons of the English faculty in the twenties lived in the same state of excitement as the physicists in the Cavendish. They saw themselves discovering a new theory of criticism that was concerned not with judgement and pontification but with appreciation and response to works of art. A few of the cleverest undergraduates began to read the subject and astonish their teachers. Richards described what happened when he found himself supervising the one who was to be his most brilliant pupil.

> As he was at Magdalene this made me his Director of Studies. He seemed to have read more English literature and to have read it more recently and better, so our roles were soon in danger of being reversed. At about his third visit, he brought up the games of interpretation which Laura Riding and Robert Graves had been playing with an unpunctuated form of 'The expense of spirit in a waste of shame'. Taking the sonnet as a conjurer takes his hat, he produced an endless stream of lively rabbits from it, ending by, 'You could do that with any poetry, couldn't you?' This was godsend to a Director of Studies, so I said, 'You'd better go and do it, hadn't you?' A week later he was still slapping away at it on his typewriter. Would I mind if he just went on with that? Not a bit. The following week here he was with a thick wad of very illegible typescript under his arm – the central thirty thousand words or so of the book.

Such was the genesis of William Empson's *Seven Types of Ambiguity*. Empson was the most remarkable technical critic among Our Age: a poet himself inspired by the metaphysical poets he loved, a skirmisher who enjoyed defending impossible positions and waging prodigious battles against Milton for believing in God, a man who, like Coleridge, believed in the power of the imagination to reconcile opposites and who was touched with Coleridge's originality and dottiness. Great literature alone concerned him, and the only discriminations he made were in his selection of passages to illuminate a poet.

The revolution in literary criticism had little influence on kindred subjects in the humanities. It was applied by Martin Turnell to French studies, and by Peter Stern to Germanistik, but this was exceptional. In classics it had hardly any influence at all. This was another field in which British scholars now led the world, and they continued the austere tradition of Housman. Denys Page, Hugh Lloyd Jones and Geoffrey Kirk showed that editions and interpretations of texts and inscriptions now had to be undertaken in the light of numismatic and archaeological evidence. (Perhaps the event which most caught the literary public's imagination was a young architect's deciphering of the Linear B Script.) We proved to be at least as competent as its predecessors in carrying on British Museum scholarship – the scholarly interpretation of ancient civilizations.

Nevertheless, after 1945, the new mode of literary criticism began to penetrate departments of English throughout the country. One after another, departments which had hitherto taught literature in terms of its history and genres capitulated. But already in the thirties Cambridge criticism was disturbed by one of its practitioners who would not play the game of pluralism. When Richards had asked his audience what the poems before them had meant, he had asked a further question. Did they think them good or bad? Once you asked *that* question you had to be clear what your criteria were for saying so – especially when Richards's audience thought Longfellow superior to Hardy, and preferred Ella Wheeler Wilcox and an army chaplain known as Woodbine Willie to Hopkins and Christina Rossetti. Eliot had proposed a revaluation of English poetry, but how was that to be justified if you lacked Eliot's authority to declare that Dante was superior to Shakespeare? It was inevitable that someone would systematize the revaluation. One of the younger dons at Cambridge and his wife had, between the wars, already begun to do so. They were Frank and Queenie Leavis.

CHAPTER 20

The Deviants – F. R. Leavis

1

LEAVIS WAS THE most self-conscious deviant of Our Age and gloried in his contempt for its pieties. A don who despised scholarship as pedantry, a critic who called for collaborative enterprise yet considered compromise as treachery, a moralist who demanded writers – in fact everybody – should be judged by a single standard – reverence, awareness and openness to 'life' – he was both reviled and revered. Reviled as the puritan who denounced fashionable pluralism, revered as the secular saint who gave the young a rule of life that owed nothing to that other enemy of pluralism, Marx.

His colleagues at Cambridge believed the key to criticism was understanding. He believed it was judgement. For him it was crucial to separate a handful of poets and novelists from the rest by demonstrating how superior they were; and from this it followed that it was a grave misdirection to the young – a betrayal of culture itself – to encourage them to waste their time reading inferior work. His colleagues, whom he denigrated in public, thought his influence in schools and the university was disastrous: he took all enjoyment, all grace, all variety out of life and literature. His admirers thought he dignified criticism by treating it as a calling not a pastime, and his pupils were captivated by his personal integrity and total intransigence.

Leavis was so influential a critic that he imposed himself upon his generation. In countless books he has been taken at his own valuation. In America in the forties and in England in the fifties and sixties he appears as the true representative of the Cambridge ethos, the only don inspired by the ideal of turning the university into a community in which criticism took the place once held by theology. Raymond Williams thought he was deeper than he appeared. Beneath the confident opinions was a man with 'a true sense of mystery, and of very painful exposure to mystery'. And it was an opponent in the last cohort of Our Age (among whom were Leavis's most fervent disciples) who said that he was 'far and away the most successful teacher and far-reaching literary-critical influence in academic circles that English culture has ever known'. He made sincerity the touchstone in judging a writer, and his own sincerity and intense seriousness was beyond question. One of his best interpreters, Martin Bell, has seen him as the analogue of

Heidegger, but it is not his criticism in all its complexity that must be analysed here: it is his dissent from the culture of Our Age.

2

LEAVIS WAS DETERMINED to make criticism seem the most important of all intellectual activities. The critic was the guardian of language; and hence of all human achievement. Arnold had made high claims for criticism, yet the very enchantment of his banter diminished the force of his claims. Henry James and Eliot made even higher claims, but each seemed to be writing criticism to defend his conception of the novel or of poetry. Leavis declared that criticism was an independent discipline of the mind. He defended it against philosophy in a famous exchange with René Wellek, and he showed conclusively that it could not be extrapolated into philosophical terms. He defended it against Frederick Bateson and the literary historians. He defended it against the marxists – literature was indeed rooted in society, but it was not a relatively unimportant part of the superstructure. He defended it against the biographers and the psychoanalysts – the life or intention of the artist was irrelevant – he reminded us of Lawrence saying, 'Never trust the artist, trust the tale.' The critic must identify the quality of 'intelligence' among writers and convict those who lacked it because intelligence is the quality that geniuses possess to the highest degree; and since we ordinary human beings also possess some, we can learn from the critic how to refine what we have got and improve ourselves and the quality of life.

Leavis was a master of Cambridge practical criticism. He had an eye for those moments when a writer transcends his own self and speaks for all humanity. Like Arnold he singled out a particular poem, or line, or even phrase, as the touchstone to the genius or the insignificance of the writer. He described his own method in these words:

> Putting a finger on this and that in the text and moving tactically from point to point, you make at each a critical observation that hardly anyone in whom the power of critical perception exists, or is at least strongly potential, wouldn't endorse (This is so, isn't it?). The ideal is (not usually for the critic, in important cases, a remote one) that when this tactical process has reached its final stage, there is no need for assertion; this 'placing' judgement is left as established.

Leavis used to say that the question 'This is so, isn't it?' expected the answer, 'Yes, but ...' In other words criticism was the very antithesis of tags like *de gustibus non disputandum*; it was a collaborative enterprise in which critic and reader establish judgements as they proceed and build up a case book of judgements. Judgement is not something you put before your reader. You force him to follow you and get him to respond himself to the text. Criticism therefore was not an elegant essay. The critic must abominate the Saintsburys and Squires who picked a rose, smelt it and threw it aside. The critic should belt beauty out of *belles lettres*. When you criticized a work, you had to begin by asking how important it was, how it related to other works by other authors; and thus you 'placed' it. You found your 'bearings' by using the theodolite of criticism to see where precisely you were. You didn't steer your ship by consulting a treatise on navigation, you steered it by taking sightings.

Modernism was making every country take new bearings. In Paris before the war Thierry Maulnier published an anthology that contained not a single poet between Racine and the Romantics; and he winnowed the Romantics to make space for Scève and some twenty other sixteenth and early-seventeenth-century poets. In England Eliot and Richards began the depreciation of rhythm, melody and sonority in favour of intellectual gymnastics: the metaphysicals and Gerard Manley Hopkins were in, the Romantics out. Fiercer and sharper on the trail Leavis followed this line. Milton, he claimed, was now finally displaced and Shelley and Tennyson banished as unthinking, immature songbirds. Leavis began as a protagonist of modernism. In his first book he wrote on Hopkins and Pound as well as Eliot, and throughout his life Lawrence and Eliot were his constant concern. In a never to be reprinted set of essays he considered Dos Passos, Dreiser, the later work of Joyce and other modernists whom he thought to have failed; and indeed it was the novel and criticism, the state of the culture of our times, that were in the forefront of his mind.

If his revaluation of poetry was not original, his revaluation of the novel certainly was. Leavis saw that with the death of the epic and verse drama the novel was the art form that expressed a vision of the world and man's place in it. No one until he had ever thought of fathoming a 'great tradition' in such an amorphous genre, still less of confining it to five novelists. Leavis contended that Jane Austen, George Eliot, Henry James, Conrad and Lawrence were alone distinguished 'by a vital capacity for experience, a kind of reverent openness before life and a marked moral intensity'. Character, plot, story were not the criteria for judging a novel. They could not by themselves sustain a novel because they had no independent existence from the novelist's conception of 'life' and morality. An author who lacked an 'adult' mind could not redeem his reputation by his talent for invention or fantasy. Leavis moved in his lifetime from praising George Eliot's impersonality and belief in a classical order in literature to praising Blake and Lawrence. These men realized we have a direct responsibility to life and demanded us to condemn industrialism and the drudgery of getting and saving.

Yet the most obvious breach which Leavis made with his own generation was his prose style. Ah, that style! How superficial the writing of other contemporary critics seemed when compared with that tortuous, strenuous prose which Leavis fashioned into a deadly weapon of attack and defence. The irony and put-down owed something to Arnold, the finality and dismissiveness to Eliot, the inwardness and obscurity to Henry James, but the voice was beyond dispute the voice of Leavis. That flat, Cambridgeshire voice reflected his austerity and the Orwellian contempt for upper-class manners and the mandarin style of the day that was fashioned by Greek and Latin. His ugly, clumsy sentences were intended to reproach Pater's 'substitute creation' or anyone who valued grace, elegance and the shine on an argument which blinds the reader to its thinness. His prose displayed 'the mind at work', a mind wrestling with the problem for all to see. Derek Brewer thought Leavis's style was the 'masterly expression of a man and his whole attitude to life'. It seemed to George Steiner that Leavis had kidnapped the words that recur in his writing – discrimination, robustness, responsibility, challenge, creative response – and made them his own. His was a rhetoric that enabled him to dodge and weave if attacked, and it was rarely possible to be quite certain what the crucial sentences actually meant as they could be given different shades of meaning. This style reminds one of the priest at Nemi in Frazer's *Golden Bough* – a man creeping through the forest with a knife in his hand ready to spring on his foe, and all the time glancing this way and that, terrified of himself being knifed. He cultivated to perfection the sneer which he used like an oyster-knife, inserting it into the shell of his victim, exposing him with a quick turn of the wrist, and finally flipping him over and inviting his audience to discard him as tainted and inedible. He would dismiss an author by naming in disparaging terms those who admired him, thus dismissing them too. Fielding 'is important not because he leads to Mr J.B.Priestley, but because he leads to Jane Austen, to appreciate whose distinction is to feel that life isn't long enough to permit of one's giving much time to Fielding or any to Mr Priestley'. He upstaged his adversaries by appearing to be more rigorous, more highbrow, more concerned about values and less willing to overlook triviality – the kind of triviality, he reminded his readers, that was the womb to evil. Occasionally the tone was of the misunderstood and wronged, sometimes of the indignant and righteous and, as he grew older, he wore the mantle of Old Testament prophets as to the manner born.

Leavis outraged his academic contemporaries by the way he used this style upon them, but in his defence it must be allowed that serious critics had a good deal to put up with in those days. Writing about modern poets in the *Evening Standard* in June 1927 Arnold Bennett had said:

> These parasites on society cannot, or apparently will not, understand that the first duty of, for instance, a poet is not to write poetry but to keep himself in decency, and his wife and children if he has them, to discharge his current obligations, and to provide for old age.

Edgell Rickword, the editor of *The Calendar of Modern Letters*, wondered whether Bennett would say that the first duty of an inventor was not to invent but to keep himself in decency, or the first duty of an explorer was to keep up the payments on his life insurance policy; and he concluded, 'Mr Bennett's attitude to literature ... is not sensible but extremely gross.' Geoffrey Grigson, very much his own man and a merciless assassin, argued that St John Ervine or Ivor Brown in the Sundays assaulted the younger poets in such terms that the only way to reply was:

> a slash with the bill-hook which was far too much my weapon and which I endeavoured to keep sharp, wiping off the blood from time to time – when it happened, that is, to catch someone in whom any blood was flowing. But the tactic was wrong. It was worse than wrong, it was foolish. I had not grown up enough to discover those lines by Dryden and to realize that the neck of a beheaded fool grows three more foolish heads.*

Yet, however great a technical critic Leavis might be, we shall never understand his influence unless we realize how his criticism rested on a theory of culture. And if we are to understand that theory, we must use the referent in English society which provides so many clues to English behaviour. We must observe class differences.

Leavis's theory of culture was directed against the upper middle class and in particular against the Oxford Wits and the descendants of Bloomsbury. According to his theory society had become corrupted by industrialism and urban polish and insincerity. Once upon a time there was a rural world in which speech was natural and vigorous, in which life was deeply felt and morality simple and unalloyed. Sometime, however, in the seventeenth century, the 'dissociation of sensibility' struck English culture. By our times men, overcome by machine civilization, suburban falsities and the glitter of polished upper-class civilities, had become alienated and brutalized. The native vigour had been sapped by cosmopolitanism, the natural robust response to language had been gelded by advertising. In the process high culture had become divorced from folk culture. No 'organic relationship' any longer existed between the two. As a result high culture had become coterie culture.

The worst coterie was Bloomsbury, whose tentacles stretched over all the important organs of British intellectual life. Through their influence in

* After the war Grigson pretended he had been too uncharitable and was no longer able to 'bill-hook my victim and sit on his corpse and enjoy a glass of his blood'. None of his victims thought this vampire had changed his habits, and there was a certain irony in the situation when he chose to bill-hook Leavis. Grigson was enraged by Leavis referring to T. S. Eliot as a bloodless, sexually crippled, nay-sayer incapable of exhibiting Lawrence's reverence for 'life'. Leavis began his reply by rebuking Grigson for his 'impertinence' and said he had always admitted that Eliot had 'that rare thing, a fine intelligence in literary criticism'. For once he did not get the last word. To assert, hissed Grigson, that Eliot was 'radically destructive' was to deny that he had a fine critical intelligence; and to say that Eliot hadn't lived was to say he was dead. 'There could be ways of saying it less sickening and foolish than Mr Leavis's.' Of pity for Eliot and his suffering during his first marriage, or any feeling for the reasons (which Pound understood so well) why Eliot played possum, neither man gave the faintest sign.

London they were able to control the organs of opinion which ought to have been in opposition to worldly upper-class morality. The British Council offered to foreign countries an image of British culture that was fashioned by Bloomsbury. The Arts Council subsidized their taste and ignored minority views such as those of the Leavises. The monster had more heads than Scylla: *The Times Literary Supplement*, the Third Programme, the Sunday papers, those Oxford dons C.S.Lewis and David Cecil, the scientists who dared speak of Rutherford as their analogue to Shakespeare, all the cosy, frivolous, elegant, suave essayists who suggested to their readers that one writer was as good as another. Chief among this brood were his own colleagues. The pioneer English dons at Cambridge came mostly from the upper to middling part of the middle class. Indeed the wonderfully absentee regius professor, Arthur Quiller-Couch, was beyond question a Cornish gentleman. The assumptions of their class, as much as their eclecticism and hatred of insularity, made them assume that any educated person spoke and read French and also probably German, and was thoroughly acquainted with Russian literature in translation. That he had read the Greek and Latin classics in the original went without saying. As for English literature and letters, they were part of the heritage of the nursery and schoolroom. It was only through the widest reading and by travel that undergraduates could learn to understand the complexity of human nature. Their students were Our Age, the new class of *revoltés* in post-1919 England. They were public school boys consciously emancipating themselves from their philistine schoolfellows when they set sail on the vast sea of European literature.

Leavis, on the other hand, was the son of a piano dealer in Cambridge. His father was a fine Victorian radical, a vigorous rationalist and republican, coming from nonconformist lower-middle-class stock. Leavis went to the Perse, the local grammar school, then under a rare headmaster W.H.D.Rous. It was to pupils from grammar schools that Leavis was to appeal. His denunciation of the metropolitan culture of Bloomsbury won an immediate response from the grammar school boy coming from the provinces to the university, sometimes from a home where books were a rarity. Such a boy was apt to be scared or depressed by the vast areas of reading that seemed to be expected of him before he was thought fit to utter a word about the literature of his own country. Now he needed to read with minute attention a handful of books, and he could imply that he had read a lot more he had discovered were not worth his time. Now he felt able to turn his back on foreign literature on the ground that the critic cannot profitably deal with a work unless he can unravel every strand of the texture of its language.

Leavis gave such a boy a new kind of self-respect. He taught his pupils that they too could belong to the elite. Not the false, fashionable elite that Bloomsbury had sponsored, but to an embattled elite fighting for intellectual standards against fearful odds. He told them that they were the true descendants of Arnold, a trained body of readers who could set the tone for the whole of society by denouncing anything that was worthless and trivial, while praising only those authors that a true critic must perceive were of lasting importance. The ability to respond only to great literature indicated your ability to live. Leavis differed from anyone before him in asserting that the elite had to be trained in literary criticism at the university, that criticism was the only discipline which defined culture and defined it in terms of morality. He went further. He asserted that the activity of criticism was the most important of all the activities in the humanities, indeed that an English faculty ought to be at the centre of every university curriculum. He went further still. He declared that only when students were taught to discriminate and place authors in relation to each other could there emerge a climate of opinion in a country which would benefit creative artists and awaken them to what is valuable or what is childish or trivial in their own experience. Thus he gave to students the sense of belonging to a dedicated minority, a minority that would in the end triumph and convert succeeding generations, a minority which held the key to establishing truth and defining goodness.

And just as Bloomsbury had won the admiration of the disillusioned and cynical young after the First World War, so Leavis spoke to the condition of a very different generation of young after the Second World War. He told his pupils not to write for the newspapers and periodicals. Despising research, he sent them into the schools – the state, not the public schools – to pass on the lessons of their master that much of what was most deplorable in English culture had been engendered by Bloomsbury. The teacher-training colleges were his most potent centre of influence; and that influence spread as the reputation of the grammar schools rose. His disciples were the outsiders, the meritocratic generation, making their way by their intelligence not through their connections and manners. They felt as superior to the other dons and their contemporaries as the young Evangelicals had felt to the High and Dry or Low and Slow fossils in the early Victorian Church.

The natural puritanism of the young – the satisfaction the marxists of the thirties had found in showing how self-serving the older generation was – appeared again in the forties and fifties expressed in Leavis's vision of the world. As a pupil of Leavis you did not argue with his premises, you accepted them. Then indeed you might suggest a variant or advance a qualification. So devoted did his most faithful pupils become that the accounts of him they gave – truthful accounts – astonished those outside his circle. Michael Black, for instance, found him 'supremely courteous in that he paid his audience the compliment of assuming they were with him'. Rebuffed for maladroit praise, cut for selling the pass by a concession to the enemy, they continued to revere him. Queenie was sometimes severer than him: she told Boris Ford he would no longer be welcome in their house, and Leavis had to slip out to see him. But others remembered her as kindly, a deft hand with plum cake. Her sympathies were wider than his. Rupert Christiansen, in flight in the seventies from a marxist teacher in King's, recalled tutorials that lasted for four hours and discovered that Queenie in her widowhood liked Trollope's novels, thought well of *Cakes and Ale* and Nabokov, and devoured thrillers. David Holbrook pictured Leavis as

> Still looking like an old corm, lissom and knowing
> Uncannily what's good, what's bad
> And probably rather hard up into the bargain.

For Donald Davie '*Scrutiny* was my bible and F.R.Leavis my prophet', 'the secular saint of the modern university', 'the last prophet we had in England', to fall under whose spell was 'like a religious conversion'. Had there been anything like this since 'Credo in Newmanum'?

Those who sat at Leavis's feet began to move into positions of influence in the fifties and sixties. Boris Ford edited the Leavisite *Penguin History of English Literature* (and later the *Universities Quarterly*). Peter Hall and Trevor Nunn became directors of the Royal Shakespeare Company. Several departments of English in the new universities were teaching versions of the Leavisite doctrine. Well before then the columns of the *Guardian* had become the preserve of Leavisite criticism. The tone of the periodicals changed and grew more serious and discriminating. How could it not when one of Leavis's pupils, Karl Miller, became successively literary editor of the *Spectator*, the *New Statesman*, the *Listener* and the *London Review of Books*? The most gifted Leavisites, such as Dennis Enright, cut the traces as they grew up. The old Scrutineers, Harding, Knights and Traversi, remained loyal and a core of hatchet men operated after Leavis died imitating his style and tone of voice.

Frank and Queenie Leavis achieved many of their objectives. They succeeded in discrediting Bloomsbury. L.H.Myers's *The Root and the Flower* was often held up by *Scrutiny* as a judgement on Strachey, and Eliot (whom Strachey admired and once tried financially to help) was praised for contrasting a passage from Joyce with the stale images and clichés of Strachey's evocation of Queen Victoria recalling the events of her life as she lay dying. Queenie Leavis did the hatchet job on Virginia Woolf, though characteristically she left it to a disciple to demolish *The Waves* and *The Years*. She did it by 'placing' Virginia Woolf. She habitually referred to her as 'the clever daughter of Sir Leslie Stephen'; and her review of *Three Guineas* stands high as an example of modern invective. Leavis had written in 1938 a genuinely appreciative essay in *Scrutiny* on Forster, though he tipped the wink to his readers that he thought him inferior to L.H.Myers. After the war when Forster lived at King's he revised his view and denigrated him. Keynes, he could hardly deny, had distinction of mind. But shortly after Keynes's death the publication of his memoir *My Early Beliefs* gave Leavis the opening he needed. In that memoir with remarkable candour Keynes had admitted that D. H. Lawrence's criticism of himself and his friends in their youth had some justice. 'I can see us as water-spiders,' he wrote, 'gracefully skimming, as light and reasonable as air, the surface of the stream without any contact at all with the eddies and the currents underneath . . . We practised a thin rationalism ignoring both the reality and the value of the vulgar passions joined to libertinism and comprehensive irreverence.'

This act of repentance brought no absolution from Leavis. Is it repentance to ignore one's real depravity? It was no excuse to argue that the money Keynes had amassed by speculation was spent on the arts. He was corrupted by the act of amassing it. Leavis indicted Bloomsbury's morality in a memorable sentence. 'Articulateness and unreality cultivated together; callowness disguised from itself in articulateness; conceit casing itself safely in a confined sense of high sophistication; the uncertainty as to whether one is serious or not taking itself from ironic poise: who has not at some time observed the process?' By the seventies hardly a good word was ever spoken of Bloomsbury in academic circles. Three Oxford critics, by that time all professors and by no means alike in temperament, John Bayley, John Carey and Christopher Ricks, echoed each other's distaste; but then that was to be expected in Oxford.

The Leavises were not only successful in discrediting Bloomsbury. They discredited their colleagues by persuading the world that they were the victims of monstrous injustice; had been kept out of posts to which they were entitled; and spurned by the university where they alone stood to preserve the true Cambridge tradition of Henry Sidgwick and Leslie Stephen – that dispassionate search for truth in the face of contemptuous good form. This story was accepted in America, and reinforced by an anthology of articles from *Scrutiny* compiled by Eric Bentley. Americans at once picked up the issue of class and saw Leavis as a victim of English snobbery. In England Leavis became a feature story for journalists and he fed them pieces about his discontents like any politician. The achievement of his colleagues – the English faculty was then at the height of its distinction – went as nothing beside the volumes of *Scrutiny*, reissued by the University Press, so dense, so serious in its animosities and so intent on saving literature from the horrors of modern civilization.

3

THE STORY THE Leavises wove about themselves was a legend. The truth was that the young Leavis, though a loner and scarred by his experience as a stretcher-bearer in the First World War, had found friends in the university. Stanley and Joan Bennett were both members of the English faculty and got work for Leavis as a teacher. Stanley Bennett had a fellow-feeling for this shy, awkward student. Like Leavis he had struggled to Cambridge by scholarships: indeed he came from working-class stock. Then Leavis met a graduate student, Queenie Roth, and she made up her formidable mind to marry him. Some people marry their opposites, others their mirror images. The latter damage themselves more, for in an incestuous marriage the virtues never seem to be strengthened as intensely as the vices.

Queenie cut Leavis off from his friends. Whereas the Bennetts were beginning to convince him that life was not a conspiracy directed against him, she did her best to make it so. She ordered Gwyneth Lloyd Thomas to choose between them and I.A.Richards. 'I don't see the necessity,' she replied. 'Then you have already chosen.' When ordered to choose between them and her husband, Joan Bennett also refused: she was then accused of stealing material from Leavis's lectures on the metaphysicals. In the thirties Ivor Richards was unwise enough to suggest to Leavis – he had been begged to do so by Quiller-Couch – that he might like to apply for a post at Leeds: instant excommunication followed.

Like sorcerers the Leavises conjured up tempests to discomfit their colleagues in the English faculty. The insults they hurled, the letters of astonishing vituperation, the monologues of unbelievable ferocity Leavis delivered in committee were to themselves proof of their incorruptibility. It emerged that the passages Leavis had set in a Tripos paper were the very ones he had taken his own pupils through. A protest had no effect: he did the same thing another year. To him it was self-evident that, if these were the best passages for critical comment, they were the best ones to test his students and the best to set in an examination – what was the fuss about? He was in fact *unkollegial* to the highest degree. To him his insults were disinterested judgements spoken in a righteous cause. When he talked of criticism as a collaborative enterprise it was an enterprise in which he alone held the equity. Just as he identified with Lawrence he identified with Pope: he saw himself flaying Colley Cibber and the tribe in the *Dunciad.*

Having attacked Bloomsbury as a coterie the Leavises were not going to lay themselves open to the same charge. They had an eagle eye for anyone, such as George Steiner, who they imagined was attempting to jump on their bandwagon; and if some wretched adherent praised Leavis in a review, Leavis would at once weigh in and point out how lamentably the fellow had missed the achievement he ought to have praised. They turned on their collaborators, L.C.Knights and Denys Thompson, or their abject admirers in the *Cambridge Quarterly.*

But if they permitted no coterie to form, the Leavises did something as damaging. They founded a sect. The sect was very strict and in the end those of the true faith were a tiny gathering with no critic of distinction among them. Only those pupils, such as Karl Miller, who left the shadow they cast could grow. For Donald Davie, a poet as well as a critic, Leavis was the god that failed. Davie accepted that Leavis was not obliged to read any contemporary literature. But then why should he pretend that he had been keeping a vigilant eye on new novels and new poetry over the past forty years if in fact he had been doing nothing of the kind? What had happened to the young don of the thirties, whom Denys Thompson remembered as 'strong, idealistic, hopeful for the future', willing to consider his pupils' variants and emendations to his own insights, how was it that he became the monologist of the sixties?

The Leavises' colleagues had cause to complain of their scholarship as well as their manners. Scholars are entitled to change their minds but it is the custom to acknowledge it. Leavis changed his mind on James, Eliot, *Lady Chatterley's Lover* and Dickens, and never said so. The case of Dickens became notorious. In 1932 Queenie Leavis declared that 'Dickens stands primarily for a set of crude emotional exercises', and in *The Great Tradition* Leavis omitted Dickens explaining that 'Dickens' genius was that of a great entertainer, and he had for the most part no profounder responsibility as a creative artist than this description suggests ... the adult mind doesn't as a rule find Dickens a challenge to an unusual or a sustained seriousness.' But in 1970 the Leavises published a rapturous criticism of Dickens, bubbling over with superlatives. There was no acknowledgement of a change of heart, only Leavis's note in the preface to say that if the omission of Dickens as belonging to the great tradition 'looked odd it was meant as an avowal ... of a deferred commitment to making the default good' – an explanation so devious that an American professor referred to it as weaselling.

Scholars also acknowledge their debts to predecessors. The Leavises, however, used to misrepresent critics who, they considered, had trespassed on their preserves. They knew that most readers do not go to the library to see, for instance, what Humphrey House or Orwell or Edmund Wilson had written about Dickens. If they had they would have found that Leavis appropriated seven of Edmund Wilson's most notable insights. When he lifted Lionel Trilling's analogy to Blake from Trilling's essay on *Little Dorrit* he made no acknowledgement. In the end one wondered whether Leavis's tactic of denigration was all that different from Strachey's. Those who remembered his denunciation of Bloomsbury, 'Articulateness and unreality cultivated together; callowness disguised from itself in articulateness ...', were tempted to rewrite that sentence and apply it to him. Portentousness issuing from inflexible self-righteousness; self-righteousness masked by unctuous humility, the hypertrophy of conscience which excluded half of what is human and poisons the mind of the critic in the act of judgement.

No historian could accept his theory of culture. Historians ignored him because his theory of culture was all too familiar. It is compounded from Rousseau, Herder, Ruskin, William Morris and Lawrence and from minor figures such as Eric Gill and George Sturt. Perhaps it also owed something to Spengler who like Leavis believed in cultural decline. It is the familiar tale of a golden age destroyed by science, industrialism, advertising and mindless vulgarity. His theory first took shape in Queenie Leavis's *Fiction and the Reading Public*, a book often praised as a pioneer work which looked back to *Literature and Society in the Eighteenth Century* by Leslie Stephen. Both Stephen and Queenie Leavis, however, ran into the same difficulty. To make the generalizations they wanted required research by generations of scholars into the actual reading habits of different social classes in the past. Stephen realized this and was diffident, Queenie Leavis did not and was dogmatic. She had read a large number of ephemeral popular books on Victorian times but not the sole scholarly monograph then available by another woman scholar, J.M.S.Tompkins's *The Popular Novel in England 1770–1800*. What, her colleague F.L.Lucas asked, are we to make of her praise of the Elizabethan masses for not being debauched by emotional orgies or lascivious syncopated rhythms (Queenie Leavis was referring to the cinema and jazz) – what are we to say, when the most choice entertainments of that time were to see men hanged, drawn and quartered, to mock idiots in bedlam and bait bears? Did journalists in the eighteenth and early nineteenth centuries have such sound sense, as she said, that they at once recognized a genuinely original author? Perhaps she thought the reception given to Keats and the young Tennyson was just?

Leavis did not read history nor would he even cross Cambridge's Downing Street. Had he done so he would have found technicians in the lab getting at least as much satisfaction from setting up an experiment with complicated apparatus as George Sturt's wheelwright of old that Leavis took as his exemplar of the fulfilled life. Nevertheless he realized after the war that his theory of culture was not wearing well, so he found a new name for our cultural decline: we were being ruined by 'technologico-Benthamism'. This was the morality of Gradgrind and Bounderby but it was also the deplorable influence of sociology, the welfare state, the egalitarian unction of the Labour Party and reformist movements in general. The second theory was no better than the first. It required no knowledge of history but simple observation to realize that the technological advances of the past two centuries had made life less harsh, less poverty-stricken, less disease-ridden, more secure, more full of choices and of opportunities for protest as well as self-expression.

Even some of those who acknowledge a debt to Leavis, such as Raymond Williams and Richard Hoggart, began to question his theory of culture. Why, they asked, did Leavis denounce the Robbins Report as a monstrous Benthamite heresy? Did he really believe that higher education should be confined to four per cent of the population? For some time the oracle of Dodona was silent. Then it spoke: no, he was not oblivious to the needs of the multitude: but they should not be at universities, there were other places ... but what other places, and what the multitude should study, the oracle did not reveal. For had Leavis been honest he would have had to refer to polytechnics and admit that on his own premises all the multitude were fit for was techno-logico-Benthamite studies.

The younger philosophers, too, were rebuffed. Clearly he was saying things of great interest to them, and Michael Tanner, a gifted philosopher and admirer of the Leavises, brought his talents to bear on the matter. But true to Leavis's practice of dissociating himself from those who sought to be his allies, he took this opportunity to say that, if there were any philosophers worth his while, they were Michael Polanyi and Marjorie Grene – not exactly names to conjure with in university departments of philosophy. Why did he not – if he was going to bother to find philosophical allies – investigate Wittgenstein? He had preened himself on having told Wittgenstein that he had behaved on one occasion selfishly, and on another inconsiderately. And yet Wittgenstein was the hammer of Cartesian thought, hostile to cleverness, aware of 'life' as an animating principle. But no; Wittgenstein was a rival in virtue. What Leavis liked were *phrases* of the kind he found in Polanyi and Grene not the philosophical *argument* he needed to establish his position.

The consequences of rejecting pluralism now became clear. Leavis believed that good ends could never conflict. A great artist must *a fortiori* be a good man, a bad writer despicable. Such a belief shows an astonishing lack of knowledge of the world. He can be seen as a vitalist picking up phrases from Nietzsche and Shaw, but above all from Lawrence: celebrating 'life'. Certain writers were *healthy*, or *affirmed life*, or were *reverently open* before life, or exhibited conscious and skilled creativity or – but the list of phrases with which he tried to describe the indefinable were legion. *Das Unbeschreibliche hier ist's getan* - but was it? Or do we agree with Wittgenstein that when we try to do so it 'is a terrible business – just terrible. You can at best stammer when you talk of it'? Leavis remained a true conservative deviant. But the forces of pluralism were too strong for him.

4

WHEN OUR GENERATION was growing up literary criticism was still in the hands of men of letters. Eliot's criticism was the most serious, but the literary pages of the *New Statesman and Nation* under Raymond Mortimer captured many of Our Age as readers and journalists. Perhaps the best of them was V. S. Pritchett who succeeded Raymond Mortimer as its literary editor. If Mortimer was a master of French culture, Pritchett knew Spain and its literature. He was Bloomsbury enough to think George Eliot puritan, but to read him was to enter the republic of letters with a short-story writer as your courier. He introduced you to writers you would not expect to find in the same room. You were brought up short by a phrase such as his description of Max Beerbohm's two wives treating him 'tenderly, if overwhelmingly, as a dangerous toy'. He would describe the characters in *Tristram Shandy* as all living 'shut up in the madhouse of their own imaginations, oysters itching voluptuously upon the pearl within'.

Victor Pritchett never bothered to confront literature with theory. Too bad if the pundits declared that character is unimportant. For him fiction was character and the plot a device to reveal it. No idea was worth a fig in fiction unless you recognized at once the way the person embodying it walked and talked. Pritchett loved characters, particularly rogues, freaks and queer fish. Comparing those two monstrous egoists Boswell and Sterne he said, 'The Scotsman is wanton, transparent and artless, haunted by the fear of the Presbyterian devil, whereas we can be sure that the devil himself was afraid that the half-Irish Sterne would drag him into bad company.' This was the kind of writing that came to be brushed aside in universities as merely celebrating literature. Years later, when Pritchett was in his eighties, Dennis Enright observed that when we read Pritchett we think we have read the books he is writing about. 'The impresssion is one we rarely get from academic critics. For the most part all we read when we have read them is them.'

But the grandest of the men of letters before the war was an American: so sympathetic to Our Age that he became part of their critical discourse. Edmund Wilson was a journalist, perhaps the last grand old man of letters, who grumbled that professors imposed their views on their pupils instead of teaching them to form their own opinions. He was an example to professors, a scholar always learning something new about the Dead Sea Scrolls or the Iroquois or the Russian language; he died learning Hungarian. He was the first to turn writers into cultural emblems, to study the cultural implications of marxism, the first to study the literature of the American Civil War. Only Wilson would have reinterpreted the story of Philoctetes and seen him as the artist armed with an unerring bow that shot an arrow into the lies and deceits of men. Instead of being grateful they shunned him because the stench of his suppurating wound, the stigma of artists, made him insupportable. To read Wilson was to realize that criticism was not synonymous with academic criticism. He did not write for an audience of students studying a syllabus. He wrote for the adult reader who lived in the world of affairs.

As Our Age grew to maturity the man of letters was superseded by the academic literary critic. At the *Times Literary Supplement* the editorial chair once graced by Alan Pryce-Jones and Arthur Crook was filled by former dons John Gross and Jeremy Treglown. Works of criticism poured from university presses and London publishers sent their scouts to common rooms to sign up new authors. One by one university departments of English capitulated as Cambridge sent a succession of its young dons to posts in the civic universities, such as David Daiches and Matthew Hodgart at Sussex, Arnold Kettle at Leeds, Brian Cox at Manchester, John Broadbent at East Anglia. It is true that in the British Academy the literary historians never lost control:

literary critics continued to be excluded unless, like Kermode or Ricks, they had an edition under their belt. But at Oxford the regime of Helen Gardner and C.S.Lewis in the end crumbled: literature later than Shelley and Keats entered the curriculum. One of the last places to hold out was University College London, but Frank Kermode eased it into the twentieth century. Kermode became the doyen of academic literary critics. His range was astonishing. He was a rare example of a critic who renewed himself each decade and absorbed whatever was the new method of reflecting upon literature, whether it was linguistic structuralism, post-structuralism or deconstruction.*

And the German Renaissance? No more than the philosophers were the literary critics prepared to alter their methods of close textual reading and analysis. There were, of course, plenty of scholars who discoursed on Nietzsche and the implications of German philosophy and criticism, Erich Heller and Peter Stern foremost among them; and much admiration for German humanists such as Curtiss and Gundolf. The contribution Lukacs made to marxist criticism was acknowledged. But one critic thought that Cambridge criticism diminished literature by its insularity. Why were British critics so unconcerned with theories of modernism and language? George Steiner considered that the critics deafened us to the greatness of the works of art they expounded. Steiner brought the ideas of the German Renaissance to bear upon literature, and considered Heidegger and existentialism as a drill to penetrate the rock-face of our experience and our predicament. His work was an exercise in allusion in which you were challenged to see the connection between the concepts, the names, the references that were at his fingertips in many languages and periods. His admirers who packed lecture rooms and watched him on television considered they were hearing profundities that would awaken us to the contradictions and perplexities of our condition – would explain, no that was impossible, would probe how such a catastrophe as the Holocaust could have taken place. His manner also created sceptics. They found his rhetoric inflated and disliked the repetition of words such as intense, urgent, exigent. What at the end of the day did these words precisely mean? 'The more strenuously he says "yes",' said John Gross, 'the more he makes you want to murmur "no".'

There was, however, another critic of Our Age who did indeed wrestle with the implications of German thought, but he was American. Lionel Trilling was par excellence a New York intellectual, but his works on Arnold and E.M.Forster and his sympathy for English culture gave him a special

* Kermode was the natural choice when the regius chair fell vacant at Cambridge where the faculty was somewhat tempest-tossed as its prima donnas refused to sing in harmony and there was no longer an effective chairman. Kermode hoped to set the faculty on course as he had done with such success in Manchester and London. He was soon disillusioned and left. Matters improved when there were three women among the professors.

place in the affections of Our Age. His referents were Freud and Marx, but the conclusions he drew from them were very different from what the readers of the *Partisan Review* expected when he looked at the wheelbarrow of progressive conclusions that so many trundle across their garden in planting ideas. Trilling defended Whittaker Chambers and shocked his liberal friends by accepting that Alger Hiss had been a spy. The theme of his first volume of essays, *The Liberal Imagination*, was that liberals had no imagination. He used the word 'liberal' in the American sense as the 'educated class which has a mild suspiciousness of the profit motive, a belief in progress, science, social legislation, planning and international co-operation'. Trilling pointed out that no major great writer had ever celebrated these beliefs and he wondered how liberals could admire those who rejected these beliefs so decisively. He questioned whether the heroes of American modern literature in those days – Dreiser, O'Neill, Dos Passos – were heroes or plodders bereft of subtlety or ideas. He said that sociologists such as David Riesman told us more about society than most modern novels. He was a liberal in the English sense – or rather of those Englishmen who were suspicious of the good intentions of the enlightened. Trilling was not disturbed by the narrowness of the society Forster and Jane Austen depicted. The fact that these societies had such exact dimensions enabled the novelist better to satirize the snobbery, meanness and vulgarity within them.

Trilling recognized, like Leavis, that the philistine culture of the Establishment, rooted in class differences, was still 'entrenched in unexamined, unpromising beliefs'; and intellectuals were right to distrust those who controlled the levers of power. But, unlike Leavis, Trilling realized that we were no longer living in the inter-war years. By the sixties what had been the struggling counter-culture of modernism protesting against the Establishment had now become a flourishing culture in its own right. The educated classes, swollen in numbers by the multiplication of universities and polytechnics and the media, lived by this second culture. They congratulated themselves on not being contaminated by making money or running any institution. Students believed they were joining a heroic maquis to ambush the Establishment. In fact they were joining a rival Establishment, well-heeled and enjoying the luxury of being in permanent opposition. They were sanctified in censoriousness. Moreover, the fact that Trilling's pupils absorbed without a qualm the shattering conclusions of modernism disturbed him. It disturbed him because modernism in rejecting jingoism also rejected patriotism. In rejecting the tyrannies of the family it also ignored the existence of love between parents and children. In rejecting the claustrophobia of class and community it forgot the need for pride in one's roots. Modernism mocked lasting fidelity between lovers and also the affection that can survive the passing of passion. Unlike Leavis, Trilling grappled with the literature of the times and accepted that the young would want to grapple with it too.

My contemporary, Graham Hough, a fine critic who wrote for the educated public, praised Trilling for examining the consequences of modernism in his last book on *Sincerity and Authenticity*. Trilling took *Le Neveu de Rameau* as his text and said that the reader naturally sympathized with the Diderot of the story, a rational being who accepted society and was accepted by it; and as naturally the reader disliked Rameau's nephew, disappointed, embittered, hypocritical and sycophantic. But Hegel had disagreed. Hegel had welcomed the disruptive nephew: for it is by such dissident, deviant sprites that the social order is changed, as change it must. Sincerity was the supreme virtue in the classic novel. But it was valid only so long as one accepted that there was a unified self, the self of Rousseau's *Confessions* or the self of the puritan who speaks plain like Leavis.

So is sincerity enough? What happens when people regard the sincere man as no more than a player of roles, a traitor who accepts the civilization of which he is a part even though it is corrupt? Anyone who tried to adapt to society and therefore play a role is inauthentic. To be authentic the artist must reject every impurity of convention or tradition. That means ceasing to regard art as something to give us pleasure and recognizing that the only authentic work of art is one in which the artist speaks only for himself and is indifferent to the public's response.

Society then comes to be regarded as an enemy of authenticity. So much so that Ronald Laing suggested that madness was not a disease or a disorder. It was a cry for help against the pressures of society, the sane response to the corrupt culture we have created. As Vendice says in Tourneur's *Revenger's Tragedy* (a play my generation at Cambridge rediscovered),

> Surely we are all mad people; and they
> Whom we think are, are not: we mistake those;
> 'Tis we are mad in sense, they but in clothes.

The most extreme forms of antisocial behaviour now become praiseworthy and authentic in the canon of modernism.

Trilling was in fact facing the impact of ideas that came out of the German Renaissance. He was a true pluralist critic, for he did so by ranging through the length and breadth of western literature in a way that recognized there can be no single overruling measure of virtue or standard of conduct such as Leavis set up. We have to seek such shelter as we can find when the rational world of the stable self prizing sincerity and honesty and anchored in society is struck by the tempestuous forces that batter and try to destroy the world for its hypocrisies and delusions. In his work we can see how important were the great insights of the German Renaissance and how much we gained from them; but also how much they needed to be mediated by the Anglo-Saxon tradition of respect for fact, inference and the Greco-Judaic tradition.

PART IV

CHAPTER 21

Was Our Age Responsible for Britain's Decline?

1

IN MARCH 1979 Nicholas Henderson, an untypical and outstanding British ambassador, sent a valedictory despatch from Paris to David Owen, then in his last months as foreign secretary of the Labour government. Henderson told him how difficult it was to be an effective diplomat when the rest of the world regarded Britain as having squandered her power. In 1955 we had been the strongest economic and military power in Europe and the leader in atomic energy. In 1979 we were not even in the front rank of European, let alone world powers. Nearly every economic indicator on growth of the gross national product – GNP per capita, percentage of world trade and productivity – showed us lagging far behind Germany and France. The one graph in which the British curve exceeded the others was for days lost by strikes – in 1977 Britain lost ten million, France two and a half million, Germany under 160,000. Our management was inefficient and there was no interchange in Britain between those at the top of the civil service, banking and industry as there was in France. What incentive was there when our top executives paid over eighty per cent in tax? How could they improve productivity when they faced a closed shop, shop floor bargaining and a process of arbitration in which the employees invariably won? How could industry compete when compelled to negotiate with a hundred and fifteen trade unions and Germany had seventeen? The rest of the world watched us cancelling major capital projects like the Channel Tunnel and the third London airport, and chafing in Cyprus and Rhodesia unable to impose our will.

The *Economist* got hold of Henderson's despatch, and Margaret Thatcher, by this time prime minister, did not hesitate to endorse it. It was all the more arresting because here was the Establishment itself speaking. Not in fact for the first time. Victor Rothschild had said something similar when he was head of the think-tank: unfortunately it coincided with a euphoric speech by Edward Heath designed to rally his party, and Rothschild was told that as a civil servant, however temporary, he should keep his trap shut. But for years the topic of Britain's decline had kept journalists busy. In 1962

Anthony Sampson began his series on the *Anatomy of Britain*, and a year later *Encounter* ran a series of articles on Britain's decline. Goronwy Rees had been a director of the family firm of his friend Henry Yorke (the novelist Henry Green). He lashed the inefficiency and gross self-indulgence of the board room, and Michael Shanks observed that the effortless superiority of the British that so irritated foreigners had been replaced by effortless inferiority. There was one dissenter – Henry Fairlie. He praised British culture for questioning whether efficiency should be the main goal in life and reproved one critic for being willing to throw into the trash can humanism, liberalism and parliamentarianism as luxuries that Britain could no longer afford if she was to become efficient. That critic was the young Correlli Barnett.

Correlli Barnett became the Jeremiah of his generation. For Barnett, as for Jeremiah, there was never any balm in Gilead: the British had sinned and would be visited by serpents and cocatrices. The myths they comforted themselves with would turn out to be moths eating through their clothes so that they would soon be left in tatters. Barnett's first coup was to catch and pin down the Monty moth. He argued that the field marshal had created a myth about himself: Auchinleck not Montgomery turned the tide in North Africa. Subsequent research did not make that charge stick, but Montgomery himself would not have disagreed with Barnett's second charge, namely that the British commanders in the desert were amateurs up against the professional Rommel. They used their tanks like chargers as if they were galloping in the cavalry brigades under Lord Uxbridge at Waterloo, while Rommel's tanks sat, hull down, and picked them off.

Barnett next set out to destroy the myth that Britain had won the war because the home front was so efficient. Delving into the wartime archives he drew a picture of British industry dependent on American supplies of tanks, lorries, steel, radar and machine tools because their own were inferior; while the production of coal, steel, aircraft and ships was interrupted by wildcat strikes and management tolerated restrictive practices. Barnett did not blame the workers. The brutality of the masters in the British industrial revolution was being visited by the children of those masters upon the eighth and ninth generation.

British industry, so the indictment continued, was managed by boards of directors drawn from the upper classes. Their ambition was not solely to make profits. It was to make sufficient profit to enable them to do what the English gentleman traditionally did: to own country houses, hunt, preserve partridges and invite their neighbours to shoot them. Some industrialists were self-made men, but they had all the more need to make themselves respectable. Gentlemen did not hustle, gentlemen distrusted management techniques as a misguided attempt to professionalize their activities, gentlemen tried to eliminate competition by mergers because competition meant hustling. When Royal Dutch and Shell merged, the Dutchman Henry Deterding became president, single-minded in his pursuit of profit. The Englishman Marcus Samuel had other ambitions: to be Lord Mayor of London and devote himself to public service.

Barnett had an American ally. Martin Wiener connected the decline of Britain's industrial spirit to English culture. For over a century the cultivated class – the clerisy – had been hostile to management and industry. Most people lived in towns, but poets and writers painted an icon of an England of hedges and dells, of rolling hills and ploughland. To become prime minister one had to cross oneself before the icon. Baldwin, the son of an industrialist, liked to be photographed scratching the back of a pig. Neville Chamberlain softened his image of a Birmingham businessman by revealing that he was a bird-watcher. Even Jim Callaghan, a town-bred boy, bought a farm. Intellectuals despised industry. From Cobbett to Leavis the guardians of culture contrasted rural simplicity with the false sophistication of London and the loathsome values of getting and gaining in Coketown.

If the object in life was to become a gentleman, the purpose of education was to guarantee that one did so. Those two great educational pundits, John Henry Newman and Matthew Arnold, ignored the need to train the country's managers and industrial workers. Newman described the University of London as a series of 'bazaars or pantechnicons, in which wares of all kinds are heaped together for sale in stalls independent of each other'. He admitted that without the 'mechanical arts' life could not go on, but they were inappropriate for the elite to study. This was one of the few occasions on which John Stuart Mill agreed with the future cardinal. Arnold identified the diversity of the godless institution of Gower Street with the failure to discriminate which was the fruit of anarchy, the enemy of culture. Sheldon Rothblatt, the historian from Berkeley, California, showed how long it took for Cambridge to establish a faculty of engineering and how few sons of businessmen went themselves into business.

Correlli Barnett disinterred in our own times a ripe example of Establishment thinking. Reporting during the war to Rab Butler on the curriculum in secondary schools, a former headmaster of Harrow Cyril Norwood and his committee opposed the teaching of any course that might be called vocational. They recommended that modern languages should be taught as far as possible as dead languages since few boys and girls would be likely to need them later in life. Three pages were devoted to the needs of commerce; seven to religion. Norwood's report, Barnett considered, was in line with the ideas of Robert Morant when he set up a system of maintained secondary schools at the turn of the century. Progressives as well as traditionalists were adamant that to segregate children in schools geared to vocations was to treat them as helots and deprive them of their birthright. (The Hadow report of 1926, which took a different line, was not mentioned by Barnett.)

As a result Britain entered the Second World War with a workforce that lacked technical skills and a management that was often ignorant of technology. In 1986 when Geoffrey Elton (a redoubtable Conservative and regius professor of history at Cambridge) snapped at the 'ignorant parrot talk' of those who blamed the country's poor economic performance upon its higher education, Correlli Barnett asked Elton why he called the grammar school curriculum 'mind-stretching' and liberal, when such a narrow part of the mind was stretched and liberal excluded anything that could be smeared as vocational. Barnett considered the educated classes were primarily to blame for Britain's decline. Instead of bracing themselves to endure a decade of austerity as defeated Germany would do, the British preferred to build a new Jerusalem on England's green and pleasant land, the high priest Beveridge offering incense at the altar of the welfare state. Like a lush with a hangover reaching for the bottle Britain returned to a life of leisure and illusion, only to see the dream of New Jerusalem fade and turn into 'a dark reality of a segregated, subliterate, unskilled, unhealthy and institutionalized proletariat hanging on the nipple of state maternalism'.

Correlli Barnett and Martin Wiener were to have considerable influence. When Keith Joseph became secretary of state for education he used to wave Barnett's book in the face of his civil servants. Nicholas Henderson quoted Wiener in his valedictory despatch. Their diagnosis in part inspired the educational reforms of the Conservative governments of the eighties. Joseph held Our Age responsible. He accused the dons and intellectuals of not perceiving that the comfortable bough on which they rested was sustained by business. Their scorn for business was a *trahison des clercs*.

What are we to make of this?

Historians did not think much of Barnett's indictment. In 1945 social reform and economic recovery were not alternatives. No British government could have withstood the demand to implement the Beveridge Report. That report had a venerable lineage stretching back to Lloyd George: it was as if the country had been sitting in committee on the matter for half a century. Had he been elected Churchill would have moved more slowly and Britain would not have had such a good health service: but he would have moved, remembering his past as an ally of Lloyd George's scheme of social insurance in Asquith's government. Nor could any government have resisted the demand for houses to replace the destruction of the air raids. Forty thousand people lived in disused army camps: yet even so the Labour government had to curtail its housing programme in 1947.

The technique Barnett applied to Britain could be applied to any country. Was indeed applied to Germany. Immediately after the war an American research team (of which Auden was a member) examined the effect of the allied bombing offensive on the German economy. It found that the civilian population had been less effectively mobilized than the British. Rival bosses fought each other over the allocation of raw materials, and not until Speer took command was a coherent system of industrial production organized. If Barnett had conducted an audit of war on the American economy, he would also have found diseconomies, muddles, overlapping and waste. He did not take account of the fact that Britain had to support not only an army and an air force but a navy as well – and a merchant fleet decimated by U-boat attacks. His strictures on the British aircraft industry came in for particularly harsh criticism by economic historians. His statistics on productivity in terms of weight of aircraft produced per man-day were not only said to be wrong but irrelevant. 'Nobody was really interested in the weight of aircraft produced, but in fighting power,' said Ely Devons: to measure the efficiency of production quite separately from the usefulness of what was produced was grotesque. Nor was it true that the workforce kept women out. The proportion of women in the aircraft industry in America and Britain was about the same. It was in Germany where the workers managed to resist dilution until 1944. Britain spent more on the war than any other belligerent, manpower was better mobilized, nutrition high, rationing fair and inflation low.

The economic historians were no kinder to Barnett's picture of an effete gentlemanly class mismanaging industry. Barnett did not refer to Donald Coleman's celebrated article on that matter which took its title from the cricket match at Lord's between the Gentlemen and Players. It was true, Coleman said, that the Victorian industrialists behaved as did those who had made their fortune in banking and commerce. Profits were the path to status and power; and status meant sending their sons to public schools and into the professions. But that should have made space for a new generation of entrepreneurs. It was, in fact, the Gentlemen who introduced scientists to industry and set up laboratories within the firm against the inclination of the Players who tended to think the lessons learnt on the shop floor were all management needed to know.

Even American historians declared that by and large the British were adequate managers. What they were not good at was exploiting innovations. British management remained too individualistic and wedded to family ownership. In America mass production and distribution created the multidivisional company in which the gain of splitting it into specialist units each with its own management was balanced by the centralized direction of a powerful head office. British business remained too small, too smug and too unenterprising: but the British were as prepared as any industrialist to get their hands dirty.

Had all British intellectuals been content to echo Newman and Arnold, they would stand justly condemned. But they did not. Scores of them over the years told politicians and industrialists that British industry was slipping behind its rivals. In the 1860s Edward Huth told the Royal Commission on endowed schools that the masters and foremen of other countries were better educated than our own. Herbert Spencer pointed out that the curriculum of the classics and the Bible left out almost everything that concerned the business of life. He was disregarded as a notorious bore. In 1880 T.H. Huxley tried to convince Arnold that science was as good a mental discipline as Latin and Greek. Barnett ignored Bevin's efforts and Bernal's attempts during the war to increase productivity and efficiency in industry; and civil servants, many of them intellectuals such as Douglas Jay, warned of our inability to compete successfully after it.

There was, moreover, a vast part of the business world that Barnett did not consider. The City – the world of banking, financial services, insurance – was one which sustained Britain with its invisible exports. There were those who held it to be more responsible than the intellectuals or the educational system for the weakness of British industry. The City was keener to invest in enterprises abroad which offered a higher and swifter return on money than home industries. But despite criticisms in the fifties of the staid unadventurousness of the older merchant banks, there were plenty of entrepreneurs of Our Age around – such as Kenneth Keith, the master of the reverse takeover bid – who made fortunes and shook up companies. There was the world of the property developers; some like Pat Matthews were battered in the recession of the seventies, others like Max Rayne and Harold Samuel moved on serene. There were the great family concerns – Wolfson, Sieff and Sainsbury: certainly retailing was a business in which British entrepreneurs excelled. Any assessment of the prosperity of Britain even in a period of declining power has to take the country's commercial successes into account.

When the termites had done their work they were satisfied that not much was left of Barnett and Wiener. The new fashion was to blame the impersonal forces of history rather than statesmen for economic decline. Biographers exculpated their subjects by demonstrating that they could not have acted other than they did. As one turned the last of the eleven hundred pages of Middlemass and Barnes on Baldwin one wondered how anyone could hold that much-wronged, kindly man to have been responsible for Britain's failure to prepare for war with Hitler. Paul Addison dismissed Barnett by saying he must be the only British historian 'whose creed was Bismarckian nationalism'. No modern nation, except Germany, had ever consciously oriented its economy to military efficiency. Any civilized government must have other goals.

Very true. And yet a doubt niggles ... How is one to explain the decline of British power, how explain that, although living standards rose, they declined relative to other nations in Europe, to the United States and Japan? Were the politicians and civil servants incompetent and was our generation to blame for choosing the wrong goals in life?

2

THE PARTY POLITICIANS among us were indignant if one referred to a post-war consensus. The venom Conservatives exuded when Churchill was rejected by the nation took one back to the days of 1910. Imprudently invited by a member to White's, Aneurin Bevan on leaving the club had his bottom kicked by some unreconstructed oaf. But then Bevan believed in his heart that Tories were lower than vermin and Dalton never missed an opportunity to taunt them. Years later, in 1987, two members of Our Age met: Decca Mitford, over from America to cover the general election, as nonchalant a communist sympathizer as ever, and Peregrine Worsthorne, a Peterhouse Conservative and faithful *Telegraph* journalist. 'Certainly there's a class war,' said Worsthorne. 'And we're winning it.'

And yet the politicians of Our Age were driven by a laudable ambition. They wanted to call a truce in the class war. That was why they put such a premium on full employment and the provision of generous social benefits without a means test. The Conservatives were embarrassed by the interventions of that national figure of fun Sir Waldron Smithers, MP for Orpington, whose ideals were not all that dissimilar from those of Margaret Thatcher. This was not to be a laissez-faire but a managed economy. Churchill was in a conciliatory mood. He put Butler and not Oliver Lyttelton at the Treasury and chose the smooth-tongued charmer Walter Monckton to be minister of labour as a sign that he wanted to live down the reputation for bellicosity that he had won during the General Strike. Until 1960 people still went along with the wartime tradition of cooperation with government as Britain grappled with shortages of labour as well as goods.

Who was to manage the economy and achieve the goals of full employment, stable prices, a stable currency and growth in the economy to pay for increased welfare? Churchill brought in businessmen to run ministries and act as overlords. The ploy failed, and he soon lost interest in his idea for reorganizing ministries. The management of the economy therefore rested in the hands of the Treasury and of the permanent secretaries in the ministries, most of them Treasury men. This was where we were to exert our influence. The civil servants from Oxbridge and the LSE met the advisers, often dons, whom ministers brought in as their ideas men or as a counterweight to the mandarins – also from Oxbridge and the LSE. Loud were the trumpetings as these bull elephants locked tusks in argument about the management of the economy. Coming into Whitehall from Oxford by Cherwell, Donald MacDougall found himself up against Otto Clarke. Clarke was untypical as he had begun his career as a financial journalist. But he became the most self-confident of the Treasury mandarins running a plan to float the pound and protect its value by blocking overseas sterling balances. MacDougall thought this crazy. So he first divided the Treasury mandarins and got the key figure of Edwin Plowden on his side. Then he won over Frank Lee at the Board of Trade to hold his flank against the Bank of England which was backing Otto Clarke's scheme. Finally he set out to divide ministers. For six months the battle swayed to and fro until Edward Bridges at the head of the Treasury was persuaded to seek Lionel Robbins's advice. Robbins opposed convertibility, and Rab Butler and Otto Clarke and his Treasury supporters retired to lick their wounds. When in 1957 the Treasury tried again to deflate, Macmillan refused to listen and in the new year the chancellor of the exchequer and the Treasury ministers resigned.

The Treasury had for long been derided by Labour intellectuals and was regarded by Tommy Balogh, Wilson's economic adviser, as staffed by Oxbridge classical scholars ignorant of the principles of economics and Keynesian analysis. Had not Macmillan complained that the Treasury was always asking him to catch trains by using last year's Bradshaw? And so Labour set up a separate Department of Economic Affairs which was to plan the economy while the Treasury kept the books. But it was the chancellor with his book-keepers, not George Brown and his economists, that had the last word: within three years the DEA was destroyed.

The politicians thereupon engaged in a more familiar dispute with the Treasury. Every government depends for its life on Treasury control of expenditure. But the Treasury found that the estimates of expenditure made by the departments were often inaccurate. Defence always overspent, and soon every department tried to match the expenditure the public expected. Ministers won their spurs only if they could show they could fight their own corner against the Treasury. Each minister took his case to the chancellor. Both Thorneycroft and his successor Heathcoat Amory became exhausted by such bruising negotiations. So a new post of chief secretary to the Treasury was established and Otto Clarke set up a committee in Whitehall where the main predators fought each other instead of ganging up on the chancellor. The problem of control was never solved. In the sixties and seventies it grew like a gigantic cancer; and even Margaret Thatcher had to establish a star chamber under Whitelaw and bring litigants to heel after they had refused to accept the chief secretary's ruling. The trade unions were not alone in syndicalizing life: government departments and institutions all took pride in fighting their own corner and knocking the financial controllers groggy.

Yet Treasury control went further than this. At the weekly meeting of permanent secretaries the head of the Treasury would get them to brief individual members of the cabinet to oppose any minister who was taking a line against the wishes of the prime minister. Indeed a permanent secretary under a minister whose policy he thought disastrous might hint to his colleagues to brief their ministers to thwart that policy in cabinet. Bernard Donoughue, adviser from LSE to Callaghan, maintained that the cabinet would suddenly find a Treasury paper put before them deflecting them from following the policy they had agreed. He called that the 'Treasury bounce'.

As Britain in the sixties began to run into financial difficulties, the managers found their job even more perplexing. In 1961 Selwyn Lloyd introduced a pay pause, cuts and a more ambitious plan. There was to be an incomes policy to make a rational judgement on the demands of the unions and to curb them: he was sacked by Macmillan the next year. In 1966 the Treasury got government to make that policy *statutory*. That plan ended with the rejection of Barbara Castle's reform of trade union law. Revived again by the head of the civil service William Armstrong in 1974, it brought down Heath's government. When Wilson took office in 1974 he minuted on a paper produced by the think-tank, 'Analysis fine, except for incomes policy'. Yet at the height of the 1976 crisis, with the International Monetary Fund officials at the door, the Treasury once again tried to slip in a statutory incomes policy. But this time the bounce failed. By now the Treasury was discredited. Having underestimated public expenditure by four billion pounds in 1974 they had overestimated it in 1976 by three billion. But much as Labour analysts made of these errors, rational forecasting had by that time become almost impossible.

The top civil servants were on the whole consensus men and it was not until Margaret Thatcher governed that consensus was dubbed 'corporatism'. But as the economy began to deteriorate, the friction between ministers and mandarins grew. The civil service, so highly esteemed by those wartime civil servants Gaitskell and Jay, lost face and lost heart. Both Conservatives and Labour accused civil servants of being obstructive. Crossman's encounters with 'The Dame' (Evelyn Sharp) were legendary: Anthony Part, Tony Benn's permanent secretary, collapsed with a heart attack. Part could not reconcile his duty as an accounting officer to Parliament with his minister's determination to sanction schemes that, if Part were challenged by the Public Accounts Committee or a select committee, would make him appear such a patsy as to merit immediate retirement. On the other hand Barbara Castle was right in regarding as an enemy her permanent secretary at Transport. Soon the civil service was put under the microscope by John Fulton's committee. Open up the intake, he said, bring in specialists, abolish the different classes in the service and replace them with a structure of grades, set up a civil service college to train staff in modern management techniques. His report was painlessly put to death by the head of the civil service William Armstrong. No ENA – Ecôle Nationale d'Administration – was established.

We were less successful than the French Enarques in planning the economy. We were not inferior to our French colleagues as negotiators but the French bureaucracy was geared to operate a plan to revive their economy. Under Labour governments the targets and assumptions were changed with such rapidity that the conception of a national plan administered from Whitehall fell into disrepute. There was, however, one kind of planning that Our Age admired. That was town and country planning. Their heroes in the past were Patrick Abercrombie and Patrick Geddes and their shrines the Green Belt and the Garden City. The new towns rose; Bill Holford planned a new Piccadilly Circus and Ludgate Hill; famous buildings were protected (and numbers demolished); and inner cities transformed. Local government exercised enormous powers, but on appeal central government might step in and hold an enquiry. This was done when the Roskill commission was appointed in 1967 to determine where a third London airport should be sited.

For some years opposition to the selection of Stansted among the well-to-do in East Anglia had been mounting . After four years the commission delivered its verdict, having spent the hitherto unheard-of sum of a million and a quarter pounds in assembling and analysing data and using the most sophisticated techniques of cost-benefit analysis. It recommended to the Conservative government that the airport should be sited to the northwest of London near the village of Cublington. True, a thirteenth-century church would have to be demolished, but this virgin farming land and its proximity to motorways and the Midlands made it the best choice in the view of the commission. The report was destroyed within six weeks. The one piece of research Roskill failed to carry out was into the whereabouts of the formidable, dynamic and attractive political hostess, Pamela Hartwell. Her country house was near Cublington. She launched a campaign denouncing the committee with such speed and vigour that the government faced a major revolt from Conservative MPs: and the minister announced that, in accordance with the note of dissent in the report (sprung on his unwitting colleagues) by the well-known planner Colin Buchanan, the third London airport would be built at the mouth of the river Thames on Maplin Sands.

Maplin Sands had indeed been considered by Roskill. It had attractions as a site. Aircraft would approach London over the sea and the noise of air traffic would be diminished. But to build there would mean demolishing large numbers of working-class houses in order to drive a rail link and motorway through to London. And where would the motorway end? Slap in the City, the financial centre of London, already choked with traffic. That was why Roskill, using cost-benefit analysis, had ruled out Maplin Sands. When the Conservative government fell Tony Crosland cancelled the Maplin Sands project. He simply announced that there would be no third London airport. That was neither heroic nor practicable. In 1987 a Conservative government announced, twenty years after Stansted was being rejected as the site for the third London airport, that this airport would be sited at – Stansted.

The débâcle of Roskill and of the Layfield enquiry into London traffic made Whitehall and the educated classes leery of such enquiries; and indeed there were several, such as the route of the Winchester by-pass, that produced not decisions but anarchy. Yet one planner at least retained his faith in the persuasive power of reason. Richard Llewelyn-Davies belonged to the old left of the thirties – to that group at Cambridge who had been influenced by Bernal to put their trust in 'scientific' socialism. He believed that for too long social problems had been tackled by applying general principles about human behaviour. Before any architectural or planning decision could be taken you should assemble and analyse quantitative data. This was what he had done when studying the design and function of hospitals for the Nuffield Foundation. In one hospital he put cotton threads of different colours into the hands of nurses so as to chart their movements. He logged 27,327 journeys made by the nurses and discovered that each was making three to four hundred separate journeys and walking on an average two to two and a half miles in her tour of duty. He was in revolt against Le Corbusier. He wanted to learn how people lived and worked, how they moved from kitchen to living room and what they did in their kitchens. He wanted to make the best guess how they would live in the future. When therefore he designed the new town of Milton Keynes he planned it on the assumption that eighty per cent of the inhabitants would own a car. Therefore there would be no need for a bus service which would be expensive and underused. On the other hand special provision should be made for the cyclist and pedestrian so that children should not be crushed by lorries. There should be no town centre clogged with shoppers and traffic and no single industrial area creating rush-hour traffic jams.

Yet as the years passed his plan of Milton Keynes was criticized not for its understanding but for its neglect of how people lived. The town council had to subsidize a bus company to provide a service along the grid roads. People complained that cosiness had vanished. The drab street in an old town with its pub and corner shop in which families gossiped was superior to the town based on research that showed how people were likely to live. The revolt against planning began. The left pilloried it as using green belts to protect property values and private interests, and slum clearance as an exercise in gentrification: the problem of the under-housed was exported to another part of the city. Garden cities were denounced as 'anti-urban escapism' ignoring the facts of 'demography and socio-economic data'. The motorist and his demand for ever more freeways was the enemy of the people. The right denounced the planners for taxing betterment, harping on development values, ensuring that no one made a profit at any point and stopping any public or private investor from breaking free from the web of red tape. On all sides planners and architects were satirized for imposing their ideas on human beings without ever consulting them. It was a strange epitaph on professionals who had prided themselves on discovering how human beings lived.

In the eighties a new generation of planners criticized us for imposing grand solutions, master plans and monuments to architects' vanity instead of asking the public what they wanted: a worthy sentiment but the public always wants many things – and they conflict. The Conservative government had other ideas. They sanctioned a vast development in London's dockland

and lifted all planning procedures. The development on this largely derelict area would never have taken place had they not done so. But the problem of the environment remained. It became the cause of right-thinking citizens. Margaret Thatcher's government, blazoning free enterprise and the abolition of regulations, became forced to impose new regulations to reduce smoke from industry that killed trees.

Perhaps rational government was failing for another reason. Perhaps the structures were wrong. The devices of Churchill's overlords, Wilson's gigantic departments of state, the Heath think-tank did not live long. Keith Joseph presided over two disastrous exercises in restructuring and seemed fated to receive bad advice from his civil servants. As a minister of housing under Macmillan he sanctioned the plans for high-rise flats even though Leslie Martin had shown how a building in the form of a ziggurat was a better way of using the permitted plot ratio for a site. As minister for local government Joseph modified John Redcliffe-Maud's report and produced a system of government that was neither local nor regional and with which voters could not identify. He reorganized the administration of the Health Service and did indeed make it more convenient for patients and their families, but he added another tier of bureaucracy. Kilbrandon's musings on the constitution ended in a defeat for regionalization and separate assemblies for Scotland and Wales. The select committees Crossman and St John Stevas nursed in the Commons did not make government more efficient. But efficiency was not always the first consideration in the mind of Our Age. Or rather it was argued that government would command more support if more people participated in it or were at least consulted. If people were to be asked to make sacrifices, you had to convince them that what government proposed was both reasonable and fair. And so government set up tribunals, quangos, boards, committees and commissions. Advisory agencies multiplied to tell these bodies what the public thought and what they might later think. Sometimes they were tiny like the 'three wise men' – Lionel Cohen, Dennis Robertson and Harold Howitt – whom Macmillan asked to advise on prices, productivity and incomes. More often they were unwieldy bodies on which sat the obligatory trade unionist and, somewhat grudgingly, the obligatory woman.

More fanciful explanations for the failure to achieve growth and run the economy with success were put forward by the old guard – that body of opinion that ranged from Quintin Hailsham to Mary Whitehouse. Had not our morals decayed and the country become ungovernable? Peter Jenkins admitted that the world of the Rolling Stones and David Bailey, of the angry young men of the fifties or of Albert Finney in *Saturday Night and Sunday Morning* riding his bicycle off to work in that insolent manner, had displaced the model of the Boy Scouts and Greyfriars; and Clint Eastwood was a very different type of Hollywood hero from Gary Cooper.

There was, in fact, a more convincing explanation of Britain's decline, and it sprang from our desire to bring harmony to society. It sprang from our desire to conciliate the working class and bring the trade unions into partnership. In practice it led to life in Britain becoming syndicalized.

3

ATTENDING A WEDDING in Norfolk in the fifties Richard Wollheim was intrigued to hear the bishop say in his address to the bride and groom, 'Until now each of you has always said "*I'm* going to do that, *I* want this, *I'm* going to take that!" Now you are going to have to learn to say, "*We're* going to do that, *we* want this, *we're* going to take that."' Every group in society fought its own corner. The professions were as ruthless as the unions. Doctors and dons alike urged their claims, nurses could expect to get a sympathetic hearing, new white-collar unions like Clive Jenkins's ASTMS spoke for the growing status group of technicians.

In the rail strike of 1953 Rab Butler expressed his concern that no inflationary settlement should be made. Churchill and Monckton met the union leaders and next morning Churchill phoned his chancellor of the exchequer to tell him they had not bothered to keep him up as it was clear that agreement would not be reached until the small hours of the morning. 'On what terms was the strike settled, Prime Minister?' Butler asked. 'On their terms, of course, old cock,' came the genial reply. Had the railways been privately owned they would have been bankrupted by the settlements of 1953 and 1955. Macleod was tougher. He not only defeated Cousins over a London bus strike but saddled Gaitskell with the blame for the inconvenience. But the militancy of the engine drivers' and firemen's union ASLEF was an alarming omen. It was a sign that the skilled worker would fight to preserve his differential over the unskilled and would not accept that new technology could mean fewer jobs. There was another omen. When Frank Cousins became the general secretary of the TGWU it was a sign that the old right-wing union leaders, Deakin, Lawther and Williamson, who, remembering the defeat of 1926 slapped the militants down, were being displaced. Full employment, that fine ideal, had strengthened the unions' bargaining power and weakened wage restraint.

Government built its defences. Macmillan's National Incomes Commission became Wilson's Prices and Incomes Board. Later came the Industrial Reorganization Corporation, the National Enterprise Board, the Industrial Relations Board and the Monopolies Commission, all designed to reassure the unions they would get fair play and that City slickers and company directors would not escape restrictions on pay. At first Wilson and Brown seemed to have got a voluntary agreement from the TUC on prices and incomes.

But as each year the government cut back its programmes the unions grew more restive. Frank Cousins never accepted the 1965 national plan based on a three per cent pay norm. Nor as minister for technology could he stomach productivity deals which caused unemployment, and he resigned. The Labour technocrats, Charles Snow and Vivian Bowden at the DES, were sacked. So at the DEA was Austen Albu, the sole engineer in the government.

Wilson's white-hot technological revolution turned out to consist of soap-suds. The Industrial Reorganization Corporation was to finance new investment and make industry more efficient by mergers. The mergers created unwieldy corporations that made industry even more overstaffed; or when they caused unemployment the policy switched to bailing out ship-builders on the Clyde notorious for inefficient management, bickering unions and thieving employees. Beeching recommended five thousand miles of railway lines making a loss should be closed: in the end only two thousand were shut down. The minister Richard Marsh recommended that the line from Shrewsbury to Cardiff should be one of them. In cabinet he heard the lilting voice of the secretary of state for Wales say, 'But, Prime Minister, this line runs through three marginal constituencies.' The line was not closed.

Investment by government came to mean waiting for the next employer to threaten mass dismissals on facing bankruptcy. In the seventies, when Chrysler was bailed out, the American managers went chuckling back to Detroit. They later sold the company to Peugeot. Tony Benn's workers' co-operatives at Meriden and Kirkby soaked up funds producing unwanted goods, and the workers refused to appoint competent sales managers. Even Judith Hart questioned whether her department on overseas aid should give up its handout from the Treasury to keep ship-building yards working when there was a glut of tonnage. Ships could not be stockpiled.

Then the strikes began. In 1964–67 2.3 million days were lost. In 1969 the loss was 6.8 million. The TUC voted 7–1 against Roy Jenkins's pay policy. George Woodcock foresaw disaster ahead and encouraged Barbara Castle when she showed him the draft of *In Place of Strife*. His successor Vic Feather rubbished it, and two formidable union commanders, Jack Jones and Hugh Scanlon, determined to see her off. The unions had no lack of allies in and out of cabinet. Callaghan behaved like Themistocles and went over to the Persians. He took his revenge for her nagging opposition to his policies when he was at the Treasury, and her old allies Crossman and Foot deserted her. Wilson sued for peace. 'Take your tanks off my lawn, Hughie.' His army fell back defeated and signed an armistice called the 'Solemn and Binding Agreement'. It was to be neither binding nor solemn.

A new army took the field under General Heath. His strategy was to set an objective of ten per cent growth by 1973 and abolish the Prices and Incomes Board and the Consumer Council. The market was to be his compass. Barber's first budget was greeted with enthusiasm by economists and the media. There were to be no lame ducks: the Mersey Docks got no reprieve. He launched his infantry in a frontal attack under Howe who introduced an industrial relations bill. The attack was hasty and ill-prepared. Heath had told his countrymen to stand on their own two feet, so Frank Chapple, the new general secretary of the electrical workers and passionate anti-communist, took him at his word and demanded a twenty per cent rise; and when the government intervened ordered a go-slow that led to winter blackouts. Meanwhile the power workers drove in their opponents' front with a startlingly inflationary settlement. On the left wing the miners inflicted heavy casualties in 1972. They won a pay award of twenty-seven per cent, a young commander named Arthur Scargill leading flying pickets and defeating the police at Saltley.

Meanwhile Heath's centre began to crumble. Scared by the risks his advance involved, leaving a million unemployed in his rear, he changed his plan of battle and ordered an about-face. He sacked his commanders John Davies and Nicholas Ridley. Lame ducks were again to be given prosthetic treatment. Once again the Clyde ship-builders were subsidized. The reinforcements for industry he was hoping to raise got diverted into a property boom and the 1972 budget was directed to the objective of full employment but the tax cuts in it were too little too late. Heath's retreat into incomes policy drove moderate unions into action. He tried in the true spirit of Our Age to parley with the enemy: Campbell Adamson of the CBI thought Heath preferred the unions to his natural allies the industrialists. Luck deserted him. In 1973 oil prices quadrupled and all commodity prices rose sharply. He resembled a general battling against floods and mud as well as a determined enemy. The miners mounted a blitzkrieg and, by using the tactic of secondary picketing, took their enemy by surprise. They overran Heath's position and accepted his surrender.

By now the tanks of the unions were fanning out over open country as they faced Harold Wilson, a general they had already once defeated, commanding an army by now divided and beleaguered. Michael Foot at the department of employment resembled a baron in the Wars of the Roses: one could never be certain which side he was on. The miners won another twenty-two per cent award and weekly wages rose in 1975 by thirty-three per cent ... But the tale of disaster in the seventies is only too familiar. When Wilson threw up his command, Themistocles took over. Callaghan was a fair and decisive chairman of the cabinet. He brought himself to back Healey his chancellor; and they stabilized the front in 1976 by getting reinforcements from the International Monetary Fund. For two years Jones and Scanlon held their forces back. What Joel Barnett at the Treasury called 'the costly years of educating Jack and Hughie' were over. But were they? The union bosses found they could not control their own forces let alone their fellow commanders of trade unions such as NALGO and NUPE. In 1979

Callaghan was defeated by the forces of the unions despite the fact that cabinet papers on the home front were being sent to the TUC for their approval. His last words to the unions when the TUC General Council met the cabinet at No. 10 were of abject subservience. 'We are prostrate before you – but don't ask us to put it in writing.' Even when another army formed under a commander who had devised new tactics to defeat secondary picketing, she had to make one or two retreats – once again on miners' pay in 1982. But by 1984 her counter-offensive was in true Montgomery style teed up. This time the external circumstances favoured the Conservatives: a world recession and considerable unemployment. Scargill met his Alamein and retreated, his forces decimated by pit closures and desertion.

The experienced politicians, no less than the intellectuals, did not realize how much the trade union movement had changed. Gone was Low's old carthorse. The authority of the general secretary diminished with each decade. On the General Council the soft left displaced the old right. The unions were at odds with each other, power workers and electricians against miners, skilled workers against low-paid workers; and branch officers were edged out by militant shop stewards. The differences between government and unions could not be resolved by reason. To Frank Chapple the agreed wage restraint in 1976 negated all his hard work in negotiating a thirty-three per cent rise over three years in return for a genuine improvement in productivity, and he was as truculent as the most unprincipled Trot. To the unions an incomes policy destroyed collective bargaining because it locked every worker on to a grid; but a flexible incomes policy was a recipe for inflation. Denis Healey made the shrewd comment that the winter of discontent in 1978–9 was not caused by ordinary workers frustrated by wage restraint; it was caused by trade union activists frustrated by a pay pause which left them unable to justify their existence.

Was Britain's decline the fault of management? Management must take part of the blame. The CBI as much as the TUC wanted to protect old industries instead of promoting new concerns. When government began to intervene, management sat back and lapped up the flow of investment. Mergers became fashionable in the sixties and seventies: the larger the enterprise the less likely government was to allow it to fail. But the larger the corporation the more likely it was to be run by chiefs who regarded dissatisfied young thrusters as a menace to them: it was safer to agree with your boss and increase the number of your subordinates. Few learnt the lesson Arnold Weinstock taught – that large concerns need small headquarters staffs to set targets and cash limits to divisions, and should let their management get on with the job.

Too often firms expected their managers to learn on the job. They said they could not afford to train them and would not pay skilled engineers salaries comparable to those on offer in the City. No wonder there were so few fliers in the metal and engineering trades which made up half of industry. Those who blamed government for refusing to pump-prime investment, or the City for going for quick returns rather than long-term investment in capital goods, forgot that it was not the supply of capital that was lacking. It was demand for it. Perhaps part of the trouble was that old imperial Britain had supplied many markets and the diversity meant shorter runs and less standardization; and since individual markets fluctuated, expansion was never at a uniform rate. Heavy industry produced one-off jobs: ships and locomotives.

The desire of Our Age to improve relations with the unions was their undoing. The productivity teams, the Neddys and national plans and investment allowances had little effect because the root of the trouble was on the shop floor where managers became accustomed to surrender to the shop stewards. Particularly on innovation: for years commercial television companies kept in cupboards modern equipment that the unions refused to allow their members to handle. Ian MacGregor, the courageous chief brought from America to rationalize the British coal and steel industries, thought managers had too often become administrators. Administrators learn the art of making existing systems run smoothly. Managers should put efficiency first, discover what needs to be changed and have the will to force those changes through. The growth of personnel and industrial relations departments insulated the managers from the most difficult part of their task: how to get the workforce to accept change. The junior managers – foremen and overseers – got bypassed by the industrial relations men who spent their days monitoring good relations with the unions, the shop stewards and the press, and little time in getting the workforce to perform better. Meanwhile there were plenty of shop stewards who enjoyed the power that went with their particular branch of management – the management of disputes. As confrontation and distrust of authority spread in the sixties, communists, Trots and anarchists appeared among them.

We prescribed two medicines to cure the British disease. The first was conciliation and was at the heart of the proposals of Alan Bullock's committee on industrial democracy. It recommended that trade unionists should be members of the boards of limited liability companies. Bullock reported at a time when Militant Tendency was penetrating the unions with some success, and his findings were derided. But the right of workers to have a voice in management was to reappear in the directives of the European Community like the genie in the bottle. The second was to reform trade union law. Victor Rothschild at the think-tank told Heath we were the only country that had no effective laws to control the unions. But it was received wisdom that the Taff Vale judgement was sacrosanct: unions could not be made liable for the damage a strike caused to employers whatever the circumstances. The political will to restore power to management did not exist until Margaret

Thatcher became prime minister, and it was recognized that management cannot manage if the cards are stacked against it. Even then received wisdom said that government ran the risk of a general strike if the law on picketing was changed. But Norman Tebbit got a law passed to sequester union funds on a breach of the law, and there was no general strike. The reform of trade union law was Margaret Thatcher's greatest achievement.

There was a third possibility. Ian Macgregor had brought back American practices in industrial relations. Why not look east instead of west and learn from the Japanese? Received wisdom at once said this was fruitless and called in the sociologists to explain that industrial relations are part of culture and those prevailing in such an alien culture as Japan could not be transplanted to Britain. But the decision of Japanese companies to set up factories and impose their tradition of management and consultation threw doubt on received wisdom. Teamwork, a stream of information to the workforce, abolition of job demarcations, keeping the production line going when a breakdown in the past would have been welcomed as a time to take a break, getting the workers instead of inspectors to improve quality, obtaining, if possible, a no-strike agreement with a single union were some of the items in the fundamental change which Japanese management introduced; and in a handful of factories the Japanese managers transformed production.

They also met with resistance. The removal of management perks was bitter to middle managers who felt they had worked their way up to eat in an executive dining room and obtain separate lavatories. There was not a flicker of a sign that such cooperation impressed the TUC. They preferred the time-hallowed punch-up; and the Transport and General Workers Union were to prevent the establishment of a new plant in Scotland which would operate on a no-strike agreement. It was clear that the British would be very slow to learn the lessons the Japanese had to teach us. Neither government nor management nor unions were receptive. Yet in the eighties one other thing was clear. In pursuing what they believed to be their interests, the trade unions split the Labour Party in the seventies. They also destroyed social democracy for a decade and the political assumptions of Our Age.

4

BRITAIN'S DECLINE WAS hastened by one further assumption made by us and even more by our elders. That was the assumption that Britain was one of the three great powers. This assumption diverted politicians' attention from the state of British industry and it destabilized the economy. The high level of expenditure overseas and on defence made the balance of payments worse.

Propelled after the general election to the Potsdam conference Attlee and

Bevin could hardly be blamed for continuing Britain's wartime role. People forgot that Bevin did not urge Britain to make an atom bomb solely from fear of the Soviet Union. He did so because the US secretary of state Byrnes was so hostile to imperialist Britain that Bevin feared Britain would be isolated and left without effective defence. As the Soviet threat grew more menacing in Berlin and Czechoslovakia, there was always a reason why Britain should spend more on defence. Yet the fact that we could not finance our presence in Germany or Greece should have made the Labour government see the writing on the wall.

Fate was against them. When the Korean war broke out, which in Europe was taken as the beginning of a third world war, Cripps was dying and Bevin ill. Under intense American pressure Attlee and Gaitskell thought it was Britain's duty after the triumph of the Berlin airlift to send troops to Korea and rearm. So Gaitskell cancelled Cripps's subsidy for re-equipping British industry on the grounds that Britain could not simultaneously rearm and both build houses and re-equip her industries.

The decision to rearm was a disaster. Otto Clarke said no chancellor of the exchequer should ever sponsor an expenditure programme. British governments should be reducing overseas commitments, not adding to them. The decision also split the Labour Party. Both Gaitskell and Bevan were to blame: Gaitskell for refusing, even when Attlee asked him, to cut a penny from his rearmament programme – which the Tories cut at once when they won the general election – Bevan for resigning in the most damaging way against the advice of all his friends except his fiery wife Jenny Lee and his deplorable disciple Michael Foot.

Had the left's objective been to curtail defence expenditure, their case would have been formidable. But their opposition was hydra-headed. One head sprang from the pacifism of the thirties out of which came the campaign for nuclear disarmament. Another head sprouted anti-capitalist and anti-American sentiments welcome to constituency activists and to the parliamentary faction Bevan led against German rearmament. The left fondled a chimera, always a favourite beast of theirs, that was as much a myth as the notion that Britain was still one of the great powers. The chimera was that Britain could be independent. Which nation does not want to control its destiny? In Greece the left pursued the chimera with great ardour; and there the left had a genuine grievance against gross American interference in their domestic politics. But geography and history denied Greece the chance to be as independent as Norway or Sweden. So did Britain's geography. In Britain the left wanted to loll in splendid isolation and build a socialist republic. Barbara Castle opposed the Channel Tunnel in the seventies not because it cost too much but because our 'island should not be violated'.

The majority of Our Age believed the western alliance was the only way to deter the Soviet leadership. Years later Denis Healey was to say he had been mistaken in thinking Stalin intended to conquer Western Europe. Possibly. Stalin used other means than full-scale military invasion to destabilize parliamentary democracies. Stalin, Khrushchev and Brezhnev moved at the first sign of irresolution in the west or rebellion in the east; and Healey was to swell with indignation when Margaret Thatcher made economies in the defence of the Falklands that encouraged the Argentinian junta to invade the islands. We disagreed not on the principle so much as on the tactics of defence. Healey spent many months devising schemes of détente more ingenious than practicable. He proposed that all foreign troops and nuclear weapons should be removed from West Germany and Eastern Europe. So, independently, did Rapacki the Polish foreign minister. Others such as Solly Zuckerman took the line that nuclear deterrents cancel each other out and only those ignorant of physics and biology could envisage their use. But understandably enough, most proposals were inspired by the desire to avoid nuclear war rather than reduce expenditure.

The Conservatives were no better than Labour in limiting Britain's commitments and hence the cost of their defence; worse in fact. Churchill, Eden and Macmillan nursed illusions of reconciling the differences between America and the Soviet Union by the benign diplomacy of the third and most sophisticated of the great powers. Cherwell argued that unless Britain could make atom bombs we would become a second-class power 'like the native levies who were allowed small arms and no artillery'. The imperial metaphor was revealing. Suez was the symptom of acting like a great power, and the pusillanimity of the military commanders, the bewildering changes of plan, the indecision and muddle were ignominious. We were almost unanimous in regarding the enterprise as a disaster and we noted the disagreeable sting in the tail. The country wanted to forget it as quickly as possible and those who opposed it suffered. Gaitskell lost the next election; and Nigel Nicolson was turned out of his seat by his constituency party. When Dean Acheson made his aphorism about Britain having lost an empire and not yet found a role, Macmillan made himself absurd: he issued a statement recalling our exploits against Philip II, Napoleon and the Kaiser.

Suez brought to a head the greatest of all issues since Munich: European Union. After the war Bevin had favoured a customs union in Europe, but the Treasury and the Board of Trade vetoed it. And then faced with the Schuman plan to integrate Europe's coal and steel, the National Executive of the Labour Party declared, 'We are closer to our kinsmen in Australia and New Zealand than to Europe.' Illness struck Bevin and Cripps. Neither the prime minister, foreign secretary, chancellor nor lord chancellor was present at the ministerial committee that rejected the Schuman plan. Perhaps, then, there was an excuse for not tying our economy to the ailing states of Europe, though the reason Morrison gave was ominous. 'The Durham miners won't wear it.' It was all the sadder because Britain and France had collaborated with great success in preparing the response to General Marshall's plan for aid.

But by the mid-fifties Europe was once again stable, and the refusal by the Conservative government to take seriously the Messina conference that was to lead to the Treaty of Rome was inexcusable. It was the most ruinous diplomatic decision taken by my generation. Many were the excuses that were made. Ministers spoke of our nuclear alliance with America; our devotion to free trade with all, not just six, European countries in the OEEC; our devotion to GATT; our commitment to the Commonwealth; and the doubts of the chiefs of staff. Anthony Eden said, 'I feel in my bones that we are not European.' 'That's a funny place to have thinking,' said Paul-Henri Spaak, the Belgian foreign minister who had been at pains to remove all supranational language from the resolutions that were to be discussed at the conference. The Foreign Office thought nothing would come of Messina. To the despair of Spaak Britain sent an under-secretary of the Board of Trade to represent Britain at the conference. Spaak came to London to see Rab Butler: the warmer Spaak became, the colder was Butler's reception. 'I don't think I could have shocked him more when I tried to appeal to his imagination if I had taken off my trousers,' Spaak said to his *directeur du cabinet* Robert Rothschild. At the eleventh hour the Europeans tried again and sent the Dutch foreign minister to Butler. To be lectured on Britain's moral responsibility to lead Europe by such a little nation was too much. 'I got very bored with him,' Butler later told Michael Charlton; and he had the satisfaction of making a little joke at an OEEC dinner in Paris about the excavations going on in Messina.

Conservatives were always to jibe at the slightest loss of sovereignty to a European body. And here the oldest members of Our Age were to blame: Harold Caccia and the Foreign Office, Roger Makins and the Treasury knights, indeed much of the galaxy of Whitehall talent were opposed to European union. Among diplomats Con O'Neill was an exception, among civil servants Frank Lee and Eric Roll, among Conservatives Christopher Soames, Iain Macleod, Edward Heath, and Bob Boothby. But Boothby – a foundation member of Our Age – was distrusted and aroused the envy of his party for his masterly television performances full of rollicking unorthodoxies; Macleod and Heath were too young. Too many of us (including myself) were in a vague way in favour but irresolute. Yet not perhaps as irresolute as Whitehall. When finally Macmillan dipped his toe in the water, the ministries stood on the bank for months arguing the pros and cons, searching for the best possible solution, as if Britain was an arbiter rather than a suppliant. The French officials, like Marjolin and Wormser, men devoted to Britain, were dismayed.

Suez was to prove a double disaster for the cause of European union in Britain. France once again felt betrayed by Albion. Within eighteen months de Gaulle did his deal with Adenauer. Both were determined to keep such an unreliable partner out of the Community. Correspondingly Macmillan strained every nerve to rebuild the special relationship with America and started silly manoeuvres to destabilize the negotiations in Rome. Still clinging to the notion that Britain was, if not one of the *great* powers, still a *special* power, Macmillan made his nuclear secrets deal with America and got Polaris. By so doing he simultaneously saddled Britain with yet heavier defence expenditure and hamstrung her chance of running in the European stakes. De Gaulle did not miss his chance. By vetoing British entry in January 1963 he inflicted a humiliation on Britain equal to that of Suez – and worse than Dakar. Edward Heath, whatever verdict may be passed on his days as premier, took the decision, as important as Attlee's to quit India, to join the European Community.

On the issue of Europe Labour resembled a calculating suitor brought face to face with a prospective bride. Labour neither liked her face nor her figure and doubted whether she was rich enough. The only ardent lovers were Roy Jenkins and his supporters, among them some civil servants accustomed to serve abroad, such as Eric Roll. He was cast down when Gaitskell in the last year of his life came out against joining the Community. In the sixties Wilson was able to avoid a decision. One made noises, of course; one toured Europe with George Brown; one posed as the restraining influence upon America, as the man who persuaded Lyndon Johnson not to drop the atom bomb on Hanoi. Tony Crosland used to excuse his lack of interest by saying that Europe was not very high on the priorities of his constituents at Grimsby. Denis Healey said he was agnostic on the matter. In opposition Wilson agreed to hold a referendum on the terms the Conservative government had got when Britain joined the Community. In one sense Wilson was right to do so. The decision to sign the Treaty of Rome was an historic one to surrender a part of national sovereignty. But the referendum disintegrated the coalition of interests that had brought Labour to power.

Labour found a convenient impediment to joining the Community. That was the Commonwealth. It did not mean much to most of Our Age except for those who had spent some years creating its universities. But it meant much to Conservative intellectuals and it certainly meant much to the Queen. Some elders of Our Age were seduced into taking the line the die-hards had always played. In March 1959 Lionel Robbins wrote in a letter to *The Times*: 'The predominance of the white man ... must continue for at least another generation. Few black Africans of the central African tribes have yet developed the qualities of leadership or the education and experience to act without control;' and this was why Conservatives, who had been willing to grant independence to West African colonies, were disinclined to do so in East Africa where white settlers were accustomed to rule. It took the disgraceful incidents in the Hola camp in Kenya – the occasion of a philippic by the astonishing Enoch Powell – to make Macmillan deliver in 1960 his winds of change speech. It was a speech which the ancient former colonial officer Leonard Woolf had been making since the twenties; and, unlike Robbins, Woolf had no illusions about the leaders of the whites – in 1957 he had denounced Roy Welensky as a villain. By the time Macleod had done his work in East Africa the old guard Tories were disenchanted with the Commonwealth. They saw it now ruled by former rebels, as ungrateful as they were (sometimes) corrupt, and too given to tribal dictatorship. For Conservatives the Commonwealth spelt immigration – and trouble. So the wheel turned full circle. The intellectuals on the left of the Labour Party became as partial to the Commonwealth as they had been hostile to the Empire. Some went to advise Nkrumah or Nyerere, and Barbara Castle and Judith Hart prided themselves on extracting from the Treasury funds for overseas development. With a true ignorance of the role of power in foreign policy some Labour ministers nursed the illusion that the Commonwealth could be an effective counter-weight to the European Community.

Nevertheless, the peaceful divestment of the Empire was the most successful political achievement of Our Age. Unlike France who fought bloody battles in Indo-China and Algeria, which divided the French nation and shook the army's allegiance, Britain withdrew from her dependencies in good order and left little resentment behind. The credit must go in the main to Attlee's cabinet who resolved to cut the Gordian knot in India. The communal massacres were terrible and no doubt mistakes were made; but the massacres would have occurred however the transference of power had been effected, and if the British had tried to prevent them by delaying independence, they would have been sucked into the maelstrom and earned the abuse of both sides as they did in Ireland. The Conservatives may have been slow to move in Africa, but move they did. Very few British lost their lives in the disengagement; and the British stuck to the adage of Gladstonian liberalism – self-government is more important than good government.

But the realism that we displayed over colonial issues was not displayed in foreign policy. Hardly had he taken office than Harold Wilson in an ecstasy of self-importance set off round the world making commitments at each whistle stop. Like the Tories he was convinced that our oil supplies would be endangered unless we had a presence east of Suez. Our frontier now lay on the Himalayas – quite an extension since the days before 1939 when it was said to be on the Rhine. Denis Healey was a fine secretary of state for defence but even he found difficulty in liquidating defence commitments by cancelling ruinous aircraft projects when the Foreign Office refused to liquidate Britain's political commitments. He was caught in a vice. Britain had put workers into factories rather than into conscript armies and at the beginning of the century six of the ten largest manufacturers in the country were recipients of defence contracts. In the twenties Britain had the highest absolute defence expenditure in the world and in 1940 it was the largest manufacturer of all types of aircraft. We found that proposals to reduce defence expenditure were countered by the argument that to do so would create unemployment by destroying our ability to sell arms abroad.

Wilson's most astonishing armaments deal was yet to come. Soon after he took office in 1974, with inflation raging after the chaos caused by the oil-price rise and with his party baying for more public expenditure, he slipped through the cabinet against the stated policy of his party what he called a 'little bit of modernization' to 'enhance' existing nuclear weapons for a mere twenty-four million pounds. Even before he left office it had cost £595 million and was not cash-limited. Joel Barnett, the chief secretary at the Treasury, had never heard of it: when he did, some years later in opposition and as chairman of the Public Accounts Committee, the cost had exceeded a thousand million pounds.

The threat of nuclear warfare had preserved peace in Europe for nearly thirty years; and the British were right to vote against those who they thought endangered their security by unilateral disarmament. But surely the total cost was too high. When Our Age was in power Britain spent a slightly higher proportion of her GDP on defence than France or Germany: the amount of money may have been smaller but that was because the British GDP was so much smaller. Reason told us that Europe was protected by America's nuclear deterrent. Britain's own nuclear weapon was negligible as a deterrent and terrifyingly expensive to update. We were mistaken to do so. We were mistaken to try to police the Middle East and form a bastion in the Far East; to finance the sterling area and pump aid into former colonies; construct every type of military and civil aircraft including Concorde; even replacing the ageing *Queens* with yet another gigantic ocean liner. What Nicholas Henderson said was true: Britain's ability to remain a power of any sort depended on her financial and economic strength, her unity of purpose too, and it was that that he called in question.

And so it was that, when we looked back at our past, we were haunted by the ghosts of our irresolution. The two great European countries had been ruined by the war: Germany by the iniquities of her rulers and by bombardment and occupation, France by the stain of collaboration, die-hard colonialism and ineffective governments. Yet they found leaders. Adenauer and de Gaulle resurrected them. Meanwhile Britain, apparently the victor in the war, had been unable to adjust to her changed condition in world politics. Led during the war by a master of rhetoric, Britain now became the victim of her own rhetoric. She fondly imagined she had won the war. She had not. America and Russia had won the war. Britain had in her finest hour not lost it. Long famed for her social solidarity Britain fell a victim to a syndicalism that divided the nation into warring factions. Every institution seemed to think it a mark of masculinity to fight its own corner and expose the weakness of central and local government. No one from the elder generation, and none from Our Age, arose to match Adenauer and de Gaulle who proved to be contemptuous enemies of Britain. They gave their countries self-confidence and pride, and the leadership of Europe passed into their hands. Sadly enough the humiliation of defeat teaches men better than the vanity of victory how to revive and inspire their own dear country.

CHAPTER 22

Our Age Reforms Education

1

WAS MARTIN WIENER right to indict Our Age for establishing an educational system that despised science and technology and deflected the brightest and best from a career in industry? In one sense he could not help being right. The culture of any country cannot fail to be reflected in its system of education. American culture in the nineteenth century was a business culture. Throughout the Middle West in the last century and the early years of this, the Land Grant colleges were set up to help farmers and businessmen. British culture was geared not to business but to governance: to producing the educated classes that were to be civil servants, colonial officers and professional men who underpinned parliamentary government. Wiener was right in maintaining that the professions, the armed forces and service in the Empire were the careers that were held up for admiration to the eyes of my generation. He was also right in thinking that the ancient universities and the public schools were perceived as a civilizing force in society – all the more necessary as the plutocracy grew in size. G.M.Young had no doubt about the matter. He took pride in the fact that Oxford and Cambridge did not become in Victorian times seminaries for parsons or seminar rooms for professors. But he also said, 'If we imagine Victorian England without Oxford and Cambridge what barrier can we see against an all-encroaching materialism or professionalism?' Or consider my own headmaster, J.F.Roxburgh, who set out his ideals in a little book called *Eleutheros*. He echoed Aristotle's words that 'there is a form of education which should be given to our sons, not because it is necessary, but because it benefits a free man and is noble'.

It is true that before the war the public schools did not value science and engineering as highly as classics or history. There were exceptions such as Oundle, which was renowned for teaching these subjects – no wonder since many boys there came from the homes of industrialists in the Midlands. But after the war the oldest cohort of Our Age, now running the Federation of British Industry, equipped the public schools with up-to-date laboratories and workshops. The school curriculum was not loaded towards 'useful' subjects. It is true that there was no subject built into the curriculum like 'shop' in American schools where at around thirteen one learnt to use one's hands; but the curriculum was not all that different from American high school studies and considerably more exacting. Nor was it so different from the curriculum on the Continent. No one could argue that a French boy going to Sciences Po or any university was being trained to be a manager or entrepreneur. The careers that the highest proportion of graduates followed were in commerce. Hardly odd in a nation renowned for trade. The British had a three-century-long tradition as bankers. What could be more natural for able graduates than to choose that as a career or one in other financial services such as insurance, commodity broking, the stock market, retail trade and the like? But the careers the young follow depend much on where they live and what their parents do for a living. For masses of boys industry was the career they hoped would be open to them when they left school.

Why then were we uneasy when we heard the kind of criticism Wiener and others made? They were uneasy because they were absorbed by quite different issues when they discussed education.

Like Faust we discovered that *Zwei Seelen wohnen ach! in meiner Brust.* The first soul, the soul of justice, wanted more children to stay on and work in the sixth form, far more to enter higher education, wanted the disparities between the public school pupils and the children who before the war left school at fourteen to be diminished, wanted them to be taught about things that make life worth living – music, literature and art. This was the soul that, analysing statistics, was shocked to see how the scales were weighted against the poor and later the blacks. The other soul, the soul of excellence, wanted the standards of entry to universities raised, and sixth-form studies to multiply but remain as rigorous as ever. This soul dreamed of a society in which merit replaced privilege, longed for boys and girls to study whatever subject stirred their imagination, and admired the high standards achieved by early specialization. This soul assumed that Trevelyan and Northcote had been right in recommending that the examinations for competitive entry to the public service should resemble those in the universities for the bachelor's degree. It was up to the professions to provide instruction – in the Inns of Court or the hospital medical schools, for example – and to monitor professional standards. And similarly it was up to industry to train its management and workforce. In all the reports on education by Crowther, Robbins, Dainton, in all the sapient articles by Vaizey, Peterson, Ashby, Mott and so on, you can see the two souls wrestling for mastery. The very documents that called for the expansion of education upheld principles that curtailed it.

2

THE EDUCATION ACT of 1944 reflected this struggle between the two souls. The Act bore Rab Butler's name, but he was its midwife not its father. Not he but several powerful officials who had served for decades in the Board of Education conceived it when they had been evacuated during the war to Bournemouth. Griffith Williams, the head of the secondary school branch, a tireless bachelor adept at manipulating committees, wanted to retain grammar schools and select children for them at eleven years old. William Cleary, the head of the elementary school branch, wanted comprehensive secondary schools. Or, if that were unacceptable, he would settle for selection so long as it was delayed until thirteen when children would go either to a grammar school or to a technical school. The third official, responsible for technical education, was not their equal and therefore technical schools died at birth. The permanent secretary, Maurice Holmes, ruled in favour of Williams. So the main sections of the Act were settled before Butler became minister. He made a little sortie against the eleven-plus principle but retired when his officials assured him that if children had been wrongly assessed they could be transferred as late as thirteen to a grammar school. He made another little sortie to abolish fees in direct grant schools, but retired again when the Conservative back-benchers insisted that every parent should have the right to buy the best education for his children that he could afford.

But Butler deserves the credit for doing what only a politician could do. He first had to win over Churchill, no easy task. Churchill's memory went back to the furious squabbles over the church schools that had marred Balfour's, and broken Birrell's, education bills in the early years of the century. Butler cracked this nut. With his Labour colleague Chuter Ede he got the nonconformist communions to accept that fifty per cent of the costs of the Church of England schools should be borne by the state on condition that their own schools got equal treatment. He did not think it his business to decide how the schools should develop or what they should teach. That never had been the business of ministers responsible for education. The British liked to mock French ministers of education who, they said, knew at any hour of the day precisely what every child in France was learning. In Britain ministers of education had barely the power of a constitutional monarch. All to the good, so people said. No politician should dictate what ought to be taught: the local worthies elected to govern the boroughs and councils and their bureaucrats, not the state, should run the schools. As a result the reforms and the expansion proceeded higgledy-piggledy.

It became customary to genuflect when the Butler Act was mentioned. But today we can see that it evaded the real problem: who should be taught what. Before the war twice as many Germans had stayed on at school until eighteen, and two and a half times as many took the equivalent of Higher Certificate (A Level). In Germany industry trained boys after they left school. In Britain few educationalists gave them a second thought. But David Eccles did. He asked his officials and insisted against their advice on providing more technical education. The reluctance of British firms to train their workforce was a scandal. He realized the Treasury would not be moved unless he could get an 'independent' view on the deficiencies of the nation's education. He therefore asked Geoffrey Crowther and the Central Advisory Council for Education (one of those enormous bodies beloved by civil servants because they represent every interest) to tell him. Crowther told him how backward Britain was. Eighty-seven per cent left school at fifteen. Of the rest only two fifths of boys and girls got full-time education from fifteen to seventeen: those who did not might get released from work one day a week to study for a vocation. Butler's Act had produced a pattern of grammar and secondary modern schools. The soul of excellence rejoiced over the boys and girls who went to the grammar schools – well, over those who in ever-increasing numbers got into the A stream and battled for the tiny number of places in universities. They certainly were emerging with high standards in their sixth-form specialism.

But by the late fifties the soul of justice awoke from its slumbers. A few dons were asking who had benefited from Butler's Act. A young Cambridge economist, John Vaizey, turned himself into an expert on the economics of education. He found the ministry of education deficient in the most elementary statistics, and his work showed that Britain was spending a lower proportion of its national income on education than it did in the depths of the Depression in the thirties. Jean Floud showed that the successful children in secondary schools were those who had literate parents; David Glass and Richard Titmuss at LSE that the main beneficiaries of the Butler Act – indeed of the welfare state – were the middle classes. Was it not typical of our rulers, asked Glass, to concentrate on the universities and despise as inferior the sector that enabled day-release pupils to get vocational diplomas and qualifications? Finally Roy Kelsall, a professor at Sheffield, analysed university intake and found that the numbers of public school boys entering Oxbridge were out of all proportion to the number in these schools.

Suddenly the very notion of a meritocracy, an elite, began to be attacked in every walk of national life. In 1958 Michael Young wrote a book that caught the imagination of Our Age. In *The Rise of the Meritocracy* he imagined what would happen when academic and intellectual merit was the acknowledged criterion for all posts and jobs, from prime minister to dustman. By 2033 everything had gone according to plan but unaccountably the manual workers began to rebel. Young's irony was not lost on the new advocates of mass education – Brian Jackson, Tyrell Burgess and Eric Robinson. Hardly any comprehensive schools had survived under the Butler Act. Now their advocates wanted them to be more than institutions of equal opportunity. They were to be institutions that made equality a reality throughout a child's school days. There should be no streaming or setting and no competition in form. No child should be made to feel inferior to another. Only when the clever and the stupid were taught together would class divisions begin to disappear.

And so began the great debate about comprehensive schooling. Those who put academic achievement first opposed it. Eric James was appalled that its advocates were so ignorant of what would happen if children of all abilities were admitted to a grammar school. The bland way these publicists compared public schools to comprehensive schools showed that they did not realize what measured intelligence (IQ) was. Numbers of thick boys and vacuous girls went to public schools – though far fewer were any longer going to the leading public schools – but even the thickest and most vacuous had an IQ of more than a hundred, i.e. 'average' intelligence. But the tide of opinion was running faster and faster against the Butlerian division of grammar and secondary modern schools. The tide was to sweep away the groyne between them, the hated examination taken by children between ten and twelve years old. Every summer middle-class parents, it was said, resembled King Aegeus sitting on the rock looking out to sea hoping that the sail would be white signalling success and entry to a grammar school, or despairing when it was black and their child condemned to a secondary modern.

Conservatives liked to pillory Tony Crosland and Shirley Williams for forcing comprehensives upon unwilling local authorities. That was propaganda. It was the middle classes that brought in comprehensive education. Conservative local authorities, no less than Labour, were not prepared to see children separated like sheep from goats at the age of eleven. When later Cyril Burt, the psychologist on whose research measured intelligence tests had been based, was suspected of having falsified his results, the exam was even more discredited. The exam was only part of a process of assessment but no matter; any assessment that suggested your children were inferior was ignominious.

In 1961 Tony Crosland looked at this stratified system of education. He noted that the public and direct grant schools taught only twenty per cent of sixteen-year-olds but accounted for sixty per cent of the Oxbridge entry. The proportion of fourteen-year-olds at public schools was so small that it did not show up in printer's ink on a histogram. Yet what a high proportion of top places in the professions and business went to their pupils! Crosland was true to his beliefs as an egalitarian. When he became secretary of state he set up a commission to recommend how the public and direct grant schools could be integrated into a national comprehensive school system.

So here at last was the chance for my generation to confront one of their symbols of snobbery and oppression. When the public schools saw the terms of reference Crosland set out for the commission, they bleated that the terms stated as a fact that the public schools were divisive: surely that was for the commissionto examine. But Crosland was stating an incontrovertible fact. The public schools divided England in a way that the prep schools of New England or the Jesuit schools in France did not; they exacerbated the class differences that every foreign observer noted. The public schools for some years had offered places to boys and girls whose fees would be paid by the local authorities, but the scheme never flourished because few local authorities were willing to drain talent from their own schools and pay disproportionately high fees for a few favoured children. So the soul of justice waited expectantly for the commission to report.

It waited in vain. Of all futile committees on which I have sat none equalled the Public Schools Commission. It was doomed from the start. Crosland had told the chairman John Newsam that he would not countenance abolition of the public schools. Such a curtailment of liberty in a democracy was unacceptable and the cost to the local authorities of taking them over (which the commission then estimated to be sixty million pounds) prohibitive. The soul of excellence within the commission stressed the efficiency of the public schools. Nearly all children who failed the eleven-plus and were sent to public schools got O Levels: nine tenths of those who went to the secondary modern schools did not. If it had been so difficult to find an acceptable scheme for integrating the public schools with the grammar schools, how much more difficult it would be to integrate them with comprehensive schools. To contemplate teaching barely literate children made Dr Arnold's successors shudder. Still more intractable was the fact facing the soul of justice that most of the public schools were boarding schools. How were children to be found to fill over half the 138,000 beds in them? The commission's research team argued that vast numbers of children were really in need of boarding education. John Vaizey was sceptical. He thought the team had confused demand with need. No measure of 'demand' for boarding could ever be devised. It was as if Henry VIII on dissolving the monasteries 'had filled them with social need cases after an exhaustive social survey of the number of people in the population who felt the need for a life of contemplation in a cell'. He concluded that it was more sensible to do nothing and told the press he was putting his sons down for Eton.

The commission's very existence had concentrated the minds of public school headmasters wonderfully. Some of these, such as John Dancy at Marlborough or John Thorn at Winchester, were pioneers of change. Our Age won some of their objectives. The grosser abuses in the schools – the beating of boys by boys and fagging – disappeared. Boys and girls had more leisure, were less regimented and absurd boy-made rules fell into disuse. Roxburgh's liberal ideals began to be accepted. The schools began to prize A Levels and enterprise rather than games. Girls were admitted to sixth forms and separate houses built for them. Soon the abyss between the state system and the private sector was deeper than it had been twenty years previously. The public schools declined to integrate with the state system. So did most of the direct grant schools; they became in effect public schools in which virtually all pupils paid fees. By the eighties Britain's membership of the European Community stopped any further attack on the public schools. They were practically all religious establishments: and the Community ruled that those who wanted to opt out of the state system of education on grounds of liberty of conscience should have the right to do so. Those in the Labour Party who regarded these schools as Carthage, meet to be destroyed, muttered without much conviction that high taxation and the removal of charitable status would bring the public schools to their knees. But though considerable numbers of boarding prep schools closed, the public schools flourished in the affluent society as never before.

3

THE EDUCATED CLASSES were divided on the issue of comprehensive schools. Probably a majority of us wanted to retain the grammar schools and later observed that West Germany had introduced the Gesamtschule without abolishing the famous Gymnasium. American academics who had spent a sabbatical year in British universities were amazed to hear that these schools, which had given their kids such a good education, were to be abolished. The dons heard stories from them of the defects of the American high school – underpaid teachers trained in the theory of education and inexpert in the subjects they were meant to teach. Would these errors spread to Britain?

But soon we recognized that America was a country where the vast majority of children stayed at high school until eighteen and fifty per cent of them went on to some form of higher education. Those like myself who believed that in the long term comprehensive education was inevitable had to face many bad consequences. The reorganization ran up against bricks and mortar: school buildings dictated and distorted many of the changes. Sometimes a school was divided between different sites, others lost their sixth forms when sixth-form colleges were created; and the growth of ethnic communities in the city centres created fearsome problems for teachers. Some authorities transferred children from elementary to secondary at eleven, others at twelve, others at thirteen. Some channelled their pupils into streams according to their ability, others regarded this as a betrayal of egalitarianism and wanted children to go at their own pace as in the primary schools.

Fortune loaded the dice against the comprehensive schools. The reorganization coincided with the cultural revolution of the sixties. The comprehensive school headteacher of the fifties wanted his new school to become as far as possible a uniform-wearing, satchel-carrying school with homework. In the sixties discipline, as elsewhere in society, relaxed. More children bunked off and the authority of teachers diminished. In a public school bullies, idlers and disruptive children existed; but they were kept in check or, if unmanageable, expelled. Whereas the brisk hum of gossip and talk in a secondary modern classroom meant that only those children from disciplined homes would keep their heads down and work at their algebra through the buzz. In some city schools vandalism, arson and assaults on teachers were no longer horrifying exceptions. The more child-centred a school became the less children were willing to accept the notion of being taught. More people scoffed at the view that school told each generation what the rules are, what things are worth valuing and what kinds of behaviour are odious, destructive and wrong.

The reorganization also coincided with the rise of union militancy. The teachers' unions had always been moderate. They conceded change by bargaining for fewer duties and more pay, but they hardly ever took industrial action. Now in the seventies the largest union became bloody-minded. The National Union of Teachers did not call a strike. They preferred the tactics of disrupting the work of the schools, now in this authority, now in that, so that only a few of their members actually lost a day's pay. Truancy among teachers became a feature like truancy among children. Graduates who would formerly have become teachers found jobs in universities and polytechnics or in the computer industry: few in the schools who taught mathematics had graduated in the subject. By 1986 the numbers of auxiliaries and bureaucrats in full-time jobs needed to service the 525,000 teachers in the maintained schools had risen by two thirds to 362,000. Local authorities, policed by the unions, would not reduce the numbers of staff. They preferred to cut the provision of school books, and soon government was blamed for providing none. Not all schools or local authorities suffered from union militancy: but a sufficient number did and they provoked a counter-attack.

The counter-attack against comprehensive education was led by two dons teaching English, Brian Cox and A. E. Dyson. They published what they called Black Papers. They and their successors in the eighties, such as Caroline Cox and Roger Scruton, may be called the grammarians. They insisted that the schools were failing to teach children the fundamental skills of grammar and arithmetic with the result that they emerged from school unemployable, illiterate and innumerate. They argued that the comprehensives were less effective not only than the grammar schools but than the old secondary modern schools. The grammarians rounded on their opponents for trying to destroy anything that differentiated one child from another, such as examinations, setting, streaming. By no means all the comprehensives taught their children in mixed-ability classes, but the grammarians accused them all of holding back those who had started with better advantages in life, better brains, better vocabulary, better habits and training, and pictured them as being made to march at the same pace as the rest of their peer group. Did this not institutionalize idleness among the better brains, so that the clever children got bored and were never taught the habits of hard work and accuracy? The grammarians seized on documents such as the Hargreaves Report written by a top bureaucrat in the Inner London Education Authority who had concluded that the many hours of teaching modern languages produced such meagre results that it would be wiser to abandon teaching French and German. It was not clear to the grammarians why the author had not made the not too arduous journey to Holland to learn how the Dutch managed, since they were the best linguists in Europe.

The grammarians also campaigned for Standard English. The progressives argued that if linguists such as Chomsky or John Lyons or David Crystal showed us that no language or dialect was inferior to any other, why not sanction West Indian creole dialect, or Cockney or Yorkshire dialect? Had not Leavis denounced the Use of English examination as a monstrous attempt to strangle living prose? Teachers who corrected a child's speech or writing were wrong: in trying to conform to Standard English the child would stumble into clichés and verbosity. What was Standard English but an oppressive instrument of a cruel ruling class? And were spelling bees likely to improve spelling? Reading improves spelling; and if children do not read at home they will not spell words correctly. But the grammarians replied that intelligent parents among ethnic and disadvantaged groups realized that to master Standard English was the first step to rising in society, or at least holding your own in it. Were we really to believe that the ability to master the calculus was irrelevant and all that mattered was whether a kid was street-wise?

The grammarians' case was both true and untrue.* Many schools all over the country bore no resemblance to the grammarians' description. Even when conditions were against them there were as ever thousands of devoted and able teachers contending with multicultural classes, children of divorced or single parents and with the new General Certificate of Secondary Education which emphasized the teachers' assessment of their pupils (like Abitur). Yet all was not well and parents knew it. Their children may have been happier at school than they themselves had been, but the average and below-average child was behind his German contemporary particularly in maths and languages: comparison with Japan would have been even more dispiriting. Jim Callaghan when prime minister called for debate in his bluff way, but debate was all he got. For the past century laissez-faire had been the ruling principle in education. The system of letting a multitude of authorities and

* There is one piece of evidence to suggest that the grammarians overstated their case. When I became provost of King's College Cambridge in 1956 nearly seventy per cent of the entry came from the public and eighteen per cent from direct grant schools; barely ten per cent from maintained grammar schools. Not that the college had any academic apologies to make. Year after year King's obtained the highest percentage of firsts in the Tripos. Nevertheless, I thought King's ought to try to attract more boys from the maintained grammar schools and we found that the headmasters of such schools rarely encouraged their pupils to try for King's because they thought that they had little chance of getting a place. Twenty years or more after I had left the college, fifty-four per cent of the entry at King's came from the comprehensive system and fifteen per cent from the few maintained grammar schools that still existed. King's no longer came top of all colleges in the Tripos results, but it often came out about fifth or sixth and never lower than thirteenth. In 1990 it again came first. The comprehensive school students could not always compete on equal terms in the first or even the second year. But by the third year they were as good as their public school contemporaries and perhaps had greater potential.

examining boards determine the form and content of education was failing the nation.

As Our Age moved towards the grave, the two souls wept in self-reproach. The soul of excellence lamented the destruction of the grammar schools. The soul of justice lamented that the pursuit of excellence had canonized a system of education in which sixth-formers discarded either maths and science or language and literature in order to specialize. And here we have probed to the heart of the matter, the centre of the conflict between the two souls. Why was it that England and Wales alone in the western world allowed adolescents to drop maths and science (or languages) at sixteen and often as early as fourteen? Why were A Levels so different from the Baccalauréat, Abitur, Matura or, in America, College Board? The reason was curious. Oxford and Cambridge still threw their long shadow over higher education even when their student numbers were only a fraction of those in higher education.

The Victorian dons believed the ancient universities existed to educate the upper classes as members of 'our happy Establishment of Church and State'; and since the sons of these classes were often indolent or thick, they made the entry qualifications to Oxford and Cambridge exceedingly modest and the pass degree unexacting. But the Victorians also wanted the talented sons of poor gentlemen to go there to read for honours despite the high cost of tuition and boarding in the colleges. And so pious benefactors and the colleges themselves increased the number of scholarships. The exacting *college* exam for these scholarships became the blue riband for the public schools and grammar schools. But the *university* entrance exams remained as modest as ever. When Oxford and Cambridge established examining boards which granted exemption from these modest entrance exams to anyone who obtained five credits in the School Certificate – an exam that could be taken by an intelligent fifteen or a clever fourteen-year-old – the schools faced a problem. What were such adolescents to do after they took the exam? The answer was to work for a scholarship in classics or maths or science or history or modern languages at Oxford or Cambridge. In due course the civic universities set up their own examining boards and a new sixth-form exam, the Higher Certificate (the forerunner of A Levels), was invented – but it followed the pattern of the Oxbridge scholarship syllabus. However much the colleges insisted that competitors for a scholarship should show proficiency in ancillary subjects, everyone knew that the prizes went to those who showed outstanding merit in the specialism of their choice. Everyone also knew that the academic prestige of a school depended on how many awards it won each year at Oxford and Cambridge.

Secondary education had got caught in a vice. There were too many with vested interests to welcome change. The system suited the dons: boys and girls arrived at the university already knowing something about the scholarly debates in their specialism. It suited the Treasury because the first degree took only three years. It suited the professions: in Britain a doctor qualified in seven, a lawyer in six years after leaving school. The British boasted that their students were two years in advance of American contemporaries and graduated earlier than those on the Continent. A German might be nineteen or even older before he passed Abitur, and in the years after the war French boys struggling to make the *concours* for the Polytechnique or the Ecole Normale would have to take *taupe* or *cagne* for two further years after taking the Baccalauréat. The British system claimed to have one merit. Why not let able boys and girls study subjects which appealed to them: what is the good of trying to force those who have a mathematical block or who cannot master languages to continue with these subjects?

But the system had two defects. Industry complained that scientific graduates had narrow interests, and commerce that arts graduates were innumerate. Geoffrey Crowther and his committee shied away from the problem. They rebuked the universities for their chaotic system of admissions and for jacking up their entry requirement even higher. Dons, they said, would do well to talk less about the education of an elite and more about training large echelons of intelligent men and women in modern skills. But they could not bring themselves to recommend that every sixth-former should be trained to be both numerate and literate. Implicitly they endorsed early specialization. A simple reform of sixth-form studies, I argued, would have ensured that all boys and girls were required to continue to study until they left school the two international languages of our time, maths and English: all must take a paper in practical mathematics and in comprehension and précis writing in English. But in Britain's academies no agreement can ever be reached on simple reforms.

But was Crowther right in thinking that there were too few places in universities for able boys and girls? The old guard had their doubts. In 1939 Walter Moberley, who thought of the university as a training ground for the professions, considered that 'something like saturation point had been reached'. In 1944 Grant Robertson, vice-chancellor of Birmingham, questioned whether, 'dredge or subsidize as you will, there is no large untapped reservoir of brains'. In the fifties Marjorie Holland, the elegant American economics don at Girton and wife of the vice master of Trinity, opposed the creation of a third women's college on the ground that there were not enough talented girls to fill the two existing colleges at Cambridge. The dons' trade union, the AUT, was sceptical. So too was a sentinel of the new guard. Kingsley Amis asked why a girl was admitted to read English literature at his university when she had never heard of metre in poetry. In 1960 he issued a warning in *Encounter*, 'More will Mean Worse'. On the other side a Fabian group calculated that by the end of the sixties there would be nearly a quarter of a million fewer places in higher education than needed and by the end of the seventies nearly half a million.

One argument in favour of expansion carried all before it. This was the contention that higher education was the key to economic growth. Turn on the tap and the next generation would be more productive as well as better educated. The more dons there were the higher production would rise because of the spin-off from fundamental to applied research and from that to industry. It would happen automatically and British industry would benefit as American, German and Japanese industry had benefited. Soon a stream of books and reports began to flow, all urging the expansion of this or that discipline: veterinary science (1944), dentistry (1945), science and technology (1946), Slavonic, Oriental and African studies (1947), social and economic research (1948).

The weather in Whitehall has a Mediterranean quality. For long the sea remains unruffled. Then zephyrs from one quarter, and then another, begin to play, die down, rise again and disappear. And then suddenly a breeze from one point of the compass sets in and begins to blow strongly. Weather-beaten mariners, the old salts in Whitehall, know almost as soon as it blows that it differs from those deceptive zephyrs. In May 1958 the chairman of the UGC Keith Murray had repeated the received wisdom that there seemed to be only a small reservoir of potential university students. Within a few months he was announcing plans to open half a dozen new universities and expand old ones. He had felt the breeze freshen. Always an expansionist at heart, receptive to student opinion, a bachelor, indefatigable, benevolent and persuasive, he had at his side a civil servant, Edward Hale, who was one of the first to see the implications of the Butler Act. Since dons lamented that many talented boys and girls were deterred from entering a university because they would be a drain on their parents' resources, Eccles set up another committee under Colin Anderson to examine which students should be eligible for grants. His masterstroke was to come. Crowther and Anderson mortared the enemy's trenches. Now he rolled his heavy artillery into place. He persuaded Macmillan to appoint Lionel Robbins chairman of a committee on higher education.

4

IN THE SWEEP of its proposals and its idealism the Robbins Report was 'one of the great state papers of the century perhaps the last of its line', in the opinion of John Carswell, the Treasury official who acted as assessor to the committee and later became secretary to the UGC. He saw Robbins as 'a bland silver lion', gentle in manner but with a 'giant paw from which a claw or two would sometimes make a carefully modulated appearance', a man who tolerated disagreement and let it make not the faintest impression on him. 'I never encountered anyone except Otto Clarke of the Treasury who was more confident that he was right.' Disgruntled humanists accused Robbins of thinking as a philistine intent on providing trained manpower for the nation's economy. They were wrong. The report was as concerned as any Victorian report with moral and intellectual improvement. And when Margaret Thatcher was secretary of state in her unreconstructed days she was to issue a white paper saying that places in higher education were not to be awarded to meet some estimate of the country's need for qualified people. Higher education was valuable because it helped men and women develop as individuals. Claus Moser and Richard Layard at the LSE provided overwhelming statistical evidence why Britain could no longer afford to admit only three to four per cent of each age group to universities. With a general election looming and almost without public discussion Macmillan announced that he had accepted the report.

Seen now in retrospect Harold Macmillan was unwise to appoint a celebrated professor like Robbins as chairman of the committee, and Philip Morris, the most powerful and wily of all vice-chancellors and architect of the report, to be his henchman. Was it right that in a report on the future of the *whole* of higher education the majority of the committee should have been *university* academics? And was it right that there was no one from the technical colleges, no toughie from industry and no engineer? Robbins knew little about scientists and their ways, or about the relation of schools to universities or technical education. Robbins and Morris were idealists, determined to give new opportunities to the children of parents who came from the same class as their own; but observing them at work John Carswell concluded that 'the university model they knew and understood exercised so strong an influence that they had little sympathy or understanding for any other'.

Why universities? Goronwy Rees argued that Britain had no need for more universities: what it needed were *Techniche Hochschulen*. It was because I sympathized with such views that I urged that the colleges of advanced technology should become universities – as Robbins was to recommend. The CATs would bring diversity: other universities, I hoped (in vain), might copy their sandwich courses or their distinctive language courses. Yet what other option had Robbins than to expand the universities? In the post-war years five university colleges (Nottingham and Leicester, for example) had blossomed into universities and Keele had been founded. Now Murray had created the new universities and in so doing pre-empted Robbins's choices. People jeered that Murray was so much an Oxford don that he sited them in cathedral towns instead of in the centre of industrial cities. There was a wisp of truth in this. When Murray asked me to become chairman of the planning board at the University of Essex, he told me he had overruled the promoters who favoured Chelmsford rather than Colchester as the site because dons would be tempted to live in London and commute to Chelmsford. Nevertheless, the criticism is ill-founded. The cost of acquiring sites in the centre of cities would have been prodigious, the delays and frustrations intolerable. The example of Edinburgh split between three sites, all by then too small, was a warning.

Robbins and Morris were also animated by a more devious motive. They wanted their recommendations to be acceptable to their colleagues in the common room. They therefore said that anyone who got two A Levels and appropriate O Levels should be eligible and would qualify for a grant subject to a parental means test if he or she got a place in higher education. If he or she got a place ... The dons of Our Age were adamant in rejecting the continental system. There anyone who had passed the Baccalauréat, Abitur or the equivalent had a right to go to a university. Was the University of Rome to be taken as a model where a hundred thousand students had to use buildings designed for ten thousand? Surely a system of mass entry and a prodigious dropout at the end of the first year was inefficient and brutal. In Britain remarkable care was taken in selecting students: many departments interviewed hundreds of students for a handful of places. The dons would not admit more students than they thought could be taught properly, and that meant a ratio of no more than one don to eight or ten students. Britain might admit fewer students but the number that graduated was far higher than that of other countries.

The dons therefore told Robbins they required more staff and buildings. So Robbins promised that nothing would diminish the autonomy of universities. No university would be treated differently from any other – parity of esteem was to be the principle whatever the reality. No don (other than professors) was to be paid on a different scale from his peers (except, regrettably, in medicine). Show your academic colleagues that expansion need not mean dilution or lower standards. Enshrine the UGC so as to convince the dons that government will do what the universities wish. Ensure that government recognizes that every teacher must be paid to research. Then your colleagues will accept expansion; and very soon – as Morris indicated in a passage he drafted – they will see that those who expand will get big rewards at the expense of those who don't. The appeal to self-interest was irresistible. But there was no need for such a surrender. The battle for expansion had been won before the Robbins Report was published.

Robbins had in fact looked across the Atlantic and once told me how impressed he had been that Tawney of all people had returned from America praising that great capitalist country for providing higher education for vast numbers of adolescents. But Robbins and those like myself who wanted expansion were guilty of not knowing how Whitehall worked. The American system accepted that institutions with the same name would have large differentials in salaries and standards. They might all be called college but everyone accepted that Cambridge, Mass. had different standards from Oxford, Miss., and both from a community college in California – even though they were all called 'college'. They catered for different ages and needs. Credit obtained for work in one could be used to obtain a degree in another.

The result of treating all universities as equal was borne in on me for the first time on the planning board of the University of East Anglia. When the headship of the school of biology was being discussed, I mentioned the name of someone I knew to be a good teacher and organizer. 'Not nearly distinguished enough,' snapped Solly Zuckerman, who had a down on Oxbridge. 'This school of biology is going to be better than that of Cambridge.' This was absurd. But Whitehall assumed without question that all universities were to have the same standard of financing. It was part of the Robbins bargain with the dons. The cost of his proposals in fact appalled the civil servants. Why should the seven colleges of advanced technology, their *Lieblingskinder*, be taken out of their control and called universities? It added millions to their costs without adding a single student. That was the devastating answer made by Toby Weaver, who was responsible for higher education in the new Department of Education and Science, to those such as myself who had wanted the CATs to become universities.

The new universities were not created to do something new. They were created to do better and more imaginatively what was already being done in Oxbridge and the nineteenth-century universities. Over the years barnacles had grown on the hulls of those graceful Victorian yachts. No new subject could be accepted until it had proved it was rigorous, every fledgling university had to teach the external London degree courses until it had proved it was respectable. When Sandie Lindsay at Keele persuaded the Labour government to abandon this obligation there were fearful mutterings in London's Senate House. These dissatisfactions surfaced in a book *Redbrick*, written by an anonymous professor at Liverpool. But his remedy – to give greater powers to professors – overlooked the fact that it was the cabals of professors that made innovation so difficult. Promotion, facilities, prospects, the curriculum depended on the single professor who ran the department.* When Charles Wilson, a powerful vice-chancellor who had experience of Glasgow, Oxford, LSE and Leicester, sat on the planning boards of Sussex, East Anglia and Stirling, he urged them to break the single-subject honours degree and the monolithic department. There was little professorial tyranny at Oxford and Cambridge. But there, since the whole body of dons was entitled to vote on any proposal for change, university reform resembled a civil war which

* At University College London a professor, who relished his reputation as a character and a boozer, thought it funny to tell a junior lecturer to take a train to the professor's home in Gloucestershire and pick up his keys which he had forgotten.

no side could ever win. As every proposal at Cambridge had to be sent to faculties and colleges for comment; as comment was unobtainable in less than a term; as the central bodies never met during vacations to consider the comments; and as no controversial issues could be put to the university between mid-May and mid-October, a reformer had to be pretty nippy to get a proposal put to the university for decision before the academic year was out. Many of the best among the dons left Oxbridge and Redbrick to found the new universities and free themselves from these frustrations. Asa Briggs at Sussex tried to create a more general curriculum by establishing schools of study rather than departments. Many experimented with inter-disciplinary studies and introduced new variations in social studies. But only too often such experiments were wrecked on the reefs of professional advancement or of sixth-form specialization.

Government departments may lose a battle but they seldom lose the war. Weaver was an exceptionally able civil servant and he fell back on a new line of defence – the binary line. Across that line, he urged like Pétain at Verdun, *ils ne passeront pas*. There must be two sectors in higher education each representing the other, the 'autonomous' university sector and the local authority sector. The advent of a Labour government gave him an advantage. He played on Crosland's egalitarian principles and persuaded him that universities were centres of snobbery – ivory towers unsuited to carrying out Harold Wilson's white-hot technological revolution. Like a general who has seen seven divisions moved from his army to another front, Weaver planned to hijack the next lot of reinforcements. He did so by persuading Crosland to set up thirty-two polytechnics. They were colleges of advanced technology but grander still with new buildings, laboratories and workshops, their degrees attested by a national council of academic awards. The teacher training colleges should swell and become colleges of education, the technical colleges be upgraded to colleges of further education. And so the binary system was established. Weaver had sensed the breeze that had blown Robbins home to port had changed direction.

The establishment of the polytechnics was the answer my generation made to Correlli Barnett and Wiener. They were a genuine attempt to turn Harold Wilson's rhetoric about the technological revolution into reality. But Crosland made the error of believing that the true egalitarian must make all institutions equal. His polytechnics were to be on a par with universities and their students geared to a level of support that emanated from Oxbridge. No diplomas for them. They too must offer a three-year bachelor degree. Between 1969 and 1982 their non-degree work fell from seventy to thirty per cent of enrolments and their part-time students to under a third. Worse was to follow. Crosland and Weaver let the polytechnics slip out of their grasp and into the hands of local authorities. The polys should have concentrated all their efforts on applied science and have been geared to make British industry more productive, more inventive, more competitive. Instead, starved by sixth-form specialization of applicants wanting to study science and technology, they taught arts subjects, and colleges of fine art were often ordered to become part of them. At one time Middlesex had a large department of philosophy. 'Am I to teach German and not to teach my students to read Goethe?' one admirable native-born old German refugee asked me. The answer should have been 'Certainly, but not until they have learnt how to read and write the German that is spoken in business and in the European Commission.'

Once again it was the teachers who were setting the agenda against the spirit in which the polytechnics were founded. The polys did not run courses on management. They set up departments of sociology. Such departments concentrated not on the production but on the distribution of wealth – a topic as legitimate as learning to read Goethe but secondary to the purpose for which polytechnics were set up. The binary system that Crosland established severed further education from higher education and polys from universities. You could not transfer with credit from a poly to a university, you could not get credit for a year's work: and therefore if you dropped out you had to start all over again. You could enrol in the Open University without qualifications, but you had to study for a bachelor's degree: it became just another elite university with open access but no open degrees. The sector that should have been given special priority was not given sufficient resources. The colleges of further education were inexpensive. Most of their students were part-time and studied for vocational qualifications. But bright students there hardly ever transferred to universities or polys as would have happened in America. Only Charles Carter, one of the few vice-chancellors with imagination about the future (and therefore regarded by right-minded professors as a dangerous man), envisaged a civic university as a planet with satellite colleges in orbit exchanging students.

In retrospect how timid the innovations of the new universities look, how traditional the spread of subjects and how marginal the institutional change that substituted schools of study for departments! These developments were excellent examples of the ethos of the dons that was to suffer signally in the eighties.

CHAPTER 23

The Dons Learn Bitter Realities

1

THE YEARS 1900–40 were the golden age of the Oxbridge undergraduate. For the clever and ambitious, to get a first – as those who study *The Times* obituaries will notice – was a permanent hallmark for life: if one missed a first it had somehow to be explained away. But no stigma attached to the average, the idle or the stupid; their passports could be stamped with a blue, or by making a mark in the Union or editing the *Isis* or *Granta*. You belonged to a place which was small enough for you to become known and, if you were lucky, there would be a young don or two who might turn out to be your guide, philosopher and friend. According to the legend these were the years when you grew up, when you learnt how to get on with all sorts and conditions of men, when the aesthetes broke the bonds of the philistines and the hearties could play while being unwittingly civilized. These were the years of laughter and the love of friends.

The years 1945–75 were the golden age of the don. The boffins had captured the public imagination: the stereotype of the absent-minded professor who had been transformed into the keen-eyed inventor in a white coat of radar and artificial harbours. The don rose in public esteem: became an indispensable back-room boy in Whitehall: became an adviser to politicians. Lady Bracknell had said of Liberal-Unionists, 'They dine with us. Or come in the evening at any rate;' and so it was that dons – at any rate from Oxford – began to be seen in London salons. To be a don became an attractive way of life. However hard they worked, however ill-paid they thought themselves to be, they 'work when they feel like it, get up late if they want to and have long holidays', wrote James Joll in 1955 rightly without shame. Like a top civil servant a don had security of tenure and with it peace of mind. Less well-off than the civil servant, he was at least his own master. He could teach what he liked apart from the occasional standard courses. Some of the best dons spent their days becoming ever more learned and never bothered to publish. But a dedicated scholar could devote himself to changing the map of knowledge by articles in periodicals or by his books, and end his days a fellow of the Royal Society or British Academy, honoured by his colleagues, the recipient of doctorates from other universities. If his special gift lay in teaching or administration he could at Oxbridge supplement his income by becoming a bursar or a senior tutor. In his college meetings a don enjoyed the delectable illusion of being an architect or a farmer weighing the advantages of a dual-purpose shorthorn herd, bred for both milk and meat, over a herd bred by a cross of Aberdeen Angus on blue grey. He could develop a nose for the balance of a portfolio or of a young claret. He might act as a consultant for industry or for an investment trust. He might administer big science for the nation, give talks for the BBC or the British Council, write for the reviews, organize experiments in education or fill a seat on countless national or local committees. In Britain dons could win a national audience: those who emigrated to America found they had only a campus audience. No wonder Belloc's lines were rewritten:

Remote and ineffectual don!
Where have you gone, where have you gone?

Like von Humboldt and Newman the dons of Our Age had their idea of a university. It existed to discover new knowledge. That it did through research. But a university differed from an institute because the finest and most productive teachers taught undergraduates as well as their graduate students. It also existed to transmit high culture. That it did through teaching its students whatever was thought to be intellectually important and made men and women more civilized. It also existed to select and certificate its students and collaborate with the professions. Most of us disagreed with Herbert Butterfield and saw no reason why, if theology and law were studied, social administration or chemical engineering should not figure in the curriculum. We never claimed that universities could teach the qualities people in politics and business need – such as shrewdness, judgement, flair, sagacity, the trustworthiness that inspires confidence and the toughness to choose the lesser of two evils when to choose neither would be worse. We did not expect the university to teach culture or wisdom any more than theologians taught holiness or a philosopher goodness or a sociologist a blueprint for the future. These virtues are acquired through example, not by precept. What then did the university exist for? Writing in 1963 I said I thought it was for

> The intellect ... the intellect ... the intellect. *That* is what universities exist for. Everything else is secondary. Equality of opportunity to come to the university is secondary. The need to mix classes, nationalities, and races together is secondary. The agonies and gaieties of student life are secondary. So are the rules, customs, pay, and promotion of the academic staff and their debates on changing the curricula or procuring facilities for research. Even the awakening of a sense of beauty or the life-giving shock of new experience, or the pursuit of goodness itself – all these are secondary to the cultivation, training, and exercise of the intellect. Universities should hold up for admiration the intellectual life. The most precious gift they have to offer

is to live and work among books or in laboratories and to enable the young to see those rare scholars who have put on one side the world of material success, both in and outside the university, in order to study with single-minded devotion some topic because that above all seems important to them. A university is dead if the dons cannot in some way communicate to the students the struggle – and the disappointments as well as the triumphs in that struggle – to produce out of the chaos of human experience some grain of order won by the intellect. That is the end to which all the arrangements of the university should be directed.

From the end of the sixties this ideal began to be questioned; and the first to question it were the students.

2

THOSE WITH LONG memories might have recalled that in 1936 a Miss Button had called on the National Union of Students (NUS) to make a 'militant defence of students' interests', and in 1963 a Mr Swindlehurst demanded students should strike to gain their ends. But after the war the NUS, now sickened by communist manipulation, concentrated on promoting students' interests; and David Eccles shocked his civil servants by inviting the NUS to meet him. Indeed when students began to ask to become members of university bodies the wise chairman of the Vice-Chancellors Committee, Derman Christopherson, drew up a concordat on participation with the then president. Next year in 1969 Jack Straw became the president. He once again politicized the NUS. After him the NUS leaders repudiated the concordat and supported every disturbance.

The aim of the tiny group of militants who fomented the disturbances was to disrupt the institution and take it over. They perfected their tactics of disruption, which were to goad the authorities into taking disciplinary action and exploit their mistakes. But the aims of the considerable numbers of students who followed the militants puzzled the dons. They no longer talked like the students E.M.Forster pictured in *The Longest Journey*, discussing whether if one saw a cow and went home the cow was still there. In those days students considered such questions were the real world and the false world was the pursuit of success and money-making. By 1970 numbers of students no longer thought the world of learning and discussion was an alternative to the world of success and money-making. They said the two were identical. What was the competitiveness of the campus – the struggle to get a first in exams, the PhD, the awards, fellowships, posts and prizes – but the rat race of society? What was the vice-chancellor with his car and driver and dinner parties for prospective donors but a fat cat? What were absentee professors off on jaunts to America and the Antipodes but part of the consumer society? These were the students who clamoured for more participation in government; and when they got it became more disaffected when they found that in academia power is so diffused that it is impossible for any group to transform the scene overnight. These were the students who rejected traditional student life – the rags, games, dances in evening dress and festivals – and were determined that no regulations should interfere with their private life. For them the university was a rock pool not a flow chart.

The majority, the 'moderate students', whom the authorities imagined would rally to their side in a disturbance, stayed on the sidelines amused by the general discomfiture – as we would have done when we were young. For some of them the sit-ins and disturbances were fun – people made friends as they had in the wartime blitz; others despised the political vocalists and got on with the job of getting a qualification. But the venom and hatred of the militants, and their methods of intimidation, shattered the spun-glass relationship between dons and students that we treasured. A generation gap opened: one side no longer wanted the other.

Few institutions emerged with credit. Oxford did. Oxford had no hesitation in expelling thirteen students who defied an instruction and broke into the Indian Institute. But most universities never learnt how to make their tribunals effective. After damage running into tens of thousands of pounds a few students would be hauled before these bodies often accompanied by barristers whose fees were paid by the students' union. The judges soon became the accused. Nevertheless, the disturbances in Britain were minor compared to the havoc that student unrest caused in America and Europe. In Britain no Drittelparität, no reforms by Edgar Faure, no academically worthless programmes to buy off black militants were inflicted on our universities. The militants in universities such as Essex, and the unparalleled intimidation and disruption at the Polytechnic of North London led by Mike Hill and Terry Povey, left the institutions they plagued in essence unaltered. But they damaged them.

Not perhaps so much as some of the dons. From the start they cut a poor figure. The die-hards were pilloried by the press – they were the sort that stood by regulations such as those at LSE that required a student to obtain permission to write a letter to *The Times*. The conciliators passed contradictory and vacillating motions on senate. But the public was more startled by the staff sympathizers. These were the dons who sided with the militants on ideological grounds. At Warwick E.P.Thompson disapproved of Jack Butterworth's plans to link the university with industry in the Midlands. At the Polytechnic of North London the staff sympathizers made it impossible to enforce any code of discipline and were abetted by some of the governors. At Essex one of the lecturers in sociology seemed to regard the sit-in with its vandalism and intimidation by the militants as an agreeable opportunity to snub the vice-chancellor and do some field work within the university itself. At LSE John Griffith and Bill Wedderburn used their professional skills as lawyers; and Griffith was the moving spirit among a group of radical dons who set up a committee to defend, so they said, academic freedom and democracy. Its members defended disruptions and justified the suppression of free speech at Sussex.

Our generation was in fact facing one of the consequences of our expansion of higher education. Britain had now acquired a new radical intelligentsia. It overflowed from higher education into broadcasting, journalism, publishing, architecture, design and a multitude of white-collar jobs of which computing was the largest. After the war marxists such as John Saville, Raphael Samuel, and later the contributors to the *New Left Review*, had been marginal men. Now in the seventies they appeared as epic figures on the campus. In 1972 some young dons in the new universities brought out *Radical Philosophy* in which existentialism, phenomenology, Hegel as well as Marx, were discussed; and British analytic philosophy was pronounced sterile and inadequate. Most of the new left intelligentsia belonged to the generation after ours. The intellectual in caricature was no longer Mark Boxer's bitchy, cowardly media pair, Joanna and Simon Stringalong. The new couple were Posy Simmonds' Weber family whose head (if George Weber could be so styled) was the mild, muddled polytechnic senior lecturer awash with family problems and encumbered by articles for publication that never got written. The university novel reflected this change of heart. *Lucky Jim* had spoken against modernism, Bloomsbury and Oxbridge and for honesty, common sense and vitalizing vulgarity. He was displaced by Howard Kirk, the archetypal staff sympathizer in the best of all university novels of the time, Malcolm Bradbury's *The History Man*. Kirk symbolized the politicization of the campus. In 1949 Isaiah Berlin had been disturbed that some dons felt guilt in pursuing knowledge for its own sake. They seemed, he wrote, to think they ought to be fighting poverty and injustice. It may be admirable (even if futile) for dons to try and change the wicked world. But should the life of the intellect dwindle into social service? Moreover in the wicked world there are some ends – power, wealth, heartless enjoyment – which function as motives for action; and out of them science and art grow. Twenty years later, however, numbers of dons in social science departments could argue that they did not need to choose between political commitment and their academic work: the two were identical.

3

WHILE THE DONS were losing their name with Westminster and the public, they were also losing it in Whitehall. It had been right to expand higher education. What had been wrong was to imagine that all students could be given a Rolls-Royce higher education. No country could afford it. No country could afford within a decade to double the number of university institutions, create thirty-two polytechnics, upgrade the colleges and finance this expansion on the principle of parity of esteem. No country could afford to run all its major institutions with staff–student ratios of one to ten or lower. No country could afford a system of mass higher education at the per capita costs of the universities and polytechnics. No country could afford centres of excellence (the equivalent of Harvard and Berkeley, the Grandes Ecôles and Max Planck Institutes) and declare that all other universities were to be given equal status – that their academic and supporting staff were to have uniform rates of pay, their students all to be supported at the same level and their degree courses in all subjects to be of the same length. Yet experts such as John Vaizey in 1972 were convinced that we could have more children in nursery schools as well as more students in higher education.

The wave of expansion gathered such momentum that when it broke it left devastation behind it. In 1956, Keith Murray's third year in office in the UGC, the capital programme was £3.8 million. In 1963, his last year, it was thirty million pounds and rising fast. The bureaucracies of higher education proliferated. The size of the UGC quadrupled; the secretariat of the Committee of Vice Chancellors and Principals mounted as subcommittees proliferated; a national system for considering student applications to universities (UCCA) and the Council for National Academic Awards for the polytechnics were set up. So were new research councils for the environment and for social sciences. Business schools were founded; postgraduate support was extended; services for health, sport and careers burgeoned; and as student unions' income shot up, their facilities grew more lavish.

The founding of the Open University added to the costs. Between 1958 and 1960 the salaries of the dons rose by over twenty-eight per cent – vastly in excess of inflation. Colin Anderson's committee, which considered grants to students, knew nothing of the UGC's plans for expansion: if they had known they would have realized that the cost of their proposals, estimated (not allowing for postgraduates) to be twenty-one million pounds in 1958, was in fact going to be over forty million. Meanwhile the trade unions got in on the act, and found individual universities a soft touch. Clive Jenkins in particular was adept at milking them for the benefit of the technicians in the labs. I once asked Robbins whether he had made any assumption about economic growth to finance his proposals. He said the Treasury had told him informally that he might assume a four per cent growth rate. No such rate in real terms was ever achieved. The report coincided with the down-turn in the British economy that was to last for years.

The polytechnics finally broke the bank, and the government moved to contain the costs soon after the expansion got under way. Each year cuts were imposed, and Eric James said if Robbins represented a great step forward he wondered what a great step backwards would look like. The government announced that no more universities would be founded. Robbins's plan to create half a dozen institutions resembling the Massachusetts Institute of Technology was shelved, and Alex Todd's Royal Commission on medical education made recommendations to buy new sites and provide new buildings for medical schools at such astronomical expense that most of them were ignored.

Then began a war of attrition that was to last for over ten years. Like Napoleon after 1813, the universities displayed great skill in fighting a vastly superior enemy. When Kenneth Berrill was chairman of the UGC he deployed all the arts he had learnt when serving in the Treasury to defeat his former Whitehall colleagues. Even after the oil crisis of 1973 and the galloping inflation that followed, government relied on the rack rather than the axe. The Whitehall ploy was to grant inadequate compensation for inflation or agreed salary increases with the result that the income of universities fell by one per cent a year in real terms. Each year government announced a grant so dire in its consequences that vice-chancellors had to engage in the exhausting process of making economies while lobbying government to relent. And then, just as the economies were due to be implemented, each spring government, like some lover full of remorse for his infidelity, laid a bouquet of flowers in the shape of supplementary grants at the feet of the siren. But if government resembled a faithless lover, then the universities resembled a *poule de luxe*. Their lover begged them not to ruin him by their demands. Like Zola's Nana they were impervious to his pleas. Shirley Williams put thirteen points for economy to the universities: they trashed some and toyed with others. The Vice-Chancellors Committee nearly always elected as their chairman one who could be relied upon to declare that since universities were self-governing no one, least of all he, could speak for them. Arthur Armitage, a man who won the affection of his colleagues and pupils for his rugged kindness, was a characteristic chairman. As a tutor at Cambridge he had fought the rationalization of college admissions until with the advent of UCCA he could fight no longer. As a vice-chancellor he took the line that to give in to any request to reduce expenditure would lead to the already inadequate grant being reduced still further. Why lay one's head on the block?

Only one observer diagnosed the fatal flaw at the time. This was Martin Trow, a sociologist of higher education at Berkeley, California, who predicted that the laudable desire to give opportunities to more of the young would be doomed if all were to be financed at the levels to which Oxford and Cambridge had been accustomed. Why should all universities be funded at the same level? Indeed why should all dons be paid on the same scale? Even more fundamental, why should the myth be sustained that the bachelor's degree is of the same standing and value in every degree-giving institution? In 1986 the vice-chancellor of Lancaster, P.A. Reynolds, urged that universities should not all do the same thing. Nevertheless he advised his colleagues that 'it is of the first importance' that degrees from different institutions should be comparable. No wonder access to higher education was so difficult – and expensive.

4

THE EDUCATION REFORM Act of 1988 was the fruit of the discontent with the schools and the universities. It was a vote of no confidence in those who ran the schools – the local authorities and the teaching profession. It was a vote to transfer power into the hands of those who were meant to care about the actual education the children received – their parents, school governors and headteachers. It was a vote to control the curriculum. Edward Boyle had set up the Schools Council to discuss changes in exams and the curriculum, but the National Union of Teachers wrecked it by using changes as a lever to obtain concessions on pay and duties. Meanwhile the unions disrupted the work of the schools in pursuit of their claims. The government had had enough. The committee for negotiating pay claims had been deadlocked for months. It was abolished. So was the Schools Council. For the first time government imposed a national curriculum in the schools, laid down which subjects formed it and how much time should be devoted to it. Weedy, incompetent teachers were to be sacked, the training of teachers reformed and the children were to be tested by the schools beginning at the age of seven. Visions of Mr M'Choakumchild's school and Dickens's Gradgrind rose before the dispirited teachers.

Meanwhile the dons were awoken from their dreams. They had been transfixed by the Grand Transformation Scene in which the Cinderella of higher education had seen her dingy redbrick fireplace disappear and found herself in a plate-glass spangled castle in the countryside of Sussex or Kent. Those tiresome students, the broker's men, slunk into the wings, and Cinderella's fairy godmother, Shirley, waved her wand. Off she went to the ball where she had eyes only for that handsome bachelor of arts and science Prince Charming. But, as the clock struck midnight in 1975 and the oil for the lamps ran dry, she forgot the thirteen points her godmother had whispered in her ear, and she found herself back in her rags forlorn. It is only in pantomime that Prince Charming comes to claim his bride. In the stark life of the eighties Cindy was deserted. She should not have set her sights on that handsome BASc. She ought to have gone to the local disco and mixed with part-time students who had few qualifications or none and got a cheap education, leaving with a diploma and with the skills that enabled them to earn a living in the world. The true Prince Charming wore jeans.

In the past universities had emerged from scrutiny of their expenditure with credit. Their administrative costs were extraordinarily low; and if the ratio of staff to students was far more favourable than that of any other country, only just over three per cent failed for academic reasons. But now the government determined to shake them up as well as shake them out. Between 1981 and 1984 universities lost fifteen per cent of their grant. But since most academic staff had contracts to retiring age, government had to give redundant staff compensation for breach of contract. It cost £285 million. No wonder government resolved to end such an inflexible system and abolish the tenure the dons enjoyed. The dons regarded the Education Act of 1988 as a ball and chain shackling the universities to the state. In fact the Act recognized that for years the UGC had not been independent of government, a mere adviser on the needs of the universities. All sorts of new ideas about the relation of universities to the state began to be heard. Conservative radicals such as Elie Kedourie, Harry Ferns and the young Tory aspirant Oliver Letwin argued that the dons who were complaining of a further extension of state control, and had sold their soul in the sixties to Mephistopheles, should redeem it by tearing up the contract with him. Give each student vouchers to go to whatever place he thought would give him the best advantage, price courses, let universities vary their length and vary the salaries of staff to respond to shifts in demand. It was clear that in the last decade of the century hitherto unmentionable questions would be asked, and that higher education was going to be organized and financed on much less favourable lines than in the golden times of Our Age.

So the dons felt slighted. It was bad enough that the grant to universities and research continued to be squeezed and pay awards were less than the rate of inflation. It was worse to hear the accusation in Westminster and Whitehall that the dons were underemployed, mismanaged their affairs and in terms of what society paid out produced a dubious return on the investment. Just in case the dons had not understood the message the government, infuriated that Conservative ministers were howled down on campus, lost its temper. It tacked on a clause to a bill going through Parliament more likely in practice to restrict than preserve free speech. Its action reminded me of Thomas Beecham, exasperated by the recalcitrant dancers of the Camargo Society, conducting the dance of the little swans at double the speed and saying, 'That made the buggers hop.' The customary dawn chorus protest at the level of government support changed into a screech. For an old Leavisite educationalist, Fred Inglis, the Education Act was exemplary in its arrogance, philistinism and duplicity; it transformed education into a commodity. Here was the 'genteel deutero-fascist managerialism which is now the manner of power'. Was the disinterested pursuit of knowledge to be sacrificed to commercial considerations? As some of the brightest dons in the humanities and medicine joined the brain drain to America (which had flowed, it must be said, throughout the years of expansion) the dons sensed they were no longer prized. Were Nobel Prizewinners now thought to be irrelevant to the nation's economy? The dons heard the accusation that their ethos, their culture, was responsible for the failure of Britain's industry and enterprise. Nothing they said could convince their masters that scholarship and learning are ends in themselves.

But in the eighties the dons began to move from the Trevelyan–Northcote assumption that the old academic subjects were all that a university should teach. Management studies sprouted, business schools were set up, even the Cambridge faculty of engineering ceased to regard mathematical elegance as the most desirable quality in an engineer. The meaning of meritocracy had changed. It was no longer an assertion that brains should take precedence over privilege. It now meant the rule of those who had learnt the knack of making enterprise profitable and efficient. Well it might, when a third of Britain's schools were judged by the inspectorate to be below standard and children spent their time dawdling; when the workforce was still far behind in literacy and numeracy that of Germany; and when too many foremen were semi-skilled and middle managers incompetent. Industrialists still neglected their own best interests and failed to train their employees, fearful that if they did their competitors would poach them. The government's scheme to develop training and technical education was improvised and under-funded. No leader appeared to tell the universities that the top priority was now to train the workforce and that, until the nation became wealthier, they would have to be content with a lower income. Nevertheless, the message was clear. In its desire to develop training, government was endorsing Correlli Barnett's sneers at the culture of the humanities and even the achievements of university scientists.

The golden age of the dons vanished into the past. Their buoyancy and self-confidence dwindled. Convinced that irreparable damage had been done to British scholarship, they saw themselves as the victims of an unnecessary catastrophe. Michael Oakeshott, the third among the Conservative deviants of our generation, looked on these academic developments with the eye of a man who had foretold it all. Meanwhile such staunch Conservative supporters among the regius professors as Hugh Trevor-Roper and Hugh Lloyd Jones fell silent as the dons' Pompeii disappeared under the ashes of their hopes. You expected to find that they had scribbled on the walls of Christ Church the quotation from the *Aeneid* 'Conticuere omn . . .'* that the excavators found some sage had written as he suffocated in that doomed city.

* 'All fell silent.'

CHAPTER 24

The Deviants – Michael Oakeshott

1

When I returned to Cambridge after the war it was not Leavis to whom one referred when discussing general ideas. It was Oakeshott. They had certain similarities – both were spare and lean and both belonged to the oldest cohort of Our Age. Both dismissed the received wisdom of the world of affairs. Indeed Oakeshott had been an early contributor to *Scrutiny*. But the contrast between their temperaments could scarcely have been more marked. Michael Oakeshott embodied the spirit of *espièglerie*. His writing twinkled with mischief and his good humour was imperturbable as he twitted and taunted his opponents. He enjoyed the company of pretty women. Serving in north-west Europe in one of those irregular units, he was entranced by the success of his young fellow officer, Peregrine Worsthorne, whose zeal in the pursuit of the enemy was matched by his zeal in the pursuit of ladies whom he induced to celebrate the liberation of their country in his arms.

Something of the same gaiety of spirit sparkled in the pages of the newly founded *Cambridge Journal* after Oakeshott took over the editorship. But he wrote as a disillusioned man whose countrymen en masse were taking the wrong turning and marching to perdition. However much Oakeshott despised socialism and the ethos of Attlee's government, his contempt for the new conservatism of Butler and Macmillan was as searing. They did not reject the central planning of the economy; they claimed to be better at it. They too wanted to be social engineers. Tory paternalism was almost as dangerous as socialist ideology. To Oakeshott post-war England provided the lamentable spectacle of 'a set of sanctimonious, rationalist politicians, preaching an ideology of unselfishness and social service to a society in which they and their rationalist predecessors have done their best to destroy the only living root of moral behaviour; and opposed by another set of politicians dabbling with the project of converting our society from rationalism under the inspiration of a fresh rationalization of our political tradition'.

What did Oakeshott mean by rationalism? The answer he gave startled the sober-sides. Rationalists could be utilitarians, marxists, fascists, liberals and socialists: people who advocated the Rights of Man, the reunion of the churches or the revival of Gaelic as the official language of Eire. Rationalists were people who worked out theories and then applied them to politics. They imagined that the entire art of ruling could be learned from a crib. Machiavelli wrote such a crib for the new prince, Locke for the Whigs, Bentham for the radicals and, in our own time, Beveridge for the progressives. Writing cribs is not confined to politics – Paley's *Evidences* was a crib for Christians. Even the anti-planners like Hayek were not beyond reproach. 'A plan to resist all planning may be better than its opposite, but it belongs to the same style of politics.' The rationalist fails to understand that experience of men and affairs is a far better guide to action than trying to apply an ideology. Surely no one ever imagined that to be a good Christian meant mastering theology. Oakeshott quoted Donne: 'He who will live by precept shall long be without the habit of honesty.'

Oakeshott's rationalist is a man who does not distinguish between theoretical and practical knowledge. He thinks of practical knowledge as if it were theoretical. He thinks of it as a technique from a book and applies it mechanically. He accordingly believes that political decisions can be deduced from an ideology. Practical knowledge can be learned only by apprenticeship to a master. An apprentice acquires knowledge by observing his master practising his craft. Technical knowledge appears to be more certain because it is there – written in the textbook; and the trouble with the rationalist is that this is the only kind of knowledge that interests him. And yet what land-owner would think that he could run his estate by consulting books on estate management, or what chef would accept that his art could be reduced to recipes? The books and the recipes can be helpful guides but only for those who have already become familiar with the practice – who have become familiar with a tradition. Tradition is made up of all sorts of knowledge of all sorts of things: ancestors, customs, relations with other people and others too many and too intangible to be reduced to a simple list. And that is why practical knowledge takes two or three generations to acquire. It cannot be acquired overnight and is perfected by being handed down from one generation to another.

So it is with morality. A morality, wrote Oakeshott (and by 'a' morality he drew attention to the fact that there are numbers of moral traditions), a morality is neither a system of general principles nor a code of rules, but a vernacular language. You can, of course, draw a set of principles from it just as grammarians can abstract the grammar from a living language. But morality is not to be had by learning rules that tell one to be charitable or fair or always speak the truth – morality consists in learning how to think and act in a good way; not in solving moral problems. Unfortunately for centuries Europeans have confused morality with the pursuit of moral ideals. The Church began the decline when it no longer defined morality as 'the custom of the Lord'. Already by the days of St Ambrose morality was categorized in virtues and vices; and the trouble with categories is that they are inflexible. Worse still the morality of ideals encourages perfectionism. Now, dangerous as it is, there is nothing wrong in an individual taking wings to reach perfection: an individual should be free to lead his life as he sees fit; he may crash or, rarely, he may end by being called a saint. But when a society attempts to make itself perfect, a few impose their interpretation of perfection upon the rest and chaos, absurdity or repression reigns.

Oakeshott was never satisfied when his opponents merely modified their mode of thinking. Like all philosophers he demanded they adopt his mode. He too chose that passage from Keynes's *My Early Beliefs* that Leavis had savaged to attack the notion of rational conduct. He admitted Keynes had acknowledged that in his youth he had too narrow a view of rationality and admitted it had excluded much of what was 'irrational' – passion, spontaneity, 'volcanic impulses', which could be valuable though they often produced evil. But for Oakeshott acknowledgment of the irrational was as misguided as belief in the efficacy of the rational. He drew our attention to the discussion in *Anna Karenina* between Levin and Sviajsky on 'rational' agriculture. For Sviajsky it means modern implements and methods of accounting. To Levin this is nonsense because the peasants don't know how to use the machinery and break it on purpose; and they will never use it until they are educated. In other words an activity – farming – consists of knowing how to behave, and until peasants are brought up learning about machinery and its workings they will not behave 'rationally'.

Oakeshott's delight in mischief inspired his best known demonstration of the distinction between practical and theoretical knowledge. He asked his readers to consider that item of late Victorian ladies' fashion – bloomers. Why did they design such a garment? The rationalist would argue it was an attempt to design rational clothing suitable for cycling. But shorts would have been much more rational. Bloomers took the shape they did because what was needed was not just something suitable for cycling but a garment which also met the demands for the standard of decency at that time current in society. One of Oakeshott's minor works was called *A Guide to the Classics or How to Pick the Derby Winner* (a book which disappointed classical scholars and alarmed devotees of the turf who imagined it must be related to the Latin texts which had defeated them at school). Of this book Oakeshott said that although it was a guide to form it could be no more than a guide. It was never intended to satisfy some of its greedy rationalist readers on the look-out for an infallible method to skin the bookmakers.

It was characteristic, thought Oakeshott, of the rationalist that he pretends tradition is just another ideology. It is in fact a guide-post not a ball and chain. The true master of politics, who is well versed in the traditions of his country, can draw on its rich materials and respond flexibly to events. He thinks of politics as diplomacy which he practises with no self-conscious purpose; and that is why government is far better in the role of referee, holding the ring for the contestants and ensuring their individual liberty so they can pursue their goals, a referee who understands the Queensberry rules of the ring, i.e. the morality of our society. Government is not the management of a large-scale enterprise. It exists to reinforce the rules upon those who are managing their own enterprise. It should not exhort. It should be pacific, it should pour cool water on those who become too excited in the pursuit of their aims. It should not impose views and certainly does not exist to make men good. Yes, it must suppress malpractices but must never attempt to realize abstract principles of social justice. Government should engage in the 'pursuit of intimations', not the pursuit of a dream or a general principle. It is the art of knowing where to go next.

Knowing how vehemently the Oxford philosophers rejected Oakeshott, people have seen him as some latter-day idealist descended from Bradley or Collingwood. In fact he shared the admiration of the Oxford philosophers for Hume. He and they admired Hume for repudiating rationality as the source of truth, the link between God and man, the faculty that defined the ends of human activity. But Oakeshott went far further than Hume. Hume revered the roles of reason and passion. He believed passion dictated the ends in life and reason was its slave devising means to reach these ends. Oakeshott denied that reason was a faculty for doing only *one* thing. It was the power of interpreting, shaping and responding to experience in a *variety* of ways. Contrary to classical or Idealist philosophers, Oakeshott considered history or poetry as 'rational' as science and engineering. Carpentry or trading (the activity of businessmen) are no more and no less rational than logic or mathematics. Like the Oxford philosophers he did not regard philosophy as the queen of the sciences promulgating the truth. But unlike them he saw it as the way of reflecting upon the whole of human experience and showing how the different things human beings do, and have done, relate to each other. The philosopher is not superior to other human beings. He differs from most of them because he deals in abstractions. But that does not mean he is qualified to give practical advice. He is no more qualified than the carpenter to tell men and women how to live. St Augustine, Montaigne and Hume would have agreed.

The 'rationalists' are wrong to think there is only one language in which everything can be discussed. There are in fact many modes of experience or 'voices' or 'language' which we use when talking about experience, and we speak them with different degrees of skill, learning, sensitivity and originality. One of the rules of language is that you cannot speak French at the same time as you are talking German. There is the language of history or of poetry. Some people imagine that science or the scientific method is an appropriate language for telling us how to act in the world of affairs. They are wrong. Science is indeed a mode of experience, but one that abstracts a quantitative interpretation of phenomena from the whole of experience.

It creates a marvellous, coherent world, but coherence is bought at a price. The price is remoteness from everyday experience. As a separate mode it cannot mate with any other. You cannot apply science to experience as a whole. As a result Oakeshott dismisses the claims of many social scientists to give us answers to practical problems.

Nor can poetry or history provide such information. Poetry (by which Oakeshott meant the arts) is a language in its own right but it could be best described as a way of dreaming about the world. Who but philistines would sneer at this mode of describing the world or demand that the arts must be useful if they are to be accepted as a rational way of speaking to others? Art too interprets what men encounter in the course of living, but like every mode an artist has to learn his craft: for him also tradition is important. Poetry contributes to the 'conversation of mankind' – it is not, as Leavis thought, coterminous with morality. History too is a separate language, but it will not tell us any more than science the laws that govern human development – because there are none. History does not tell us how we came to be what we are. It is a language which can be used only to describe events as they are known to us through historical evidence. And to trace the connections among these events. We may find knowledge of the past useful when we think about the present, but history as such gives no guide to the politics of today. It is not scientific as some positivists maintained. The historian interprets evidence and in so doing imposes a pattern on events. But *qua* historian he has no licence to pass judgements on the past. There is no purpose in history.

Religion is no more than another voice. It is not a commandment carrying an ultimate sanction. Christianity was not a set of liberal propositions to be turned into the practical politics of banning the bomb or supporting the miners' strike. Nor was it synonymous with the programme of a social worker or probation officer. Today priests appeal to Christ's praise of the poor and the meek to justify socialism. Do not be deceived. Recite the Beatitudes and you will see that they cannot be applied to the world of affairs: they are God's judgement on that world and its pretensions. Religion helps to reconcile man to the pains of mortality and the dissonances of life. Faith is a voice that does not speak in the same language as other kinds of experience. But religion is no more than another voice; and, if it presumed to tell human beings how to order their affairs, could be as presumptuous and dangerous as any other form of rationalism.

No, the language we use when immersed in the world of affairs is the mode of practical experience. It is neither more nor less important a mode than poetry, history or science; but most of us use it more often. Whether or not we know it, we speak this language whenever we exert our will. To act is to exert our will. Each of us in society tries to get pleasure, or love someone, or find God, or rule others, or find solitude. Each of us tries to change our present state into a more agreeable state and hence, in doing so, we encounter others whose desires and activities may frustrate or conflict with ours. The only way to avoid such frustrations and conflict is for everyone to submit to the same rules.

2

BY TRADITION CAMBRIDGE was the university of the Whigs, but that tradition had for long become threadbare. Like Oxford it received the recommendations of the three Royal Commissions for reform with ill grace. Certain colleges, such as Corpus Christi under that arch-Establishment figure Will Spens, or Magdalene, or Jesus, were notable Tory citadels, but the great colleges of Trinity and St John's were no less than the rest well to the right of centre. Almost as soon as the left celebrated its triumph in 1945 the pendulum began to swing to the right. The historians were not going to allow a version of socialist history to be imposed on them in which the one far-off divine event to which the whole creation moved turned out to be the incarnation not of Christ but of clause four of the Labour Party's manifesto. The younger historians of Our Age were by no means men of the left. Denis Mack Smith was telling us not to read Gladstonian liberalism into the Risorgimento: Elton, Chadwick, Hinsley and Ullmann were notable Conservatives. Oakeshott began to be recognized as the leading theorist in the Conservative revival. With that sallow face and those darting eyes he appeared like an intelligent collie on the look-out for self-righteous predators on the left.

He was not himself in fact at the most radical of all Conservative colleges in Cambridge. This was Peterhouse. It acquired the reputation under Paul Vellacott who, first as tutor and then as master, promoted the careers of those students and fellows who found his brand of conservatism sympathetic. The most remarkable was a Yorkshire boy, a Methodist from a grammar school, in whom Vellacott saw his successor: Herbert Butterfield. By 1950 Peterhouse had become a notable centre of historical studies in Cambridge: three of the professors in the faculty, Knowles, Postan and Brogan were there. So was Butterfield's favourite pupil, Brian Wormald; Desmond Williams, the Irish iconoclast; and Denis Mack Smith (who to Butterfield's chagrin was elected into the fellowship he had hoped Williams would get). Butterfield was in fact more provocative than Oakeshott. By 1943 he was advocating a separate peace with Germany and saw nothing odd when visiting Dublin as external examiner at the university in going to parties at the German Consulate. In the first number of the *Cambridge Journal* he lamented that the outcome of the war had been to give Russia all she had wanted (except Constantinople).

Butterfield's denunciation of modern self-confidence ran in tandem with Oakeshott's political philosophy.

When Oakeshott left Cambridge for Laski's chair at LSE, Laski's students were appalled. They listened with horror to his inaugural lecture which told them their hopes of a better world were false and their guides wiseacres. He teased them by saying that politics were *nur für Schwindelfreie*. The world they inhabited 'is the best of all possible worlds, and *everything* in it is a necessary evil'. But W.H. Greenleaf remembered that whereas at the end of a lecture by Laski he departed filled with noble sentiments but soon had no very precise impression of Laski's argument, he left Oakeshott's puzzled but with three or four chains of argument that had disturbed his preconceptions. Laski always knew all the literature on any topic and his graduate students were told what to read, how to handle their subject and what the themes and indeed the conclusions should be. Oakeshott conducted a rambling conversation, but it taught Greenleaf what was involved in trying to understand the past; and his thesis came to very different conclusions from those Laski had dictated.

At LSE Oakeshott found colleagues who understood him and used his perceptions to enlighten their own work: such as the historian Elie Kedourie, or the sociologist David Martin, or the political theorist Kenneth Minogue. Oakeshott dedicated *On Human Conduct* to Shirley Letwin. His name was often invoked by the journalists of the *Daily* and *Sunday Telegraph* – T.E. Uttley, Colin Welch and Peregrine Worsthorne and later in the *Spectator* of Charles Moore. A considerable number of the neo-Conservatives in America such as Irving Kristol and his wife Gertrude Himmelfarb spoke of him with approval. But many of those who wanted to enlist him in their ranks vulgarized his ideas and tried to produce a doctrine, a set of propositions and directions to find their way across country, whereas all Oakeshott offered was a way of thinking or an outlook.

There are those who maintain that he was the guru inspiring Margaret Thatcher's revolution in conservatism; and certainly he preferred the classical economics taught by John Jewkes in Manchester to the planned economy. In his essay on Henry Simons he made the connection between the market economy and his notion of civil association. Civil association is the form of political order that does not impose any one language or enterprise on all its members. It confines itself to making non-instrumental rules – such as the rule of law – which will allow each member to pursue his own projects in peace or cooperate as he chooses with others. Its members do not perform functions: they pursue their own choices and are protected from collisions and conflict by the law. Government exists to give a push here, or remove a mischief there, and hold the ring for the conflicting pressure groups.

But when in the eighties the tide turned against planning and demand economics – and when he himself was in his eighties – Oakeshott considered monetarism as much a heresy as Keynesianism. On a visit to England, shortly after Margaret Thatcher had formed her first government, Hayek had said that unless inflation was reduced to zero in six months she would have lost the battle. That was crude ideology. But it was Hayek and Friedman, rather than Oakeshott, who inspired the new conservatism. Their message was spread by the Institute of Economic Affairs where Ralph Harris, Anthony Seldon and John Wood worked to persuade the publicists of the advantages of a market economy. Oakeshott played no part in Keith Joseph's Centre for Policy Studies although occasionally he attended a meeting. He never allowed himself to dwindle into the role of the house philosopher of the Conservative Party.

3

INDEED IN NOTHING did Oakeshott show the virtues of his deviancy and his detachment from party politics more than in his writing on education. He was beyond everything a teacher. To him a university was a place of learning: not a place to 'push back the frontiers of knowledge' – one of Edward Boyle's favourite phrases – not a place to obtain qualifications, certainly not a place where learning was degraded into research. A don who published little or nothing but read enormously was more valuable than the author of a myriad of articles, all trivial variations on some unimportant theme. A university was a meeting place of minds who engaged not in vulgar controversy but in conversation – the conversation in which scholars engaged each other on his own line of enquiry or concern, exchanged views and spoke in his own voice. The university had not developed in order to submit society and itself to ceaseless self-criticism. '*Ceaseless* criticism never did anyone or anything any good: it unnerves the individual and distracts the institution.' The university was not *for* anything, it had no self-conscious purpose. Dons did not exist to give answers to 'the burning questions of the day' or construct courses to explore 'the unsatisfied demands of social justice'. The best dons are not those giving 'dynamic lectures'. Anyone, commented Oakeshott, who knows anything about a university 'knows that even the meanest has room for a dozen different sorts of lecturer. And when I look back upon the great teachers I have heard . . . none of them was dynamic and none cared a straw about a *Weltanschauung*.'

Nor was a university a place that should concern itself with meeting national needs. If it does so it will castrate itself. The real enemies of a liberal education are relevance and manpower planning in which each student is seen as a role-performer in a so-called social system. Almost as bad is the cliché that students should learn to think for themselves. That degrades education into teaching aptitudes. A don should teach the man or woman and concern himself with his or her quality of mind. In an unforgettable passage Oakeshott defined the time the student spent at a university as a blessed interim:

> Here was an opportunity to put aside the hot allegiances of youth without the necessity of acquiring new loyalties to take their place. Here was an interval in which a man might refuse to commit himself. Here was a break in the tyrannical course of irreparable events; a period in which to look round upon the world without the sense of an enemy at one's back or the insistent pressure to make up one's mind; a moment in which one was relieved of the necessity of 'coming to terms with oneself' or of entering the fierce partisan struggle of the world outside . . .

Give students time and freedom to learn. Do not cram them, do not overload syllabuses, do not command them to attend this course or make this or that attainment compulsory, allow them to choose what they want to study by setting examinations in which they have to answer only a few of the questions set. Oakeshott's recipe is a boon to the diligent – and to the idle. It was the finest evocation of 'the idea of a university' since Newman; and more subtle and persuasive.

His idea of a university was matched by his notion of what school should provide. Education was an initiation into the discipline of the various languages and voices that constitute civilization. So Oakeshott contrasted true education with training for industry. He was not so foolish as to decry the latter. Vocational training was necessary for those, and they would be bound to be the majority, who had not had the good fortune to be brought up to inherit the traditions and culture of their country. Let children learn a craft and be taught to use their hands because manual work has a dignity and delight all of its own. Teach them manual work because it is valuable in itself – and particularly to intellectuals so they can learn just how difficult such skills are to acquire and just how inept they may well be in trying to acquire them. But do not teach children to do such work because it will be of use to the state. They should be thought of as apprentices not as statistical fodder for this or that calling. Apprenticeship – learning by example from a master and acquiring the inside knowledge of a trade – is a sensible alternative to education. An alternative. For it is quite distinct from education itself.

School is the place where children are educated and education means initiation into the inheritance of sentiments, beliefs, understandings and activities: an inheritance that is at once intellectual, moral, imaginative and emotional. Children learn to study; and that is hard and they have to develop a formidable list of virtues to do so: attention, concentration, patience, exactness, intellectual honesty and courage. School detaches children from their home and the brute forces of existence, a place where they find they have to answer questions that had never occurred to them. A child has already learnt to communicate at home: at school he learns things far more subtle than merely making himself understood. A school is nothing unless it has teachers who impart not so much knowledge as the inheritance, a transaction between the generations. This kind of a school – embodied in the Lycée, the Gymnasium, the grammar school (and the ancient public school) has always been recognized as being different in kind from the vocational training given in schools designed to 'socialize' the poor and ignorant, to make them literate and numerate and capable of earning a living – the Communaux schools and the Realschulen. Even as recently as 1926 this valuable distinction was recognized in the Hadow Report which addressed itself to the problem of what should be taught to children who were to leave secondary schools at the age of fifteen.

And it was the school that educates, Oakeshott declared, which was now being ruined by the educationalists. Bowing down before the ideal of educational equality of opportunity they wanted all schools to teach children of all abilities: and that meant depriving those of limited ability of their apprenticeship and the intelligent of education itself. Then there were the progressives. They argued that so vile were the restrictions and disciplines imposed on innocent children that school should be abolished; and children should learn only what they wanted to learn. Or they wanted learning made easy by language laboratories or calculating machines. Or they substituted videos and tapes for teachers. These were enterprises 'for abolishing man, first by disinheriting him and secondly by annihilating him'. Worst of all were the fanatics who, wanting to abolish disparities in opportunities in order to produce a 'fully-integrated' society, determined to make all schools the same and ensure that 'none should be "school"'. Schools did not exist to make children well-informed or acquainted with the different points of view of their elders. They existed to give children seclusion to learn and acquire the treasures of mankind.

Oakeshott's sense of outrage at such pronouncements as the Robbins Report, and at the malaises that have struck schools, carries his readers along on the crest of a wave until it breaks on the sands; and then, as it recedes from the mind, we look around and recover our senses. It is not that his ideal or even his indictment is at fault. But when we come to look at the beach on which we have landed we realize that the same waves have been pounding it for many years. How odd to find him agreeing with that least intellectual and most philistine of dons the tutor of Jesus, Claude Elliott, who subsequently became headmaster and provost of Eton! Like him Oakeshott distrusted science. Science, he says, might have entered education as a benign addition to what was already being taught – as an introduction to intellectual adventure and a component of our intellectual inheritance. But it did not. It belonged to the alternative to education proper, dealing with objects not ideas, observations not thoughts. With some difficulty it detached itself from vocational training. 'In the course of time something has been done to give it recognition as one of the great intellectual pursuits of mankind: but without notable success.' His condescension is breathtaking; and to the scientists of his own university laughable. How scientists work and think seems beyond his comprehension. He did not anathematize an actual branch of science as Butterfield did when he said chemical engineering was the sort of scientific development that ought not to sully a university. But such a thought was never far from his mind; and some specious reasoning was employed to absolve the most ancient of applied sciences – medicine – from his dismissal of vocational study.

Nothing could be further from the intentions of the Conservative ministers of education – Keith Joseph, Kenneth Baker and Robert Jackson – than Oakeshott's ideals. He might have been pleased that their reform of school education was a response to his contempt for the educational follies of the left. But the remedies of a national curriculum, the concentration of educational policy in Whitehall, the emphasis not upon teachers but upon bureaucrats who were to inspect examination results and set syllabuses, would hardly have been to his liking. Indeed the contempt for teachers that Conservative fiscal policy displayed did not chime with his belief that they were at the heart of education. Moreover, nothing that Robbins proposed was as hostile to his idea of a university as the Conservative conception, inspired by Correlli Barnett, that British universities should be geared to increasing national productivity.

Yet in Oakeshott's writings there is a relentless refusal to acknowledge the facts of life. In 1949 when he wrote his essay on the universities he deplored the overcrowding, the influx of students, after the war years. It was an illusion that 'there was any large untapped reserve of men and women who could make use' of the kind of university he held up for admiration. Marjorie Holland could not have said so more succinctly. That there should be universities which fulfilled a different but as necessary a function he did not allow to cross his mind. He remained oblivious to the shortage of teachers at a time of full employment and growth of the polytechnics and colleges, or to the difficulties of teaching different ethnic groups, or maintaining classroom discipline in city-centre schools – indeed to the multitude of problems that any headteacher or director of education in a local authority wrestled with daily.

His defenders declared he was an egalitarian in believing that everyone could and should acquire some education in the strict sense and pointed to his eulogy of 'School'. But he ignored the tension in the minds of those who cared about education as intensely as he did – the tensions of knowing that there were tens of thousands of children who, given the opportunity, could rise from the status of helot which Oakeshott's acceptance of technical schools would have allocated them; and the tension of knowing that there were thousands of parents who were not prepared to see their children stamped with the mark of second-rate citizen. It is true that a village school with a handful of devoted teachers may give a better education than a town primary school with large classes whose staff spends more time on keeping the children occupied than in teaching. But Oakeshott makes one feel that parents who demand more for their children are selfish and stupid. Not all parents share the sentiments of the wife of the head of an Oxford college who, in sending her children to the local school instead of to a public school, said, 'Second best is good enough for our family.'

The fact that parents will not accept second best creates a political problem insoluble in Oakeshott's terms. This was a point made immediately after the appearance of his essay on 'Rationalism in Politics' by a young graduate student, Dorothea Krook, who admired both Leavis and Oakeshott and later became a distinguished critic of Henry James and of seventeenth-century thought. She protested that his pathetic little upstart of a rationalist bore no relation to those who had not only high hopes of changing society for the better but high expectations. They knew that they would be disappointed but were prepared to pay the price for not abandoning their ideals. By failing to recognize that such people existed and by failing to recognize that the moral tension in their minds was an honest response to experience, Oakeshott was exercising his negative capability at rather a cheap rate.

Oakeshott was, of course, a prickly pear for the analytic philosophers. Ayer gobbled like a turkey cock and declared Oakeshott unfit to hold any chair of philosophy. Just when Idealists and their bastards had at last been exposed and expelled from our universities, here came sidling in another misbegotten creature. Oakeshott's method of reasoning had been identified by the American analytic philosopher C.L.Stevenson: he called it persuasive definition. You define a rationalist and by skilful rhetoric persuade your reader to accept that definition. But the definition owes nothing to any logical process. You are playing the old game the German philosophers played to sidestep Hume. For the Oxford philosophers the solving of individual problems of logic, perception or communication came first. To them Oakeshott was another of those charlatans who constructed a philosophic system (his modes of experience) and then argued by assertion referring back to the system when challenged. They did their best to ignore him.

But Oakeshott presented a far more serious challenge to the social scientists, and he was answered by the scholar who just before the war captured the minds of some of the most intelligent undergraduates who studied history at Cambridge. Munia Postan was a voluble and cultivated conversationalist and a fascinator. His speciality, improbably, was the system of land tenure in medieval England and in particular the effect upon society of the commutation of services into monetary payments or rents, a subject which the Russian economic historian, Kosminsky, had made his own. But Postan was no narrow medievalist. The lectures he gave before the war on English economic history were the most stimulating in the faculty, replete with allusions to the history of ideas, and he spoke as a European at home in the culture of many countries. When Clapham retired from the chair of economic history there was only one other candidate, Postan's collaborator, Eileen Power, whose contributions to the subject were more numerous and better known than his. Postan's method of eliminating this competition was original. He married her.

Postan realized that Oakeshott, for all his disclaimers, was planting a mine under the social sciences. He began by putting Oakeshott's attacks on rationalists in historical perspective. Were they not the lineal descendants of the ogres that every reactionary invents when he detects dangerous thoughts threatening the established order? Reactionaries always appeal to history, intuition and tradition. That was what happened after Montesquieu and his followers constructed new systems of law and Napoleon enacted some of them. This disturbed Savigny and Puchta, and they countered by arguing that law could not be reduced to a code because it is the creation of history. When de Maistre and Bonald appealed to the ancient wisdom of the church and hereditary monarchy, they did so because they believed them to be the best barrier to the ideas of the French Revolution. The disembodied rationalist was a familiar figure in conservative demonology – yet how many men who use reason in fact conform to that stereotype? Bentham? Beccaria, perhaps? Certainly not Rousseau or Adam Smith. Even Marx was shot through with sentimental liberalism, and Soviet propaganda resounded with appeals to heroic example in education and personal leadership. Oakeshott surely was playing the old Kantian game of dividing reason into two: the scientific method that gives us answers about things; and 'practical reason' which accepts we can never predict uniformities in the world of affairs because we have free will and God exists, so therefore those who presume to plan merely waste their time proposing things that God alone disposes.

Social scientists know this is rubbish. They know that, however imperfect their inquiries, they can gather positive knowledge about the world of affairs, some of it actually of practical use. What determines what we make of a social phenomenon is the question we ask about it. Newton could have treated the apple as a phenomenon in time and written the history of the apple. But he chose to ask a generic question. He asked why apples fell. He therefore produced a theory of gravitation: the decision was Newton's, not the apple's. Rational enquiry can tell us little about social reality as a whole, but it can tell us more than a bit about discrete parts of it. Nor are there any parts wholly inaccessible to reason. What is theology but the application of reason to the nature and purpose of God?

Oakeshott would not have disagreed with much of this but in his eyes it was irrelevant. He was not interested in applying theory to practice. Robert Mackenzie remembered asking him at LSE in the early sixties, after Oakeshott had taken the chair at a public lecture on British entry to the European Community, where he personally stood on the matter. Oakeshott looked at him and said, 'I do not find it necessary to hold opinions on such matters.' Mackenzie thought such Olympian detachment on the part of a professor of political science excessive. For even on Oakeshott's own premises theory cannot ignore practice at every turn. However sceptical Oakeshott may have been about his colleague Karl Popper's belief in social engineering, some theory is needed to sustain any policy. Policy has to be underpinned to some extent by arguments derived from economics or social administration. Politicians need to justify their actions, and even if the scholar exposes their justification as humbug they cannot act unless they cocoon themselves in humbug. Nor need we be so cynical. Some consequences are bound to flow from Christian doctrine. Loving your neighbour as yourself does not entail subscription to the full programme of nuclear disarmament, minority rights and unlimited aid to the Third World, but it is bound as a commandment to raise questions of conduct, as Oakeshott admitted when he included religion as one of the voices which speak to men in the world of affairs.

Oakeshott held a romantic view of education. Perhaps he recalled the story of the dominie giving his son, who is to compete for a bursary at Edinburgh University, a final word of advice on the pitfalls in the examination in Greek translation. The examiners, he warned, had an unholy habit of setting a passage of the New Testament and leaving out a couple of verses somewhere in the middle, 'and you're just the one to tumble head-first into the *lacuna*. (I ken ye, Robbie.)'; or the college don in weekly conversation with his pupils, one by one, the discourse disturbed only by the rumble of horse-drawn vehicles. His ideal is not unrealizable: it is realizable for a tiny number. In the *politikos kosmos* it defies realization for the many.

The key to Oakeshott is to be found in that little book on the Derby. He rejoiced that life was a gamble. There was no device, ideology, method of reasoning, ruse, by which men could bet on a certainty and forecast how to turn fate to their advantage. He felt a faint contempt for those who want such certainty – even for those who think that by putting their trust in some economic theory they can shorten the odds. Why should they expect a political philosopher to predict which horse will win? All he can do is to warn them not to bet on some horse whose breeding makes it unlikely it will win the race; and if a philosopher sets up as a tipster, you can be sure he is out to grab power. The rule of the course (law) and the institutions (the Jockey Club) are there to check a particular owner, trainer or jockey getting too much into his hands. Men need nerve in the race of politics rather than ideas. Oakeshott was the Pascal of political theory – *il faut parier*.

On one count he was of his times and no deviant. He was an uncompromising champion of pluralism. But as he entered the lists to do battle he saw at the other end another champion of pluralism who was not at all inclined to sit at the same Round Table. This was Isaiah Berlin. Both knights were the soul of courtesy. Oakeshott scarcely ever mentioned by name those he sought to overthrow and, while Berlin regarded Oakeshott as an adversary from Collingwood's camp, he issued no challenge. But the fact that these two were prepared to fight for the same lady was no guarantee that one would respect the other. Meeting Oakeshott soon after the war Berlin suggested he should write a book on Hegel – on his thought, his influence, his culture, in a word the sort of book Berlin himself might have written. The proposal fell on stony ground especially as Berlin in his exuberance said the need for such a book was so great that better one written by a charlatan than by no one at all. Some years later Oakeshott was chairman on the occasion when the LSE had invited Berlin to give the first Auguste Comte Memorial Lecture. In introducing him Oakeshott spoke at such length and, so Berlin thought, in tones of such silky hostility – praising him as the Paganini of lecturers – that Berlin was unnerved. He abandoned his customary practice of speaking extempore, referred to his script and gave the worst lecture of his life. Devoted to the cause of pluralism as both champions were, neither desired to splinter a lance.

CHAPTER 25

Our Political Leaders

1

QUITE A NUMBER of Our Age believed they had the wrong leaders. At the age of twenty-seven Hugh Thomas edited a book on the Establishment. This popularized the notion that society consisted of interlocking circles each controlled by public school men, in particular by Etonians, who were neither experts nor trained to manage and ran institutions confident that common sense and social status alone were required for success. In this book Thomas Balogh blamed Attlee, Dalton and Cripps. They had excluded economists like him and had appointed the worst examples of the old guard to key posts in the economy and nationalized industries. How could Attlee have appointed that hardened reactionary Rayner Goddard to be lord chief justice? Or Fisher to be Archbishop of Canterbury – who treated the Church of England as if it were a public school going through a bad patch?

In 1958 an event took place which enabled analysts to put flesh on the bones of the Establishment. A tribunal had been set up to investigate how an impending rise in the bank rate had been leaked and Tom Lupton analysed the antecedents of those before the tribunal. He found the percentage of those who were educated at the same places and belonged to the same upper-class clubs to be:

	Eton	The Big Six Public Schools	Oxbridge or armed service colleges	London, Other Univs or None	The Crust Clubs
Ministers of the Crown	32.4	50	73	23	60
Senior civil servants	4.1	19.2	68.5	31	9
Directors of Bank of England	33.3	66.6	50	50	50
Directors of Big Five banks	29.7	48	55	31	32
Directors of the merchant banks	32.7	43	41	14	60
Directors of 8 insurance companies	30.9	47	44	20	48

The City magnates intermarried. That was hardly surprising. What was significant, however, was the exclusion of interlopers on the ground that those with no social ambitions were to be preferred to those who had worked their way up and had no inherited capital. Why should respectable merchant banks hustle? They could make enough by the business that came to them by tradition, such as new issues. Only hot firms like Warburg's or Philip Hill needed to be aggressive. When after the crash of 1974 Oliver Poole at Lombard's was asked how he avoided lending money to the fly-by-night property dealers he replied, 'Quite simple: I only lent money to people who had been at Eton.' But then Oliver Poole, who had been Montgomery's quartermaster, enjoyed a tease.

Many of us regarded Macmillan as the arch-Establishment man. His apologists remind us that he brought middle-class men into his cabinet, Charles Hill, Maudling, Heath; and Marples who was working class. The aristocrats, such as his nephew Andrew Devonshire, filled junior posts. Nevertheless, most of Macmillan's ministers exhaled an upper-class Oxbridge fragrance; and after his notorious 1962 reshuffle nearly half the cabinet were Etonians. In the nursing home, considering whom he should recommend to succeed him, he consulted nine colleagues: eight were Etonians. He did not consult Macleod even though he was leader of the House and chairman of the party. Anthony Sampson became fascinated by the way British institutions interlocked – from schools and television, to trade unions and the police. He anatomized Britain in three volumes (1962, 1971 and 1982), and exposed his disillusion with the top people for failing to persuade the workforce on how chilling Britain's prospects were. He too dissected the Establishment and found the chairman of the BBC, the editor of *The Times*, the foreign secretary, the heads of both foreign and civil services and two of the chairmen of the big four banks were Etonians; and the home secretary, the chancellor, the director-general of the BBC, a bevy of judges and the other two chairmen of the big four banks had been at Winchester. In her first cabinet Margaret Thatcher resembled a film star in the studio encircled by producer, director, cameraman, gaffer and grips – with Norman St John Stevas as best boy: all of the seven Etonians in the cabinet were supporters of Macmillan and Heath.

But long before this the Establishment had been changing and new faces from our generation appeared among its ranks. The change came when Wilson took office, and a new set of businessmen, financiers, dons and scientists were appointed to public posts. The old Jewish families which bred men like the law lord Lionel Cohen or Louis Gluckstein – the Samuel, Montefiore, Behrens families – were part of the old Establishment. Now they were joined by families such as Wolfson, Sieff, Weinstock and Clore. The most remarkable of the new arrivals was Wilson's lawyer Arnold Goodman, whose large face, mobile eyebrows and expression of amused expectation reminded one of portraits of David Garrick – magnified. He was the most skilled conciliator of the day achieving his successes by elucidating in great detail with frankness and courtesy what each side could afford to give and where their hands were genuinely tied. He transformed the notion of what the chairman of a public institution should do. As chairman of the Arts Council he considered it was for him to argue the case of cultural institutions with government and persuade Whitehall and Parliament what art can do to make life more civilized and stimulating. To help the distressed he also became chairman of the Housing Corporation and of Motability, which helped the disabled to get about. At one time there seemed scarcely to be a dispute or a delicate negotiation in which he was not involved.

Harold Wilson had no difficulty in finding civil servants and economic advisers who sympathized with Labour's objectives. Frank Kearton, Peter Parker and David Ezra were willing to try to make state investment in industry work and nationalized industries efficient. Dons pullulated in Whitehall. Perhaps the most original attempt to get a member of Our Age to give a lead to government was Heath's invitation to Victor Rothschild to set up the Central Policy Review Staff. Rothschild's dry, wry, account of the think-tank's existence explains some of the difficulties facing those who want to make Britain more efficient.

Victor Rothschild had left biological research as a don at Cambridge to become head of scientific research in Royal Dutch Shell. He was by nature a superior technocrat – someone who is interested in analysing why things are working badly and suggesting how they could work better. He first of all collected sixteen clever youngish men and women: among them the future ambassador Robin Wade Gery who supposed that the task of the tank was to 'sabotage the over-smooth functioning of the machinery of government'; the economist Dick Ross who thought it to be 'thinking the unthinkable'; a fellow of All Souls' and future Conservative minister, William Waldegrave; a future secretary of the cabinet, Robin Butler; William Plowden, a future expert in public administration; and Kate Mortimer who had shared digs at Oxford with three other clever girls, Marina Warner, Caroline Elam and Rothschild's daughter Emma.

The tank did what no one in a government department had time to do. It concerned itself with long-term problems such as energy in all its forms. It warned of the impending oil crisis; it was severe about government research and development; the computer industry, nuclear reactor policy, race relations, electric cars, current headaches such as Concorde involving three or more government departments. The tank also second-guessed the reports to cabinet coming from individual ministries: not a popular assignment. A critical eye from within government service on a product of that service is galling to those who come under its gaze. Even less popular were the terseness and brevity of the tank's reports which contrasted with the mellifluous prose of civil service drafting. Rothschild had been told by the secretary of the cabinet that he should never admit the think-tank had ever written a report on any subject, but he might admit it had taken an interest in one. Rothschild took considerable care to work with the top civil servants: he knew if he tried to buck the system he would be frozen out by devices at which civil servants are adept. But he reiterated what the Fulton Report had said: too few top civil servants had professional qualifications as managers, scientists, engineers or accountants. To Rothschild's regret the tank never had time to consider how to tackle the nation's housing, or the desirability of nationalized industries, or the level of secrecy in government, or services for the elderly, or whether there would be enough fresh water in ten years time, or climatic change.

Shortly after Wilson became prime minister again in 1974 Rothschild resigned as it seemed evident that Wilson had neither the time nor the desire to consider any question which was not coming up next week. But there was another reason. In the seventies he became despondent. Had the nation's leaders the will to make the sacrifices necessary for tackling inflation and getting us to behave as we had at the time of Dunkirk? Technocrats have the greatest difficulty in not losing hope. Their country's diseconomies and indifference to its efficiency is dispiriting.

Who, then, were the political leaders of my generation who might have recognized the nation's dilemmas, even if they could not cure them?

2

THE FIRST DID not belong to our generation. And yet Harold Macmillan was so identified with it as to be almost part of it. He had an authentic Our Age childhood, unhappy at Eton and the object at Oxford of Ronald Knox's chaste passion. Between the wars he was regarded as a bit of a bore, something of a prig and on the pompous side, receiving no very warm welcome from his wife's kinsmen at Chatsworth. One of the few Tories before 1939 with genuine pity for the poor, he rebelled like Lloyd George, Mosley and Leo Amery against the orthodoxy of the Establishment and suffered the irony of holding political views almost identical to those of the dashing buccaneer who became his wife's lover. Like Boothby, Macmillan despised the policy of appeasement and put himself beyond the pale by refusing the Tory whip.

Yet the war transformed him into an Oxford wit. The middle-class squaretoes emerged as the patrician statesman, enchanting Andrew Devonshire who now ruled at Chatsworth, an acceptable gun on the grouse moors in August, a chancellor who, sympathizing with his fellow citizens in their liking for a flutter, introduced into his budget Premium Bonds (a con on a scale that W.C.Fields would have thought exorbitant). Indeed, his most notable piece of legislation as premier was the Betting and Gaming Act. By the time he became prime minister he was flippant and unflappable. He regarded Gaitskell as having been during the war an embusqué Wykehamist and over Suez little better than a traitor unworthy to receive the customary intelligence briefs sent to the leader of the opposition. When Eden went only one of his cabinet colleagues preferred Butler. His fans considered his decision to despatch aircraft and troops to the Emirates in the Gulf against American and Arab subversion cost Britain less than it earned in revenues from oil and engineering contracts. When his Treasury ministers resigned he convinced his party that they had made a miscalculation characteristic of clever men. When Salisbury gave trouble he accepted his resignation with indifference.

Our generation associated him with the end of restrictions on foreign travel, the advent of labour-saving devices in house and kitchen and the growing ease of life in the fifties. We recognized in the authorizer of university expansion a cultivated man, well-read for a politician, with Churchill's feel for the sweep of history and the historic moment. We saw how the indifferent speaker of pre-war days, and the over-elaborate one after it, perfected a style which at the age of ninety enabled him to deliver the finest oration of his life. Had he lived a little longer he would have had the last laugh: inflation after ten years of Margaret Thatcher as premier was higher than it was in any year of Macmillan's premiership. No wonder many of us admired him.

And many did not. Gaitskell distrusted him for much the same reasons as Gladstone detested Disraeli. His U-turn over Suez ('first in, first out', as Harold Wilson observed) offended the upright. There was also something odious about Macmillan's surprise over Profumo lying to the House of Commons when he and Selwyn Lloyd had lied like troopers denying that there had been any meetings with the French and Israelis before Suez. To his opponents he seemed to exhibit the affectations of the upper class and the portentousness of an old buffer. The member for Stockton (the seat he lost in 1945) vanished and the member for Bromley, dapper in grey top hat, replaced him. Like an aged general he fought the war of the economy by applying the lessons of the war before last. Unemployment in the days of world consumer shortages and limitless demand was not the problem. The problem was inflation, the balance of payments, prices and incomes. He asked the ship-building bosses to improve their offer to the workforce though the industry was the most inefficient in the country. When his ministers tried to rein in the economy, he gave it another flick of the whip.

Was there not something complacent in his acceptance of union power and industrial weakness? It was not Labour but Selwyn Lloyd who first had to go cap in hand to the International Monetary Fund when he borrowed more than half the fund's lendings for the year. For his detractors the rot set in with Macmillan.

There were not many reflective politicians on the front bench of Churchill's or Macmillan's governments who were interested in principle as well as policy, and looked at politics in the light of history. Ministers governed by rule of thumb, good plain cooks, some with a lighter hand than others. Shrewdness, good judgement, a sense of the appropriate, what the party would wear were the qualities of the fare. Heathcoat Amory, Anthony Barber, John Boyd-Carpenter, Alec Home, Geoffrey (but hardly Selwyn) Lloyd, Christopher Soames (but not Duncan Sandys), David Renton and Peter Thorneycroft were the most able. The ablest was David Eccles, arguably the best minister of education since the war. He possessed the successful politician's instinct for the direction in which public opinion was moving and for moving wheels in Whitehall. Opinionated, self-assured, a Wykehamist with the manner (so Etonians said) of a Harrovian, he was a manager. Far more effective than the laid-back, self-indulgent Maudling.

Some would hail Rab Butler as beyond question the most important and the greatest Conservative of his generation; and certainly his continuous record as a minister or shadow minister from 1932 to 1964 is a tribute to his endurance. Helped by his young lieutenants he rebuilt the Tory Party; he taxed his countrymen's income less than any other chancellor; he abolished wartime controls; and under him began the prosperity for which Macmillan claimed the credit. His admirers thought the title he chose for his memoirs exemplified his exact understanding of politics: *The Art of the Possible.* And yet for all his reputation among us as a liberal Conservative who had re-educated his party after 1945 as Peel did after 1832, for all his patronage of a generation of clever young Conservatives in Central Office, for all his amusing deviousness, afraid to strike yet willing, well, not to wound but to scratch, he was so cautious, so much a man of Munich that few major initiatives came from the succession of departments where he presided. He had a record that looked fine as home secretary, chancellor and foreign secretary and, of course, as minister for education: hardly a foot put wrong. But, then, some of us considered, his feet had not moved all that far. If you stride you may put a foot wrong, and Butler failed to stride into the European Community. He and Eden reinforced each other's scepticism. 'Whenever I met Anthony, the sort of conversation was, "Simply nothing doing, you know".' On major issues he hardly ever questioned the wisdom of his advisers. The paradox remains. He could have won the 1964 election for the Tories but was the only contender for the leadership towards whom his colleagues felt lukewarm.

It was the combination of complacency and caution that made the Macmillan–Butler age so dispiriting to myself and others in Our Age. Change was conceded so slowly and so unwillingly: imagination was at a discount.

It seemed as if government could not understand how fast things had to move if Britain was to prosper and become less divided. This was what made Gaitskell and the Labour Party for all its divisions seem preferable to this creaking Establishment.

The most formidable minister among the Conservatives was certainly not an intellectual. Iain Macleod did not expound conservatism as Quintin Hailsham did. Macleod was a gambler: before 1939 he reckoned to win two thousand pounds a year at bridge. He possessed the art, Roy Jenkins once said to me, of insolence: like Canning, Disraeli and Joe Chamberlain. Always talking and working in politics, he was a deadly opponent at the despatch box, sarcastic, biting, rude yet with a fondness for opponents such as Bevan. (He had caught Churchill's eye in 1952 by demolishing Bevan in debate and within six weeks Churchill made this young man of thirty-eight minister of health.) He was of Our Age in recognizing that the colonies had to be given independence. As this was inevitable, the quicker it was done the fewer the recriminations.

There were, however, recriminations from the white settlers in East Africa and his relations with Welensky became so acrimonious that Macmillan replaced him with Maudling; but he did not lose Macmillan's support – Macleod became leader of the house and party chairman. Too clever by half, Salisbury called him. He enjoyed drinking others under the table at White's, but the clubs he enjoyed – Crockford's and the MCC – were not those of Macmillan's circle. Harold Wilson taunted the Tories by telling them Macleod was the opponent he most feared yet caused him least alarm because they would never elect him their leader. He knew Macleod had offended both the stuffy back-benchers and the golden Etonian circle when he refused to serve under Alec Home, and then explained why when he became editor of the *Spectator*.

That was as much an error as Roy Jenkins's resignation as deputy leader of Labour. Both were right to stand on their principles but wrong to dramatize their stand. It lost him all chance of the leadership when Home threw in his hand. He was determined in 1970 to reform the tax structure. Not to help the rich, but he realized that punitive taxation on higher incomes destroyed incentives for middle managers. The Barber budgets of 1970 and 1971 were constructed on his proposals for taxing spending rather than earnings. His death in 1970 was a disaster for the Conservatives.

And yet would Macleod have followed Heath in burying Selsdon man and monetarism? The odds are that he would. Heath was almost as much a disappointment to his side as Wilson. He had the great achievement of presiding over Britain's entry to Europe, the terms of which he had largely negotiated under Macmillan. In his long, bitter recriminations with Margaret Thatcher he argued that everyone supported his expansionist budgets and determination to cut unemployment – which fell from one million when he took office to half a million. Everyone backed him when he reduced taxes to a lower percentage of the GDP than Margaret Thatcher ever achieved. But he did not face the charge that by turning his back on Selsdon man his economic policy became meaningless. Heath was exceptionally honest. He acknowledged that throughout his regime his first priority as an orthodox member of his generation was to reduce unemployment. He blamed inflation on the fourfold increase in oil prices in the autumn of 1973, but it had been mounting for some months. He was beyond question a leader, and at a time of crisis guessed wrong. Like Mihailovich in Yugoslavia during the war, he got blown away by the winds of history.

There were, of course, Conservative ministers among us who reflected on politics. Among the elders Quintin Hailsham mused on the nature of his political creed; but reflection is not the word that comes first to mind in describing that rumbustious character. There was Edward Boyle, for whom we had a special affection after his resignation over Suez. Macmillan brought him back but held him back, and Boyle's notorious tolerance, open-mindedness and undogmatic temperament lost him his name with his party when he would not oppose comprehensive education tooth and nail. Heath would promise him nothing so he left politics. He was a better vice chancellor of Leeds University than he was a politician, but his departure was a blow to the kind of conservatism that Macleod stood for. He was, perhaps, the one politician of Our Age who was transparently good, disinterested and devoid of personal ambition.

The supreme intellectual among the Tories was their supreme rebel: Enoch Powell. Powell was a true intellectual, more of an intellectual than any Labour politician: for he was also a scholar. No other politician had the ability to translate the law book of a medieval Welsh king, edit Greek texts with a dryness that made Housman look gushing, master the intricacies of the medieval House of Lords, and reinterpret the New Testament; and this extreme analytic frame of mind, schooled in exactitude, induced him to assault unscalable mountains and cross Serbonian bogs where armies whole had perished.

Unlike Crossman he was moved by passion. He was a true puritan dedicated to his principles which he believed were confirmed by the march of events. He had become convinced in the fifties that the Conservatives had taken the wrong turning in two matters near their heart – the Commonwealth and the management of the economy. He considered the Commonwealth not to be the glory of progressive colonialism; it was a decaying corpse poisoning Britain with coloured immigrants. If that was true, why not say so? Powell thought his opponents hysterical and was amused when Crossman's diaries showed Labour fiddling the registrar general's statistics on immigration which supported Powell's case. The management of the economy, he considered, was a delusion. Fundamental to prosperity, in fact to any civilized life, was sound money. He egged on Thorneycroft to resign, yet the gap between what Thorneycroft asked should be taken out of the economy and what Macmillan and the cabinet would settle for was at the end only one per cent of a year's expenditure.

Powell shared with the left of the Labour Party their hatred of America, their rejection of nuclear deterrence and their illusion that Britain could be independent. He was as romantic as Michael Foot in his devotion to British sovereignty and the supremacy of the House of Commons; would not surrender a jot of it to the European Community nor to Eire; and preferred to leave the Conservative Party and stand as a Unionist in Ulster rather than accept the right of Dublin to supervise affairs in the province. For him Margaret Thatcher's firmness in refusing to reflate the economy in 1981 and 1982 vindicated his resignation in 1958. For him Jehovah spoke in the racial riots of Toxteth, Brixton and Bristol. He himself spoke like a man possessed. He was a formidable speaker, logical, precise, incandescent, as fluent as Benn but more ordered, more gifted in his use of metaphor and in the balance of his sentences. He resembled the prophet Amos, who not only pronounced the doom of all surrounding kingdoms but foretold the doom of Israel itself, and was banished for his pains to Judah. It was as if he wanted to set himself beyond the pale and languish in exile. But that was not how he saw matters. To him the relentless pursuit of his principles, wherever it might land him, was the justification of his life. He took satisfaction from being idolized – but no more; he scorned the execration.

Our generation considered him the embodiment of all they feared, the man who roused the lumpenproletariat and inspired the London dockers to march in support of his thundering against black immigrants. His curious classless voice, his staring eyes that might have been transplanted from Rasputin, his clear incisive sentences, made him a demonic figure for his contemporaries. The left lifted their skirts, the right praised him for the lead he gave to reintroduce a market economy while muttering a prayer of thanksgiving that such a high-principled and unbending ideologue no longer had to be humoured as a colleague. Powell himself was content to await the verdict of history, certain that that verdict would prove him to be the most far-sighted man of his times.

The most influential convert to the free market economy came not from Cambridge but from All Souls' Oxford. After the war A.L. Rowse had excoriated his college for being the shameful headquarters of appeasement before 1939. When John Sparrow was elected warden the college once again symbolized reaction and skilfully evaded reform by double-crossing the Franks Commission and conceding only the creation of some visiting fellowships. On one point only was Sparrow defeated. As colleges became mixed he was heard to say, 'There'll be women here before you can say Joan Robinson.' And there were – one or two. The college's reputation for conversation was, however, unimpaired. (After dinner I once heard a spirited discussion lasting for over half an hour on how many fellows might have been harmlessly tickled by A.L.Rowse.) There was no question of either Isaiah Berlin or Bernard Williams being elected warden; and by the eighties the college had again become a nest of thrusting young Conservatives, among them Robert Jackson, the minister for higher education and scourge of the dons. The mother bird in the nest was Keith Joseph regurgitating digestible lumps of monetarism.

Joseph had been an orthodox member of the One Nation group to which Macleod, Heath and Powell belonged. He cared as much for the relief of poverty as ever the young Macmillan had. Whether Ralph Harris or Alfred Sherman first persuaded him that Hayek was holy writ is in dispute, but he joined a group that included Jock Bruce-Gardyne, John Biffen and Sam Brittan who were determined to liberate the economy. When he became minister, Joseph found this more difficult to do than he had imagined. No sooner was he at the department of trade and industry than horrible ghosts clanking their chains haunted his waking hours demanding further government subsidies – the perennial British Leyland and British Aerospace among them. When he moved to education he turned what had been a mere cost-cutting exercise in higher education into a crusade to boost applied science and dethrone the set of studies that went by the fraudulent name of social science. He was not a successful minister: he wore a hair shirt for inept reforms of local government and the administration of health in the days before his conversion, and Kenneth Baker found ways to revise the curriculum in the schools that had eluded him. But it was he who altered the tone of the debate about education, and he was redeemed in the eyes of his colleagues for the fervour with which he embraced the intellectual revolution of the right.

3

NO GOVERNMENT HAD ever contained so many former dons and intellectuals as the Labour administrations of the sixties: Wilson himself, Crosland, Crossman, Dell, Gordon Walker, Healey, Jay, Jenkins, Longford, MacDermot and Shirley Williams. Michael Stewart had been a teacher and WEA lecturer, Evan Luard became a don, Harold Lever was a financial wizard (and as good a bridge player as Iain Macleod), and Peter Shore had been head of the Labour Party's research department. Who could deny that Michael Foot and Barbara Castle were intellectuals in the sense the word was used in the Labour Party? Tony Benn publicly announced on being elected member for Bristol at the age of twenty-five that he must lose the stigma of being an intellectual and was told by his former Oxford tutor Tony Crosland, 'You'd better acquire the stigma before worrying about losing it.'

Before 1939 Cripps had been expelled for advocating a popular front. The division was now not solely about foreign policy. It was a contest between social democrats and socialists. The bitterness of the fight over nationalization, German rearmament and the bomb was intense. It was also baffling. At first the right had all the heavy guns, the old trade union leaders and many of the up-and-coming intellectuals. But the ranks of the right were often in disarray: in 1956 Attlee demanded the removal of American bases from Britain; and in the last years of his life Gaitskell came out against entering the European Community. The ranks of the left were even more divided. Its great leader was the slave of his emotions. Sitting in the smoking room Bevan would turn on his cronies: a phrase had scraped his vanity, some proposal had aroused his contempt for those who liked moving resolutions and counting heads. He would explode in anger, entreat, charm and when he met resistance (which he preferred to sycophancy) sulk and fall idle. The left appealed for unity: why not accept resolutions that salved the conscience of pacifists and fundamentalists? The right replied that such fudges would bring the party into contempt throughout the country. Crossman denounced Gaitskell as a pig-headed pedant, the Gaitskellites regarded Crossman as treacherous as well as dishonest, his compromise drafts intended to trick Gaitskell into rejecting them and thus win support for his removal as leader. The hatchets were never buried. The left's memories of the injuries and humiliations they suffered at the hands of Gaitskell's young lieutenants festered: suspicion, back-biting, intrigue and appeals to remain loyal to 'the left' or to Gaitskellism continued for the next twenty-five years.

So a new principle began to dominate Labour that was to have as debilitating an effect as the pacifism of the thirties. The unity of the party must come first. At all costs. And Harold Wilson was the man to preserve it. The gloom lifted as the party saw Wilson score point after point off Macmillan in his summer of discontent, and then follow it up with a flurry of combination punches that had Alec Home reeling on the ropes. Here was the Cheeky Chappie, not from Hoxton but from Huddersfield, reminding this unrepresentative cabinet that ordinary people did not speak or think like them. Here was a classless, competent hustler, a professional in the house and in his handling of the press, who picked advisers from the ranks of the intellectuals of his generation. He seemed to understand the deeper needs of the nation as well – the need for a technological revolution. Here was the technocrat in a white coat replacing the aristocrat in tweeds.

Disillusion could hardly have come quicker for us. We thought Labour was (in grand prix parlance) in the pole position. The Maudling boom provided full employment but it had fuelled inflation and left Labour with an enormous deficit in the balance of trade. The strategy of the Labour economists was to impose an incomes policy at once to ensure that growth did not lead to inflation; a payroll tax to stop over-manning. If labour could be shaken out and wages held, for a time, there could be more jobs and higher wages. The overvalued currency should take this strain. But they believed Wilson, Brown and Callaghan blew it almost on election night. Dog-tired they took no advice from cabinet or their experts and decided not to devalue. As a result every few months there was a new round of cuts and every department geared to improve the welfare state got its programme disrupted. When the pound was at last devalued, Roy Jenkins had to institute another and yet more drastic round of cuts that really hurt in order not to lose industry the advantage devaluation brought. Whenever Wilson declared he would stand, retreat followed: that took the heart out of the party. There would be no devaluation: we devalued. Britain must stay east of Suez: in the end we left. Britain would join the EEC: we didn't – and since this was yet another issue on which the party split, new equivocations were prepared. The young asked why Wilson was so subservient to Lyndon Johnson over the detested Vietnam War and why he dickered so long with Ian Smith over majority rule in Rhodesia. Soon the young no longer regarded Labour as their government. Our Age expected less, but they too were disillusioned.

The greatest disillusion was with Wilson himself. Harold Wilson was kind-hearted, genial to his old cronies of the left and as loyal as he knew how to his senior colleagues on the right. But he was not a leader. He was a manipulator. To read the diaries of his old friends Crossman and Castle is to sense their despair at his failure to grasp what policy is. He had no sense of perspective or of the need to hold a line. Politics was one damn thing after another. One might have expected him to be clear whether or not Britain should enter the Community. He crossed the Channel with George Brown; but a talk with Kosygin so impressed him that he said he was no longer persuaded. Then sensing opposition on the left he accepted the device of a national referendum. When the day came to hold it, he comforted Barbara Castle by saying, 'The decision is a purely marginal one ... I have never been a fanatic for Europe.' He and Callaghan stood aside ostentatiously and let Jenkins incur the odium of campaigning with Heath and Thorpe to endorse British entry.

Was he prepared to modernize industry even if it meant more unemployment? He would never say. Ostensibly backing his chancellor, he would undermine his attempt to reduce public expenditure by backing policies that must increase it. Preserving the unity of the party meant for him the clever balancing of portfolios in cabinet, giving the left the hard-slogging administrative ministries and keeping the Treasury, foreign policy and defence in the hands of the centre and right. He prided himself on the subtlety of his ministerial reshuffles. 'When it is all over,' he said to Barbara Castle in the post-referendum reshuffle of July 1975, 'you will say that the old boy has not lost his touch. It is pure poetry.'

She was unimpressed. 'He subordinates all considerations, not only of principle but of administrative effectiveness, to his balance of power manoeuvring.' He presented defeats as clever victories. 'This doesn't mean, of course, that the pound here in Britain – in your pocket, or purse, or in the bank – has been devalued.' In 1974 he ignored the oil crisis. Having scraped into power he subordinated everything to winning a quick election that would give him a working majority. Inflation roared ahead. Wilson saw politics as a giant slalom race, getting through the gates: the fact that he and country were going downhill was irrelevant.

Cabinet under him presented a curious spectacle. Crossman misunderstood how Wilson used his cabinet. It was Crossman's ambition to supersede Bagehot as the interpreter of the British Constitution. Bagehot had told the Victorians that the cabinet had replaced the Crown as the executive. Crossman told Our Age that the prime minister had replaced the cabinet. Operating through the cabinet secretariat and the cabinet committees which the prime minister appointed, and suppressing in the cabinet minutes any mention of alternative policies put forward by ministers, in much the same way as a mortician massages away disfiguring injuries from the face of a corpse, the prime minister exercised limitless power – power that was reinforced by the vast range of patronage at his disposal.

Crossman was mistaken. As a description of Margaret Thatcher's cabinets in her second and third administrations it could hardly have been bettered. But in Wilson's cabinet there was no waspish Attlee, no heavy-weight trade unionist such as Bevin, no elder statesmen such as Morrison and Dalton. Harold Wilson's cabinets were young, self-confident and talkative. In the case of George Brown and Barbara Castle much too talkative. She used cabinet as a place to clear her mind. When Jenkins announced cuts in 1967, she spoke for an hour arguing that her ministry of transport should be exempted. Crossman depicted her maundering on, outlining her third or fourth draft bill on industrial relations and actually reading out proposed clauses from it in cabinet. If she could not get her way by coaxing, she tried tears. The fact that a cabinet meeting lasted for three hours was not a sign of crisis but normality. Cabinet meetings resembled seminars; and indeed the appetite for meetings of some ministers was insatiable. 'Tony loves meetings,' Joel Barnett said of Benn. 'He had so many, I often wondered when he found time for real work.' After a morning in cabinet he and Barbara Castle would spend the afternoon in the National Executive Committee of the party complaining that cabinet had deviated from NEC policy.

Wilson added to the triviality when cabinet met by trying to identify the leak in that morning's newspapers, although his colleagues knew that his kitchen cabinet engineered most of the leaks. Wilson encouraged loquacity. If everyone talked themselves out, it was easier for him to get his way. He hated confrontation in private even more than in public: that was where his kindness undid him. But like all prime ministers he wanted to get his way, and he would often introduce an item on the agenda by saying that he wanted a preliminary discussion – no decision today – just an exploration of views: and by the time cabinet had passed to the next item, they found that some sort of decision had in fact been taken. This was one way he exercised his famous sleight of hand. He evaded the attempts of his cronies to set up an inner cabinet. He was accessible to his ministers, but he hated to see one of them praised in the press; and when that happened his kitchen cabinet at No. 10 fanned his fear of conspiracies, and devised punishments for those who spoke out of turn.

The determination to hold the party together weakened what discipline there was. Tony Benn, even after demotion, continued in the seventies to advocate an alternative policy yet remained in the cabinet. On Healey's crucial 1976 finance bill one would have expected the whips not to put die-hard left-wingers on the committee and the Labour members of the committee to vote with the government. But no. This unwillingness to confront opposition spread through the whole labour movement. Shop stewards defied branch secretaries in the unions and MPs feared to speak out against the changes that the hard left brought about in the constitution of the party in 1980–81.

'The Labour Party always goes mad after losing a general election,' that fine old battle-axe Barbara Wootton once said to me. 'But it recovers.' The constituency activists and the trade unions had a simple explanation for defeat at the polls. Socialism had been betrayed. Every potential leader came to realize that in order to stand a chance of succeeding Wilson he must embrace the principles of the left. Jim Callaghan saw that opposing Barbara Castle's mild measures for trade union reform would enable him to climb back into favour; and when Wilson retired he had the support of the unions as well as of the moderates and the right. He proved to be a more skilful prime minister than Wilson; he took decisions and won his colleagues round to support them. But a nemesis of Greek proportions overtook him when the trade unions in the winter of discontent proved how right Barbara Castle had been.

After the defeat of 1970 both Tony Crosland and Tony Benn had got the message and begun to move to the left. Crosland was the most serious of the Labour intellectuals, but that was not at first his reputation. In the army he had waged his own war, teasing and snubbing brass hats, bowler hats and high hats. After it girls and uproar diverted him from the more painstaking duties of political life until he married Susan Catling from Baltimore, whose biographical portrait of her husband is as like him as it is loving. Nothing pleased him more than to take the mickey out of the Establishment, and indeed out of anyone who was advising him. No politician of Our Age ever said more forcibly to the world *Je m'en fous*. He despised official banquets, the social whirl, gossip: no white tie or morning coat for him. No austerity either: plenty of drink and Sunday afternoons reserved for making love at home. He was famously rude and difficult and as self-assured as Eccles. He was a genuine egalitarian who preferred his Grimsby party workers to fellow intellectuals. The intellectuals who worked for him respected the dedication with which he applied reason to practical problems; but others wondered whether it was ideology rather than reason that he applied.

Yet unlike Eccles he found it hard to make decisions as a departmental minister. At education it was easier: there he could concentrate on one problem at a time. But at the department of the environment where he had half a dozen major problems coming at him, he often could not bring himself to give a ruling on more than one. He had no base within the party because he could not bother to build one. Callaghan was his base, and he infuriated George Brown, who offered him his first post in the DEA in 1964, by saying, 'I'll have to clear this first with Jim.' In cabinet he spoke little, but when some absurd ploy was put forward by Tony Benn his habit was to rubbish it but finish by saying it was of so little consequence that it would be a pity to divide cabinet. So ploys which others thought catastrophic edged through. 'There's nothing the matter with Jimmy,' he used to say of Benn, 'except that he's a bit cracked.' But there was a great deal the matter with Jimmy. By the seventies Benn's articulate, good-tempered oratory in the house or on television was winning plenty of adherents in the party, as he set himself up after 1970 as the new messiah. Crosland shut his eyes to the consequences of the party's shift to the left.

Or perhaps he opened them to see the best way of following it. One of the tests of socialist purity was your attitude to public expenditure. The Treasury was regarded by the left as a devious opponent and the ministers in it little better than traitors. There was no crisis. It was engineered by the IMF, and public expenditure should remain as high as ever. That was what Crosland's book on the future of socialism had said and when foreign secretary he did not hesitate to oppose Healey's 1976 showdown. He argued in cabinet that Britain should continue to borrow. By 1980, when North Sea oil would have come on stream, the pound would again become a strong currency and the debt could be repaid. At one time it even seemed as if he could carry Callaghan with him, though in the end he backed Callaghan and Healey against the anti-deflationists. Crosland had by now shed his indifference to success. He calculated that he could succeed Callaghan. His rival Jenkins had burnt his boats. Denis Healey had maddened the left who hurled insults at him in the house as he fought for the IMF deal ('They questioned my paternity,' he said of one exchange of obscenities, 'and I praised their virility.'). Since Healey got within ten votes of defeating Foot for the leadership, Crosland would have won it.

* * *

The intellectual who was a caricature of intellectuals and combined in himself almost all the contradictions within the Labour Party was Dick Crossman. The pleasure other men got in seducing women he got in seducing minds. Like a hearty pirate chief he boarded your ship and waving a cutlass drove you to walk the plank if you disagreed with him. He won friends by his insatiable delight in gossip, affairs, events, policies, the way he slashed away with his cutlass, scarring friend and foe alike, firing off shot after shot of indiscretion. The very quality that made his diary so enjoyable was his undoing in politics. He could not keep his mouth shut. He was, as Jenny Lee said, a compulsive communicator. And yet he was surprised that Wilson did not treat him as a confidential adviser. He genuinely wanted to inform and enlighten those he met, his colleagues, constituency workers, pressmen, the nurses he met as secretary of state for health and social security, miners on their summer outing. Not for him the dreary platitudes so often handed out to the faithful. His speeches fizzed with ideas, new ideas, ideas that had just come into his head that morning, ideas which often appeared not to square with what he had said the day before. He was incapable of being dull because he could transmit even on such a sombre and technical subject as pensions his belief that the scheme he propounded was the best and most ingenious that could possibly have been devised. He disliked royalty, despised most ministers and his deep hatred of Europe and Germany went back to the twenties as well as the thirties.

He never could understand why others thought him devious. In 1955 he supported nuclear weapons as an alternative to German rearmament. When he failed to prevent it, he opposed British nuclear weapons on the ground that they would weaken Britain's influence in NATO. Both the right and the left considered Dick Double Crossman had betrayed them. He voted for Gaitskell in 1955 but could never get over the fact that Gaitskell had outstripped him. 'If you were at school with someone who seemed innocuous and insignificant through your school life, it is difficult to believe in his greatness.' What a shadow the public schools threw over political life in the times of Our Age.

Roy Jenkins never failed to irritate him. He disliked him for being a 'literary man' (being a journalist Crossman presumably thought was all right), for playing tennis, for being competitive, for being ambitious, for caring about personal success, for wanting to be a successful chancellor of the exchequer yet keeping the Treasury at arm's length, for being an 'extraordinary mixture of ingenuousness, feminine petulance and iron determination', for being concerned with his image, for being at once inscrutable and indolent. What vexed Crossman was that with all this indolence Jenkins got results which he himself failed to get. He simply could not imagine what it was to relax; to ruminate; and then, by using instinct, flair and political *Fingerspitzengefühl*, to come to conclusions which should, Crossman thought, be achieved by brutal work. Like a British general in the Great War he believed the only tactic was the frontal attack: victory could be gained by battering in a war of attrition your colleagues, your civil servants, and the party. Unremitting hard work and loyalty to the party were the test; not the enjoyment of rotten London literary parties. Jenkins writing biographies and moving in circles quite remote from politics and the party faithful, was as bad as Gaitskell enjoying dancing.

Yet in 1970 Jenkins looked likely to succeed Wilson. He was deputy prime minister and someone whom Wilson was unwilling to cross. His reputation as the first liberal reforming home secretary in living memory was immense. Without his support none of the reforms, most of them initiated by private members – abolition of capital punishment, the reform of the law on homosexual acts, of abortion, of censorship – could have succeeded. His penal reforms were somewhat handicapped by the escape from gaol of the spy George Blake, but he showed how quick-witted he was by getting Mountbatten to head an enquiry. No post-war chancellor, not even Rab Butler, was his equal. He understood that in the British economy you had to juggle with half a dozen balls; to throw one of them up too high in the air meant dropping one of the others.

There was only one other minister as forceful as he: Barbara Castle. She was an intelligent, articulate radical, who assembled a team of advisers to help her build the new ministry of overseas development and to defeat the Treasury mandarins. Tough and courageous, she imposed when she was transport minister a seventy m.p.h. speed limit, made seat belts in cars compulsory and introduced the breathalyzer test. Which male minister would have done so? But she was too self-obsessed and too small-minded to compete with Jenkins. Roy Jenkins was the one minister with a feel for history who saw how the past was linked to the present, who saw issues such as the European Community and the American alliance in perspective because he knew in detail the history of each country, its aspirations and its difficulties. He regarded his fellow statesmen with the eye of a veteran trainer at Newmarket, marking their good points and their weaknesses with a friendly eye, aware how elusive success is and how luck determines reputations. A few ministers emerged with credit in 1970, such as Denis Healey at defence or the upright Michael Stewart who held out against the powerful Biafra lobby in his own party during the Nigerian civil war. But Jenkins was the only one whose reputation was enhanced.

Did he throw it away? He once said to me that he would have liked to *have been* prime minister and to survey in the tranquillity of old age his achievements and measure them against his predecessors in the past. He accepted the presidency of Europe when Callaghan rewarded Tony Crosland, and not him, with the foreign secretaryship, because he was not prepared to accept every compromise to achieve his ambition: he would accept some, yes; but not those he thought demeaning. Perhaps he was too much one of his generation. What mattered was the good life. His house at East Hendred was as modest as that of any of the other contenders for the leadership, but he was not willing, as Crossman and Castle, to address and conquer in argument almost any audience however insignificant. He had formed his style and tastes in the fifties and saw no reason to drop his upper-class friends just because the trends in the sixties were changing the style of his party. It was not for nothing that he was Asquith's biographer. Asquith was his hero, loyal to the radical tradition, willing to take on the howling ranks of the Tories on reform of the Lords and the unification of Ireland, unalterable in support of Lloyd George's new welfare state. But Asquith saw no reason why he should not be a benevolent presence in the tohu-bohu of Margot's world. Jenkins's appetite for the beau monde was undeniable; and the presidency of Europe enabled him to combine work for a cause near to his heart with observing the crowned and uncrowned heads of Europe. Yet he was the most imaginative, skilful and balanced of all the Labour leaders. He had flair which his mentor Gaitskell lacked: and on nearly all important issues he was more right than wrong.

The only other credible leader of the Labour Party was even more conspicuously an intellectual. Denis Healey too valued a private life, devouring modern novels, collecting recordings by young conductors, playing Chopin and translating the classics. He also was at home on the Continent, fluent in Italian and French, an ebullient figure at seminars on international politics and an expert on nuclear and orthodox defence systems. He got results by brute force, not by Jenkins's more subtle means. He enjoyed power and kicked his enemies in the teeth, whether generals or civil servants, but he expected them to answer his bellowing and treated them as equals. Other secretaries of state treated them as lackeys.

Jenkins had become convinced that no sane economic policy could emerge from a party so dominated by the trade unions as Labour. He returned home from Europe hopeful of forming a social democrat party; and numbers of our generation after the winter of discontent followed him. I was not one of them. I could not believe that a fourth party could ever detach sufficient numbers of Labour voters in perpetuity. In British politics an occasional wave of disgust with the two parties sweeps across a constituency as it did for Dick Taverne at Lincoln or at Orpington when the Liberal Eric Lubbock broke the Conservative vote. But a mass movement sweeping the country and breaking the mould of politics . . . ? Had proportional representation operated then change could have come, but neither Conservatives nor Labour would put such a curb and snaffle in their mouth. Denis Healey determined to stay in the Labour Party and fight for the leadership. In the fearful recriminations after 1979 he made the mistake of not opposing the proposal to set up an electoral college for the leadership and alienated supporters who drifted off to join Jenkins. He was prone to make such mistakes. Perhaps his greatest was not to build a political base within the party by using his talent of joviality. He did not suffer fools gladly, but he did not suffer even the well-meaning gladly. Geniality with intimates, yes; but with the back-benchers he seemed to find it a torment. Like so many of those talented intellectuals he found alliances difficult; and at crucial moments he came to the wrong decision.

Had the public been asked who was the most typical Labour intellectual, they would have answered Michael Foot. No one who knew Foot could dislike him. Gentle and charming to his friends, a cultivated bookman, as passionate a parliamentarian as Enoch Powell and as egalitarian as Crosland, he saw himself as a descendant of the Levellers – indeed of the Ranters – and the man to whom the dying Bevan threw his standard. People of my temperament underestimate the passion that sustains the left; nor is it ignoble. Foot loved to recall Byron and Shelley denouncing in smouldering verse the iniquities of Castlereagh, the massacre of Peterloo, and the years of Tory repression. Hazlitt was his most sympathetic literary figure. For him there was only one issue: defeating the Tories. At the time of the vote that would decide whether Britain joined the European Community, he pleaded with Roy Jenkins to persuade all his followers to vote against the motion and thus with the votes of dissident Conservatives bring Heath's government down. That Roy Jenkins would consider Britain's entry to the Community a national decision far more important than the fate of Heath's government was beyond Foot's comprehension. 'We're being governed by the most reactionary government since Lord Liverpool,' he said. Presumably he revised that judgement during Margaret Thatcher's premiership.

Foot burned with the sense of injustice that made Marx write with such violence. That was why he permitted all sorts of marxist groups to enter the Labour Party and why he opposed what he and his confrères called witch-hunts. As a rebel he sympathized with other rebels and wanted to protect them. He had spent twenty to thirty years on the back benches and knew what it was to be treated as a public nuisance. That was why to his credit he opposed Benn's demand that every Labour MP should sign a declaration of loyalty to the manifesto. But he was also the friend of the unions and as secretary of state for employment had passed to the TUC all major home legislation for their approval. And it was to his discredit he backed the National Union of Journalists' demand for a closed shop on newspapers that would include editors and give the union control over the news.

No one among our generation had a more malign influence upon the Labour Party and no leader was more calamitous. Michael Foot fed on his own rhetoric. He loved to stand in Trafalgar Square, arms flailing, locks flowing, voice rising, the reincarnation of a Victorian radical. It was he who egged Bevan on to resign and kept plucking at his conscience to stand upon his principles and deepen the division in the party. He belonged to the soft left – he did not oppose NATO – but as the veteran of many a CND march he could never go along with any coherent Labour foreign policy. He was no administrator, had never faced the kind of decisions ministers have to make that go against what the party wishes. Vanity and his wife's promptings made Foot stand for the leadership. Many moderates, obsessed by the issue of preserving the unity of the party, convinced themselves that Michael alone could preserve it. His election was in fact the last straw.

As leader Foot looked like, and behaved like, an old sheep. Having abetted for years movements against the leadership he now found himself undermined by Benn and the Militant Tendency. In 1982 the sheep began to bleat; but the excesses of the hard left continued to the end of the decade and were to plague his successor. Not until the nineties did Labour begin to look electable and only then did the spunky but ignorant Kinnock begin to emerge from emotional unilateralism and show signs that the long process of educating him in political reality had been accomplished: just as Jack or Hughie had to be educated in 1976.

The comparison was often made between Enoch Powell and Tony Benn, rebels who ended disowned by their parties. The analogy is false. Powell was an obsessive classical scholar, Benn a decent schoolboy. The Wedgie of the sixties believing all the stuff about technology became the Tony of the next two decades backing workers' control and participation instead of incomes policy and wage restraint, backing planning agreements instead of entrepreneurial initiative. He signed the hard-left prospectus, too naive to see that it was being promoted by a bucket shop. He was loathed by right-wing trade union leaders for intervening behind the backs of union officials, endorsing meetings of shop stewards, steaming up one track today and reversing fast down it the next, arousing contempt for his opportunism, deviousness and gerrymandering. And yet he had prodigious political gifts. He was unselfish and tireless and raised the temperature throughout the Labour movement. He could talk with radiant lucidity, never lose his temper and in an instant justify, with a flow of reason, policies that were wholly unreasonable. The diary he published was excellent. Even his comical mannerisms – the tape recorder and the tin tea-mug – exemplified his unselfish desire to be the people's tribune. He was among those of Our Age who, finding themselves in the sixties being out-distanced by the young, sprinted to catch them up. To some that meant drugs, happenings, and longer hair. To Benn it meant the adoption of neo-marxist programmes and sharing the outrage of the young over Vietnam and Rhodesia and the capitalist conspiracy which deflected Labour from its destiny. It meant abolishing the House of Lords, Aldermaston, and the Stock Exchange. He wanted open government and the security services to be as democratized as a caucus run by militants. Yet he considered it reactionary to propose that the Labour Party should elect its leader on the principle of one member one vote, or for trade unions to ballot their members before striking. Benn's version of democracy was caucus democracy.

A party that elected Foot as its leader and failed to elect only by a whisker Benn as deputy leader deserved to be humiliated at the polls.

In 1983 and again in 1987 it was.

4

EVERY DEVELOPED COUNTRY was plagued by the same dilemma. How was it possible to get economic growth to pay for the increase in social services and welfare and at the same time preserve full employment and convince its citizens that each class was getting a fair share of the new prosperity? How to do this and at the same time ensure adequate defence, help poorer nations that were in difficulties and not destroy by pollution, overcrowding and rapacity the countryside, historic sites and buildings and the blessings of nature? Our Age did better than may first appear in realizing some of these aims, in particular the structure of social benefits for the disadvantaged, though this structure was greatly weakened under Margaret Thatcher's government. Britain had a better record on pollution, ribbon development and overcrowding than another small country, Japan. That was the price Japan paid for its astonishing growth and brilliant industrial performance. Bad as was the performance of British car production, it was not set much of an example by the American automobile industry which in the sixties got flabby, overmanned, badly managed and unresponsive to public demand.

The two great communist regimes were no exception. Soviet Russia year after year failed to get the growth that their state plans decreed. The economy improved but the queues grew longer for all kinds of consumer goods that were on sale in the West. The vast budgets for defence and for space travel (a morale booster) distorted the economy, and in the technology of the computer age the Soviets fell further behind until the stagnation and corruption of the Brezhnev years became intolerable. In China the pursuit by Mao of social equity took such bizarre forms that on his death Deng made a dash for growth and praised the entrepreneurial spirit. America was able to export its deficit and European countries, if they had ups and downs, were more successful than Britain in squaring the circle. They regarded Britain as the equivalent of Turkey in Victorian times – the sick man of Europe.

Britain had problems other countries did not face. It is a small country with a home market smaller than that of Japan and Germany, and its old overseas imperial markets inhibited managers from concentrating on long runs on the production lines. The regius professor at Oxford, John Elliott, spelled out in his work on the decline of Spain the psychological and administrative difficulties a country encounters in winding up an empire. The British have a long tradition of practical democracy and an intense determination to use the law to delay, and if possible defeat, the proposals of ministers, councillors and their bureaucrats. Kipling thought this peculiarly English. In his pride he pictured the dying Norman baron saying to his son and heir:

> You can horsewhip your Gascony archers,
> Or torture your Picardy spears;
> But don't try that game on the Saxon;
> You'll have the whole brood round your ears.

Still, it was much easier for the descendants of the Picardy spearmen to accept the dislocation of the Channel Tunnel in the wide spaces of the Pas de Calais than it was for the descendants of the Saxons and Jutes in Kent to do so. Anything new was opposed: it was upsetting. Not until November 1959 was the first section of the M1 built. The enormous conservatism of the British in every profession, from the lawyers and the doctors to the dons and the teachers, found its parallel in industry. Even accountants were slow to abandon the delicious intricacies of double entry for the techniques that detect true profit under inflation and expose the problems of cash flow.

It was not for want of trying that the political leaders of my generation failed to reinvigorate Britain and diminish this aversion to change. For thirty years they tried one device after another to realize the dreams of their youth. The remedies they suggested may have been wrong, the goals they set themselves too many, too contradictory, too idealistic. But they tried.

During the war the temporary civil servants, the scientists and the dons, had warned the politicians how perilous was the state of British industry. Our generation could boast of its achievements in science and scholarship, and some of our compassionate political ideas were realised in practice. No doubt we were at the mercy of external forces, the impersonal forces of history – what Machiavelli called Fortune and the ancient Greeks the gods. But Our Age cannot opt out of its responsibility in part for Britain's decline and failure to remedy the ills we had identified.

Then in 1980 the most remarkable leader our generation produced tried a different set of remedies – determined, as she put it, to turn the country round.

CHAPTER 26

Our Vision of Life Rejected

1

AS EACH GENERATION turns to make its exit from the stage it hears a disagreeable sound. People in the audience are talking, not listening; they are indifferent to what their elders are saying on stage, worse they are uttering heresies. That is the inescapable penalty of growing old. Imagine the indignation of the generation of Kipling who lived to see the Empire derided and the war, in which their sons and friends had perished, stigmatized as criminal and pointless. Or go back to the radicals of the 1860s. The blind MP Henry Fawcett, postmaster-general in Gladstone's government, believed in a Simon Pure version of laissez-faire. Keep public expenditure to a minimum and oppose 'any scheme, however well-intentioned it may be, since it will indefinitely increase any evil it seeks to alleviate, if it lessens individual responsibility by encouraging the people to rely less upon themselves and more upon the state'. Abolish any institution, including the monarchy, that rests on hereditary right; abolish 'landlordism' and hereditary wealth because they inhibit free competition; open every post to 'intellectual merit and moral worth' – and to women. By the end of the century such radicals found their party committed to various forms of collectivism and opposed to women's suffrage. How melancholy must Fawcett's ghost have been as it wandered over the face of the earth hearing his principles spurned. And then, a century after his death, it found rest at last when a woman prime minister exhorted her countrymen to practise manly individualism, thrift and responsibility, and praised the market economy.

Margaret Thatcher belonged to the last cohort of Our Age, but in the choice and pursuit of her goals she exhibited the hard-headed professionalism of the undergraduates of the 1950s. Why were the educated classes of my generation so incensed by this remarkable woman, far less hollow than her predecessors, elected and re-elected to lead her country, the victor over Argentinian militarists and trade union militants – why did they hate the prime minister with a bitterness that had not been seen since the days of Neville Chamberlain?

2

THE SIMPLE ANSWER is this: she rejected practically all their beliefs and practices. It was she who led the hissing as my generation made their exit from the stage.

We believed in government by discussion. Out of discussion came policy, a policy which was further modified by more discussion. Bargains and trade-offs were not considered signs of weakness, they were considered sensible compromises. If agreement could not be reached, the dissenters must not be alienated.

Margaret Thatcher thought this nonsense. She hated the word consensus. To her it meant weak-kneed compromise. There could be no consensus with the IRA or the National Union of Mineworkers. To achieve anything you must form a policy and see it through. Harold Macmillan was shocked that she referred to the miners as the 'enemy within'. Had not the fathers of the Durham miners, he said with a catch in his voice in his maiden speech in the House of Lords, fought in two world wars? There was hardly a dry eye in the house when he sat down. He did not mention that Arthur Scargill insisted that no pit should close without the permission of his union, refused to allow his members to vote on the strike and then tried to intimidate the Nottingham miners who had broken away. Margaret Thatcher rightly regarded Scargill and his flying pickets as an insurrectionary mob trying again to bring down an elected government by naked force. Those of us who accused her of breaking consensus in government forgot that whatever consensus existed had been broken in the sixties and seventies by the militants in the unions.

We felt guilt about unemployment – we remembered the Jarrow marchers. She felt none: she was then a schoolgirl. When unemployment rose to four million she did not recoil as Heath had done. She put the rise down to poor productivity, poor salesmanship and vicious unionism that had already destroyed a large part of British industry. We put the destruction down to her imposition of monetary policies during a recession. But she would not subsidize ailing industries. That would be to throw good money after bad. The only remedy was to expose them to the Arctic winds of competition. If businesses went bankrupt, too bad. New businesses manned by leaner and hungrier men would replace them. Some at least of the unemployed could get jobs if they showed initiative or, as her henchman Norman Tebbit said, got on their bikes. Her hero was not the dedicated administrator, the brilliant lawyer, the cultivated intellectual, nor even the scientist or engineer. Her hero was the entrepreneur.

The educated classes were dismayed that she rejected their interpretation of politics. They saw growth and full employment as two sides of the same coin. She said she didn't believe government could promote growth. The old wisdom was that growth would materialize at whatever rate was necessary to finance the level of public expenditure that politicians determined was 'right'. She replied that the appetite of politicians and pressure groups was limitless. Three hundred and sixty-four economists told her that Geoffrey Howe's 1981 budget would bring disaster and maintained it had done so. She maintained it had made industry more effective and productive. Denis Healey sneered at her for being a 'handbag economist who believed you pay as you go', and Harold Lever thought she did not realize that free enterprise is built on borrowing. She suspected borrowing meant all too often printing money. She knew that Keynes believed in sound money and had advised the Treasury during the war to clamp down on the money supply: she thought the Keynesians had abused his name.

Her opponents swore she lacked compassion. Look at the niggardly level of supplementary benefits she permitted: put them up and you increase the purchasing power of the poor and create employment. She said that was a disincentive to finding work and would increase unemployment by inflating labour costs. They urged her to create jobs by financing public works: why not repair the crumbling sewers rather than leave men idle? She said that spelled inflation. They observed the harsh way the benefit was administered and her drive to reduce the number of claimants. She said she was after the wide boys who turned up to claim the dole while round the corner stood the taxi they drove on the black economy. She thought her opponents were too lazy to analyse what was happening to the welfare services. Were there not since the last Labour government 6,700 more doctors and dentists? She recognized that this increase of over thirteen per cent was necessary because the aged had multiplied and treatment grown ever more expensive as medical science advanced. As it advanced so did people's expectations of being cured of ailments that twenty years ago would have been thought incurable. So she set about yet again reforming the health service to make it more cost-effective.

Determined to bring inflation down she came up against local government. She argued that the boroughs and counties had become so improvident, and in Labour-controlled cities so rigged and so riddled with political vendetta, that central government could check the abuses only by reducing its subsidy. That would compel the local councils to put their house in order. Many of Our Age swept this aside. To them the fact that schoolchildren had no books and the London streets were potholed was further evidence of her contempt for local services. Her harsher policies on housing and child benefit brought her into conflict with the parsons. The Church of England, many Roman Catholic bishops and priests, and ministers of the Church of Scotland accused her of creating a society that considered covetousness and greed virtues and praised competition and self-interest. She remembered the Methodist adage 'get all you can, save all you can, give all you can', but her childhood communion waxed hot against her; and her address to the

General Assembly of the Church of Scotland led to much bandying of texts. The favourite parable of the clergy was the Good Samaritan. She reminded them that the Samaritan would not have been able to put up at the inn the man who fell among thieves unless he had had twopence and his credit had been in good standing. She found a religious leader more to her taste in that stern moralist the Chief Rabbi whom she ennobled. Immanuel Jakobovitz praised work not welfare and told other ethnic groups to follow the example of the Jews and work their way up in society. He had no truck with homosexuality, nor did he express compassion for deviants. Margaret Thatcher admired his principles more than those of the Archbishop of Canterbury who had been born under a more merciful dispensation.

She was not interested, as intellectuals are, in discussing what to do. She thought she knew what to do and needed no advice. Bill Pile, who had been her permanent secretary at the department of education, noticed that she never once said 'I wonder whether'. It was rather, 'Why do we have to have all these meetings?' She was interested not in what to do but in how to do things; and that was a subject in which intellectuals are seldom interested. She considered her civil servants and think-tanks could supply that advice. But an old Whitehall mandarin, Kenneth Clucas, thought that the ministries and think-tanks churned out programmes that ignored published research. In his opinion the civil service needed to be buttressed by non-political research institutes.

She thought such bodies produced rubbish. Time was when intellectuals held posts on public boards and were appointed to head royal commissions and committees of enquiry, which examined social problems and the causes of discontent or injustice. Ah, those committees of enquiry! Was there any subject during the sixties and seventies that was not covered by such committees – sexual conduct, obscenity, juvenile delinquency, prison reform, abortion, race relations, medical education, gambling? Among their members had to be at least one woman, one member of an ethnic minority, one trade unionist and hence one representative of management, one Scotsman, one Welshman; and nestling among the members could be found at times a philosopher or an economist like some wise old toad with the jewel of wisdom in its forehead. The committees were balanced and expected to be detached and objective. They took evidence, travelled, cogitated and after a gestation of three years delivered a voluminous report stuffed with appendices. On their report the government would issue a white paper and prepare legislation. Or more usually it would not. It would not because the issues were too contentious, or because there was no parliamentary time, or because its supporters were divided on the recommendations, or because the committee itself was divided or had been composed of owls. Or government had never intended to take any action and had set up the committee as a device to silence criticism. Nearly always such committees recommended spending more public money to remedy matters.

Margaret Thatcher believed she came to power to stop that. One of the few committees she did set up was on broadcasting. Loaded towards free enterprise it was expected to follow her lead and recommend the BBC should take advertising. Alan Peacock's report must have confirmed her distrust for such bodies because, although it was full of heresy regarding public service broadcasting, it did not recommend that the BBC should take advertising. Another committee in the safe hands of Brian Cox, the author of the Black Papers, which had been set up to advise how children should be taught English dared to declare that they should not spend time on formal grammar. Typical of a professor.

Her determination to put every institution that drew support in whatever form from the state under the microscope, and likely enough under closer control, outraged our generation. They said she wanted to curb any independent institution – the BBC, the universities, the churches – and any individual – ministers, civil servants, lawyers, doctors and dons alike – who expressed views differing from hers. Roy Jenkins said such concentration of power in the hands of central government was unparalleled in the West. But some sagacious critics took a different view. Had not the bodies which were supposed to make public institutions accountable to the public failed to do so? Had not the UGC, the councils of universities, the trustees of museums, the governors of the BBC become the mouthpiece for the dons, the museum directors or the broadcasters? That was now to be changed. Teachers and medical consultants were to be judged on their performance, dons on the contribution they made to the nation's need for trained manpower. No longer would the don be the sole arbiter on the length of a degree course or the subjects to be taught in his institution. No longer would teachers decide what and how to teach. No longer would only surgeons decide what number of operations to perform or physicians what to prescribe. To the intellectuals Margaret Thatcher's policies looked like monstrous interference with professional standards of excellence: they and they alone could set the standards required in scholarship or medical care or good schooling. But to her supporters the professionals had been allowed for too long to identify their own self-interest with that of the nation.

She offended us by slighting our mission to civilize Britain. That was to reverence the arts and redeem our country from the charge of philistinism. We could claim some success. It was no longer smart at school to kick the bottoms of those who read or wrote poetry, played and listened to music or pottered in the art school. In 1957 the trustees of the Gulbenkian Foundation asked Edward Bridges, Diana Albemarle, George Barnes and myself to advise them how to spend their funds. Bridges, the son of the poet laureate, has been head of the Treasury. His report, recommending that the foundation should concentrate on supporting the arts, was not a masterpiece of prose.

But through the platitudes one could sense his passion that none should be deprived of the chance to understand and love the arts. When Keynes had set up the forerunner of the Arts Council he did something more than create a channel to distribute funds from the state to the arts. He made Britain part of the Continent. European nations had long traditions of state patronage for opera, music and the theatre. Each year the queues at the National Theatre, the Royal Shakespeare Company, the Royal Opera House and the Coliseum, the museums and galleries grew longer.

Margaret Thatcher preferred the American model. She told the National Theatre, Royal Shakespeare Company and Royal Opera House that more of their budget should come from subscriptions and gifts from business. The director, first of the Royal Shakespeare Company and then of the National Theatre, Peter Hall, a grand master in the art of compelling government to increase his grant, mouthed abuse. She then offended the fine arts lobby by cutting the purchase grants of museums and galleries. Their trustees were told to charge for admission, as was done in France and Italy. The trustees believed that free entrance was a hallowed British tradition, but the more dilapidated and the less popular museums like the Victoria and Albert and the Maritime Museum were forced to raise money at the gate. Meanwhile to their horror the intellectuals heard a new set of publicists asking by what right had Our Age, these Whigs, these self-appointed guardians of the public's taste, exercised their power? Whom did they think they spoke for? Why should any tax payer be fleeced to finance the rubbish that the Tate Gallery bought or the snobbery of the *stagione* system of opera at Covent Garden? Twenty years earlier such sentiments could have been voiced only in the tabloids. Never once did Margaret Thatcher express regret that state subvention to the arts had to be reduced: that incensed the intellectuals.

But before all those indignities were heaped upon them, the intellectuals had taken their revenge. Every Oxford graduate who had become prime minister could expect to receive an honorary degree from his alma mater and it was unthinkable that the first woman ever to hold that office would not be so honoured. The unthinkable was thought; and the proposal in 1985 to confer the honour was voted down. It was an unparalleled snub.

3

OUR AGE PINNED their faith upon rational inquiry. Reason would deflect government from making irrational, chauvinistic, biased, emotional decisions. Living by this belief some intellectuals among us could not forgive Margaret Thatcher her triumph in the Falklands. To them the whole affair was madness. Nicholas Ridley had negotiated an agreement to transfer sovereignty of the islands but with a leaseback possibly for fifty years. The House of Commons had been mad to allow the islanders and their lobby to reject the proposal.

Margaret Thatcher had been mad to insist on such cuts in our naval forces that HMS *Endurance* had been withdrawn – a decision that the Argentinian junta took to be a sign that the British had lost interest in the islands. Maddest of all was the decision to send the task-force. Did that not convince our European colleagues that the British were sunk in the anachronisms of her imperial past? These intellectuals considered that the House of Commons had fallen into a characteristic fit of hysteria, and Foot had lacked Gaitskell's courage and independence of mind over Suez. The cost of the expedition, and worse still the aftermath of creating Fortress Falklands, was prodigious at a time when welfare services were being pruned. The cost undermined her attempts to rein in public expenditure: the navy not only defeated Galtieri, it defeated her. It would have been cheaper to have given each islander a million pounds to resettle elsewhere. And were not the deaths of soldiers and mariners – and of the Argentine combatants – a final indecency? Dr Johnson's pamphlet destroying British claims to the islands was unearthed. And Malcolm Muggeridge quoted the Norwegian captain's answer to Hamlet when he asked him why young Fortinbras was marching to Poland:

> We go to gain a little patch of ground
> That hath in it no profit but the name.
> To pay five ducats, five, I would not farm it;

But Muggeridge forgot that when Hamlet exclaimed, 'Why, then, the Polack never will defend it', the captain told him the Poles had already sent a garrison there. It is at this point in the play that Hamlet realizes resolution is a virtue. If Fortinbras and his men are ready to die for this little patch of ground, how can he not revenge his father's death?

Other intellectuals such as myself remembered the summer of 1940. Reason dictated then that peace should be arranged with Germany. There was no possible hope of winning the war, and the probability was that we would lose it. Sensible men in the cabinet thought so. Sensible men in 1982 knew that Galtieri and the other thugs were no reincarnation of Hitler any more than Nasser had been. But sensible men often neglect something that cannot be measured which is of immense importance to any country in peace as well as in war. National morale. De Gaulle restored France's morale after Algeria: that decent, sensible, uncorrupt politician, Mendès-France, could not have done so. No statesman was ever more criticized by intellectuals than Adenauer: yet by refusing to do what sensible men thought right – to grovel in repentance for the bestialities committed by his countrymen during the war – he won a settlement first with the West and then with the Soviet Union. Even more galling for sensible men was the sight of Ronald Reagan, a man with the slimmest of pretensions to statesmanship, rallying the United States when Americans were shaken by the débâcle of Vietnam, the shame of Nixon's resignation and the humiliations inflicted by Carter's moralistic foreign policy.

The reaction during the Falklands war to the sinking of the *Belgrano* revealed how fanatical some of Margaret Thatcher's opponents could be. They declared she had ordered the battleship to be sunk so as to abort the President of Peru's peace initiative. Tam Dalyell and John Hatch refused to accept that the president's proposals could not have been considered in London before the British submarine struck. They seemed to have forgotten that the sailors and soldiers in the task-force were already being attacked by Argentine aircraft when the *Belgrano* was sunk. In fact no man could have handled the war better than she did. Unlike Eden at Suez she did not change her mind, unlike Churchill she did not plague her generals and admirals with impracticable plans. She told them to get on with the job and backed them when the going got rough.

Many of us believed she did not understand Britain's role in Europe. She had a good case for asking that Britain's grossly inflated dues should be reduced, but the way she did so appalled them. In November 1979 she opened her offensive. Roy Jenkins, then president of the Community, thought she understood only four of the fourteen points in the British case and repeated them twenty-seven times. Giscard d'Estaing and Helmut Schmidt (who compared her to a female rhinoceros charging) tried to overcome her. In vain: for seven months she threw the affairs of the Community into confusion. In April she at last got a highly favourable offer. She rejected it. In May she accepted with ill grace the same offer, dressed up by Peter Carrington to spare her blushes. Yet would a subtler negotiator have done as well?

She refused for long to join the European Monetary System. She distrusted the Brussels bureaucracy even more than her own, and she had a nightmare of the ghost of Napoleon nodding with pleasure as Western Europe submitted to French notions of *droit administratif.* She endorsed the Single European Act in 1986, Geoffrey Howe at her side, so it was said, with reluctance. And perhaps she sacked Howe as foreign secretary in 1989 when she realized its implications. She put her country into the impossible position of adhering to political as well as economic union and then repudiating it in her speech at Bruges. When England lost the last of her lands in France Mary Tudor said, 'When I am dead and opened you will find the word Calais lying in my heart.' If an autopsy were ever performed on Margaret Thatcher, the word lying on her heart would be America.

She offended another lobby among the intelligentsia: the Third World lobby. She felt no guilt about imperialism. In her bones she resented, as she saw it, emotional blackmail and crude self-interest which Third World countries exerted to extract aid from Britain. On this issue Margaret Thatcher called in one of her economists, Peter Bauer, who argued that if people want to send aid to the developing countries they should do so through agencies such as the Red Cross and other private organizations for famine and poverty relief. State or IMF aid should be stopped because it was diverted into the pockets of politicians who used it to reward themselves and their families by creating vast bureaucracies for them. Dump the food surpluses of the West upon families living on the barest subsistence and the livelihood of peasants who produced food was ruined. On South Africa she was notorious in the Commonwealth for her opposition to sanctions, and some of Our Age and their successors of the sixties and seventies were outraged by her intransigence. But they did not carry public opinion with them, not even in their own generation. When the neighbouring African states admitted that sanctions would ruin them, some of us did not see why Britain should add to its unemployment and surrender its markets to less scrupulous foreign adventurers.

On only one issue did the intellectuals give Margaret Thatcher grudging support. Even they had to admit that measures to curb the trade unions were overdue. Some mocked the new laws. Did the government and the Coal Board apply all the new provisions during the miners' strike? They did not. In fact it was unemployment rather than the new laws that made the automobile workers throw out their militants just in time to save their industry from extinction. But those who carped and quibbled forgot that the policy of putting full employment first and placating the unions had been a failure. Her most popular measure – that enabled tenants to buy their council houses – they passed over in silence.

4

MARGARET THATCHER WAS at odds with another part of Our Age and it was a set in her own party. Most of the genial old guard among the Tories – those she called the Wets – were not intellectuals but some of them were shrewd men of affairs. Even so they did not realize that in the seventies opinion in both parties had become more extreme on the back benches. Upset by the U-turns forced upon their leaders by events, Labour back-benchers moved to the left and voted in Foot. Conservative back-benchers moved to the right and voted for the woman who shared their ideals and values. One of them, George Gardiner, said the revolt began when they tried in 1975 to stiffen Prior's employment bill. They were defeated then; but when the old guard whispered in 1981 that the party wanted Howe to reflate, the back-benchers signed a round-robin saying they wanted no such thing. The well-meaning paternalists thought they had a function to reconcile the conflicting interests within the party. But there were so few to reconcile: only one Conservative MP went over to the Social Democrats. Margaret Thatcher and the back-benchers could rely on a new army of voters whose fears she assuaged. With such a power base she knew she could weed her cabinet at will. By 1990 only one of the original members remained.

The old guard resented that elected to govern she governed. Wilson spoke of the smack of firm government but it was his government's face that was smacked. She announced at the outset that cabinet was not to be a forum for discussion, and she arranged for most disputes to be settled in cabinet committee. When challenged by Michael Heseltine over the trivial matter of the future of the Westland helicopter company, she isolated him in cabinet and shifted the agenda so he could not bring matters for decision there. The old guard fumed that she did not regard herself in cabinet as *primus inter pares*, taking the voices and leaving ministers to get on with their own job and exercise their own patronage. But she regarded herself as the managing director of Great Britain plc, responsible for checking that every minister was doing his job.

Nothing escaped her. Every minute of the day, of weekends and holidays was spent on her papers. Her capacity for work was so formidable that she could criticize the papers they sent to cabinet with authority – and with that degree of rudeness that managing directors use with their subordinates. 'Who wrote this paper? Oh well, I should have known. What else could you expect?' 'I read the paper most of the night. You should read things before you put them to cabinet.' 'I'm sorry, Prime Minister,' said a minister on another occasion. 'That was an error.' 'Not an error. Total incompetence.' When Willie Whitelaw met his new chief in 1975 to discuss tactics in opposing a bill, she saw at once he had not mastered his brief. She was furious. 'I have never been spoken to that way in my life,' he said – though he must have experienced as an ensign in the Guards the observations of the regimental sergeant major.

She despised the old Tories' belief in muddling through. The old Tories were clubbable and fixed things before meetings over drinks. Excluded from this male world she was no fixer. She reached for her bludgeon. Or she took her revenge through her press officer, putting the frighteners on her ministers by leaking from No. 10 that they were on their way out or being watched for stepping out of line. She was aware of men, particularly of bold, handsome, smooth men. But she was not in love with men. She was in love with power and her own success.

Her whole life was politics. So was Harold Wilson's; but wheeling and dealing, plotting and counter-plotting were not her line. She was not vain like Eden nor adroit like Wilson, she did not possess Butler's reflective mind or Churchill's imagination. She used every device to get her way and destroyed those who impeded her will. Like many managers she worked through confrontation. Macmillan was exasperated. 'That woman is not just going to ruin the country, she's going to ruin us.' Alec Home was wiser and remembered what a grasp she had of every subject. 'She was never caught out, ever, by any question asked. I came back one day and said to my wife, "You know, she's got the brains of all of us put together, so we'd better look out."'

Another critic, Allan Massie, who regarded Rab Butler as the greatest Conservative minister of the century, reminded his fellow Conservatives that his party had a long tradition of opposing unrestricted competition and used the power of the state to correct the inequities of the unrestricted market. State action had clogged the markets but the time would come when Conservatives would resort to it again. He quoted from a review George Orwell wrote of Hayek's *The Road to Serfdom*:

> He does not see, or will not admit, that a return to 'free' competition means for the great mass of people a tyranny probably worse, because more irresponsible, than that of the state. The trouble with competitions is that somebody wins them.

To Margaret Thatcher that fear of facing the inevitable realities of life was responsible for the decline of Britain's fortunes.

There was another group in her generation who found themselves under fire. They were the top civil servants. She did not trust them. She never wanted to delegate anything to her staff, even the job of buying the kind of streaky bacon her husband liked. Margaret Thatcher noted that there was no incentive to make civil servants more efficient; they could simply tell their minister that the Treasury grant to their ministry was inadequate to do what the minister wanted. The management and delivery of services, as in practically all state bureaucracies, were often deplorable because the top civil servants regarded such work as beneath them; and they connived in covering up delay and deceit quite often caused by politicians surrendering to lobbies. So in 1979 she brought in Derek Rayner, of Marks and Spencer, to introduce efficient management into civil service departments. Rayner concluded that top civil servants loved to write minutes on policy but were indifferent to the managerial problem of getting that policy implemented. The Treasury set the tone. It was interested in how much money was spent, not in whether value was got for money. When he asked a top civil servant in the ministry of defence to set up an efficiency committee in each department, the mandarin reported that all departments were satisfied the present arrangements were highly efficient. Rayner got him moved and tried again.

This time a team of young men went out to look at obscure warehouses and sub-departments. Everywhere they found waste and directors who did not know what their operations cost or how their materials compared in price to those in the free market. This time action was taken. But some of the young men found their promotion blocked. They found they were regarded by the civil service personnel department as being 'unreliable'. Margaret Thatcher sacked its chief, closed the personnel department and centralized control, as in the days of the powerful Normanbrook, under the secretary to the cabinet. Not for nothing was one of her favourite television programmes Anthony Jay's series *Yes Minister* that delighted audiences on the Continent as well as in Britain for the accuracy with which it satirized the vanity and weakness of politicians and the deviousness of top civil servants. And yet the most experienced of academic observers of politics, David Butler, remarked that after all its buffeting the civil service still remained in the hands of an Oxbridge elite, was still not politicized, still honest and uncorrupt. Perhaps the top civil servants – the 650 in the top three grades or the less than one per cent of all civil servants in the top five grades – had compensations for their pains. From 1945 to 1987 their pay rose by a factor of twenty. Prices rose by a factor of fifteen.

She could not have challenged her ministers and civil servants without help. So she set up a court at No. 10 whose costs rose from £4.4 million in 1986 to nearly six million pounds in 1990. Her opponents noticed that when the Queen's household got a rise of five per cent, her court got ten per cent. The policy unit at No. 10 superseded Heath's think-tank, regarded as too academic and containing dangerous subversives. Some were career diplomats and civil servants like Charles Powell and Bernard Ingham. Alan Walters and John Hoskyns were economic pundits, the pious Brian Griffiths a marginal don. Her advisers tended to come from her own background: able grammar school boys from the provinces. Her advisers shadowed her ministers and enabled her to challenge them in cabinet, particularly when she thought they had fallen beneath the spell of their civil servants. Wilson's kitchen cabinet concerned themselves with intrigue. Her kitchen cabinet concerned itself with policy. Being 'one of us' did not save you from the block. Biffen, Tebbit, Brittan, Howe and even her chancellor Lawson all went to the scaffold. She refused to sack Walters who openly ran a policy counter to that of Lawson. Such hubris in a prime minister rivalled Chamberlain.

The constitutionalists among Our Age were outraged. Mark Bonham-Carter in particular was incensed by her selective use of patronage. He was right. Her defenders might claim that she stuck to Callaghan rules in appointing bishops and rarely fingered an appointment to a regius chair, even if vice-chairmen of quangos like himself and Richard Hoggart were not reappointed. But Bonham-Carter was wrong to claim that things were so different under Wilson. After thirteeen years of Tory rule Wilson and his ministers brought into Whitehall and on to the quangos considerable numbers of political advisers; economists as committed as Hoskyns or Walters; libertarians to serve Roy Jenkins; and social administrators such as Brian Abel-Smith, trained by Titmuss, to help Barbara Castle. When the broadcasters gave trouble, Wilson made Charles Hill chairman of the governors of the BBC and put Bert Aylestone at the head of the IBA. Some of the Wilsonian Establishment had always been Labour supporters such as Jack Donaldson or Harry Walston. Others, like its most prominent member, Arnold Goodman, were cross-benchers. Mark Bonham-Carter himself, though a Liberal, was not likely to adopt a policy on the Race Relations Board that would be right of centre. Labour's favourite High Court judge to head an inquiry was Leslie Scarman: in the fifties the Conservative choice would have been Cyril Radcliffe. The membership of committees of enquiry was balanced but gently skewed to come up with suitable answers. Gradually some of the older hereditary peers and other *bien pensants* from Macmillan's days disappeared from boards and were replaced by dons. When I was asked in 1978 to join the board of the National Gallery trustees and become their chairman, seven of the ten members held academic posts and only one was an active businessman. Not a well-balanced board.

But there was a difference between Margaret Thatcher's and Harold Wilson's Establishments. The new Establishment was expected to put a specific policy into effect – the policy of diminishing state expenditure and returning concerns wherever possible into private hands. She was a reformer in a sense that Wilson never was. Nor, for that matter, the aristocratic wing of the Tory party among Our Age: according to them, a touch on the tiller here, a shortening of the sail there, was all the ship of state needed. She knew how hard it was to change anything in Britain. Prince Philip used to astonish institutions that invited him and expected to bask in royal approval by asking why they did not do this rather than that and move with the times: how many of them took his hints? She did not rely on hints.

But were there not more subtle reasons why the Wets and the intellectuals hated her?

5

IN JANUARY 1988 a freelance journalist interviewed a number of intellectuals to discover what they thought of Margaret Thatcher. Graham Turner, who came from the working class, sympathized with her aims, and a gleam came into his eye as he listened to their unbridled denunciations. Mary Warnock, an Oxford philosopher, life peeress and Mistress of Girton, said Margaret Thatcher's patronizing voice reminded her of a primary school headmistress. Why did the prime minister have to shout people down? Her husband, one-time vice-chancellor of Oxford, had told her that when the prime minister came there she did not listen to the dons, as Shirley Williams would have done, but lectured them and was extremely rude. Those shirts, each with a tie bow, were obscene, those neat packaged clothes and groomed hair-do were 'not vulgar, just *low*', Margaret Thatcher had no respect for culture, would regard Wittgenstein as worthless instead of a figure of intellectual glory and could not understand there were values other than her own dear to many intelligent men and women.

The reason why people loathed her was self-evident, said Jonathan Miller. 'It's the same as why the bulk of the human race is hostile to typhoid.' She was a philistine of odious suburban gentility and saccharine patriotism catering to commuter idiocy. Peter Hall (another of Miller's aversions) thought that ninety per cent of those in the arts and education were hostile to her. Alan Bennett called her a typical lover of opera, a genre which absolves you from thinking, and – most subtle of insults – a typical Chichester Festival Theatre attender. Peter Porter considered her bullying and stupid, David Gentleman arrogant, tactless and vain, Peter Nicholls saw her as speaking for taxi-driver Tories – the rising working class Conservatives. Jonathan Raban thought she was too crude. Intellectuals appreciate paradox, irony, ambiguity. Harold Wilson was a man who respected complex ideas and intellectuals, but she had the mind of a second-class graduate in chemistry incapable of making adjustments between economic and social goals.

I thought some of these criticisms inept and was puzzled by their virulence: until I remembered how I had hated Neville Chamberlain when I was young. But one saw Chamberlain as a blinkered old man who by his folly would land our country in war. It was Margaret Thatcher's personality that some of Our Age and many of the succeeding generation of intellectuals disliked. Was she a philistine? Margaret Thatcher probably read more poetry than most prime ministers though she was not as well-read in novels as Macmillan – but did one want another Stanley Baldwin endorsing Mary Webb's *Precious Bane*? Francis Bacon said it was beside the point whether politicians liked or disliked painting. Kingsley Amis praised her for not pretending to be what she was not. She made bold, brash statements and the intellectuals picked up one: 'There is no such thing as society. There are only individual men and women and there are families.' One of her junior ministers was fly enough to track down the quotation. He found it in *Woman's Own*: not, as he said, required reading among periodicals for intellectuals. In that article it was clear that she meant no one can escape moral responsibility by transferring it to a reified abstraction. She had gone on to say that it was right sometimes for government to intervene, but 'too many people have been given to understand that if you have a problem it is the government's job to cope with it'. The intellectuals' response to Robert Jackson's elucidation of the article did them no credit. A professor of divinity sneered and another critic said how happy he was that a minister for higher education had time for such research. Not a very warm welcome for accuracy. The dons examined her and gave her beta double minus query alpha. She was the eternal scholarship girl always wanting to get on: no conceptual sense, give her a problem and she is as happy as a Girl Guide. No humour or subtlety and mistakes politeness for weakness. As a pluralist I was intrigued that her critics would not acknowledge that the virtues she espoused were virtues; they insisted that self-reliance could be a synonym only for private greed.

* * *

Her critics were convinced that she was determined to curtail liberty, in particular the freedom of broadcasters to put out programmes expressing their own version of events. The charge was partially true. Our Age had loosened the bonds on broadcasters. The vigorous but fair interviews conducted by Robin Day and Robert Kee were matched by uninhibited drama and political revues. But the injunctions of due impartiality and overall balance still operated; and Hugh Carleton Greene, the director-general of the BBC, to whose regime broadcasters always appealed when they felt their liberties threatened, had taken off *That Was The Week That Was* when it ignored these injunctions. The next generation of broadcasters shut their ears to the warnings which the Committee on the Future of Broadcasting gave them. They would not admit there had grown up a broadcasters' orthodoxy in their response to current affairs: the knee-jerk reaction of the progressives. It did not help their cause when programmes promoted by writers who challenged that orthodoxy were strangled at birth.

But some of the criticisms were just. It was maladroit to ban union membership at Government Communications Headquarters, the secret organization that had succeeded wartime Bletchley where Ultra was produced. Even though a strike there provoked her action, Margaret Thatcher could have got a no-strike agreement. Her outrage at Peter Wright's breach of confidentiality about his career in MI5 not only led to a humiliating series of defeats in the Australian courts and the discomfiture in the witness box of the secretary to the cabinet. It also led to the government's revision of the notorious catch-all section two of the Official Secrets Act being less liberal than it could have been. She did not hesitate to vote for the return of capital punishment. It was Auberon Waugh, not a Liberal, who accused her of creating the nanny state. Over numbers of issues of liberty the shadow of the IRA and world terrorism fell; and also the shadow of the CIA and FBI and Britain's anxiety not to forfeit its partnership with foreign intelligence organizations.

She had a defect that we thought would in the end prove fatal. She lacked a quality they rated so highly. She lacked a sense of humour. She was obsessed with morality. She seemed determined to put her countrymen in the schoolroom to learn by heart the copybook headings. She turned everything – everything – into a moral message. For instance everyone agreed that the antiquated system, the rates, of raising money for local government should be replaced. In other countries people paid for local services through some form of income tax. But Margaret Thatcher insisted on moralizing the system and bringing home to people that it was their responsibility to decide how high local taxes should be. Everyone except the destitute should pay something so that people would vote against pork-barrel bonanzas of the kind Ken Livingstone handed out on the Greater London Council. Even her sanguine supporters feared her poll tax or community charge would reap the whirlwind. No wonder when a mass of citizens paid for local government for the first time, and the rich would pay less than they used to pay in rates. 'No representation without taxation' was not a good election slogan.

She banged on about Victorian virtues: prudence, diligence, temperance, self-reliance, responsibility. They are indeed virtues, however dispiriting intellectuals find them. But in pursuing thrift, people can become avaricious and mean; in pursuing prudence stiff-necked and reactionary; in pursuing diligence they can end by condemning merry-making and all the harmless relaxations that make life supportable for the poor and enriching for the rest of us. In pursuing temperance they condemn spontaneity: if you have never experienced excess you cannot understand to the full the merits of the golden mean. In pursuing self-reliance men may ignore the unfortunate and weak and begin to take a delight in trampling on them. Every merit has its defects. But did my contemporaries appreciate that exactly the same criticism could be made of the virtues they prized?

Peter Pulzer was probably right when he judged it was her style as much as her opinions and policies people disliked. One of the beliefs nearest to the heart of Our Age was that morality is inseparable from style. By the clothes we wear, the way we wear them, by our preferences and tastes we show whether or not we are in a state of grace. Style becomes more important than beliefs. A man's beliefs may be unexceptionable but, if he is uncouth and insensitive, they lose whatever force they possess. Actions can be impeccable but they lose their glory if the will that ordered them is perceived to be gross, dictatorial, conceited, self-important. In the fifties and sixties this insight became debased. As the profession of public relations and advertising advanced, the editors and authors of fashion magazines and cooking books, the promoters of pop stars and media events, performed prodigies to persuade people what was smart and what was in. Not to be with it became a sin, a failure of nerve, an admission of hardening arteries.

And yet style is inseparable from personality. Margaret Thatcher's critics thought she had the same vices as Mrs Miniver who could never be put down because she always had a happy riposte to everyone. 'Top drawer but one' E.M. Forster called Mrs Miniver. Mrs T. like Mrs M. was out to impose her will. Were her critics snobbish? How much is style a euphemism for snobbery – the snobbery of looking down at a woman who was the daughter of a small-town grocer, a member of that class which Marx and Matthew Arnold so disliked, the *spiessbürgerlich* lower-middle class? John Vincent was right to see her as being at 'the point where all snobberies meet, intellectual snobbery, social snobbery, the snobbery of Brooks's, the snobbery of arts graduates about scientists ... the snobbery of men about career women.'

Although men hated her for being a woman and sneered at the masochism of her cabinet and colleagues, it was her female critics who were most vindictive. Their heroine was Shirley Williams: late for every appointment because she cared so much for the problem she was tackling and the people she was talking to; hair in a mess, wearing old serviceable clothes; the soft voice and its genuine inflexions; the possessor of a heart of gold, striving against none, not because they were not worth her strife but because she believed in the power of reason to convince them. But Shirley Williams had the reputation of being reluctant to come to decisions. She could see so many sides to the question that she used to call for more research before the matter could be resolved. Yet this was regarded almost as a point in her favour.

Against this Margaret Thatcher's waddle of a walk and the voice manipulated by elocutionists to coo in sympathy as she visited the victims of a national disaster, made the Maudie Littlehamptons, the Joanna Stringalongs and the Wendy Webbers throw up. These women did not like her because she did not care for them. What had she done to make it easier for women who had not (as she had) married a well-to-do husband to get on in the world? Nothing. By her economies nursery schools had closed. The qualities that women can display to make life less brutal and obsessed by power she despised. Yet it was not by her doctrine but her manner and style, by the way she said things, by her tone and her glance that they judged her. What other premier took such pride in being in the driving seat and bossing her ministers? What other premier displayed so little sense of magnanimity?

There was certainly nothing magnanimous about them. Of course women may argue that it is only men who attach importance to achievement. Yet I could not help thinking of Victorian heroines such as Florence Nightingale, George Eliot and Josephine Butler who endured obloquy but by their character overcame male prejudice. Or the humble example in our own time of Virginia Woolf's physician, Octavia Wilberforce, great-granddaughter of William and granddaughter of Samuel, who was disinherited when she insisted on qualifying as a doctor. Nancy Astor maddened people but she was acclaimed as the first woman to sit in the House of Commons. Yet women who were honoured in their profession – great actresses, fine novelists, excellent scholars, professionals in every field – could not find a good word to say for the first woman who had climbed to the top of the greasy pole and in courage had emulated Disraeli.

Not all intellectuals despised her. Anthony Quinton and Hugh Thomas proclaimed her virtues. Shirley Letwin was an even more effective admirer because her dissection of her own side was as merciless as her dissection of Dworkin's jurisprudence. One convert came from the left and belonged like her to the last cohort of my generation. This was John Vaizey, who thought politicians should implement the predictions social scientists made about the level of employment and welfare. The inflation of the seventies killed his belief that social scientists could predict anything. He crossed the floor of the house and became as much a maverick on the

Conservative side as he had been on the Labour benches of the House of Lords. Before he died he wrote with genuine affection of five men he had known and admired and whose views he had once shared. The problems they had agonized over seemed now to Vaizey to be either of their own making or irrelevant. Among the five, Boyle had backed comprehensive schools against the instincts of his party, Crosland created the expensive and wasteful binary system and rejected for no logical reason the market economy in housing and health care. Titmuss, believing that the market, if left to itself, would generate unequal distribution of resources, concluded that the state must tax the rich to subsidize the poor: but since the rich would evade taxation, an army of civil servants must be mobilized to frustrate them; and since doctors prescribed expensive drugs, the pharmaceutical industry might have to be nationalized. Vaizey was mercurial, erratic, ingenious; his friend Frank Field, as dedicated a Christian as Vaizey, stayed in the Labour Party; but true to his reputation as someone always trying to find new solutions to the old problems, John Vaizey declared that he and his generation had got it wrong and they should shake out a reef and sail on a new tack.

But who was that booing as Our Age came to the front of the stage to take their bow? The catcalls came from the Cambridge neo-Conservative dons from Peterhouse. They booed because they believed they had enlisted to fight in a war to control the nation's mind. An 'intelligentsia' had captured that mind and had amused themselves by indulging their theories and experimenting on the body politic. The Peterhouse dons intended to give offence just as the young John Henry Newman had done when he was trying to save the National Church from Laodiceans, Erastians and infidel Liberals. Their leader was Maurice Cowling who for years had been growling in his lair at Peterhouse against the liberal Establishment. He was a devoted teacher, father-confessor to generations of undergraduates, an old-style bachelor who used his college, not to advance his own career, but to fashion scourges for the backs of the benighted enlightened. When Herbert Butterfield died Cowling caught Elijah's mantle as it fell from the skies. Butterfield maintained that the best explanation of the meaning of history was to be found in Christianity; and to those astonished by this revival of apologetics Cowling replied, 'Historical writing is an instrument of doctrine whatever historians may imagine.' Unfortunately Butterfield was in error, so Cowling considered, in seeing Christianity as a religion of reconciliation and consensus. Even more disappointing was Oakeshott in being so resolute a secularist. Enoch Powell was nearer the truth. He recognized that Christianity is a religion that sits in judgement on this world. To try to square the Beatitudes with politics which are about power is to defile Christianity.* The City of God was not

* Powell, like Butterfield, came of nonconformist stock as did Margaret Thatcher, Rhodes Boyson and Ralph Harris.

to be realized in this world by raising the level of child benefit or easing the lot of the single-parent family.

Cowling intended to dethrone 'the unbearably self-satisfied authors of the fifties and sixties: Snow, Plumb, Koestler, Spender, Ayer and Berlin'. It was a difficult task because so many Christians – T.S.Eliot, Knowles, Ullmann and Owen Chadwick – who might have been expected to be useful allies were, in Cowling's judgement, such indecisive, polite souls that they failed in their duty. And that duty was to show their resentment of the pretensions of liberalism and to remember what an effective weapon rudeness was. How sad, he thought, there were so few clergy like Cowling's colleague the Dean of Peterhouse, Edward Norman, who had no truck with the humanism of archbishops and the socialism of bishops.

Implicit in Cowling's programme was the rewriting of British history, and one of his adherents Jonathan Clark, who had left Peterhouse when he was elected to a fellowship at All Souls', set about the task. Clark wrote an erudite work that was an undisguised attack on Jack Plumb's interpretation of the history of the Stuarts and Hanoverians. Clark found himself in the company of Tony Benn when he was engaged to debunk the celebration of the Glorious Revolution of 1688. It was not glorious but infamous. That was the time when, according to Clark, the English aristocracy betrayed the principle of the legitimacy of an anointed sovereign. The succeeding century was not an age of reason whose apotheosis was the flowering of Hume and Gibbon. It was a century of theological dispute, a century when many men of principle were Jacobites. But it ended in another betrayal by the aristocracy, this time of the Anglican Church, when in 1828 they emancipated Roman Catholics and passed the Reform Bill. It was then that that ugly child liberalism was born, so rightly cursed by Newman. How well he knew the brat – mouthing that religion cannot be true unless it conforms to reason; that everyone may profess what he believes to be true, even if it is evil, so long as he pleads freedom of conscience; and that the only source of political sanction is the people's will.

Cowling himself took the occasion of another anniversary to explain why the declaration of war in 1939 was an act of folly. It did not promote British interest and there was no need to take a moral line that could not be honoured and offer guarantees to Poland and later Greece. There was no proof, rather the contrary, that Hitler wanted war with Britain. There was much more evidence that he intended to attack the Soviet Union; and that would have suited Britain's interests. Why should a Germany dominant in Europe have been worse for Britain than a Europe dominated by America and the Soviet Union? Chamberlain was at error, not in trying to make Germany a contented European power but in getting involved in the dispute between Czechoslovakia and Germany. As a result the British Empire, which Chamberlain went to war to preserve, broke up and presented Britain with an immigration problem. America finally destroyed Britain as a world power at Suez, and the disaster of liberalism in Ireland, and of socialism in industry, produced the malaises of the seventies.

Three research fellows of Peterhouse took up the tale. Roger Scruton, who edited the *Salisbury Review* and became professor of philosophy at Birkbeck, saw society as governed by some who dominate the rest. Books and articles poured from his rooms. When Ayer died he dismissed him as a philosopher of no account – a man who had to admit in middle age that the verification principle on which his most famous book was based had been found inaccurate and useless.* Isaiah Berlin he censured for not standing up to be counted when liberty was threatened by the left. Why did he not anathematize Hobsbawm, Hill and E.H. Carr for 'polluting' the world of scholarship? Scruton thought Berlin's sensibility shallow, and Jonathan Clark asked where in Berlin's four essays on liberty did one find suffering, sinful humanity.

The most sprightly of the Peterhouse iconoclasts was John Vincent, a professor at Bristol. A master of paradox he praised Margaret Thatcher as the first politician to have the guts to swim against the tide and for being neither subtle nor amusing. While other prime ministers tried to look better than they were, she chose to look worse. Why was she attacked for her code of morality yet no one attacked the Chief Rabbi or the Jewish ethic of work? She had brought courage back into politics and did so 'without uncommon abilities or uncommon advantages and despite the Tories'. But he was sad. She had not the imagination to challenge from her middle and lower-class political base 'the Lib-Lab Venetian oligarchy'.

And so Our Age began to hear a chorus of opinion-makers challenging their ideals. A good number of the neo-Conservatives were not intellectuals in the old-fashioned sense of that word but publicists. The furious young editor of the *New Statesman* in the sixties, Paul Johnson, had become the furious elderly columnist of the *Spectator* in the eighties. His heroes among modern statesmen included Coolidge, Nixon and Pinochet. He wrote a book on intellectuals proving what despicable characters most of them had. He chose Rousseau, Tolstoy, Shelley and Marx. No chance of him choosing Diderot, Montaigne, Arnold or Tawney. The truth is that when men and women with imagination and originality and drive rise to the top, whether it is in art or politics, they are often selfish and ruthless to those who loved or depended on them. And when Jonathan Clark, a respectable scholar, described Johnson's book on intellectuals as brilliant, one realized that the neo-Conservatives were not much interested in serious analysis of ideas and events. The reading public who had gone to the theatre to see a Greek tragedy and ponder on its cosmic implications had been regaled as the curtain rose by a troupe of acrobats.

* Richard Wollheim rebuked Scruton for lèse-majesté, but Ayer had recently reviewed Scruton's book on sexual desire with, well, not rudeness, but with dismissive severity.

6

BUT HAD MARGARET Thatcher turned the country round?

Within five years the Britain Nicholas Henderson had described when he retired from the embassy in Paris had certainly been transformed. Britain had the highest growth rate in Europe, inflation fell and so a little later did unemployment. Every foreign country recognized Margaret Thatcher's feat. She herself saw the fifties as a false dawn prefacing years of stagnation, overmanning and poor management. Manufacturing's share of the GDP declined in the eighties, but so it had in every country. Now Britain was learning to compete. What was wrong with Britain when the Japanese chose to build their factories here? She was certain she had turned the country round.

We recognized that the fifties had looked very different ... in the fifties. We then radiated effortless confidence. We told the young Neal Ascherson at Cambridge that the problems which had defeated their elders had been solved. Full employment had been achieved, growth assured, life was becoming easier, more interesting and rewarding, and poverty was receding. All that was required was to spread benefits wider still. Keynes stood at the gate of heaven looking down at the Satanic Marx tumbling into hell, banished for ever. A touch on the brake now, then change up and put your foot down. The mastery of the economy had been achieved. Ascherson was unconvinced.

Certainly we were no longer so confident that the planned economy was the other side of the coin to a higher standard of living. How many still believed that the first priority was to restructure our schools and other institutions to diminish the deadly class divisions in our country rather than improve the level of education? Although most of us still believed that the state should maintain a level of welfare that would not shame a decent person, they were much less certain that the way to obtain the level of welfare was solely by the redistribution of wealth through taxation. And they were even less certain, downright sceptical, that the state should run all welfare services, still less industries, through bureaucracies accountable to Parliament. The nationalized industries with which ministers could tinker at will were not an advertisement for good management. We could no longer read the future as we once thought we could. Perhaps we had lived in a period between the post-Darwinian 1880s, when Herbert Spencer published that bible of free enterprise *Man and the State*, and the new era of the 1980s when the goal was to free enterprise from regulations.

But rosy as the sky looked in the mid-eighties, the clouds gathered in the nineties. Like a skin disease the familiar symptoms reappeared. Inflation rose and the balance of payments tilted against Britain. Margaret Thatcher's obsession with defence made it cost over a quarter more than when she became prime minister. The fundamental problem on which all others depended –

the efficiency of British industry and a revolution in industrial relations – remained unchanged. All the familiar solutions for industrial relations hung like rotten medlars on the tree: mergers of unions to avoid disputes over demarcation and to ease plant negotiations; schemes such as Bullock's for participation with trade unionists on the boards of companies; rationalization of rule books; share-holding employees (Margaret Thatcher's favourite). High unemployment might make strikes less likely but a fall in real wages, whatever the level of employment, made them more likely. Management, apart from large enterprises, was still lackadaisical about training the workforce.

Not all industrialists endorsed Margaret Thatcher's policies. Toby Aldington, a former Tory minister and chairman of a select committee on industry, considered that Britain had been hit far harder than her competitors in the recession of 1981–2 by her monetarist policies. How could David Young, the secretary of state for trade and industry, appear so breezy when the manufacturing trade account that had been two billion pounds in surplus until 1983 went into deficit which in 1989 reached fifteen billion? Manufacturing capacity did not climb back to the level of 1974 until 1988 – by which time other countries had long surpassed that level. Productivity and efficiency had certainly increased in the eighties but not Britain's share of the market. No sooner did industry improve its performance than it was penalized by high interest rates brought in to regulate inflation. By 1990 it was being garrotted by a rate of fourteen per cent. Corporation tax was double that in France and Germany. Electricity and water charges had risen by ten per cent. What would happen when the North Sea oil revenues declined?

David Young's belief that manufacturing industry could be allowed to decline because it could be replaced by service industries was indeed debonair. Were hairdressers combing out American matrons in their hotels likely to replace in dollar earnings capital goods exported to the United States? Conservative policy seemed to be as curious as Nikky Kaldor's view that selective employment tax could bankrupt hairdressers and drive them into factories. Nor was Conservative policy towards industry the only matter on which people remained unconvinced. Question them and they said they favoured increased taxation to pay for a better health service, better education and higher social benefits. People did not welcome the entrepreneurial state; they still put job security first, and they still believed that the state should intervene to improve the quality of life. Meanwhile uglier symptoms appeared. A third of the schools were judged to have poor teachers and inadequate books and equipment. Crime increased, the public no longer had simple confidence in the police; the homeless living rough were a feature of the streets, and the streets in cities were potholed. The symptoms recalled New York rather than Tokyo. The rich were richer, the poor poorer; and the increase in productivity not matched by a comparable increase in output.

Certainly there was one institution Margaret Thatcher had turned round. That was the Labour Party. In 1990 it produced a manifesto to which, it is true, some strips of the old socialist skin it was sloughing off still adhered, but which accepted the market economy as the only practicable arbiter of choice and efficiency. It could almost have been accepted by those who left the party in 1980.

Turn the country round? Suddenly the shore appeared littered with broken-backed Conservative reforms: the poll tax, the privatization of nuclear energy, the reform of the legal profession, the reorganization of the health service, and loans for students. Some thought that those old-style committees of enquiry gave better answers than the reports of Conservative think-tanks because they canvassed a variety of opinions. But the real cause of the disarray was more curious. Margaret Thatcher was even more the prisoner of her ideology than the socialists she despised. To each problem she applied ideology like emulsion paint to the fretwork of society with a broad brush. No wonder the fretwork got clogged and the paint lumpy and cracked.

Turn the century round? Significantly one of the favourite quotations that was bandied about by journalists in the last decade of the century was Disraeli's advice a few weeks before he died to the socialist H.M.Hyndman. Britain, he said, 'is a very difficult country to move, Mr Hyndman, a very difficult country indeed, and one in which there is more disappointment to be looked for than success'.

CHAPTER 27

The Sixth Age Shifts

IN THEIR LAST years Our Age looked at where they had left their country. The spectacle that greeted their eyes was odd. Britain appeared to be a reluctant member of the European Community and had still not grasped the implications of the Single European Act of 1986 and its predecessor the draft treaty of 1984 adopted by the European Parliament. The British still continued to believe that the Community was only a large free trade area in which goods, services, capital and people could move without internal frontiers. But the Continent regarded economic cooperation as a step towards political union.

Few indeed of us realized that the three bodies that made law in the Community – the council, commission and parliament – were going to rule the lives of our successors through their regulations, decisions and directives. The Community's political practice ran counter to British constitutional practice. The bureaucrats in the commission drafted laws without the supervision of ministers whereas in Britain ministers had to justify the detailed provisions in legislation before lobbies and public opinion. Not only did ministers have no voice in the commission, they were not heard in the European Parliament. Parliament gave its views on the commission's proposals, and it was only then when the council of ministers met that ministers could intervene. As a result they found themselves forestalled – they had lost their voice and a rubber stamp had been placed in their hand.

Few of us had grasped that the Westminster Parliament would become the equivalent of a state or provincial legislation in America or Canada. Britain's foreign policy would often be decided in Brussels. Ministries such as defence, agriculture and industry would disappear; public health, immigration, environmental controls, pensions and industrial relations would be governed by the regulations and directives of the Community. We had not understood how the European Court of Justice would interpret the wording of the treaties. The court operated on a legal system based on Roman Law in which judgements were made not on precedent but on principle. As the ultimate object of the treaties was the integration of all states within the Community, the European Court ruled that the exact wording of the treaties was not paramount. It was the promotion of integration that was paramount. The ruling principle in deciding cases was whether the action was likely to bring about the political union of the member states. Indeed the Van Duyn judgement gave citizens of the Community rights whether or not their own state acknowledged these rights.

Stalwart Europeans such as Edward Heath and Roy Jenkins were unperturbed. They welcomed this brave new world. They said there was no alternative. Britain had to belong to one of the three great trading blocs. Since half our exports went to Europe we had no other choice; just as Japan had no other choice than to tie her economy to that of America. Moreover, the old Europeans added, change would be very gradual; and who could say how many compromises and modifications might be made on the way to union? But those who dreaded political union, and the old enemies of the Community, found new possibilities to stand outside. What would happen if the Scandinavian or the Alpine states or Turkey were admitted to associate membership in which they accepted the rules of the free-trade zone but were able to opt out of the political and legal system? Why not have a loose free trade area open to Eastern European states? These hesitations and backsliding reflected the fact that Britain with her system of common law, her judiciary independent of any ministry of justice was always going to find difficulty in accommodating herself to the Napoleonic forms of administration that had taken root in Europe two hundred years ago. When Monnet, Spaak and the others had begged Britain to join the Community as it was forming, they had in mind Britain's reputation for individual freedom and the judicial tradition that had shone among the British judges and advocates in the Nuremberg trials. But whatever happened in the next century we would have to endure the reproach that our failure to join the Community when it was forming was the gravest of all political mistakes we made. Was our last cohort led by Margaret Thatcher going to make the same error?

Yet even odder was the break in the cloud that had hung over my generation ever since they came to power. The sun now shone through it. The West had won the Cold War. We had been divided on the tactics needed to fight that war. Some had even denied the need to fight it. But we all held our breath as we watched the movement of reform in the Soviet Union growing and the Communist regimes in Eastern Europe being overthrown. We had been right to hold Berlin in 1948 and to rebuild the economies of the West behind the defences of NATO. The nuclear deterrent had worked. The strain it had put on western finance was as nothing to the strain it had put upon the economy of the Soviet Union. Perhaps it was even the threat of star wars Reagan had conjured up that brought about Gorbachev's démarche. The Iron Curtain was rent. Of course the signs of genuine political change could well be false. Gorbachev's reforms could be reversed and he could fall by a coup engineered by apparatchiki, the military or indeed the voters. The history of Russia did not give much comfort to optimists who foretold the end of autocracy. Pessimists murmured that the leaders of an autocracy that shows signs of disintegrating have been known to launch an attack against a neighbour as a way of rallying their people.

Few intellectuals, however, think the way professional politicians do. Despite their passion in the thirties the intellectuals did not warm to those whose whole life was dedicated to the game of who's in, who's out, and the moving of amendments. Nor did many of them understand business. They pitied those who found their life's work in their work. Certainly you worked hard and hoped to take delight in it; but you did not feel guilt if you took time off to enjoy yourself. You earned money to lead the good life not to make yet more money. Most of them still found it difficult to understand that making yet more money could also be enjoyable. Their greatest error was to neglect – and some even to despise – the need for their country to become more efficient, more productive in business and industry; and their greatest failure to persuade organized labour to join in that enterprise.

They saw life more as a comedy than a tragedy. Even when moved by the wretchedness of so many of their fellow men and women, they considered it unenlightened not to be able to see the absurdity as well as the degradation of their own times. They put a high premium on cleverness and irreverence. They wanted to be amused and amusing. They were puzzled – and amused – by their solemn successors insisting that humour was tolerable only if it was ironical. High Victorian seriousness and pessimism were not for them. One of their younger critics, Roger Scruton, chided them for being so incorrigibly liberal and lacking 'experience of the sacred and the erotic, of mourning and of holy dread'. They thought they had done rather well by the erotic, but were prepared to admit they were a bit short on holy dread. Like Heine they thought *Dieu me pardonnera; c'est son métier*.

But the critics who considered them shallow and trivial knew little of their inner life. They were a generation who lived through poetry. Many of Our Age read the poets in as many languages as each could master, they translated poetry in dead and living languages, they anthologized, they read poetry for consolation and to stir their sense of wonder. They read and reread the classic novels too; but it was poetry that spoke to their heart in a way which – though they may have misjudged – it did not seem to speak to their successors. They grew up when Hardy and Housman were still living or only recently dead; when Yeats was reminding them of the mysteries of life, when Eliot's exquisite ear kept his revolution in prosody within the poetic tradition. To those who accused them of not understanding the profundities of life they might have replied, pointing to their volumes of poetry as the dying Adrienne Lecouvreur did pointing to the bust of her lover the Maréchal de Saxe: '*Voilà mon univers, mon espoir, mes dieux.*'

Whatever may have been their sense of holy dread, they had their share of profane or secular dread – dread of the bomb and of the hazards to nature and mankind on which pundits delivered sermons. Yet they were sceptical of prophecies of doom. When they were young pundits had foretold the annihilation of the population in the next war by poison gas and bombs. It had not happened. John Boyd Orr had warned them that in India hundreds of millions would starve unless Indians controlled their breeding habits: in fact India had saved herself by teaching her peasants to grow more productive strains of wheat and rice.

The defence of liberty still puzzled them. If utilitarianism was inadequate, should they fall back on rights? But might not the very insistence on rights diminish liberty? They acknowledged that cruelty to animals was bad. But the rights of animals were now invoked to stop research that might prevent deformed babies being born. Why should women who bought furs be pilloried? Were farms rearing mink more vile than those rearing sheep or chickens? The rage to do good by legislation could lead to a paradise for censorious busybodies and lawyers. And yet it was necessary to protect children, adults, animals, nature – to keep rivers pure and the landscape green and the air fresh – to protect the ionosphere itself. Some among them recognized that although the entertainment industry might insist on total freedom to meet the material, erotic and aesthetic appetites of the times, the spectre of AIDS, drugs, violence and alcohol stoked the fears of thoughtful people who saw children taking third place as the number of divorces mounted.

To handle such matters, as Matthew Arnold said of literary taste and criticism, 'there is needed a poise so perfect that the least overweight in any direction tends to destroy the balance. Temper destroys it, a crochet destroys it, even erudition may destroy it.' Perhaps the reforms Our Age had made in extending the liberties of the individual might last for a while. Perhaps not: who in the times of the Regency would have forecast the change in public morality that swept England during Victoria's reign?

The collapse of communism in Europe forced them to consider the realities of power. Germany and Japan, their defeated enemies, were now the most powerful economies. America, like Britain after 1918, had become a debtor country. Power always evaporates in debtor countries and passes to their creditors. Would a united Germany, with considerable military power and financial clout, be a benevolent master in Western Europe? No treaty restrictions or demilitarization would impede her will any more than they did in the period between the wars. Japan was far more threatening – a country that ruthlessly had undercut her competitors by deceit and broken promises, a country psychologically as aggressive and arrogant as in 1941, a country as secretly, as it had once been openly, convinced it was the master race, now contemptuous of America, buying up American property and poised to teach her a lesson by selling its technological know-how in electronics to Soviet Russia. Would the twenty-first century show a *renversement des alliances* far more sensational than that of Maria Theresa – in which the West once again as in 1914 was allied with an autocratic Russia?

But such speculations were no longer for them. By 1990 only a handful of them were still able to imagine that they might mould the future. We were dying. I found myself going to memorial services, sometimes speaking at one. For us the owl of Minerva had folded its wings. All we could do was comfort ourselves with Shakespeare's reflection that, though there was never yet philosopher that could endure the toothache patiently, a few of us had 'writ the style of gods and made a push at chance and sufferance'.

We sat as the fire burned low and remembered Thomas Hardy's Ancient addressing first his own generation and then the next.

> We have lost somewhat afar and near,
> Gentlemen,
> The thinning of our ranks each year
> Affords a hint we are nigh undone,
> That we shall not be ever again
> The marked of many, loved of one,
> Gentlemen . . .
>
> And ye, red-lipped and smooth-browed; list,
> Gentlemen;
> Much is there waits you we have missed;
> Much lore we leave you worth the knowing,
> Much, much has lain outside our ken:
> Nay, rush not: time serves: we are going,
> Gentlemen.

Index